PU

Pursuits of Wisdom

Six Ways of Life in Ancient Philosophy
from Socrates to Plotinus

John M. Cooper

PRINCETON UNIVERSITY PRESS

Princeton and Oxford

Copyright © 2012 by Princeton University Press

Published by Princeton University Press, 41 William Street, Princeton,
New Jersey 08540

In the United Kingdom: Princeton University Press, 6 Oxford Street, Woodstock,
Oxfordshire OX20 1TW

press.princeton.edu

Cover art: Francesco Rustici detto il Rustichino, *Wisdom and Prudence*, c. 1620, courtesy of Scala/Art
Resource, NY.

Third printing, and first paperback printing, 2013

Paperback ISBN 978-0-691-15970-6

The Library of Congress has cataloged the cloth edition of this book as follows

Cooper, John M. (John Madison), 1939–

  Pursuits of wisdom : six ways of life in ancient philosophy from Socrates to Plotinus / John M.
Cooper.

    p. cm.

  Includes bibliographical references (p.   ) and index.

  ISBN 978-0-691-13860-2 (hardcover)

 1. Philosophy, Ancient.   2. Wisdom.   3. Conduct of life.   I. Title.

  B111.C67 2012

  180—dc23   2012002204

British Library Cataloging-in-Publication Data is available

This book has been composed in Garamond Premier Pro

Printed on acid-free paper. ∞

Printed in the United States of America

10 9 8 7 6 5 4 3

For G.E.L. Owen and Michael Frede
In Memoriam

CONTENTS

My first idea for a book on ethical theory in ancient philosophy came in the 1970s: at that point it was to encompass Plato, Aristotle, and Hellenistic philosophy. My friend Jerry Schneewind, then a colleague at the University of Pittsburgh, proposed a joint project of a three-volume "history of ethics": ancient ethics by me, post-Renaissance ethics by him, and someone (to be discovered) to deal with the intervening late ancient, medieval and Renaissance periods. Jerry eventually published his remarkable and ground-breaking *The Invention of Autonomy* (1997)—not exactly the envisaged general history of "modern" ethics, but quite close enough. Later, other friends, notably Myles Burnyeat and Michael Frede, insisted that the expanding field of ancient philosophy really needed a comprehensive study of ancient moral and ethical theory, and urged me to fill this gap. I agreed with them about the need (this was in the early 1990s, before Julia Annas had published *The Morality of Happiness*). But what theme could one use to weave a truly comprehensive, philosophically live history of the ancient tradition, which by this time had to include late ancient Platonism? I didn't have the stomach for a traditional critical report on what current scholarship in the field says about Socrates' ideas about virtues, Plato's accounts in the *Republic* of virtue and happiness, and about pleasure in the *Philebus*, Aristotle's ethical theory, the controversies surrounding Stoic and Epicurean ethics, and Plotinus' spiritualist and Platonist conceptions of the human person and the human good. So, while I continued to write scholarly articles on topics in ancient ethics, moral psychology, political philosophy and related matters that struck me as interesting and needing attention, the book languished inchoate.

I found my theme about ten years ago through reading English translations of the late Pierre Hadot's remarkable and highly stimulating work on ancient Greek philosophy as a way of life: *Philosophy as a Way of Life* (1995) and *What Is Ancient Philosophy?* (2002). Fascinating and even inspiring though I found Hadot's ideas, his understanding of ancient philosophy, and of in what way it *could* be a full and complete way of life for its adherents, seemed to me to omit virtually altogether the central and indispensable place in philosophy (in Greece and ever since) of rigorous analysis and reasoned argumentation. As the first fruit of my liberating encounter with Hadot's work I published an essay in 2007, in Dominic Scott's festschrift for Myles Burnyeat, on "Socrates and Philosophy as a Way of Life," in which I explained my dissatisfaction with Hadot's conception of philosophy, and marked out my own new path toward conceiving, not ancient philosophy itself as a way of life (as if ancient philosophy were a unique and special genre of philosophizing), but specific ancient philosophies—in fact the six to which this book is devoted—as *ways* of life.

In writing this book, my ambition has been to discuss, both as a unified tradition and as a set of widely diverging individual philosophies, the main ideas and theories of pagan Greek moral philosophy as a whole—in a continuous tradition from Socrates, the originator of full-blown ethical theory in our Western tradition, down to the Platonists of late antiquity. I hope to show my readers both how wonderfully good and, above all, *interesting* the philosophies of antiquity are, both individually and in the full sweep of this tradition's history, when considered as offering ways of life. I want to show first, how good and strong these philosophies are in strictly philosophical terms—as carefully, coherently and plausibly reasoned sets of all-inclusive proposals for understanding human nature, human values, and the best way of living a human life—but also, second, how clear, and even compelling, these philosophies are as potential guides to living, for anyone who has any inclination to live their life on the basis of reasons they can understand and approve, after critical reflection of their own concerning what reason itself tells us about how we should live. It is true, of course, that our own cultures and historical circumstances differ in many ways from those of antiquity, and we see in ancient philosophy some basic assumptions that we cannot easily accept in the climate of twenty-first century philosophy. But we can set those aside, and consider the ancient theories, nonetheless, in the light of them. My own experience, which I hope my readers will share, is that these theories open up illuminating and clarifying perspectives that can both enrich our contemporary philosophical thought, and open the prospect of new self-understandings that might allow us to embrace philosophy as a way of life, in the ancient manner—to some extent, at any rate—even in our very changed modern circumstances.

With these ambitions, I have attempted to make the ancient philosophies that I discuss accessible to philosophers, and students of philosophy, with little or no familiarity with specialist scholarship within the now burgeoning philosophical sub-field of ancient philosophy. But I have hoped to make the book equally accessible to readers interested in philosophy, and in the idea of philosophy as a guide to life, with little formal background in the academic field. I have avoided unexplained specialist terminology, untranslated Greek words, and technical or quasi-technical terms of philosophy, in favor of as direct and plain contemporary English as I was able to manage. Even though many of the ancient philosophers' ideas are unfamiliar and even surprising to a twenty-first century reader, and their arguments are often complex and difficult, I hope to have made good and clear sense, even for less philosophically adept readers, both of what these ideas actually amount to, and the philosophical reasons that the philosophers in question rested their theories on.

With the interests of non-specialist readers in mind, I have excluded from my main text discussion of scholarly details and scholarly disputes (including interpretations alternative to my own), as well as all specific references to texts of ancient authors that I rely on in my presentations and critical discussions. Such textual references are liberally provided in the footnotes, where I also inform the reader (sparingly) about alternative interpretations and approaches from my own, and cite the work of other scholars and philosophers. I also provide in footnotes what seemed essential background information concerning ancient authors and texts, including English translations where available; this is followed up in the lists of Readings for each chapter that are assembled at the back of the book. Longer discussions, particularly those of special or exclusive interest to ancient philosophy experts, are relegated to Endnotes. I hope this somewhat unusual division of labor—footnotes for the most essential information readers should take into account as they proceed through the book, plus endnotes for more extended discussion of particular points that arise—will prove easily manageable and convenient.

I am grateful to many institutions for financial support during the long gestation of this book. Princeton University supported my research and writing during five paid leaves beginning in 1992–93, with additional support coming from the Center for Advanced Study in the Behavioral Sciences and the A.W. Mellon Foundation of New York, the American Council of Learned Societies, and the Princeton University Council of the Humanities, in which I was an Old Dominion Professor in academic year 2010–11. During the spring of that year I delivered the John Locke Lectures in the Philosophy Faculty of Oxford University on the topic of ancient philosophies as ways of life, as a Visiting Fellow of All Souls College. I am grateful to the Faculty for inviting me to give these lectures at such an opportune moment—just as I was putting the book chapters into final form—and to All Souls for its hospitality and the comfortable housing and first-rate facilities that a visiting fellowship there entails. Discussions with many Oxford philosophers and philosophy students, at the lectures and seminars of the series and informally, helped me greatly to clarify and sharpen my arguments. Over these years I also gave papers and lectures at a number of universities using material that eventually made its way into the book (becoming, in many cases, free-standing articles as well). I thank those from whom I learned in discussions, too many to recall here, on those occasions: at the Universities of Athens, California at Davis, Canterbury, Chicago, Kentucky, Maryland College Park, Memphis, Oslo, Oxford, Paris-Nanterre, Paris-Sorbonne, Pittsburgh, São Paulo, Toronto, and Virginia; Australian National, Boston, Bowling Green State, Columbia, Cornell, Florida State, Fordham, Georgia State, Hamburg, McGill, New York, Northwestern, Ohio State, Otago, St. Joseph's, Stanford and Uppsala Universities; Franklin and Marshall, Haverford, and Middlebury Colleges, and the City University of New York Graduate Center.

Jerry Schneewind's encouragement from early on in my work on the book, and his comments chapter by chapter as I completed penultimate versions of my text over the last twelve months, were invaluable to me. My Princeton colleagues Hendrik Lorenz, Benjamin Morison, Alexander Nehamas and Christian Wildberg each read and commented extremely helpfully on different chapters of the book at the same late stage of preparation (Nehamas had, as always, read drafts and discussed with me my ideas as they took shape at earlier stages); their generous sharing of their expertise, especially when it came to Hellenistic and late Platonist philosophy, saved me from errors and helped me greatly to sharpen and clarify my ideas. As the book was already in press, Lorenz and I gave a joint graduate seminar, attended also by Morison and Wildberg, on the topic of ancient philosophies as ways of life, in which we read and discussed relevant ancient texts in the light of the book chapters. Lorenz's acute and deep exploration in the seminar of central points in the moral philosophies of Socrates, Aristotle, Epicurus, Chrysippus, Sextus Empiricus, and Plotinus, and in the detailed examination of related texts, helped me to make many final corrections and improvements to the book, as I revised copy-edited texts and at the page-proof stage. I got efficient and intelligent assistance from Corinne Gartner and Samuel Baker in preparing the lists of Readings appended to the individual chapters, and very helpful comments from Arudra Burra on penultimate versions of the first chapters of the book. I am extremely grateful to all these friends for their generous help and support. Finally, I would like to thank my Princeton University Press editor, Rob Tempio, for his patience in waiting for the book to be finished, and for his good judgment and advice concerning issues in both the preparation and the production of the book. I also thank Bruce Tindall for his expert and thoughtful preparation of the book's Index.

As I indicated above, in writing the book I have drawn upon material I have published already in scholarly articles, in all cases, however, thoroughly reworked for presentation in a book intended not primarily for co-practitioners in the specialist sub-field of ancient philosophy, but for a wide readership. In footnotes I frequently refer readers to these articles for detailed explanation and scholarly support of various points of interpretation. However, I repeat verbatim or in close paraphrase from three of these articles sufficiently so that I should acknowledge and thank their publishers: "Socrates and Philosophy as a Way of Life," in *Maieusis*, ed. Dominic Scott (Oxford University Press, 2007) (used in chapters 1 and 2); "Political Community and the Highest Good," in *Being, Nature, and Life in Aristotle*, ed. James Lennox and Robert Bolton (Cambridge: Cambridge University Press, 2010) (used in chapter 3); and "Stoic Autonomy," in my own *Knowledge, Nature, and the Good* (Princeton University Press, 2004) (used in chapter 4). I would also like to thank my sister-in-law Dora DeGeorge for taking the author's photo, showing me sitting before my olive tree, named Athena after the goddess of wisdom and donor to Attica of its marvelous and characteristic plant.

I dedicate the book to the memory of Gwil Owen, whose unheard of, brilliant, and amazing lecture course at Harvard in the spring term of 1960 on *The Logic of Physics and the Logic of Metaphysics in Aristotle* burst open for me the world of ancient philosophy, who sustained my enthrallment during my subsequent graduate studies at Oxford and Harvard, and who was my colleague at Harvard and intellectual model in all my subsequent work in the field; and Michael Frede, whom I first met in Owen's B. Phil class on Aristotle in Corpus Christi

College, Oxford in October, 1962, and who became my close friend, colleague at Princeton, and constant collaborator: in fact, he sometimes seemed a co-conspirator, as we pursued, and tried to promote, the study of the texts of ancient philosophy, and their interpretation, in the terms of ancient philosophy itself—without coming to them from contemporary philosophical problems so as to see what the ancients might have to say about those, but seeking to understand ancient philosophy "as it actually was"—and thereby to expand the contemporary philosophical imagination. Both of them are sorely missed.

Princeton, December 2011

CHAPTER 1

Introduction

On Philosophy as a Way of Life

1.1. Philosophy Ancient, Modern, and Contemporary

Philosophy is a subject of study. In this, it is just like physics, mathematics, French language and literature, anthropology, economics, and all the other established specialties in contemporary higher education. Undergraduate institutions everywhere have departments of philosophy offering degrees in the subject. These departments are staffed with lecturers and professors with advanced degrees certifying their preparation as teachers and as professional philosophers—as people who pursue research in the field and write articles and books of philosophy and on philosophy, just as physics lecturers do physics and write on physics, or anthropologists do and write on anthropology. In fact, this book is just such a book of philosophy, written by a professional philosopher and teacher of philosophy.

But, even as a subject of study, philosophy is different from all these others. One indication of this is the fact—often a cause of frustration, even irritation, in professional philosophers when confronted by it—that in the popular imagination, and even among many beginning students, a philosopher is often conceived simply as someone who has a wide and deep experience of human life and insight into its problems. On this view, a philosopher is supposed to be a wise person, full of good advice on what to value in life most and what is worth valuing less, on how to deal with adversity and how to develop and sustain a balanced and harmonious, properly human, outlook on life, one's own and others'. So professional philosophers are often vaguely thought of—until closer acquaintance dissipates this idea—as especially wise people, with deep knowledge of human life and its problems. Moreover, the connection of philosophy to wisdom about human life is also reflected in the prevalence nowadays of the idea of a "philosophy of life," and in the attribution of a "philosophy" to pretty much anyone who seems to have some consistent set of ideas about what to value and strive for in life, and can at least claim they are guiding their own choices and courses of action with them. But people speak of their own "philosophy of life" with no thought of professional philosophy, or of philosophy as a subject of study, as any sort of source or foundation for it. On the contrary, a "philosophy of life" is felt to be such a personal thing that its status as a philosophy might seem degraded if it were subject to validation by—let alone if it resulted from—rigorous study within an intellectual discipline having its own principles and its standards of evidence and argument. Your personal commitment and your resulting strength in leading your life are proof enough, or so people seem to feel.

Even so, there are ties linking these popular ideas about philosophy to the subject of study that is pursued and taught in philosophy departments by professional philosophers. Indeed, I believe that these ideas reflect something deeply ingrained in philosophy from early on in its origins (for us in the European intellectual tradition) in ancient Greece, even if this may not be prominent in contemporary philosophy today. In antiquity, beginning with Socrates, as I will argue in this book, philosophy was widely pursued as not just the best guide to life but as both the intellectual basis and the *motivating force* for the best human life: in the motto of the U.S. undergraduate honor society Phi Beta Kappa (even if ΦBK never understood it in quite the ways the ancient philosophers did), for these philosophers, philosophy is itself the best steersman or pilot of a life (βίου κυβερνήτης). Over most of the one thousand years of philosophy in ancient Greece and Rome, philosophy was assiduously studied in every generation by many ancient philosophers and their students as the best way to become good people and to live good human lives. That history has left its mark in these popular ideas.

Indeed, one aspect of ancient philosophy as a way of life has survived intact in philosophy nowadays: the prominence among philosophy's varied subfields of ethics or moral philosophy. When Socrates introduced this ancient ambition for philosophy, he notoriously did so by shifting his focus away from the study of the world of nature in general to specifically that of human nature and human life. He established ethics or moral philosophy as one part of the subject (for him, in fact, his sole interest). As it has been practiced since the Renaissance—and things were not so very different for philosophy in ancient Greece and Rome—

philosophy is traditionally conceived as composed of three branches, namely, metaphysical philosophy, natural philosophy, and moral philosophy.[1] It is true that these traditional terms, especially "natural philosophy," are somewhat out of fashion nowadays. Philosophers today speak of philosophy of science instead.[2] In fact, it is not uncommon to hear a different threesome mentioned, namely, metaphysics, epistemology, and ethics. Other established specialties not easily brought under any of these principal headings are recognized, too (logic, philosophy of language, philosophy of art, and so on). In ancient philosophy, from the time of the Stoics and Epicureans, the standard threesome διαλεκτική, φυσική, ἠθική prevailed—that is, dialectic (which included logic, philosophy of language, and epistemology), philosophy of nature ("physics"), and ethics. What stands out in all these divisions of the subject—the ancient, as well as the traditional modern and the contemporary ones—is the enduring presence of ethics, or moral philosophy as it is also called, as one of the three principal components of philosophy.

In the ancient scheme "ethics" or ἠθική meant the philosophical study of human moral character, good and bad, and of the determinative function in structuring a person's life that their character was assumed to have—character being their particular, psychologically fixed and effective, outlook on human life, and on the differing weight and worth in a life of the enormously varied sorts of valuable things that the natural and the human worlds make available to us. In fact, the alternative term "moral philosophy" itself has its origin in Cicero's decision (in the first century BCE) to render the Greek ἠθική with his own coinage, *moralis*, meaning in Latin essentially the same thing: the philosophical study of moral character.[3] Contemporary moral philosophy or ethics is different, as a result of the long development of human cultures since antiquity, and correspondingly of changed bases for philosophical reflections upon our human circumstances, and as a result of changed conceptions internal to philosophy itself as to what philosophy can, and cannot, reasonably hope to accomplish. The ancient philosophers all agreed in assuming, as I have implied, the centrality of moral character (good or bad) to the conduct of individual human lives; ancient literature (history, drama, poetry) and many cultural practices, both in Greece and

[1] See *Random House Dictionary*, s.v. "philosophy."

[2] In early modern philosophy "natural philosophy" denoted natural science (including astronomy and physics); the field of philosophy of science is a recent creation.

[3] See Cicero, *On Fate* I 1. As Cicero says there, the customary translation into Latin of the Greek word for character, ἦθος, was (in the plural) *mores*; all he had to do was form an adjective from this noun, in parallel to the corresponding well-established Greek adjective.

later in Rome, supported them in this. People of outstandingly good character were held up as models, both in literature and in life, or, more commonly, those of bad or flawed character were the focus of fascinated attention, in both daily life and high-cultural contexts.

Among the other changes that modernity has wrought in our ways of thinking, the focus in moral philosophy or ethics has shifted—away from good and bad character and toward morally right and wrong action. Current ethical theories do indeed include something called "virtue ethics," indebted to the ancient writings in the central role assigned within it to moral character. But more prominent, indeed dominant, in the field are other familiar theories, in particular those of two types. First, there is utilitarianism, or in general what are called consequentialist theories of ethics, in which moral requirements are related to and justified in terms of their supposedly good consequences for self and others. Second, we find theories indebted to Kant's ideas about a supposed "categorical" imperative as establishing the priority of "moral reasons" (ones deriving from other people's needs and interests, together with one's own, and others', human powers and status as rational agents) over concerns (otherwise legitimate, of course) for one's own pleasure or material advantage, or simply over one's particular desires—likes and dislikes—or special relationships one may stand in of love or family, and the like.

Again, some theories give special prominence to individuals' "intuitions" about what is the right thing to do in given specific sets of circumstances, or more generally in recurrent ones. And, indeed, some current work by psychologists on the psychological basis of human morality, and its grounding in evolution, starts from the assumption that morality is nothing but a specific, widely shared, set of such intuitions about right and wrong.[4] And some philosophers, too, in what they call experimental philosophy do surveys of ordinary people to see how they report their intuitions about various "scenarios," drawing conclusions from the often surprising results about the contents and structural features of the "ordinary morality" of perceived right and wrong actions.[5] And there are many other types of theory too: "divine command" theories, and one based on so-called natural law, for example. One striking common point, though, for all these theo-

[4] See, e.g., Hauser, *Moral Minds: How Nature Designed Our Universal Sense of Right and Wrong*, also published in paperback under the title *Moral Minds: The Nature of Right and Wrong*.

[5] Joshua Knobe, Shaun Nichols, Jesse Prinz, and John Doris have done prominent work of this sort. On the severe limitations on experimental philosophy's contribution to ethical theory, see Appiah, *Experiments in Ethics*.

ries is their principal focus on the question of right versus wrong action (not, as for the ancients, good versus bad character). Contemporary theories concern, and offer different proposals about, which actions in given circumstances are right, and which wrong, and what the ultimate basis is for deciding that question. In general, then, one can say that contemporary ethical theory (i.e., what is called "normative" ethics)[6] concerns centrally and primarily right versus wrong actions, and how to explain and, perhaps, justify assigning this or that action to one or the other of those classifications. Ancient moral philosophy, by contrast, as I have said, starts from and focuses on goodness and badness of character: rightness and wrongness of action comes into ancient ethical theories, to the extent it does at all, as the expression, respectively, of good and bad character.

Nonetheless, as noted above, despite these differences between modern and ancient philosophy, and leaving aside the vast array of differing approaches to ethical questions in contemporary moral theory, as just summarized, ethics is and has always been one principal component of philosophy. That fact establishes the difference that I claimed above between philosophy as a subject of study and any of the other specializations offered in universities as undergraduate majors and for graduate training. Whether one is trying to arrive at a satisfactory result concerning the bases for deciding right and wrong, or thinking and learning about good human character, as grounded in judgments concerning what is valuable in life, moral philosophy deals with questions about how one (how anyone) ought to live. Since everyone has a life to live, this subject professes to concern everyone, and not in some incidental way, or in some way that can be left to others (to experts) to see to. Other subjects may and indeed do have much to teach that can have practical value, beyond whatever may be intrinsically interesting about the questions they take up and the ways in which they pursue them. But moral theory takes as its subject something that concerns everyone directly. (At least, it does so if it can return the investment of time and energy required.)[7] Moral philosophy, and so philosophy taken altogether, does propose itself as having a different intellectual standing, in this respect, from other subjects of study. It is inherently a practical subject, at least in part, one

[6]I set aside here "meta-ethics," concerned with the analysis of moral language and the sociology and psychology of ethics, and other studies of ethics from the outside.

[7]This does not mean that everyone, if rational, must or even ought to study moral philosophy: one might reject the idea that philosophy can achieve what it sets out to achieve, or not think it sufficiently worthwhile to spend time thinking about how to live, instead of just proceeding with doing it, in light of where one already stands in life at a time when the issue of how to live might arise. After all, life is short, while art—especially this art of living—is long.

that engages directly with universally applicable questions of how to live and what to do—whereas, it seems, none of the others has such a status of mandatory universal personal concern.[8]

Only in antiquity, however, did philosophy realize to the fullest extent all that moral philosophy's combination of theory and practice might involve. Nowadays, normative ethical theories, or normative political theories, attempt to tell us what we should do or not do, personally or politically, where questions of what we owe to one another simply by living in the world together arise (i.e., questions of moral right and wrong)—but only there. So contemporary philosophical argument, analysis, and theory, of a highly intellectual and to some extent abstract kind, offers itself as guiding us to correct practical decisions and actions, telling us about certain actions or policies as right or wrong, and on that basis as to be done or enacted, or not.

But beginning with Socrates, as I mentioned above, ancient philosophers made philosophy the, and the only authoritative, foundation and guide for the whole of human life, not just as to questions of right and wrong action—a limited part of anyone's life.[9] For these thinkers, only reason, and what reason could discover and establish as the truth, could be an ultimately acceptable basis on which to live a life—and for them philosophy is nothing more, but also nothing less, than the art or discipline that develops and perfects the human capacity of reason. No one can lead their life in a finally satisfactory way without philosophy and the understanding that ideally, anyhow—when finally successful and "complete"—only philosophy can provide.[10] And, to speak positively, when one does possess a completely grounded philosophical understanding of the full truth about how to live, by living one's life through that understanding one achieves the finally and fully satisfactory life for a human being. In this way, for these ancient Greek philosophers, philosophy itself became a way of life. Socrates himself, in setting the pattern for all later thinkers in this tradition, made the activities of philosophizing (philosophical discussion and argument) central ones of that best life: so in this tradition philosophy was indeed a subject of study, with basic principles, and theories and arguments and analyses, and refutations of tempting but erroneous views, and so on. But the whole body of knowledge that, when finally worked out fully, would constitute the finished result of such philo-

---

[8] On "literature as a way of life," see endnote 1.

[9] For Socrates, and my reasons for regarding him as the philosopher who initiated the ambition to make philosophy a way of life, see chapter 2.

[10] On the special status of ancient skeptics within the Greek philosophical tradition, see endnote 2.

sophical study, was also not only the best guide to living (by telling you how to live, and what to do or not do, in all aspects of life), but one's full grasp of that knowledge was to be the very basis on which the best life would then be led. Philosophy was not merely to guide one's life. One was to become a good person and live a good human life not as a mere result of philosophical study and by following its precepts; rather, precisely in and through one's philosophical reasoning and understanding of the world, of what is valuable in life, and of what is not so valuable, one was supposed to structure one's life continuously, as one led it, and to keep oneself motivated to live it. One was to live one's life from, not just, as one could put it, in accordance with, one's philosophy. Your philosophy did not just guide your life, it steered your life directly, from its implanted position in your mind and character. Philosophy would be the steersman of one's whole life. My aim in this book is to explain and explore this ancient tradition of philosophy as a way of life, as it was founded by Socrates and as later thinkers, adopting Socrates's ambitions for philosophy, successively applied and elaborated his conception in their own individual ways. This tradition lasted unbroken from Plato through to the eclipse of ancient pagan philosophizing and its ultimate replacement as a way of life in the Greek and Roman world by the Christian religion.

Philosophy conceived as a way of life encompassed, if not for Socrates (for reasons special to him that I will explain in the next chapter), then for his successors, the whole subject, not only philosophy's moral part. All the major thinkers in this tradition regarded the subject of philosophy in all its parts, and gave good reasons for so doing, as a completely integrated, mutually connected and supporting, single body of knowledge. The "moral" part was not something separable and could not be fully comprehended except along with the philosophy of nature (including the theory of the divine), logic, the theory of knowledge, philosophy of language, and, above all, metaphysics. So in our exploration in this book of the ancient Greek tradition of philosophy as a way of life, we will be occupied not only with ethical theories of Plato, Aristotle, the Stoics, Epicurus, the ancient Pyrrhonian skeptics, and the Platonists of the imperial period, but also with their metaphysical theories and philosophy of nature, and, though less centrally so, with their logic, epistemology, and philosophy of language, as well. We will need to grasp in each case the whole worldview proposed by each of these philosophies, as the context necessary to understand and fully ground what they propose about the best way of leading a human life. Each of the ancient ethical theories simply expresses a particular moral outlook, on the basis of an all-encompassing, particular philosophical worldview—different for each of them, in important regards. Each ethical theory presents a certain conception of the place and role in human life of the whole vast array of different sorts of goods and bads, or more generally of things of positive and negative value, that our nature as human beings makes available to us. Despite various points in common, the Platonist worldview differs from the Aristotelian, and both differ from the Stoic, from the Epicurean, and from the Skeptic. And in each case the moral outlook expressed in the respective ethical theories derives in crucial ways from that worldview—and so, those differ correspondingly, too. For that reason, it is entirely appropriate to speak, as Socrates and others in this tradition did, of philosophy, as they conceive of it, and not instead only moral philosophy or ethics, as proposing and constituting a way of life.

It is not my intention to offer an account of the ways that later philosophy—medieval, early modern, nineteenth century, twentieth century, and contemporary—differs from ancient philosophy in this regard, much less to attempt to explain such differences in historical or in substantive philosophical terms. That would require much knowledge that I do not possess. But it may help to set the ancient philosophical tradition in sharper focus if, before turning to further preliminary remarks about it, I offer some brief, admittedly speculative comments on philosophy in these different other philosophical worlds.

The late Pierre Hadot, distinguished French scholar of Plotinus and late ancient Platonism, has given a persuasive account of the transformation of philosophy from a way of life into what it is today: no more than a subject of theoretical study. Hadot argued that this transformation actually began in a decisive way not within pagan philosophy itself, but rather with transformations during late ancient times within Christianity—a major opponent of pagan philosophy at that time.[11] For Hadot, the transformation in philosophy was completed, and the new, purely theoretical conception of philosophy firmly established, in the inclusion of philosophy in the medieval universities' curriculum as just such a study. In his influential books published in English with the titles *Philosophy as a Way of Life* and *What Is Ancient Philosophy?*, and in the French articles and books from which these derive,[12] Hadot explains how the new religion of the followers of Jesus Christ, as it expanded to encompass Greeks and Romans of all

---

[11] For further discussion of Hadot's account see below, pp. 20–22.

[12] Hadot, *Philosophy as a Way of Life* presents a rearranged and expanded translation of *Exercices spirituels et philosophie antique*, and in Hadot, *What Is Ancient Philosophy?* Chase translates, with some corrections by Hadot himself, *Qu'est-ce que la philosophie antique?*

classes, itself claimed also to be a philosophy—that is, a way of life grounded in a philosophical, but also religious, worldview. Indeed, Christianity claimed to be the one true and valid philosophy—all the pagan philosophies were rejected as inadequate and false.[13] Of course, the doctrinal content of this religion-cum-philosophy, corresponding to the philosophical tenets of a straight or pure philosophy (such as Plato's or Aristotle's), had its ultimate basis not, as with the pagan philosophies, in rational insight and reasoned argument, but in the Christians' holy scriptures. It did not derive, ultimately and completely, from philosophy, allegedly giving the results of philosophical reason's own judgments. Nonetheless, if the new religion was to succeed in recruiting Greeks and Romans of the educated classes, it had to equip itself, in claiming the title of a philosophy—the true one—with philosophical elaboration of its basic claims.

Increasingly in Roman imperial times the revived Platonism of Plutarch, Numenius, Plotinus, and Plotinus's successors, came simply to be Greek philosophy: Aristotelianism, Stoicism, Epicureanism, Skepticism simply ceased, or (with Stoicism and Aristotle's philosophy) were absorbed into and reshaped as components of a comprehensive Platonism. And Platonist metaphysics, with its focus on a triple set of immaterial and intelligible world-creating divinities (the One, Intellect, and Soul), was readily co-optable by Christian thinkers for this purpose (even though the second and third gods were derived from and not co-equal, even in what came to be the Christian way, with the first).[14] So, as Hadot shows, pagan philosophy did have a large, even in many ways decisive, role to play in the elaboration of Christian theological doctrine in the early centuries of the new Church, as well as later when Aristotle became the main intellectual authority in the Western Church. But this role was a strictly subordinate one. Philosophy was recruited so as to aid in the explanation and working out of doctrines of the faith whose acceptance as true rested on their claim to have been authoritatively asserted in those scriptures as true. The Christian way of life of later antiquity and medieval times was thus grounded in the scriptures, or anyhow in the authoritative interpretations and elaborations of them recognized officially by the hierarchical Church. Thus, however much Christianity in the early centuries claimed also to be a philosophy, the Christian way of life was one of religious devotion and faithfulness in all aspects of one's life to Christ's mes-

---

[13] See *Way of Life*, esp. chaps. 4 and 11, and *Ancient Philosophy?*, chaps. 10–11 (where Hadot amends some of his former views: see p. 254, n. 3).

[14] The Platonist system was in formation already in the first century CE; it reached its (more or less) authoritative form with Plotinus (third century); on Plotinus see chapter 6.

sage of love. It was not a philosophical way of life, in the sense that the ways of life of the ancient Greek philosophies were—it was not a way of life grounded in philosophy, or rather, in reason (philosophical, argumentative, analytical, deductive reason) itself.

What then about philosophy, once Christianity at last eclipsed its rival pagan system of thought and way of life, the late Platonist one? What could remain of philosophy—this pagan invention—within the Christian community? Philosophy had claimed to be reason's authoritative cultivator and spokesman, but in the religion-dominated world of late antiquity it was deprived now of the pagan Greek philosophers' further claim that reason is authoritative for all aspects of human life. Philosophy did survive, for example, as I mentioned, in the medieval universities, but only as a handmaiden of theology in the task of explicating and supporting scripture-grounded items of belief, and the corresponding way of life. As such, it could be only a body of argument, and in general a form of discourse, that could be studied for its theoretical and clarifying interest—and needed to be, if reason were to be given its due. But philosophy could have no direct practical value for life, but only this indirect one, in supporting the theology and religiously sustained doctrine that gave life its direction. The Christian way of life was anchored elsewhere than in philosophy, directly in the scriptures, accepted as divinely inspired.

Hadot's account, just summarized, does not claim to do justice to the many currents of philosophical thought between the end of paganism and the origins of modern philosophy in the Renaissance.[15] Nonetheless, there seems no doubt that in its principal embodiments philosophy after antiquity, and ever since, is no longer widely conceived as a way of life. And Hadot's account surely does properly highlight one central component in the explanation for this state of affairs. Once, with the help of Platonist philosophy, Christianity had refashioned itself from a popular movement of the lower classes and became a formidable intellectual force that could appeal to educated people, and once philosophy became, in the Middle Ages, a purely theoretical study subordinated to religion, philosophy was surely unlikely to regain the status of an independent way of life so long as the Christian religion was dominant, as it remained for several centuries after medieval times. An enormous expansion of philosophical work began as philosophy regained a tenuous autonomy in the Renaissance, and

---

[15] Hadot acknowledges and sketches some countermovements, and counterconceptions, both in medieval philosophy and in later times, in *Ancient Philosophy?*, chap. 11.

continued as philosophy ceased to be located exclusively within universities during the seventeenth and eighteenth centuries. Given the many currents of thought this expansion generated, such large-scale cultural generalizations as I have been indulging in become too hazardous even to embark upon, and of doubtful explanatory value in seeking further light on the fate of philosophy as a way of life during the sixteenth to nineteenth centuries. If one looks within philosophy itself, however, that is, into the internal and substantive development of philosophical ideas over this time, one might be able to cast some useful light. To be sure, the very great complexity and the play of strongly contrasting, even contradictory, ideas on fundamental principles that characterize modern philosophy throughout its history leave room for important exceptions to any generalization one might hazard. Still, there are three closely connected points I wish to make here.

First, the major ancient philosophers from Socrates onward, without exception, share one fundamental assumption that post-Renaissance philosophy, continuing to the current day, came to reject. At any rate, even if some philosophers accept a version of this assumption, in modern and contemporary philosophy it does not figure as any sort of basic principle for ethical analysis, as it did for the ancients. Socrates's philosophical quest, the essential forerunner in this regard of all later Greek philosophy, was founded on the assumption about human reason—the power of inquiring into and recognizing truth as such—that it is also, psychologically speaking, a power of motivation for action.[16] Those beings that possess this power are moved simply by it (or by themselves through that power) to seek to know, and to try to discover truths. Moreover, where these truths concern what is good, or in general of value, for themselves, those who possess this power are moved by it to obtain and make value-directed use of things that they recognize in their own thinking, for reasons that they give to themselves implicitly or explicitly, to be good for them. They may make mistakes in their reasoning and come to hold something to be good for them that is not good in fact. But whatever the quality of their reasoning may be, reason, by its very nature, is, for all the Greek philosophers, such a motivating force in any human being's life. As

---

[16] The "British moralists" Samuel Clarke (d. 1729) and Richard Price (d. 1791) in England, as well as Kant in Germany (d. 1804) and Thomas Reid in Scotland (d. 1796), are among the modern philosophers who also assign motivational force to the deliverances of reason. So far as I am aware, however, none of them see Socrates, or the ancients in general, as their forerunners in this, nor do they, in the manner of the ancients as detailed below, connect this part of their theories of human motivation with both theories about the sole authority of philosophical reason for the establishment of truth in practical matters, and a conception of the overriding motivational power of philosophically grounded knowledge.

we will see in subsequent chapters, some of these philosophers, unlike Socrates, adopt analyses of human psychology that recognize other internal sources of motivation in the same sense—additional powers within the human psyche with which we can move ourselves toward action, independently from reason and even in opposition to the impulses generated by our own reasoned judgments of value. And all these philosophers are clear in recognizing that sometimes what one may hold, for reasons one takes as valid (rightly or wrongly), to be the best thing to do, is not what one actually does: various psychological mechanisms, depending on further details of their theories about the human psyche, are invoked to show how this possibility can be realized in a human life, and is depressingly often realized in fact. We will explore these details of theory at many points in this book. For the moment we can leave such differences to one side, since they do not affect the general point, relating to this whole philosophical tradition, which I want to emphasize now: that for the whole tradition of Greek ethical philosophy the capacity for reasoning does have an inherent power of moving us to action.

It is by adopting this assumption that the ancient philosophers are able to make plausible, and to work out, in their different theoretical constructions, their conceptions of philosophy as a way of life. For they all share a second fundamental view. They think that philosophy, in being the pursuit of wisdom and ultimate truth, is the intellectual accomplishment (in ancient terms the "art" or the form of knowledge)—the only one—whereby reason is made perfect.[17] As such, it is the final and sole authority as to what really is true. Accordingly, given the motivational force belonging to reason, once those who pursue philosophy have perfected their power of reason by coming to possess a reasoned, articulated philosophical understanding of, among other things, everything of value in a human life, they will be moved, simply by that knowledge, toward living in such a way as to realize in their life that correct scheme of values. But merely being motivated to live in a certain way, and being motivated for that by one's philosophical knowledge of values, is not sufficient to make one's philosophy one's

---

[17] As often, it is the Stoics who officially formulate this idea, basic to the whole Socratic tradition of ancient philosophy during the classical and later periods. Clement of Alexandria, a second to third century CE Christian opponent of pagan philosophy, quotes the following Stoic definitional account of philosophy: it is "the devoted practice of correctness in reasoning" (ἐπιτήδευσις λόγου ὀρθότητος) (see J. von Arnim, *Stoicorum Veterum Fragmenta*, vol. 3, fragment 293). The same definition occurs again in a text preserved on a papyrus from Herculaneum that von Arnim argued ("Über Einen Stoischen Papyrus") might be due to Chrysippus himself (vol. 2.131, p. 41, lines 27–29). (Hereafter I cite the von Arnim collection with the abbreviation *SVF*.)

actual way of life. It must not merely provide an authoritative guide for it that might nonetheless not always be followed. If one's philosophy is to be lived, it must function, as I put it above, as precisely that from, as well as on, which one lives. By this I mean that one's philosophical thought or understanding must on its own, and directly, provide the motivation (or an essential and indispensable part of it) on which one actually lives one's life in just the way that one does. Hence, if one's philosophy is to be one's way of life, those who possess the full knowledge that philosophy promises must be moved simply by having that knowledge and through its power (or rather, through the power of their reason so equipped) to live consistently on its basis. Thereby, the ancients think, they will achieve the human good.[18] This achievement is due to philosophy itself, and, indeed, for the ancients, it is unachievable without philosophy.[19]

We are thus led to recognize a third basic principle that I believe the Greek philosophers shared—and one to which, again, as I will suggest below, modern and contemporary philosophers do not subscribe. The character Socrates in Plato's dialogue *Protagoras* asserts this principle when he speaks of the psychologically decisive power of knowledge. In his extended debate with Protagoras over the possibility of acting against one's better judgment, Socrates lays out his own position on one crucial aspect of this issue: "[K]nowledge," he says, "is a fine thing, capable of ruling a person, and if someone were to know what is good and bad, then he would not be forced by anything to act otherwise than knowledge dictates."[20] A little later in the dialogue Socrates says of this knowledge that "by

---

[18] As Chrysippus, the greatest theorist among the Stoics, said, the "goal of philosophy is living in agreement with nature" (ὁμολογουμένως τῇ φύσει ζῆν), which is to say "happily," since this phrase expresses the Stoic principle that the human highest good or happiness consists in living consistently throughout one's adult life in just that way (*SVF* 3.5). (We will examine below, in chapter 4, how this formulation is to be understood.) The consequence is that for the Stoics, and indeed for the whole of this tradition, philosophy itself has as its inherent and definitory aim to achieve for us the highest human good, or happiness.

[19] It is this strong commitment of the ancient philosophers to the claim that philosophy itself is not only necessary for the full possession of the human virtues, and through that for happiness, but also sufficient for virtue and happiness, that most sharply marks ancient philosophy off from modern and contemporary philosophy. Perhaps as inheritors of the Christian idea that all human beings are equally children of God, the canonical philosophers of our modern tradition all hold that the knowledge necessary for a morally good life (one in which, as for Kant, one is at least deserving of happiness) is available to all of us, without any elitist philosophical study being at all necessary. And, as for sufficiency for happiness, as just indicated, not only Kant but the basic thrust of the whole modern tradition are strongly against any such idea. These commitments survive in the contemporary context, though for the most part without any close tie to ideas derived from Christianity.

[20] *Protagoras* 352c. (Strictly speaking, Socrates does not assert, but rather asks Protagoras whether he accepts, this view—but he goes on to confirm explicitly the impression he gives here that this is his own view, too.)

showing us the truth, it would give us peace of mind firmly rooted in the truth and would save our life."[21] So we can give this Socratic principle of the power of knowledge the alternative and equivalent title of the power of truth—that is, the power that possessing the truth through knowledge gives a person, with the effect that he or she is completely safe from ever doing any wrong thing, and therefore inevitably lives a completely secure, consistently and thoroughly good life. Now, in Socrates's case, this principle is accompanied by a number of specific further philosophical views, some of them peculiar to him within ancient philosophy and in any event by no means shared by all his successors. Yet, as we will see in subsequent chapters of this book, all these successors show themselves, upon examination of their philosophies, to adhere to some version or other of this principle of the power of truth and knowledge, one framed in terms of their own detailed, overall philosophy.

It follows from Socrates's commitment to the power of truth that he thinks there is only one set of philosophical views that, constituting knowledge, will save our lives. Other views of other philosophers definitely will not save anyone, he must think; any other philosophy will not possess this power, since power belongs not to views or opinions as such about what is good and bad, but only to knowledge and truth. It may even be that Socrates, and his successors, might hold that if one's philosophical views do not constitute, or are not fully grounded in, the truth, then there is no guarantee at all that one will live fully in accord with them, or, as I have put it, from them. The weakness of one's views, in terms of falsehood or philosophical inadequacy, might render them such that no one could stick to them, no one could fail to waver in their commitment, and to harbor doubts that might rise up on occasion to prevent them from living fully and consistently from that philosophy. On the other hand, each of our philosophers, and all the full adherents of their philosophies, hold that their philosophical views do rest upon and do express the truth. Even if they may be mistaken (and at least some of them must be, since these philosophies are in conflict at many points), they are fully entitled to adopt and put forward their philosophies, in light of the fully articulated and defended analyses and arguments on which they rest them, as being fully grounded in reason. So they can hold that by living from the Stoic, or the Epicurean, or the Platonist or Aristotelian philosophy, they are living the life of perfected reason—and so are living happy and completely and unassailably good lives.

---

[21] *Protagoras* 356e. On these Socratic ideas, see further section 2.2.

I suggest that modern philosophy and contemporary philosophy lack the ancient conception of philosophy as a way of life because these three large-scale, interconnected assumptions of the ancients have not been part of the accepted intellectual landscape for philosophical inquiry at any time since the Renaissance (nor, for that matter, in medieval philosophy). The ancients assume a seamless connection between philosophical views, or in general philosophical convictions, about what is good and bad for a human being, and the actions—as well as the life made up of those actions—of anyone who holds those views. The classical philosophers of the modern tradition, and also contemporary philosophy, have developed theories of human motivation that greatly complicate any connection there might be between one's philosophical views on life and how it is best led, or on what is right and wrong to do, and one's actual way of living and one's actions. The result is that even if moral philosophy in modern and contemporary terms could be taken to present itself as a guide to a good life and to right action, by working out theories about these matters and presenting them as true, and therefore to be followed, there remains a psychological gap to be bridged. The question remains how to link these philosophical views to whatever it is in one's psyche from which actual felt preferences and actual decision making derive. Philosophy alone—reasoned understanding of practical truths—does not suffice, in the modern and contemporary philosophical climate, as it did in the ancient one.

To this one could add that philosophers in antiquity, after Socrates, as I have emphasized, were able to conceive and present the whole of their philosophies, and not merely some separate ethical part, as not only guides to life but ideas from which a life might be led, by contributing in some important way to what motivatingly steers it. As I have said, the ancient philosophies insisted on the complete unification and interlocking, mutually self-supporting, character of ethics, physics, and dialectic (or however else one might divide up the totality of philosophical discourse). That, too, is a feature of ancient philosophy that is lacking, certainly, in contemporary philosophy, and arguably in most of post-Renaissance philosophy through the nineteenth century as well.[22] Nowadays

[22] Here too there are exceptions: certainly both Spinoza and Kant have a strongly unified set of views linking their moral philosophies very closely to their theories of metaphysics and epistemology, and politics too. Descartes, as well, and even John Stuart Mill, not to mention Hegel, are strongly systematic thinkers whose views across the whole spectrum of philosophical topics form a unity. Others could be mentioned, also. Nonetheless, with the sole exception of Spinoza, it seems that for all these thinkers their moral philosophies were meant to stand on their own, in the sense that you could fully comprehend their first principles as well as the conclusions drawn from them without venturing into metaphysical or other

people work on logic or metaphysics or epistemology or philosophy of language, taking up the questions that interest them in isolation, or at any rate with no concern to integrate their answers to them with answers to a full range of other contemporarily pressing philosophical issues. One can hold interesting and engaging views on the metaphysics of personal identity or the metaphysical analysis of physical objects, or adopt a fallibilist epistemological analysis and, again, a Humean theory of motivation, without seeing any necessary connections among any of these, or any significant consequences for normative ethics. Or so it appears to me, from where I sit and work as a philosopher concerned to understand the history of ancient philosophy. Hence, even if moral philosophy nowadays might be approached and presented as offering guidance for life, one cannot think of philosophy as a whole as having even that function. Most of philosophy today is truly an exclusively theoretical discourse, with no direct connections to the conduct of one's life.[23]

What then is someone to do who comes to academic, seriously argumentative philosophy with the idea that it is a uniquely vital subject, one that, if one succeeds in it, will alter one's life directly for the better? There seems to be no viable alternative except to study ancient philosophy—or rather, the ancient philosophies, in the plural—in the spirit in which they were written, that is, with a view to one's own self-improvement. As for those governing philosophical assumptions that, as I have suggested, made ancient philosophy conceived as a way of life possible, maybe they are actually true, even though they are not made part of contemporary approaches to ethics. Many considerations favor them, all emphasized by philosophers in the ancient tradition, and these may still have some force with us, if we consider the matter carefully. At any rate, they may be plausible enough to encourage someone brought up in our modern intellectual milieu to follow out, and weigh for the constitution of one's own life, the varied philosophical theories, in all areas of philosophy, that the ancient philosophers constructed on the basis of them. As I turn now to make some further preliminary remarks about how we should understand ancient philosophies as ways of life, and in subsequent chapters, that is what I invite the reader to do.

---

areas of their thought. For the ancients, as I argue below, the connection from moral theory to metaphysics and physical theory, as well as logic and epistemology, was such that one cannot fully grasp either its first principles or conclusions in separation from these other subjects.

[23] I should emphasize that I am speaking here of recent and contemporary philosophy. In the tradition of modern philosophy one could see Spinoza as a philosopher who like the ancients presented his work as something to be lived as well as grasped intellectually, or lived when and because it was understood intellectually; it was not something purely theoretical.

1.2. What It Means to Live a Philosophy

In speaking of ancient philosophy I have been assuming that for the ancients with whom I am concerned, exactly as with us, the essential core of philosophy is a certain, specifically and recognizably philosophical, style of logical, reasoned argument and analysis. Anyone who has read any philosophy at all is familiar with this style, whether it takes the form we find in the question-and-answer dialectic of the character Socrates in Plato's Socratic dialogues, or in the medieval disputation, or in Hegel's elaborations of his system of Absolute Idealism, or, again, in the writings of a contemporary analytic philosopher. The idea of philosophy as constituted essentially by devotion to rigorous, sensitively logical and disciplined thought, in pursuit of a philosophically grounded, ultimate truth about the world and our place in it, goes back, in fact, to Plato.[24] And Plato, in his dramatic presentations of Socratic thought, holds Socrates up as its devoted exemplar. This is not to say that there were no philosophers, in this Platonic sense, before Socrates (one may think of Parmenides, or Heraclitus, or Anaxagoras and Empedocles as instances). But, if we follow Aristotle, who characterizes all the "early" philosophers as "lisping" in their thinking, we can think of these predecessors of Socrates as saying things without paying serious enough attention to what the things they say mean, to the philosophical implications and bearings of what they seem to announce as philosophical theses of theirs, so as even to make coherent sense—as Aristotle thinks philosophers beginning with Socrates and Plato all tried to do quite self-consciously.[25]

In considering the ancient view of philosophy as a way of life, we must bear constantly in mind what this thing, philosophy, on which one is to hang one's life, is supposed to be. One must take with utmost seriousness that what the ancient philosophers, following Socrates's innovative lead, are proposing is that we live our lives from some set of argued through, rationally worked out, rationally grasped, and rationally defended, reasoned ideas about the world and one's own place within it. They propose that we live from these ideas precisely on the basis of just that reasoned understanding. A philosophical way of life is therefore in fundamental ways quite a different thing from any religious way of life. This is so whether we take as our paradigm of religion contemporary Christianity and other contemporary religions, or the ancient civic religion of classical Greece,

---

[24] On Plato as origin of this restricted conception of "philosophy" (φιλοσοφία), see endnote 3.

[25] See Aristotle, *Metaphysics* I, 985a21–10 and 993a15–25. On early philosophy's "lisping" see Cooper, "*Metaphysics* A 10: Conclusion—and Retrospect," pp. 15–18.

whether we think of it as enriched with mystery cults or not. The key here is the idea of reason—an idea, if not quite introduced, then purified by philosophical inquiry beginning in pre-Socratic times, and crystallized in the work of Socrates and Plato. To live a life of philosophy is to live committed to following philosophical reason wherever it may lead. The promise is that by doing so—but only by doing so—one will achieve the best possible human life. But, given what reason—philosophical reason—is, this promise can be made good only through one's own deep and complete understanding of the reasons why the way one is living is best.[26] In leading such a life you cannot, as in leading their lives from religious conviction people can and do, accept what any text that you regard as authoritative tells you about how to live, just because you regard it as sacred. That is so even if you think you have excellent reasons for assigning authority to that text, or to that tradition if tradition takes the place for you of a text. If you follow a text at all it is because of your independent rational assessment of the truth of what it recommends. You must understand everything for yourself. A mere feeling of conviction that some way of living is the right one, induced for example through prayer or through a sense of having a personal relationship with a higher than human power, will not do. These characteristics of a religious way of life—living on the basis of a sacred text or tradition, validation through an intense personal feeling—distinguish that way of life from the philosophical one.

To be a philosopher in this ancient tradition, then, is to be fundamentally committed to the use of one's own capacity for reasoning in living one's life: the philosophical life is essentially simply a life led on that basis. This is the basic commitment that every true and full philosopher made in adopting philosophy—in choosing to be a philosopher—whatever ancient school they belonged to. Pierre Hadot, whose writings on ancient philosophy as a way of life are fundamental reading on this subject, speaks of an "existential option" as needed when anyone becomes personally aligned with the doctrines of any specific school.[27] But that is incorrect. Any specific philosophical views and orientations

---

[26] I speak here of the views of the "mainline" philosophies (of Socrates, Plato, Aristotle, the Stoics, and Plotinus and his successor late Platonists): Epicurus and the Pyrrhonian skeptics (see chapter 5), in their different ways, do not require so extensive a grasp of the reasons why the Epicurean or skeptic way of life is the best. Nonetheless Epicureans and skeptics lead their life on what they present to themselves as a *rationally* worked out grasp of the truth about human nature and human values, or, in the skeptic's case, on an appropriately qualified commitment to such reasoning.

[27] On "existential choices" or "options" see Hadot, *Ancient Philosophy?*, pp. 102, 103, 129, 132, 176, etc. Hadot begins to use this terminology only with his chapter on "The Hellenistic Schools," but he makes it clear from the first occasion (p. 102) that he thinks that Socratic philosophizing, and Plato's and Aristotle's schools too, were characterized by such a fundamental option or choice. However, there is no reason

that might characterize an ancient philosopher (as a Platonist or Aristotelian, or Stoic or Epicurean or Pyrrhonian skeptic) do not result from anything "existential." They result simply from coming to accept different ideas, all of them supported by philosophical reasoning in pursuit of the truth, that these philosophical schools might put forward about what, if one does use one's powers of reasoning fully and correctly, one must hold about values and actions. One's "option" for any one of these philosophies in particular, far-reaching as the consequences might be for one's way of life, does not deserve to be called an "existential" one. The only existential option involved is the basic commitment to being a philosopher, to living on the basis of philosophical reason. The choice to be an Epicurean, or a Stoic, for example, depends—certainly, by the standards of these philosophical movements themselves, it ought to depend—on rational arguments in favor of the fundamental principles of the philosophical school in question. It is crucial for a correct understanding of what ancient philosophy is, or was, that one sees the central force of the fundamental commitment to living a life on the basis of philosophical reason. It is this that set philosophers off as a single group from the rest of the population.

Pagan Greek philosophy was continuously practiced for a very long time, of course—more than a thousand years. Philosophy itself, as well as the rest of ancient culture, underwent progressive changes over these centuries, many of them momentous in their proportions. We will see, however, in investigating the major ancient philosophies in subsequent chapters of this book, that the pagan philosophers remained committed to this central idea of philosophical reason, and to its power to generate and shape the best possible life for a human being. Only in late antiquity—long after the heyday of Greek philosophy, in classical and Hellenistic times (fifth to mid-first centuries BCE)—did the way of life of philosophy begin to share the features of a religious way of life that I have just drawn attention to. This is only one part of what Hadot has incisively and illuminatingly described as the progressive mutual contamination of pagan philosophy and the Christian religion, beginning roughly in the second century CE.[28] One aspect of this contamination is the presence in late ancient philosophy and reli-

---

to think any ancient philosopher made a choice first to be a Stoic and live a Stoic life, or any other specific philosophical life. For one thing, many of them studied at more than one of the Athenian schools, simultaneously or in sequence, before finally settling in one philosophical milieu or another. First came the decision to live a philosophical life (perhaps, of course, under the influence of the attractions of some particular version of it)—to live according to reason. Even if at the same time one decided to live as a Stoic or an Epicurean or a Platonist, that specific choice is logically subsequent.

[28] See "La fin du paganisme," in his *Études de philosophie ancienne*, pp. 341–74, esp. pp. 369ff.

gion—indeed the very conception—of those "spiritual exercises" that loom so large and strikingly in Hadot's own account of ancient philosophy as a way of life, and which he claims belonged to it from the beginning, in Parmenides and other philosophers before even the time of Socrates, and which allow him to assimilate it to Michel Foucault's ideas about "the care of the self." The earliest evidence Hadot can cite in ancient philosophy for the presence of such exercises—his name for them seems to derive from St. Ignatius Loyola's sixteenth century handbook *Exercitia Spiritualia*, urging meditations on sin and on Christ's life and passion for the sake of one's spiritual improvement as a Christian—is in Seneca, in the first century CE.[29] In one passage of his *On Anger* Seneca cites the nightly practice of self-examination on one's day's behavior as something particular to a certain Sextius, a now-obscure Roman teacher of philosophy at Rome in the reign of Augustus. This citation is evidence of the novelty of such a practice at Seneca's time. So even if Seneca does refer to the daily bedtime examination of conscience with approval, saying that he adopts it himself, the passage counts not in favor of, but against, Hadot's idea that such practices (or any associated one of "spiritual strengthening") were common or standard even in the Hellenistic schools, much less in ancient philosophy as a whole, from Socrates's time or even earlier.[30]

Moreover, one of the new features of life in late ancient times to which Hadot points, as making possible the contamination of which he speaks, is what he calls a "psychological phenomenon" increasingly widespread among intellectuals of all stripes from perhaps the second century onward, as Christianity spread from its original home among uneducated Jews to the upper classes everywhere both in the Greek-speaking East and in Rome and the Latin West. This is a new conception of one's individual self-consciousness—the "I" at the center of one's experiences that people began to worry about—as constituting in some way one's very self, the *person* that one is, the subject of one's actions. Long before this conception began to show itself, the earlier ancient philosophers had well-developed conceptions of individual persons, with "selves" as the object of their fundamental and regulatory practical concern. The way of life of philosophy for these earlier, as well as all later, ancient philosophies was a life for individuals, conceiving themselves as such, and seeking the best life possible for themselves individually, as embedded in a rich and full physical and social life. In fact, a self might, as for

[29] For more on Hadot's ideas about "spiritual exercises," see endnote 4.

[30] For a discussion of "spiritual exercises" versus philosophy as ways of self-transformation, see endnote 5.

the Stoics, be a mind and nothing but—but such a mind was conceived unproblematically as part of the natural world. In short, no philosopher until the late
Platonists conceived of a person's bare *consciousness*—the "I" at its center—as
such a self, as the object of fundamental concern, the thing whose life was in
question when one sought to live the best life possible for oneself. And in conceiving of consciousness in this way these philosophers were integrating into the
philosophical tradition to which they belonged—the pagan one, deriving from
Plato—an idea about the self that lay at the base also of Christianity, as it became
transformed from a local Jewish cult in the late first century CE into a world religion by the end of antiquity. (We will consider in chapter 6 the intricate maneu-
vers of interpretation by which Plotinus was able to find this conception already
fully present in Plato's works, especially or most prominently, for Plotinus, in the
Phaedo.)

Hadot acutely describes how this new understanding of the self carried with
it a psychological crisis that characterized this whole epoch—a "spiritual tension, an anxiety," even a "nervous depression."[31] What is the origin of this mysterious thing, this "I" of consciousness, itself no part of the natural world, the
world we learn about in significant measure through the use of our senses?
Where did it come from? What is its destiny? That is to say, what is one's own
origin and destiny? Thus arose, for those who became Christians as well as for
those who became Platonists, not only an anxious concern about our origin and
ultimate destiny, but a deep-seated feeling of not belonging to the natural world,
not being at home in it, of being an alien interloper. And this led to an intense
need to find personal salvation—not the saving of our lives that Socrates speaks
of in the passage of the *Protagoras* I have cited, which we achieve by ensuring that
we live and act well, but the salvation of our very selves, first of all, from the in-
tolerable anxiety caused in us by this way of conceiving who or what we are.
Christianity offered one resolution, Platonism another. I will explore these issues
further in chapter 6.

For now, it is enough to say that along with the rapprochement of these two
spiritual rivals went a change in the way the life of philosophy itself came to be
conceived. The sharp separation ceased between, on the one hand, the life of
philosophy as grounded in an individual's personal grasp, through fully articulated reasoning and argument, of the true reasons why a certain way of life was
best, and, on the other hand, a religious life grounded in sacred texts and vali-

---

[31] See "Fin," 346ff.

dated through intense feelings of conviction generated in prayer or in the sense of having a personal relationship to a higher power. Those nonrational practices that Hadot describes as "spiritual exercises"—meditation, self-exhortation, memorization, and recitation to oneself of bits of sacred text, causing in oneself devoted prayerful or prayer-like states of consciousness and mystical moments—had, and could have, at most a secondary and very derivative function in the philosophical life during the heyday of ancient philosophy. The promise of a happy, fully good life that philosophy held out required not only the achievement of that full personal understanding but the use of it as the ultimate basis from which all the actions of one's life themselves directly derived. But once the late Platonist philosophers adopted this conception of a human consciousness as a self, an "I," and conceived of that as what our life derives from, nothing was easier than to suppose that, in order to improve oneself and so one's life, what one really needed to do—more than to improve one's grasp on reasons for acting—was to turn inward, to focus on and attempt to purify, and thereby strengthen, that consciousness. So spiritual exercises came to occupy a more central place in the way of life of philosophy.

Accordingly, in the successive chapters of this book, as I discuss the Socratic, Aristotelian, Stoic, Epicurean, and Pyrrhonian skeptic ways of life, I will leave aside altogether any consideration of spiritual exercises as forming part of those lives. (It is in fact only in the Epicurean life that anything of that kind has a place, and that is for reasons deriving from specific philosophical views of Epicurus, primarily his empiricist account of what knowledge and understanding requires and is.)[32] I limit myself to examining those philosophies as philosophies, that is, as systems of philosophical thought. Only when I come, in the last chapter, to the philosophy of Plotinus will I, in addition to examining it as such a system of thought, make room for any consideration of the spiritual exercises that are so emphasized in Hadot's conception of ancient philosophy. Even with Plotinus it will be crucial to see that and how specific philosophical theories he adopts, explaining and arguing philosophically for them, make it possible for such exercises to become central or essential parts of the Platonist philosophical life. If his Platonist successors, of the fourth through sixth centuries (Iamblichus and Proclus and their successors), import into philosophy and into the philosophical life further aspects of late ancient Christian and pagan religion, that is further evidence of the contamination of philosophy by religion of which Hadot speaks. By their

---

[32] See section 5.4.

time, the assimilation of philosophy to religion, and of the Christian religion to philosophy, is reaching its final point—the total extinction of philosophy as an independent force in the life of late antiquity. Once pagan philosophy has transformed itself in these ways into something not easily distinguishable from a religion, it no longer has a reason to exist as an alternative to Christianity.

CHAPTER 2

The Socratic Way of Life

2.1. Ancient Philosophy as Intellectual Pursuit vs. as Way of Life

Not everyone in antiquity whom we (and the ancients themselves) classify as philosophers conceived of their work as aimed at providing them, or any "disciples," with a whole way of life. Vast numbers of philosophical writings from all periods, beginning with the sixth century BCE, when the first philosophers lived, had effectively been lost already by the last years of the Roman Empire. Hence many authors mentioned in ancient writings that have come down to us have been little more than names for more than a millennium. Nonetheless, for many philosophers of almost all periods of antiquity we have no evidence to suggest that their philosophy was considered as offering, or being, a way of life.[1] Their work seems to have been motivated by nothing more than what motivates most philosophers nowadays. They seem to have found philosophical ways of thinking, and the questions philosophy addresses, simply interesting, even engrossing. They enjoyed logical analysis and argument, and were fascinated by logic and paradox, as philosophers of all ages have always been. They found some of the questions of philosophical debate at their time fascinating and worth thinking about, for their intrinsic intellectual value. In their approach to their work they did not differ from such other intellectuals of their time as mathema-

---

[1] I say "almost all" because as later antiquity advanced and philosophy came to be limited to Platonist philosophy, it does seem that all those pagans who claimed to be philosophers and were recognized as such did regard and treat their philosophy as a way of life; they were motivated in their philosophical work by the urge to save their souls thereby (see section 1.2). I discuss these developments in chapter 6.

ticians or medical researchers, even if we, and they, might agree that those other sorts of work could have more immediate practical applications and so were less purely theoretical than theirs. Also, of course, they found doing philosophy rewarding: they seemed to be good at it, and others' reactions to their work confirmed them in this impression.

Consider the very earliest philosophers we hear of, such as Anaximander or Anaximenes, or somewhat later ones such as Parmenides or Zeno of Elea, or, later still, Anaxagoras or Diogenes of Apollonia, or even Democritus (a slightly younger contemporary of Socrates). We read about their philosophical views, and find quotations from their work as well, in many surviving authors (as far back as Plato). We cannot responsibly read back onto them the ambitions for philosophy as guide, and unifying component, of a good life that we do find already clearly articulated in the work of Socrates (d. 399) and exemplified in his own life (at least, as that is reported to us by Plato and others who knew him personally). You could not make a life from thinking what Anaximander or Anaximenes did about the origins and current composition of the natural world, or about the orderly processes by which the seasons succeed one another and the world order holds together. Nor could you use for that purpose the metaphysical reflections of Parmenides, through which he concluded that the real world is in fact quite different from how these earliest philosophers (and ancient and modern common sense, too) think it is—and then went on to propose a set of first principles of his own as what control these cosmic appearances. Such abstruse matters of high physical and cosmic theory do not and could not define for them, or any followers they might have had, any conception of how to live a full human life. And there is no chance at all that, unbeknownst to us, any of them extended their physical and metaphysical theories into additional, related, ones about such matters of human concern. Aristotle and later writers who had available to them these philosophers' writings and traditions about their teaching, would have told us about these, if they had. With only the exception of Democritus, the philosophers I have mentioned had no theories, or even any developed philosophical conceptions, about what is good for a human being—about what is good, or bad, in a human life and why it is good or bad.[2] Apart from their fascination with philosophical thinking and their striving for recognition, or even fame, in that connection, whatever gave structure to their lives lay elsewhere. The range of their philosophical thought was simply too limited to offer

---

[2] I return to Democritus below (p. 31), where I explain how his philosophy too fails to be conceived as a way of life.

guidance, and too distant from any concern for questions about how to live a human life.[3]

Even in post-Socratic times not all interest in philosophy and not all philosophical teaching or writing were grounded in ideas about philosophy as a way of life. This is true even of some of those who turned to philosophy under Socrates's influence.[4] One fellow devotee with Plato of Socrates in Socrates's last years, Euclides, wrote Socratic dialogues similar in form to Plato's. He also taught philosophy in his native city of Megara. But the tiny amount we are told about Euclides's philosophical views leaves the strong impression that he acquired from Socrates an interest in argumentation and analysis concerning ethical and other questions of philosophy, but no devotion to philosophy as a way of life.[5] At any rate, among the many aspiring philosophers who, we are told, went to Megara to hear Euclides was Euboulides, the famous originator of the well-known Liar and Sorites Paradoxes that engage logicians to this day, as well as other paradoxes (the Horned One, the Veiled Figure, the Bald Man, etc.) that were also much studied by subsequent ancient philosophers, including most notably by the Stoic Chrysippus in developing the first complete system of propositional logic.[6] Euboulides's successors in the study of logic included Diodorus Cronus (creator of the famous "Master Argument" that Aristotle and Chrysippus and others were much occupied with in their work on the logic and metaphysics of possibility) and Philo ("the Dialectician"), who proposed an analysis of the truth conditions of "if . . . then . . ." statements, in relation to the truth or falsehood of the two component propositions. This preoccupation by numerous philosophers of the fourth century (contemporaries, near enough, of Aristotle)—an exclusive one, so far as we are told—with logic and philosophy of language matches the limited scope of the work of the pre-Socratics noted above. It was left to Chrysippus, in

[3] Nor could the philosophers mentioned have thrown themselves into physical, cosmic, and metaphysical philosophy as a way to personal salvation, with the idea that their self was a bare consciousness that could be purified and saved through concentrated intellectual thought. No one before late antiquity had any such idea about their own identity, and no one before then had developed theories of salvation on that basis. See section 1.2. (For Pythagoras and Empedocles, see below, pp. 31–32.)

[4] For an account of the "Socratics" who wrote dialogues see K. Döring, "The Students of Socrates," pp. 24–47.

[5] On Euclides, see Diogenes Laertius, *Lives of Eminent Philosophers* 2.106–112. The followers of Socrates also included the philosopher Antisthenes (see Diog. Laert. 6.1–21), about whom see below, section 2.5.

[6] Diogenes says that these and all Euclides's followers, together with their own successors, constituted a distinctive set of "Megarian" philosophers (a Megarian "school"). But he also reports that, in particular, Euboulides and his own successors early acquired an additional, separate designation as the "Dialectical" (i.e., "logician") philosophers.

taking up these "Dialectical Philosophers'" logical inquiries and pursuing further their analyses of those paradoxes, to integrate their specialties of logic, philosophy of language, and epistemology into a complete philosophical system
that did present itself as defining and directly supporting a total way of life.[7]

Even much later, after the tradition of philosophy as a way of life had long
been well established, some who valued philosophy highly, studied it assiduously, and recommended it to others, did not approach the subject in that spirit.
Take, for example, the medical writer Galen, living in the second half of the second century CE. Galen maintained, in the title of one of his writings as well as at
many places in his works, that *The Best Doctor Is Also a Philosopher*. Similarly,
Cicero (in the mid-first century BCE) held that eloquence, the orator's ultimate
accomplishment, was unattainable without a close and extensive study of philosophy, especially moral philosophy.[8] Both authors give remarkably similar accounts of the ways in which knowledge of philosophy contributes to excellence
in their respective professions. Both maintain that all three of the then recognized "parts" of philosophy (dialectic, physical theory, ethics) must be thoroughly mastered.[9] Moreover, Galen himself wrote a number of works specifically
of philosophy (many of which have not survived), some in each of the three traditional areas. And Cicero, of course, is well known for his Latin philosophical
writings, again in each of the three areas.

But both for Cicero and for Galen the interest in philosophy, and what they
recommend it to their professional colleagues (and others) for, is of a strictly
theoretical kind. Knowing philosophy is needed for pursuing a particular career
successfully—that of physician, or orator in the law-courts and speaker and

---

[7] On Chrysippus, see below chapter 4.

[8] This is a recurrent theme in all Cicero's works of oratorical theory; see, e.g., *Orator* 14–16. Cicero
repeatedly insisted (see, e.g., *Orator* 12) that he himself owed his skill in public speaking and the law courts
most of all to his philosophical studies in the skeptical Academy at Athens, the "school" of philosophy
that he thought most suited for ambitious members of the Roman ruling class to devote themselves to;
since Academics trained their pupils in negative examination and debate concerning the positive philosophical theories of other philosophers (Stoics and Epicureans, primarily), a student necessarily learned,
from a deeply critical perspective, the whole prior Greek philosophical tradition.

[9] Compare Cicero *Orator* 15–16 and *On the Making of an Orator* (*De oratore*) III 55 with Galen, *Doctrines* sec. 3. Elsewhere Galen makes one exception to this requirement: metaphysical questions, for example concerning the soul (whether it is an immaterial substance, existing independently from the body,
and immortal—as his generally favored Platonist orientation in philosophy maintained). About these
questions he always expresses himself as unable to reach a decision; moreover, nothing in the knowledge
and practice of medicine requires taking any position on such matters. Knowledge of logic (dialectic) and
logical theory and knowledge of general physical theory as well as human psychology, as well as of ethics,
are another matter, and in Galen's opinion these are indispensable for an adequate grasp of medical theory
and practice.

writer in public life generally—and for doing the good for others and for the larger community that that career makes possible. And it is intellectually reward-ing besides. There is no thought in either author of learning philosophy in order to make from it a way of life. Even Cicero's main, comprehensive work of moral philosophy, *On Moral Ends*, is presented in a theoretical, dialectical spirit, in which he examines and debates which set of philosophical views seems the most acceptable, rationally and morally. He conducts his inquiry from the point of view, to which he has already become morally committed in advance of all philo-sophical study, of an upstanding, serious, ambitious Roman aristocrat. And he assumes a reader like himself in this respect. Cicero is far from wanting himself, or his son to whom he addresses one of his writings in ethics, *On Duties*, or any of his other Roman readers, to use any of the philosophies he examines, or any other philosophy, for living their life.[10] It seems highly likely that even many Stoic and Aristotelian philosophers, during the long lives of these philosophies in antiquity—not to mention many of their pupils—approached philosophy in this same spirit of intellectual adventure, with no idea of its use as a way of life.[11] And they did this despite the fact that the "founders" of these philosophies actu-ally present them in that life-guiding guise. Perhaps the important first century BCE philosopher Posidonius was such a Stoic. It seems that also Alexander of Aphrodisias, the famous Aristotelian philosopher and commentator on Aristo-tle of the late second century CE, approached philosophy in the same, purely theoretical way.

Nonetheless, there can be no doubt that before, after, and during Cicero's life-time both Stoicism and Epicureanism, and Aristotle's philosophy, too, did pres-ent themselves as bodies of thought "from" which (to use again my terminology of the previous chapter) one should live one's life. This is also true of the new Pyrrhonist school of skepticism, established in Athens by Aenesidemus in the first century BCE (it was apparently unknown to Cicero), as well as of the re-vived Platonism that came to prominence beginning more than a century later. Yet, as I have explained, this was not true of the earliest philosophers of Greece

---

[10] As an Academic skeptic, Cicero abstains, as a matter of principle, from endorsing any philosophical system at all; when he concludes *On Moral Ends* by judging the system of Antiochus of Ascalon the most plausible, he still does not commit himself to it or adopt it as his own. And in relying for his guide to life on the traditional Roman upbringing he received and endorsed, he is not acting on his philosophy of Aca-demic skepticism, as in similar circumstances a Pyrrhonian skeptic could be doing (see chapter 5 below).

[11] Perhaps, for different reasons special to those two philosophies, this would not apply to Epicureans or late Platonists. See chapters 5 and 6 below.

(the "pre-Socratics," as we call them), and not true even of many of those influenced by Socrates. This is enough to show that it is by no means, as Pierre Hadot
thought, "of the essence" of ancient philosophy—part of its fundamental character, distinguishing all of ancient philosophy from modern or contemporary philosophy—that it was pursued and taught as a way of life.

So, when did this conception of philosophy originate? What can explain it?
One thing seems clear: the figure of Socrates, as he is presented in some of Plato's
dialogues, and with particular force and vividness in Plato's *Apology of Socrates*, is
the model for the whole subsequent ancient tradition of a philosopher who understands philosophy in this way, and who tenaciously lives his philosophy, and
lives "from" it. Since Socrates wrote no philosophical works, it is, however, a difficult question to what extent the historical Socrates's activity as a philosopher,
his conception of and ambitions for philosophy, and his life matched Plato's representations. To guide us in assessing Socrates's place in the history of philosophy
we have not only Plato's dialogues, but ones of Xenophon, a contemporary of
Plato's, as well as some remaining fragments of dialogues written by other "companions of Socrates," including Euclides, mentioned above; and there are other
literary accounts, such as that of Aristophanes in his comedy *Clouds*. But these
do not coincide on all essentials with one another, and Xenophon's dialogues
even contradict Plato on some points. In fact, it is possible that one ought not to
look to such literary presentations (which are all we could have to go on) for reli-
able pictures of Socrates's professional and personal life (apart from various
straightforward biographical facts). Such writings, both the theatrical and the
philosophical dramas, seem not even to have aimed at historical accuracy; the
conventions for such writing may have allowed or encouraged a much freer play
of ideas, with the result that what we find attributed to the character Socrates in
Plato's and others' dialogues is the authors' invention, possibly with only a slen-
der relation to whatever the man Socrates may have said or thought in his own
philosophical discussions.[12] Under these confusing circumstances it seems best
not to attempt to solve the "Socratic problem" of how the historical Socrates conducted himself as a philosopher and what he stood for. Better to restrict oneself,
for our purposes, to working out and presenting interpretations of the philosophical views of a notional person. That is what I will do in discussing the philosopher called "Socrates" in this book. Our interest will be in the philosophy

---

[12] See Kahn, *Plato and the Socratic Dialogue*, chap. 1.

that the later philosophical tradition, on the basis of these writings, and especially on the basis of Plato's, attributed to the historical Socrates.[13] We can do no
better, I suggest, in seeking an origin for the idea of philosophy as a way of life,
than to suppose that this notional Socrates—the historical person as refracted
through the writings of Plato and his contemporaries, the authors of Socratic
dialogues—is the ancient Greek philosopher who first conceived of philosophy
in this way.[14]

In fact, the words for *philosophy* and *philosopher* were gradually introduced
into Greek only during the historical Socrates's lifetime. Most of the philosophers we call "pre-Socratic" did not know these words and did not present their
work under the conception they imply. They did not think of it as carried out "in
the pursuit of wisdom," where wisdom was to be understood in Socrates's way as
a complete, rationally worked out account of reality. Indeed, originally the Greek
word *philosophia* could be used to indicate, rather indiscriminately, a person devoted to intellectual and general culture and to the expression in speech and
writing of opinions deriving from it. It was not restricted specifically to philosophy, conceived as self-consciously devoted to rigorous reasoning and rationally
disciplined inquiry, as we, following my notional Socrates, conceive it. Nonetheless, among our earliest recorded uses of the term are some that do reflect such a
narrower conception—initially, the usage of the term was somewhat fluid, and
could encompass both the wider, cultural, application and this narrower one. As
I have already mentioned, Plato, following the historical Socrates's lead, insisted
firmly on the exclusive correctness of the narrower conception, along lines that
remained fixed thereafter both in Greece and in medieval and modern times, at
least in academic circles. In this conception philosophy involves a commitment
to logical reasoning as the fundamental method for the formation of respectable
beliefs. It also involves a broad scope for specifically philosophical beliefs. These
include results of inquiries into logic, the physics of the natural world, and metaphysical issues; it is not limited to the questions of practical life and politics that
Socrates—my notional Socrates, I mean—devoted himself exclusively to. Hence
all the pre-Socratics came to be classified retrospectively, but reasonably enough,
as philosophers.[15] One prominent aspect of philosophers conceived in Plato's

[13] See further Cooper, "Socrates and Philosophy as a Way of Life," p. 22 and n. 3.

[14] From what I have just said it follows that we cannot rule out the conclusion that, really, Plato is the
responsible one.

[15] Many modern scholars, also reasonably enough, emphasize the rather indeterminate mix in early
Greek philosophy of (as this was later conceived) rational philosophy and other cultural elements (literary, religious, even magical ones). It does not properly place the earliest philosophers within Greek culture

narrower way, which is already evidenced in texts from the fifth century, is that they engage in logical argument and trust to reason in pursuit of the truth to such an extent that if the pursuit of truth requires it, they unhesitatingly disregard and override experience and convention. They stick to what reason shows them (or what they think it shows), no matter what.[16]

I mentioned some of the early philosophers above, and explained why their philosophies could not have been a way of life for them or for any followers, because they neglected questions about what is good for a human being—about what is good, or bad, in a human life—and why it is good or bad. Among the philosophers whom we conventionally cast as pre-Socratics, Democritus, the famous early defender of atomic physical theory, stands out as an exception in this respect, and Heraclitus too might be pointed to. But though, to judge from the evidence available to us, Democritus did indeed have a broad, if somewhat inchoate, philosophical theory of human life and values, he did not put forward the idea of living on the basis of the philosophical reasoning that leads to and supports those conclusions. Heraclitus's notorious obscurity prevents us from judging him any differently.

The only predecessor of Socrates whom one could reasonably suggest as a philosopher who conceived his philosophy as a way of life is Pythagoras (along with Empedocles, whom ancient writers class as influenced by him). In fact, however, we know too little about Pythagoras to say anything firm about his own philosophical views (he wrote nothing). Still, before and during the historical Socrates's lifetime there were Pythagoreans in southern Italy and later in mainland Greece, at Thebes and Elis, and they plainly constituted some sort of cult or "brotherhood" with some sort of common life together, whether in a political community as at Croton and Metapontum in Italy in Pythagoras's own day (last half of the sixth century BCE) or in private organizations ("schools"). This life combined what we can recognize as philosophical ideas with dogmas, ritual practices, and dietary and other taboos, all allegedly inherited from Pythagoras. Murky as the whole history of early Pythagoreanism is, however, it nonetheless seems doubtful that the philosophical ideas in this mix (say, ideas about the immortality or transmigration of souls, or anything to do with the importance of numbers in constituting reality) functioned in a way comparable

---

as a whole to speak of them simply as "philosophers," or to focus exclusively on their philosophical analyses and arguments.

[16] On the linguistic and historical matters reported in this paragraph, see further Cooper, "Socrates and Philosophy as a Way of Life," p. 23, n. 4. See also section 1.2 and n. 24 there.

to the role of philosophy in Socratic and later conceptions of philosophy as a way of life. One may allow that the Pythagorean brotherhoods could have offered some suggestion or model for Socrates in his own life devoted to philosophy. But it seems fair not to count them as more than suggestive forerunners. For a full-blown, self-conscious conception of one's philosophy and the reasoning on which it rests as grounding a whole life, we have to look, as I have suggested, to my notional Socrates. The Pythagoreans of the historical Socrates's time do seem to have had a philosophy, and also a way of life. Unclear is the extent to which the two may have affected one another.[17]

2.2. Socrates in Plato's *Apology*

Plato's *Apology of Socrates* was written not long after the events it dramatizes— Socrates's trial and conviction, at an advanced age, in an Athenian popular court, on the charge of violating the law against impiety by publicly offending the civic divinities and corrupting the morals of young Athenians by his teaching (the charges did not need to specify what the accusers thought this teaching concerned).[18] In the speeches making up Plato's version of Socrates's response to these charges, Socrates presents himself as having been devoted over many years to what seems to be full-time engagement in discussions in the public places of the city with various fellow Athenians and visitors to Athens. Some of them were young men who flocked round to listen to him, some of them adult persons with settled positions and reputations in Athenian society. These discussions were philosophical in character. They consisted of questions Socrates would ask about some matter of importance for human life, to get the discussion started:[19] What

[17] It is quite possible that Pythagoras and the Pythagoreans, and Empedocles too (to judge from the remains of his poetry), and maybe even Heraclitus, did regard, and pursue, cosmological knowledge as crucial for the salvation of one's soul (in a way somewhat similar to the late ancient Platonists). But they seem not to have developed philosophical analyses, integral to the rest of their philosophies, to explain and ground this idea. And in making that pursuit central to their lives (and recommending it to others), they did not extend their metaphysical, cosmological, and mathematical work in such a way as to develop thereby ideas about the overall human good and virtue on which one could pattern the whole of one's life.

[18] On Plato and Xenophon as writers of Socratic dialogues, and on Socrates in Plato's works, see endnote 6.

[19] In the *Apology* (19b–d; cf. 26b–e) Socrates insists (and offers witnesses to this) that he never investigated or discussed the sorts of questions then associated in the public mind with philosophy—questions of a "pre-Socratic" kind, about the origins or constitution of the natural world or how to explain natural processes. In Plato's *Phaedo*, a discussion Plato sets as occurring on the historical Socrates's last day, the

do you think courage actually is (*Laches*)? Or modesty (*Charmides*)? Or friendship (*Lysis*)? Is virtue one thing, or are there some number of separate and distinct virtues (*Protagoras*)? Is oratorical skill a good thing? What even is it? What does it do (*Gorgias*)? He would then direct further questions to the respondent about his answers.

Socrates would emphasize in his further questions (and in ancillary comments) logical relations of implication, inconsistency, and the like, as he tried to work out between himself and the respondent what the respondent actually thought—and then, whether, once you think of it in light of these further developments, the initial idea can continue to seem as attractive as the respondent at first thought. The requirement was always borne in heavily on the respondent that he was to take himself seriously as someone who cared about the truth on the subjects under exploration. Socrates made it clear that he would not bother to hold such a discussion with anyone who was not serious about the truth, or was not willing to adopt that stance for the duration of the discussion. To hold opinions about what is true, Socrates assumed, is to be prepared to explain and defend them, by appealing to reasons that in fact do support them as being true, and to be committed to accepting as further opinions (or as parts of the initial ones) any logical or other consequences that could plausibly be drawn from them. His discussions, moreover, were always confined to issues about human life, about how to lead it correctly and well, about how to conceive and appreciate the value of the various highly rated traditional virtues, in comparison with other things apparently also of value (such as bodily health, physical strength, wealth, bodily or other pleasures, social and personal relationships, and so on).

The *Apology* offers two neat samples of such Socratic question-and-answer discussions.[20] Socrates uses his right, as the accused, to question Meletus, the spokesman for the three Athenians who swore out the complaint charging Socrates with impiety, as an occasion to make him answerer in such a discussion. Meletus and the others have made two claims against him, and Socrates treats these as two "theses" on a moral subject comparable to the philosophical claims

---

character Socrates claims (96aff.) to have been quite interested in such questions in his youth, but soon to have become disenchanted with them, since they seemed beyond our human capacity for grasping the truth. The truth about human life and the human good, however, lay nearer to hand, and so he thereafter limited his inquiries and discussions to those topics, as he reports in the *Apology*. So even if Socrates (either the historical or my notional one) did have a fling at philosophy of nature in his youth, that can be left out of account for our purposes.

[20] *Apology* 24d–28a.

with which his discussions regularly begin. So Meletus is assumed to present the two charges (that Socrates corrupts the youth, that Socrates does not believe in the civic gods), as two things he firmly believes or even knows to be true. He is assumed to be (in the Socratic sense) serious about them. Then, upon Socrates's relentless questioning, in the second case (atheism) Meletus contradicts himself, and in the other (corruption) he is reduced to saying highly implausible things that he cannot explain, or defend as true, despite the implausibility. These two failures—self-contradiction and being reduced to saying implausible things in order to maintain one's thesis, without being able to explain how the thesis can be true in light of the implausibilities—are the two failures that, over and over again, show, according to Socrates, the inadequacy of his interlocutors and of their views on the moral questions he investigates with them. Here, Meletus is shown up as frivolous in making his charges, since he hasn't paid enough attention to what he is charging Socrates with even to be able not to contradict himself when explaining how the charge applies to Socrates. And though these failures do not prove that Socrates is innocent of the charges, they do show that Meletus really had no business bringing them against him, a fellow citizen entitled, as such, to special consideration. (Alas, this is not how the 501 Athenian male citizens making up the jury react to Socrates's "demonstration" of Meletus's inadequacies: at any rate, they found him guilty by a vote of 280–221.)

Later on in Plato's *Apology*, Socrates famously maintains that one's soul and its condition, whether good or bad, is the most important thing for anyone: that, he says, is what he has gone about the city of Athens all his life trying to convince his fellow citizens of, both old and young.[21] This is something about which he is quite confident (though, as I will explain below, like all his substantive views in philosophy, it is not, in his opinion, definitely and finally established as true). It is the crucial claim on which Socrates's philosophy, and the Socratic way of life, is grounded. It became a foundational principle for the whole later tradition of ethical philosophy among the ancients. For Socrates, the soul is vastly more important than any of the other valuable things mentioned above, indeed so vastly so that it makes them not just pale by comparison but, in their very value, totally dependent upon it. When your soul is in its good condition, you have something of unconditional value, Socrates claims—whereas all other goods (money, pleasure, good relationships with others, power over them, whatever it might be) are only conditionally good: their value depends on how they are used, how they are

---

[21] *Apology* 30a–b.

fit into your life. They are dependent as goods upon, and make a positive contribution to our lives only because of, what we ourselves make of them, how we regard them, how we react to having or lacking them, and what we do with them.[22] That is because the soul is that with which we live our active lives: our assessments of value, our decisions, our desires, our choices—all these depend upon it. So long as the soul is in its good condition, which Socrates calls its "virtue" (whatever more precisely that may be—that remains to be considered), we will live well, because, if we have this most importantly valuable thing in good condition, all other potential, or commonly agreed, values (wealth, health, good social connections, etc., even bodily pleasure) become actually valuable for us. With a good, well-conditioned, soul we can make proper and good use of these other valuable things, and so live good lives. With a bad soul we will have bad desires, make bad choices, misvalue and misuse such other potential goods, and, as a result, make a bad life for ourselves.

Moreover, for Socrates, this good condition of the soul is, ultimately, entirely a matter of developing and maintaining a firm grasp on, a firm understanding of, fundamental truths about human nature and, as a consequence of that, about the nature of what is valuable for a human being; the good condition of the soul is, in his terminology, wisdom. The reason why, if you possess "virtue" in your soul, you will live a good and happy life is that you will then know the true value of every possible sort of thing you might want to have, in comparison and in relationship with all other things similarly of value. You will, in other words, know the truth of Socrates's own claim about the preeminent value of the soul, and the merely conditional value of money, position, power, personal relationships, bodily pleasure, and all the rest. Since you will never value anything else more highly or even at anywhere close to the same level as the state of your soul, you will never value at more than their true worth either "external" goods, such as possessions, social position, and the like, or "goods of the soul" other than virtue, such as a good memory or sense of humor or native friendliness, nor yet "goods of the body" such as health, strength, bodily pleasure, physical ease.[23] Their true worth is that of something to be used "virtuously," and none of them have any value apart from what accrues to them through that good use. Accordingly, whether or not you are lucky as regards those other goods, whether or not you

---

[22] Socrates argues this in Plato's *Euthydemus* 278e–282d.

[23] For this distinction among three classes of goods, see *Euthydemus* 278e–279b and *Meno* 87d–88b. The distinction became a canonical one in subsequent philosophy: see, e.g., Aristotle, *Nicomachean Ethics* I 8, 1098b12–16.

have plenty of such traditionally highly valued "resources" for life, you will find that your soul's good condition will govern your real life, that is, your active life consisting in your choices, actions, reactions to and evaluations of what happens to you, in such a way as to make it happy and fulfilling. Pains and failures as regards these external and bodily goods, and the various superficial goods of the soul, do not diminish the fine quality of your life at all: they only pose special, even perhaps interestingly challenging, circumstances in which the power of your soul, given to you by your virtue, can show itself, as you smoothly respond to and accommodate whatever your "resources" may be, in the actions you undertake, or leave aside. The value (for you) in your life is achieved solely in the actions that make it up.

For Socrates, then, whatever else it may include or imply, virtue is wisdom. Virtue, the good condition of the soul, is this state of mind in which one does firmly grasp and understand the full system of human values, in comparison and relationship with one another. With wisdom, he maintains, one will always live on the basis of that system of values, and so one will live completely happily and fulfilled. That implies, of course, that understanding the truth about what is good or bad for you inevitably and necessarily leads you to act in the way that is indicated in that knowledge, in whatever your current circumstances may be, with their prospects for the future and relationship to the past. With wisdom and understanding you will always act in what is in fact the right way. Moreover, the fullness of your understanding will enable you to give good and sufficient reasons why that was in fact the right thing to do in those circumstances (given what could be known about them—even a wise person isn't clairvoyant). Knowledge—knowledge of values, of what is good and what is bad for a human being—has, then, an extreme power in Socrates's view: if you have it, it will not just unwaveringly and irresistibly govern your life, but it will make it a good and fulfilled one, too. Socrates explains and defends this claim about wisdom's power—it is a claim about human psychology—in Plato's *Protagoras*.[24] It isn't that Socrates thinks all possibly countervailing psychological powers—powers in the soul with possible influence on your choice of which action to do, or refrain from, in any circumstance—will miraculously disappear once you become wise. He recognizes the power of pleasure and pain, or sexual and other states of passion, as possible influences even on the choices and actions of the wise person: pleasure

---

[24] See *Protagoras* 353c–358d. (All translations from Plato are from Cooper, *Plato: Complete Works*, sometimes with unspecified alterations.)

and pain, or their prospect, or anger or fear or sexual arousal, and so on, can alter the way things appear, valuewise, to any agent. And so, these feelings might lead them to act wrongly. However, Socrates argues, this "power of appearance" to mislead us is always weaker than the power of value knowledge—if, that is, we really do possess this knowledge fully, and are completely wise. How so?

Here we meet a fundamental insight or assumption of Socrates, one that some subsequent philosophers, including both Plato (in dialogues other than his Socratic ones) and Aristotle, will oppose, while others, most notably the Stoics, will strenuously agree with him in accepting. It belongs to human nature, Socrates thinks, that when we are grown up and in charge of our own lives, any and every action we do is done with, and from, the thought that it is the best thing (taking into account everything it occurs to you to take into account) for you to be doing then. You may be ambivalent or uncertain, to some extent, as you at first reflect on the situation (if you reflect at all), but when you act, you necessarily are committed in your thinking to the idea that this (despite whatever may count against it) is the best thing to do. If your mind remained unmade-up, you would not (yet) have acted. This follows from the fact, which Socrates thinks belongs to human beings by their nature as rational animals (the only rational ones among the earthly animal kingdom), that we can act only on reasons that we accept, at the time when we act on them, as sufficient to justify the action. Only the acceptance of such reasons can possibly move an animal with a rational nature to action. Thus, for Socrates, our power to see and give ourselves reasons for acting is the only psychic source of motivation within us that can actually set us upon the movements that constitute or produce our actions—with their particular goals and nuanced, or merely gross and unnuanced, embedded appreciations of what we may be doing. Possessing a rational nature entails, for Socrates, acting always, in a sense, rationally. We always act "subjectively" rationally, that is, we always act for what we take to be adequate reasons. As Socrates puts it in the conclusion of his analysis in the *Protagoras*, "[N]o one goes willingly toward the bad, or what he believes to be bad; neither is it in human nature to want to go toward what one believes to be bad, instead of to the good."[25] Many people may regret what they have done immediately after doing it, just as they may waver and be uncertain just before acting. But everyone, in acting, does what they then hold to be best, because otherwise, given our rational natures, we would do nothing at all (we would not even refrain from acting).

[25] *Protagoras* 358c–d.

From this thesis about human psychology, Socrates's claim of the power of value knowledge follows directly. Value knowledge gives its possessor an unfailingly complete basis for evaluating situations and circumstances as one becomes aware of them. This leads to a clear apprehension of the best thing to do under the current conditions (as one understands them to be). If it is part of human nature always to do, if anything at all, what one thinks is best, the possessors of such knowledge will always and only do what they think is best, at the time when they act. And because knowledge makes them always right about what is best, they always live well, happily, and fulfilled, in the way I described above. Other people, ones not possessed of this knowledge, will very frequently be governed by the power of appearance—it is a second fundamental feature of human nature to be constantly bombarded by value appearances. Just like the wise person, they will always do what they think is best as they act, but the power of appearance can affect them in such a way that, because of feelings of anger or sexual passion, or the presence or prospect of pleasure or pain in the near future, they form the opinion that something would be an overall good thing to do that in fact is not. Due to the power of the appearances that such states of feeling can induce, they may even act against their considered judgment about what is best—a considered judgment that might be correct but that, when one is in thrall to the appearances, one overemotionally displaces with a judgment based on the appearances. None of this can happen to a wise person. Even the wise may still be subject to appearances that present the options differently to their consciousness, because of angry feelings or some other emotional distortion, but their value understanding is so complete, and in that sense so deep and strong, that these contrary appearances, and the feelings that give rise to them, cannot affect their action in any way.[26] Knowledge—value knowledge—will save our lives, and nothing else could reliably do so.[27]

Wisdom, then—the good condition of the human soul, in which the soul performs to perfection its function in giving rise to all the actions of which a

[26] Though Socrates does not go into this in the *Protagoras* or elsewhere, presumably he thinks that the wise person will not even have many of the misleading feelings and appearances that most people get. Nonetheless, it is part of his conception of human nature that everyone remains subject to such feelings and appearances, in some degree and force. That he thinks this follows from his comparison of value appearances with the appearance to sight of things at a distance. Once you know how far away something is, that knowledge does not by any means rid you of the appearances you get of it as if nearer; all it does, as Socrates emphasizes—and that is enough—is to prevent you from being taken in by them.

[27] Socrates refers to this knowledge as our savior at *Protagoras* 356e, under the title of an "art of measurement"—measurement of immediate potential goods of action against future good and bad consequences.

human life consists—is the highest objective for any reasonable human being. "Wisdom and truth," Socrates says in Plato's *Apology*,[28] are what we need above all else. Earlier, however, in explaining his life of philosophy to his fellow Athenians at Plato's version of his trial, he has expressed a deep suspicion that, alas, there are not, and are not likely ever to be, any wise human beings. His own long experience, to which I will revert below, in seeking wisdom himself has left him with the strong impression that wisdom must remain for us a goal to be striven for, but one that will never finally be achieved. Human nature—our nature as rational beings—does make wisdom in principle possible for us, but it is too difficult, for reasons we will discuss more fully below, for anyone to achieve in practice. However, on a religiously nonstandard, philosophical conception of divinity that Socrates himself has devised (we see this conception on display in the *Apology*), the divine nature is totally and perfectly rational. Hence, only god, he suspects, is or will ever be wise—and, given the divine nature, god is wise necessarily and without effort. To explain this, Socrates tells the tale of his friend Chaerephon's consultation, at some unspecified point in Socrates's philosophical career, of Apollo's famous oracle at Delphi, in which Chaerephon asked whether anyone was wiser than Socrates.[29] To Chaerephon's enthused satisfaction, the oracle's priestess replied that no one was wiser. Socrates, however, was sure that his own understanding of human values—he assumes those are the concerns of wisdom as the oracle, too, understands it—does not measure up to what wisdom requires. So what could the oracle mean, in declaring that no one is wiser than he? That seems to imply that he does have wisdom. How so?

To arrive at an answer, we need to ask what exactly Socrates thought he lacked. To see this, we need first to examine more closely Socrates's conception of wisdom, and to see how his own practice of philosophical discussion, as described briefly above,[30] is connected to the pursuit of wisdom, where wisdom is conceived as (practically speaking) an exclusively divine possession. A central component of Plato's strategy in writing his version of Socrates's defense speech is to refute the charge of impiety and corruption by establishing a close and positive relationship between Socrates's philosophical discussions and his own personal piety. It is an exquisite refutation of the charge if Socrates can show that the very activities on which the charge was principally based were divinely authorized and, in some way, carried out in god's service. So Plato has Socrates sup-

---

[28] *Apology* 29e.
[29] On Xenophon's evidence about the oracle, and more on its implications, see endnote 7.
[30] See section 2.2 above.

press all reference to philosophical discussions that took place before he heard the priestess's response; Socrates also leaves in the dark any discussions after that carried out directly among himself and his young men. (One thing he says later perhaps leaves room for them, however: he speaks of holding discussions with all and sundry, at any rate with anyone he met whom he thought might be wise.)[31] In referring to the oracle and his reverent response to it, he speaks as if his whole career had been given over to holding discussions with other mature men with a reputation for wisdom, who also thought of themselves as wise, or with other mature men who claimed to care for their souls and for wisdom and truth. Socrates implies that his total aim was to demonstrate to these people, and, more significantly perhaps, to any bystanders (including his young men), that these allegedly wise men were indeed not wise at all (or, in the other case, that the people in question did not care about their souls and wisdom, as they had claimed to do). And this he did in service of, and on implicit instructions from, Apollo, when Apollo's priestess answered on his behalf by saying that no one was wiser than Socrates. On this account, Socrates's aim was to show that no one else was wise at all, so that since he was not wise, and did not claim to be, he could show the world that no one but god was wise and thereby do honor to Apollo and to god generally. The superior wisdom that the priestess attributed to him consisted solely in this self-knowledge that he was not wise.[32]

We need not think of Plato's Socrates as dishonest or disingenuous in giving this distorted or misleading account of his work as a philosopher—misleading as to when he began his philosophical discussions, with whom he carried them on, and what his motives were in doing so.[33] When people tell narratives of their lives in old age we expect them to see in retrospect aspects of their lives, and connections among events in them, that make sense of them in ways they may not have done while they were being lived. And in any event, no such narrative should be taken to indicate a preconceived pattern according to which from the beginning the people led their life. Still, the fact remains that we must disregard many details that the *Apology* conveys if we are to recover and understand Socrates's methods and his practice in philosophizing in one-on-one question-and-answer discussions such as I have described above. These were certainly not,

---

[31] See *Apology* 23b, 29b.

[32] See *Apology* 21b–23b.

[33] Socrates was surely not guilty of the charge of impiety (even given the loose standards of legal interpretation that prevailed in the popular juries of Athens), so if he had succeeded in winning an acquittal by making these distorted (or even literally false) claims, he would, at least, not have perpetrated any unjust evasion of the law.

either before or after the oracle's pronouncement, carried out exclusively with alleged and self-conceived wise people, or else aimed at disabusing someone who claimed to care most about wisdom and truth of that false opinion of themselves. They did not start only in response to the oracle, in order to find out, as Socrates insinuates, what the god could have meant by seeming to say that Socrates is wise.[34] Nor was the motivation of serving the god by urging people to realize (or conjecture, as he himself does) that no human, but only god, is wise, more than a secondary one. In fact, this motivation might well belong simply to the retrospective narration of his life that he (Plato's Socrates) addresses in the *Apology* to himself as well as to others, provoked by what he thought an outrageous charge of impiety. At the end of his life, as with other people under similar stimuli, he may see new motivations in the way he has been living, or overemphasize barely operative ones.

In any event, there is one thing that it seems we certainly can say about Socrates's discussions from the beginning, right through to the end. Whether he was talking with one of his young men or deflating the puffed-up intellectual ego of some established older person, Socrates was engaged in his own pursuit of wisdom—the greatest good, as we have seen he thinks, for a human being. Near the end of the *Apology* Socrates tells his fellow Athenians that "it is the greatest good for a person to discuss virtue every day and those other things about which you hear me conversing and testing myself and others."[35] Pursuing this good was clearly his principal, if not single-minded, task in all his philosophical work: for him, as we have seen, the pursuit of happiness, which is equivalent to the pursuit of wisdom, must be for all reasonable persons their highest objective. That is why he tells his fellow citizens he would refuse to give up his daily practice of such discussion even if they promised to acquit him on condition that he ceased. Effects on others were secondary aims, which is not to say that they were not important to him—whether effects on his young men, who might accept from him the same conception of the human good and adopt his own ambition to acquire wisdom through philosophical inquiry; or on the allegedly wise, who might realize their own deficiencies and join him in recognizing their need for intellec-

---

[34] See endnote 6. At 21b Socrates traces the origin of the "slanders" against him—that he claimed a highly specialized philosophical wisdom, allowing him to reject the traditional gods in favor of purely natural explanations of natural phenomena, and to teach young people for a fee—to his decision to respond to the oracle by going about examining and refuting self-conceived wise people. He conveniently disregards any reputation for wisdom that might have sprung up from the prior philosophical discussions he must have been having, and must have been fairly widely known in the city to be having.

[35] *Apology* 38a.

tual improvement, or at least benefit by reconsidering the issues that were in dispute; or on entrenched opponents of his regard for philosophy and his conception of moral rightness; or merely on observant bystanders, who might come to regard his skills with awe and increase his own reputation, and/or might heed his implicit call to care most for the good condition of their souls, and not to devote themselves instead to gaining wealth or social and political power. Socrates says in the remark just quoted that he is testing not just the others with whom he carries on a discussion, by examining their opinions and, as it always turns out, bringing them to find fault with what they have previously thought or taken for granted. He is also testing himself; it is in that second testing that, it seems, his pursuit of wisdom is primarily to be found.

2.3. Socratic Dialectic, Socratic Knowledge, and Human Wisdom

In his philosophical discussions in Plato's Socratic dialogues, as I have mentioned, Socrates always takes the role of questioner of others' opinions, specifically on issues concerning what is of value in a human life.[36] He never presents, argues for, or explains any such views of his own—or his philosophical reasons for holding them—as he would have to do if he were the answerer instead. He has a reason of principle for this.[37] He always asks and never responds because he has "nothing wise" in him, he says once—echoing his disclaimer of wisdom in the *Apology*.[38] When Socrates raised a question for discussion—What is courage? What is justice? What does oratory accomplish? What benefit do you promise (if you are a sophist) to bring to your pupils? Is it better for you to be punished if you have done wrong, or to get away with it? and so on—he evidently thought that those who did respond implied, in setting forth their opinions, one or the other of two things about themselves. That is because he always gave his interlocutors the credit of being serious people, concerned for the truth of their opinions—they were at least not willing to look frivolous and merely

---

[36] On differences in this respect between the Platonic and the Xenophontic Socrates, see endnote 8.

[37] Thrasymachus in *Republic* I refers with contempt and outrage to this feature of Socratic discussions, 336b–337a: Socrates, Thrasymachus says, does nothing but ask questions and then refute the answers, just to show his own superiority, but he won't answer questions himself—something much harder than to ask them—and will use any ploy (such as ironical praise of the greater competence of an intending questioner, who therefore ought to speak and then answer instead) so as to avoid having to do that.

[38] *Theaetetus* 150c6: this is a dialogue of Plato's that does not count as Socratic, but in the passage cited the character Socrates speaks about his persona as we find it in Plato's Socratic dialogues.

self-absorbed by answering and then just walking away: as serious people, they were opening themselves, by responding, to having to answer any of the sorts of questions Socrates would go on to ask. So, perhaps, as a first option, they thought they already knew the answer they gave to be true (and thought they were wise on the subject). This first possibility applies to the people he went to so as to test the oracle,[39] as well as to some of his other interlocutors in the Socratic dialogues: the expert on religion, Euthyphro; perhaps Critias in the *Charmides* (when he intervenes to propose what he is convinced is Socrates's own view about the virtue of temperance or moderation); the generals in *Laches* (alleged experts on courage); Protagoras (teacher for a fee to young men of what he thinks is wisdom); the rhetoricians in *Gorgias*; Meno, who has confident opinions on the nature of virtue in general; Hippias in the two dialogues named after him; and the Homeric expert Ion, who claims to have artistic knowledge.

Or else, as a second option, they were at least ready to present an answer as something they had thought about sufficiently (maybe only then for the first time, when Socrates raised the question), were convinced of, and so were prepared to defend in discussion and argument, with a full commitment to its being true—even though they were far from claiming wisdom in the matter. At any rate, they were ready to explore the consequences of their answer with an advance commitment to its rational acceptability and defensibility. This would be the situation of any of Socrates's young men when he engaged them in a discussion, asking for their opinion on some matter to do with human life, and going on to explore with them the philosophical difficulties that then arise for their view.[40] We see this exemplified by many of his interlocutors in Plato's dialogues, not all of them among his young men: Crito (a contemporary of Socrates's) and Charmides and Lysis (both young men) in the dialogues with their names, the young Alcibiades in *Alcibiades*, Clinias in the *Euthydemus*, Polemarchus in *Republic* I.

Socrates did not think he was in either of these positions. Certainly he had thought hard and long about all the matters he questioned others about (in part precisely through prior such examinations of people's opinions). Certainly he had views on all the subjects on which he conducted such discussions: this you can tell from the follow-up questions he asks, and the direction in which he leads the discussion once it is under way (I will have more to say about this below).

[39] See *Apology* 21b–23c.
[40] On Socrates's reasons for omitting reference to philosophical discussions with his young men, see endnote 9.

Often, these were well formed and carefully articulated, as we can see from the way in which he formulates the criticisms implied in his further questions. The crucial inhibiting factor for Socrates was that he adopted and held all his own opinions in a spirit of open inquiry. Even after he might have reached what seemed to him some solidly based conclusion on some matter of moral importance, it remained for him ultimately still tentative. He was not convinced; he was not fully satisfied with his current understanding. His attitude was one of openness to the need for further thought before one could declare any of these conclusions with final certainty. That attitude, he felt, was incompatible with occupying the answerer's role in philosophical discussion—he could not claim to be wise, and he also could not put forward a view of his own as something of which he was convinced, and therefore prepared to put forward and defend as something to whose truth he was intellectually fully committed.

First of all, as for not being wise, for Socrates, to be wise meant to have a completely firm grasp of the truth in the subject matter one was wise about (arithmetic, geometry, carpentry, medicine—whatever it might be), and a grasp that was settled and permanent in one's mind. At any time when in normal possession of their powers, a wise person would be prepared to answer—and they could know in advance that their understanding made this possible—any and all questions that connected, however remotely, with the matters in question. Wisdom about human life, which is not a technical subject but one we all are concerned with and informed about, is such that a person wise on this subject could answer any such questions in a highly plausible and satisfying manner, bringing more illumination to the topic, not less, and by all means without obfuscation.[41] Moreover, such a wise person is prepared in advance to respond, again with plausibility and increased illumination, to every objection anyone, however clever and intense in their scrutiny, might pose. This complete grasp of the truth on any matter to do with the human good—given the interconnectedness and mutual implications from one part of the subject to others—would require the total grasp of the whole vast subject of human nature and the human good, knowing the true value of every possible sort of thing you might want to have, in comparison and in relationship with all other things similarly of value, which I have described above as the Socratic virtue of wisdom.[42]

If we are to believe his account of himself in the *Apology*, Socrates had repeated and extended experience with the most illustrious of his contemporaries

[41] On the wisdom Socrates sought versus craft wisdom, see endnote 10.
[42] See section 2.2 above.

with reputations for wisdom, and in fact not one of them could ever meet this most demanding of intellectual tests—not when Socrates's own was the scrutiny to which they fell victim. In effect, then, knowing his own skill at Socratic cross-examination, Socrates was intensely conscious of how hard it is to reach wisdom. Could he himself, in relation to any of his own considered philosophical opinions about human values, withstand the intellectual onslaught that some equal of himself might launch in putting him to this ultimate test? Was there not perhaps something he had not yet thought of that, if brought up by such a person, might reasonably give him at least momentary pause? Were there not perhaps circumstances of life so far unanticipated by him in which his own favored view about justice, or about courage, or about any other important moral issue, would seem to indicate a response that, in all honesty, he would have to say seemed wrong? That would require him to reconsider, and elaborate in new ways, his old view. To him, it seemed clear that he very well might not pass this test.

For one with such an attitude it could very reasonably seem that the right stance to take in philosophical argument was the one that Socrates did assume. He questioned others, and continued to think and rethink his own opinions in the course, and as a result, of doing so. Since he was not actually convinced about anything—that is, not fully and finally certain of any specific philosophical thesis taken together with all its ramifications, many of them as yet unconsidered—shifting to the position of answerer would carry severe intellectual discomfort.[43] This discomfort would remain, even if, like his young men who were willing to put forward a view as their own, he agreed to say why he thought what he thought on what courage, or temperance, or justice is, or whether or not it is better to get away unpunished for injustice if one happens to do some, while making it clear that he did not think himself wise on any such matter. Even so, he felt, one should advance theses as one's own only if one thinks it certain that they are true, and is prepared to show that they are true, if challenged: seriousness in serious discussion about the most important matters seemed to him to demand no less in self-conscious restraint. Indeed, part—a major part—of what he hoped

[43] There could be moral discomfort as well. Socrates reports in the *Apology* that those who were witnesses to his examinations of the wise regularly inferred that he must be (positively) wise himself on all the matters on which he refuted the views of others (*Apol.* 23a). If, then, with this reputation, despite his insistence on the unsoundness of that inference, he put forward views of his own, and undertook to explain and defend them before others (even in conversation just with his young men), there would be a great danger that others, especially the young men, would just take his word for the truth. They would not adopt the attitude of openness and need for further thought that he regarded as appropriate, and so they would not think the matter through for themselves. Yet that, if anything, is what he wanted to teach them to do.

his young men might learn from their experience with him, whether as witnesses of his debates with conceited, allegedly wise people, or as answerers themselves, was this very principle. Having started from a position of confidence in some view, but failing to sustain their position, then thinking the matter over further on their own, and trying a new idea on Socrates at a subsequent time, only to find that that fails, too, they might gradually learn for themselves the severe hazards of advancing positive views in philosophical argument. At last, they would turn, with Socrates, to investigating moral questions and thinking and rethinking their own ideas through questioning others who have not yet learned this prime lesson—or who never will learn it.

Wisdom, then, is a permanent, deeply settled, complete grasp of the total truth about human values of all sorts, in all their systematic interrelationships, primed for ready application to all situations and circumstances of human life. Socrates says he knows about himself that he is not wise, and he suspects that only god is wise, because he has never met anyone else after all his years in the philosophy business who has such a permanent understanding of values. The divine nature, for Socrates, includes knowing all this, so of course god's knowledge is permanent. What it is to be god is to know all this. Human nature, by contrast, makes human beings at best know how to behave in right ways temporarily, on the basis of a temporary full grasp of all the reasons why some particular action is right and best. Human beings at best act well and do fully good actions only for some time, or at some points, in their lives.[44] They always fall away and lose that grasp, with the result that they become bad—that is to say, they act badly then. To act fully well requires acting, at the time when one acts, on a full grasp of how the circumstances of one's action, and all the things of value that are at issue or are affected by one's action, interrelate, so as to make this action the right and best one to do then. It often happens, of course, that one does the right thing, but not for the right reasons. Equally, one can do the right thing for the right reasons, but not while seeing them in full relation to the whole system of human values that a person with knowledge would relate them to. And because, or so it appeared to Socrates, no human being has ever consistently and throughout their adult life acted with that knowledge, any actual human goodness is precarious and unsteady. It does not amount to the true and full goodness that is wisdom—and that, apparently, belongs solely to god. Even acting in that fully

---

[44] Socrates explains this when he interprets a poem of Simonides in Plato's *Protagoras*: for his interpretation of the poem see 339a–347a; and for his remarks on the impermanence of human goodness, see 343d–345c.

good way at some times, or for a period of time, is quite an accomplishment, and is surely a rare one. To possess and use even once this full grasp of all the reasons why some particular action is right and best—that is, to know its rightness—is very hard to achieve. Wisdom is all the harder, since it requires knowing the rightness not only of similar actions whenever similar circumstances arise, but of all actions in all circumstances, whenever those may arise—and possessing this knowledge, to boot, as a deeply seated and permanently continuing feature of one's mind.

Given this distinction between knowledge and wisdom—closely bound together as we have seen they nonetheless are—Socrates can say of himself, as he does at his trial, that he knows some moral truths. As to death, which he might face if found guilty, he suggests that neither he nor anyone knows whether it is a bad or a good thing, in general or for himself, at his time of life. But he does know, he says, that it would be a bad and disgraceful thing if he voluntarily gave up his current way of life—that is, his daily discussions and self-examinations concerning virtue and the human good. (He fantasizes, for effect, that the jury might offer to acquit him if he would stop.) To stop would be to trade a known, very great good in order to avoid something not known to be bad, but only speculatively considered so. He would be opting for continued mere life, as if that were an important enough value to justify abandoning his pursuit of the good of his soul. He would be abandoning the essential activity that, as he understands, is the sole way for actual human beings to substantiate in their lives their commitment to the preeminent value of the soul's goodness over all other values. For him, this is the sole way to do that, given that, as it seems, none of us will actually attain wisdom, but we can all pursue it with all our energy and all our powers.[45]

---

[45] See *Apology* 28d–29d. Here Socrates places his commitment to what he refers to later as his "examined" life (38a), in preference to avoiding death at all costs, alongside his courageous behavior as a hoplite, or infantryman, with the Athenian citizen army when he remained at his appointed place in the line, following the commanders' orders, at risk of death. In fact, Socrates cites at first the general principle that "obeying one's superior, be he god or man" (29b6–7) is what he knows to be good. I will return below (section 2.5) to this principle's application to a human superior's orders; the divine commander he refers to here is Apollo, the god of the Delphic oracle, whom he interprets as ordering him to live this life. Plato is continuing his strategy of refuting the charge of impiety by portraying Socrates's life in philosophy as commanded by god. Since for Socrates the divine nature just is the reification of wisdom and knowledge about values, to disobey god is simply to abandon the true system of values, which places the good of the soul ahead of all other goods, even the good of life itself. To disobey by abandoning the committed pursuit of wisdom would be to prefer some lesser good to the greatest one, divine wisdom itself. (It is true that Socrates also recognizes god as communicating with humans more personally and directly, for example through his own notorious "familiar sign," or δαιμόνιον, a kind of inner voice that he says warned him occasionally not to do something he might be contemplating. See *Apol.* 31c, 40a; *Euthyd.* 273a; *Phdr.* 242c;

For Socrates, then, knowledge is the grasp of the truth of some fact or group of facts on the basis of a comprehensive, complete understanding of the whole system of facts, and relationships among them, that constitute some distinct area of intellectual inquiry. In the case of the human good and what is bad for human beings, such knowledge is a grasp of what to do in particular sets of circumstances, where that grasp derives from and depends upon a complete understanding of the whole realm of human values. Wisdom goes beyond that knowledge by requiring that, once acquired, it be so deeply and firmly settled in one's mind that one would be prepared, for all future time, when in normal possession of one's powers, to apply that knowledge, with confidence and demonstrable authority, in any and every circumstance, so as always to do what is right and best, with a complete and fully grounded justification in mind for what one does. Wisdom requires, as I put it above, being always able to answer any and all questions that connect, however remotely, with the matters in question, and to do so in a highly plausible and satisfying manner; wise people are always prepared in advance to respond, again with plausibility and increased illumination, to every objection anyone might pose to their judgment or course of action. Nonetheless, it remains possible for someone, at some time, to have even that perfect knowledge, and all the more something only approaching it, without being wise.

2.4. Socratic Philosophy as a Way of Life

That, then, is what Socrates thought he lacked, when he insisted, in his puzzlement on hearing the oracle, that he was not wise. And no wonder he thought he lacked wisdom, if that is what it requires! For Socrates, the complete good condition of the soul is entirely a matter of one's ability, unfalteringly and with an inexhaustible thoroughness, to understand, explain, and successfully defend by argument and analysis, to others and to oneself, one's own values and commitments. This good consists, therefore, in the perfection of the ability to understand and argue well about values. It is the condition in which that ability is made absolutely secure and permanent. That is what Socrates understands by wisdom. But, as it seemed to Socrates, and surely not unreasonably so, human beings never do, in practice, achieve this condition. One must be prepared to

---

Euthyph. 3b; *Rep.* 496c; *Alc.* 103a–e, 105e, 124c. It may be unclear how to relate that divine function to, or reconcile it with, the Socratic divinity's essential identification with perfect reason; in any case, because of the "sign's" negative powers it is irrelevant in the present context.)

face up to challenges anyone might raise against any of one's ideas that one had carefully examined and felt quite persuaded of. But how can anyone, with all the limitations there manifestly are on human intelligence and individual human experience, ever be confident that they have already fully considered and found good reason to reject every possible challenge? Or how can they know that any remaining, so far unconsidered, ones could immediately upon presentation be turned aside on the basis of adequate reasons already found among those on the basis of which they have become confident of the idea in question? In fact, how could one be absolutely sure (given one's current state of belief) that no unheralded future experience of one's own or others, or some unfamiliar situation for decision, could possibly provide what one ought rationally to consider, even if only for a moment, to be an acceptable basis for doubting the truth of some cherished belief? No human being can already know about all possible relevant experiences people might have, and all grounds of possible objection to any view on what is best or right to do that they might have arrived at. Wisdom must be unshakable; but it would be extremely rash of anyone—and so, it would go counter to reason itself—to claim to know anything about human good and human bad in that unshakable way.[46]

Moreover, Socrates thought his lack a permanent condition: as we have seen, his experience in philosophical discussions fairly early in his career had forcibly borne in upon him the strong suspicion that, while the divine nature made god wise automatically, human nature, while opening wisdom to us too in principle, brought with it other defects that rendered wisdom practically unattainable, so that it was never actually attained by any human being. Perhaps in his early days he threw himself enthusiastically into philosophical discussion in the somewhat naïve hope that with enough concentrated effort and devoted attention to the good of his mind and soul he could eventually win his way to that goal. Once he had achieved it, he could use his hard-won wisdom, no doubt not without continued philosophical thinking and philosophical self-direction, to organize and

---

[46] Hence it is a mistake to think that Socrates is "ironical" or feigning when he says repeatedly in the *Apology* and other works of Plato that he has no wisdom. When he denies that he is wise in the way other prominent Athenians were held to be, Socrates is registering his considered view that he is not in a position to withstand any and all such requests for explanation and defense of any of his own values and commitments. He was aware that he might well, if questioned extensively enough, contradict himself or fall into implausible and unreasonable-looking assertions without always being immediately able to dispel or explain away that appearance: this is what his puffed-up allegedly wise interlocutors always ended up doing, under his prodding. That inability is what showed them to be unwise, and the same applies to himself.

lead his life. He would achieve thereby the maximally fulfilled, happy, good human life. Having attained from then on a permanent grasp of the whole system of human values, he would confidently and gracefully conduct his life from the knowledge that that wisdom would provide him.

But by the time of the oracle, Socrates had begun to suspect strongly that his existing lack of wisdom was never going to be overcome, however hard and devotedly he worked. His subsequent experience, especially in discussions with the most illustrious "wise" men of Greece, only deepened this suspicion into a near conviction. What began as a devoted but—he must have hoped—temporally bounded pursuit, through philosophical discussion, of goodness of the soul as the preeminent and controlling value in human life, became a permanent commitment. As I said above, he now understood that philosophical discussion was the sole way open to any actual human being to make real in their life the fundamental Socratic commitment to the goodness of the mind and soul as the preeminent value in human life. And given the constraints that prevented him from engaging in discussion from any position except that of questioner, this commitment led him to a lifelong practice of the particular sort of discussion that I have outlined above. He would raise a question concerning human values for discussion, and then would follow up the respondent's initial answer with further questions, with follow-up questions on the further answers, until the respondent was unable, even to his own satisfaction, to defend his position successfully, and had no further idea to propose. Engaging in Socratic question-and-answer dialectic is the key and indispensable means by which to sustain this commitment to care for one's own soul.

For Socrates, then, philosophical reflection and analysis concerning the human good, as well as concerning human deficiencies, dictate a quite particular way of life. This way of life is, practically speaking, though not in theory, the best for a human being. It is a life in which the practice of philosophical discussion is itself the central activity. Philosophical insight and knowledge show us that the good of the soul is the highest good, and that this good is wisdom—a permanent, deep, and complete grasp of the whole system of human values, in all their ramifications and applications to the varying circumstances of life. Philosophical insight and knowledge also establish that god possesses wisdom automatically and by a necessity of the divine nature. However, an assiduous and self-critically demanding philosophical investigation of existing views on questions about human values, including one's own, leads to the conclusion that, though human nature opens the possibility of wisdom to us, wisdom is too demanding a goal for us to attain in practice. Hence, though in principle the best life is one in which we possess and live on the basis of wisdom, in practice the best human life—the best life any actual human being is ever going to live—is the one in which, like Socrates, we constantly and ceaselessly pursue wisdom through philosophical inquiry and discussion. The practically best human life is a life, not of wisdom (*sophia*), but of philosophy (*philosophia*), wisdom's love and pursuit.

To be sure, in a Socratic "dialectical" discussion, the key activity in the Socratic pursuit of wisdom, all the opinions expressed—all the commitments intellectually undertaken—are the answerer's, none the questioner's. It is answerers who initially advance a thesis on the nature and value of justice or courage, for example. It is answerers who have to respond to subsequent questions by either accepting or rejecting some further premise offered to them for their consideration by Socrates, the questioner. And if some consequence is deduced from these assembled answers that is incompatible or at any rate not in good harmony with the initial thesis, it is the answerer's position that suffers. The answerer's initial thesis is shown not to consort well with his additional views as elicited by Socrates. Likewise, if the questioning leads the answerer to say things in defense of his thesis that are quite implausible—hard to believe—and he cannot find anything to say in order to do away with the implausibility or make it seem acceptable, that is his responsibility. Nonetheless, even though Socrates is the questioner, in such discussions he is engaged in an unrelenting effort on his own part to widen, deepen, and refine his understanding of the vast realm of human values. He aims to make his understanding as comprehensive and as clear and precise as possible. In these discussions he learns a wide variety of opinions on a wide variety of such questions, examines them in the presence of and together with earnest persons who begin by at least favorably regarding them. He learns about the strengths and weaknesses of each of these viewpoints, and its implications and defensibility, in a wide-ranging and open-ended examination of its consequences in relation to issues of human values generally.

Ultimately one who practices Socratic philosophy learns of the need for revision, extension, limitation, and the like, if any of these views are to be sustained at all. In all this one is reaching preliminary positive conclusions oneself, or confirming one's own ideas—one's own critically examined values—by seeing how well they stand up to the test, when one pits them against different conceptions, even sharply contrary ones, by criticizing these conceptions from the point of view of one's own ideas. However, though Socrates's ideas do stand up well, and though in doing so they show their greater intellectual strength than those of his interlocutors, they, too, need greater and deeper defense than Socrates realizes he is capable of giving them. In all his discussions so far, and also (as past experience teaches him) for any future in philosophy that might remain to him, he engages in philosophy in the spirit of a searcher for the truth; he may possess it already, at some point, but he does not have the full and complete, deepest possible grasp of all the reasons why it is true that he seeks as the highest human good. For Socrates, the philosophical discussion that stands at the center of any actual well-lived human life is always one in which one seeks the truth, never one in which one speaks from its possession.

Thus by unrelentingly applying his mind and developing his powers of thought and argument, Socrates constantly improves his understanding. In all his discussions he is testing, while expanding, the range and adequacy of his own grasp of the moral issues on all sides of difficult and debated questions about human nature, human virtue, and the particular virtues of courage, temperance, justice, piety, wisdom, and the rest, which his daily discussions and debates concerned. Eventually Socrates, or any Socratic philosopher, can hope to come as close as possible to possessing the wisdom that belongs to divinity by its very nature—without however, as one may predict, ever reaching it. By following reason where it leads them in these discussions and in their subsequent reflections upon them, they can reach a critically examined commitment to certain ideas about the nature and value of virtue, the nature and value of specific virtues, and the nature and value of the different classes of things other than the good condition of the soul, in relation to the preeminent value of wisdom itself. Reason will lead them ever closer to the truth in these matters—to the truth that god knows, because it is the body of knowledge about human values that constitutes god's connatural wisdom. They will become ever better at articulating to themselves the reasons that support their value conclusions as true, and at defending them against potential objections—even though they do not offer to do this as answerers themselves in such dialectical discussions. They refuse that role, as we have seen, because they remain still not totally convinced of any of their conclusions, however justifiably committed they are to their truth, at least for the time being. They confirm and strengthen this commitment day by day by spending as much of the day as they can manage in discussing, debating, and examining themselves and others on the all-important Socratic questions about human good and human life. And in leading this life of Socratic philosophy, as we have seen, they are constantly assimilating themselves to god, so far as that is practically possible for a human being.[47]

However, the centrality to the Socratic life of open-ended philosophical discussion and inquiry is only one of two ways in which Socratic philosophy not only defines and establishes, but partly constitutes, a way of life. Socrates thinks anyone who repeatedly reasons through, as he has done, all the issues about human nature and the human good that he has kept on addressing, will find their thoughts converging upon a certain determinate set of conclusions. Like him, they will conclude that god is wise in virtue of the divine nature, and that the highest and controlling good in a human life is wisdom, or, in practice, its pursuit. They will reach other conclusions as well, since these also concern issues of human values, but ones affecting, in many practical details, the conduct of our daily lives. They will reach conclusions about the nature of justice and its value, the nature and value of courage, the particular nature and value of other virtues such as piety and temperance or moderation in one's capacities for bodily pleasure and indulgence in it (I will say more about these below). All these conclusions (which I will also go into in more detail below) stand firm, based on strong and systematically deployable reasons that establish them as much more true (if one may speak that way) than any of the alternatives we might hear about from others, or think up ourselves, concerning these questions.

Hence, Socrates, and anyone else who has thought as assiduously as he has about human life and human values, will have strong, self-critically developed reasons for thinking that we should lead our lives on the basis of just these conceptions: we should be courageous, just, temperate, and wise people, and should consistently act courageously, justly, temperately, as well as wisely, according to a specific set of conceptions as to what these virtues are and what they require of us. Thus besides adopting a central place within the well-lived life for philosophical discussion, we must, if we are Socratic philosophers, follow Socrates in the ways we live our daily lives, in the full amplitude that normal social and political relationships provide for them. In fact, we must lead our daily lives not only with such philosophical guidance, but *from* our grasp of these philosophically derived conclusions about human nature and human values. Socratic philosophy not

[47] This motif, of both philosophical activity and virtuous action constituting the maximal assimilation of a human being to god, is inexplicit and only implied in the dialogues of Plato and Xenophon that form the main basis on which we can learn about our notional Socrates. It becomes explicit for the Socrates of Plato's *Theaetetus* (176a–b), and, through that passage, a major component of late ancient Platonism (see chapter 6 below). It is evident too, though not so emphatically presented, in Aristotle's and the Stoics' ethical theories (see chapters 3 and 4 below).

only gives us principles and guidelines telling us how, in considerable detail, we should lead our daily lives (viz., virtuously), and why. For Socrates, as we have seen, all human actions derive from an agent's views about what is good or bad. Those views give her or him not only the reasons, but also all the psychological motivation, on which they act. Hence, in living according to those principles, we are at the same time constantly exercising our philosophical understanding, not just in selecting, but also in performing, the actions that make up our Socratic lives. In short, this understanding—this philosophy—directs and infuses both our philosophical inquiries and our daily choices and actions.

The most important of Socrates's conclusions, from the point of view of moral theory, is his claim of the "unity" of virtue. Wisdom itself, as we have seen, he conceives as a single, tightly unified, comprehensive knowledge of the whole realm of human values. But Socrates holds that that same unified condition of the soul is, in a certain way, also a number of other virtues as well.[48] This knowledge constitutes not just wisdom, but also justice, courage, temperance or moderation as regards bodily pleasures, piety, and perhaps other related moral perfections as well. In ordinary life we do recognize what we intuitively regard as a number of different psychic conditions that we think are perfections of human nature: we think practical wisdom or knowledge is one of these, but we also think a fully good person and a completely well lived life require justice and the other virtues I listed. Because we think of these as distinct and separate perfections, we also, however, tend to think a person who possesses one of them might lack others. Just people can lack courage, we think, and might even be a bit cowardly: they recognize injustice when they see it, and are moved thereby to help correct it, but may hold back, out of fear of the consequences to themselves or their families. Courage in battle, but also courage in the face of illness or hardships of other kinds, seems not inconsistent with overindulgence in drink or drugs and sex, and with bad attitudes about the importance of bodily pleasure generally. Even those whom Socrates's contemporaries regarded as wise (the leading politi-

---

[48] Socrates argues for this view in his debate with Protagoras in Plato's *Protagoras*. Early in the discussion, at 330b, he has undertaken to show Protagoras that the various virtues are not, as Protagoras has claimed (following the common opinion that I explain below in this paragraph), distinct and separate perfections, attainable one by one, with or without one another. Instead, as Socrates says at the inconclusive end of the dialogue, he has throughout the debate "attempted to show" that "everything is knowledge—justice, temperance, courage" (361b). He has attempted to show this by driving Protagoras, through his questioning, to agree with that conclusion—that is, with the thesis of the "unity of virtue." This is a noteworthy place where, though Socrates takes the questioner's role in the discussion and never advances any "thesis" of his own to answer for and defend, he nonetheless announces the unity of virtue (of the virtues) as a philosophical thesis of his own.

cians of Athens, or the most important tragic or other sorts of poets of the Greek tradition), were not thought immune from injustice or other vices in their private lives. These people might know and have outstandingly good judgment about what the city needs and how to achieve it, or even know, and be able to express movingly and effectively, important ideas about human life in general, without themselves being paragons of good living.

But once we follow Socrates in recognizing that true wisdom belongs to the divine and, it seems, solely to the divine, we see that his contemporaries (and perhaps we ourselves too) have very inadequate ideas about what wisdom is, as well as about who has it. If wisdom is the complete knowledge of values that Socrates thinks it must be (since, he thought, god could hardly have only a partial knowledge of values), then not only do even the wisest of humans apparently lack it, but the separateness of other apparent virtues from wisdom is also called in question. This knowledge must encompass whatever values courage specially concerns, and whatever the ones are that fall under the special purview of justice—or of temperance, or piety, or any other virtue there may be. Each virtue enables its possessor to identify or recognize good or bads things that need to be protected or advanced, or guarded against or warded off or otherwise attended to, in some area or recurrent set of circumstances in human life. And so long as we accept, with Socrates, that knowledge of the value of something is sufficient to motivate us appropriately in relation to it, the comprehensive knowledge of value that is wisdom must also contain all that is needed to make us just and courageous and temperate and pious, and indeed possess any other human virtues there may be.

But we can go further. This single knowledge does not contain—as it were as separate components—the knowledge of courage's, justice's, temperance's, and piety's values. If permanently lodged in someone's mind, as it is in god's mind by the divine nature, this single knowledge, taken as a whole, is, in fact, not only wisdom, but also true justice, temperance, courage, and piety as well. Human values—the goods of the soul, the goods of the body, and external goods, of all the many varieties there are of each class—are not a mere collection of independently worthwhile things for a human being to possess and use in shaping their life. They are a mutually integrated, multiply related, set of good things (or bad ones), the true and full value of any one of which cannot be encompassed through any isolated understanding of it alone, or of it and others of its same class taken on their own. They are all interrelated, as I have put it in discussing wisdom above. Knowing, for example, the true value of the goods one must advance or defend in courageous action, under some given circumstances, requires knowing in a completely open-ended way their comparative worth in relation to any and all other values, of whatever class; hence it requires reciprocally knowing each and every one of those other values, too. It is not merely that courageous or just or temperate or pious action in some circumstance or other will have some impact on values not among those that the virtue in question normally makes us alert to—values that, in applying that virtue's knowledge, we need to take into account in our action, if it is even to be an act of virtue, and not a mistaken and ultimately bad action instead. The knowledge of the value of anything good for us in any way at all consists in part of knowing its value in comparative relationship with the value of each and every valuable thing. There is a system of human good, and any element in it is fully understandable as the good that it is only by seeing it in its systematic place in the network of human goods. Thus, having the knowledge that is justice not only requires having the full knowledge of the totality of good, that knowledge (the knowledge of the goods of justice) is, ultimately, the same knowledge that is also wisdom. That is, being just not only requires also being wise, it is, ultimately, the same thing as wisdom. And the same holds for courage, temperance, and piety.

What then distinguishes justice from courage, and both of them from wisdom? Or is there no distinction at all to be maintained? Well, justice is permanent knowledge specifically of one range of human values, and courage of another. Just people's justice enables them to know about the value to themselves individually of living in harmony and cooperation with others, in mutual respect of one another's private domains (their property, their individual family interests, their political rights and obligations). Through justice, they know the value to themselves of their own private domains alongside the value to others of theirs, and they know the higher value to themselves of the harmony and cooperation with others that comes from attending to these with mutual respect. In the classical formula, just persons know the value to themselves of "leaving to each their own." By contrast, courage enables courageous people to know the value to themselves of all manner of good things specifically when the possession or use of them comes under threat of one sort or another, from one source or another. With courage, one knows how and when to yield some good in the face of a threat, and how and when not to, but to resist. One knows also how, and how not, to resist, as well as how to behave in case one loses the good despite one's efforts. And the same holds correspondingly for temperance (in relation to bodily pleasures and physical comforts) and piety (in relation to respect for the divine, and loyalty and respect for parents and country).[49] Wise persons' wisdom makes them know all these things, too, but it is nonetheless worthwhile to recognize courage, justice, temperance, and piety as distinct, though not separate, virtues, both from wisdom and from one another. While any fully courageous person is, as we have seen, necessarily also wise, and just and pious and temperate as well, normal individual human beings differ widely in their knowledge of these different ranges of human values. Some are much closer to having a full knowledge of the values of justice than they are to knowing those of courage, and vice versa; and similarly for knowledge of the values of piety, temperance, and such other qualities as we may see the need to recognize as distinct virtues. Some people choose to behave justly much of the time, but they often do not act courageously when courage is morally called for. They are more nearly just than they are courageous, and we—and they—need to recognize that difference in both praise and criticism of them.

For Socrates, then, the care of the soul as the most important thing in human life requires two things. It requires the pursuit of wisdom through constant philosophical discussion about matters of human value, and through constant self-examination of one's own views on the fullest range possible of those questions. But it also requires the pursuit of justice and all the other human virtues through the constant practice of just, and temperate, and courageous, and pious, and all other virtuous actions in all the varied circumstances of daily life, as the kaleidoscope of life turns. However, just as we are to pursue true wisdom—wisdom as that is itself conceived after and through philosophical reflection on what wisdom must contain and entail—so likewise we are to pursue true justice, true courage, true temperance, and true piety. That is, we are to pursue and practice these virtues as we come to conceive them, and understand the actions they require of us, through philosophical thought and argument. It is philosophy and only philosophy that both reveals and demonstrates to us the system of values from the knowledge of which just action as well as courageous, temperate, and pious action all equally follow. If we could possess that knowledge permanently, we would know always how to reach, given the circumstances so far as we can know them, the proper comparative assessment of the worth of all the different good and bad things our possible actions might affect, whether positively or

---

[49] I have argued for the foregoing interpretation of Socrates's views on the unity of virtue in "The Unity of Virtue" in Cooper, *Reason and Emotion*, pp. 76–117. See esp. sections II–III. My presentation of Socrates's thought on this topic expands greatly on the meager details the text of Plato's *Protagoras* gives us. The reception of the Socratic view in later Greek philosophy suggests this expansion.

negatively. We would know just which balance of interests and concerns, our own and others', would be just and would lead us to the just action in given situations. And the same holds also for action where courage, or temperance, or piety is called for. Even without knowledge, however, our philosophical reflections can lead us to a wide range of fully and well considered views on many of these questions. We can have well-reasoned views on the just balance of interests and concerns in given situations, and act accordingly. We can hold, with good reason, to the idea that some particular action is the one that justice requires of us. Our Socratic inquiries into the nature of justice and the other virtues can result in a significant degree of confidence in our resulting moral judgments, as well as confidence in the rightness of our actions. This confidence, which does not, as I said above, amount to final conviction and absolute certainty, is sufficient to lead us to vigorous and morally (if not absolutely) committed and firm action.

Plato's works include dialogues devoted to each of the major virtues I have mentioned. There are Socratic dialogues wholly devoted to the virtues of piety, courage, and temperance (σωφροσύνη), as well as to the quasi-virtue of friendship;[50] the quasi-Socratic *Republic* I addresses the nature and value (to the just person) of justice. Wisdom is the focus of Socrates's attention in his discussions with Clinias in the *Euthydemus*.[51] In all these dialogues, Socrates is for the most part the questioner in a standard Socratic question-and-answer investigation of an answerer's ideas. Formally, all the philosophical claims made are the answerer's. Nonetheless we can easily identify views about these virtues and their value that Socrates shows at least sympathy for, while using them as the basis from which to develop his lines of question. Given what we have learned about how, on Socrates's view of virtue, a virtue like courage is to be distinguished from justice or temperance or piety, we would expect his inquiries into the "definitions" of particular virtues to lead, eventually and if successful, to a focus on the specific values, as I put it above, that that virtue normally concerns. The core of what courage makes the courageous person know is the value of those specific goods (and bads), in their full comparative relationship with all other good and bad things, of the same and of different classes. So, as Socrates understands the matter, knowing what courage is should include knowing these compara-

---

[50] *Euthyphro, Laches, Charmides,* and *Lysis,* respectively.
[51] See above, section 2.2. Xenophon's *Mem.* also contain dialogues on temperance (II 1), friendship (II 4–6), justice (IV 4), and self-control (IV 5).

tive evaluations and the reasons on which they ultimately rest for their correctness and truth.

In fact, of course, Socrates's discussions in these dialogues never reach a successful conclusion. They end in both Socrates's and the answerer's frustrated sense of puzzlement. The discussions, in the end, are abruptly and inconclusively broken off. And before that, they mostly do not concern the specific values that need to be considered and weighed, and any principles there might be to guide that process, in deciding what is the courageous or just thing to do, whether in general or in particular types of situations. Instead, we learn a great deal about issues of moral psychology—how emotion and feeling are, and are not, involved in the practice of the virtues, how knowledge and the concern for virtue as the good of the soul should, and can, govern our lives, and the like. I have discussed those issues above. There is much else of great interest in these dialogues that, if our concern were to discuss Socrates's moral theory as a whole, in all its aspects, we would want to investigate. The *Euthyphro*, for example, presents us with much valuable food for thought about the relationship of the religious virtue of piety to secular ones such as justice, temperance, and courage. True piety, true "service of god," consists, Socrates suggests at the end of the dialogue, simply in living according to these other virtues: the moral life, lived with a sincere commitment to moral values, conceived nontheologically, turns out to be, in itself, just what true respect for the divine requires of us. Worth mentioning also are the discussion in the *Charmides* of fascinating issues about self-knowledge as a crucial basis for living a good life and the puzzling aspects of the goodness for human life of having friends and being a friend that Socrates pursues at length in the *Lysis*. But for our investigation of ancient philosophies as ways of life, these ideas are of peripheral interest.

In conclusion, let us return to Plato's presentation of Socrates as a person, and of his way of life. We have already seen Socrates described in the *Apology* as an outstandingly courageous man, in refusing to stop parading his philosophy in public, even when stopping would save his life. And his friends all regarded him, as one of them says upon his death, "of all those we have known the best, and also the wisest and the most just."[52] With his views about the difficulty for actual human beings of attaining wisdom, Socrates would surely deny that he possessed any of these virtues. But his courageous and just life did consist of a multitude of courageous and just actions, and, on his own account of what moti-

---

[52] These are the last words of Plato's *Phaedo*.

vates action, those derived from views about the specific values that courage and justice concern that he had worked out through philosophical reflection and self-examination. Plato's and Xenophon's dialogues leave us largely in the dark as to what these were. Nonetheless, however fully or incompletely worked out was the detailed knowledge of human values at which Socrates arrived in his discussions, he lived his philosophy not only through his daily discussions about the virtues and the good life, but also through all the courageous, just, temperate, and pious actions that made up the rest of his life.

The strength of Socrates's commitment to living according to philosophical standards of courage, justice, temperance, and piety, rather than by following unexamined cultural norms of these virtues, is nowhere more striking than in his refusal to allow his friends to arrange his escape from prison after he had been condemned to death for impiety, because it seemed to him clear that to escape and run away would be an injustice.[53] Many others, including many of his contemporaries, might think otherwise. But to him the fundamental importance, as required by justice itself, of respect for law—even flawed or mistakenly applied law—morally demands the willing acceptance of any legal judgment once it has been finally authorized, and so long as it is in force. Justice, for Socrates, requires that no one, not even someone unjustly condemned under the law, may simply set the law's judgment aside and follow his own private wishes and private judgment, instead of the legally authorized orders of the court. Universal reason takes precedence over the particular judgments of single individuals. When finally authorized as applying to an individual case, the laws' commands must be followed, as a matter of justice, just as much as those of a commander in battle.

2.5. Socrates and the Subsequent Tradition

The central feature of Socrates's philosophy is his abstention from all claims to have arrived, with permanent certainty, at the truth in philosophical matters. In Plato's dialogues, he repeatedly declares his lack of wisdom, and just as frequently emphasizes his own love of it. To everyone he meets he urges the love of wisdom as the guide to a well-lived life. Accordingly, the Socratic philosophy as a way of life is, first of all, a life of constant and continued examination of the moral opinions of others, and self-examination in the process. It is also, as we

---

[53] See Plato's *Crito*.

have seen, a life committed to just, courageous, temperate, and pious actions, but without claims to have reached a final and permanently endorsed view about the precise content of the system of human values that guides such actions, if they are to be truly just, courageous, temperate, and pious. It is a life of continued and, in principle, open-ended search for the truth, both in the theory and in the practice of life.

The committed open-endedness of Socratic philosophy marks the Socratic life off sharply from all its successors in the ancient tradition of philosophy as a way of life. Socrates's life and the personal effect of his teaching on those who took part in or witnessed it were powerful influences on his immediate successors, the so-called Socratics, of whom, of course, Plato was one. However, not all the Socratics, from what we know of them, adopted Socrates's conception of philosophy as a way of life as part of their Socratic heritage: I mentioned above Euclides and the "dialectical" philosophers of Megara.[54] Antisthenes, another important Socratic, frequently mentioned in later reports of early philosophers and their lives, seems to have had striking if obscure philosophical opinions in logic and metaphysics. He also lived, and promoted, a rigidly ascetic life, cultivating hardihood and indifference to pain. Diogenes Laertius, in his *Lives of Eminent Philosophers*, makes Antisthenes the "founder" of the Greek "school" devoted to a cynic "back to nature" life of flouting the "conventions" of civilization. (Diogenes of Sinope, the famous Cynic of the fourth century BCE, was alleged to have been Antisthenes's "pupil.") But, however much Antisthenes's life of hardihood may have imitated Socrates's own notorious indifference to bodily comforts and adornments, and the general simplicity of his lifestyle, we have no evidence connecting Antisthenes's ascetic style of life to the philosophical views he is reported to have held. Nor, so far as we can tell, was it in any way a life led from rationally worked out philosophical views that might support it: the lack of connection between life and philosophy in Antisthenes's case mirrors the situation with the fifth century Pythagoreans, as described above. In fact the whole subsequent ancient tradition of a Cynic way of living (modeled on Diogenes's) seems not properly to be counted an instance of philosophy as a way of life at all.[55] Diogenes Laertius himself reflects this when, having discussed for many pages the lives of the famous Cynics one by one, he goes on (with some strain) to

[54] See above, section 2.2.

[55] Readers interested in learning more about Diogenes the Cynic should read the accessible and amusing, but philosophically acute, account given by Raymond Geuss in his *Public Goods, Private Goods*, chap. 2.

assemble a single page of "philosophical views" he alleges were common to the "school." In fact, he admits that some authorities deny the Cynic movement was a philosophy at all; it was just a way of life (ἔνστασις βίου)—though one with a sharp "philosophical" point.[56]

Among the Socratics, our evidence seems to suggest, it was Plato alone who followed Socrates in conceiving of philosophy as a way of life; indeed, as I have argued, his Socrates, the Socrates that Plato fashioned in his Socratic dialogues, is the originator of this conception. But there are striking differences. In Plato's philosophy (as expressed in his *Republic*, which, at least after its first book, is not a Socratic dialogue) we find the conviction that one actually can come to know, and, under ideal conditions, can educate a whole (small) group of political rulers so that they too will know, the full truth about the human good.[57] There is an intelligible Form of the Good, and philosophical argument and discussion, if assiduously enough pursued, will lead us to grasp its full nature. We can also be trained to live our own lives constantly from that knowledge, once we have grasped it. So, according to this and other non-Socratic dialogues, some human beings will in practice, and not only can in principle, possess all the virtues (including wisdom) that Socrates thought no human being would ever in fact attain. The completely fulfilled and happy life is seen as actually attained by human beings—of course, only by a naturally gifted few, and then not without strenuous personal effort, in not only intellectual but also moral self-training, and (notably), even for these gifted few, only within a carefully constructed social and political world that will offer constant assistance, both early and late in life, for their personal efforts. For Plato in the *Republic*, it is possible to be brought up and educated so that one unfailingly lives according to the virtues and on the basis of the philosophical understanding that lies behind them: the Socrates of the *Republic* specifies in considerable detail what that education will contain.

Accordingly, if we count the theories of his non-Socratic dialogues as constituting Plato's philosophy, then a Platonic way of life would be one led on the basis of actually possessed knowledge and wisdom. It would differ sharply in this respect from the Socratic life of searching for the truth, without ever fully find-

---

[56] See *Lives of Eminent Philosophers*, VI 103. Taking this cue from D. L., I think it is better to treat the long-lasting and fascinating movement of Cynicism in ancient Greece and the Roman Empire as aspects of social history, rather than as part of the history of philosophy. The cynic way of life was a popular off-shoot of philosophy, not a philosophy of its own, i.e., a life based on sustained philosophical analysis and argument. For that reason it does not deserve inclusion in our list of ancient philosophical ways of life, or discussion in this book.

[57] See *Republic* II–X, esp. V, 474-VII.

ing it. As just noted, the Platonic happy way of life differs also from the Socratic in the crucial importance for Plato, if (leaving aside some one-off exception, such as Socrates himself) the happy life of philosophy is to be attained by human beings at all, of the assistance provided through an ideal social and political system. This system itself is defined and regulated on philosophical principles, and aimed at making both possible and actual the most happy lives of the philosophers, alongside the less happy lives of ordinary, nonphilosophical people, as well.[58] The wisdom of the founding philosophers of Plato's ideal city will show itself in the moral and political principles that provide its constitution, and will be replicated, generation by generation, in their successors. For Plato in the *Republic*, the wisdom that these successor philosophers will possess, and will exercise both in helping to direct the life of the whole city and in their own continued philosophical research and contemplation, is conceived as one of pure philosophical insight into basic metaphysical truths about physical reality and its relation to a higher reality of true being—the eternal, intellectually graspable Forms of Platonic metaphysical theory. So the happy life of the *Republic*'s philosophers will be a life of philosophy in the strictest and narrowest sense: it is a life in which devotion to intellectual activities of philosophical analysis, argument, and contemplation of the truth is at the center of their way of life. Nonetheless, this life also involves active participation by the philosophers (each taking their turn, in fair rotation) in the political activity of constant oversight of the institutions of the ideal city.[59]

That the philosophically happy life is one of full knowledge, actually possessed, and not merely sought, as it was for Socrates, is assuredly true, as well, of the Platonist way of life advanced by Plotinus and others in late antiquity, on the basis of their reading of the *Republic* and other dialogues of Plato.[60] The same is true of the whole tradition in between Plato and Plotinus of philosophy as a way of life, with the sole exception of the skeptical thinkers, Academic and Pyrrhonist. Aristotle, the Stoics, and Epicurus disagree sharply among themselves, and

[58] Plato's emphasis on the necessity of a proper social and political context if the happy life of philosophy is to be attained is taken up and developed in his own ways by Aristotle in his *Nicomachean Ethics* and *Politics*: see below, chapter 3.

[59] As we will see, for Aristotle, Plato's closest follower in ethics and political theory, because he varies from Plato in recognizing a second form of wisdom, practical as distinct from theoretical, the *Republic*'s single happy life, grounded in the pursuit of wisdom, becomes two lives: a life devoted to philosophically theoretical thinking led by thinkers who do not undertake political rule or oversight, and another life, devoted to the exercise of practical wisdom, led by the political leaders of the happy city, in overseeing the happy—though not happiest—daily life of the rest of its citizens.

[60] See below, chapter 6.

with the views put forward in Plato's dialogues, on many important points of philosophical theory, as we will see in subsequent chapters.[61] But each of these philosophers (or philosophical systems) propounds his own theory of the full nature of the human good. They believe they have arguments that establish once and for all just what the good is, and what it requires of us in the organization and living of our lives. Philosophy, for them, is in each case a well-defined way of life, in which one's philosophy tells one with assurance what is best in any circumstance, and puts that knowledge into effect in one's choices and actions. For them, as for Plato, and late Platonists, this is a life of constant and continued engagement in philosophical study and thought, but also one of confident, philosophically grounded virtuous action. Perhaps, as in the case of the Stoics, it is thought to be an exceedingly rare accomplishment to acquire this knowledge and wisdom. But the Stoics seem to have thought that Socrates, at least, despite his own denial, had actually achieved it. So, they think, perhaps others have done so, and we might do it too, if we think hard enough! Nonetheless the crucial point of difference stands. All these successors propose a philosophical way of life in which one actively knows the human good and through that knowledge lives virtuously throughout.

The Pyrrhonists, philosophical skeptics of the first century BCE and later, do, of course, doubt whether knowledge of the truth, in these or any other matters, is actually possible even in theory. Their philosophy, like Socrates's, consists in inquiry into the truth by examining the opinions and arguments of others— namely, all these other philosophers'.[62] But unlike Socrates—and this is a deep and crucial difference—they not only suspect that no one knows anything; they have no faith that there is any objective truth to be known, whether on any issue of philosophical dispute or on any other question. To be sure, they do not hold, as a matter of philosophical doctrine, that that there is no truth. But their experience with the practice of philosophical inquiry, insofar as that is grounded in the assumption, common to Socrates as well as all these other philosophers, that there is an ultimate truth, a truth lodged in the nature of things or in god's mind, has led them to be very much inclined to believe that this assumption is a philosophical delusion. It is deeply harmful, too, they think, since it causes other philosophers (the ones who accept this assumption) needless and pointless anxiety, once it is discovered, by the Pyrrhonists' own insistent, but noncommittal, phil-

---

[61] See below, chapters 3 and 4 and section 5.2, respectively.
[62] See below, section 5.5.

osophical inquiry, that no positive result of any philosophical inquiry has ever yet been established, securely and once and for all, as true. So the Pyrrhonists' commitment to the value of philosophy—that is, to their own noncommittal philosophizing, by examining and rejecting all positive philosophical doctrines—is much weaker than Socrates's. So is, as we will see, their commitment to the principles, derived from their skeptical philosophy, on which they live their daily lives.

Thus, the Socratic way of life stands markedly apart from all the others in this one respect. Socrates's passionate but tentative commitment to exploratory, open-ended philosophical reasoning as the grounding for the whole of one's life is unique to this one ancient way of life. Despite this momentous difference, however, Socrates bequeathed a very great deal to all these successors. To begin with, as I have argued in this chapter, Socrates's powerful new conception of philosophy as not merely an intellectual pursuit but a way of life, and the power of his personal commitment to it, established that conception deeply in the whole subsequent ancient philosophical tradition. Moreover, the priority among goods that he assigned to the good of the soul in determining the goodness and happiness of one's life became axiomatic for later philosophers. Socrates's focus on the good of the soul also stamped the moral philosophy of the ancients with its characteristic eudaemonist orientation: virtue, as the good of the soul, will make us live happy and fulfilled lives. Likewise, as for Socrates, so for the subsequent tradition of ancient moral philosophy (setting the Skeptics aside), philosophy and philosophy alone, since it is the acquired expertise at reasoning in pursuit of the truth, has the authority to determine what virtue truly is, and what it requires of us. For the whole philosophical tradition going back to Socrates, social and religious traditions are secondary phenomena of the moral life, subject to the critical authority of philosophical reason to correct them where they may go wrong (as they certainly do, at many points). Finally, Plato and Platonists, Aristotle, the Stoics, even Epicurus, an opponent of all religion—that is, all the main philosophical schools and movements of antiquity except, of course, the Skeptics—follow Socrates in making the philosophical life the best for human beings by also making it the most divine or godlike.

As inheritors of this common Socratic ethical framework, the major subsequent Greek philosophers also followed Socrates in his independence of mind and his insistence on thinking all things through for himself. It is true, as I have brought out in my discussion in this chapter, that Socrates's mode of philosophizing, through question-and-answer discussions in which he is never the answerer, often leaves the reader and interpreter with a difficult task in trying to uncover, or indeed even in conjecturing the philosophical reasons on which he may seem to have rested all his conclusions. In reading a Socratic dialogue of Plato's you always have to think through for yourself all the reasons that might support the positions staked out and critically discussed, as well as their implications. This applies even to Socrates's commitment to the supreme value of the good of the soul, as also to his views on what virtue is and, for the most part, what particular virtues require of us, and on the life of philosophy as the most divine or godlike one. Subsequent philosophers, beginning with Plato and running all the way through the Greek tradition of moral philosophy, philosophize in a different way. They present positive arguments in their own voices (or, in Plato's case, in those of his principal speaker) for all their conclusions, both when they follow Socrates, developing theories that will justify his philosophical commitments, and when they depart from him. The result is a whole series of elaborate, intellectually striking, original, and in many points mutually conflicting sets of ideas about human nature, the nature of the universe, the human good, and the human virtues—not to mention myriad theories on particular questions falling within this broad scope, all argued out and justified by carefully considered reasons of a philosophical kind, presented openly as such. Ancient philosophy is not a way of life; it is many quite distinct ways of life—not only the Socratic, but also the Aristotelian, Stoic, Epicurean, Pyrrhonist, and Platonist ways. We will examine these ways in the subsequent chapters of this book.

Readers may wonder why I do not include also a detailed discussion of the "Platonic way of life," but limit myself to the brief summary account provided above. A detailed account would require close attention not only to the *Republic* but also to Plato's *Laws*, in whose city philosophy and philosophers play a quite indistinct role, even though the citizens willingly live their lives on the basis of philosophical principles. Other dialogues (or specific passages in them, such as ones in *Phaedo* and *Theaetetus* that I will be concerned with in chapter 6, when we turn to the Platonist way of life proposed by Plotinus and other Platonists of late antiquity) would be required as well. We would also need to address the *Statesman*, with its subtle accounts of the rule of law and the role of philosophical insight and judgment itself as an alternative basis for an ethical and happy life. My principal reason for not including a chapter on the Platonic way of life, alongside those on the Aristotelian, Stoic, Epicurean, Skeptic, and Platonist ways, is this: unlike all Socrates's other major successors discussed in the chapters of this book to follow, Plato famously always presents his philosophical ideas in dialogues. This is one important heritage of his experience with Socrates and his admiration of him as a teacher and as a person. If the historical Socrates taught Plato anything, it was an abhorrence of dogmatism in philosophy. One must always be open-minded, even when one thinks one has arrived at some truth, and, accordingly, true Socratic philosophers, even ones who do have elaborate philosophical theories to present, as Plato decidedly does, must not present them to others (whether in their writings or in any other forum) except as something for them to consider, think and rethink, mull over, and make up their own minds about.

Hence, in Plato's dialogues, some character or other, an invention of the author even if they bear the name of a historical personage, speaks every word that Plato writes (and, unlike in Cicero's dialogues, there is never even a character named "Plato"). Plato never speaks directly to the reader, as author of a straight presentation of arguments and ideas as ones that he accepts and defends philosophically as his own. All the other philosophers I discuss below wrote philosophical treatises in which they expounded their ideas and arguments, and they offered them to readers as the truth, backed up (as they thought) with invincible arguments and analyses, duly presented as such to their readers. Plato wrote no philosophical treatise. I would not dispute that there is a "philosophy of Plato," but in order to reconstruct and discuss it, an interpreter must attempt to locate in his works some set of philosophical ideas, with supporting arguments and analyses, and present those as the author Plato's own, conveyed somehow from within and behind the dialogic text as prepared by him. The scholarly and philosophical hazards presented by such an effort introduce a level of complication for any honest account of Plato's contribution to the tradition of philosophy as a way of life, that the straightforward contributions of the other major figures in this tradition do not present. Moreover, there are unresolved conflicts and contradictions in the varied texts that would have to be somehow negotiated, if one should attempt to reconstruct a "philosophy of Plato" from such dialogues as *Republic*, *Laws*, *Theaetetus*, *Phaedo*, *Statesman*, and *Philebus* (among others), as well as a single "Platonic way of life" based upon it. Everything one said would have to be too hedged about with qualifications and reservations. For these reasons, it seems best to limit our detailed discussion of ancient philosophies as ways of life to the presentation and interpretation of the views set out and advocated by philosophers as their own views, in writings of theirs that we can consult for ourselves, or can reconstruct from reports by ancient authors about them.

Plato's importance in this tradition is nonetheless enormous. As I indicated above, he was the philosopher who most clearly and persuasively elaborated, for the whole later tradition, the very idea of philosophy as a way of life: it is the Socrates of the Socratic dialogues that Plato wrote who articulates and presents in such an inspiring light that conception of philosophy and of its power to reform and elevate human life. Moreover, as we will see below, different elements in his work lie behind and inspire to a very considerable extent many of the developments that we will see within this tradition, beginning with Aristotle and carrying right through to the uses made of Platonic ideas by the Platonists of late antiquity. Aristotle's theory of the moral virtues and his moral psychology were developed to a great extent through thinking about the views expressed by the Socrates of the *Republic* and those of the Athenian Visitor in the *Laws*; I mentioned above Aristotle's endorsement of ideas of Socrates in Plato's *Republic* about the social and political context necessary for philosophy as a way of life to be even a hoped-for achievement. The Stoics' adherence to Socratic ideas about the power of reason to direct our lives, without the aid of emotions or other nonrational powers, derives largely from their reading of Plato's Socratic dialogues. In addition, fundamental parts of the Stoics' view of the world as a divine creation, and of the place of human beings within that creation, derive from Plato's works (the *Timaeus* primarily). I will be making extensive, though piecemeal, reference to these points of influence as we proceed.

Let me conclude this chapter with one note of caution. As I pointed out early in this section, the main subsequent exponents of their own philosophies as ways of life—not only Plato, but also Aristotle, the Stoics, Epicurus, and Plotinus—all hold that full personal perfection and a fully happy life, based on fully accomplished philosophical knowledge, are realistically within many, or even most, human beings' sights, even if that achievement is a relatively rare achievement. So they focus their discussions of ethical matters upon working out the details of the life of the fully virtuous, fully happy person: "the wise man," as it is often put. On the other hand, they are well aware, as their recognition of this relative rareness indicates, that most of their readers will not end up succeeding to live that best and perfect life (just as they themselves may well not do, and with full knowledge of that fact). However, it is at least implicit in their work (for Epicurus, as we will see, it is almost explicit) that, according to them, the moral and intellectual improvement that comes from studying and learning the truths, as they see them, of their philosophical theories is by no means limited to those who fully master them and make them their own. Every forward step toward the goal brings a steady improvement in the life that one leads through the effort to live the Aristotelian, or Stoic, or Epicurean, or Platonist way of life, as that is defined in the ideal terms of the comprehensive theories on which these philosophers' accounts of it are focused. If readers are to use, and benefit, in their own lives, from the examination of the philosophies of the Greeks in my subsequent chapters, they must constantly bear this point in mind. The "ideal" character of Greek ethical theory does not deprive it, when properly grasped, of the most complete, universally applicable, and fully practical consequences for the way we can individually decide to live.

CHAPTER 3

Aristotle
Philosophy as Two Ways of Life

3.1. Introduction

For Aristotle, philosophy itself and the life of philosophy are much different and much more complex than they were for Socrates. Aristotle's philosophical activity included writing (and presenting in lectures) whole treatises, fully elaborated and extensively argued. In these he advanced, as philosophical theses of his own, many positive conclusions on all sorts of subjects. As a philosopher, he did not rest content, as Socrates did, with full and careful exploration of his own or other people's ideas about human life and how to lead it. He developed, argued for, and defended elaborate theories not just on ethics and how best to lead a human life, but he certainly included ethics prominently in the topics that he did investigate. Aristotelian philosophical argument and analysis encompassed topics in logic and the methodology of argument, some of them directed toward the sort of question-and-answer discussion that Socrates specialized in. But included also were the general theory of nature: how all the kinds of matter there are are constituted from physical elements; and the natures of time and place, the laws of motion, as well as theories about the "soul," which he regarded as the physical (and metaphysical) basis for the life of any living thing, including not only human beings and other animals, but plants, too. Aristotle made extensive investigations of a very wide range of animals aimed at developing a methodology for understanding central features of animal life. Included as well were special studies of varied psychological processes, such as sensation and its varieties, memory, dreaming, sleep and waking, aging and death, and the varieties of the self-movement from place to place among the different species of animal. His studies extended to metaphysics, too: the importance of the distinction between a physical object's essence and its additional properties, the constitution and the bases for identity over time of physical objects themselves, among other metaphysical questions, and the nature of god, who (or which) on Aristotle's analysis is a living being, not the creator of, but in crucial ways the causal origin for, the whole universe and its organization.

A full account of how Aristotle conceived philosophy as a way of life must pay heed to some of the results of his wide-ranging studies in areas other than ethics and moral and political philosophy, particularly in the general theory of nature and in the metaphysics of divinity. On the other hand, as we will see, Aristotle developed a powerful conception of moral philosophy as a separate and essentially freestanding part of philosophy as a whole—separate from such "theoretical" philosophical topics as those concerning nature and divinity. Still, at crucial junctures he draws upon results of his physical and metaphysical studies in developing his ethical and political theory. Moreover, his overall conception, deriving from those studies, of human nature and our place in the world at large, stands always as an essential background against which we must place his ethical and political thought if we are to understand it properly. Nonetheless, in addressing Aristotle's conception of philosophy as a way of life we must focus our attention on two main works, his *Nicomachean Ethics* and *Politics*. Along the way, we will occasionally need to draw into our account some aspects of these other studies. In the next chapter, in discussing Stoic ethics and the Stoic way of life, we will seek further illumination concerning Aristotle's conception of human nature itself and our place in the overall world order in which we live, by comparing it with the markedly different views of the Stoic philosophers of the centuries following Aristotle's own.[1]

Aristotle's *Nicomachean Ethics* presents itself as the first part of a single enterprise, the second and concluding part of which we find in his *Politics*.[2] For Aristotle, ethics and politics, as philosophical studies, are not just related externally to one another, so to speak. It is not as if we must first study, in the *Ethics*, personal ethics and individual happiness as something self-contained (even if perhaps with implications for political involvement), before going on next in sequence to study, in the *Politics*, the principles of a correct social and political order for people living a good human life, as individuals—the two added to-

---

[1] See section 4.3.
[2] See endnote 11 for information about Aristotle's other works on ethics.

gether constituting a complete "philosophy of human affairs."[3] From the outset (*Nicomachean Ethics* I 1–2) Aristotle describes the concern of ethics as, indeed, the highest human good (human happiness)—something that individuals, alone, can possess, as individuals. But he is at pains to make that a part, the most fundamental part, of the study of what in these chapters he calls political knowledge or science. For Aristotle, understanding the highest human good (just by itself, so to speak, as a good of individual persons—the function of the *Ethics*) is, in an essential and fundamental way, part of acquiring the political capacity or power. This capacity is, as he puts it, the "most controlling" or "most architectonic" science or knowledge. Its province is to know, and so to tell us about, and put into its proper place, every aspect of human life—on the assumption, which Aristotle articulates at a number of places in his work, that human beings are by nature drawn to, and need to, live within a politically organized social context if they are to realize their full nature. Full knowledge about any and all activities of the good and happy human life (and of all the not-so-good and happy ones) is, on Aristotle's view in the *Nicomachean Ethics*, found exclusively in political knowledge. And this knowledge by itself constitutes the fully accomplished capacity or power to engage expertly in political affairs, the affairs of state. Thus, for Aristotle from the outset in the *Nicomachean Ethics*, ethics or moral philosophy must be understood as an undertaking in pursuit and as part of political knowledge.

This political aspect of philosophical ethics as Aristotle pursues it, though plainly there for all who read the *Nicomachean Ethics* to see, is often left to one side by commentators, after obligatory mere mention. That may be due to the fact that Aristotle carries out his subsequent discussions in the *Ethics* (in the remainder of book I and in books II–X, chapter 8) without making the political dimension of ethical knowledge that he begins by insisting on an explicit topic for extended discussion. He does not explain in just what ways he thinks ethical knowledge is somehow, and indeed fundamentally, political. In sum, in the rest of the work, he offers a summary sketch of human happiness or the highest human good in book I, and goes on in subsequent books to fill in this sketch. He gives us extensive accounts of the "ethical" virtues governing the activities of a happy person's daily life—not merely virtues concerning how we treat one another, but others governing other more personal (as we would speak today, "nonmoral") parts of our lives. He also discusses the virtues of thought that complete

---

[3] Aristotle uses this expression once, in the last chapter of *NE*, X 9, at 1181b15.

these moral virtues but also complement them, by introducing into the study of the happy life the cultivation of our theoretical powers and attention to their special intrinsic value. Aristotle completes the project of the *Ethics* with further accounts of the nature of human action, self-control and its lack, the nature and varieties of pleasure, the forms and value of friendship, and, finally, the ideal life itself. But, in the separate discussions devoted to this series of special topics, he only glancingly takes notice of any connection of these topics to political knowledge or the political capacity or power.

At the very end of the work, however, Aristotle returns to the political theme introduced in the first two chapters of book I. He tells us there that, despite having gone through all the topics I have just listed in my summary, we do not yet know all we need to know in order to fully grasp the highest human good, happiness. He points his readers forward to the study of political constitutions and systems of laws (the very stuff of political science as we would ordinarily think of it) as what we must take up in order to complete our knowledge of the highest human good. We need, then, to turn to the final chapter of the work (*NE* X 9) in order to understand in just what way ethics is a political subject for Aristotle. Once we grasp that, we will be well on our way to understanding also how, and in what different ways, knowledge acquired through philosophical reflection— as exemplified in the *Ethics* itself—is a key resource for living a good life, according to Aristotle. Not only that, we will begin to see how, for Aristotle, the activities of philosophical analysis and study themselves are crucial components of the well-lived human life's most distinctive activities.

Two main ideas control what Aristotle says in *Nicomachean Ethics* X 9. The first concerns his conception of ethical and political knowledge (the sorts of knowledge to which his studies in both *Nicomachean Ethics* and *Politics* are intended to contribute) as (in a way I will attempt to explain) essentially practical, and not at all theoretical or "contemplative" in character.[4] This Aristotelian conception of moral philosophy as, in a special sense, aimed at practical knowledge is, like its connection to political science, clearly marked in Aristotle's text. But, again, this is neglected or ignored by commentators. As we will see, the specifically practical character, for Aristotle, of the knowledge that moral philosophy aims at achieving is a key element for us to take fully on board, in discussing Ar-

---

[4] Aristotle's Greek term θεωρητική, applied to "theoretical" knowledge, is indeed the origin of our word "theoretical," but its root in Greek indicates an act of viewing, and there is a suggestion of spectatorship—as at the theater, hence the tendency of translators to characterize Aristotelian theoretical knowledge in English as "contemplative."

istotle's philosophy as a way of life. It enables him to claim that one crucial role for philosophy in human affairs is to establish a certain way of life as the best one for human beings, a philosophical way of life. In fact, for Aristotle, philosophical inquiry and thought play a central and ongoing part in this life. The basic idea here is that the knowledge that those who engage, in a proper way, in reading and thinking over what Aristotle has to say in his *Ethics* are attempting to acquire, will necessarily affect, indeed control, the way those who have acquired it lead their whole life. This knowledge may consist of what we might reasonably call "theories" of ethics (and of politics), but knowing these theories, Aristotle insists, is not a theoretical kind of knowing at all, but instead "practical" knowledge. This is a special kind of knowing. It is not merely knowing one particular subject matter, the human good, rather than some other—say, the mathematical intricacies of the planets' movements, or the nature of the soul, or details of the structures of animal bodies and their relation to animals' life activities. This subject matter, the human good, when known in this special sort of way, one that Aristotle thinks is intrinsically suited to it, comes to provide the guiding oversight and direction for a person's whole life—in fact, for all the actions and activities that make it up. In that respect, this "practical" knowledge of the human good is unique among all the branches of human knowledge.

The second controlling idea in *Nicomachean Ethics* X 9 concerns Aristotle's view that happiness or the highest human good, the ultimate object of these studies, is of such a nature that it cannot fully be achieved except in a political community—a community of people who lead their individual lives as parts of a common project of living happily and well as a whole group. It is through this understanding of the human good that Aristotle (as I will explain) establishes the essential connection that, as I have mentioned, he establishes between knowing the human good and knowing about systems of laws and political constitutions, both good and bad.

3.2. Practical vs. Theoretical Knowledge

First, then, let us consider Aristotle's conception of practical knowledge, as a unique kind of knowledge. Aristotle refers to this at the beginning of X 9, after raising the question of whether the preceding discussions, in books I through X, chapter 8, do or do not completely fulfill his and our (his readers') intentions in engaging in them. He reminds us that, where it is a question of actions and activities that are, or are to be, done (τὰ πρακτά), our goal in our studies is not to develop theories (θεωρῆσαι) and to know (in that "contemplative," theoretical way) about the various points concerned.[5] Rather, our purpose is to come to act, ourselves, in all the relevant ways. This echoes what he said back in book II, as he began his discussion of the ethical virtues:

> The present undertaking (πραγματεία) is not for the sake of developing theories as our other ones are (for we are not inquiring so as to know what virtue is, but so as to become good people).[6]

As this earlier passage implies, Aristotle does think that it is a necessary, or anyhow an especially effective,[7] means to becoming a good person (i.e., a fully good one, one who actually does fully possess the virtues) to engage for oneself in the philosophical thinking and argument involved in studying ethics with him, in the progression of discussions that make up the *Nicomachean Ethics*.[8] I will return to this later. But for now we need to bear in mind that, according to Aristotle's analysis in book I (which is the accepted point of reference for all the subsequent discussions), the highest human good, happiness, itself consists in "virtuous activity." It consists in the activities that express in a person's life possession of those qualities of mind and of character that qualify as the human virtues. (I will return to this later, too.) So in saying that in our undertaking in the *Ethics* we have been seeking to become good people, he implies also, in effect and more fundamentally, that we have been seeking to achieve our highest good, our happiness, through these studies.

In these passages of books X and II Aristotle contrasts "developing theories" (θεωρῆσαι) about other matters with thinking about "actions that are to be done" (τὰ πρακτά). Following his lead, we can state the difference between moral philosophy, on the one hand, and his studies in, for example, metaphysics or phi-

---

[5] 1179b1.

[6] 1103b26–28. This itself echoes and expands what Aristotle said already in I 3, 1095a5–6: "the goal" in political studies "is not knowing but acting." Here and elsewhere in my translations from the *NE* I have consulted those by T. H. Irwin, *Aristotle: Nicomachean Ethics*, and Christopher Rowe, *Aristotle: Nicomachean Ethics*. I mostly follow one or the other of them, usually Rowe, but always freely and with alterations that I do not note explicitly.

[7] See further p. 90f. below.

[8] Being fully good means possessing all the human virtues for action, including the one he calls φρόνησις or practical wisdom—a virtue of thought, not an "ethical" virtue. Aristotle implies in this passage that, even if it might be possible to become practically wise (and therefore fully good) without philosophical study, the study of ethics he is engaging his readers in aims at the goal of making them practically wise. See *NE* VI 13, 1145a1, referred to below.

losophy of nature, on the other, by saying that the understanding sought in moral philosophy is, as I put it above, not a theoretical (or "contemplative") but a practical understanding—one that immediately or directly leads to one's "practices" in the living of one's life. We can begin to understand why Aristotle is so insistent that an understanding of human actions must be sharply distinguished from the understanding of other matters if we bear in mind that, as he frequently says, actions are always done for the sake of some good—in fact, some human good. The understanding being pursued in these studies, but not the others, is therefore an understanding of what is of value to a human being, *as* being of value to them. This understanding is one that does not merely know that what is valuable is valuable, but knows it *as* valuable—that is, it sees and embraces it as valuable. Aristotle reasonably thinks, it seems, that one cannot attain an understanding of such good things in this way, as being of value for us, just by knowing in a non-committal, theoretical, way what these good things are, or even what is good about them. Someone who could go through all the arguments and who understood on their own behalf, and could explain and defend with full articulateness (and not just by repeating what some teacher has said), all the reasons offered for the value of virtue and virtuous action for a human being (i.e., for oneself, among others), but who was left indifferent by those reasons, could not properly be said to understand the value of virtue. Understanding human goods, including virtue itself as the most important of all goods, as being of value to us, must include a motivation for becoming and being virtuous.[9]

It is important to see, however, that for Aristotle this practical understanding of virtue, which includes this motivation, really is simply an *understanding* of it as valuable, and nothing more.[10] It is a full, explicit, articulable grasp of what is good about virtue, and how virtue relates as a value to other things also similarly grasped as good. (I will have more to say about this later on.) Such a grasp, he thinks, simply in and of itself, moves us to embrace virtuous activity as our highest good. No feeling of attraction to virtuous activity, as something separate from the understanding, needs to be added in order for the motivation provided directly in this understanding to be present and at work in one's psyche.[11] Because

---

[9] Indeed, this motivation must be decisive; that is, it must lead to one's acting in accordance with virtue—but that is another matter.

[10] See endnote 12 for further discussion on practical knowledge in relation to desire.

[11] This is not to deny that in virtuous people there will also be some additional feeling of attraction for virtuous activity, something emotional in character, as we could say; my point is only that for Aristotle practical understanding of values, as values, in and of itself provides its own, separate, sort of motivating push or pull toward virtuous activity. See below, on the "love of the fine," about which Aristotle speaks in

of the essential connection to motivation implied in the very act of understanding something good as good for a human being, which is lacking in other cases and other sorts of argued or articulable understanding, this counts as a unique sort of understanding. For a human being, Aristotle thinks, to understand something as being of value for a human being is to be moved thereby toward it. The understanding here in question is what Aristotle identifies as one of the "intellectual" virtues, or virtues of thought (διάνοια),[12] as opposed to the virtues of habituated states of feeling (ἦθος). It is in fact φρόνησις or practical wisdom. By having acquired that understanding, that practical wisdom, once we also have the fully habituated relevant virtuous states of feeling, we become fully or simply or without qualification good and virtuous, on Aristotle's account—ἁπλῶς ἀγαθός.[13] So, when Aristotle says in *Nicomachean Ethics* X 9 that our purpose in going through the investigations of the *Nicomachean Ethics* is to come to act in certain ways—virtuous ones—he is reminding us that our study just being completed is aimed at making us fully good people by giving us this sought-for practical understanding of virtue.

Here we need to take into account Aristotle's notorious insistence that no one is to take part in the philosophical study of ethics and politics without first, through their earlier upbringing and education, having acquired good and virtuous habits of feeling.[14] Having achieved such habits of feeling enables them to go forward, if they are otherwise sufficiently gifted, so as to grasp the philosophical principles that ground the further virtue of practical wisdom. In fact, they will thereby turn those early habits into fully virtuous states of character. These habits are sufficient to give them an intuitive attraction to proper behavior and to the values it serves, and an intuitive dislike of the opposites. Without such intuitive feelings, he thinks, one is not open to grasping the reasons why the one sort of behavior is such a good thing for oneself, and the other so bad. One just will not listen if someone tries to explain them, or won't understand if one does.[15] Only by having these intuitive feelings is one now ready to pay attention to what reason says. Such a person is not led, as people not well brought up are, simply by the passions (especially those related to untutored immediate pleasure and dis-

---

this connection: this is just such an emotional attraction, and all virtuous people experience it, in addition to the purely rational motivation provided by the understanding itself in grasping the value of virtuous activity.

[12] Cf. 1103a5.

[13] See *NE* VI 13, 1145a1.

[14] See I 3, 1094b28–95a11 and 4, 1095a30–b13.

[15] Cf. X 9, 1179b26–29.

like) that proper behavior places restrictions on. Hence, as Aristotle says,[16] the knowledge of philosophical ethics and politics would be of use to such a person, as it would not be for those without those prior habits of feeling (assuming counterfactually that they could ever acquire this knowledge).[17] Such people would be in a position to be improved by it, as the others are not. It would give them a full understanding—a practical understanding as I have just explained it, involving reasoned motivations—of what is good and what is bad for human beings, quite generally, and so of the consummate value of the virtues in giving shape to a human life.

It is important to emphasize that such neophytes, first coming to the study of ethics, are not good and virtuous people already, despite their habitual practice of virtuous behavior, and their intuitive love of the values that such behavior constitutes and promotes. Here we can profit from observing an important distinction that Aristotle occasionally notices, and, in fact, marks out in the last chapter of the *Nicomachean Ethics*.[18] This is the distinction between a good person (an ἀγαθός, someone who fully possesses the virtues of character) and someone who is merely decent (ἐπιεικής). The latter sort of person has decent habits of feeling and behavior, but lacks the knowledge and understanding, and other refinements, of the truly good. In terms of this distinction, the well brought up young (or youngish) men whom Aristotle thinks qualified for the study of ethics and politics, and whom he permits at his lectures, are basically decent, young-adult, but still somewhat unformed people.[19] Having made a good start through their upbringing and their experience of life so far, they might come to possess well-settled characters, and so to be decent fully mature people, even without engaging in philosophical study of ethics and politics. But their incipient characters are so disposed, and their intelligence is such, that they can acquire the understanding that philosophy provides. They can thereby become more than de-

---

[16] *NE* I 3, 1095a8–11.

[17] I take Aristotle's thought here to be this: people with bad habits of feeling will tend strongly toward actions that gratify those feelings, even if they might (counterfactually) acquire the knowledge that would provide them some motivation away from those actions and toward ones that are more decent. The long-engrained habits of feeling and action would provide them with what they would regard as stronger, and sufficient, reason to believe the bad actions they keep on performing are the better ones, and not to trust what they have "learned" through having this knowledge.

[18] At 1179b4–10.

[19] At I 3, 1095a2–4 Aristotle emphasizes that adolescent boys (who might be ready for other philosophical studies; see *NE* VI 8, 1142a11–23) are not suitable students of ethics and politics, in part because this study presupposes considerable experience of life. Only adult people have all the qualifications he requires.

cent people. As the copestone to the development of their merely instinctual feelings into that condition of settled, fully adult decency, they can add, through philosophy, a cultivated and informed, argued and articulate, grasp of the whole realm of human values. Their practical reason, and its special motivations, can be brought in to clarify and support their developed, merely intuitive feelings— and thereby to make them good, and not merely decent, people. Hence, when Aristotle says, in the passage from book II quoted at the beginning of this section, that our undertaking in the philosophical study of the virtues aims at our becoming good people, he is taking for granted that anyone engaging in these studies is already a basically decent young adult, destined to become a decent, fully mature person in the normal course of events—and without philosophical study. He is saying that by learning what philosophy has to teach us about ethics (and politics) we acquire the virtue of practical wisdom and become fully good.[20] Thereby, we come to live the happy life.

3.3. The Highest Good, Happiness, and Virtue

In section 3.2, then, I have tried to give a preliminary understanding of the first of the two ideas, mentioned at the end of section 3.1, that control Aristotle's discussion, in *Nicomachean Ethics* X 9, of the political character of ethical studies— his insistence that moral philosophy is a "practical" inquiry in the strong sense I have explained. We cannot, however, proceed immediately to the second of these controlling ideas. This concerns Aristotle's reasons for thinking that no one can complete the studies needed in order to provide the practical knowledge of the human good I have just been explaining, without going on to supplement what they have learned through investigating the topics covered in the *Nicomachean Ethics*. They need further studies of systems of laws and political constitutions. That is, they need to take up additional lengthy studies in what we usually think of as political science, in a narrow or strict sense of that term. We must postpone the discussion of why Aristotle thinks all this until section 3.9 below. We must first take up, in the following six sections, several issues arising from what I have said in the previous section. These issues concern the study of ethics (and politics) as a practical inquiry, aimed at making us fully good, and happy,

---

[20] See endnote 13 for further comment on practical wisdom as the result of learning moral phlosophy.

persons, possessed of the virtues of habituated feelings but also of practical knowledge of the human good. First we need to consider further a central point of Aristotle's conception of the human good that I have so far simply taken for granted. What are Aristotle's reasons for thinking that, indeed, the happy life is the life of virtue? Why does he think that, if we know the human good, and live in full pursuit or even attainment of it, we will lead ethically or morally good lives? We need also to consider, more deeply than I have so far been able to, how he can think that acquiring a philosophical understanding of ethics (and politics) does have the effects for specifically moral improvement that we have just seen he does think. Those are the two topics I take up in this section.

I mentioned in the previous chapter that a central component of Socrates's commitment to the good of any human being's soul as being the most important good for them, decisive so far as the happiness of their life is concerned, was a further commitment. Part of Socrates's devotion to wisdom as his soul's most fundamental good was a commitment to living justly, and virtuously in every other way, as well. I said then that, so far as we can tell, Socrates really did not have a well-developed system of philosophical ideas that could support this identification, or essential association, of wisdom with justice and other social virtues. However, it became an urgent matter for later philosophers in the Greek tradition to develop philosophical analyses of the human soul and human nature that would underpin these Socratic convictions. What we need now to consider is Aristotle's contribution to this effort.

For the Greek context as well as in our own terms, Aristotle holds an unusual view about the soul. He thinks that not only human beings, or even only animals, have souls. He does not associate a soul exclusively with conscious states of mind or feeling. He regards the soul as the essential basis or source of any living thing's being alive at all, in any way. Hence, for him, plants of whatever type, as well as animals, have souls;[21] this applies to insects as simple as grubs, as well as to large mammals such as cattle and dogs; also to sea creatures whose life is as limited as a sponge's or an oyster's, as well as to dolphins and swordfish—plus human beings and even, as we will see, eternal or immortal beings such as the stars, the planets, and the god whose acts of thought are ultimately responsible (as Aristo-

---

[21] See his treatise *On the Soul* (*De Anima*). He agrees in this with Plato in *Timaeus* (see 77a–c, and *Theaetetus* 167b–c, where however Socrates speaks for Protagoras), though he departs from Plato in not attributing conscious experience to plants (Plato thinks plants perceive pleasure and pain). The Stoics, following ordinary Greek usage, treated soul as the seat of animal, and human, consciousness only.

tle thinks) for the ordered life of the whole world. Each living thing's soul (different for each different kind, keyed to its particular way of being alive) is the basis or source of all the things any of these living things does that are aspects of its being alive, of its life. This means that, for Aristotle (remarkably, and unusually), all the vegetative and other automatic functions of cell replication, metabolism, heart beat, breathing, and the like—all of which are encompassed within being alive as a human being—derive from our souls, just as much as our conscious sensations, thoughts, and decisions. They are all aspects of our being alive, and all are among our life activities—the activities we engage in (though, in some of the cases just mentioned, involuntarily) that constitute, as a whole, the life we lead. Taken as a whole, therefore, a human life will be better or worse in some way or respect depending on how well any and all of these life activities are carried out. An inhibited or diseased functioning of any of the life activities, even one of the physiological or some other automatic type, will mean that the overall life of the person goes badly, to some extent and in the particular way indicated. This is so, whether or not the malfunction results, as one would of course expect, in other inhibited, burdensome, or even painful activities—perhaps more palpable ones—of, as one might put it, a higher order. A life just is the living thing's life activities, so if any of those go badly, then, to that extent, the life goes badly. But since, through our voluntary efforts, we humans can sometimes correct such malfunctions, or compensate for them to some extent and perhaps completely, activities of a higher order, and in particular our voluntary ones, are vastly more significant components of a human being's life. Aristotle recognizes this when in the *Ethics* he turns to discuss the human good.

I have already said that Aristotle organizes his *Nicomachean Ethics* and *Politics* around the highest human good as their central topic, a good to which, early in the *Nicomachean Ethics*, he gives the name (in itself, as he admits, not very informative) of happiness (εὐδαιμονία). He establishes this organization when, at the beginning of the second chapter of the first book, he says,

> If then there is some end of the things that we do[22] that we wish for because of itself, while wishing for the other things we wish for because of it, . . . it is clear that this will be the good, i.e. the best good. So for our lives

[22] Or, that we are to do. The Greek term being translated here, τῶν πρακτῶν, has the suggestion not so much of what we do do but of what we have good reason to do (in case there is a difference between these two things). This nuance need not be insisted on here.

too won't knowing it have great weight? Like archers with a target we would be more successful in hitting what we ought to do. If so, then, we should try to grasp it, anyhow in outline—what it is.[23]

The highest good postulated here (whatever it turns out to be: that is a matter for subsequent investigation) is to serve as the organizing goal of any well-lived human life. As he puts it, this good is wished for because of itself, and everything else wished for is wished for because of it, as the single and constant ultimate end of all one's life activities (anyhow, of those that one controls by one's own decisions).

One should observe that Aristotle speaks hypothetically here: *if* there is some single end. He does not argue here, or indeed anywhere else, that there is some single thing (whether an activity or something else) that is, or deserves to be, the organizing goal, or that anyone who wants to live in accordance with reason will set up such an end for themselves, or recognize one as valid for human life.[24] He seems rather to take this for granted—and the whole subsequent tradition of Greek moral theory follows him in this. Most notably, the Stoics, like Aristotle, make being happy (εὐδαιμονεῖν) "the end, for the sake of which all actions are done, while it is an action done but not done for the sake of anything [else]."[25] Again, Cicero's famous dialogue *De finibus bonorum et malorum* (*On Moral Ends*), reporting and criticizing the ethical theories of Epicurus, the Stoics, and Antiochus of Ascalon (a first century BCE philosopher in Athens), is written from the same perspective. What sense can we make of this strange-seeming idea that in a well-lived life we do all of our actions for the sake of some single end? One might rather have assumed that, given the complexities of human nature, human needs, and human interests, and of any reasonable way of taking them into account in your life, there would be many distinct ends jostling for attention, and needing some other basis for organizing your pursuit of them than recognizing some single one as the final arbiter. It might seem to help us to un-

[23] 1094a18–25.

[24] He does offer some confirmatory considerations for this conclusion when he takes up the topic of the highest good again at the beginning of I 7, but those do not amount to a full and independent argument in favor of this way of going about organizing a life. In one passage of *Eudemian Ethics* I 2 (1214b6–11) Aristotle does say that not to live this way would really be foolish—apparently because any other life would have to be simply disordered. He does not there or anywhere else consider whether there might be other ways of living an ordered life than by having a single highest end.

[25] So the first century BCE writer Arius Didymus tells us (as preserved in the fifth century CE anthology by Stobaeus, i.e., John of Stobi; see Long and Sedley, *Hellenistic Philosophers*, 63 A. My translations from the Stoics are based on Long and Sedley's, in cases where their book contains the text in question, but with significant departures of my own, as here.

derstand Aristotle's assumption if we think, as Aristotle and the Stoics do, of the highest end as happiness, since it might seem at least initially intelligible to think of all that a person does as done for the sake of their own happiness. But that depends upon a misleading idea of what the Greeks had in mind in speaking of "happiness," as we shall see. And, in any event, even one's own happiness (unless so abstractly conceived as to be a purely formal end, having no role independent of one's other ends in giving direction to one's life) seems only one among the plurality of ends jostling for one's attention.

However that may be, on this ancient conception, we organize our lives, if we should take control of them for ourselves at all (a big if), by looking to some overall highest goal for our life and for its constituent activities. Other goals there will of course be, long-term ones as well as others that are temporary, salient only from time to time, in special circumstances. But these other goals will be regulated and given their overall sense (their individual weight and importance), as goals suitable for us to pursue, because of their relationship to the highest goal (whatever it might be) that we have set up or accepted as our highest good. Everything that we do, why we do it, indeed how we do it, how it relates to other things we do—all this will ultimately make sense only in terms of this orientation to a highest good. (It will be better to postpone further examination of this conception until we can see how it works out on Aristotle's own formulation.) Aristotle's quest in the *Nicomachean Ethics*, then, as he says in the passage just quoted, is first of all to figure out what, given human nature and all our human needs, is the correct ultimate end to organize our lives by—that is, which is the one that conforms to our nature, the one that is our end *by* nature. After that, he will raise specific topics for more detailed treatment, because of their connection to that natural ultimate end. It is in that sense that the highest good, or εὐδαιμονία, is the central, organizing topic of the whole treatise.

Aristotle holds strongly, but does not assume as part of the general understanding of the term εὐδαιμονία (happiness) among his contemporaries, that happiness or the highest good for a human being is some human activity. He allows that many people, unreflective and unserious ones especially, do think that happiness is simply having a lot of money or experiencing frequent and intense bodily pleasure (without lots of corresponding pain), or other passively received pleasurable payoffs from doing or accomplishing things (the doing or the accomplishing not being conceived as of any value in themselves, apart from generating these payoffs). But that view, he thinks, is silly: it is just too plain on any reasonable assessment of human nature and human possibilities that our good, and so our happiness, must consist fundamentally of some or other activities, some or other of the activities that make up our lives (as I explained above). We are essentially active beings. If money or pleasure, passively received, is good at all, it must be because of some relationship to other, more basic goods: in the case of money, as an instrumental good, enabling us to engage in activities that in themselves have value for us, or to accomplish other more important goals; pleasure is good perhaps as a superficial but welcome indication, impressed upon us through our powers of sensation, of the prior and more basic goodness of whatever gives rise to it, and, most importantly, of the activities it accompanies. In any event, for Aristotle, happiness or the highest single good for a human being has to be some human activity. By having that activity, that happiness, in one's life, and by effectively organizing the whole of one's life (i.e., all of one's other activities) with a view to it, one will attain a happy life.[26]

The question for Aristotle then is, which activity is, or constitutes, happiness? Which activity is by nature, and by our nature, the correct end for us to pursue as the one for organizing and regulating our whole lives—all the other activities, and also, of course, all the other goods of a nonactive sort that our nature and our natural needs make it right for us to wish to have, and therefore right for us to pursue?[27] He offers a sketch of his answer in *Nicomachean Ethics* I 7.[28] His first step is to point to the decisive difference between us as human beings from all animals (and a fortiori all plants), namely our possession of reason (λόγος). Even if our own senses, not to speak of the more automatic biological activities I mentioned above, differ systematically from those of other animals (species by species), what is truly distinctive and uniquely human, in comparison with the plants and animals that, like us, inhabit the planet Earth, is our rational powers. Aristotle reasonably thinks that our highest good, being an activity of ours, must be something distinctive of human beings as a species, some activity that no other living thing can engage in. What we are looking for, then, must in some sense be a rational activity, an activity we engage in insofar as we possess the power of reason, and that we engage in by employing it.

Human reason is, however, a complex phenomenon, a single and unified capacity but with many aspects—or so Aristotle thinks (the Stoics, as we will see

---

[26] The reader should notice here that in Aristotle's terms we have to distinguish happiness from a happy life: happiness is some single good activity, and a happy life is one made happy by containing it.

[27] In the remainder of this and the next four paragraphs I give what I take to be the main force of Aristotle's argumentation in *NE* I 7. I do not enter into the details of this much written about and much disputed chapter.

[28] See *NE* I 7, 1098a20–26.

in the next chapter, differ profoundly from him in this). Taking his lead from the character Socrates in Plato's *Republic*, he recognizes three distinguishable powers belonging to the human soul that can in some significant way be called rational: what in Plato are called appetite and spirit, and thirdly reason, in a strict and narrow sense, itself. As Aristotle (admittedly somewhat obscurely) puts this, these constitute "what has reason" (τὸ λόγον ἔχον):[29] by this, he means the rational aspect of the human soul, as distinct from its vegetative and sensory or sense-related powers. The three powers referred to "have reason" in one or the other of two ways or senses. Some of "what has reason," so to speak, is rational in a derivative sense, that of having the capacity to obey what reason in the nonderivative sense of having thoughts and actually thinking things out, has to say. Appetites such as hunger and thirst and the other desires for bodily pleasure, and spirited impulses of a competitive and aspirational sort, are not in themselves powers of thinking, at all. So they are not rational powers in that sense, the basic one. Yet as both Plato in the *Republic* and Aristotle hold (we will have much more to say about this below) these powers can be developed and trained so that they fall into line with the judgments of value that one comes to hold through reflection and rational planning as to what is best for you to have appetites and aspirations for, and as to what it is best for you to do on the basis of those motivations. If one judges, for example, that a certain amount of certain sorts of food is the right amount to be eating on a regular basis, one's appetites may be habituated, anyhow in principle but no doubt only within certain limits, so that they come to conform to one's reasoned judgment about this matter. Then one has appetites that drive one with their own power to eat only so much as one's judgment has declared is the right amount, and to eat only those foods one has decided on: in this way, they can be rationalized so that they "obey" reason (in the strict sense of the word "reason," viz., the power to think things out). In that derivative sense such an appetite deserves to be called rational too.

However, just because these powers are only derivatively rational, it is clear that the active employment of the rational powers of this second type—appetitive or spirited desirings when thus trained—are not acceptable, on their own, as candidates for the rational activity in which our highest good can be achieved. Clearly, the power of rational thinking that gives rise to the judgments of value from which, through training, those desires get established is not merely rational in a prior sense, as noted above. Its activities, in reaching and maintaining these

---

[29] At *NE* I 7, 1098a4–7.

judgments, are obviously, for just that reason, more fundamental goods. In order to locate the rational activity that is entitled to be counted as our highest natural good, we need to look to those activities that are rational in the nonderivative sense. One such activity is the one just noted, the activity of practical thinking, in which we ponder (whether as philosophers or not) our own good, and make plans for achieving it. But there is another one too, distinct from this one, or so Aristotle thinks: the power of thinking, not about the human good and how to achieve it in our lives, but about purely theoretical matters, of physical theory, or logic, or biology, or mathematics, or metaphysics and theology. These are all subjects of theoretical study in which, as I indicated above, Aristotle thought philosophical thinking (in a broad use of the term) allows us to achieve solid results in pursuing the ultimate truth of things.

In each type of rational activity, of course, both the derivatively rational ones of feeling (and acting on feelings), and the ones in which we think practical and theoretical thoughts, our full natural good can be found, if at all, only when the relevant powers are developed to and exercised in their own naturally best condition—in effect, when they are exercised with their proper virtues. In which, then, of these two sorts of nonderivatively rational activities—the practical or the theoretical—should we take our highest natural good to be found? Or should we regard our good as encompassing both—so that our good would be, as it were, a single activity of reason, consisting of these two different ones in some sort of tandem? And how is rational activity in the extended sense, of feeling and acting on rationally approved feelings, to be fit into a proper account of our good? It is a remarkable fact about the *Nicomachean Ethics* that in his sketch in book I of the highest good or εὐδαιμονία Aristotle does not even raise these questions. In fact he does not even clearly distinguish the derivative rationality of well-directed appetite and spirit as something secondary in relation to our good, in comparison to rational activity in the stricter sense. He speaks of the human good simply as "rational activity of the soul in accordance with virtue or excellence," rather mysteriously adding, without any explication at all of how to understand this, "or if there are more than one [relevant] virtues or excellences, [the human good] is rational activity in accordance with the best and most complete[30] virtue or excellence."[31]

---

[30] Or, on a different understanding of the Greek, most final or end-like.

[31] 1098a16–18. He also famously adds "in a complete life," indicating that the activity in question is our highest good when understood as extending over a whole lifetime, not as something achieved only at some moment or short period of time, while being absent from the rest of one's life. It is not entirely clear

It seems that Aristotle thought it adequate for his purpose in giving this initial sketch of the human good, for later filling in, that he draw attention simply to two basic features: first, that it has to be a rational activity (for the reasons I have already explained) and, second, an activity in which relevant virtues or excellences (virtues or excellences, in one or another sense, of "what has reason") are expressed in, and in fact control, what is done. As for this second condition, his idea seems to be that rational activities, whether appetitive desirings (and actions so motivated), or practical judgments and consequent actions, or theoretical thoughts, if they are to rise to the level of constituting or helping to constitute our highest good, must be such as to derive from a power of reason that has been brought to its perfection in doing its tasks. The rational power for theorizing will have developed so that it reliably discovers and so knows, or comes to know, the truth about whatever subjects the person studies. The rational power for practical thinking and knowing will have developed so that it reliably discovers in all circumstances that may arise, and so knows, what is good and what is bad for one to want, to decide, to pursue, and to do. And appetite and spirit have been brought to the condition where what they obey or fall in line with, when practical reason says something about what is good and bad for one to desire appetitively or spiritedly, is only something truly good. They have not just been trained, but trained correctly— in accordance with the truth about what is good and bad for a human being. (In fact, the condition of training for these feelings that I mentioned above, in which they conform to the values that practical reasoning affirms, is to be understood as one in which practical reasoning, too, has achieved its specific virtue, practical wisdom.) In all these cases the power of reason in question has acquired specific qualities, now inherent in it, that constitute the condition of its perfection. These are the virtues or excellences that Aristotle is referring to when he speaks of "[rational] activity of the soul in accordance with virtue" as constituting the human good.

In this preliminary sketch, then, in *Nicomachean Ethics* I 7, Aristotle is satisfied to propose an undifferentiated or inclusive conception of "the" activity that is the highest human good. It is inclusive in that "the" activity referred to includes activity of the virtues of all three of the powers of reason that his theory of the human soul recognizes.[32] So far, this is not so much an activity, a single

what will count for him as a "complete" life: presumably it will be one that has lasted long enough for the person to grow to maturity and experience a normal range of opportunities and difficulties in relation to which to engage in the activity.

[32] This may be so even in his mysterious addition about "the best and most complete or end-like of the

one, as a particular sort of activity. His proposal, so far, is simply that our natural good consists in the exercise, over a normal mature lifetime, of our power of reason, when that is perfected by the possession of its virtues or excellences. That sort of activity is our highest good. We are to treat that as the organizing goal for our whole life. From the point of view of that goal, we are to judge the ultimate value of everything else, including all our other active interests, our other goals, and all our possible or actual possessions, personal relationships, and so on. It is by reference to this activity that we are to see them as being good for us at all. In order to grasp fully the implications of this proposal, we need to examine more closely the three different sorts of virtue I have alluded to: the virtues of theoretical reason, those involved in practical knowledge, and the virtues of the derivatively rational powers of appetite and spirit. Aristotle distinguishes and discusses all of these sorts of virtue in subsequent books of the *Ethics*. Shortly I will say more also about the manner of guidance this highest good of virtuous activity provides for us in recognizing and pursuing or (as the case may be) practicing other good things—material goods, friendships, other social relationships, bodily and other pleasures of life.

Even before proceeding to Aristotle's filling in, in subsequent books, of this initial sketch, we can appreciate his special contribution to the Greek philosophers' efforts to develop theories that will justify Socrates's commitment not only to wisdom and philosophy as very great human goods, but also to the moral and social virtues of justice, courage, temperance, and so on. Aristotle has drawn upon the explicit and detailed philosophical account of the human soul that he gives in other works, as being that in us by which we are alive and live our lives. He has brought us to see how and why our highest good cannot reasonably be conceived in any other terms than as some activity of our own: health, material possessions, honored status in our communities, bodily or other pleasures of passive feeling, victories in competitions, and achievements of our other goals (simply as such—as victories and successful efforts), must all be secondary goods. To the extent that (and when) they are good at all, they are good only because of some way that they contribute to the higher good consisting in the active use of our soul's powers. Furthermore, he has drawn upon philosophical principles to

---

virtues": that refers ambiguously either to the activity of some single virtue, to the exclusion of all others, or to the undifferentiated "activity of virtue" as including, in particular and with emphasis, the activity of the best virtue—that one, above all, must not be absent, if we are to speak of the human good as achieved in someone's life. In the present context (whatever might be true once one has read through the last chapters of the work; see the next paragraphs) the second reading is the more salient.

give us reasons why our highest good must be, in particular, some activity that we engage in with powers of our souls that belong to us alone among the other things that live on and around the Earth. Against this background, we come to see our powers of reasoning as properly the central focus of our lives. Our lives will go well, or badly, in the first instance, depending on whether our rational powers are used well or badly—and that must mean, whether or not they are used through the possession of their specific virtues or excellences. If justice and the other commonly recognized virtues of the human soul are among these specific excellences, then we can now see that they must be important components of our own highest good. As for which powers these "rational powers" are, Aristotle has drawn upon his philosophical theory, one version of which is argued for at length in Plato's *Republic*, of two sorts of rational powers that we possess, one set rational derivatively from the other, by being trained to obedience to the latter's determinations.

It is true that in this sketch in *Nicomachean Ethics* book I Aristotle has not yet gone into questions about which qualities are the virtues or excellences of the three powers thus indicated; he does that only later in the treatise. But he expects us already to see, as I have suggested, that among them will be the moral and social virtues that are commonly recognized, or something corresponding closely enough to them. Others will be qualities of mind whereby the essential function of reason in all its guises is carried out. This function is to discover and hold onto what is correct and right, or the truth, in whatever matter is being rationally thought about, whether theoretical or practical. This complex philosophical analysis and series of philosophical arguments give us a perspective on our lives, supported by philosophical analysis and reflection, from which to see that living virtuously (however we finally come to conceive that, after further philosophical investigations) is simply one essential component of living with a justified focus upon the exercise of our rational powers (when perfected) as our highest good. From this perspective, we can readily see that, and understand why, if anyone ever acts in such a way as to express a preference for or give a higher ranking to any of those other putative goods I have mentioned—health, money, bodily pleasure, achievement of what one wanted, etc.—above virtuous action itself, they are abandoning a concern for the true goodness of their own life—a concern for their *own* good—in preference for something whose manifestly lesser value to them has been established, again, by careful philosophical reflection. And acting in that misguided way, of course, is precisely what Socrates said so many of his Athenian contemporaries were doing all the time. The remedy for that, Socrates thought, was philosophy. We have now seen how Aristotle draws upon and develops philosophical principles of his own so as to reach essentially the same conclusions, in this regard, as Socrates had reached, though Socrates reached them, as we saw in chapter 2, without openly and fully presenting the arguments needed to establish them.

It deserves special emphasis that Aristotle's whole train of thought here is philosophical in a very strong sense. He lays down or justifies in philosophically theoretical terms basic principles, and reasons from them to his conclusions. Those who grasp Aristotle's arguments and act in accordance with them, understanding themselves and their good in Aristotle's terms, depart markedly from the ways of thinking and the ideas that any ordinary upbringing would lead any ordinary decent person to have. The habituated training of a person's instincts and emotional feelings can bring a child or adult to feel intuitively disposed against, say, stealing some item in a shop. They would enjoy having or using the thing, but they feel it would be disgraceful and low-minded to opt to get hold of something that would give such pleasure, when it was properly up to another person to use or release it at their option. If asked why that really was low-minded or disgraceful, whatever they might say, if anything at all (rather than issuing a contemptuous and dismissive snort at the very idea that it wasn't low-minded), would surely not include philosophical theories about the human soul as the basis of all our life, about the special place of our powers of reason in human life, and about the principles concerning goodness that lead one to see virtuous activity as one's highest good. It might include some uninformative reminders, to others with the same trained feelings and outlook, about what low-mindedness and disgrace involve, or about attractive features of high-mindedness and honor. But mere verbal articulation of these mere feelings would be the limit of what one would expect from someone with only an ordinary good upbringing into decent ways of feeling and thinking. Someone like that would not even so much as conceive of a highest good as something under which to organize and regulate the whole of their life. Indeed, as I indicated, they might very well not feel any need or wish to develop any line of thought at all about such matters: the very distinction, a specifically philosophical one, that Aristotle draws between mere decency and true and full virtue would hardly be intelligible to them. Such a distinction is no part of what being well brought up, in terms of feelings and love for the noble or honorable, itself includes.

It is possible, of course, that some well-brought up person who had not studied philosophy with Aristotle or anyone else might, simply through curious reflection on their daily experience—on their habits of feeling and acting and their own intuitive sense of the goodness of these feelings and actions—hit upon ideas of their own to propose if asked my question about why pilfering a shop is low-minded. But, of course, one can be a philosopher without having studied the subject with any teacher. The more such a train of thought, in for example explaining what is low and disgraceful about pilfering, had the structure of an organized theory or set of theories, with comprehensive scope, the more one would be inclined to count such a person as someone with a philosophical nature—one who was able to acquire something close to the knowledge contained in the virtue of practical wisdom without formal study of philosophy.[33] As it is, as I have said above, what we see in the trains of thought, such as the one I have summarized in the last paragraph, that make up Aristotle's *Nicomachean Ethics*, are so many elements in the body of knowledge that constitutes the basis of understanding of the human good that underlies both the virtue of practical wisdom and (on Aristotle's conception of it) political science. Practical wisdom really does add a lot in extending and deepening the basis for decent and good living that mere training of the appetites and spirit provides for the merely decent person; the thought, provided by practical wisdom, on which fully virtuous persons live their life, is much better structured and much more articulate and comprehensive than any train of thoughts ordinary decent people might associate with their own behaviors. As we learn details of Aristotle's account of the moral virtues, we will be uncovering additional trains of philosophical thought that form part of practically wise people's understanding of their own life and its basic principles. The way of life that Aristotle wishes to establish in this treatise as the best one for a human being differs in fundamental and clearly marked ways from the way of life of a merely decent, ordinary, nonphilosophical person, raised with what Aristotle would recognize as good moral habits and a decent moral outlook.

3.4. Two Happy Lives, Two Happinesses: The Contemplative and the Practically Active Lives

In his sketch of happiness or the highest human good in *Nicomachean Ethics* I 7, then, Aristotle alludes only briefly to the three types of virtue, and the three powers of reason that they are respectively associated with. He first speaks ex-

---

[33] For more on why, according to Aristotle, pilfering a shop is low-minded and disgraceful, see below, section 3.6.

plicitly about these classes of virtues (the moral virtues of correctly trained feeling, of practical wisdom, and of the wisdom shown in the perfected power for theoretical knowledge) beginning in the last chapter of book I, and continuing on in books II through IX.[34] Having filled out the preliminary sketch of book I through that long series of discussions, Aristotle can then return in book X 6–8 to take into account what we have learned about all the virtues of the different types, so as to provide a final, less sketchy, but, as he insists, still sketchy, account of the human good.[35]

In that final sketch Aristotle distinguishes again two sorts of activity of virtue. First, there is the activity of reason in thinking about theoretical matters in a theoretical way, when that power possesses the various virtues that are needed in order to ensure that, in using one's power of reason, one does unerringly and correctly conceive, and fully understand, as the ultimate truth about some matter, what in fact is the truth. Aristotle has discussed these virtues already, in book VI 3, 6–7, where he lays particular emphasis on the virtue of σοφία (wisdom—theoretical, as against practical), as the copestone of these virtues. This wisdom not only ensures correct and full understanding of all other theoretical matters when the wise person looks into them, but it also includes full and correct understanding of "the objects that are highest by nature."[36] These are the divine and eternal first agents of the whole world order, including the sun, planets, and stars, but extending also to the cosmic god whose thoughts, on Aristotle's theory of metaphysics, are the ultimate source of these divine entities' orderly and fostering behavior. This first sort of activity of virtue, accordingly, is a contemplative exercise of these virtues for theorizing. In particular, and most fundamentally, it is an exercise of wisdom in understanding the metaphysical, and theological, first principles of the whole cosmos.[37]

One sort of activity to which Aristotle draws attention in X 6–8, then, is activity of the virtues for theory—in short, the active exercise of the theoretical virtues. The second sort of activity combines that of practical knowledge, as described above, with the activities of appetitive and spirited desire when the powers of appetite and spirit have been trained by habituation to the point where they function perfectly correctly, by producing just the right states of feeling and

[34] I postpone detailed discussion of any of the virtues until sections 3.5–3.7 below.

[35] On the sketchiness of even this final account, see X 6, 1176a30–32.

[36] 1141b3.

[37] On Aristotle's understanding of god as metaphysical first principle, and in some way responsible, ultimately, for the being and existence of the orderly world of nature, see my discussion below in section 4.3, pp. 13ff., where I compare Aristotle's view to the very different one of the Stoics.

emotion to suit the varying situations and circumstances of life, as practical knowledge dictates.[38] More specifically, these latter activities, of appetitive and spirited desire, are exercises of the virtues of character as standardly recognized in Greek culture (and our own as well), such as courage, temperance, and justice—when those are engaged by a person who possesses them all in the fullest degree, and who has a perfected understanding of what they truly require us to do and not do under varied circumstances. We can clarify Aristotle's intentions here if we introduce a bit of terminology of our own, and speak of practical virtue or virtues, in contrast to the theoretical virtues just briefly canvassed: these combine the virtues of practical thought with the virtues of feeling and emotion into a unified condition involving both of those sorts of virtue. The basis for treating in combination, as Aristotle does here, these two sorts of virtue (those of practical thinking and those of nonrational desiring) has been laid out in book VI 12–13. Up to then, Aristotle had discussed separately these two types of virtue, leaving implicit—anyhow, not taking explicit account of—their relationships to one another. But now, in the last two chapters of the book on the virtues of thought, book VI, Aristotle explains that these virtues of feeling and character, on the one hand, and practical wisdom (consisting in full practical knowledge), on the other, are by their natures found always together and cannot be found apart. His main idea, or claim, is that these virtues, respectively of mind and feeling, cooperate, and that both are needed, in producing the virtuous actions that each sort of practical virtue is directed toward in its own distinctive way, through its own activities of thought, or of nonrational feeling.[39] For example, for a just act, or a courageous one, to be an act respectively of the virtue of justice or courage—the act of a just or courageous person, one who opts for the action from a fully virtuous disposition and commitments—it must be the joint product of the right ways of feeling, in spirit and appetite, about everything involved in the action and in its circumstances, and of the right understanding of the pluses and minuses—of the true value, in relation to one another—of all the things of any concern at all to the agent at the time and in the circumstances.[40]

---

[38] Aristotle refers to this in the first line of X 8, 1178a9, when he refers to a life devoted to activity deriving from and expressing "the other sort of virtue"—that is, other than the activity of theoretical wisdom, discussed in the immediately preceding lines, at the end of X 7.

[39] See endnote 14 for detailed discussion of this cooperation.

[40] In VI 12–13 Aristotle does not give this as one of his reasons for holding that the two sorts of virtues always go together; he writes briefly and in fact not entirely clearly on this point there, since his discussion is "aporetic," by offering answers to objections against the practical usefulness of practical wisdom. However, on his view of practical reason as the legitimate authority in determining our actions, it is also part of

Corresponding to these two different sorts of virtuous activities, theoretical and practical, in X 6–8 Aristotle also distinguishes two sorts of "happy lives," what we may accordingly refer to as the contemplative and the practically active lives. These lives are characterized as happy because of the presence in them, as their highest organizing good, of the one or the other of these activities as the εὐδαιμονία or happiness in it.[41] In his discussion of these two lives, then, we find Aristotle's completion of his preliminary sketch in book I 7 of εὐδαιμονία as an undifferentiated sort of activity, as I described it above—that is, as an activity inclusive of all the activities of the virtues of the human soul insofar as it possesses reason. Now he separates these virtues into two sets (theoretical and practical, as I have suggested that we call them) and speaks separately about the activities of each. He indicates that though both activities qualify, as the generic account from book I implied, as εὐδαιμονία or happiness, one of them ranks ahead of the other under this common title. He argues explicitly and clearly that the life organized under the pursuit and practice of the virtues of theoretical reasoning is "happiest," the other life being happy or happiest in only a secondary way or in the second rank.[42] Thus, in completing his sketch he maintains that, in all strictness, εὐδαιμονία is not a mere *sort* of activity (virtuous activity), but, in fact, one specific activity, the activity (as organizing principle for a whole life) of the theoretical intellect's virtues. That activity, as he puts it, is, all by itself, complete or final or end-like happiness (τελεία εὐδαιμονία). By contrast, the activity of the practical virtues (the virtues of character as overseen by practical wisdom) is a secondary happiness, when it is made the organizing principle for a whole life.

---

reason's proper function to see to the correct disciplining and training of the desires of appetite and spirit. On this view, it follows that no person's reason could yet have inherent possession of the qualities that perfect it, in doing its tasks, if their appetite and spirit were not correctly and fully trained so as always to support reason in its value judgments, or at any rate never to oppose them. In the end, moral training has to be self-training, that is, training deriving from one's own efforts, through exercise of one's powers of rational understanding, directed at making oneself have correct nonrational patterns of desire. That this is Aristotle's view about training for virtue is clear, if less than fully articulated, in his account of habituation to virtue in book II.

[41] Aristotle speaks at 1178a21–22 of "the εὐδαιμονία according to" the virtues of character and practical wisdom, that is, the one consisting of morally virtuous activity as highest organizing good, as a distinctively human happiness, and of the life defined by it as a distinctively human life. Compared to this, the other happy life, the one according to the theoretical intellect's virtues, will be a divine life, because the intellect, being in some way separate from, and certainly superior to, the bodily needs and social functions supervised by the practical virtues, is something "divine in us" (see X 7, 1177b26–31). The activity of the intellect's virtues, in a complete lifetime devoted to it, is "complete (or final or end-like) εὐδαιμονία or happiness" (1177a16–18, 1178b7–23).

[42] See 1178a7–9.

It will take us most of the next section to unravel all the intricacies of Aristotle's distinction here between two levels of happiness. But it is clear, to begin with, that the first of the two lives just referred to is the one that Aristotle sometimes (but not explicitly here) describes compendiously as the "theoretical" or "contemplative life."[43] He uses that term in *Nicomachean Ethics* I 5 for one of three "prominent" types of life, the others being the vulgarian's life devoted to bodily pleasures and the life of a political leader, the "political" life (πολιτικὸς βίος). There he says he is going to examine the contemplative life somewhere in what follows, and if he makes good on this promise, it can only be here, in X 7–8, that he does it. Not surprisingly, in I 5 Aristotle immediately sets aside the life of pleasure as not worth taking seriously as a candidate for the happy life, but (though, again, he does not make this explicit) it seems that the second of the two lives set apart from one another in X 7–8 is the one he refers to in I 5 as the political life—the life of someone devoted to the practice of the moral and social virtues in the active life of a good and expert political leader.[44] This is surprising: why should a well-lived life devoted to the practical virtues, where practically virtuous activity is conceived as the agent's highest good, require one also to be a politician, a political leader in the community where one lives? We will need to consider later Aristotle's reasons for thus selecting good and expertly qualified political leaders, in particular, and not also or instead ordinary citizens living good and virtuous private lives, as the ones who exemplify, or perhaps best exemplify, the happy life organized under the pursuit and practice of the practical virtues as its highest good. But for now, let us pause to consider the manner in which the two virtuous activities—those of the theoretical and the practical virtues—do provide organization for these respective lives. This will give us the opportunity also to examine Aristotle's conception of the practical virtues themselves, and of how the knowledge of and about them that he is attempting to convey in the *Nicomachean Ethics* is intended to play a role in helping to make us

---

[43] He once calls it the "life of the intellect" (ὁ κατὰ τὸν νοῦν βίος, 1178a6–7, cf. 1177b30), but he repeatedly refers to the person leading it as one who contemplates or theorizes (ὁ θεωρῶν, 1178b3) or whose most devoted activity is theoretical study or contemplation (θεωρία), and he contrasts the happiness of this life with the other one's as being "contemplative" (θεωρητική). Significantly, in *Politics* VII 1–3, in discussing which is the most choiceworthy life he contrasts the "political life of action" (trans. Reeve) with a "contemplative" one (θεωρητικός), saying that some people hold that the latter is the only life befitting a philosopher (1324a25–29). I return to discuss this *Politics* passage below.

[44] At 1178a26–7, in discussing the need for material resources by people in leading the two lives, he refers, rather abruptly but casually, to the political leader as the one leading the second life. Earlier, in discussing the merits of morally virtuous activities as against theoretically excellent ones, he speaks similarly about morally virtuous activity as "the activity of the political leader" (1177b12).

good (virtuous people) by strengthening our motivation for being virtuous and living virtuously.

3.5. Theoretical vs. Practical Virtue as Highest Good

The contemplative life differs in obvious ways from any other virtuous life, whether the political life of the expert political leader or that of people occupied for the most part solely with ordinary business or professional concerns, as well as with private personal interests and the daily and weekly flow of family life and social life in their community. This is the life of people who have the natural talent and disposition for philosophical (and related mathematical and scientific) study and learning, and who have (presumably) devoted many hours when growing to adulthood, and continually afterward, to reading, discussing, listening to lectures, and thinking hard for themselves about the most difficult intellectual questions. They possess firsthand, extensive, experience of the very great good for any rational being that, according to Aristotle's analysis of human nature, is contained in the exercise of one's intellectual powers, when they have been sharpened and deepened through such practice. These people love those activities—reading, discussing, thinking, exploring, and comprehending all aspects of solid, fully vindicated theories of higher mathematics and of metaphysical philosophy, as well as their logical consequences and application. They love engaging in such activities more than anything else that one can do or enjoy. That is not in the least to say that they do not also love plenty of other things in life: this is only their first love. And, as we have seen, Aristotle has provided us, and them, with clear and persuasive analyses of human nature that show they are right to love these activities in that way. The rest of us can also know, on Aristotle's same grounds, that these are indeed the best and most lovable things a human being can do. But, with us, that is only abstract, merely theoretical knowledge. Lack of talent or disposition has kept most of us from more than a partial and passing firsthand acquaintance with the good that these activities bring a human being; our knowledge of this good is not practical knowledge. Those who live the contemplative life, however, have the fullest practical knowledge of these truths, and that knowledge forms a powerful and central part of their motivation (their desires), not only for engaging in these activities for their own sakes, but also for making them, in a full practical sense, the highest and organizing good of their whole lives. As with anyone else with a consuming passion, these people mostly spend their days largely absorbed in these activities, so far as other needs and pursuits permit, and within the limits that the nature of these activities, and that human nature itself, impose for not overdoing a good thing and spoiling it, or getting exhausted and bored, or obsessively and frenetically overengaged.

But these people know full well, and in the same practical way, that excellent or virtuous rational activity, which is the distinctive good for human beings, a good limited among mortal animals to us alone, has a wider scope. There are other virtues of rational activity, too—the practical virtues of mind (practical wisdom) and character (the moral virtues). Those leading the contemplative life know the value of these other virtues, too, as values for themselves. Their knowledge of this value is full practical knowledge, and so it carries with it a motivation, belonging to that very knowledge, to engage in the corresponding activities. Thus, it is part of their practical knowledge that theoretical interests are the best and most lovable that these other activities are good and lovable, too. Thus they know also that their own, just like any human being's, daily life in family and community, including the social connections and political requirements that go along with it, can and ought to be governed by the full development and exercise of these other virtues of the human rational power. My remark just above that they pursue their passion for theory only so far as other needs and pursuits permit points to this. The practical virtues, as we will see in some detail in the next section, provide the right evaluation for all the human goods involved in daily life, and in life among a community of people with varied special interests and pursuits but similar material and social needs. This is the sort of life that is natural for human beings—all human beings. And our contemplatives are human beings, just like the rest of us. Their passion for theoretical philosophy makes them highly unusual persons, from the typical human being's point of view. It will lead them, under normal or expectable conditions of life, to keep out of public sight to a larger extent than the norm in their wider community. But they will, like everyone else, belong to a family and live within and as part of a normally mixed and varied human community. So in addition to possessing—abnormally or even uniquely—the virtues for theoretical study and knowledge, they will possess the practical virtues as well.[45] In living their daily lives in their

---

[45] Thus as *Pol.* 1253a3–7, 27–29 and *NE* 1178b5–7 make clear, Aristotle's contemplatives will not (since they are neither superhuman nor actual gods) live a life of separation from the rest of the human community, or from the essential political context for anyone who, on Aristotle's view, has any hope of living happily. See also, on the need of every human being for external goods and goods of the body, including

families and communities, they will be constantly exercising those practical virtues. Their love and pursuit of the virtues of study and theory provides a more distant ultimate organization even for their ordinary daily activities and social concerns, but they organize these directly through their love and pursuit of these other virtues of the human power of reason.[46]

The difference, then, between the contemplative life and other (lesser) good and happy lives is simply that in the contemplative life, besides the love for and active devotion to practically virtuous activity, this further love not just plays a role, too, but in some sense a more ultimate and fundamental one. (I will have more to say about this below.) Nonetheless, all these happy lives will have a very great deal in common. They involve a shared outlook on what is most important in human life in general and, in particular, on the conditions under which things of value for a human being, other than the virtues of the soul's power of reason and their exercise, are good for anyone. In exploring this aspect of even the contemplative's life, therefore, we can turn now to consider Aristotle's second happiest life, the political life. This is a life led with the exercise of the practical virtues as its highest good, that is, as the highest good actually achieved within it, and in fact as the highest goal pursued in it as something to be realized. Aristotle spends four whole books of the *Nicomachean Ethics* (II–V) giving his account of the virtues of character. He includes therein his discussion of voluntary and involuntary actions as they affect praise and blame, of decision (προαίρεσις) as the immediate psychological cause of virtuous and vicious acts, and of wishing as a form of desire that belongs to the power of reason itself. The other side of practical virtue, the virtue of practical wisdom, is the topic of a major portion of book VI. Furthermore, both the lengthy discussion of the "semivirtue" of self-control and its lack in VII 1–10,[47] and the much lengthier one of friendship in VIII–IX,

---

these intellectually specially gifted persons, 1178bb33–1179a9. The need for goods of body and external goods is (see further section 3.6 below) the arena for exercise of the most fundamental practical virtues. The contemplatives, like every other human being, need these virtues if they are to live happily, on Aristotle's analysis.

[46] I do not enter here into obscure and disputed details of how, on Aristotle's theory, the two principal virtuous activities—those of theoretical thinking and practical action—relate to one another, so to speak in their internal qualities, insofar as the former alone is, on a correct final view, εὐδαιμονία or the highest human good. That implies that the exercise of the practical virtues is less good, but in what way? Moreover, if it too, as a lesser good, has to be pursued for the sake of the exercise of the theoretical virtues, what does this "for the sake of" relationship come to? Our present purposes do not require us to enter into these intricacies of Aristotle's theory. But see Gabriel Richardson Lear (*Happy Lives and the Highest Good*, esp. chaps. 4 and 8) and my own discussion in "Plato and Aristotle on 'Finality' and '(Self-)Sufficiency,'" chap. 11 in *Knowledge, Nature, and the Good*, sections 5 and 6.

[47] In discussing lack of self-control in VII 10, 1152a17, Aristotle calls such a person "half wicked." His

though formally distinct from the treatment of the practical virtues contained in II–VI, illuminate Aristotle's views on that topic in many ways. So it is quite fair to say that the greater part of eight of the ten books of the *Ethics* concerns these virtues, and the political life that is governed by them as its highest (achieved) good. But that is not to say these books do not also concern the contemplative life, since the contemplative life, as I have explained, is one in which all these other values are achieved and sustained, as well as the values of contemplation itself.

3.6. The Practical Virtues: General Account

In turning to Aristotle's second happiest life, we need to attend first to his account of the virtues of character—those of nonrational desire and feeling—in II through V; the other virtues, those of practical thought, involved in every virtuous action, discussed in VI, can be addressed later. Many readers feel disappointed by the extremely abstract and formalistic character of Aristotle's discussion of these virtues, especially in his lengthy general account in book II of virtue (viz., of character) as a "mean" or intermediate condition between two extremes. This general doctrine, of moral virtue as "lying in a mean," has the result, which Aristotle evidently thinks quite an important one, that each moral virtue has not one but two vicious conditions of character opposed to it, at opposite extremes of one or another continuum of some sort of feeling and acting, with the virtue in question occupying the center of that range.[48] This is, in fact, quite a novel account, and Aristotle is particularly concerned, as he goes through his discussion, later on, in books III–V, of specific virtues, to show that when you consider them case by case, simply on their own, you can vindicate this general theory fully. Indeed, one could suspect that the desire to vindicate his novel general account, presented in book II, is no small part of his motivation for going into

---

general account, of course, is that self-control is a quite distinct condition of character from virtue, not strictly speaking something psychologically like it, but an incomplete or half finished stab at virtue. At the end of book IV he calls self-control not a virtue (of character), but a "mixed" condition (1128b34). It is something like a mixture of virtue and vice.

[48] The virtue of justice is something of an exception, both in its basic conception (as Aristotle points out, it has only one opposed vice, injustice) and in the organization and content of the chapters devoted to it. But the crucial notion in "the doctrine of the mean," that reason always seeks to balance and impose rational order on whatever it touches, is still at the center of the discussion. Competing claims of justice and competing values have to be balanced and ordered both in considering general questions of justice and in considering the justice of each particular act.

details, in III–V, about so many particular virtues in the first place:[49] we will see shortly just why this is such a matter of concern to him, and why his concern is legitimate. As for its novelty, unlike what in ordinary life one might routinely think or say, Aristotle argues, courage (physical and moral), for example, has not just the vice of cowardice as an opposed and vicious condition of character, but also that of rashness and overconfidence. Aristotle also departs (without so much as mentioning the fact) from Plato's concentration in the *Republic* on the four "cardinal" virtues of wisdom, justice, courage, and moderation or temperance, as if any others there may be (piety, for example?) might be reducible to these four.[50] Aristotle does recognize and gives due attention to justice, courage, and temperance (wisdom of course is a virtue of intellect, not character, so it gets dealt with later, in book VI). But he insists that they are only three of the eleven virtues of character (apparently to be regarded as coequal both in moral and in theoretical standing) that he distinguishes and discusses, one after the other.

It is true that Aristotle may often seem to apply the threefold scheme to his eleven virtues in a rather mechanical way. But, as he goes through the virtues, he also advances challenging ideas owing little or nothing to that framework, and one must not allow any tedium induced by his mechanical procedure to lead one to miss these ideas, as I think readers often do. Among these challenging ideas, one might note the following. First, consider Aristotle's restriction of courage (and cowardice and rashness) to citizens' feelings and conduct when on the civic battlefield during Greek cities' almost annual wars with their neighbors.[51] Or, more edifyingly, one could note his inclusion, as one important arena in which serious issues of moral character and moral fault arise, of the daily round of interactions of all sorts (shopping, passing in the street, minor business dealings, etc.) among people who do, and have to, live and deal constantly in some reciprocal way with one another, as well as at parties and social interactions of all sorts. Aristotle describes in detail three different virtues covering these matters (none of which is clearly recognized as a virtue in popular thought, or is even given a

---

[49] He mentions this point about vindication twice, once in the initial overall account of the moral virtues (II 7, 1108a14–16) and again in IV 7, 1127a14–17, in the middle of his detailed discussion of the virtues governing daily interactions with one's neighbors. Both times he gives it as his justification for including these states of character on his list of virtues to be gone into in detail.

[50] As we will see in chapter 4, the Stoics accept the Platonic scheme, ranging under one or another of these canonical four all of the enormous number—vastly more than Aristotle's eleven—of distinct virtues that they recognize.

[51] The sharp contrast here with the views of Socrates on courage (ἀνδρεία) in Plato's *Protagoras* and *Laches* must have been much in Aristotle's mind as he wrote his chapters on courage.

name). Commentators sometimes refer to these, perhaps disparagingly, as "minor social virtues," but Aristotle himself gives no indication that he regards them as minor at all, not even comparatively. For Aristotle, "morality" is by no means limited to justice or abuse of power and status, or other violations of civic or other rights and duties, but extends equally right through all aspects and circumstances of life, including even how one conducts oneself in eating, drinking, and carrying on conversations at the dinner table. In the next section, as I discuss detailed points in his discussions of his eleven virtues, we will see other striking and morally interesting points arising in Aristotle's presentations of these virtues.

In fact, there is much more than mechanical tidiness in Aristotle's development and application of his tripartite scheme for displaying and discussing the moral virtues and vices. As he explains it, the fact that each virtue has a pair of opposed vices, which are themselves opposed to one another in a different way, as "excesses" and "defects," has a relatively deep philosophical explanation. It is due to the general fact that nonrational desires and feelings, and actions done partly as a result of them, are essentially continuous quantities. They can (given particular circumstances) be great or much, or small or little in those circumstances. Here we must remember that, from the outset, Aristotle has described the human virtues as belonging to the rational part of the soul (as opposed to the "vegetative" and other automatic life functions, not controlled by our desires and wishes). The moral virtues belong to appetite and spirit, as we have seen, insofar as those powers can conform through habituation to, and so can obey, the dictates of practical reason. The function of reason in all its aspects is to get things right, to judge and decide correctly—and in so doing to find the underlying order, balance, and harmony, in the phenomena being thought about. So here, where feelings and actions range from small to great or little to much, the function of virtue (as a perfection of our power of reasoning, in one of its aspects) is to lead a person to have the right strength or level of feelings (in the given circumstances) and act just as much as is right. The right feeling and the right action will be ones that are properly measured, so to speak, in relation to the circumstances; they are not more, nor less, than is right, and so, in that sense, they are intermediate. We will see in some detail in the next section how Aristotle's theory of the virtues as intermediate conditions is worked out in particular cases. Further clarification can await that discussion. For now, the main point to emphasize is that, as a product of reason, moral virtue or virtue of character reflects the underlying power of reason, in discovering the truth, to find the order and pleasingly appropriate balance in the objects of its concern.

Thus the intermediacy of a moral virtue is itself a function of the fact that virtuous persons, in any specific area of life, regularly or always have the right, that is, in that sense, the intermediate, feelings, and as a result they act intermediately. Thus, they feel and act in a way that is perfectly well ordered, in relation to the particular circumstances for action that they face. The intermediacy of the virtue in each case reduces to the intermediacy of the nonrational feelings with which the relevant virtuous agents act, and the intermediacy of the actions that they do (partly) as a result of those feelings. It is in this prior intermediacy that the virtue's pedigree as belonging to a rational part of the soul, and so itself an intermediate thing, displays itself. It is in the intermediate feelings and actions belonging to or constituting the virtue that reason's essential function of getting things right, by discovering good order and proper balance, consists.[52] The vice of "excess" in each case is the condition of a person's habituated feelings, and resulting actions, in which he or she habitually feels and acts with excesses of some relevant feeling or desire: they habitually overfeel and overdo in certain ways and circumstances. Mutatis mutandis for the vices of "defect." By contrast, the virtue itself is a standing condition from which the agent regularly and always feels and acts, as I said, in an intermediate way. In taking pleasure in morally virtuous action, then, as Aristotle famously insists any morally virtuous agent must do, these agents are taking pleasure in the exercise of their reason in which these intermediacies are recognized as such, and felt and enacted. They are taking pleasure in the exercise of the capacity of their nonrational desires and feelings to be, through rationally self-directed training, in whatever is in fact the intermediate (and correct) condition, the well-ordered one, under each of the fluctuating circumstances of daily life. Likewise, they take pleasure in the intermediate (and right) action, as that condition is defined by practical reason to be the intermediate one, as these trained feelings lead them to it. The good of, and in, moral ac-

---

[52] Aristotle draws attention to this essential feature of morally virtuous feeling-cum-action, and emphasizes its importance in his overall conception of the moral virtues, in his frequent reference, as he discusses the individual virtues in turn, to "the fine" as being the constant and distinctive aim of all morally virtuous actions. "Fineness" (τὸ καλόν, in some translations "the noble"), on Aristotle's understanding of the term, belongs to whatever exhibits rational order (see Cooper, *Reason and Emotion*, chap. 11, "Reason, Moral Virtue and Moral Value," sec. v, 270ff.). Given the importance in his account of the fine as the special aim of virtuous actions as such, it is odd that Aristotle does not introduce and explain this aim already in his initial, general account in book II, but mentions it for the first time only somewhat incidentally in his chapters on courage (1115b11–13). That morally virtuous actions possess fineness is mentioned in passing or implied several times already in book I (see 1099a18, 1101a14, 1104b32), where Aristotle treats it as part of the common conception of virtue for which he intends his treatise to provide a philosophical explication and support.

tivities and actions is due to—indeed, it consists in—that exercise of the human power of reason. The universal pleasure that the morally virtuous take in engaging in such activities and doing such actions is just one way that that good displays itself to them. (Of course, depending on the particular case, they may and will experience other pleasures too, in doing their morally good acts.) It seems, then, that Aristotle is so concerned to use the tripartite scheme in going through his eleven virtues, case by case, because of his need to establish, once and for all, that, when properly conceived and articulated, the virtues really are functions of reason. They are not some arbitrary, or merely socially derived, set of approved conditions. Their intermediacy and the good order that that displays show this.

Readers are sometimes disappointed in a second way than the one mentioned above in which Aristotle's discussions of the moral virtues are abstract. And, here again, Aristotle has good reasons of theory for writing as abstractly as he does. He never even attempts to tell us about the morally virtuous person's feelings and thoughts about any particular cases—even any specific recurring type of case, such as the famous one Socrates discusses in the first book of the *Republic*, of what to do if you have borrowed someone's knife and he asks for it back when in a deranged state, in which he might well harm himself or someone else.[53] Comment on or resolution of conflicts of moral values in particular circumstances plays no role in Aristotle's account, either in the general account of book II or in the particular and detailed ones of the later books. He has a good deal to say about the sorts of things that the various types of virtuous people feel, or do not feel, concern for—the sorts of things they decide and feel correctly about, feeling neither too much nor too little, doing neither too much nor too little. But he gives no guidance at any level of detail that might provide a concrete picture of the particular ways of feeling or thinking about specific practical circumstances that distinguish the virtuous person from the various sorts of non-virtuous ones. He tells us, for example, that it is wrong to fear poverty or sickness or other such bad things, except when they might arise from having lived viciously, or be due to some moral fault of our own. And he also says that, though such fear has nothing to do with courage, every decent person will fear a merited loss of good reputation, because lack of such fear connotes the absence of any sense of shame—something that is a fundamental feature of decent, as well as fully virtuous, people.[54] Other such general remarks about the psychology and

[53] See *Republic* 331b–d.
[54] See *NE* III 6, 1115a10–18.

moral attitudes of the virtuous person in general, or belonging to particular virtues, occur quite frequently as one reads through these books. I will say more
below about their place within the knowledge about virtue that Aristotle means
to be conveying in this part of his work. But specific judgments of what is right
to do, or what feelings and desires it is right to have, in what strengths, in any
given concrete circumstance, with reasons supplied in explanation and support,
are altogether omitted. Aristotle does not enter into moral "case studies," of the
sort that are described and discussed with "scenarios" about trolley cars and the
like in our contemporary philosophy.

Aristotle restricts himself in this way for reasons of philosophical principle.
Early in the first book he includes some comments on the degree and sort
of precision that apply to the political studies he is embarking upon.[55] He says
we should be satisfied if what we say provides the sort of full clarification
(διασαφηθείη) that conforms to the standards for precision appropriate to the
subject matter. And he adds that fine and just actions, as well as good things, even
virtues like courage, have a sort of "wavering" quality, in that what counts correctly as fine and just varies to a degree from place to place and (I take it he also
intends) circumstance to circumstance, and in that good things do not always do
good, but sometimes also harm, instead. Such wavering does not show that fine,
just, and good have no natures of their own that one can subject to study and
provide full clarifications of, but are only categories made up by human beings in
their interactions with one another. Their natures are such, however, that in
order to clarify them to ourselves we must speak in terms of what is "for the
most part the case," but might sometimes be absent, or may apply differently
from one case to another. At the end of book II, in concluding his general account of the moral virtues, and again well along into his discussion of the particular virtues, Aristotle applies these ideas to specific judgments about what in
some circumstance constitutes the "mean" or intermediate feeling or action.[56]
Because these concern particular cases, which are so and so only for the most
part, the judgment must be given by perception, he says. How angry to get, and
for how long, against whom (whoever it is who has done something that normally merits anger), and what does merit anger—all these are matters on which
virtuous persons do constantly get things right, but neither they, nor we in our
philosophizing, can provide clarifications of their getting it right that can ex-

---

[55] I 3, 1094b11–22.
[56] II 9, 1109b14–23; IV 5, 1126a31–b4.

plain exactly why the right answer to such questions in any particular case is precisely what it is. The nature of virtue is simply such that that kind and degree of precision cannot be achieved, and ought not to be expected, in the description of virtuous actions.

However, that these assessments are provided by the virtuous agent's trained or experienced power of perception by no means implies that for Aristotle moral judgment is altogether intuitive—either you "see" what is right or you do not; you do "see" it if you have been brought up well; if not, then not. On such a view nothing can be said to cast light on any substantive reasons virtuous agents may have for reaching those particular assessments, because there are none. At most they might say something vague and truistic, aimed simply at leading another virtuous agent who had temporarily lost their way back into the light—allegedly the light of "reason," but reason understood as inarticulate, moved by mere strong feelings of conviction that something is the right way to feel or act, but without being able to say at all why. But as we have seen, in the passage of I 3 cited in the last paragraph, Aristotle speaks not at all of the moral agent's, or moral philosophy's, having no clarification to give. Quite on the contrary, he speaks of full clarification—however, a full clarification given, necessarily, at a certain level of generality. At that level of generality Aristotle does offer many clarifications of the state of mind and feelings of the virtuous agent. I have already mentioned two of these: the intermediacy, and the fineness of virtuous feeling and action. Among these clarifications are many further remarks about the ideas on the basis of which such an agent decides in particular cases how to feel and how to act, in determining in particular circumstances the application of the general notion that virtuous actions always fall in an intermediate zone between two extremes. When one attends closely, and attempts to construct from these remarks an overall account of the practical stance and attitudes of virtuous agents toward themselves and others, and as regards all the sorts of things that are in one way or another of value for a human being, a quite substantive picture clearly emerges. To see this, let us turn to Aristotle's detailed accounts of his eleven particular virtues.

3.7. The Specific Practical Virtues

Morally virtuous persons, because, as we have seen, they necessarily also possess practical wisdom (φρόνησις), the virtue of practical reason, are able to deliberate well about the things that are good and of advantage for oneself, not in specific contexts, e.g. what sorts of things conduce to health or to physical strength, but what sorts of things conduce to living well in general. . . . [Their virtue of practical wisdom] is a state of mind grasping the truth, involving reason, concerned with action about things that are good or bad for a human being.[57]

These "things that are good or bad" Aristotle classifies into three groups: goods of the soul (virtues of all three types, plus talents, acquired skills, dispositions of personality, bodily and other pleasures, etc.); bodily goods (health, strength, manual dexterity, physical attractiveness, etc.); and external ones (material resources, friends, social connections, political power, etc.), plus their opposites or lacks, in comparison with the normal human being.[58] Virtuous people, then, because they have this knowledge about how to deliberate concerning all these goods, have been trained (indeed, they have trained themselves, along the way while acquiring the knowledge) so that their nonrational desires and feelings concerned with all the goods of these three categories always conform to practical reason's correct judgments as to their actual, true importance and worth, in relation to a well-lived human life—indeed in relation to a properly directed *human* life altogether.[59]

The key point, as we have already seen Aristotle argue, is that some goods of the soul, namely the virtues (of any of the three types he distinguishes), rank first among goods. The role of the practical virtues (the moral ones taken together with practical wisdom) is to provide the proper basis for evaluating (both in judgment and in feeling) the place and worth of all the goods of the other sorts, and therefore for acting in relation to them. The practical virtues evaluate the goods of the soul other than virtues, and bodily and external goods, both among and in comparison with one another, and in relation to themselves and to other virtues (e.g., those of the intellect). All the actions and activities of human life evidently involve deciding and acting in relation to goods and bads (at least to things taken by the agent to be such), and it is always possible to judge and feel about these rightly or wrongly. The practical virtues are the states of mind and character that guide a person to the right, and away from the wrong, judgments and feelings, in any and all of the actions and activities of life. That is why, for

---

[57] VI 5, 1140a26–28, b5–6.
[58] For this classification, see, e.g., *NE* I 8, 1098b12–14.
[59] See endnote 15 on the virtuous person, as described by Aristotle, as an ideal type.

Aristotle, as for the other philosophers in the Greek tradition, these virtues cover so many aspects of human life that in our modern ways of speaking and thinking do not count as concerning morality at all.

This means that in all the feelings and actions of their life virtuous people are aware, at least implicitly, of the fundamentally subordinate value or disvalue of all other goods and bads except virtues and vices of soul—money, pleasure, social power, prestige, friendships, even mere peace and quiet, and all the other principal objects of pursuit and competition in any human community. Despite this lower ranking, these other things may indeed remain good or bad, as the case may be, and be good or bad for even an agent who does not feel and think about them in that virtuous way, but overvalues them. Indeed, most people (either now or in Aristotle's time) do not feel and think about these other goods in that virtuous way. They regard them as the primary aims of life, the determinants of whether or not, and to what extent, a life goes well and is happy (even if they also assign some important value to behaving decently and fairly to other people, perhaps as a mere side constraint on the pursuit of these allegedly more fundamental values). On Aristotle's conception, however, the virtuous feel and think quite differently. Virtuous people regard all these other things as good (even ones that are good or bad simply on their own, in some way independent of their involvement in the active exercise of practical virtue) primarily for their use or other value in virtuous actions and activities, or bad because they prevent or conflict with virtuous action. Pleasure taken in eating or sex, for example, certainly may satisfy an appetite and be good for the person enjoying it, in part, simply for that reason. But, for virtuous persons, any such pleasures they take are found good, and are good, only as and because they are pleasurable responses to activities of eating and sexual contact that are themselves properly and rightly done. Pleasures one might get outside that context of virtuous action are not ones that virtuous people would regard as good at all; indeed, they would not take any pleasure, even of that bodily sort, in the activities that would give rise to them.[60] Aristotle himself has given good reasons to show—and these are among their own reasons for thinking it—that a human life would not be improved by any amount by adding any such illicit pleasures to it, given that one would also have to add disorderly appetites to be satisfied in experiencing these pleasures.

In this way, virtue is not quite a condition that has to be met if any other type of potentially good thing is to be good at all, and do the one having it any good.

[60] See *NE* III 11, 1119a11–15.

But it is a condition for any of those other goods being worth having, everything considered. In all their feelings of nonrational desire or aversion, in relation to bodily and external goods and bads, then, virtuous persons desire them as being only, in the way indicated, conditionally good or bad. They are good or bad conditionally on their use or other value in relation to virtuous acts and activities. For example, the pleasure of satisfied appetite while one is eating is a worthwhile good only in that such pleasures naturally accompany well-done acts of self-maintenance or of socially valuable meal sharing. And this feature of virtuous persons' nonrational motivations in acting then affects and shapes the actions themselves and the ways in which they carry them out. Their sense of the subordinate value of these things is felt in the very desires they may have for them, and it shows itself, to an attentive eye, in the actions that they then take, and the ways they do them. Saying only so much still leaves mostly in the dark the terms on which the virtuous judge the pursuit, or enjoyment or use, of these goods to be appropriate and right. Although as I have already said, Aristotle thinks these terms can be clarified only at a certain level of generality, he does clarify them significantly at many places in his discussions of the particular virtues. In doing so he constructs a philosophical account of his own of the feelings and attitudes of the virtuous agent, that is, of the truly virtuous person, who possesses both the habituated virtues of character and the articulated practical understanding given through the virtue of practical wisdom. He also develops and explains what he thinks are the good reasons why one should hold that these feelings and attitudes are the right ones for human beings to have as they lead their daily lives. These are his reasons why these feelings and attitudes constitute the right overall and general evaluations of all the human goods, in comparison and ranking with one another. It is, then, this understanding and this set of feelings and attitudes that guide morally virtuous persons in deciding what, in any given set of circumstances, the mean or intermediate way to feel and to act actually is. These reveal the reasons they have for so deciding, so feeling, and so acting.[61]

---

[61] In what follows down to the end of this section I draw upon and bring together somewhat dispersed remarks of Aristotle's. I also engage in some extrapolation from the things he says explicitly in some particular context, so as to apply and develop them in other contexts. I provide specific textual references at many points, but I do not wish to claim that what I say about each of the virtues is contained, or highlighted, in the specific chapters devoted to it in III–V. The understanding of and outlook on human affairs that I indicate that Aristotle means to be conveying to his hearers/readers requires each reader to reach their own full understanding of the virtues, and that can never be simply a matter of learning just what Aristotle says in each few pages about each virtue. The sort of extrapolated construction I provide is precisely what a proper reading of his work by his intended hearers/readers demands, if they wish to use it, as he intends it to be used, in helping them to become independently good moral agents.

For example, Aristotle clarifies the virtuous person's attitudes to the routine pleasures of eating, drinking, and sex when he refers to "natural appetites" as ones that, in parallel to the other animals, we experience because of recurrent physical lacks—lacks of food or drink for example—or other physical needs, when our bodily constitution requires nourishment or other restorative adjustment, if we are to continue our proper physical functioning in good health.[62] All animals get pleasure from the activities involved in seeing to these needs.[63] But of course it is quite possible to seek, and get, these pleasures even where there is no natural need to be responded to, or well beyond anything those needs require. Virtuous people see, and feel about, these pleasures in light of the natural role of such pleasure in helping to motivate us to maintain our physical constitutions and well-being; for them, these natural needs provide the measure of excess, or deficiency, in caring about and pursuing these pleasures. Those who like these pleasures more than anything else, and who seek and enjoy them with an intensity that does not correspond to their natural place and role in our lives, overemphasize the purely animal aspect of our lives (the "beastly" one, as Aristotle puts it): they "like them more than they are worth."[64] Temperate people (those with the virtue that instills these right attitudes of feeling) "get no pleasure from the things that overindulgent people most get pleasure from—on the contrary, those things revolt them; nor . . . do they get intense pleasure from any source of such pleasures, nor are they distressed when such pleasures are absent."[65] Their appetites for these pleasures are always only moderate, as befits the pleasures' relatively unimportant, however recurrent, place in a properly conceived human life. That does not mean they will not want and would not enjoy a suitable variety of interesting and wholesome food, drink, and sex: they will, as Aristotle says, seek and enjoy in this moderate way any sort of pleasant food, drink, and sex, provided it is no obstacle to fitness and health—and, importantly, so long as it does not exceed their financial means.[66] If your means do not allow it, you will not feel desires for, and will not worry yourself to any degree over, certain varieties of food, drink, and sex that you might very well take an active interest in, and see to it that you could regularly enjoy, if you were richer—provided, that is, that you do possess the virtue of temperance. You will have trained your appetites,

---

[62] See endnote 16 for discussion of the varieties of pleasure in the use of the senses.

[63] See *NE* III 11, 1118b9–11, 15–19.

[64] *NE* III 10, 1118b4 and 11, 1119a19–20.

[65] *NE* III 11, 1119a11–14.

[66] 1119a16–19.

and reinforced them with the reasoning I have just gone through, so that such desires do not arise.[67] Aristotle advances this philosophical conception of how these bodily appetites relate to our health and fitness for life (i.e., for the rest of life) as an essential part of fully virtuous persons' understanding of themselves and their life. Taken together with consideration of their financial means, this understanding leads them to whatever, for them individually, and in individual circumstances, is the right and intermediate way of feeling and acting in regard to these pleasures. To exceed one's means would clearly betray that one valued them at more than their true worth.

As for external goods in general, and wealth in particular—the continuing or renewable sources of income that provide financial means beyond the necessary minimum for sustaining a civilized life—Aristotle's basic principle finds expression early in his discussion of the virtue of justice. This principle has two parts. First, all external goods (ones he also calls "goods of fortune") are indeed goods (within very broad limits), if considered just on their own and in relation simply to human life in general. Their opposites or lacks are bad things in the same way. But, secondly, they are not always good for particular people.[68] Neglecting this distinction, people typically wish for and indeed actively pursue these things as if they were absolutely good, good come what may. But, Aristotle says, what they ought to wish for and ought actively to pursue instead is that these goods should be good *for them*. They should want to make themselves the sort of people for whom such goods would be good, come what may.[69] For, as he explains at one point in the *Politics*, virtuous persons are the sort of persons who make "unqualifiedly good" things good for them. It is their virtue that makes those in-themselves goods, good also for them.[70] Virtue does this because it guarantees that everything done through or with these goods—every activity that they enable—will itself be a good activity, in fact one of the constituent activities of

[67] It may be that Aristotle and Plato before him have an overoptimistic view about the degrees to which these appetites can be altered through training and habituation, and about the possibility of this sort of close cohesion between trained appetites and reasoned views about what is good and bad. We will see that Plotinus thinks they are overoptimistic (section 6.5). But the general phenomenon they appeal to surely cannot be doubted.

[68] Not all the goods Aristotle has in mind under these headings are "economic" goods. Included are friends, or having friends, social standing and the political influence it brings, and even physical attractiveness. (See *NE* I 8, 1099a31–b6.) For my discussion here and in what immediately follows, however, I leave the noneconomic goods of fortune aside.

[69] See *NE* V 1, 1129b1–6.

[70] *Politics* VII 13, 1332a22–23. Compare what Socrates says at Plato, *Apology* 30b2–4 (as translated in the main text of Cooper, *Plato*, p. 28); and see my discussion of this passage above, section 2.2.

their εὐδαιμονία or happiness. It will be an activity of virtue. The nonvirtuous, for whom these may well not be good in any way or to any degree at all, chiefly benefit from them passively, to the extent they benefit at all. They cannot benefit in the active way that the virtuous do. Thoroughly bad people may not be made worse by possessing a large disposable income (though of course that could happen). But their attitudes to the value of money and the things that it can buy will make the activities in which they use these resources, or which these resources enable them to engage in, pretty worthless. At most these resources will contribute to increased comfort, or bodily and other pleasures of recreation, as well as an increased or more secure sense of (nonetheless flawed) self-esteem. But compared with the worthlessness of the activities themselves, any such good effects will count for very little so far as the improvement of their lives may go. Of course, not all nonvirtuous people are thoroughly bad; accordingly, they may benefit not just passively (through comfort and so on), but to some extent and degree actively too, in the expanded range of interesting and good virtuous (or decent) activities such good fortune would enable.

Accordingly, the virtuous will not seek wealth or material goods and resources except for their uses, first of all, in making possible a virtuously well-lived daily life for themselves and their family, and at a relatively high material level. They will have no regard for conspicuous consumption and for the admiration or envy this might evoke in others, or any other effects of heightened social standing that resulted. But Aristotle explains that, secondly, they will wish for a degree of wealth that will go beyond supplying their and their family's needs. This will enable them to give money and goods away, especially to friends, but also to others in their community who may be in need, or who could themselves make good use of them.

This follows from a second principle that Aristotle relies on in relation to these external goods. For in fact, as Aristotle thinks, the correct basis for judging who merits or deserves external goods of any type is a person's virtue or decency—precisely because the true value of these goods is in the virtuous or decent activities of life that they enable.[71] Hence in discussing the virtue of

---

[71] In his discussion of the virtue of magnanimity or greatness of soul (μεγαλοψυχία; sometimes rather unfortunately also rendered in English as "pride") Aristotle announces that worth (or desert: ἀξία) is worthiness to have external goods (*NE* IV 3, 1123b17); and, because of their exceptional virtue, the great souled (as their name implies) are worthy of and deserve great such goods, including especially the greatest of them, which Aristotle says is being honored. Even though they have no concern for even more than ordinary levels of other external goods (they disdain both them and the concern for them, in their higher

ἐλευθεριότης, usually given in English as generosity,[72] Aristotle emphasizes that generous people know, among other ways of being intermediate in their actions and feelings, to whom they ought to be generous in giving their financial assistance. It is to those whose characters are decent (μέτριοι τὰ ἤθη) that they will give: they will not enrich people who ought to be poor because their characters are bad, any more than they would give to those who would flatter them and might help to spread their good reputation.[73] What they would most value is their own actions of generosity, together with the concern for the good of others that motivates those actions—and, of course, the good of others that their actions aim at, if as intended it results. They are not concerned to promote their reputation, even if their actions merit a good one, and although they do call for a grateful acceptance on the part of the one benefited. Likewise, they would take care not to provide assistance that would deplete their resources to such an extent that they would not be able later to continue their practice of giving where it might do this sort of moral good. They give in accordance with their means.[74]

If it should so happen that they possess extraordinary wealth, then besides such relatively minor generosity, aimed at advancing the morally good or decent lives of private persons who are their friends, or acquaintances in their community, they will use their resources in philanthropic endeavors on behalf of the whole city and its citizens in common. In describing these (the principal concerns of the virtuous person that Aristotle calls "magnificent" or "munificent"), Aristotle understandably presupposes a person living in the context of ancient Greek civic culture, but it is easy enough to apply his ideas to other cultural contexts, including our own.[75] Regarding wealth and what it can provide as very subordinate goods, in the first instance of use in engaging in or promoting activities of virtue, extremely rich virtuous people look to the common good of their community and its citizens, and they seek ways of contributing on a large scale to that. Large-scale contributions to the common good are especially salient indications of the generous lack of concern exclusively for the material context of one's

---

concern for great affairs of state and great deeds), nonetheless they do deserve them and, morally speaking, ought to have them.

[72] It is sometimes also translated as liberality, or (so Rowe) open-handedness. See *NE* IV 1.

[73] See *NE* IV 1, 1121b5–7.

[74] See *NE* IV 1, 1120b2–9.

[75] See *NE* IV 2, on μεγαλοπρέπεια. "Munificence" is Rowe's translation; it suits Aristotle's emphasis on the active concern of this sort of person for public buildings and facilities and major civic enterprises requiring expenditures of the sort that only people like themselves can afford. But it does less well when it comes to the houses befitting their riches that they build, as suitable adornments, and the magnificent weddings they give their daughters, and their impressive death monuments (1123a1, 6–10).

own life, and even one's own private acts of virtue, that characterizes moral virtue as a whole. Aristotle mentions temples to the gods, splendid productions of plays at the drama festivals, the outfitting of warships, and communal meals on special occasions of celebration.[76] These are all central institutions and practices where moral education and the support of moral attitudes, and of civilizing, moral activities among all the citizens, are very much in focus. It seems to be with those moral functions in mind that Aristotle describes the magnificent person as someone possessing an important moral virtue.[77]

Both generosity and magnificence focus on providing material goods for the use of others in their own moral activities. As I have emphasized, through these virtues virtuous people show their interest in the good of other people—others' moral good, not merely whatever good there may be for them in having material resources otherwise at their disposal, though of course that good is included within the concerns of the virtuous in their generosity. They willingly and gladly, and with pleasure, concern themselves in that way with the good of their fellow citizens. This is only one way in which, on Aristotle's account, virtue entails a concern for the good of the other people among whom one lives—even, and especially, of those who may not be morally very good themselves, as is the case with the mass of citizens who are the objects of the magnificent person's munificence. Aristotle's account of the more mundane virtues of "mixing with others, living in their company and sharing with them in conversations and the business of life"[78] provides insight into how he conceives the virtuous person's attitudes toward other people in general. This important background for generosity's and magnificence's much more extensive concerns for the good of other people shows that the latter are simply extensions of a fundamental and active goodwill that characterizes the virtuous. This goodwill, which is displayed most clearly and fully in Aristotle's account of these virtues of social and commercial interaction, is the (so to speak) default attitude that virtuous people bring to their relations with other people. We can come to understand Aristotle's, and (on his

---

[76] NE IV 2, 1122b19–23.

[77] Aristotle does not draw specific attention to these moral functions in his discussion of magnificence, but he does emphasize that the magnificent person's activities are aimed at the common good of a city and all its citizens (see 1122b21, 1123a5), and he is entirely specific throughout the treatise about what the good of human beings consists in. And since Aristotle explains magnificence as the specific virtue that accompanies generosity in a person of extraordinary means, the same focus on good character that we find in the case of generous benefactions will apply in the case of the grander virtue of magnificence, through provision of public means for building or reinforcing good character.

[78] NE IV 6, 1126b11–12 (trans. Rowe).

account of them) virtuous people's, reasons for holding this attitude through attending to his discussion of these additional virtues.

It is clear, though Aristotle does not point this out in his discussion, that the attitudes and feelings of the virtuous that he clarifies under the heading of these virtues of communal and social life, reflect and develop an underlying positive and embracing attitude to the essentially social and mutually cooperative life that Aristotle regards as belonging to human beings by nature. Human beings are of such a nature that they need to, and do, live together with and among other people, in groups of larger than family size, whose members live interconnected, and in many ways interdependent, lives. They are essentially communal beings, and every normal human life is lived as part of the more inclusive life of some community.[79] Aristotle's virtuous people know this, and embrace it: they do not resent or begrudge it, or try to avoid or minimize its consequences for them. They take the communal basis of human life seriously in the ways they feel about other people, and think about and live their own lives, individually. They think, and feel, that it is right to treat anyone and everyone that they come into contact with in their daily activities around the city as they would if they were their friends—as if they were themselves moved by the same goodwill that they feel, and that they think it right to feel.[80] Such goodwill is owed, they think, to others with whom one shares one's life, as befits cooperating partners. This goodwill, and the assumption of its being mutually returned, is the default attitude that they bring to all their daily interactions with their fellow citizens. Hence, they are not cantankerous and demanding, or abrupt and inconsiderate, nor of course fawning or overfriendly and intrusive: these are not actually good personal friends, so it is right to keep a certain distance. They want to take pleasure mutually with the other person in whatever their business together involves; they avoid giving unnecessary or unreasonable pain or annoyance. And when it is time to relax over a drink or in some game or other pastime together with strangers or slight acquaintances, they know not to allow their jokes or funny remarks to become offensive, or crass—and they know how to give others the pleasure of a welcoming and suitably amused reception of their own.[81] All this

---

[79] When he says that "the human being is a political (or 'city-state') animal" (e.g., at *NE* I 7, 1097b11 and *Pol.* I 2, 1253a3) he goes further than this minimal claim, but it is of course implied (cf. *NE* IX 9, 1169b18–19). I will have more to say about Aristotle's understanding of what a community is, and the importance of the specifically political community, and of the communal life of a city, in section 3.9 below.

[80] See *NE* IV 6, 1126b19–28. My reference to goodwill here draws on Aristotle's account in VIII 2, where he makes it the central motivation in friendship (see esp. 1156a3–5).

[81] See *NE* IV 8.

they think, and feel, is what suits casual interactions with others with whom one's life is bound together in many ties of mutual dependence and cooperation, and for whom therefore one feels goodwill.

But there is a second side to these virtues. They also involve attitudes to or about oneself as those may affect the quality of one's interactions. The virtuous know not to present themselves as condescending or to put on airs when they engage on this common field of daily civic life. They do not boast about themselves or their family, or lay claim falsely to status and accomplishments that do not belong to them. They present themselves on the basis of open honesty about themselves, and without pressing on others even their true status or accomplishments, if those are remarkable, as if thereby to win favored treatment or propagate an exalted reputation. They acknowledge, and do not hide, their own other virtues, and any other goods they may legitimately lay claim to; but they leave these aside, unspoken, and without in any way drawing attention to them. Behaving otherwise is a shameful intrusion into the properly casual and equal context of such daily interactions among those who cooperate together in living their lives in a community.[82] They object to such behavior when they confront it in others, and by their own behavior and in other ways too they encourage everyone to share their own attitudes, in helping to structure with them the generally approved and expected modes of interaction in the public sphere of daily interactions in their community. Their assumption of mutual goodwill, and these consequences of it, are, they think, rationally dictated by the shared life that naturally suits human beings, and that, therefore, human beings have good reason to want to lead.

On the other hand, the virtuous also understand that the naturally appropriate badge of their virtue is honor, praise, and general esteem among the members of the community.[83] Being held in honor and treated with special respect is merited, and properly merited only, on the basis of one's virtuous states of mind and feeling, and the actions in which they are expressed.[84] That is because it is virtue

---

[82] See *NE* IV 7.

[83] On the virtues concerned with honor see *NE* IV 3 (on "greatness of soul," deserving of great honors) and 4 (on the nameless virtue of those deserving of minor or medium honors).

[84] In his account of honor as a human good in the *Rhetoric* (I 5, 1361a28–b2) Aristotle says only that honor comes to people famous for having done good (for others). He does not clearly mention virtue as what merits it. This is only one indication of the ways in which Aristotle's own philosophical account of matters to do with the human good departs from conventional ideas of his time. For honor as the badge of virtue (and so, a merited badge only for virtuous benefiting of others) see *NE* IV 3, 1123b34–6. Presumably, at least one part of the value of honor (when it has value at all, i.e., when given as a badge of true virtue) is that it helps to spread the idea of the goodness of virtue among the population.

and virtue only, among all accomplishments in life, that shows anyone to have applied themelves in a rationally fully defensible way to the most important and most difficult of tasks, the living of a full and good human life. Anything else that one might be properly honored for should be good things one does in part with and on the basis of one's virtues. So the virtuous expect to be honored in some ways or other, appropriate to honoring someone first of all and primarily for being a good person, and to be deferred to accordingly. They do not, of course, care about honor in itself or on its own; it is honor based legitimately on their virtues and their virtues' expressions in action that they desire and feel entitled to. They do not wish to be honored for the wrong reasons, or by those whose own appreciation of true virtue is too limited to be of any consequence. To seek to be honored in other ways and on any other basis is a mark of vice, not virtue—it betrays attitudes that are excessive or defective, and not intermediate and fine ways of feeling and acting.

Hence virtuous people do not demand to be shown deference or special respect (even though it might be merited) in their daily interactions. Indeed, they do not take offense and become angry or irritated at petty surliness or slights, or even at major but inconsequential insults: they are ready to make allowances and are not touchy, or bent on revenge for any and every offense.[85] They can and do take offense, but not at slights to the special honor and esteem their virtue merits, since, as we have seen, they do not in any event demand esteem or its signs from others, though they do feel entitled to it. Clearly, what do offend them (though Aristotle does not say this explicitly) are serious insults of the sort that betray an attitude of disrespect and abusive disregard of one citizen toward another. These violate the norms of easy goodwill that they hold are rationally demanded for the conduct of one's relations with the others with whom one shares a common life. Because they value the life defined by those norms far more than they do any pleasure in avenging such an insult, they will not respond in kind and will not become extremely angry or remain angry for long; they will not harbor grudges. Their overriding aim will be to restore and help to maintain decent relations of mutual respect, and mutual regard, with all their fellow citizens. This point of view provides the due measures of their anger—whom to get angry with, how angry to get, how long to stay angry. It defines what is appropriate to the circumstances.[86]

---

[85] See *NE* IV 5, 1126a2–3.
[86] On the virtue of mildness or good temper, see *NE* IV 5.

3.8. Practical Knowledge and Ethical "Theory"

This, then, is a sketch of the ways of thinking and feeling about themselves and others, as members of a human community, that Aristotle attributes to morally virtuous persons.[87] These are thoughts and feelings about the place and value in a human life of bodily and other ordinary human pleasures, and about economic goods in general and wealth in particular, and about having and maintaining good and friendly, supportive relationships with all with whom one comes in contact. In attributing these to virtuous agents, Aristotle clarifies for us the nature of these virtues.[88] As I mentioned earlier, these are the attitudes with which both the contemplatively inclined person leading Aristotle's contemplative life as well as the politically gifted and trained leader leading Aristotle's political life approach all aspects of their daily lives. Into them they fit their work devoted to their special respective passions of philosophical study and theory, and political leadership. These attitudes also ground and give shape and structure to the lives of every other decent or virtuous person who lacks either of those passions and lives a private life, pursuing some ordinary profession or other work. Like the expert politician, such people treat practically virtuous activity as their highest attainable good. As we have seen, decent people (which is the best that most of us could aspire to be) will have approximately the same feelings about things, in general and in concrete situations, that the fully virtuous person would have. Their understanding of why these are the right ways of feeling would, however, be not nearly so complete and detailed, or as philosophically deep, as that of the fully virtuous person described above: they live with a settled sense of what is fair and decent, but with not much more than that. When properly conceived, as we saw earlier, Aristotle holds that the moral virtues of feeling and character, and the virtue of practical wisdom, cannot exist except in a single unified condition

[87] In the previous section, following an order of my own devising, I have drawn especially on Aristotle's accounts in books III–V of the virtues of temperance, justice, generosity, magnificence, the three virtues of social intercourse, and "greatness of soul." I touched very briefly also on the virtue of "good temper," and I said something about courage in section 3.6. I have not attempted a thorough discussion of any of Aristotle's eleven virtues; my focus has been on general features of the evaluative outlook of Aristotelian virtuous person, as regards virtue itself and the other goods (and bads) of human life, as shaped by their understanding of human nature itself.

[88] In preparing this sketch I have omitted most of the clarifications he provides in discussing the virtue of justice, in *NE* V. They mostly concern details not closely related to my purposes in the sketch. I have also not drawn much on his accounts of friendship in VIII and IX, which likewise raise many interesting points of detail that go beyond anything needed for present purposes. But on justice and friendship see further below, section 3.9.

of mind and character. Hence, for him, the morally virtuous person, if correctly conceived, requires to possess practical wisdom. And, as we have seen, on Aristotle's understanding of practical wisdom, since it is the same (as it were) body of knowledge as the political expertise that he is helping his hearers and readers to acquire, through attending properly to his ethical treatise together with his political one, this means that true moral virtue, strictly conceived, requires the grasp of a considerable body of philosophical analysis and argument. It embodies a philosophically derived and explained systematic view about human nature and human life, with prescriptions for how to lead it. Ordinary, decent people cannot be expected to meet those demanding conditions, however firm, good, and even admirable their way of life might be.

We see this clearly in my sketch above. I have assembled my account of virtuous agents' thoughts about the reasons for feeling and acting as they do from a number of texts. In reference to certain details about several of the individual virtues, it goes beyond anything Aristotle himself says explicitly in his specific discussions of them. However, I believe, and have presented evidence as I have gone along, that this account is one that ancient readers or hearers of Aristotle's lectures who not just listened, but tried through independent reflection and understanding to put together a conception for their own use of how to be a good person, could assemble for themselves, thinking it to be what Aristotle himself had in mind. On this account there are many quite specifically philosophical ideas, and others that, though in themselves they might not have to be so conceived, owe a lot, in the context of their presentation, to specifically philosophical (as we would call it) ethical theory. Aristotle, as I explained in the first and second sections of this chapter, distinguishes sharply "theory" and theoretical understanding, as something distinct from the practical understanding needed for leading one's own life, and for helping to direct the communal life of a city. And his version of what we, without his reasons for avoiding the term, would call "ethical theory," does indeed operate to a great extent with highly refined conceptions of the human being and of human life that are, at all events, not simply part of ordinary ways of thinking, handed down to us through our upbringing and moral education—however well connected these philosophical ideas may be with some of the latter. So he is requiring of truly and fully virtuous people a considerably refined philosophical understanding of themselves and of human life. This may derive from study in a school (or department) of philosophy, but it might be arrived at through natural philosophical talent, from general reading and reflection on one's experience of life as it has presented itself.[89]

I pointed out already above how nonordinary, how fully philosophical, are Aristotle's arguments in *Nicomachean Ethics* I 7 (derived from Socrates) about the human soul as the basis of our life, and about our soul being the most important concern for us if we really do care whether our life goes well or badly.[90] Likewise for his ideas about the special place in a human life of our powers of reason, as well as his division of those into the (two or) three kinds we have been considering for these past many pages, and his account of the virtues and their active employment as our highest good. These are not ideas that any nonphilosopher would arrive at, or that anyone comes away from a good upbringing, and moral education in childhood, holding to. Yet they are the very foundations for the more specific ideas about the practical virtues I have presented in my sketch of the previous two sections. To summarize these, consider first Aristotle's "theory" (as we usually speak of it) of the moral virtues as lying in an intermediate condition. As I explained that, it rests on important philosophical reflections of Aristotle's (owing a great deal to Plato's ideas in the *Republic*) on reason in its theoretical applications as aiming always at grasping the inherent good order and harmony in the universe and all its aspects, in terms of whatever the first principles are that determine that order in any particular area of study. The search for truth, which is reason's function in all its guises and applications, is, these reflections show or suggest, the search to find the good order in things. The "doctrine of the mean" is a direct application of these ideas specifically to the operations of practical reason. That virtues of character (dispositions of soul for nonrational feeling and action in specific areas of life) lie in an intermediate zone with two opposed vices on either side is a consequence of the continuous spectrum of relevant feelings and actions that are possible, together with the fact that order and balance are always to be found in the middle range on any such spectrum: to find that middle requires seeking the appropriate balance among competing, or at any rate alternative, values and interests at work in the given situation. Virtuous people, because of the perfection of their practical reason, always see, and respond appropriately in their feelings to, these values and the objects of these interests, in a well-balanced, well-proportioned, rationally ordered way.

[89] I suggested above (section 3.3) that this might be possible in unusual cases.
[90] See section 3.3.

None of these ideas about the soul, reason, and the mean are ones that anyone who has not engaged in philosophical thought ever possesses. Someone who lived solely on the basis of the traditional ideas conveyed to young people while they are being raised well, and given good training in their habits of response and behavior, would never think in these terms at all. In fact, until Aristotle himself propounded the doctrine of the mean, probably no one at all, not even any philosopher, had thought in those terms. Thus, on Aristotle's account, the virtuous person has ideas about virtue itself, and about its place in a well-lived human life, that no one could attribute to good people simply by observing and reporting the ideas on these subjects of people with good reputations in one's own community. Certainly no one reporting on what the most highly regarded Greeks of the fourth century BCE thought about virtue itself and its place in human life would say that they held the intricately detailed account of the ways that all other goods (goods of the soul other than virtues, bodily goods, and external goods) are subordinated to the good of virtue.

Further effects of philosophical theory are found at every stage in the description I have given of the thoughts and practical attitudes of the morally virtuous agent. To continue my summary, the idea that the bodily pleasures of food, drink, and sex are to be sought and enjoyed in relation to the natural needs for engaging in the activities that give rise to them is perhaps, in itself, something that someone well brought up in habits of feeling about, and pursuing, such things might formulate for themselves. But the detailed account of some appetites for these pleasures as natural that Aristotle provides, and his theory of their proper subordination to the pleasure of virtuously engaging in the underlying activities, and of virtuously enjoying the pleasure given by them, provides a rich and illuminating—even transformative—philosophical context into which these ideas might be placed. Likewise, the idea that money and economic goods in general are truly of use only in supporting various activities, and that they might not be and do good for some people—that that depends on what one does with them—is quite possibly just common sense to the well brought up. But the elaboration of this idea and its grounding in Aristotle's argument that it is only virtue that can, and does, make these "unqualified" goods good, come what may, clarify and strengthen the point. Similar effects are seen in Aristotle's account of friendliness as the appropriate and virtuous stance to take in all one's daily interactions with one's fellow citizens, and in the underlying attitude toward the naturally communal circumstances of human life that I argued it rests upon in

Aristotle's account. The vision that, according to Aristotle, the virtuous have of a community permeated by decent relations of mutual respect and mutual regard of all citizens for one another, as something demanded by reason itself, given these facts about human nature, and virtuous people's conception of wealth as appropriately consumed, in great measure, for providing resources to be used in the virtuous activities of other good and decent people, who by their decency or goodness deserve them—these too are ideas with a deep philosophical pedigree.

These considerations point to just one way that Aristotle's discussions of the specific moral virtues are based in philosophical ethical theory, and go well beyond any simple, lightly rationalized descriptions of the ways of feeling and thinking about action that he found prevalent among the conventionally virtuous in his own society. Noteworthy also is the very fact that he includes in his list of traits to be discussed the three social virtues I have myself discussed above. Aristotle says that these are all nameless, which is a sure sign that the conditions he describes were not clearly marked off in the popular mind, or in Greek social traditions, as among the virtues to be striven for by the morally ambitious. Another virtue he tells us is nameless is the one discussed in *Nicomachean Ethics* IV 4, an intermediate condition that concerns minor recognitions and small honors. In all these cases it is Aristotle's own philosophical analysis of the natural conditions of human life, and of what a properly virtuous outlook would most prominently consist in, that lead him to discover virtues that he regards as important to recognize and discuss. It is very far from true, as one famous philosopher who greatly admired Plato and Socrates used to say, that Aristotle's ethics, by contrast with these other Greek thinkers' bold and revolutionary moral and political ideas, is conventional and conservative. In fact, it is full of innovations, all deriving from a clearly conceived and comprehensive philosophical account of human nature and human communal life, if it is lived in accordance with reason's own prescriptions. If most of these are a matter of deepened psychological insight and do not rival for audacity Plato's bold and revolutionary proposals for overall social organization, or Socrates's unconventional turn-the-other-cheek purity, that should not obscure the creative power of philosophical reflection and insight that gave rise to Aristotle's sketch of the morally virtuous agent's attitudes and outlook.

It is while having firmly in mind this philosophical understanding of everything of value for a human being, and of its proper place and order in a properly lived human life, that Aristotelian practically virtuous persons organize and conduct the whole of their lives. As I said, this is so, whether they are contemplatives living Aristotle's contemplative life (the absolutely happiest one); or political leaders making activities of political leadership their highest aim (thus living the secondarily happiest life); or even ordinary private persons, living virtuous and so happy lives, though neither of the two happiest ones. It is clear, then, that in all happy lives, for Aristotle, philosophy and philosophical knowledge are key elements. Both theoretical and practical philosophy are at work in the contemplative life, while in the other lives, knowledge of practical philosophy plays a preeminent role. So we can now begin to see how it is that for Aristotle, philosophy, rightly conceived and rightly practiced, might be a way of life—differently in many respects from how it was for Socrates, and indeed differently within each of these three happy lives.

But before we can pursue these questions further, we need to return to our opening inquiry into Aristotle's reasons for claiming, in *Nicomachean Ethics* X 9, that the study of laws and constitutions is a necessary second step, after completing the studies of character, pleasure, and virtue, and the other topics of the *Nicomachean Ethics*—a step we need to take before we can become fully good persons and so be able to live any of these happy lives.[91] Obviously, one would need to have undertaken this further study in order to live as an accomplished political leader: any competent politician needs to know about law, and about general issues for the formation and conduct of states and their affairs. But why are such studies needed in order to live virtuously as an ordinary citizen, much less as a devotee of the activities of theoretically philosophical study and contemplation that Aristotle thinks are, on the final accounting, εὐδαιμονία or the absolutely highest human good? Our first task is to understand why the knowledge of these apparently unnecessary, more or less technical, political matters should be needed even by the ordinary citizen, in leading a virtuous and happy life. We need, after that, also to consider why Aristotle thinks the life of the fully virtuous political leader is the happiest of lives aiming at the activity of practical virtue as the highest good, a happier one than that of the noncontemplative, fully virtuous, private citizen who engages in political activities not significantly more than any other responsible citizen generally does. Finally, we can return to our account of the contemplative life as including a life also of moral virtues, to see why even the contemplative needs to know what the study of politics, as Aristotle conceives, has to teach us. I pursue all these questions in the next section.

---

[91] See above, sections 3.1 and 3.2.

3.9. Political Community and the Highest Good

So far, in presenting and discussing Aristotle's account of the virtuous outlook on life, I have regarded morally virtuous agents as individuals, each living alongside and in cooperation with one another, but each acting separately. This is how Aristotle presents them in his own account in the *Ethics*. Following Aristotle, I have emphasized that virtuous people embrace the necessarily social conditions of any normal human life, and I have drawn attention to some of the consequences that follow. I drew attention to virtuous people's conception of decent friendly relations among those who live together as the right footing on which to conduct one's daily commercial, social, and political interactions with others. And I explained the virtuous attitudes of generosity and magnificence as involving a commitment to aid one's associates and fellow citizens in their own lives of decency and virtue. Those aspects of the virtuous outlook clearly imply that, however much they might live as separate individuals, the virtuous nonetheless are not concerned merely with their own actions and their own virtue and happiness. They feel an interest and concern also for the good of the others with whom they live. That interest and concern is an integral component of the attitudes that their virtues, and their concern for themselves, create in them. We need however to widen our perspective on Aristotle's moral philosophy, and extend the account of the *Ethics*, by looking into his *Politics*. As I have said, Aristotle himself tells us at the end of the *Ethics* that we need to read about and learn the principles of good legislation and political constitutions, if we are to achieve our goal in attending to the *Ethics*—to become good people ourselves. But equally, modern readers of Aristotle, who are presumably not so committed as he is to the idea of practical knowledge as our objective in studying moral philosophy, need to take into account the perspective of the *Politics* on moral virtue, in completing their understanding of Aristotle's theory of the virtues.

When we do turn to the *Politics*, we discover that Aristotle regards moral virtues, and morally virtuous activities and lives, as in a crucial way social (indeed, specifically political) accomplishments—a conception that hardly shows itself in the *Ethics*. They are only partly due to the choices and decisions of the individual agents who are their immediate possessors and sources. That is because (in a way that I will explain) they are, for him, parts of a communal enterprise. He envisions an undertaking by a whole polis or "city" (i.e., a citizen body), individually and collectively, to live lives of virtue, or at any rate of full decency, through a shared commitment that makes each and every single agent's decent or virtuous activities at the same time part of an overarching shared activity of virtuous living by the whole polis. Each person lends their own support to the individual contributions of the others. Hence, each person's good virtuous life is not solely their own accomplishment; it is a joint achievement, in ways that we will see as we proceed, of the whole group's efforts in living virtuously. It is in this conception of the virtues that we find the basis for a response to the questions I posed at the end of the last section. The reason why Aristotle thinks anyone wishing to become a good person has to learn first about systems of laws and political constitutions is that, for him, to be good is in part to be engaged in the sort of communal life of shared virtues, and shared virtuous living, that I have just briefly described. In order to understand properly the foundation and essential elements of this communal life, one needs such "political" knowledge. And this same conception is the key, as we will see, to Aristotle's view that the happiest of the lives making practical virtue their highest good is the political life of the virtuous political leader.

In order to understand this political and communal aspect of the practical virtues, we need to consider, first, Aristotle's understanding, in the *Politics*, of what a κοινωνία (conventionally translated as "community") is. It may come as quite a surprise, especially when one is thinking in terms of modern communities, to learn that for Aristotle κοινωνίαι are, at bottom, in each case a set of *shared activities*. We see this in the first sentences of book I of the *Politics*. Aristotle says that the polis,[92] because it is a koinonia, in fact the one that contains within itself and regulates all the others, aims at some good. The adjective from which this noun is formed, κοινόν, means "common," in the sense of some common possession. A koinonia therefore is something shared by a group of people, as something that is theirs in common, but not as a pooled sum of separate parts produced or maintained privately by each. It is a whole belonging in common, as a whole, to the whole group. This thing—this koinonia—that is common in that sense to a group of people turns out, on Aristotle's analysis, as I just said, to be some set of actions or activities. This is implied by the reason he gives in this passage for saying that all koinoniai do aim at some good. He says that this is because "everyone does all their actions for the sake of what they take to be some

---

[92] I leave this Greek word for "city" untranslated, or adopt it into English, because of the special features of an ancient city, which occupy so significant a place in Aristotle's work: its sovereignty and its wide territorial bounds. I will also hereafter adopt or transliterate into English the Greek word κοινωνία, rather than always rendering it, in our discussions, by the English word "community," which is not well suited to capture the features of an Aristotelian koinonia that I go on here to explain.

good."[93] Taken strictly this clearly implies that, for Aristotle, a koinonia, at bottom, is some actions (in fact, some activities): all actions or activities, he is saying, including the ones that constitute koinoniai, aim at some good. Indeed, a koinonia is some activities that the individual people making up the group engage in in common, in the way I just explained. These are activities of theirs, as individuals, but not with each acting on their own merely in some coordinated way so as to produce some "common" product. Rather, these activities are theirs as group members; they are activities of the whole group (in some way that needs explanation, which I provide below), at the same time that they are, more specifically, the immediate activity on each occasion of some one person, or perhaps some smaller group of individual members.

We will understand better what it means for the activities of virtue to be engaged in as common activities of the whole group of citizens if we consider at some length the common activities that constitute the "communities" that Aristotle mentions as contained in and regulated by the polis. In the *Politics* Aristotle discusses in turn three subordinate "communities," before turning to the final "community" of the polis. In order to see clearly and well in what ways the polis "community," when structured and conducted according to human nature, involves a shared life of virtue, we need to give close consideration to these subordinate "communities." Two of these make up a household: first, the "community" of the property owner and the slaves, or workers who are maintained on the property, and do manual work, under the master's direction, in agriculture, minor crafts, and running the household; and second, that of the immediate family whose household it is. Third, there is the "community" of the village or local neighborhood. In describing these below, I follow Aristotle in his own discussion by speaking of them as they are "according to nature," that is, as they are according to the nature of human beings (generally, and group by group), and according to the nature of the human good. They are according to nature when they are properly constituted and conducted, in accordance with the natural place and point of each sort of "community" in providing for a truly good (i.e., decent or virtuous) life for the citizens of whatever city they are parts of. It is to be taken for granted that most and even possibly all the actually existing such "communities" have been in greater or lesser degree perversions of this natural ideal. Certainly, many actual master-slave relationships in ancient cities, maybe

---

[93] *Pol.* I 1, 1252a2–3. In this and all my translations from this work I follow C.D.C.'s excellent translation, but with many departures (usually unmarked).

all of them without exception, were perversions of Aristotle's ideal conception. In discussing the other "communities," too, of the family, the village, and indeed the polis itself, I should be understood to be discussing these only as they are according to nature. Nonetheless, Aristotle reasonably thinks, by learning about what these "communities" are like, when they do exist and function according to nature, we learn something that can and ought to regulate our own ambitions, as well as our basic self-conception, as we approach our lives in the communities (defective at all levels) in which we presumably all live.

Aristotle discusses first the "community" of master and slave. This is of less interest for our purposes than the "communities" of the family and the village are. It is worthwhile considering it briefly, however, in order to bring out a significant contrast between the ways the master-slave activities are common to the two sides of the relationship, and what is in common to the members of the family, village, and civic relationships to be discussed next. A slave for Aristotle is simply a laborer who, being stunted by birth, is capable of only a narrow range of human activities. Not only that, in doing them, slaves (but not other people) require some more fully endowed human being (a master, or his representative) to give them direction and keep them focused on what they are doing.[94] Aristotle says that slaves are living tools for action, namely for certain activities of their masters.[95] These activities—for example, sweeping the floor, or plowing a field, or preparing a meal for the family—are, on Aristotle's analysis, activities done by the individual slaves (who as we would think are the primary agents, if not in fact the only ones), in common with the master who directs them (and who Aristotle thinks is in fact the primary agent). The master sweeps the floor, and so on, using the slave as his living, self-moving tool. Both master and slave are active whenever the slave works as a slave, and the actions making up the work are common activities of the two.

As Aristotle conceives them, then, these activities have two agents; they are done by two people in each case, a slave and the master. It is those activities that constitute the master-slave "community." That "community" extends precisely,

---

[94] Aristotle's view is that ("natural") slaves share in reason only to the extent of understanding what is said to them, but not so far as to use reason themselves in planning and leading their life (*Pol.* I 6, 1254b22–23). Thus they lack the power of deliberation (I 13, 1260a12). I take it that this need not mean that for Aristotle they cannot figure out how to get anything done, using their own thought and planning, but only that anything extremely complex, or requiring concentrated attention over any significant period of time, is beyond their natural capacities. Their minds are always apt to wander off in pursuit of more immediate gratification.

[95] See endnote 17 for explication of slaves as tools.

and only, so far as those activities do. It includes only the work activities that the slave engages in, but that the master himself also engages in together with the slave, in the way I have indicated. Accordingly, very many activities that go to constitute the lives, respectively, of the master and the slave are no part of the master-slave "community." Now, notably (and this is where the contrast with the common activities of family, village, and polis comes in), the good aimed at in the master-slave common activities is entirely the good of the master (and, derivatively, that of his family). The good aimed at is not at all that of the slave, though incidentally, on Aristotle's view, slaves achieve their good in doing these activities, insofar as, being stunted human beings, they are capable of achieving a personal good at all.[96] All the slave's work is aimed at making the daily lives of the master and his family go well, both by providing the materials and the material conditions needed by the family to sustain their lives, and by assisting them in engaging in some of the activities that make their own lives up, but in which the slave does not engage jointly with them.

The common activities constituting the other subordinate "communities" (those of husband, wife, and children, and of the village where the household is situated) are importantly different. In addition to being done by more than one agent, as with the master-slave activities, all of these are aimed at a good common to all the participants. This added feature means that these further activities are done in common in a deeper way by the members of these communities—they aim at a common good. But these activities too, like those done in common by master and slave, make up only some relatively small part of the activities of the individual lives of the people engaging in them. It is only when we reach the level of the polis that, on Aristotle's analysis, the common activities of a "community" (one "according to nature") coincide with all the life activities of the individuals participating in it.

The "community" of the Aristotelian family includes a married couple and their children, but its foundation is the parents, who Aristotle says form a couple (and so institute this "community") for the sake of procreation. They do this out of the desire, arising naturally in human beings as in other animals, to leave behind offspring like themselves. The activities of the couple, as a couple, will include their sexual activities as marriage partners, and all the activities of raising

[96] See 1254b17–20 (slaves are "people whose work [ἔργον] is to use their bodies," this being "the best thing to come from them"); 1252a30–34 ("the same thing is beneficial for both master and slave"); and 1278b30–37 (rule by a master is "rule exercised for the sake of the master's own benefit, and only coincidentally for that of the slave").

and educating the children, even if those are performed primarily by only one of the parents at any given time (in some instances, with the use of slaves). Raising and educating their children is a common project, undertaken by the parents together. When the mother, say, is helping a young child to learn to play fairly, and with due consideration of the other children he is playing with, it is an essential component of what she is doing, implicit though not normally self-conscious, that this is part of a whole series and set of activities that fit together to constitute a larger and more extended activity that she and the father are engaged in together over many years, of raising the child to adulthood. Some of the other components of this single activity are performed, in the first instance, not by her but by the father; and all of these, whichever the primary agent may be, are endorsed, and actively supported, by both parents. Other activities, too, are included in the family "community": all the activities of daily life together within the household, the meals taken together, the conversations, the games played, and, of course, with particular emphasis, those of these into which the moral virtues (as Aristotle understands them) are integrated, since those are the center and substance, for him, of a well-lived human life. (I return to this moral component below.) While it would not be easy to specify more exactly which the activities are that constitute this Aristotelian "community," they clearly make up, still, only a relatively small part of the activities constituting even the daily life within the household of its individual members.

All the activities that do form part of the family community aim at the good of all the participants, and at a good held in common by them all, in two different ways, or at two levels. First of all, the activities themselves are good, because they are well conceived and well carried out (remember, we are discussing a family according to nature), and this good—the good of the activities of child rearing, the good of the conversations and other shared activities—belongs to, and is achieved by, both or all of the participants simply in doing them. It is furthermore an indissolubly common good, consisting not (or not only) of a pooled sum of individual goods, achieved separately in or by the actions of the separate agents. It is a single good belonging in equal measure to each of the participants, because it is a good achieved by the pair or group of participants, acting together. In this sense, the mealtimes, and the conversations, are taken up with an activity that the family members all engage in together, as a common undertaking—well conceived and well carried out by all members in their own individual ways, each doing something different that fits together with, and is (at least implicitly) understood by them all to be a contribution to, something they are doing in common. The good therein achieved is a good common to them all.

But many of these activities are also aimed at goods external to the activities themselves, and some of these are common in a different way. The meals are aimed, among other things, at obtaining daily sustenance. Relaxation and stimulation are further external goods provided at mealtime, as well as through conversations at other times, and through games and other pastimes. These external goods may, and mostly will, be distributed individually to the individual members, and will not be something indissolubly common. In this case, to say that the good is a "common" good means only that the provision of these respective separate shares to all is part of what the activity consists in, what it is for. The relaxation and stimulation of games and daily social interactions, as well as the sustenance provided at meals, are for all the members of the group—but one by one. Some such external goods are, however, aimed at as common goods in a stronger sense, instead. Most notably, the parents' activities in raising the children aim (as an external objective) at making them good human beings, and at enabling them to live good human lives as adults. But one's children being good and living well, as good human beings, when adult, is part of the good of any parent.[97] So, in this case, the external good is something that belongs, when it is achieved at all, to the parents in common, not in a divided way.

Aristotle says extremely little about Aristotelian village "communities." Almost all he says is that, whereas the household is "naturally constituted for the everyday," the first koinonia (in the analysis of a polis from the simpler to the more complex) "constituted for the sake of other than everyday needs" is the village, constituted out of some number of households.[98] I take this to mean the following. Villages make possible a social life, with a wider and more interesting range for conversation, and other leisure-time interaction, than single households do. By introducing local cults with priesthoods, and festivals (with poetry readings and drama performances), and the like, they also expand the range of human activities. These new human activities belong specifically to village communities and are not possible within a separated household. They satisfy other than everyday needs. With the reciprocal exchange of surplus production, how-

[97] See NE VIII 12, "parents feel affection for their children as being something of themselves" (1161b18), they "love their children as being themselves, for the ones coming from them are as it were other selves of theirs" (b27–29).
[98] See Pol. I 2, 1252b12–13, 15–16.

ever, that villages introduce, they also make possible the satisfaction of everyday needs more easily than life in an isolated family could, and more satisfactorily, too, because of the resulting greater variety, and higher quality, of materials and material goods they make available for consumption and use. We should also take account of the fact that, for Aristotle, village communities are made up of household ones. This means that (as I have just implied) the common activities of the household receive a wider context that makes them involve the pursuit of a wider common good than just that of a single family. Parents are raising children to live well not just in their own households, but in the villages of which their households are parts, just as the householder is directing his agricultural slaves and his farm animals for sustaining the life not only of his own household, but in part also (reciprocally) for sustaining the life of the other households in the village. The life-activities definitory of the household will, in general, also become, in this altered form, activities of the village community as well, since the life of the family and its household now becomes part of the life of the whole village. That means that these activities are implicitly conceived as part of an enterprise of living well, both in terms of everyday and other needs of life, engaged in in common with all the neighbors making up the other village households.

Finally, we reach the koinonia of the polis. Aristotle says that the polis "has reached the limit of total self-sufficiency" for human life, making possible, and itself actively supporting, a life for its citizens in which human nature becomes fully developed, and human capacities for action are completely fulfilled. He famously adds that "it comes to be for the sake of living, but it remains in existence for the sake of living well."[99] "For the sake of living well" (τοῦ εὖ ζῆν χάριν) here means for the sake of a life by its citizens that is governed by their possessing the human virtues as a whole—at any rate, by possessing them all as nearly fully as is realistically to be hoped for in any polis-sized human population. The citizens structure the lives they lead through exercising their virtues, as a matter of individual independent judgment, on a constant and regular basis, in all that they do. So, according to Aristotle, the polis comes into being through the union of a number of villages in some self-contained territory that possesses a city center, external trade relations, and large-scale cultural and religious institutions. Hence the (so to speak) mere life (as opposed to the life of virtue, the "living well") that it makes possible is far richer and more interesting, more completely fulfilling of human natural capacities, than that of an isolated village—in just the ways that I

---

[99] 1252b27–30.

said above that village life is richer than an isolated household's could be. This enrichment consists not only in new aspects of life belonging explicitly to the level of the city, and carried out in the city center (most notably overtly political institutions and activities), but also in the expansion and enriched content of the activities definitory of household and village "communities" that result from their being fit into this new context. It is the needs felt by people living in households and villages for the richest possible such mere life that, as Aristotle implies, explains the coming into existence of cities. As I said, this mere life, when led now in the context of a polis life, also includes, as was the case with the village, completely new activities as well, most notably the activities of the shared self-government of the citizens, through specifically political institutions and activities. But included also are all the wider social, religious, and cultural activities, plus the wider range of work opportunities, and interesting personal relationships, that come from the foreign trade and larger-scale economic activities that the polis makes possible for its citizens.

The enrichments I have mentioned so far concern only the "mere" life that a polis makes possible. But the polis community once formed exists for the sake of a life lived by the individual citizens that is governed by the human virtues, and in the first instance by their virtues of character and practical intellect. They will all be at least decent people; some will be fully virtuous, through having acquired practical wisdom, presumably from extended philosophical studies aimed at achieving full practical understanding of the human good. It is crucially important to notice that, when Aristotle says the polis is for the sake of living well, he is conceiving living well (i.e., virtuously) as the central common activity of the citizens of a polis (i.e., of a polis that is constituted and functions according to nature). As we have seen, an Aristotelian "community" simply is, at bottom, a set of common activities, and, when he declares that a polis is for the sake of living well, he makes virtuous activity the central common activity defining the polis-community. Living virtuously corresponds for the polis to a family's shared daily activities in the household and the other than daily ones shared in the "community" of the village—the local religious and cultural and social and economic activities of the village. But in this case, as part of the polis's total self-sufficiency for human life, all the actions and activities of the polis members are included in the resulting "community." The life of virtue that the polis aims at and makes possible is a person's total life (insofar as that consists of actions and activities freely engaged in). This life is all the activities making up one's life (including but not limited to the shared household and village activities), now conducted

throughout in accordance with the virtues of character and practical intellect—
or, at least, conducted in accordance with the decent, well-habituated, and self-
endorsed, nonrational feelings and desires that all normal human beings can
achieve, and that establish the common baseline for the citizens of a city constituted according to nature.

Aristotle conceives these activities of the virtues, central to the life of a polis,
just like the household and the village activities, as common ones, as activities
engaged in in common by the whole group of adult persons who take part in
civic life, in the way we have seen in those other cases. They are a common enterprise pursued, in the first instance, for the sake of the good inherent in those very
activities (the activities of exercising the virtues), conceived as a common good
for all the participants, and not a divided one, of which each citizen would get
only a private share.[100] In the polis as it is according to nature, the citizens conceive of themselves as each pursuing (and, indeed achieving) their own good
(the highest good of living constantly in the exercise of the virtues) at least at the
level of decency, in all their individual actions, choices, practical judgments, and
attitudes. But they do this, and conceive of themselves as doing it, only through
pursuing that good as a part of the common pursuit of the virtuous life of the
polis itself, that is, the common pursuit of the virtuous life of and for all the citizens. Aristotle is conceiving this common good, of which the good realized in
each person's own virtuous actions is a part, as achieved by all of them together.
How are we to understand that?

To begin with, they think of their own scheme of values, contained in their
virtuous outlook on life with its assignments of relative and comparative value to
all the goods available to a human being, including virtuous activity itself, as not
just something they have come to understand as correct through their own personal experience and education—as a matter of their own private moral insight.
They and their fellow citizens have made a common and mutually agreed decision to support this scheme of values, as something they all, individually and
collectively, have come to understand (at some level) as the correct one for
human beings to live by. It forms the basis of their city's legal system, and grounds
their agreed and common conception of what is just and unjust in the designing
and implementation of institutions of self-government. Second, with the increased strength of commitment that comes from seeing one's neighbors not just

---

[100] As with the household and village activities, many of these will also be aimed at achieving external
goods for those participating in them, but these will often be common only in the sense that each is intended to get their own private share in each case. See my discussion above.

espousing as correct their own scheme of values, but actually themselves living according to it, in a common way of life, they can be assured (as assured as any human being could ever be) of the truth of their own moral beliefs. Other human beings, one's fellow citizens, not only say they see things the same way, but show they believe it by the way they live. That widespread agreement in practice is strong evidence that these beliefs, and this scheme of values, do derive from a correct use of reason itself, and are not some merely social invention or some other aberration. With that assurance, they can count on themselves, as they might well not otherwise be able to do, to carry out unwaveringly their commitment to acting always virtuously, whatever the difficulties or pressures of circumstances might be. They see their own views as not something private to themselves and a few other people like them, or something merely a matter of how "we" in a certain family, or of a certain class, live. These represent a whole polis-sized population's shared reflective judgment about human life. By manifesting in their own actions and steady way of life their common moral convictions, therefore, each of them lends support to each of the others, when one's own personal efforts in the common enterprise require some significant personal cost, or loss. Thus, each one is right to think that the good they achieve for themselves in their own virtuous actions is the product of a joint effort also by the others.

Education in this system of values, and in living according to it, begins, of course, in the home. The raising of the children by their parents to be morally well-functioning adults is at the center of much of the daily life of the household. But, as Aristotle once says,[101] children and others in a household must be educated "with an eye to the constitution," since whatever virtues they acquire, and whatever virtues they exercise, in their household life, must be calibrated to the larger life in the political "community" of which the household is the smallest and, in one way, the basic part. This is one important aspect of what Aristotle means by saying that the polis community contains within itself and controls or regulates the other ones. Insofar as the educational activities within the household are an education in the virtues, they must not be seen as directed merely toward the goods of daily life with one's intimates in an extended family. That life is indeed the essential province of the household community. But all the educational activities of the household must be carried out as activities taking place, no doubt, within the household, but belonging to the life of the specifically political "community" of the polis itself. Their aim is to bring the children

[101] *Pol.* I 13, 1260b14–17.

to conceive of the decent way of life they are being habituated to want to live as a communal undertaking, in which each person in all their own decent behavior is also giving support to, and reciprocally benefiting from, the decent behavior of others.

This communal, or more specifically political, conception of the practical virtues and virtuous activities is scarcely to be observed in the presentation of the outlook of the morally virtuous of the *Nicomachean Ethics*. But when we expand his ethical writings' scope to include his *Politics*, as Aristotle himself has clearly indicated we should, both in the first chapters of the first book and the last chapter of the last, we learn of this further aspect of virtuous agents' self-conception and their conception of the well-lived human life. We also learn from the *Politics* that it is because practically virtuous agents do conceive of their virtues and their virtuous activities as belonging to the communal life together of a whole body of similar persons living in a political "community" organized to make it possible, that Aristotle insists that anyone who wishes to become fully good must acquire a full practical understanding, not only of the matters investigated in the *Nicomachean Ethics*, but also of those studied in the *Politics*. The practical knowledge needed, in order to be a fully good person, includes a solid understanding of what a "community" in general is, and what the points and purposes are of the different specific forms of "community" in which a complete and self-sufficient human life, with political self-determination by the citizens, can be sustained. It also requires knowing how it is that the moral virtues (whether at the level of decency or a more complete level) structure a whole communal life. (Even someone living virtuously at the level of mere decency needs to grasp basic elements of this knowledge.)

Quite a lot of what Aristotle's *Politics* actually contains, however, may seem to go beyond what any citizen except the semiprofessional virtuous politician needs. One thinks here especially of his detailed studies of unsatisfactory constitutions and associated systems of law (bad ones like democracies, oligarchies, and tyrannies; acceptable but still unsatisfactory ones like monarchies and traditional aristocracies), and of his attention to the various principles to be followed in preserving existing constitutions, or shifting toward better forms of government. But Aristotle makes no such exceptions. He speaks unqualifiedly of knowledge of "political science" and the full "capacity for politics" as needed by any fully virtuous person. Not only the fully virtuous person who is going to take up the "political life" needs to know these details. Aristotle seems to think that even people leading the "contemplative" life, and those who because of temperament or personal interests (or the lack thereof) intend to use their completed practical knowledge in living a private life of virtue, away from both the political and the intellectual limelight, must have this large body of knowledge ready for use. It may be needed at some points for grasping and deciding some aspects of right action, in some situations that might arise: all fully virtuous persons must constantly maintain the widest possible perspective on their own lives and on the lives of all the others they live among; knowledge of intricacies to do with less good forms of government, or with the support for good ones required from all the citizens, might be needed at some point in any virtuous person's life. If one thinks of the matter in this light, then perhaps Aristotle's strong demands may seem not unreasonable, given that he is discussing what one needs to know, in order to be truly and fully virtuous.

In the preceding I have been speaking for the most part of the fully virtuous person, the person possessing both the moral virtues of habituated character and the philosophical virtue of practical wisdom. But it is important to notice that the communal and political character of the Aristotelian practical virtues, which comes so clearly to light in the *Politics*, applies equally to the purely habituated characters of the decent citizens who live good but not fully virtuous lives. Precisely because the habituation they have undergone in their education is aimed at producing the right sorts of feelings that I have described in the previous sections, which are one component of the total outlook of the fully virtuous agent, they too will conceive of the decent way of life that they live, and that they want to live, as a communal undertaking, in which each person in all their own decent behavior is also giving support to, and reciprocally benefiting from, the decent behavior of others. Merely decent persons do not have a full grasp, and might have little grasp at all, of the philosophical analyses of human nature and human virtue that supply the reasons why it is good for them to live that way. But, as I have said, they do share the emotional outlook, including feelings of attachment to the others among whom they live, of the fully virtuous agent. And, in their own thinking about human life, and about their own lives, they fully endorse the attitudes that they have formed on that basis.

It is one thing, however, to observe that Aristotle's conception of the practical virtues includes this communal or political component, and to appreciate its significance for what he considers a well-lived life (whether one of Aristotle's three truly happy ones, or a merely decent life of someone who lacks full practical knowledge of the human good). It is another to consider why Aristotle thinks that the practical virtues do need to be understood, and to be grasped by virtuous people themselves as they lead their virtuous lives, in this communal way. He surely would not regard the life of someone who had an adequate practical understanding of the virtues and of the human good without this political addendum as a bad or even a seriously unhappy one. Evidently, however, he thinks that, although one might live a virtuous life without conceiving it in that way—thinking of oneself instead simply as a single person aiming at one's own single happiness through living virtuously—that would be a defective life of virtue. For a full and secure, fully realized virtuous life, he seems to think, one does require to live virtuously in the communal way we have been exploring. What can we say to clarify, and to the extent possible offer some defense of, Aristotle's thinking on this point?

Partly, it seems, Aristotle thinks that all human beings, however well developed in the virtues, retain the human tendency to act for immediate pleasure or to avoid short-term discomfort. This is the tendency that training in virtue seeks to overcome. This liability is found particularly among the young, but also among Aristotle's "many" (the unregenerate mass of human beings). But he thinks it applies even to one who has acquired sufficiently good habits to be living a committed decent life. Hence, even decent people, if left entirely to guidance by their private judgment, would inevitably sometimes lapse. They would fall away into unvirtuous choices and acts.[102] However, if their personal and private virtues are expanded so as to become part of the psychological basis for a communal life devoted to virtuous activities, as I have described it above, then the support from the community that I mentioned would give them an added psychological boost. This would enable them to more nearly overcome this apparently permanent tendency of human beings to yield to the attractions of immediate pleasure, even when it is not decent to do so. Hence, a life of decency led in that communal way would be a less defective way of living virtuously than if one led it thinking of oneself only as a single person, aiming at one's own single happiness through living decently. It would be a psychologically more secure one, and therefore also one with fewer lapses from virtuous action. And, of course, that would make it a more nearly happy life.

But we have now seen that Aristotle seems also to hold that even people (if there are any such) with a depth of understanding that would give them a strong and constant enough inner psychological commitment to their life of virtue so that no such boost was needed, would still need to learn the principles of politics, and use them in engaging, if circumstances made this possible, in a commu-

---

[102] See endnote 18 for explication of how this might happen.

nal life devoted to virtue. The wider and more complex good such people would be pursuing, in living their own life of virtue as part of the good of a whole communal group of similarly motivated agents, would constitute a finer and so a very much more worthwhile goal for their life.[103] One could even say that their virtue would be more completely realized, when linked in this way to the virtuous (or decent) life and happiness of a whole community. Their virtues would include within their scope the added effects of being exercised in cooperatively helping to encourage and support the right actions of others, and the fine rational evaluations and intermediate states of feeling concerning all the subordinate goods shown in those actions. Each single virtuous agent would in this way greatly expand the fine things that their virtue concerns itself over and that it helps to produce. This would be so even if they intended to use their practical knowledge only in living the life of an ordinary private citizen. But it would also hold, to a greater degree, for a life of virtuous active political leadership (Aristotle's "secondarily happiest," political life; *Nicomachean Ethics* X 7–8). Such politicians exercise their virtues on behalf of the community's good not merely in the oblique way I have just indicated, but quite actively and overtly as well. They do this on a daily basis, in organizing and conducting the public political business of the community. This includes most notably, of course, their attention to the provision and application of good laws, aimed knowledgeably at educating the populace in the virtues, and providing large-scale aids and encouragements toward the citizens' own conduct of as fully virtuous a life (and in any event, a decent one) as they are individually capable of. This additional direct exercise of their virtues for the public good expands yet further the scope of their virtues' activities. The good of virtuous activity reaches here its widest and richest realization. Accordingly, this is the happiest of lives aimed at the activity of the practical virtues as highest good—a happier life than even the fully happy one of the private citizen living outside the political limelight. Still, as Aristotle insists, even it is only the secondarily, or second-happiest, happy life.

3.10. Conclusion: Philosophy as Two Ways of Life

As we have seen, for Aristotle the absolutely happiest life—happiest without any qualification at all—is the contemplative one. Those living a contemplative life

---

[103] See *NE* I 2, 1094b7–10, cited above.

do put the practical virtues in control of their daily lives, and of all the ordinary interactions in family and social and political contexts that they, like everyone else, engage in. When they eat their meals, or do any other ordinary daily task, or tend to citizenly or family obligations, or take time off from their work in all the ways that every human being must, and wants to do, they engage those virtues, and follow their prescriptions. And they do that, as their fellow citizens do, too, in a social structure that is according to nature, in the communal way discussed in the previous section; they pursue the good of their own morally virtuous way of life as a shared contribution to the similarly virtuous life of the whole community. But this life also includes the best and most end-like of virtues, the virtues of theoretical wisdom and understanding, together with the active employment of these virtues on the highest and best objects of knowledge, the divine entities that are the first principles of all of reality. The activity of theoretical wisdom alone is aimed at, by one living a contemplative life, as the absolutely highest good, and it is also achieved in that life. The contemplatives' whole life is focused on, organized by, and aimed ultimately at that activity and at the good that it constitutes. To be sure, that does not mean that Aristotle understands this sort of life as one spent primarily simply in rapt contemplation, with the mind's eye, of the divine entities (or in fact of a single one of them—the "prime mover," whose whole life and whole being is itself pure, fully actualized, and eternally active contemplative thinking).

Rather, this is a life devoted to theoretical inquiry and theoretical work of all philosophical and philosophical-mathematical kinds. It includes studies in physics and the philosophy of nature in general, biology prominently included, plus logic and theory of knowledge, as well as all the rest of metaphysics, not just the knowledge of its first principles. Contemplative knowledge of the highest object, the "prime mover," is the culmination of theoretical knowledge as a whole, and it is presupposed in all theoretical knowledge (when final and complete) of other matters. Even in these other theoretical activities the knowledge of the divine first principles is constantly being engaged, at least in the background of the contemplator's thought. But because of the contemplative's devoted and passionate involvement in time-consuming activities of theoretical thinking and discussion, of all these kinds, the contemplative life excludes the sort of commitment to political leadership that characterizes the second-happiest life of the virtuous politician. And because the person leading the contemplative life lives with firsthand experience and knowledge of the goodness of these highest virtues—those of the theoretical intellect—and recognizes in the activities of thought that exercise those virtues the absolutely highest good for a human being, this is, as I said, the absolutely happiest human life. Even if in this life the practical virtues lack the widest and richest scope for deployment that, as we have seen, the virtuous politician's life achieves, the inclusion in this life of the higher good of this wholly fulfilling and excellent theoretical knowledge does not so much compensate for the necessary scaling back of that sort of activity, but rather simply and firmly outranks it in any such calculation.

It is important not to overlook the role that the recognition of this highest human virtue as the highest good plays even in the political life, as well as in the life of a private virtuous citizen. The virtuous political leader and the virtuous private citizen possess the virtue of practical wisdom, and hence, on Aristotle's account of that virtue, they know what Aristotle has explained about the three sorts of human virtues and their mutual ordering. They know, though not first-hand—through having acquired the virtues of the intellect and experienced, and enjoyed, their active use—that that activity is the absolutely highest human good. For various reasons of personal predilection, as well as a deficiency of sheer intellectual ability, they do not pursue this good in their own personal lives. But they do join together with the contemplative people themselves in recognizing and organizing their common political life in such a way as to make possible, and to actively support, the theoretically virtuous activities that the contemplatives will engage in in their midst, as their fellow citizens. Aristotle's discussion in *Politics* VII 1–3 of the "most choiceworthy life," and of whether the same life that is most choiceworthy for an individual person is also most choiceworthy for the whole community of people living in a polis, implies this. That discussion has the intended (though somewhat muffled) upshot of saying that the most choiceworthy life is the contemplative one, and that this applies both to individuals and to polis communities. Hence, the political leaders of a polis functioning according to nature, knowing that that is so, and aiming at the most choiceworthy life for their own community, will adopt such policies in administering the city.

Thus every fully virtuous agent (contemplatives, political leaders, virtuous private citizens) knows that the activities of contemplation are the highest good for human beings, and that the most choiceworthy life for a polis is a contemplative one. Even merely decent people educated in a city organized according to nature will have learned to accept and endorse this, too. This means that Aristotle's account of how the people of a polis, which is completely self-sufficient for human life, will live, includes the provision that among them will be a group of citizens who live the contemplative life, and who, though (for the reasons we have seen) they possess in full measure the political knowledge Aristotle has been conveying in that work, will not be active politicians or political leaders. The political leaders themselves, because they know that the contemplative is the most choiceworthy life for their community, will do all they can to see that this life is lived by some people in their city. Thereby they will ensure that the community itself, to which these people belong as fully participating virtuous members, will include in its own life, shared in the way we have seen by all the citizens, this highest activity. The community's life will also, of course, include the political and the private virtuous lives led by others also belonging to it. Even the private citizens who are fully virtuous, since they also have the complete practical knowledge I referred to in the previous paragraph, are aiming in their own virtuous activities at the flowering of this highest good in their community. They are aiming at making the communal life, to which all the citizens consciously contribute, one that includes this highest human good within it. The totality of the shared, common life of the citizens will therefore include the absolutely highest good within it, even if the individual lives of most of them, in their immediate personal contributions to the common good, are limited to the secondarily highest good of the practical virtues. In that way, their city will live the absolutely happiest life for a city.

Let us now, in conclusion, return to our discussion, postponed at the end of section 3.8, of the role of philosophy in these happy lives. If we consider, and compare together, Aristotle's second happiest and happiest individual lives, it is clear, first of all, that the happiness of the happiest life, that of the contemplative, consists in the constant, active philosophical reflection, thought, argument, and analysis that it contains. That happiness makes the whole of the contemplatives' lives, including their morally virtuous daily activities, happy and constantly fulfilled; but the happiness in and of this life is found in just this one activity. In a clear and straightforward sense, then, in this case, we can see that and how philosophy for Aristotle is a way of life. The contemplative's way of life is philosophy. Philosophy is at the center of the contemplative life, as what ultimately gives it all its direction and shape. The philosophy I am speaking of here is, of course, theoretical philosophy. It is theorizing aimed at the full truth about reality, considered as an object of detached study. This is theorizing aimed at knowing the truth just for the sake of knowing it. Clearly, the philosophy here in question and the philosophical life it defines differ enormously from the Socratic life of philosophy discussed in the previous chapter. Not only is its subject matter different—the divine first principles, and the rest of reality as following from them, rather than, with Socrates, the human good—but in addition, Socrates's dialectical, critically probing way of proceeding as a philosopher has now been replaced by a constructive, quasi-deductive, tracing back of various phenomena to dependence, first, on certain first principles relevant to the specific area of reality being examined. Ultimately everything is traced back to the absolute first principle of all, the divine entity on whose activity of pure thought Aristotle thinks the very being of everything whatsoever depends. Nonetheless, one can easily see that in his conception of the absolutely happiest life of contemplative philosophy, Aristotle continues Socrates's conception of philosophy as itself a way of life, not just a subject of academic study. Theoretical philosophy, correctly conceived and practiced, demands, for Aristotle, a whole way of life devoted to it as our highest human good, and including the full possession and employment of the moral virtues in all aspects of our daily and our social and political lives—just as, for Socrates, a life of constant philosophical inquiry into the human good is the best life we can achieve, and just as for Socrates that pursuit carries with it a full commitment to honoring the moral virtues in the lives we lead when not engaging in philosophical discussion.

Theoretical philosophy is not all the philosophy there is, however. For Aristotle, Socrates's topic of the human good forms the subject matter of a second branch of philosophy. As we have seen extensively in the preceding sections, Aristotle places a very high value, in relation to achieving the human good, on practical understanding and knowledge about what is valuable for a human being. This is a knowledge, based in and produced by philosophy, that is articulated, carefully thought through, and systematically developed. For him, this philosophical knowledge is the linchpin of a practically virtuous and good human life. And this knowledge is in Aristotle's focus, precisely as a philosopher, in his investigations of the human good in both *Nicomachean Ethics* and *Politics*. At one point in discussing the most choiceworthy life in the *Politics* he mentions with palpable disapproval that "some people" think that the contemplative life alone suits a philosopher.[104] In thus keeping his distance from this opinion, Aristotle is indicating that in his own view, while the contemplative life certainly is a philosopher's life, it is not the only life that suits a philosopher. It may well be that no complete philosopher can safely omit from their interests what Aristotle counts as theoretical studies. But it is evidently quite possible (and this seems to fit Aristotle's own conception) to focus one's philosophical interests very signifi-

---

[104] *Pol.* VII 2, 1324a28–29.

cantly on human life, as Socrates did exclusively. One can be a philosopher specifically or especially of human affairs.[105] This description fits the practically virtuous person Aristotle tells us about in the *Nicomachean Ethics* and *Politics*. Such a person has the full philosophical knowledge of the human good that Aristotle wishes to assist the readers/hearers of these works to attain—a knowledge that, unlike Socrates, he has no doubt at all can be attained by human beings. In attaining this knowledge, his readers are presumed to have studied in a theoretical way such obviously not irrelevant subjects as theoretical psychology only "so far as is sufficient for what they are investigating," namely, human virtue, the human good, and human happiness; "to treat the subject with greater precision is presumably too demanding."[106] "Politics" does not need many if any of such "scientific" results under its conceptual control in proceeding to its practical studies.[107] What this knowledge does need, indeed what it consists in, is a complete practical, not theoretical, understanding of human affairs. The practically virtuous person is, for Aristotle, also the philosopher of human affairs, the one who possesses this fully articulated and systematic practical understanding of what Aristotle classes as "politics," that is, human affairs.

For Aristotle, this second philosopher, or kind of philosopher, lives a second philosophical life, not the life of the contemplative but the life either of the political leader or of the ordinary private citizen. Both of these make their practical virtues, conceived as a communal good, the organizing focus of their lives. Philosophy does not just, so to speak, lie behind this way of life, supporting it from the outside. It is actually in this life, as (theoretical) philosophy also is for contemplatives, who devote major portions of their time to theoretically philosophical work. For Aristotle, the philosophical work of "philosophers of human affairs" is not isolated in that way as some one set of activities, set off from the rest,

---

[105] I allude here to Aristotle's intention in the last lines of the *Nicomachean Ethics* to complete "the philosophy of human affairs" (ἡ περὶ τὰ ἀνθρώπεια φιλοσοφία) by adding the lectures on *Politics* to those he is there bringing to an end (*NE* X 9, 1181b15).

[106] See *NE* I 13, 1102a18–26.

[107] In the passage just cited, Aristotle proceeds (1102a26–b2) to draw not on results achieved in his own treatise on the soul but rather on the broad division of the human soul into one part or aspect that possesses reason and one that is nonrational that he says is familiar from more popular writings not further specified; he eschews any inquiry into whether these are in any strict sense parts, or how else they relate to one another and to the whole soul, as not mattering for present purposes, that is, for the study of human virtue and the human good. Aristotle does take this question concerning parts seriously, and devotes some pages to it, in the *De Anima*, III 9. So it does matter for a more complete and precise understanding of the soul than he says is needed for "politics."

as it was for Socrates. Their philosophy consists in practical understanding and knowing, and the proper exercise of that philosophical knowledge is in the discriminating evaluative thinking that goes into and informs each and every virtuous action making up their fully virtuous lives. It is true, of course, that such philosophers might devote some of their time to teaching, as Aristotle did in preparing his lectures, and to engaging in discussions with successive groups of his own students of ethical and political philosophy. But even if they did not, and also did not regularly give time, as the contemplative does, to philosophical reading, discussions, and inquiry, whether in theoretical or in practical philosophy, they would be engaging in philosophical thought and analysis and argument on a nearly constant basis, as they proceed through their daily and weekly round of activities of business, family affairs, politics, and social life. They might, of course, on occasion face difficult or merely novel matters for decision, where their developed and articulated understanding of the human good would be called upon for more explicit exercise than they would usually need to give it. But it is not only in those instances that they will engage in the activities of philosophical analysis and argument. They are engaging in them all the time.

Given Aristotle's distinction, then, between practical philosophy and practical knowledge, on the one hand, and theoretical philosophy and theoretical knowledge, on the other, philosophy for him is not a way of life, as it was for Socrates. It is two distinct ones. Aristotle's contemplatives are, of course, complete philosophers. They lead lives of practical virtue in just the way the other private citizens who possess those virtues in full measure do. The contemplative is both a philosopher of human affairs and a theoretical philosopher. Contemplatives live their philosophy in a double way. Still, for reasons we have seen, the life they lead is correctly called a contemplative one, not one of practical virtue. It is one of the two ways that for Aristotle philosophy is a way of life. But for those "philosophers of human affairs"—virtuous political leaders, fully virtuous ordinary citizens—who are not also accomplished theoretical philosophers, philosophy is nonetheless just as much their way of life. The thinking and analysis and systematic argument, and systematically organized understanding, that belong to philosophy as a whole, both practical and theoretical, as its defining and distinctive characteristic, are engaged and expressed in all the thoughts that give rise to and direct all the choices, actions, and activities constituting the whole of their lives.

CHAPTER 4

Stoicism as a Way of Life

4.1. Introduction: The Three Hellenistic Philosophies

Schools of philosophy—organized places for study and instruction in philosophy and related matters—existed in Greece at least since Plato founded his famous Academy just outside the Athenian walls. That was not long (perhaps only fifteen years) after Socrates's death. Aristotle studied and taught in the Academy during almost two decades at the end of Plato's life. He opened some sort of school of his own in Athens ten years or so before his own death in 322 BCE—outside the walls on the other side of town, at or adjacent to a public exercise ground, the Lyceum. These schools continued after their founders' deaths. At first they were centers for ongoing philosophical research, and related instruction, along the lines of the founders' own work and carrying it forward. Their successors pursued, to a large extent, some of the founders' own philosophical interests and worked within an intellectual ambience colored by the founders' work and leading ideas. But even during Plato's and Aristotle's lifetimes and the first generations afterward, these schools were not at all places where one went merely to learn "Plato's philosophy" or Aristotle's, or to be an apprentice in a specifically "Platonic" or "Aristotelian" way of life—if anyone then thought there was such a thing. New work, new ideas, were the focus of everyone's attention.

However, already in the last decade of Plato and Aristotle's century there did begin to take shape schools of philosophy in a more doctrinally committed sense. Epicurus, who had had a school for a few years in the Aegean island of Lesbos and the city of Lampsacus in the Hellespont, and had already attracted followers, whom he brought along with him, acquired property in Athens and opened a school in the garden of his house.[1] This was in about 306. Probably a few years later Zeno, of Citium in Cyprus, established his Stoic school in a public portico on the edge of the central marketplace of Athens, the Painted Stoa or Porch. Ancient sources indicate only that Zeno came from his home city around this same time to take up residence in Athens. He first became exposed to philosophy there, partly from lectures and discussions in the Academy under its third post-Plato head, a man named Polemon. By the end of the first quarter of the following century these two new institutions were known not only as places where one might learn systematically developed, complete rival worldviews—Stoic and Epicurean—but as sponsors of rival ways of life. One went to these schools to learn the doctrines of the Epicurean or Stoic philosophy and, equally importantly, for many of the students, to enroll oneself in the Epicurean or the Stoic way of life.

Not long afterward (in about 268), the philosopher Arcesilaus, a generation younger than Epicurus and Zeno, became head of the Academy, after teaching there for some years. He established in the Academy the third of the three famous schools that dominated philosophy for the next several centuries: the school of Academic skepticism, which continued for close to two centuries under other famous teachers, including Carneades (d. 129). Arcesilaus modeled himself on Plato's Socrates. He adopted Socrates's noncommittal, but philosophically rigorous, questioning of his interlocutors' opinions on moral subjects. Arcesilaus devoted himself to a critical examination and questioning of the doctrines taught in the other two schools, not however only in ethics but in physics, metaphysics, and especially epistemology as well. His effort was to show that neither school had satisfied Socratic standards for knowledge in any area. Rather than betray Socratic care for one's soul through premature acceptance of either set of doctrines, and either way of life, true devotion to one's own highest good, and so to philosophy itself, required, for Arcesilaus, continued inquiry and examination—and a skeptical, philosophically carefully uncommitted, approach to life, not an Epicurean or a Stoic one.

These three new philosophical movements dominated the life and work of philosophy throughout the Hellenistic period—the three centuries after Alexander the Great's conquests (he died in 323) initiated a vast expansion of the Greek language and culture throughout the Eastern Mediterranean, and their

[1] Like Socrates and Plato, Epicurus was an Athenian citizen, though born on the Aegean island of Samos. His parents had taken up residence there as part of an Athenian settlement on the island.

transformation under these new international conditions. Indeed Stoic, Epicurean, and skeptical philosophers continued to teach and have disciples, well after the Roman conquest of Greece and the East—and not only in the Athenian schools, but also in many other cities besides Athens. Thus, for approximately two centuries before and approaching two after the turn of the millennium, educated people all through the Greco-Roman world knew philosophy as consisting primarily of just these three philosophies:[2] the Stoic, the Epicurean, and the skeptic.[3] And all three of these were known as sponsoring distinctive ways of life, under the aegis of their specific set of philosophical principles (and with allegiance to their specific founders, who were treated as authorities in all matters philosophical)—for skepticism, at least in the later centuries.[4]

In this chapter I discuss the philosophy of Stoicism, before turning to Epicurus, and then to the Pyrrhonian skeptics and the skeptic way of life, in the next chapter. I will explain as I proceed how features of Epicureanism and the skeptical tradition—different ones for each—set them off from Stoicism. Each of these three philosophies does in fact stand on its own, with an independently motivated outlook on life and the world. But the fact is that Stoicism was philosophically dominant throughout this period, so that, inevitably, these other schools were seen, and saw themselves, as figures of the philosophical opposi-

---

[2] By the middle of this period, and with acceleration toward its end, Platonism as a "dogmatic" philosophy (no longer the skepticism that had come to be espoused in the Academy beginning with Arcesilaus) began to be revived. But it was only with the third century CE that it became a serious competitor to the other three schools—eventually in fact driving them out of existence. (On these developments see further chapter 6 below.) The Peripatetic school, maintained by Aristotle's successors in the Lyceum at Athens, appears to have had a continuous existence during these times, but rather unproductively, and without the life-orienting ambitions of the three principal ones—or, in consequence, their influence. Aristotle's own philosophical works, like Plato's, began to receive renewed serious attention from philosophers (often Stoic or skeptic ones) in the last century BCE and the first two centuries CE—increasingly, however, as time went on, as part of the curriculum in the Platonist schools, and not as the independent life-orienting force that one might think it could have become. On this, too, see chapter 6. Also, see endnote 19.

[3] On varieties of philosophical skepticism in antiquity and details about its history, see endnote 19.

[4] Our reports on Antiochus (see endnote 19) do not suggest that his school had the ambition to define and ground any special way of life; it seems rather to have been, in the way now familiar for philosophy and philosophers, a place for intellectual inquiry exclusively (these were philosophers in battle with other philosophers, as Aenesidemus famously put it). It also appears that Aristotle's Peripatetic school was such a place—despite, as we have seen in the previous chapter, Aristotle's understanding, explained in his *Ethics* and *Politics*, of the role of philosophy itself within any virtuous and happy life. That may be one reason why we hear so little of Peripatetic activities during these centuries. (Also, as I explain in section 5.5, it was only the later Pyrrhonian skeptics, not the earlier Academic ones, who sponsored their philosophies as also ways of life.)

tion. So our engagement with Epicureanism and skepticism in exploring the ancient tradition of philosophy as a way of life can best be pursued by attending specially to their differences from the Stoic school, though, I hope, without thereby obscuring the power of their own independent ideas.

4.2. Stoicism: Tradition and Texts

In addressing Stoic ethical theory and the Stoic way of life we face a problem, or set of problems, that we have not met in earlier chapters, in dealing with Socrates and Aristotle. We have Aristotle's own writings to rely on in offering our interpretation, as I have done in chapter 3. Though Socrates did not write books, we have ample near-contemporary accounts of his philosophizing (those found in Plato's and Xenophon's dialogues, plus some fragments of others'). These are not altogether of a piece with one another, but they do allow us to speak, as I have done in chapter 2, of the philosophical views of a single person—the historical figure as refracted through these writings. They also allow us to assess Socrates's considerable influence, much of it mediated by these same writings, on later philosophers' work. They give us something authoritative to read and interpret for ourselves, as best we can. But in discussing the Stoics, we are dealing with a whole centuries-long tradition of philosophical writing and teaching (in the first centuries, almost always in a single location in Athens). We are entitled to speak of a single tradition here, since, as it seems, these philosophers all (with the exception of Zeno himself, of course) grounded their own philosophizing on basic principles that (as they thought) had been first discovered, laid down, and argued for by the person they regarded as founder of their school, Zeno.[5] They thought of themselves as working out in detail, and arguing in a comprehensive way for, a single, complete system of philosophical ideas that they traced back to basic principles and to a fundamental philosophical outlook laid down by Zeno.[6]

However, none of Zeno's own works, and none of the works of his successor-teachers in the school in Athens, survived into the Byzantine and Latin Middle Ages, from which our modern editions of ancient texts almost entirely derive. Later writers, in either Greek or Latin, who had access to the original Stoics' writ-

[5] On the unity of the long tradition of Stoic philosophers and their individual independence as philosophical thinkers, see endnote 20.

[6] On Chrysippus as establishing the "orthodox" version of Stoicism, see endnote 21.

ings, and whose works did survive, give us quotations, paraphrases, and reports of their opinions.[7] Reading and pondering these, as best we can, is all we can do. This is a sad situation. It is particularly unfortunate because we have lost access to the contexts of the quotations. And the paraphrases and reports by these writers are given from the perspectives of their own authorial interests. Those rarely if ever include a serious, independent philosophical interest, whether sympathetic or critical, in the philosophical reasons lying behind the specific point of doctrine being reported. The Stoic writers must, of course, have presented points of doctrine as justified by their following from or being decisively supported by particular philosophical arguments. Without hearing those arguments we can often not really know even what, in their own minds, these points of doctrine amounted to—much less what their philosophical reasons were for maintaining them. Yet the Stoics' arguments and philosophical analyses, supporting and (they think) justifying their doctrines, are for the most part simply omitted from the accounts that have come down to us. This is especially harmful when it comes to important sources, such as Plutarch (first to second century CE), whose relevant writings are tendentious outright attacks on Stoicism.[8] But it applies equally to many of the later Christian writers who provide us with snippets and reports. Plutarch's two principal writings containing Stoic materials are titled *On Stoic Self-Contradictions* and *On Common Conceptions: Against the Stoics* (i.e., on how Stoic doctrines undermine themselves by violating common sense—even though Stoics claim that only their own doctrines adequately present and preserve the truth perceived in commonsense conceptions). In writings with such polemical intentions one should not perhaps expect much if any account of the reasoning offered in support of the "doctrines": the focus, one rightly expects, is on finding superficially embarrassing clashes of opinions with one another, or with what people ordinarily think. But even the "doctrines" are very often quite distorted in Plutarch's often uncomprehending presentation.[9]

---

[7] J. von Arnim collected what he offered as the corpus of these excerpts (in the original Greek and Latin), so far as they concern Zeno, Cleanthes, and Chrysippus and their immediate students. He distributed them under an elaborate schedule of topics in the three volumes of his *Stoicorum Veterum Fragmenta*. For fragments in English one could consult Long and Sedley, *The Hellenistic Philosophers* or Inwood and Gerson, *Hellenistic Philosophy: Introductory Readings*.

[8] Plutarch wrote as an Academic in the last part of the first century CE and the first quarter of the second, as the movement toward making Plato one's principal authority in all philosophical matters was gaining momentum. Stoicism needed to be dethroned. Plutarch's anti-Stoic writings are conveniently available in Greek and facing English translation in the Loeb Classical Library series of Plutarch's *Moralia*.

[9] Another, at least equally important source, Sextus Empiricus's skeptical examinations of "dogmatic" philosophical opinions on virtually all subjects, presents somewhat different problems for the modern

In other, more neutral sources, there is, again, a serious paucity of information about the philosophical reasoning supporting the various, so to speak, bottom-line Stoic theories. Writers like Diogenes Laertius and Arius Didymus, who are among our most important sources for Stoic ethical theory, are zealous in assembling and reporting, in a fairly systematic way, the principal opinions (and many of the more minor ones) of Chrysippus and Zeno and the other leaders of the movement.[10] But they show little or no interest in the processes of reflection and analysis that led the Stoics to their conclusions, or that they would call upon to justify them. Cicero—an adherent of Philo's very relaxed version of skepticism[11]—gives a fair-minded and careful, though selective, exposition of Stoic ethics, matched and balanced by his critical rejection of its principal tenets. But for the most part even he eschews discussion and evaluation of the reasoning supporting the bottom line.[12] Seneca too, another important source, writes as an independent-minded lay Stoic—but in literary, not technically philosophical works. He often ignores or downplays philosophical argument in favor of other ways of encouraging his readers to embrace a Stoic way of life.[13]

For two reasons, then, our task is significantly different in approaching Stoic ethical theory, and Stoicism as a way of life, from our task in discussing Socrates and Aristotle in the previous two chapters. We are dealing not with a single philosopher's views, but a whole tradition, extending from the late fourth century

---

reader who wants to understand and appreciate Stoic theories as deeply as possible, on an independently philosophical basis. Sextus (second to third century CE) is very thorough and apparently fair-minded in his presentation of the doctrines, but he is often much too quick to see inconsistency. He leaves aside more favorable possible interpretations, and responses to his objections.

[10] Diogenes Laertius, who is usually thought to have written in the third century CE, perhaps in the first half of it, composed a long work, in ten books, on *Lives and Opinions of the Eminent Philosophers*, in which the life of Zeno contains an invaluable, extended account of Stoic ethics (7.84–131), alongside similar accounts of Stoic "logic" (epistemology and philosophy of logic and language, plus logic itself) and physics (7.41–83 and 132–60 respectively). This is readily available in English only in the unsatisfactory translation (with facing Greek) of R. D. Hicks in the Loeb Classical Library series. Arius Didymus, an associate of the Emperor Augustus, wrote an *Epitome of Stoic Ethics* around the turn of the millennium. It was preserved through being included in a fifth century anthology of John of Stobi (Stobaeus, as he is usually referred to) of Arthur J. Pomeroy. Recent translations of Arius Didymus's *Epitome* include that (with facing Greek text) of Arthur J. Pomeroy.

[11] See endnote 19.

[12] See his dialogue *De Finibus* or *On Moral Ends*, books III and IV. The Latin text is most readily available in the Loeb Classical Library series, with facing English translation; there is a somewhat better translation by Raphael Woolf. Others of Cicero's philosophical writings are of value too for assessing Stoicism, most notably, so far as concerns ethics, his five books of *Tusculan Disputations* (available in the Loeb Classical Library series).

[13] His *Moral Letters to Lucilius* and *Moral Essays* are available (each in three volumes) in the Loeb Classical Library series.

and the third century BCE to some indeterminate point in the second century CE, or even somewhat later, in the third. That was when the school petered out, effectively overwhelmed by the advance of spiritualist metaphysics and spiritualist ethical aspirations under the banner of a revived Platonism. Secondly, in interpreting and evaluating the Stoic theories we have to proceed not from the original Stoics' writings, which established the "doctrines" of the school, and argued extensively for them, but from other writers' quotations and reports. That means that we must attempt our own interpretations and explications of their views without much direct knowledge of the philosophical arguments and analyses that led them to their conclusions. In what follows I concentrate primarily on what scholars call the "old Stoics" of the end of the fourth and the third to the early second centuries BCE—especially Chrysippus, the greatest and most systematic of them. I will also take into account, but where necessary as a separate matter, the Stoics of the Roman period, writing either in Latin or Greek, who carried the old Stoics' system into the life of the imperial elite in the early centuries of the new millennium: Nero's tutor and adviser Seneca (mid-first century CE), the freed slave and Stoic teacher Epictetus (late first and early second centuries), and the Emperor Marcus Aurelius (121–180). As with Socrates and Aristotle in earlier chapters, in offering my account of Stoic ethical theory and the Stoic way of life, I attempt to go behind the bare set of doctrines that our sources present us with. Through engaging philosophically with our evidence concerning their views, I try to work out an account of the supporting reasons or analyses that it seems most likely that they offered in justification (and defense) of them.

4.3. Stoic Eudaimonism

Stoic ethics rests upon an elaborately articulated conception of happiness (εὐδαιμονία) as the single, constant goal or end for a well-lived human life. In their focus on happiness as the single goal of life, they carry forward the tradition of Socrates, Plato, and Aristotle. But, as we will see, they fill out this common structure for human life and action in remarkably new ways. Their famous, or notorious, insistence, at the center of their moral theory, on moral duties and on doing one's duty strictly for duty's sake, itself rests on this foundation—paradoxical as the idea might seem, at first sight, of duty strictly done, but also done for the sake of happiness. Furthermore, ethical theory, for the Stoics, becomes the central component of a rigorously constructed, fully integrated philosophical account of the whole of reality, in which they postulate a single creator god, inherent in the world of nature, as the source not only of the progress of all the world's events over all time, but also of all our own moral duties: it is because this god imposes upon us the requirement to act virtuously that virtuous activity becomes synonymous with duty for them. This is a momentous innovation in the Greek tradition, and one with immense historical repercussions. The all-inclusiveness and vast coherence of their philosophical system, with ethical theory at its center, is an important source of Stoicism's, and the Stoic way of life's, appeal, both in antiquity and even today. And, in any event, in order to understand properly the Stoic way of life, and its philosophical bases, we will have to learn a good deal about their metaphysical and physical theory, into which, as I have said, their ethical theory is set as the centerpiece of their whole philosophical system. Doing that will occupy most of this and the following section.

I have already mentioned that the Stoics followed Aristotle in declaring "being happy" (εὐδαιμονεῖν) to be the "end" (τέλος), or highest good for which all actions are done: itself an action, but one not done for the sake of anything else.[14] And, again like Aristotle, but as committed heritors of Socrates, they specified this action as "living in accordance with the virtues." Thus, for them too, as for Aristotle, happiness is a specific, single activity, or type of activity: the activity in which virtues that one possesses are expressed in all the different actions one performs in the course of living the best adult life. It is by governing one's life, and all the actions that make it up, through possessing and applying the outlook on life provided by the virtues that, according to the Stoics, as for Aristotle, human beings achieve their own highest good and live happily.

But the Stoics added two further characterizations of this activity of the virtues: it is the same as living "in agreement" (ὁμολογουμένως) and as living "in accordance with nature."[15] These are new ideas, not present in Aristotle's account. When we attend closely to them we can see that the starting point the Stoics share with Aristotle—that living happily is the end and highest good for human life, and that this is the same thing as possessing and applying the virtues in all that one does—rests upon significantly different philosophical foundations. To

[14] See chapter 3, n. 25 and the main text to which it is attached. On whether Zeno and Chrysippus had actually read Aristotle's treatises, see endnote 22.

[15] The quotations in this paragraph and the next all come from section 6e of Arius Didymus's *Epitome of Stoic Ethics*. To these three specifications of "living happily" Arius Didymus adds that Zeno himself (followed in fact by all his successors) "defined" happiness as "a smooth flow of life." That seems to capture in psychological terms what it feels like to be living in agreement (with oneself, and with the world-mind: on this see below, in my main text).

begin with the first characterization, the somewhat strange phrase, living "in agreement," seems meant, in the first instance, to indicate that fully virtuous living, or, equivalently, happy living, involves, crucially, agreement with oneself. Those who live that way have none of the divided thoughts and feelings about how one is living, or what one is doing at any moment, that at least intermittently characterize most, if not all, people who are vicious to whatever degree, however slight, or large. So understood, "in agreement" indicates something that we too, with our modern concepts of happiness, might recognize as an essential feature of any happy life: no one leading a happy life can be conflicted in their feelings, divided in sentiments and attitudes, toward themselves, their actions, and their way of life. Happiness requires, we might well agree, undivided commitment to our values and to the way we are pursuing and implementing them in our lives.[16] And, as I presented Aristotle's view in the previous chapter, this is something that Aristotle's own conception of virtue and happiness also includes.

But "in agreement" meant more than that to the Stoics. The term so translated has the word "reason" (λόγος) as its root. It means literally "having reasoned thoughts that are the same or in common" (this sameness or commonness is the force of the prefix ὁμο-). But it is not just with oneself that, for the Stoics, one thinks the same thoughts, if one is virtuous. As Chrysippus, and perhaps Zeno himself, made clear, living in agreement meant that one thinks in some way some of the same thoughts as the world itself does—the world of nature, under the governance of the world-mind or of the god Zeus (as they usually speak of the world-mind), who is indeed for them nature itself, according to one usage of the term "nature."[17] If one lives virtuously, for the Stoics, that means that one thinks some of the same thoughts about one's life, its circumstances, its successes and failures—about how one is leading it, and what one is doing at any moment in so leading it—as Zeus himself thinks about it, both in terms of one's general orien-

---

[16] I do not mean to say that, on our modern views, a happy life has to be altogether free from regret over how things have turned out for us, or from second thoughts about things we may have done, once we see how things have turned out. But that is another matter from the unity of vision I am referring to here.

[17] Zeus, in Greek religious tradition, is the leader and commander among the gods living on Olympus. He is in some vague way in charge of the world's climate and guarantor of human morality through prophecies, interventions, punishments, etc. In taking over and reinterpreting this tradition so that it accords with a properly philosophical understanding of the world, the Stoics make "Zeus" the name of a single entity (the world-mind, or the reason at work and causing all that happens in the world). This entity can also be given the names of what in the tradition were regarded as distinct divine agents (Hera, Aphrodite, Ares, Apollo, etc.), in the light of its different functions and accomplishments, in causing all the world's events and sponsoring human morality. The Stoics are, in their philosophical theory, clear and strict monotheists, not polytheists at all, as later Christian writers, in their battle against the pagan Greek traditions in thought and sentiment, obfuscatingly and self-interestedly made them out to be.

tation, and with respect to the particular actions one does at any moment.[18] So, living in agreement means living, in one's own thoughts that direct one's life and actions, in agreement with the thoughts of Zeus, the world-mind, as he or it controls and rules over all that happens in the world, through its own thoughts and decisions. Living in agreement means having the thoughts with which one directs one's own life in full agreement with Zeus's thoughts, as those direct the whole world's life, so far as these affect one's own life. In effect, in the way one lives, and in each of one's actions, one is following the wishes of Zeus as to how a human being ought to live. That is to say, one is obeying his injunctions, and so, always doing all of one's god-given duties. Thus, as we will see more fully below,[19] for the Stoics, the life of virtue, which, like Socrates, Plato, and Aristotle, they regard as our highest good, comes to be characterizable also as a life devoted to doing our moral duty.

When, according to Arius Didymus, the Stoics add that living in agreement (with Zeus or nature) is also living "in *accordance* with nature," they are not re-peating themselves. In this second phrase, the nature referred to is not the world-mind itself, in causing by its thoughts, and ruling over, what happens in the course of nature. Living "in accordance with nature" means living in accordance with the natural outcomes themselves, caused by Zeus's thoughts, as we can ob-serve them occurring over time, together with the inferences we can draw from them about the thoughts of Zeus or nature as to the proper behaviors of the liv-ing things (including human beings) that are involved in them, and that have partially led to some of those outcomes. We could think of living in accordance with nature as living on the basis of normative principles deriving from our ob-servation of how nature itself operates, in directing the lives of animals and plants—things without reason of their own to direct how they grow and develop and live—as well as what happens in human life under ordinary conditions. (I

[18] The qualification in "some of the same thoughts" is needed for two principal reasons. First, Zeus thinks thoughts about any given individual person and what they ought to do that include a full account of the history of the whole world, specifically in relation to that individual, at each and every time of its existence; of course no human being can be thinking all those thoughts. What all humans can think, if they are perfectly rational and virtuous, are Zeus's thoughts about their own situation insofar as it relates to them individually, and to their needs, choices, decisions, etc., that is, as to what they should do and for what reasons. Secondly, as we might say in contemporary philosophical terms, each of us will have lots of "first-personal" thoughts that we will formulate by referring to ourselves as "I." Zeus cannot have such thoughts, i.e., I mean, ones in which, for example, I think what I should do, in those first-personal terms. (Still, any such thoughts any virtuous individual may think will not be out of agreement, in the sense of in any way opposed, with Zeus's.)

[19] See below, section 4.7.

will say more about this later.) This idea of living in accordance with nature is the basis of the ethical "naturalism" to which the Stoics commit themselves. Thus, living virtuously, conceived as living in accordance with nature, is a second way in which, by living virtuously, one follows the wishes of Zeus for how a human being ought to live.

On this Stoic conception of human beings, we are the sole nondivine possessors of a power of reason with which we make our own choices and direct our own actions. With our own individual minds we stand in relation to a divine mind that is actually and actively present within the world of nature, causing and producing the events it contains, through its own plans and decisions. Either we live in agreement with, and obedience to, it (and so, virtuously and happily), or we do not (and so, viciously and miserably). Here we meet with a conception of divinity and our relationship to it that departs markedly from the conception we find in Aristotle. For Aristotle the natural world and its principles of operation (which are the objects of study in natural philosophy) are a self-standing realm of facts and events. This realm is constituted to a great extent of teleological processes, belonging, however, to a natural and inherent teleology that does not involve the presence of a mind to activate it, whether from within (as with the Stoics) or from outside (as with Christian ideas). It belongs to the specific natures, for example, of given types of animal that they grow to some standard range of sizes and sustain themselves thereafter by teleologically oriented natural processes of ingestion and metabolism, and so on.

For Aristotle these teleological processes are simply among the given facts of nature. The world of nature is a self-sustaining, eternal realm of plants, animals, seas, rivers, lakes, land masses, mountains, all made of material stuffs (rock, gases, metals, other solids and other fluids than the ones already mentioned) that are reducible ultimately to four "simple bodies," each uniform and not further reducible (earth, air, fire, and water).[20] Each of these different components operates on its own, given its own nature, and combines with others according to principles distinctive of and inherent in it, as the kind of natural thing it is. These principles do not derive in any way, or include, any thinking (apart, I mean, from the thinking that goes on in the human beings who are only one part of the natural world). For Aristotle, the divine mind stands outside this system altogether,

[20] Aristotle argued for a fifth "element," as well, for the sun, moon, other planets, and the stars to be made of. He holds that this element, and the things made of it, by nature go round in circles and lack weight altogether. See his *On the Heavens*. But we can leave that aside, limiting ourselves here to the world of nature considered as just the "sublunary" world of the earth and its immediate environs.

even though this system (and everything else that has any being at all) depends for its very existence upon the divine mind's thinking. The divine mind does not create the natural world (that world is eternal), and it does not direct natural processes by teleological thinking of its own. It affects those processes only through activities of thought that are most closely paralleled by our own theoretical thinking at its highest and most metaphysical. The Aristotelian divine mind notoriously thinks itself, with no other direct concerns than for this thinking, that is, for itself. God's effects on the natures of things, and on natural processes, derive (somehow) from the beauty and excellence of this thought as a model for the eternal, self-maintaining processes at work in the natural world.[21]

For Aristotle, as reasoners ourselves, we are indeed related to the thinking of the divine mind, as we are for the Stoics too, but only through the divine mind's being the ultimate and highest object for us to grasp and understand through our own processes of reasoning. As such, the divine mind is the object at which, as we saw in the last chapter, the activities constituting our highest good are directed. It is true that in understanding the divine mind's thought we are also engaging, so far as a human mind can, in an activity of thinking that is most like the very best thing there is, period. This best thing is the divine mind's activity of thought. This is the basis for Aristotle's view that this human activity of understanding is our highest good. On Aristotle's theory, we can reasonably be said to "assimilate" ourselves to god in the exercise of our highest virtues (those of the theoretical intellect). But the thinking involved in our *practical* virtues operates quite apart from any such assimilation. The virtue of practical wisdom is knowledge of the human good, not of god—god's activity—as a good beyond us. Of course, if we are practically wise, as we saw in the last chapter, we must always bear in mind that the highest human virtues, which bring us in close relation to this good beyond us, are intellectual, not practical, ones. But practical wisdom, though it does include holding that thought constantly in mind, does not include actual knowledge, so to speak hands-on knowledge, of that good—either the good in theoretical thinking, or the divine good that is beyond us. Practical wisdom includes only knowledge of the existence and high value of these higher goods. The principles of practical wisdom are derived, as we saw, from reflection on human beings as members of the self-standing realm of nature. If we are possessed of the human practical virtues, we see ourselves, through that reflection, as mutually dependent and mutually cooperative persons, in seeking the best life

[21] See Aristotle's discussion in *Metaphysics* XII (Λ), chaps. 7–9.

shared in common with like-minded other human beings that human nature makes possible for us. It is through that reflection that we also come to realize—as practical agents—that the best life includes activities that are not practical, but purely theoretical.[22]

The Stoic understanding of the world of nature is quite different. As a result, so is their understanding of our relation, even in our practical virtues (to speak for the moment in Aristotelian terms), to the divine mind and to divine thoughts about how we are to live. As we will see, on the Stoic view, we humans have the capacity, simply because we possess the power of reason, to cooperate with and thus participate in the divine thought that governs the world order and causes all that happens within it, in accordance with its own teleological thinking and planning for the world's progress. Human practical virtues—the ones through which we govern our lives and cause all our actions, if we are good people—are the very conditions of our minds in which we realize and perfect this capacity. Hence, in the activities of virtue—practical virtue, to continue to speak in Aristotelian terms—we do not merely assimilate ourselves to god, while falling short of the same thinking that he/it engages in; we quite literally think god's thoughts, insofar as they concern ourselves and our lives.

It will take us all of the next four sections to unravel sufficiently all the consequences for Stoic ethical theory of this momentous shift away from the Aristotelian view of nature as a free-standing, self-governing realm, to one in which all that happens in the world happens in a quite direct sense through the operation within it of the teleological thinking of an inherent divine mind. We can begin by noting that the Stoics' different understanding of the world of nature seems to be derived from views developed in certain dialogues of Plato, in particular the *Timaeus*. In fact, Aristotle had considered these views, and rejected them. On the *Timaeus* account, revived and refashioned by the Stoics, in defiance of Aristotle's objections (to whatever extent they knew of them), it is divine teleological planning and activity that both create and govern the natural world, which is itself as a whole conceived as a single living thing (an animal). We might ourselves think that Aristotle showed better philosophical judgment in rejecting this view than Zeno and the other Stoics did in reverting to the Platonic outlook. However, as we will see more fully in chapter 6, it was the Platonic-Stoic view that dominated the thought of Hellenistic and later Greek and Roman philosophy and science. The Aristotelian view was, surprisingly to us (or, at any rate, to me),

---

[22] On Aristotle's theology and its connection to his ethical theory, see further below, section 4.7.

an outrider among philosophers and scientific writers of antiquity. Evidently, post-Aristotelian Greek philosophers did not agree with us on the superiority of the Aristotelian conception of the universe. It was Aristotle's view, not the, to us, flamboyantly picturesque and "unscientific" one of the *Timaeus*, that seemed archaic and out of touch with "modern" thought. In fact, in late Greek philosophy, Aristotle's self-standing, nonreasoning nature was relegated to a subordinate status, as a kind of admittedly very useful intellectual make-believe, within a Platonic-Stoic universe consisting of a world-animal possessing a world-soul with which to think about and direct all its "life"—that is, to direct all the main processes and events in the natural history of the world. This world-animal contains as parts all the other animals, with material bodies and with souls of their own. But it consists in part also, most importantly, of a group of human animals possessing souls with rational minds of their own, with which they direct the aspects of their lives that consist in their own voluntary actions and reasoned thoughts— even, of course, their reasoned thoughts that are mis-reasoned and bad, wrong thoughts.

Thus, like Plato in the *Timaeus*, and the Platonists of late antiquity, the Stoics conceived the physical world (which for them, unlike for the Platonists, was all the world there is) as a single animal, with a life of its own, and a soul to cause all its movements. This soul is the locus, in Stoic theory, of the divine reason or Zeus, spread everywhere through it, and thereby through the rest of the world, too, since the soul is spread everywhere through the world. Reason or Zeus is thus in contact with all the materials making up the world—both with this soul and with all the compound and complex material bodies that this soul itself passes through.[23] Reason or Zeus in fact, on Stoic theory, contacts all parts of the world however small (indeed at what we would call infinitesimal levels). By that contact the divine mind is able to cause all the states and conditions of matter itself, and all the states and conditions of all the different kinds of material things, as well as all the changes over time, that constitute the world and its history over the whole of time. Strange as this conception may seem to us now, there are, in fact, powerful arguments in its favor, and the Stoics, following Plato's lead in the *Timaeus*, devoted considerable efforts to explaining and justifying it.[24] As we proceed, we will have occasion to see some details of these efforts,

[23] The soul, for the Stoics, is itself a material body. It is not a spiritual, nonmaterial, and nonbodily (as it were) substance, as it is for Plato and the Platonists. On this see below, section 4.5.

[24] These arguments are most readily accessed in Cicero's dialogue *On the Nature of the Gods*, book II, available in translation in the Loeb Classical Library.

even though, for our purposes in discussing Stoic ethical theory and the Stoic way of life, we do not need to enter into a full discussion of their philosophical reasons for holding to their metaphysical and physical doctrines.

4.4. Stoic Moral Psychology and the Human Virtues

So far as ethics and our ways of life are concerned, here is the main question that arises, on the Stoics' overall view of nature and of our place in it: What does the fact of our unique rationality, in relation to god's more complete and powerful mind, mean for a correct understanding of human nature and of the human virtues? That is, what does it imply about the ways of thinking we must follow if we are to perfect our own reason, and thereby live good and happy lives? This is the question we will pursue in this and the next section.

As we have seen, for the Stoics, human happiness consists in living virtuously, and therefore in living in agreement both with ourselves (in our undivided thoughts about ourselves, our actions, and our way of life) and with Zeus's or nature's own thoughts about our individual actions and our overall way of life. Here we meet with a major clash and disagreement between the Stoics and Aristotle—not just a difference, even a radical one, as before. Let us begin by discussing this clash. For Aristotle, the virtues (or rather, the practical ones) combine two distinct though intimately and essentially related conditions of the soul. On the one hand there is practical wisdom, a virtue of the mind, and on the other there are the varied moral virtues or virtues of character, consisting in a "mean" disposition of our nonrational feelings of appetite and spirit. But as part of their adherence to the Socratic heritage from which Zeno had started out on his philosophical journey,[25] the Stoics rejected this division of the soul, expounded by Plato in the *Republic* and *Timaeus* and systematized by Aristotle in his ethical treatises.[26] According to the Platonic-Aristotelian theory of human psychology, there are in us three separate and interactive powers, those of reason, spirit, and

---

[25] Diogenes Laertius (VII 2–3) tells a story of Zeno's having become seized with the desire to follow men like Socrates upon reading the second book of Xenophon's *Memorabilia* in a bookshop in Athens while on a business trip there. The bookseller sent him off to the Cynic teacher Crates, a devotee of Socratic virtue as the highest good who took that to involve complete indifference to all social conventions and conventional goods. Later, again according to Diogenes Laertius, Zeno had more strictly philosophical teachers. The first century BCE Epicurean philosopher Philodemus reports in his *Index of Stoics* that the first generation of Stoics, including Zeno, were happy to think of themselves as Socratics.

[26] I discuss below, section 4.7. the Stoics' special reasons for agreeing with Socrates on this point.

appetitive desire. For Plato, virtue therefore involves three separate, but unified, conditions, one for each of these parts or aspects of the human soul. For the Stoics, and as they thought for Socrates,[27] human virtue is psychologically a much simpler affair. It is a condition exclusively of our minds, of our practical thoughts about our actions and about the potential goals of action, and about human life. That is because, on the Stoic analysis, the only sources of motivation (i.e., of actual psychic "impulses" toward moving any parts of the body voluntarily, in actions of any kind) are found in the mind, that is, in our thoughts about what to do or avoid doing, or about what is worth acting to achieve or obtain and use, or worth avoiding if we can. There are no separate appetites or spirited desires, as on the Platonic-Aristotelian moral psychology. Appetites and spirited desires become, for the Stoics, themselves aspects or products of the single, materially embodied, reasoning power that constitutes, all by itself, the human soul, insofar as that is the source of our voluntary actions.

The Stoic theory does not at all deny conscious bodily feelings, for example those caused by hunger or thirst or sexual arousal, or the inclinations toward eating or drinking or sex that they often give rise to. But, on the Stoic analysis, those inclinations do not constitute, any more than the bodily feelings of hunger or thirst do, full-blown motivations toward doing any of those things. They are not psychic impulses, moving us in our souls toward action. Such impulses arise only when—no doubt, often enough, under the strong influence of these prerational feelings (which are not, as with Plato and Aristotle, nonrational desires)—we accept in our rational thinking the idea that we then have some good enough reason to eat or drink something or engage in some sexual activity. These bodily feelings, and the way they work on our consciousness, may give us the impression (φαντασία) that it would be a good idea to eat, or drink, or have sex, if possible, right away or pretty soon. But that impression is only a felt inclination to act in such ways; it is not yet a movement in the soul toward doing any of those things. It is not even a movement subject to being overruled by some higher capacity in the soul (reason, as Aristotle and Plato conceive it). In every case, the Stoics hold, it is only when we accept that we have some good reason to act, but not before, that we are set—that is, that we set ourselves—in motion toward action. So, in cases where we are subject to the influence of prerational feelings, and of the impressions they give rise to, it is only when, due to that influence, we accept in our minds that we have some good reason to act, that we proceed to gratifica-

---

[27] We saw in section 2.2 that they are right about this.

tion. The psychic motion—the "impulse"—toward action can, but need not, be an "appetite" or "appetitive desire"—as it might be if we brought it into existence through thinking, on the basis of feelings of sexual arousal, that it would be a really good thing to have sex right away. There are other reasons to think it a good idea to do something than that it would give us bodily pleasure.

Thus the Stoics hold that what Plato and Aristotle call "appetites" (active desires driving us to bodily gratification in eating, drinking, or sexual activity) are in fact a particular set or kind of thoughts, thoughts to the effect that there is some good enough reason to have such gratification (then). Given the basic nature of the human soul, they think, this is all they can possibly be.[28] These thoughts are influenced by prerational feelings, say of hunger or sexual arousal, and by impressions that we can have and feel, as a result, which present the relevant gratification in a graphically attractive light. But those feelings and those impressions, however much a causal background seamlessly integrated with our thoughts about acting, are not in themselves desires. Only the thought that it would be a really good thing to have the gratification, contained within the overall experience, rightly should be counted as a desire, that is, as an actual impulse to act. (I will have more to say below about these appetitive desires, on Stoic theory.)

The Stoics also do not deny other, less overtly bodily, feelings similarly entering our consciousness and affecting our actions. Again, however, they think, these affect our actions only through having an influence (in this case always a distorting one) on how we think about what to do and what to try to get and enjoy. Feelings of irritation or disgruntlement or disappointment, or pleasurable or painful anticipation, or dislike and even contempt and hatred of other people (or ourselves), can arise, on their understanding, through prerational feelings (or impressions that constitute inclinations) that we have learned (or even been taught, by social conditioning) to experience on various occasions about various types of person, thing, and event. But those prerational feelings do not constitute full-blown movements in our souls toward action—desires moving us to act. At best, they constitute only evaluative impressions about how things are. They are or give rise only to inclinations to act. We may have become accustomed, for example, to feel irritated under certain circumstances—that is, to get a certain sort of vivid impression about the meaning, for us, of being in those circumstances. But that feeling, a disturbed and upset one, no doubt, is not yet anger, if

---

[28] In speaking of the nature of the human soul here and elsewhere, according to Stoic theory, I am referring to the human soul as it is in adult humans. As explained below, section 4.5, the souls of children are different, more like those of nonhuman animals.

we understand by anger a movement of the soul moving us to lashing out in some way. Full-blown psychic movements to action come into being only when, perhaps under the influence of these impressions or felt inclinations, we have the thought, and assert to ourselves, that there exists some good reason for acting in an irritated or disgruntled or disappointed, or pleasantly or painfully anticipating, or contemptuous or hating, way. These are rational thoughts, in the minimal, but sufficient, sense that they reside in our capacity for thinking things for reasons—whether rightly or wrongly, whether reasonably or not. Hence, again, the Stoics hold that what Plato and Aristotle think of as "desires" of spirit—emotions such as anger, or contempt and hatred—are, and can only be, certain sorts of thoughts about action, and reasons for acting. These thoughts may be influenced by irritated or disgruntled feelings that themselves are graphic impressions of things or circumstances affecting us. But however much they may be a causal background (even an essential one) seamlessly integrated with the thoughts about acting that constitute the anger or other emotion, these are not in themselves desires. Only the thought that it would be a really good thing to lash out, contained within the overall experience, rightly should be counted as a desire, that is, an actual impulse to act.

Hence, for the Stoics, there is no room within a theory of the human virtues for the second sort of practical virtue, one establishing the proper condition of the "nonrational desires" that on other theories motivate us to action, independently of and sometimes contrarily to the motivations of reason toward the good. There is room only for a single sort of virtue, one consisting in a well-trained mind that has been brought to understand all the actually good reasons there are for or against given pursuits, interests, commitments, activities, ways of living. With such a well-trained mind we will know not to, and never will, behave in bad or wrong ways. We will never have thoughts about action that declare something not worth doing to be worth doing. (Impressions or inclinations to that effect are another matter entirely; I will say something below about the possibility that virtuous people might nonetheless experience those.)

This moral-psychological analysis of the capacities and activities of the human soul is the necessary ground for understanding the notorious Stoic rejection of "emotions." For reasons we will explore later,[29] the Stoics declare that all of the feelings that we ordinarily classify as "emotions" are bad, mistaken, ways of feeling and desiring; emotions are therefore totally incompatible with, and can

---

[29] See section 4.8 below.

never be found in the mind of, any person of truly virtuous character. Thus they reject, and banish from the fully moral life, all feelings of anger, grief, fear, elation, contempt, hatred, love, confidence, envy, joy, yearning, pity, emulation . . . and so on. On their view, no action should ever be done in any way, to any degree, out of any of these feelings, that is, out of any emotional desire to do them. As I have said, this is a notorious doctrine, and it was notorious already in antiquity: a huge paradox, as many other philosophers thought, and an affront to human life as it is actually lived, and indeed as it is when lived well. What can we, or should we, make of it?

Certainly, one must not attempt to criticize the Stoic rejection of emotions, as often happens, while simply assuming the correctness of the Aristotelian-Platonic moral psychology that the Stoics consciously rejected, and rejected for reasons, as we have seen, that they thought were persuasive: they agreed with Socrates's reasoning, and his conclusion that the human soul is, so far as the active life of voluntary action goes, a fully reason-based thing.[30] This cautionary note has special force for us today, since in our "folk," as well as our "scientific," psychological theory, we take for granted a watered-down Platonic-Aristotelian moral psychology. We automatically think (with Plato and Aristotle) that there are emotions, such as anger, grief, fear, elation, envy, joy, pity, that are indeed states of the soul that motivate us to action (whether in the end we act on them or not), and that derive from a nonrational aspect or part of our souls. They arise in us, we think, under various stimuli provided through perception or memory or imagination, independently of any rational judgments we may hold or make, as to the goodness or badness, rightness or wrongness, of these ways of feeling, or as to the value or disvalue to us of the external objects or events that give rise to them. They arise independently of any rational judgments we may hold as to the value or disvalue of any actions they push us toward taking. They push us blindly forward. On the occasions when we experience them, we think, we do not control through reason and reasoning whether to experience these conditions, nor do we control which ones arise and affect us—though, perhaps, we can train ourselves so as not to feel them, or not to feel them in ways that, without that self-attention, our original natural dispositions would lead us to feel. Emotions are, in short, a permanent feature of human life, we think, grounded in human nature itself. How easy it then is to think that, when the Stoics reject these as bad states of mind, under any and all circumstances, they are making demands on us

---

[30] For Socrates's analysis, see above, section 2.2.

that overstretch human nature. They want to eradicate a whole aspect of our natures! Or, at any rate, they would perversely reduce us to unfeeling and humanly unresponsive automatons of "reason," with our lives uncolored—and un-enlivened—by such responses in our feelings to the ebb and flow of human life, whether or not we think it right in given instances to follow their lead in our actions. Assuming as we do the Platonic-Aristotelian outlook on human nature and human life, we cannot fail to find ourselves shocked, upon first presentation of the Stoic total rejection of emotion.

However, when we understand the alternative Stoic moral psychology, we can quickly see that, to begin with, their demands do not at all entail the eradication of a fundamental or permanent aspect of our natures. To be sure, like Plato and Aristotle, and everyone else in the ancient philosophical tradition, they take for granted that anger, grief, and all the other "emotions" I have listed, are in fact (whatever else they may involve by way of agitated feelings and other affects) states of the soul that do motivate us to action: anger includes an impulse to express itself in actions of retaliation, grief an impulse to moan and beat one's breast and lament one's loss and one's fate, and in general to show how badly one feels, in loyalty to the one who has died. But, on their analysis of our moral psychology, such states of the soul—ones that do motivate us to action expressing them, whether we then go on to act on them, or not—can derive from, and belong to, only our power of reason. They cannot belong to some part of our souls separate from reason, since there are none that do contain anything that motivates our actions (to any degree or in any way). Hence, in declaring all emotional states bad, they may very well be demanding that we give up feeling moved in certain ways that we are used to feeling and do feel regularly and often. Anger, grief, envy, pleasurable anticipation, joy at our successes, disappointment, and other emotions are staples of most of our lives. It may be, too, that we preen ourselves on our vulnerability to being so affected, and so do not want to be rid of these tendencies. Perhaps (having been brought up in the Platonic-Aristotelian outlook) we regard that vulnerability as a cherished mark of our humanity. But the Stoics hold, and argue with considerable plausibility, that there is nothing permanent, or belonging to human nature itself, in any of this, however widespread it is in the lives of all ordinary people, ourselves included. Once one understands how these sorts of feelings and motivations are based on distorted and false value judgments, they reasonably think, one should and can come to see them not as enlivening or enriching, in a properly human way, a life otherwise thinly rational and even automaton-like, but as serious obstacles to a truly full, specifically human, life. As for their reasons for thinking emotions do always involve such erroneous judgments, we will see those as we proceed in this section, and in section 4.5.

In my account above I have distinguished sharply between the prerational feelings of irritation, depression, elation, and the like, and the emotions, themselves often influenced by such prerational feelings and impressions of anger, grief, joy, and so on. Thus, the Stoic rejection of emotions as bad states of feeling and desires does not amount to or involve the moral banishment of these feelings.[31] That is because these feelings are not motivating states of the soul. Anything that deserves the name of anger or grief, or any other of the names of emotions, must be a condition of our reasoning power that we fall into when we have accepted and agreed to the idea, proposed by such nonrational feelings or impressions, that something has occurred that is properly worth reacting to with the behaviors of retaliation or breast beating, and so on, that go along with these emotions. In fact, as we will see shortly, the Stoics reject the idea that anything at all can ever happen to anyone that in fact is worth reacting to in any of these ways. They think, for reasons connected to our role as the sole nondivine possessors of reason in a divinely and rationally governed world, that even very irritating things that are done or happen to us, and even great losses of friends and other loved ones, and all the other things that give rise in some or even most people to other emotional states of motivation and action, are not in fact worth those reactions. When they reject emotions they are rejecting such motivating reactions. They are not declaring that we should violate human nature by eradicating or unfeelingly and inhumanly suppressing an aspect of our nature that consists in having such motivating responses (whether or not they are then acted on—reason having to step in to decide what is the right thing to do). That is the Platonic-Aristotelian view of human psychology, and the Stoics follow a different analysis. For them prerational feelings and impressions of loss or irritation may, for all we have seen so far, accompany even quite good people's avoidance of emotions. So the Stoics are not demanding that we eradicate a whole aspect of human nature, the feelings and impressions inclining one toward emotions and emotional actions.

As to the "impressions" and prerational feelings of irritation or loss the existence of which their analysis does recognize, these too, as we will see, are argued by the Stoics to be inappropriate, at least if at all extreme, however natural and

---

[31] We will see below that, nonetheless, they do find something morally problematic about even these inclinations.

inevitable it may seem to us very imperfect observers for any human being to experience at least some of these extreme feelings. But that is another matter. The Stoic "cure" for emotions is to understand the reasons why actions of retaliation and breast beating, and exultation and spite, and contempt and hatred, and enraptured love and joy, or ones expressing fear or pity, are not at all justified, and are not to be taken. The "cure" for these impressions, and for the prerational feelings that engender them, requires a lot of further work on our tendencies to respond prerationally to things that happen to us in ways that our upbringing and the surrounding culture have led us to respond.[32] Plato and Aristotle (especially Plato)[33] certainly agree that many times when people do get angry or grieve, or experience other emotions, that is inappropriate: as we have seen, virtuous people for Aristotle do not experience any emotion in some contexts where nonvirtuous people do. In others, they do not experience as much emotion as most people do. Aristotle thinks that it takes a lot of early training in habituation of the feelings to reach the condition of virtue, in which one feels the correct degrees of emotion on only the correct occasions for feeling the emotion in question at all. The Stoics hold the more extreme view that even the impression or feeling (for them, a prerational one) that would incline one (but not motivate one) to act emotionally, to whatever degree, is inappropriate. (As I said, we will consider shortly their reasons for thinking this.) What will take their place are correct impressions, and accompanying prerational feelings, which reflect the true value and worth, for practical purposes, of whatever is being reacted to.

In light of their negative moral evaluation even of nonmotivating inclinations to act emotionally, one could think that the Stoics might, or even ought to, have recognized a second kind of practical virtue, after all, besides the virtues of correct rational evaluation. This would be a different thing, of course, from the Aristotelian virtues of control by reason over independent, nonrational, sources of motivation. It would be a kind of virtue consisting in the achieved condition in which one's tendencies to feel prerational inclinations to act emotionally would

---

[32] See Seneca, *On Anger* II 18–36 and III, of which there is a modern translation in Cooper and Procopé, *Seneca: Moral and Political Essays*; this must contain materials partly derived from the "therapeutic" book of a lost work of Chrysippus, *On Emotions* (unless this book was a separate work on its own). See Cooper and Procopé, p. 13 n. 17.

[33] I am thinking here especially of Plato's severe rejection of lamentation and grief in *Republic* 387d–388e. He makes a special exception (in the *Symposium*) for ἔρως ("erotic" love), but, in Plato's hands, that becomes an etherealized "love" having for its objects not only and not primarily other people's bodies, or even their minds and characters, but rather mental engagement, and, in the end, love of the beauty of the Forms that he thinks govern the world as objects of thought and of impassioned aspiration for properly developed human beings.

be permanently eliminated—in which, in other words, the early habituation we receive in experiencing, and the surrounding cultural approvals of, these feelings/impressions, would be overcome, and indeed the effects totally eliminated. It does seem that they may have held some special sorts of counterhabituation as needed. But only as a preliminary. They seem to have thought that the fully achieved understanding of the reasons why emotional actions are not right, under any circumstances, will, simply on its own, bring with it the alteration of a human being's tendencies to experience emotion-inducing impressions and prerational feelings.[34] Either, as a result, they will no longer experience them at all, or else, by possessing that understanding one reduces those tendencies to a level at which they pose no appreciable obstacles to virtuous action, that is, to action that is never emotional at all. Either way, impressions that might arise cease to be felt as significant inducements to emotional action.

In any event, it was quite natural for the Stoics, given the philosophical context in which they worked, to concentrate on rejecting any idea, along Platonic and Aristotelian lines, of a second kind of practical virtue involving the training of an allegedly nonrational sort of emotional and motivating states of the human soul. Given their moral-psychological analyses, there can be no need, or room, for any such virtues. That is, for them, the main point to insist upon. Any training needed for our tendencies to receive emotion-inducing impressions could be regarded as a minor matter, not requiring the serious recognition that would follow from speaking of a second sort of virtue in connection with it. The only human virtues are virtues of our minds, that is, of our capacities for considering and deciding, on the basis of reasons we can discover, and can approve as good ones, for acting in one way, or some other, in specific circumstances that arise in our lives.

4.5. Virtue: Agreement with the World-Mind's Plans

I will return to consider further this momentous disagreement in moral psychology between the Stoics, on the one side, and Plato and Aristotle, on the other.[35]

---

[34] The feeling and impression of, say, illicit sexual pleasure on some occasion, as something good and worth having, is a modification, in perception, of one's rational soul (on Stoic psychological analysis). If one's understanding is complete and perfect, as to the reasons why it isn't and couldn't possibly be good to any degree at all, one could suppose that that would have the permanent effect that one's soul couldn't even be modified in any such way, however temporarily.

[35] See section 4.8 below.

But first, in this section and the following one, we need to pursue the question I raised at the beginning of the last section. What are the implications, for a proper understanding of the human virtues, of our relationship, as the only other rational beings, to god or nature—the divine mind—inherent everywhere in our world? If living virtuously means, as the Stoics think it does, living in agreement both with ourselves and with the universal mind that governs nature, what does living in agreement with that mind involve for us? I said earlier that this mind is spread everywhere through the world of nature (the material world), down to its smallest parts, and that it causes all its movements. This mind is contained in the world's soul, which for the Stoics is not a spiritual substance (as it is for Platonists) but a material one; the soul serves as the first physical and material instrument used by the world-mind (god, or nature) in causing all the world's movements, thus giving rise to the world-animal's outer life—the movements and other changes that the material world undergoes. In order to understand the implications of this conception for the Stoic theory of the virtues, we need to pause briefly to survey some fundamentals of Stoic metaphysics and physical theory.

Like the soul itself, mind is not a spiritual substance, either. (This applies to both this divine mind and our individual ones.) At least it is not, if a spiritual substance is some otherworldly kind of entity deriving from or existing in some realm beyond space and time, even though somehow tenuously related to things that do exist in space and time. But, on Stoic principles, mind is also not a *material* body. In this, it differs from the soul that it is first spread through and uses as its instrument. Mind for the Stoics is one of two paired basic principles of all of reality. Mind is paired with matter as the second of the two "first principles" of all that has being. Everything that has being is composed of mind and matter: matter being entirely passive, mind entirely active. All the qualities of matter anywhere are imposed by the actions on it of the world-mind in thinking its thoughts as regards that particular matter and how it is to be physically constituted.[36] But in order to be able to have any such effects, the Stoics are convinced,

---

[36] One can think of the different sorts of matter, and the different sorts of inanimate material things, as having differential causal powers of their own, according to their kinds, on account of possessing their particular qualities (of heat and cold, lightness, solidity, fluidity, etc.). But these powers are given to them by the world-mind. Ultimately, or, if you like, metaphysically, only mind has causal powers. Metaphysically, matter and (nonrational) material things have no causal powers (of their own). As the sole active principle (matter being completely passive), mind is responsible for all that happens in the world: directly, for some of it, more remotely for those events that happen directly through the differential causal powers that the world-mind has endowed different sorts of matter with.

mind must be a corporeal, or bodily, thing (even if to our ears this sounds not only weird but almost self-contradictory). Platonists do not blanch at the idea of a spiritual substance (God, or mind, or soul in general) being able to cause movements in matter (even perhaps to create it), while nonetheless existing, in fact exclusively, in some realm beyond space and time. But the Stoics find that inconceivable. And, if inconceivable, then also impossible. There cannot be any miracles of unintelligible action of spirits on bodies, or there would be arbitrariness and, in fact, chaos at the base of things, which, it certainly seems manifest, is not the case. Hence, the Stoics develop a concept of body that includes, but is not limited to, bodies that are made of matter (as are all the bodies we can see and otherwise perceive). Minds (both the world-mind and our individual ones) are also bodies, because of their active powers to cause movements in material things. But minds are not *material* bodies, bodies made ultimately, as all material things are, of earth, air, fire and water (the Greeks' physical elements).

Next, we need to consider one point that the Stoics, along with Socrates, Plato, and Aristotle as well, take as a fundamental fact about reason itself (even in human beings). This is that, inherent in reason, is not just an interest in truth, but an attachment to, and motivation in its activities by pursuit of, the good. We have seen this in Aristotle's attribution to human reason of a special desire that all human beings have in virtue of possessing reason, separate from desires of appetite and spirit, for what each person regards as good for themselves. The Stoics reasonably take this to imply that the world-reason or Zeus, both in all its formative activities, in giving their physical properties to the various kinds of stuff, and to the various kinds of material objects the world contains, and in causing their subsequent movements, is aiming at producing a maximally good product. Its thought is fundamentally teleological in all its operations. Hence, the world's structures and contents will take shape, and interact over the whole history of the world, in ways that will constitute an external life history of the world-animal that consists in a series of events that is maximally complex, but well ordered, integrated, and efficient in sustaining the organism as a well-functioning single system, over time. A human mind, even assuming that it pursues the good, can mistake what actually is good, and can aim at results that are bad. But the world-mind has no sources, either internal or external, of any such corruption or error. Hence, it does aim, as I just said, at a maximally good product, consisting in this maximally complex, well-ordered, and integrated external life history of the world. But not only that. Whereas, of course, even a human mind that makes no mistake and aims only to produce what is truly good can be frustrated in its efforts, the world-mind faces no external obstacles at all to achieving its purposes: matter, being purely passive, can be made by the world-mind to take on any qualities it thinks best to impose. Hence, the actual history of the world, including all the stuffs and objects it contains, with their particular natures and properties, and their actions and interactions over time, does actually constitute that maximal good that I have said the world-mind, by its very essence as the mind that it is, is aiming at producing.

Our question, then, concerns what all this means for us, with our individual minds. If we consider our relation to this world-mind, as individual minds of the same substance as itself, with the same basic power of activity that it possesses in shaping and causing movements in matter, though with a greatly more limited scope, what should we think about our own place in this world? What conditions in our own minds, what principles for using our capacities of thought and action, will provide for us virtuous living—living in agreement with nature and with ourselves individually—and so a happy life? As we have seen, there are good reasons to suppose that the world-mind, in causing the world to be the way it is and in causing the events making up its history, is pursuing and achieving a maximally good result. But we ourselves contribute something to this history, too, through our decisions as to what to pursue and what to do in causing our own actions and shaping our own lives: we, as minds, have the power to move those parts of our own physical substance that we directly control, namely the parts of our souls that initiate all our actions, and in which our plans for our lives and our conceptions of what is good for us are lodged. Of course, a lot else has to happen favorably in order for us to carry out any particular decision: the world-mind, not we individually, is responsible for the state of our bodies at any time (anyhow, it is much more responsible than we may be through our earlier decisions). It is also responsible for what goes on in the outer world in which we wish to act, both before and after we initiate an action.[37]

But we, not the world-mind, are immediately responsible for our decisions and for the movements of our souls that initiate our actions. In possessing the power of reason we have ideas about what is good and bad, and what is worth doing or avoiding, and so on, and, moreover, there are standards for deciding which ideas are the right such ones to have, standards that we can recognize and

---

[37] Human beings, including ourselves through our past decisions, are partially responsible for some of our circumstances for action at any time, but, again, the world-mind has the overwhelmingly dominant role in making those be however they are, as well, of course, as in determining the consequences for us of what happens next in the outer world.

acknowledge if we think correctly. And it is up to us whether we do think correctly: just because we are rational beings, we all have the power to follow arguments and to discern the truth, at least where nontechnical matters to do with human life are concerned. In fact, it is about those standards, and their application to the way we should lead our lives, that we are now inquiring. We make our decisions on the basis of how we individually think about what is good or bad and about how as a result, in our given circumstances, we ought to, and how we will, act. To repeat, we, not the world-mind, cause our decisions and (to that extent) our individual actions. The complete history of the world, then, is the joint result of what we humans decide and how we act, and how the world-mind determines the structure of, and events in, the outer world (over most of which, of course, we have no control whatsoever).[38]

The first thing that should strike us when we consider all this background theory is that, through our rationality, we, as individual human beings, have a remarkably high calling. We are partners of the world-mind (god, Zeus), who work within Zeus's amazingly complex cosmic plan aimed at achieving the maximally good whole sequence of world events. Part of the amazing complexity of that plan is the creation of human beings as independent minds, deciding for themselves individually, on the basis of reasons they propose to themselves and recognize as valid, how they will act. Therein they make their own contributions to the achievement of this maximally good sequence. Our very nature, then, is to live and act as partners of Zeus in the carrying out of his plan. That is what we are here for. The amazing beauty and fantastic good order of the world, playing out over time in accordance with this cosmic plan, is therefore something that concerns us directly, insofar as we are by nature partners of the world-mind (indeed, subordinate parts of it) in carrying that plan out. In that way, the world's good is our good too, just as much as it is god's or the world-mind's.

Which actions of ours, then, and which ways of acting, will contribute as fully as we can to this beautiful and well-ordered sequence?[39] Each of us is concerned,

---

[38] On the Stoic theory of "fate," see endnote 23.

[39] It is irrelevant that, given the Stoic doctrine of fate (see the previous note), we will contribute fully to this sequence no matter what we decide to do. Our task is to decide what is the best thing for us to do at any given time, so far as we can determine that, given how, so far as we understand, the world works, and given our circumstances so far as we are aware of those—and to decide in what way to do it. We cannot shirk that task: whatever we do do, we will have done it for our own reasons and for our own purposes, and so, in effect, we will do it having decided to do it. The only question is whether we had good, or good enough, reasons for so deciding. Those reasons are ultimately to be assessed against the standards of beauty and good order in the world as a whole: that decision, and action, is best in any given circumstances that fits together most coherently with all the other decisions and actions in one's life and, in fit-

of course, first of all and primarily with our own needs and other concerns, as the individual animals that we are, and with our own actions. What, more specifically, are the individual concerns and interests that we should have, on this basis, as partners with Zeus in implementing his divine plan by arranging and seeing to our lives as the individual animals that we are? In what ways should we go about pursuing them? With what thoughts and attitudes should we pursue these concerns and interests, in seeking thereby to contribute as fully as we can to the good of the whole world? I explained above the distinction that Stoic analysis draws between acting in agreement with nature (in the sense of universal reason), and acting in accordance with nature (in the sense of the way natural events usually play themselves out).[40] We need to combine both these aspects of virtuous action in working out an answer to these questions. In so doing we will be able to see how, according to the Stoics, the world-mind wishes for us to act and to live—that is, how it wishes us to act and to *try* to live: as I have mentioned, whether or not we succeed on any occasion in achieving the outer goals of the action we undertake, because the world-mind wishes us to act for those outer goals, depends upon what else the world-mind wishes to achieve at the given place and time, in its own vast, overall plan for producing the maximally good and rationally coherent whole order of world history. Besides seeing how the world-mind wishes us to act—and for what outer goals—we will also see the reasons the Stoics have for thinking that living that way will best achieve our own personal good. After all, as they argue, it is a world-mind with those intentions that has created us, giving us a nature as rational beings such that living that way is the complete fulfillment of our natural work.

In order to know what interests and concerns of ours (as adults) would be in accordance with nature, we have a rich source of information to go on. We need only look to how nature itself normally conducts the lives of the plants and animals that are wholly governed by its own thought processes (because they do not possess reason). This governance, and these processes, are, of course, expressions of the world-reason's wishes and decisions in forming the world's various and variegated animal and plant life and in causing, at least in these specific cases, their growth and their life activities stage by stage, from birth right up to their deaths. By considering what goes on in the life of a normal plant or nonrational animal, we can discover what the world-mind's intentions are for the contribu-

---

ting together with them, makes the most positive contribution possible to the larger beautiful order of the whole of world history, by fitting that whole life into that history.

[40] See above, section 4.3.

tion of these plants and animals themselves, and of the sequence of events making up their lives, to the beauty and good order of the total sequence of events that constitutes the external life of the whole world-animal. Now, in fact, among the nonrational animals are included all human beings before they reach adolescence and have acquired the full use of their developing rational powers. The Stoics think observation shows us that this is a period during which human beings have desires, and impulses for doing things in pursuit of their desires, in just the way that other animals (notably, other mammals) do. Their behavior derives from a basis of instincts given to them at birth that gets transformed as they gain experience, for the most part through gradual developments that are purely natural. During this period, their behavior, changing over time, does not depend at any point on reasoned decisions of the children themselves, but only on pressures of the circumstances, given that initial natural endowment of instincts and perceptual powers.

In the case of the other animals, this develops into a steady, stable pattern of desires arising and subsiding over time, and in relation to external perceptions. This pattern gives rise to the set of life activities characteristic of a mature member of the given species. For humans, however, the processes of control of their actions, and so lives, by natural instincts and perceptual responses extends only so long as they are still growing up, and indeed only to something like the age of fourteen.[41] At that point, the "age of reason," the desires on which they act all come instead from their own reason's conclusions about how it is right to feel and to act (as I explained above). As they develop, the young of adult human parents do, of course, also exhibit in their behaviors the influence of human rationally derived customs and their parents' or other adult humans' ideas about how they should behave. Some of their behavior will certainly betray feelings of

[41] As Diogenes Laertius reports the Stoic view (VII 86), they hold that at first (in the womb) even animals' movements are directed by nature only in just the way that all the activities of plants are—vegetatively, without perception and without urges toward satisfaction of conscious desires. For animals, once born, however, nature adds "impulses" to manage them by, and much of their bodily movements are generated by those, as the animals seek, through these impulsive feelings, what they need and what is appropriate for them to eat and drink and otherwise do. In the case of human beings (i.e., when mature), nature bestows upon them their own reason "as a more perfect mode of management." Reason is added in their case as "the craftsman of their impulses": i.e., nature no longer directs any of their behavior by the natural instincts with which it directs the lives of the nonrational animals, including the young of human parents. The child's natural, instinctive impulses are replaced by reason-produced ones in causing their voluntary behaviors, and (this at least seems the best guess about something our sources are silent about) the old instinct-based desires (to the extent they survive at all) are demoted to mere bodily feelings generating at best the mere "appearances" (φαντασίαι) of which I spoke above—mere "inclinations" to act that do not rise to the level of full impulses.

attachment and aversion that do not derive simply from the natural endowment of instincts and perceptual powers, but are due to the ideas that adult humans with whom they interact hold about attachments and aversions one ought to feel. Relying on children's responses to what they perceive that do derive from that natural endowment, adult humans have great influence on how the young that are in their care come to feel, and to form, desires. The results of that influence have to be taken into account (and, to a great extent, discounted) in assessing, from observation of human infants and children, what is in fact according to nature in their behavior. Nonetheless, for the Stoics, ideas about the "natural" life of adults are importantly to be derived from the study of the actual lives (and instincts) of young, prerational human beings—instincts and behavior caused by external nature itself, and therefore directly by the world-mind, as part of its plan to produce a maximally ordered and beautiful world.

Considering the lives of plants and other animals, under conditions normal for members of their species, together with the behaviors of human infants and young children, as just sketched, we can derive important principles for how, as adults, we need to live, if we are to live according to nature. We need to eat and drink the right sorts of foods, and only in the right quantities, to maintain our physical constitutions in a naturally strong and healthy condition. We need to exercise our bodies and our mental capacities of perception in ways appropriate for keeping our natural powers sharp and strong, through games and other pastimes of a sort suitable to that end—games and pastimes in which, in addition, those powers get exercised in ways satisfying to us for their own sakes. Furthermore, we can see that animals of virtually all species give special recognition to members of the same species, and normally and naturally congregate with and cooperate with their congeners in living some sort of shared life. Hence, we can infer, we also need to establish and maintain mutually cooperative and helping relations with at least some of our fellow humans—the ones we live in community with. Likewise, we have reason (at least unless we are in some way physically abnormal) to form sexual unions with members of the other sex for the purpose of generating successor human beings. Since in the human case upbringing takes so long and is so complicated, these unions have to be enduring and stable. Further, we need to learn and pursue some mode of productive work, in maintaining the ongoing life of our communities. In all these ways, we adopt a mode of life that allows us to contribute through our individual actions, and the ensemble of actions so produced, to the beauty and good order of the whole world-animal and its life. If we are to be virtuous, and live in agreement with nature, we do these things because we understand that this is how the world-mind wishes and indeed intends us to live, using our own powers of reason to govern ourselves "more perfectly" than nature itself governs the lives of plants and nonrational animals, but following the same basic patterns, and objectives, that we see nature itself exhibiting—as I have just explained.

Most adult human beings already find themselves with natural inclinations in favor of many of these actions of a "natural" life: people, I suppose, feel naturally inclined toward marriage, and childbearing and child rearing, or of course at least toward eating and drinking many foods that are healthy and wholesome, and toward many other of the normal activities of life indicated above.[42] It is surely rarely or never, however, that these inclinations would lead us, if simply followed, toward some appropriately limited indulgences in food and drink and so on, as virtue requires. Here we see the corrupting influence of our upbringing in communities dominated by adult humans with very unnatural ideas about the value of food and drink and bodily pleasure in general in our lives. But since virtue requires acting not just in accordance with nature, but in agreement with its thoughts and intentions too, it is not virtuous ever to use our reason in producing our impulses, and our consequent actions, only to the extent of accepting and acting on whatever natural inclinations we happen to find ourselves with. Those inclinations are, indeed, in part, a residue from our management by nature earlier in our lives through natural instincts, and so are to that extent healthy and natural for us to feel. But in addition, we will certainly have some inclinations deriving from that earlier time that reflect the bad ideas introduced into our ways of feeling as we grow up through the influence on us of the bad ideas of our elders. These latter inclinations may *seem* to us to be equally "natural," but they are not; they must be eliminated or restrained.

In any event, the full use of reason in crafting our adult impulses, for which the world-mind bestows reason on us, involves our not forming our impulses directly through the acceptance of any inclination, whether in fact natural or not, as if simply having such an inclination gave us any reason to desire or to do anything. Rather, we only use our rational powers fully through our own critical reflection, reaching the conclusion that the world-mind does indeed wish and intend for us to form any given impulse in favor of any given objective, whether or not it is also the object of any such inclination. It is those reasons that we en-

---

[42] Perhaps these inclinations, consisting in impressions of such things as being of significant value, are in part residues from premature nonrational desires, arising naturally during one's upbringing and growth to maturity.

dorse, if we act not only in accord, but in agreement with, and obedience to, the world-mind. If we are virtuous, we have to be aware that, and why, the world-mind wants us to have these impulses, and wants us to act on them when and to the extent that it is right for us to do so—whether or not, again, it is also part of the overall and total intentions of the world-mind that we also achieve the external objectives that we adopt in having those impulses, or making those decisions, as to what to try to bring about. We have these reason-generated impulses, and we act on them, as *our* contributions to the overall fantastically beautiful and well-ordered sequence of events that constitutes the life history of the world-animal of which we are crucially important parts. In fact, it often happens that it is correct to want and decide to bring something about in the outer world, to want to achieve something specific—yet, we do not succeed. That means, but it only means, that the maximally good history of the world required something else to happen there and then. There is no reason to think that *our* (or our wishes') being therein frustrated was itself any inherent part of what might make the world history including instead this other event, maximally complex and well ordered (and so, more complex and well ordered than if our wished-for outcome had been included). Hence, if we are to live in agreement with nature we must accept gladly this event, even if it does go against our antecedent wish and our antecedent efforts. Both our wishes and efforts, if correctly adopted and pursued, and this outcome are parts of the same maximally good order of world events.

There is another way that the requirement that one's impulses and actions be in agreement with nature shows itself. This comes to a focus in the difficult and even infamous Stoic doctrine of the "indifference" (in a certain way that I will explain as we proceed) of all things other than virtuous action itself (and its accompanying states of mind). That doctrine implies that all ordinary objectives of action (when an action brings about some state of affairs) are "indifferent"— that, in some way that I will explain, it does not matter, and should not matter to the agent who pursues an external objective, whether it is actually achieved. Only the effort matters. This is one important basis for the Stoic rejection of all emotions, which I discussed briefly above but postponed for further discussion, in section 4.8 below. For now, the point to notice is that if our impulses and decisions are to be kept in agreement with nature, they must be formed in such a way as to treat the external objectives of all our actions as "indifferent."

We can best approach this doctrine by comparing human life with the lives of plants and animals of other species. Obviously, one thing the study of the course of nature, when we observe plant, animal, and human life, tells us, is that it certainly does not always happen that when an animal does behave normally and naturally, and so forms a desire to do something, it succeeds in getting done what it desired. Likewise plants, while behaving normally and naturally, do not always achieve the natural goals at which those behaviors are aimed. Plants wither, dry up, and die before developing into flourishing members of their species and living out their normal life span. Nonetheless, we can, by such observation, determine that there is a normal life span, and there is a fairly specific set of ongoing, orderly and ordered, well-connected activities that constitute flourishing for such a plant. Analogous points apply for nonrational animals too. We can tell that what the world-mind intends for the different species of plants and animals, under normal conditions and circumstances for a plant or animal of its kind, is precisely a flourishing life for that kind of living thing, over the normal life span for the given species. That is the contribution of this species to the beauty and order of the world-animal's life. However, for reasons that of course we have no clue about ourselves, it sometimes, even perhaps often, happens that the contribution required in the case of some particular plant or animal is some departure from the norm for its species. Nature does not give a plant sufficient water or nutriment, or causes it to contract some disease. Here the norm for the species is being violated. But we know that nature always works for the best. It always works to maintain the steady flow of events that taken as a whole constitutes the maximally good life history of the world. Hence we know, though only in extremely vague and general terms, that in the case of that particular individual plant its best contribution to the life history of the world was to wither and die, exactly as and when it did. That is so even if it is quite clear that a flourishing healthy life over a given life span—denied to this individual plant—is what, for each type of plant, constitutes that species' contribution.

Corresponding things happen with nonrational animals and their lives. This includes, as a special case, the nonrational animals that are young human children. Sometimes, even perhaps, to us, surprisingly often, nature maims and destroys these beautiful things that it creates; in the human case, children do not grow into healthy adolescents, ready to take over their own self-management through their own developing rational powers, but die or become disablingly diseased or are maimed in some way or other. With our very limited understanding of the overall life of the world-animal, and of just what the good order and beauty of that life consists in over time, we might tend to expect that a fully flourishing life, led over a normal span, would be the overwhelmingly frequent outcome, produced by nature itself, for all the members of all its nonrational ani-mal creations. To be sure, when we take rational animals into account and their effects on animal life, we might be prepared to find that, with human minds producing some of the events in other animals' lives, all kinds of disasters would occur. Humans, we know, are capable of doing horribly bad things to plants and animals. Observation shows that disastrous deviations from natural norms cer-tainly do sometimes occur in the lives of pampered domesticated animals, as well as wild animals when frivolously hunted or otherwise interfered with by hu-mans. (We see disasters in the lives of human beings themselves, too, from the same source.) But with the enormously more powerful world-mind, possessing, of course, hugely greater rational understanding, we might expect otherwise. But we see that it is not so. It is merely naïve sentimentalism to think the world-mind aims at a flourishing life over a normal life span in all or even any large majority of individual cases. There is nothing in that to be surprised about; the world-mind is concerned always about the overall beauty and good order of the totality of events constituting the world-animal's life, not in any preferential way about the life of any individual animal.[43]

Bearing in mind these features of plant and animal life, as directed by the world-mind on its own (even if often enough interfered with by misguided human beings), let us turn now to the case of human life. We adult human be-ings, unlike plants and the other animals, plan and lead our own lives, as inde-pendent causes of our own decisions and actions through our possession of rea-soning minds. But the world-mind behaves always in that same, nonpreferential way in relation to us; nor could we at all reasonably expect it to behave other-wise. People are often born maimed, they fall debilitatingly ill, die from unavoid-able natural causes, or from landslides or floods or other natural disasters; they

[43] Cicero reports Chrysippus (*On Moral Ends* III 67) as saying that "everything else was created for the sake of men and gods," i.e., not also for the sake of any other living things, or for the sake of lifeless materi-als or objects and any beauty they might provide, simply on their own; but men and gods exist "for the sake of their own mutual community and society." The material world and all the plants and animals were created in order that reason (in god and in rational animals) would have an arena in which to express it-self. On this Stoic view of divine providential concern for human beings alone, for their own sake, provi-dence does not extend to anything about individual human beings except their provision with the powers of rationality. That is all that is needed to enable humans to participate with the gods in the running of the world-order, through the mutual community and society of gods and humans, which is the ultimate pur-pose for which a cosmos was ever formed in the first place. It is vicious sentimentalism, antithetical to Stoic ideas about divine providential concern for humans, to suppose that god has any special concern for how any human being's life goes, so far as bodily or material or social advantages may go. If someone gets what he wanted and tried to get, or does not suffer some ordinary "disaster," for the Stoics it would be vi-ciously sentimental of them to want to thank god for that.

frequently fail in their most ordinary efforts to sustain lives of normal physical and social flourishing, comparable to the flourishing lives of plants and nonrational animals. Accordingly, we find ourselves in what to us can seem an awkward position. On the one hand, if we are virtuous, we can understand what pattern of life we ought to live, and even, in given circumstances, what activities and actions, aimed at achieving what external objectives, to decide on. These are the ones that are according to nature, that is, according to the natural norm for members of our human species. We will want to be and remain healthy, and otherwise live a fully "natural" life for a member of our species, as sketched above. We also know that all that we ourselves—our minds, that is—control is how we think and decide, and how we act, to the small extent to which acting consists simply in the initial movement in our soul's "command center" caused by that decision. After that, the world-mind controls what happens: various of our internal bodily parts have to move in ways that will lead to our limbs moving in such ways as to constitute the outer action intended, if we are to do what we wish to do, and have decided to do. The world-mind controls those processes. And, even more crucially, the causal structures in place, on which our outer bodily movements act as we attempt to carry out our intention, must cooperate with us, if we are to succeed in achieving our objective. This too is not at all under our own control,[44] but under the direct control instead of the world-mind.[45] We know full well that in all the world's species the world-mind very often does not operate so as to allow outcomes to be achieved that would contribute to a naturally flourishing life for an individual plant or animal.

On the other hand, we know that for every individual plant and animal the world-mind sets under way from the beginning and maintains even up to its death natural processes that aim in each case at a well-defined sort of life as their natural ends. (That is what happens even when, after growing properly for a time,

---

[44] Except to the extent that we may reasonably have anticipated the effects of specific efforts of our own upon that environment, given reasonable understandings of the causal principles at work in it, and have taken steps in advance to alter it.

[45] Except to the extent that other human beings may be involved, with their own decisions and the consequences thereof. It is up to us, if that matters, to attempt by persuasion, etc., to coordinate our own decisions with those of others. But for present purposes we can ignore or bracket these effects of other human rational agents, since even in their case any results in the outer world of their decisions will have a huge cooperating component coming from the world-mind's thoughts and decisions. Effectively, we can regard all that happens after we have decided and acted (in the minimal sense of causing the needed movement in our soul's "command center"), and especially all events out in the common world, as caused by the world-mind.

a plant withers.) So in our case too, we can make our decisions, and make our efforts to produce given outcomes that we have decided—entirely correctly—are the ones that living according to nature calls for us to bring about, if possible, in the given conditions and circumstances. But we also have to bear in mind, even as we make the decision and attempt to carry it out, that whether that outcome is achieved depends upon whether the world-mind has intended it, in this individual case, as a contribution to the overall maximally beautiful and well-ordered sequence of world events. Whatever does happen will be the outcome jointly of our own and the world-mind's decisions, but just which outcome results depends overwhelmingly greatly on the latter decision, not on our own. And we know practically nothing about what the world-mind can see is needed in any individual case; the total history of world events and its beauty is well beyond our ken, at this level of detail. So, having decided on the course of action to undertake, and having undertaken it, we have no clue as to what now ought to happen, that is, what is the best result of our efforts. However, we know (as I have explained already) that no matter what does happen, it will be a member of the fantastically beautiful and good sequence of events making up the world-animal's life. So, as rational animals ourselves that are devoted to this overall good in all our actions, and concerned to apply proper standards for determining how, in light of this devotion, it is rational for us to desire any given outcome, we cannot desire it in any absolute way. We must decide on, and desire, the specific action, and the objectives of that action, as the thing to do now. Yet we must decide on it, and want it, not in any absolute way, but, so to speak, only if Zeus or the world-mind also wills it. We cannot regret or be disappointed in anything that does happen, even if, in advance, it was what we had correctly decided to prevent, by aiming at some exclusive alternative, which we had tried our hardest to produce.[46] If we are virtuous, our overriding desire is always to help produce the best possible next stage in the overall life of the world; we correctly thought that some particular outcome was the one that living in accordance with nature required us to aim at. But we were wrong that that was also the best next stage in the world's overall best life, as we were, however, right to think it would be when

---

[46] By regret or disappointment here I mean simply a judgment or sense that one's desire and action have been frustrated by events, or have failed of fruition. One might go beyond that, and experience an agitated feeling (an "emotion," or in Stoic terms a πάθος) that might also be called regret or disappointment, instigating or including recriminations, outrage, a sense of having been offended, etc. That is a further matter, however; see my discussion of emotions below.

we aimed at it, and in aiming at it. Regret or disappointment at the actual out-come, or at our failure to achieve the one we were aiming for, would be entirely inappropriate, in light of the full character of our desire.[47]

This is undoubtedly, as I have said, a delicate and an awkward position to find oneself in. Just consider a couple of examples. First, there is the hackneyed, and somewhat maudlin, case of a virtuous mother or father whose young children die an excruciating death in a house fire despite their vigorous efforts to save them, and despite grave risk of serious bodily harm to themselves, or even death. On the Stoic theory, once it has happened, the virtuous person must greet this event as one among the truly beautiful ones in the fantastically beautiful overall se-quence of world events (even if they have little or no real idea how it does fit in so beautifully). Hence it would be a serious error to regret it, and a virtuous per-son could not regret it. That sounds shocking. A virtuous person, we would or-dinarily think, must not lightly dismiss such a loss; only a hard-hearted cad could react that way. Moreover, as we have seen, in deciding to make those efforts, the virtuous person has to embed in the decision, implicitly at least, the reservation "if, but only if, this salvation is also being willed by Zeus." Stoic theory requires that, in order to be fully virtuous, we learn how to combine a before-the-fact extremely strong, fully committed intention and desire, based in one's love of one's children and devotion to their welfare, to save them from death in the fire, with an openness to joyfully greeting the adverse outcome. Many people when learning of the Stoic theory feel (and this was so also already in antiquity) that this is an impossible combination. Such a conditional intention can seem too weak for fully virtuous people who love their children to act from in such a case.

These apparent difficulties may be felt less dramatically in other sorts of case, but they are present in even the most mundane actions and events of virtuous persons' daily life. They may decide, as part of the particular work they do, to spend the day in some interesting and challenging task. But before they get far into it something may arise that takes them off, into some routine and fairly bor-ing aspects of their position, on which they have to spend the rest of the day in-stead. The advance decision to spend the workday in the more interesting way reflects the agent's view (and, being virtuous, they are right about this) that, given the combination of their particular talents and personal interests, the par-ticular work they have decided to do is not just personally quite, or most, satisfy-

---

[47] One might, I suppose, regret that one has turned out, despite one's best judgment, to have been wrong about which outcome would constitute the world's best next stage. But that is, again, another matter.

ing, but that, partly because it is satisfying to them, its activities constitute a particularly well-ordered and fine contribution to make to the world's overall good order and beauty. Moreover, so far as they can see at the moment of decision, these are the ones to opt for spending their time on during that day, in order to make their optimal contribution to the world's good order. Part of the beauty of the world consists in the interlocking combination of many different human activities of many different sorts, all done by different people especially suited for each. Yet, when they are interrupted and have to abandon that work for some more mundane and boring routines, they do not merely undertake the latter gladly enough (in the spirit of accepting the inevitable). They do so with the thought that, contrary to their first impression and decision, the activities they can now engage in that will make the best contribution to the world's life are these alternative ones—in themselves, less well-ordered and beautiful, rather boring and routine activities.

It is easy for those of us who have not learned to lead our lives in the Stoic way to feel that impossible demands are being placed on us. We may feel that we cannot both have the commitment required to embark on the day of interesting work in a spirit that reflects the initial judgment about its worth, and then undertake the alternative work with the idea that, no, something else instead in fact has that worth. However, we must be careful here. As I mentioned earlier, our feelings about these cases may simply reflect the Platonic-Aristotelian moral psychology that has become so deeply ingrained in our modern cultures (and so, in our modern philosophical theories). Perhaps we cannot envisage such a possible combination only because we look at ourselves and our lives through the lenses of that psychological outlook: we think of the original decision as involving, on our part, an emotional attachment to engaging in certain activities with zest, which cannot not give rise to a corresponding feeling (at least somewhat agitated) of regret or disappointment or slight depression or annoyance or exasperation, when we must abandon the decision. Our shock felt at Stoic virtuous persons' reaction to the loss of their children in a fire may be due to the same phenomenon. I will return below to consider the philosophical strengths and weaknesses of Stoic versus Platonic-Aristotelian theories of moral psychology. For the moment, however, we need simply to realize that, on the Stoic theory of virtuous action, as action in full agreement with the world-mind's thoughts and decisions, any virtuous commitment to the value (in itself, and in relation to the agent pursuing it) of any objective of human decision and action is hedged about in such a way as to make it a matter of indifference whether that objective is actually achieved by one's decision or action. One is to be equally content either way things turn out. We ought not to be too quick, simply on the basis of prejudices deriving from our unthinking adherence to the Platonic-Aristotelian moral psychology, to believe that such hedging about must necessarily render the commitment too weak to support a full moral pursuit of the values that are at stake when we act, as morally virtuous people, to protect or advance some important objective for our action.

In fact, the world-mind's responsibility for everything except human beings' decisions, together with their "basic actions" of causing movements in their souls' "command centers," has a further consequence. Virtuous persons must have no differential regard at all for any external circumstances or bodily conditions affecting their lives—even without regard, as in my discussion so far, to these being possibly unattained or aborted objectives of their action. Whether one is poor rather than rich, or handsome rather than ugly, healthy rather than sickly, a slave rather than a free person, or, on some occasion, subject to insurmountable pain as against great bodily pleasure; whether one is famous or obscure, or honored or despised (or just ignored and dismissed) by the people among whom one lives; whether one has a happy, harmonious, mutually supportive family life, with an admirable spouse and lovely, good children, rather than (through no fault of one's own) messy and ugly personal circumstances— all this must be recognized as establishing conditions for one's life that the world-mind has decided upon for its own good reasons (reasons, it should be carefully noted, having nothing to do with any special wishes, one way or the other, about oneself). By deciding and acting virtuously within the given such context, whatever it may be, one can be confident that one will be making the best-ordered and most beautiful contribution to the life of the whole world that one possibly can. Virtuous people according to the Stoic analysis must be morally indifferent as to which of these sorts of conditions for their life they are presented with. The task of acting virtuously may require different specific decisions and actions depending upon the conditions, but it remains in essence precisely the same.

However, we must not forget that observation of nature teaches the virtuous that the positive members among these and other such alternatives are "according to nature" and the negatives contrary to it—in general. That is because, as I explained above, the world-mind or nature itself operates with a set of norms for human beings and human life, that establish the contours of a "natural" life that includes bodily health and strength, cooperative and mutually supportive relations with other people, a harmonious family life with good children developing into serious, decent adults, and satisfying work to do—all carried out in the conditions of political and social freedom. This indicates that the world-mind's plan for the members of the human species includes the judgment that, unless some other considerations override this in given cases, the virtuous life of persons living under those favored circumstances is more complex, richer, better-ordered, more beautiful, than virtuous ones not lived in that "natural" way. Virtuous human life under circumstances of the contrary sort is only exceptionally a contribution to the maximally good life of the whole world-animal. The normal thing, and therefore the one for any human being to prefer, and so to bring into existence for himself or herself if at all possible, is to live under the "natural" circumstances, on the basis of the positive elements in the sets of alternatives sketched just now.

Thus it is not true that virtue, for the Stoics, calls for absolute indifference, either as to the circumstances and conditions of one's life, or as to whether or not one's moral efforts succeed in achieving the external objectives that they are from time to time directed toward achieving. Stoic virtuous persons have well-reasoned preferences as to the circumstances and conditions of their lives, and if they happen to find themselves living in substandard conditions or circumstances, as measured by those preferences, they will undertake vigorous efforts to remedy them. Likewise when they decide on objectives to pursue in their virtuous actions—saving the life of a child in danger, enjoying a suitable meal, devoting their work time to the more interesting and challenging aspects of it, and all the host of other actions they will decide on and do, as the kaleidoscope of daily life situations turns itself—they definitely do pursue those with a fully differential pursuit, rejecting alternatives as not to be pursued then, either in addition or instead. They have excellent reasons for wanting the outcomes they are trying to achieve, and they give them the fullest force of psychological commitment possible for a human being in pursuing them. They do, however, have a psychologically complex set of attitudes as regards these preferences, as we can call them, both as to conditions and circumstances, and as regards these objectives of their actions. They are always ready to accept substandard conditions that they have not been able to change, and they are always ready to accept (indeed to rejoice in) outcomes that go against their advance objectives and against their efforts to achieve them. Whenever they have to accept them as out of their control, that results from what they recognize is a decision by the world-mind that selects them because they form part of the fantastically well-ordered and beautiful progress of world events.

So Stoic "indifference," as to the circumstances of our lives, and as to whether or not we succeed in achieving our morally approved objectives, is by no means absolute. There is one further step to take, however—the final and theoretically crucial one—before we can complete our understanding of the Stoics' view about how everything except virtuous action itself (together with the states of mind that accompany it) really is (in a way) a matter of indifference. Once, in the next section, we take that last step, we will be ready to see how and why, for the Stoics, the best life for a human being is one in which one does all one's moral duties, for their own sakes, and one, indeed, in which the goodness wholly *consists* in dutiful actions.

4.6. What Is Good vs. What Is Merely of Some Value

We are accustomed (since this practice seems embedded in all human cultures, and certainly in the one in which we have been brought up) to count our experiences, or things we possess or acquire, or events that happen, as good (for us), anyhow to some extent or in some way, if they satisfy or fulfill desires that we happen to have. Perhaps this applies to any desires whatsoever, or, at least, it applies to all desires with only the exception of those that seem outright depraved or thoroughly evil. Other things can be good too, we think—things that may not satisfy any desire of ours directly—insofar as they positively affect the satisfaction of some of our desires. One might go so far as to say that for the "folk" theory of ethics—the theory that expresses the view embedded in ordinary people's prephilosophical or pretheoretical ideas—good just is, at bottom and in the last analysis, satisfaction of desire. That seems to reflect, in turn, a perhaps deeper "folk" ethical view. This view holds that, ultimately, the quality of a human life, for better or worse, is simply constituted by the degree and balance of desire-satisfaction or desire-frustration that it contains. On this understanding, good is done us, and our lives go better, simply—and, at bottom, exclusively—insofar as we get something we want (and, perhaps, continue to want after we get it). It goes badly insofar as some desire of ours is disappointed or frustrated. If you enjoy what you are doing, if you succeed in any undertaking (provided, of course, that you continue to want whatever it was after achieving it), if you are pleased with your circumstances and conditions—then, your life is going well. And contrariwise, if you are dissatisfied or disappointed in any way, then, to that extent, your life is going badly. On this view, many external and bodily conditions we may find ourselves in, as well as many psychological states—ones that enable, or interfere with, the satisfaction of desire—count as good or bad for us. So do everything we may have wanted to possess and use or, simply, everything we wanted to happen, provided of course we continue to want it.

Thus, the quality of a human life, as good or bad, depends, directly or indirectly, and in either case essentially, upon how we stand in relation to those other goods, the ones that satisfy or frustrate our particular desires. Bodily health and pleasure, wealth, warm and otherwise comfortable physical surroundings, all kinds of prized accomplishments and victories, more or less innate psychological conditions such as overall cheerfulness or resilience, many acquired physical or mental abilities and skills—all these count as goods for us, and affect our lives for the better, by being present, or for the worse, by their absence, simply because of their relation to the satisfaction or frustration of our desires. In any event—whether because of some implicit commitment to the satisfaction-of-desire theory of the good, or not—it does seem to be a fundamental "folk" idea that health, and wealth, and bodily pleasure, and all kinds of sought-after external accomplishments and recognitions, are in themselves good things for a human being.

It is a central contention of Stoic theory that such "folk" ideas are mistaken—root and branch mistaken; they are fundamentally on the wrong track. In order to capture correctly important facts about human nature and, in consequence, about what is good or bad so far as a human life is concerned, the Stoics think we must distinguish sharply between things that are merely "of some value" for us (as we concern ourselves, as we all do and ought to do, with our individual personal lives and interests), and those that are actually "good" or bad.[48] They are well aware that that is an unfamiliar idea: we normally think of "valuable" and "good" as more or less interchangeable terms. It goes strongly against ordinary usage, and ordinary thought, to declare that all the things counted in the previous paragraph as good or bad for us are in fact only (at most) of some positive or negative value in relation to us, and for our lives—but, nonetheless, not good or

---

[48] Cicero gives a reasonably clear account of this difference in *On Moral Ends* III 33–34 (see also 21–23), but without offering much help as to the Stoics' reasons for thinking that there is such a difference. See also Diogenes Laertius VII 101–6, and Arius Didymus 7f and 7g (excerpts in Long and Sedley, 58D and E), for some additional details.

bad at all. What could the intended difference be between (mere) value, and goodness or badness? What reason do the Stoics have for thinking that all these things that are ordinarily valued as being good or bad, at least to some degree or in some way, have some other—lesser—status as things (only) of value? What value could anything have, if it was not by being good or bad, in itself, and/or for any good or bad effects it might have?

In order to answer these questions we need to revert to our earlier discussion.[49] There we saw that on Stoic theory human beings, through their rationality, are called to the high task of living in agreement with the rationality of god or nature. Reason, or god or nature, is spread through the whole world and everything in it, but reason is present in a self-conscious way only in human beings, among the vast creation laid out for our scrutiny and for us to voluntarily interact with in leading our lives. We are, by our natures as rational beings, and through our creation by the world-mind, partners of that mind (god, Zeus). We can work, within Zeus's amazingly complex cosmic plan, to achieve the maximally good whole sequence of world events—this is the good at which Zeus's reason constantly aims—through the contribution made to that sequence by our own thoughts, choices, and voluntary actions, all of which of course count as among those events. What however does the goodness of this sequence consist in? And what makes for goodness in our own thoughts, choices, and voluntary actions (if they are good at all—i.e., if they are correctly aimed at helping to achieve the maximally good sequence of world events, in cooperation with Zeus)? As we have seen, on Stoic principles our highest good as individuals is achieved in, and depends solely upon, a lifetime of such actions. So in asking, in the same question, about the goodness in the maximally and fantastically good life of the world-animal at large, and the (potential) goodness in our own much more modest lives, we are assuming that there is a single characteristic or property of goodness that is realizable in these two different contexts. Given what we have learned about our own natures as rational beings, and the nature of the world at large as a rational nature as well, this is as it should be. Whatever, given our natures, we ought to aim at, as our own fulfillment, should be of the same kind as what the rationality of god or nature itself aims at.

Here the Stoics, apparently following inexplicit hints in Plato's discussions of the good in the *Republic*,[50] propose the following idea. As to the world as a whole

---

[49] Section 4.5.

[50] I am thinking here of Socrates's account of the nature of the good in *Rep.* VI, 504d, to the end of book VII.

and its total history, from beginning to end, they identify the good in it with the overarching and interlocking orderliness of the world and its parts, and the strictly interconnecting and mutually supporting order among all the activities that make up its life, over time. Anything that happens anywhere in the world, as the seasons and years proceed in their orderly way, has some connection, some causal relation, to everything that happens anywhere else, or at any other time. In the orderly, developing life of the whole world-animal, from its creation to its eventual destruction, we see a beautifully and intricately connected, mutually supporting progress of processes and events. That is what is so good about it. So likewise, then, for us, our good must consist in the similarly interconnecting and mutually supporting order both among our actions themselves, in making up our lives, taken one by one (if and when we do indeed act in full agreement with Zeus's thoughts and intentions), and taken together with all the other events making up the world-animal's life.[51] Thus we reach the vision of a possibility for our own lives. On this possibility, all the daily round of activities and interests that constitute the basis for our lives as we live out our given life spans, through maturity to old age and finally death, all our desires, all our actions fit together and produce (given the constraints we face coming from natural events outside our control) a maximally well-ordered and beautiful unity. Goodness just is rational order—perfected, complete, rational order, in whatever it belongs to, the whole world, or our own lives as part of it.

Hence we can see that not only is living in agreement with nature our highest good; it is the only good that we can achieve, on our own, and for ourselves. Every other good in the universe—however much, as rational beings, we may be pleased by it, and even rejoice in it—is produced by Zeus himself in governing the life of the world. To be sure, when, as virtuous people, we live in agreement with Zeus's plan, we always have some more particular objective in any of our actions—as well as the objective of living in agreement with nature, and so of achieving our own personal good. The particular objective, not the constant goal of living in agreement, gives each of our actions the particular shape and sequential structure that it has. Indeed, a considerable part of the interconnecting order among our actions, taken on their own as making up our single life, as well as their orderly relationship to the order of the rest of the world's events, consists in the way that actions can all fit together, over time, though shaped and sequentially structured differently, to suit different circumstances as they arise. But the

---

[51] Cicero attempts to expound this part of the Stoic ethical theory in *On Moral Ends* III 21 and 33, not perhaps, as it seems, with much success in explaining it and its philosophical foundations.

good of and in our actions consists solely in that order among the given action, its circumstances, and prior and subsequent actions of our own, plus the actions of Zeus himself or itself. The more particular objective of the given action is not itself anything good: some bodily pleasure we might correctly pursue, or some accomplishment or outcome we might rightly work to obtain, does not seem even to be the right sort of thing to qualify as good (or bad, either). Nor is the action, considered as an act of pursuing or obtaining that objective, the right sort of thing to count as good. That follows from the fact that what it is to be good—the essence of goodness, as we could say—consists in the overall fit of one action to others, one's own and Zeus's. Taken on its own, the action, for example, of saving one's children from death or severe injury by fire, considered simply as done for the sake of that salvation (or with wider consequences also taken into account, such as continuing one's life with them as their parents, or their grow-ing to maturity, enjoying life with their friends, and so on) cannot be good; nor can the salvation itself, as such, if achieved.

On the other hand, correctly selected objectives, and actions insofar as they are done for the sake of them, clearly do have some value, for the agent, but also, very likely, often enough, for other persons concerned. A well-planned and nu-tritious meal must have some value for those who eat it (assuming they are of normal health). In my earlier example, what can we say about the value, to the parent or to the children, of the salvation, and of the act itself of saving consid-ered on its own? As we have already seen, the particular objectives of each of a virtuous person's actions are given by norms for living a human life that are pro-vided by the study of nature and by well thought-through inferences as to na-ture's general plans for the flourishing physical and social life of each natural kind of living thing, and so of our human kind. These objectives, and achieving them, are therefore in fact valuable (objectively valuable) just insofar as they do conform to those norms. Put otherwise, they are valuable to or for any human agent, or for any human beneficiary there might be of their action, just insofar as they are in accordance with nature—in the way I have explained.[52] As a virtuous person, one is attached to these objectives, and to the actions of pursuing them (simply as such) because one sees in them the patterns of living that realize to their fullest nature's intentions for members of our natural kind—a pattern that will in general be the one that fits best with the rest of the world's actions over time, and that in itself constitutes the special beauty of this species' contribution

---

[52] See above, sections 4.2 and 4.5.

to the overall beauty of the ongoing life of the world-animal as a whole. This pattern establishes norms for our ways of relating to our bodies and what goes on within them, and to our changing external circumstances. It establishes norms also for our interests in the inanimate or nonrational living things around us, for profit or pleasure, for example, and for our interests in the human beings as well, as potential partners in social life in our human communities. Health, money, and other material resources, bodily pleasure and the avoidance of bodily pain, enjoyable and challenging work and leisure-time activities—in fact most of the sorts of things people generally do care about most, even exclusively—are things we have very good reason to concern ourselves over. They are part of an ideal of life for a member of our species that nature establishes for us. These all have quite a bit of value, and their absence or negation quite a bit of disvalue, for each of us.

If we are virtuous, we hold this ideal of a natural life before ourselves, as something worth achieving (if possible) and something we have reason to care about, something in fact that we do care about. None of these things is good, either in itself or for us, but each of them is a valuable thing to have in a human life. A life lived without any of them or with their opposites is lacking in something of value, and in something that we rightly value. Being part of that ideal, they fulfill our aspirations as finite rational beings, whose first concern is, and must be, with the physical, psychological, and social conditions of the life of the specific individual that one is. One could call these things naturally valuable for us, valuable for us as belonging to our specific natural kind. Accordingly, the Stoics are able to argue that what I described earlier as the awkward position that virtuous human beings are in is nonetheless quite sustainable.[53] Virtuous people desire on each occasion some naturally valuable thing as the objective of their specific action at that time,[54] and they pursue whole courses of action grounded in what they rightly see as the value for themselves of the elements of this natural ideal of life. They genuinely do value them, do care about having them, and do care about whether they do have them, or do not. They do their best to obtain and enjoy these things of value.

If they fail, on some occasion, in their effort to achieve them, they recognize that something of value is lacking, and they are ready, if occasion should present

[53] See section 4.5.

[54] This is generally so, but as we can see from a remark of Chrysippus, quoted by Epictetus (*Discourses* II 6, 9), if one does (exceptionally) have sufficiently good reason to think that what the goodness of the world order requires is that one should undergo something in fact naturally disvaluable (e.g., one's own death), the virtuous will desire that, instead. Chrysippus uses the amusing illustration of the human foot: if it had a mind, it would have a desire to get muddied.

itself, and other circumstances make this seem possible, to rectify the lack. They do not, however, confuse this level of value—the value of things belonging to the natural ideal for human life—with the quite distinct sort of value that consists in the goodness of rational order and orderliness in the actions of one's own life, or of the world's life, of which one's own life is but one part. This means, as I said, that they do not regret it if their own efforts fail to produce the valued outcome they were aiming for. But that does not imply any weakness in the initial, before-the-event, desire or concern for the valued thing. It is a full-strength commitment to the natural value of whatever it might be that they correctly judged to have that value. And the after-the-fact acceptance of the contrary outcome, and indeed, it may be, the joy they take in it (for the way that it fits into the fantastically well-ordered and good life of the world), does not imply any retrospective devaluing. The ideal for human life that the virtuous hold before themselves, as they go about living their daily lives, remains unchanged; they continue to recognize the value of the thing now lacking, and continue to be committed to its value, and its value for them. They will take any and every future opportunity that might present itself to them to rectify the lack. They accept not having any of these naturally valuable things that might be denied to them, but that does not at all mean they do not continue to value them—at their true value, their value as being of naturally legitimate interest to them, but not any part of their good. In both respects, in fact—in desiring preferred outcomes as they initiate and sustain efforts to achieve them, and in reacting after the fact to the success or failure of their efforts—the virtuous *feel* (and don't just recognize in thought) the real value of these things for them and for their lives. I will say more, in the next two sections, about the nature and character of these ways of feeling.

4.7. Consequences of the Stoic Theory of Value

It is a consequence of the Stoics' analysis that a human life is not better or worse, happier or less happy, by the presence or absence of any of the naturally valuable or disvaluable things. Nor is a human life made more or less good and happy by either the success or the failure of the actions that make up that life, in obtaining and making the proper and intended use of such valuable things. Goodness or badness of life is solely determined by whether or not one lives in agreement with Zeus's plans. As we have seen at length already, people can (and the virtuous do) live in agreement with Zeus's plans, however they and their lives stand in these other respects. These naturally valuable or disvaluable things are by no means indifferent so far as the natural ideal I have referred to goes: the ideal includes plenty of the valuable ones and does not include many of the disvaluable. But the naturally valuable or disvaluable things are strictly indifferent so far as the goodness and badness, and the happiness or unhappiness, of a life goes. In our cultures today, as well as in ancient times, almost everybody grows up having developed for themselves the mistaken idea (as the Stoics argue that it is) that happiness and the good life are largely (even perhaps exclusively) determined by a preponderance in them of naturally valuable aspects, objects, and experiences. They have imbibed this view from their cultural surroundings, where it is rampant. Holding to this traditional and culturally approved idea is, on the Stoic view, the fundamental error that all vicious people make, which leads them to their mistaken and vicious ways of life. This same error is made even by many whom we might regard as decent and upstanding people, who treat others with respect and due regard for their interests and needs, and refrain on principle from all grosser forms of immorality. Eradicating this error—the error of mistaking the natural ideal as providing a guide for judging the good and happy life—is the central task of Stoic moral training. In fact, for the Stoics, the natural ideal, and the norms that define it, give us only a guide to what to *try* to achieve. The only correct guide to good living, and to our own happiness, given that we are by our nature rational agents, is to live in agreement with Zeus's plans.

Hence, as I have said, on the Stoic analysis, living in agreement with Zeus's plans is not only our highest good, it is our only possible good. And living out of agreement is not only our "highest" bad, it is our only bad. The bad of living that way is not to any degree compensable by any pile of naturally valuable things, or made any worse by any addition of disvaluable things to it. For the Stoics, then, there are no degrees of happiness or unhappiness, nor indeed of virtuousness or viciousness. Either one is living in agreement or one is not; all who are not, no matter how far out of agreement or how near to agreement they may be, are in an equal position, so far as being virtuous or vicious and living unhappily or not is concerned.[55]

[55] Cicero (*On Moral Ends* III 48) and Plutarch (*On Common Conceptions* 1063a) report the Stoics' use of the striking image of a man who drowns in the sea, and drowns equally, whether located only a few inches from the surface, or too many feet below to give him any chance that he might get to the top in time to survive. This does not mean that one person might not be closer to living in agreement, or farther, than another. Nothing in this Stoic doctrine implies any ban on judging people differentially in this respect, and treating them differently, too (punishing some of them, for example, either legally or socially,

It is worth noting the sharp divergence of the Stoics in this respect from Aristotle. Aristotle and the Stoics agree that our highest good lies in living virtuously, with the result that those who do live virtuously also live happily, no matter how they stand with respect to other things of legitimate interest to a human being. But for Aristotle, since he agrees with Socrates and Plato in counting as goods not only virtue but all the mental, external, and bodily conditions that the Stoics only count as naturally valuable, one happy life can be better than another one. If one virtuous person has better luck than another as to their circumstances and in their material successes, then, though both are happy and both live happily, the first person lives more happily than the second, because of the extra measure of mental, bodily, or external goods. In the later Aristotelian tradition, a distinction was made, to mark this difference, between living (merely!) happily and living altogether blessedly.[56] In other words, there can, on Aristotle's analysis, be more total good in one virtuous life than in another. But that is not so on the Stoics'. For the Stoics, what is added in the one life and lacking in the other is no good at all; it is only some set of naturally valuable things, which, as the Stoics carefully explain, cannot correctly be counted as good. Their presence or absence does not affect in one direction or the other the quality, or quantity, of the life, as regards its goodness or badness, and its happiness. It may make things easier or harder, more or less welcome, more or less pleasant; it may make life more or less bearable, more or less of a challenge, more or less interesting. But it does not make a life happier or less happy.

This divergence is based in—certainly it dramatically reflects—the Aristotelian and the Stoic divinities' different relations to the world of nature, and to human life as part of that world. The Stoics recognize a designing god, itself inherent in the world, as the power of reason that shapes all the material things that exist, and instills in them the laws of their natures and behaviors. Aristotle's transcendent divinity (an immaterial, incorporeal, pure "form") engages only in contemplative, theoretical thinking. Its activity is at a much higher and purer

---

and commending others). Not living more virtuously or less viciously than another does not imply not being closer or farther from virtue or vice, or happiness or unhappiness—living better or worse.

[56] See, e.g., Antiochus of Ascalon, as reported in Cicero *On Moral Ends* V (see especially sections 79–95), who distinguishes between happiness itself (the exercise of the virtues) and a higher degree of the same, a blessedness that includes also the full development of every aspect of our nature (physical and mental), and a full provision of all the natural goods. In marking this distinction, Antiochus and other later authors were obviously influenced by Aristotle's discussion in *NE* I 8–10 of what happens in good persons' life if they suffer terrible "blows of fortune," such as Priam, king of Troy, suffered when the Greeks conquered the city. Aristotle himself, however, seems not to have made such a distinction between (mere) happiness and blessedness.

level than any designing, teleological thinking, directed toward the messy material, sensible, world of nature, could possibly be. For Aristotle, all the teleological relationships actually found in the material, sensible world—and these are very extensive, even if not so absolutely pervasive as they are for the Stoics—exist as part of its eternal constitution. No divine thought imposes them upon it as part of any "plan" that it has.[57] Aristotle's cosmic god has no plans for anything. As a result, the practical virtues (for Aristotle, those of habituated character and practical thought) have to be seen as grounded in a conception of human beings as members of a self-standing realm of nature. Our rational powers of self-management do not derive from, reflect, or include (if properly developed) the contents of any divine thinking about how we should live. There can be no use in our own ethical thought for ideas about how to align our intentions, choices, and actions with the thoughts and actions of any cosmic god. In living virtuously, to the extent that we manage that, we are not following the wishes of, or fulfilling any duties imposed on us by, any divine being. We learn about what truly is of value, including what is virtuous, for us through careful attention to ourselves and to our natural needs, as we find them at work in this self-standing natural realm. It is from that process of reflection that we come to realize that our own highest good consists in "assimilation" to the divine nature, through contemplative, theoretical thinking about god and god's activity as the cause of the being of all else that has being. We do not follow any divine plan in reaching that conclusion.

There may be, indeed there definitely are, as Aristotle shows us, hierarchies among things of value, that is to say (for him), among goods. Virtue and virtuous activity are the highest of values, and, of virtuous activities, activity of excellent theoretical thinking ranks as the absolutely highest. But all values for human beings are on a par, so far as being values at all goes. They are all fulfillments of our nature, as we find that existing in the free-standing natural realm. Our natural needs, in terms of bodily states and functions, our needs for enjoyment of appropriate foods and drinks and for interesting and challenging leisure-time activities, and work, as well as for family life and friendships and other naturally appropriate social relations, together with our natural needs in terms of external resources for achieving and maintaining high levels of such functioning and virtuous activity itself—all these establish a large variety of human goods. All these goods make some contribution to the overall goodness,

[57] See above, section 4.3.

and happiness, of any human life. Our nature, although a rational nature, has other needs than, and alongside, the need for high levels of excellent, truth-attaining thought, both practical and theoretical. Our bodily health, all sorts of (true) external goods (i.e., things truly of value), good social circumstances and social relations, useful and productive work, and so on, all make a contribution to human flourishing. Our complex natures require a complex fulfillment, even if, as Aristotle argues, our happiness, the highest good through pursuing which we properly control all our other pursuits and interests, is secured even without the fulfillment of other than our rational capacities—our capacities for rational practical thought and reason-controlled states of nonrational feeling and desire. The Stoic perspective on human nature and human life, as I have explained, is radically different.

The Stoics diverge from Aristotle's point of view in ethical theory in a second major way, as I have already noted (section 4.4 above). This concerns their rejection of the Platonic-Aristotelian theory of moral psychology, with its three distinct kinds of human desire. As we saw above, this preference is the basis for their notorious rejection of all "emotions" or "passions" as bad states of mind, to be avoided under all circumstances. The virtuous person, on the Stoic account, will never experience such states of mind and feeling, whereas Aristotelian virtue (i.e., moral or habituated virtue, on Aristotle's account) consists in states of mind or feeling in which emotions are felt, but in a moderate way, so as to be (allegedly) keyed correctly to what is appropriate to the specific circumstances and context of action. In close alignment with his acceptance of a wide range of types of goods that human nature (he thinks) establishes for us as goods, Aristotle holds (as does Plato) that part of our permanent natural endowment, as human animals, is capacities for appetitive desires for pleasure and spirited desires for self-assertion, or for competitive self-expression and self-esteem as agents. These are the psychological bases in human nature for all the emotions or passions—sexual love, anger, grief, envy, fear, gnawing disappointment and regret, elation at successes, and so on. These natural powers or capacities have a legitimate claim to fulfillment, as fundamental aspects of human nature (understood, as Aristotle understands it, as part of a self-standing realm of nature). They are the original, natural, bases for our attachments to many of those human goods, and for our avoidance of the bad things, that I have mentioned above: suitable food and drink, sex, achievements in social life, avoidance of bodily harm, and so on. For Aristotle, our total fulfillment as human beings requires the due fulfillment of these capacities through satisfying their desires in obtaining these goods, or avoiding these bads, in due proportions and in due circumstances. And along with that goes his acceptance of the value, and indeed goodness, of emotions of many sorts, all, of course, in due proportion, and all in due relation to our circumstances. It is good (and a significant part of the good human life) to feel appropriate emotions and appropriate appetites for pleasure, simply because these (nonrational) emotions and desires are our natural basis for being attached to, and for caring about, a very large number of the types of things that are naturally good (or bad) for a human being, on Aristotle's account of the good.

As we have already seen, the Stoics reject the Platonic-Aristotelian tripartite psychology of desire, and deprive themselves of all these seemingly attractive consequences for moral theory. They reasonably think that Socrates (as presented in Plato's and Xenophon's Socratic dialogues) provided them with a precedent for rejecting the Platonic-Aristotelian theory of human desires as coming in three kinds, two nonrational and one rational. According to what seemed to be Socrates's view, all actual desires of adult human beings (full psychic impulses to action, not mere inclinations to be so moved) derive from and reflect the person's judgment, as a rational agent, in favor of whatever it is that is being desired, or against what is being avoided. In adult human beings, there are no nonrational desires, for bodily pleasure or spirited satisfactions, for example. Desires for bodily pleasures or self-esteem and competitive success, when they do arise in mature human life, derive from the agent's judgment, on the occasion, in favor of pursuing and experiencing those things. In short, of the three types of human desires postulated by Plato (e.g., in the *Republic*) and Aristotle, Socrates thought there was only one: the rational type. There were, for him, no nonrational desires at all that arise in the minds or souls of a mature human being (small children and animals are a different matter). Unfortunately, we do not learn much about Socrates's reasons for adopting this view. People like us, who have been brought up to think of, and experience, ourselves in the psychologically more complex terms of Plato and Aristotle, may, as I indicated above,[58] find Socrates's view simply naïve, even grossly implausible psychologically. We might think that introspection into our own experience shows that we do experience plenty of nonrational urges and desires, and act from them quite a lot of the time, rather than, or in addition to, from rational ones whether based on our considered ideas about what is good and bad for us, or on temporarily maintained, rash, and self-indulgent ones.

[58] See section 4.4.

But the Stoics were not merely following the precedent of a distinguished philosopher (and disregarding Plato's analyses in the *Republic*) in opting for the more unitary Socratic psychology of human desire and action. They seem to have found it a more persuasive account. This was at least in part because it fits extremely well with their prior commitments as regards divine reason, and the human relationship to it—while the Platonic-Aristotelian one clashes badly. Zeus, the cosmic reason, designs the world and is responsible for all its events. Our own individual powers of reason are parts of that cosmic power. Zeus is an agent that causes effects simply through deciding on them, that is, simply by the inherent, and essential, power of his thought. Reason, in basic Stoic metaphysics, is the purely and entirely active power, whereas matter is pure passivity, pure readiness to take on qualities imposed by reason's decisions. Zeus decides in each case on grounds that refer the thing or event decided always to a single overall objective: namely, to cause that world to exist, and that series of events in its life, that will constitute the optimally complex, mutually adjusted and supporting, and fully ordered, world, and history of world events. Our minds are subordinate, though much less comprehending, parts of this whole. Each of our minds is associated with some single living, material body that exists only for a limited time. Our (natural) concern is, in the first instance, with the well ordering of our natural substance and its life during that time, however long it turns out to be, in accordance with the standards provided through the guidance of the natural ideal for human life that I have referred to. In the second instance, in the way I have explained, our natural concern is also with carrying out these functions in agreement with the cosmic reason's other plans, that is, in agreement with its overall plan for the whole world. In carrying out these functions, the same power of agency, as minds, must belong to us as belongs to the cosmic mind, of which we are parts. We too must act on decisions that we arrive at for reasons having to do with ideas of what is good, however limitedly perceptive our ideas might be. No more in our case than in Zeus's can there be other forces within us capable of producing actions, and causing events, in the world. Mind—the power of reason—is the only ultimate, the only nonderivative, causal source of any event in the world. So also in our individual lives.

It is true, of course, as I just noted, that we can only affect, and must have primary concern only for, some single organism's behavior. Our responsibility is (in the first instance) only for sustaining and advancing our own individual lives, both as animal organisms and as rational beings. But that limited focus for our exercise of our rational powers, in contrast with the cosmic mind's unlimited concerns, provides no reason to think that Zeus's decision in designing human beings included imposing on us additional forms of desire or aversion (additional types of impulse to action occurring in our consciousnesses), so to speak as mere animals, in addition to the one coming from our own decision-making power. If as adults we sometimes need food or the pleasure of eating, as of course we do, there is no reason to think that in addition to a desire to eat coming from our recognition of that need as something worth satisfying, we must have a further impulse moving us to eat, of another kind and with another source within us (within our souls) than reason—what Plato and Aristotle call the power of "appetite." It is sufficient if, as is, in any event, indisputably the case, our bodies generate feelings that give us signals in this regard. Likewise with all those other valuable and disvaluable things that we have solid reasons for pursuing or avoiding, and which Aristotle classifies (wrongly, the Stoics hold) as natural human goods and bads, for which, then, natural, nonrational desires are the appropriate basis for our interest and concern. To any extent to which we may need prompting, and may not always be able to recognize that action is called for, simply through our own observations and thoughts, we certainly do not need nonrational desires with an independent power to set us in motion. Instinctual feelings and other naturally arising ways of drawing and focusing our attention are all we need. That, at any rate, is arguably the case for human adults. And that is what, surely not at all unreasonably, the Stoics maintain.

It must be recognized that as children, from birth, we did have desires and feelings of aversion of some nonrational sort, since of course at that stage of our lives we did not yet have any power of reasoning, and so we had no power of deciding what to do on the basis of reasons we recognize, and critically evaluate, as such. The desires of children or adolescents, before the onset of the age of reason, were produced directly by nature, as they also are for all the permanently nonrational animals—they were produced by the cosmic mind itself, in designing and directing the lives of such creatures. The capacity for those sorts of desires constitutes a natural endowment established and kept going by nature's own operations, through the mechanisms that it has established for the arousal, and for the effects on the animal's organism, of such desires. But, of course, during the period when, as children, we did experience those desires, and our voluntary behavior derived from them, we were not yet experiencing rational desires. It was not the case then, nor is it the case later, once we have become rational animals, that we experience two kinds of desire, with powers to produce actions and cause changes in the world around us, one an exercise of our rationality and the other something completely nonrational.[59] Once we are grown up, and do possess the power of reason, our desires are all of a rational sort. That is, they are reason based, and always represent evaluative thoughts that, in having those desires, we are thinking about what it is suitable to do (or to avoid), if possible, or to undergo or experience.

Such is the account of children's and adults' desires that the Stoics reach, starting from their commitment to a designing reason operating from within the world, of which our own minds are parts. It is this commitment, I suggest, that leads them to accept the Socratic moral psychology, and to reject the Platonic-Aristotelian one that we are more familiar, and indeed in intuitive sympathy, with. Accordingly, they think that whenever virtuous people desire food, or some bodily pleasure or comfort, or opt for any other objective among all the naturally valuable objects or outcomes that, following nature's lead, they desire on any occasion, their desire is a reason-generated one.[60] They desire the food, or whatever else it is, thinking—as the case may be—that this is something worthwhile to consume, or to have or use in some other specific way, or to accomplish. In the desire for it, they are thinking of it in that way, and are psychically moved toward it, so conceived: their desire includes, or rather is constituted by, that thought. Moreover, their thought and desire are supported, implicitly or explicitly, by considerations derived from that natural ideal for human life that I explained above, and from how they conceive that ideal applying to their given current circumstances. For the Stoics, these desires do not derive from an Aristotelian or Platonic power of appetitive or spirited desire that functions independently from reason, and that therefore can naturally be conceived as carrying with them more or less intense levels of felt attraction for their objects—feelings that might, willy-nilly, be more or less intense than reason might judge appropriate (as Aristotelian theory explains).

[59] On Stoic views on the transition from being nonrational animals to being rational ones, see endnote 24.

[60] Indeed, of course, all adult human beings, not merely any virtuous ones there may be, have desires exclusively of the reason-generated sort. Ordinary, in fact bad sorts of people, will want different things, and act differently from virtuous people: for example, in desiring to eat they will think the food or the experience of the pleasure they will get from eating it is actually good for them. They may depart from the truth in other ways too, by for example wanting more of it than the natural norms specify, and so on. In adopting such morally unsound attitudes, and in experiencing such bad sorts of occurrent desires on various occasions, they are misled by habits they have fallen into of getting false evaluative impressions about the objects of their desires: these object "appear" to them as being of more, or a different kind of, importance in their lives than they actually possess. In forming their reason-generated desires, such people yield to these false impressions, i.e., to the inclinations they feel toward those desires' objects; they accept the impressions as true. On these impressions, see above, section 4.4.

We must not, however, misconstrue these reason-derived desires as cold and affect-less. Just because they are products of reason, they are not necessarily void of any feeling of attachment for the object, or of anticipated satisfaction or relish in the desire's fulfillment—as if the functioning of reason in delivering its practical conclusions about what is to be desired and done is as cool and quasi-mechanical, or merely calculative, as it might very well be in cases of seeing how some abstract, theoretical truth of mathematical or physical theory, or other simple matter of fact, follows from certain accepted premises or other evidence. What our sources tell us about Stoic theory does not make this point explicit or absolutely clear, but what they tell also does not require that we interpret the Stoics as being so humanly insensitive as to think of virtuous persons' desires (which are the proper models for human desire in general) in such a light. In any event, the basic framework of their theory of values, as the account I have provided shows, does clearly demand this more engaged, humanly sensitive conception. The Stoic virtuous person does care about all the ordinary things a normal human life is centered round, just as much as the Aristotelian one does. In Stoic theory, then, virtuous people like their food, desire the pleasure of it, and are as one may say "turned on" for it, when they virtuously desire it. The same applies to all the other objects of their desires, in doing their many and varied virtuous actions. As I will explain more fully just below, these ways of feeling attached to things are features of the desires that their reasoning recognizes as appropriate for them to experience, when they pursue these immediate objectives of their actions.[61] Their desires follow upon and accept, as being true and right, evaluative impressions of these objects that graphically represent them as desirable and as satisfying for animal creatures such as ourselves. In accepting those impressions and approving them, one's consequent desire becomes infused with feeling.

In giving illustrations of things that are naturally valuable in human life (and are therefore worth desiring in this way, either to bring into or to preserve in existence), the Stoics seem, not surprisingly, though somewhat unhelpfully, to have limited themselves to listing physical, psychological, and social conditions and circumstances that standardly provide a favorable context for one's actions. Thus, standard lists of these (as they called them)[62] "preferred" indifferents (indifferent

---

[61] Also, their desires arise perfectly spontaneously; these features of feeling simply and directly express the thought, contained in the desire, that these are worthwhile objectives, in the circumstances, to act for. Thus it is not as if these agents somehow artificially induce such feelings, having decided that it would be appropriate to have them. They have them because they see the appropriateness.

[62] Zeno introduced special terminology for referring to the naturally valuable or disvaluable things: προηγμένα and ἀποπροηγμένα, usually nowadays translated as "preferred" and "dispreferred" things, a

in the sense of being neither good nor bad) include being alive, health, pleasure (i.e., pleasurable sensations), good looks, strength, wealth, good reputation, noble birth, sharp senses, natural ability, making moral progress, good memory, quickness of mind, knowledge of useful arts and crafts, having one's parents alive, having children.[63] The contraries of these are listed as "dispreferred"—in my terminology, naturally disvaluable. But the list of naturally valuable or disvaluable things is much wider than any set of favorable physical and social circumstances and conditions for living. We can see this from the connected Stoic theory of "appropriate acts."[64] These are acts that the virtuous person performs unfailingly, while others of us do them at least some of the time, namely, whenever we do the right thing in our given circumstances (even if we do not do it with the full understanding of all the good reasons why the action is to be done that the virtuous unfailingly bring to their actions). Thus, on Stoic theory, all virtuous acts (i.e., ones done from a fully virtuous state of mind) are also appropriate acts, but not vice versa.[65]

This connected theory is based on the idea that appropriate acts are all the ones aimed at (as they say) appropriately "taking" or "selecting" for use or enjoyment, or for simple attention and concern, any of the things that are in accordance with nature (in the way I explained above).[66] These include suitable food and drink, and people to have sex with, on suitable occasions, plus all sorts of other ordinary concerns and activities of a productive and decent human being. The desires to do and enjoy these things, if those desires are to be naturally appropriate to the point and place of such concerns in a human life, must themselves reflect and contain an enlivened feeling for the particular value in a human life of the various aspects of these objects, and for the appropriate use and enjoyment of them that is the basis of the rational attraction to them. When virtuous

---

practice I occasionally follow. See Diogenes Laertius VII 105, Cicero, *On Moral Ends* III 51, and Arius Didymus 7b and 7g.

[63] See Diogenes Laertius VII 102 and Arius Didymus 7a–b, cited in Long and Sedley, *The Hellenistic Philosophers*, 58 A and 58 C.

[64] For explication of this bit of Stoic terminology, see below.

[65] The Stoics distinguish between appropriate acts and what they call κατορθώματα, defined as appropriate acts done "with all the measures" (of thinking and decision) for a well-performed act of the given kind (eating a meal, helping a friend, whatever it may be). Only virtuous persons do κατορθώματα or perfectly right acts; others may do merely "appropriate" ones, "right" but not perfectly so. See the texts cited in Long and Sedley, *The Hellenistic Philosophers*, 59F and K.

[66] Cicero explains these (*On Moral Ends* III 20, 22; see also 58) as based on initial natural impulses aimed at self-preservation and at normal and natural behavior for a young animal of the given kind. These natural and nonrational impulses get gradually expanded as a human being grows up, so as to include, among the aims of such "appropriate" behavior, everything that is "according to nature."

people opt for a boiled-lobster meal, with a well-matched white burgundy wine, as what is appropriate for them to eat, among the meals available on the occasion, they not only do so with the idea that this is the sort of thing nature itself designed us for, and out of a desire to help implement nature's plan in that respect. They choose the meal also with a special feeling of attachment to, and anticipation of, the flavors and textures of the food and drink, and their combination in making a specially satisfying way of maintaining one's bodily constitution and health. Not to feel that way in undertaking the meal would show a failure to have wanted it in the naturally appropriate way. And that would be the mark, not of a virtuous, but of some sort of viciously insensitive or unperceptive person.

On Stoic theory, then, when virtuous persons eat their meals or do any of the other actions of ordinary daily life (including their acts of kindness to others and the dutiful discharge of their daily obligations), or when they do any of the more demanding acts of moral duty (such as saving children from fires, to revert to my hackneyed earlier example), the reasoned desires they act on are infused with feeling—different ranges and ways of feeling in the different cases. It is part of reason's task in generating these desires to make the reasoned impulse include such feelings, simply because those feelings are naturally appropriate, in light of the natural value to a human being of the objects that the given desires pursue.[67] Hence, Stoic virtuous parents love their children, and, in caring for them and taking an interest in their activities and projects, they feel and express a warmth of affection and concern for the children's progress toward moral maturity. They have (appropriate) feelings of pride as this process goes forward successfully. When the morally right thing to do (i.e., the appropriate action) involves kindly and helpful attention to some stranger or near stranger, the desire from which they act is (at least typically and often) infused with a warmth of respect and affection for the other person. They do not live, in these or other aspects of their moral lives, in an affect-free, as it were mechanically rational, way, simply judging this or that the appropriate thing to do. They also recognize, as I explained above, certain ways of feeling attached to people and things (certain affects) as appropriate. And, of course, they feel exactly as they judge it appropriate to feel: these

---

[67] These desires and desiderative attitudes replace the ones we used to have as children, under nature's own governance, and those, of course, even when not excessive or misguided, were richly accompanied with feelings of liking and interest directed to particular qualities of the experiences to be had in achieving the objects of desire. These new, reason-generated desires ought, if properly formed, to carry forward into our adult lives similar feelings of liking and interest.

feelings are parts of the desires that reason itself in them generates. Nonetheless, these feelings are not, as on Platonic and Aristotelian theory, products of some separate, nonrational source of motivation that therefore lies out of reason's direct control. They are feelings that reason itself makes part of the desires that it forms.[68]

Virtuous "appropriate actions," then, being aimed at achieving or maintaining in one's life as many as possible of things that are "preferred" (what I have called the ones that are naturally valuable in any human life)—and at eliminating the "dispreferred"—derive from naturally appropriate, reason-derived desires of differing types to suit the varying circumstances of life. But there is another aspect of these actions that deserves notice. My term "appropriate" here is the usual translation of a semitechnical application made by the Stoics, beginning with Zeno, of a Greek present participle used as a noun: τὸ καθῆκον. Literally, this means "what comes down on" or is incumbent upon a person, what it is their place to do.[69] It must be sensitivity to that etymology that led Cicero to offer Latin *officium* (a service rendered, an obligation or duty) as his translation (universally followed in subsequent Latin writing) for this Stoic term. Behind this lies the idea (explained above) that nature (or the world-mind, or Zeus) created human beings for a certain sort of life, which is therefore incumbent on us to live (as best we can), as something prescribed to us, as our place in the creation of the world and in its developing life over time. By the same token, as we have seen, that life "suits" or "fits" us, and our nature, so that the actions making it up are naturally "appropriate" to us. Hence the normal English rendering in terms of "appropriate acts" is not misleading, even if it does not capture (as the standard Latin *officium* and French *devoir* do) the etymological connection to duty or obligation. Appropriate acts are also duties that we perform, and for their own

---

[68] As explained above, it seems that, on Stoic theory, this comes about because human beings in general always form their desires on the basis of experiencing and accepting impressions (φαντασίαι) of the objectives of their actions that constitute felt inclinations, or attractions, to them. In the case of the virtuous person these impressions present the objects as desirable in the required ways.

[69] In Stoic theory the term is not restricted to the human case. It is applied also to all the natural behaviors of any other animal, and even plants (see Diogenes Laertius's explanation of the term, VII 108). Thus when a plant grows leaves and then fruits in the way normal to a plant of the given species, at the normal times of year, it does "appropriate acts," that is, ones that are "incumbent" on things of its nature: Diog. Laert. in VII 108 immediately after he gives this etymology says a καθῆκον is "an action that suits the arrangements of (a thing's) nature." The official Stoic definition of καθήκοντα is of "acts that, once done, have a well-reasoned defense" (Cic. *On Ends* III 58, Ar. Did. 8, Diog. Laert. VII 107), as of course anything done in attempting to implement the naturally ideal life for members of our species that I have explained would do. A standard list of such acts is given in Diog. Laert. VII 108–9.

sake, if we do them in the way that virtuous persons do, because they are what universal reason or Zeus demands and requires of us.

Thus, despite the awkwardness of calling, on the Stoics' behalf, all kinds of naturally appropriate human acts (e.g., eating a relaxed meal, reading a book enjoyably, carrying on a seemly conversation) duties, there is good reason to emphasize this meaning of the term. For the Stoics, what is naturally appropriate for us derives from decisions and prescriptions of god, the creator and sustainer of the world order; if we act virtuously, we act appropriately not only because doing that suits our nature and is good for us, but because god has imposed on us just those actions as things for us to do.[70] We do them in obedience to this divine command. Contrast in this respect Aristotle's theory. One could, not inaccurately, think of his theory, too, as specifying virtuous actions as the ones that are appropriate to us, because they suit our nature and are good for us to do. He, too, thinks of virtuous acts as actions we ought to do, and ones that reason prescribes to us as the actions to be undertaken.[71] But for Aristotle there is no authoritative agent, whether god or any other, that lays the law down to us in these respects: it is our own reason that gives these orders, solely on the basis of its (our) own understanding of what suits us, as elements in the free-standing realm of nature to which our own nature belongs. Without an authority to follow, or disobey, as we lead our moral lives, it seems unjustified to speak of that life as involving doing our duty. Through their concept of the καθῆκον act, then, the Stoics introduced into philosophy the idea of (moral) duty. For them, the virtuous life, and our highest good, is, equivalently, life lived always doing our duty, for duty's sake.

4.8. Stoic vs. Aristotelian Conceptions of Emotions or Passions

I have promised, at some point in each of the last four sections, to take up again and round off our discussion of the famous, shocking Stoic rejection of all emotions as bad states of mind and feeling. That is the aim of the present section. As I have mentioned, on Stoic psychological theory it is no less true for adult people who are not virtuous that their desires are—all of them—reason derived, too.

---

[70] One way in which the Stoics formulated the "end" for human life includes a reference to "the law common to all things, that is to say, right reason, which is the same thing as Zeus" and to refraining from doing any of the actions normally forbidden by that law. See Diog. Laert. VII 88.

[71] He frequently speaks of virtuous persons as acting "as one ought" (ὡς δεῖ) (see *NE* III 7, 1115b12, among other places) and as reason orders or prescribes them to (see, besides the passage just cited, *NE* VI 10, 1143a8, and elsewhere).

But in nonvirtuous adults' case, the feelings that their reasoning about the objects of pursuit infuses their desires with may, and usually would, not be of this completely appropriate kind and level. Most often their desires are excessive in one way or another. People who are not virtuous do not desire the ordinary objects of daily pursuit solely insofar as it is in accordance with nature to have and consume or use them. They do not desire them in every respect correctly, on the basis of the natural ideal of life that I have described—and often they desire them with no thought at all about that natural ideal. Even when they desire objects that are appropriate, and desire them in suitable circumstances, their desires do not reflect a completely accurate conception of them as naturally valuable, or at any rate not as naturally valuable in the way, and to the extent, that they are in fact of such value. And, of course, quite often, they desire objects that are not at all naturally valuable, in the circumstances they find themselves in. Their desires are always defective and wrong—and that shows up in the feelings with which their wrongly reasoned evaluations of their objects infuse their desires. Much of the time, indeed, their desires are outright deviant: they want too much, or the wrong sorts of food, sex, social recognition, power, entertainment. Whether merely defective, or outright deviant, their desires are products of a misused power of reason. They are disordered, ill-directed thoughts. As such, whereas the desires of the virtuous are uniformly good states of mind (because well ordered), the desires of the nonvirtuous are uniformly bad. They make the lives of the nonvirtuous bad, unhappy lives (some of them, of course, less fully bad than others: that depends on the type and degree of the errors).

The Stoics seem to have assumed that the badness of ordinary people's desires, including the deviant strengths, focus, and objects of these desires, always reflects a quite specific mistake. Defectiveness of desire, in all its aspects, they hold, reflects the pervasive mistake of supposing that the objects, or the experience of achieving and enjoying them, are actually good for the agent who pursues them with these desires. Logically, of course, there would be room for someone who agreed with the virtuous in conceiving these objects of daily pursuit as only naturally valuable (and not good), nonetheless to experience desires for some or all of them that were overblown and excessive, or misdirected—that is, directed at objects wrongly thought to be naturally valuable. This would be a mistake about how important something only of "natural value" was for a life led in pursuit of the natural ideal as described above, or about which things do have this value at all. But, psychologically, the Stoics may have thought, any such departure from the natural norms would have to be due to a greater error than that.[72] It would have to reflect a very seriously erroneous judgment made by one's power of reason, in forming such desires, to the effect that the objects being pursued were actually good, that having and using and enjoying them, if one's desires came to fruition, would contribute directly to the quality of one's life as good (or bad, in the case where the desire was frustrated). Accordingly, the Stoics seem to have classified all defective desires as instances of "passionate" or "emotional" attachment. They are all of them excessive desires, in the sense that they desire something as if it were good—possessed of a higher value—when in fact it is, at most, only something possessing the value of being "preferred." They overvalue these merely naturally valuable things, as if they were good (or their opposites bad). We have seen already why this is such a serious mistake—how deeply it misrepresents the true state of affairs for human beings, as rational animals, in living their lives. Defectiveness of desire or aversion (or of other impulsive movements of the soul toward action) is associated universally in Stoic analysis with the mistake of taking whatever the impulse is driving us toward or away from as itself something good or bad—something the having or lacking of which will make our lives better or worse, happier or the reverse. All the desires, then, of nonvirtuous persons are, in principle, excessive. As such, they can be classified as "emotions" or "passions."

Chrysippus worked out an extraordinarily systematic and elaborate theory of such desires, in attempting to help people recognize how really bad it is—how unhappy, how miserable, how thoroughly bad, it makes one's life—to be affected by them. Or rather, given the Stoic account of adult human desires as all reason based, how bad it is to make the unnecessary mistake of affecting oneself with them.[73] Seneca's *On Anger* is only the most complete surviving Stoic essay of dis-

[72] If so, this does seem to me a mistake on their part, perhaps simply an oversight: the varieties and vagaries of bad human motivation seem not to have interested the Stoics very much. They were content simply to rigorously insist that all human desires are rational in character, and none are nonrational—and that only the virtuous ever have fully correct desires for anything. They seem to assume that if one did not make this great mistake, one would see no reason to judge concerning the natural norms in any way except the correct way that the virtuous do. At any rate, they do disregard this other logical possibility.

[73] See Arius Didymus, *Epitome of Stoic Ethics* 10–10d, Diogenes Laertius VII 110–14. There is a more systematically detailed account of the virtually endless varieties of passion in a little work titled *On Passions* and attributed in our manuscripts to Andronicus of Rhodes, the first century BCE Peripatetic editor of Aristotle's treatises, excerpts of which, in the Greek, are contained in von Arnim, *SVF*, beginning at 3.391. Galen devoted much of two whole books of his long work *On the Doctrines of Hippocrates and Plato* (4 and 5) to a rather uncomprehending but contemptuous "refutation" of Chrysippus's theory (available

suasion from allowing one's life to be disturbed and disfigured by the horrors of anger (or of grief or pity, or exultation, or terror or gripping fear, or passionate, possessive sexual attachment or other overintense desires for bodily or psychological pleasure, and malicious or envious or other vexed states of mind). The root error, involved in all cases of emotion or passion, is, as I have said, to suppose that something that is in fact (on Stoic theory) only naturally valuable or disvaluable is instead good or bad. Once you do suppose such things are good or bad for you, you inevitably form attitudes of pursuit or avoidance, or reactive attitudes in relation to obtaining them or suffering their loss or absence, that incorporate the idea that your very life depends on them: that your life is made actually a lot better and happier, or marred and severely damaged, by getting or undergoing these things. Moreover, given the deep, and indeed fundamental, concern we each must feel for ourselves, for our lives (without that, we can't do anything at all), desiring these things with that idea in mind cannot fail to make one's concerns in relation to these things fraught with intense and worried anticipations, or intense and self-congratulatory pleasures of gratification, or distress, or other agitated states of feeling—given the ebb and flow of uncontrollable circumstances. If you hold such views, you rarely or never know, for sure, when, and whether or not, your life is going to be made hugely happier than it was, or deeply marred or ruined, by events that are out of your control. So, by having the idea that these things are good or bad, you subject yourself to mental or psychic upheavals, distress, trepidations, uplifts of exultation, and other such (as the Stoics therefore insist) sick states of mind.[74] Holding the views you do about the value, for yourself and your life, of these objects and outcomes, you cause the desires and reactions you then experience to be filled with such sorts of feeling.

On Chrysippus's account, then, in feeling the essentially passionate, defective desires of the ordinary person, one is being disobedient to the very standards of reasoning that it belongs to one's own nature as a rational being to follow. One is systematically misevaluating as good, things that are only of a lesser value. If, instead, one did follow the correct standards of rational evaluation, one would recognize that all these things, as we have seen, though certainly of real and important value in the design and pursuit of a human life, are by no means either good

---

in Greek with English translation). Long and Sedley, *The Hellenistic Philosophers*, chap. 65, contains excerpts from some of these, and other, testimonia.

[74] As the Stoics put it, you think it right for your soul to become expanded and puffed up in the hopeful prospect, or the presence, of these goods, and shrunk up and tense in the prospect or presence of their opposites. (See Ar. Did. 10b, with pseudo-Andronicus chap. 1 [=*SVF* 3.391].)

or bad to have or lack. Having or lacking them makes no difference to the quality of your life as in any way either better and happier, or worse and more miserable. Accordingly, the desires with which you pursue or avoid these things, and your reactions to events relating to success or failure in your efforts, are, in the deviant case, infused with passionate feelings, but in the other with calm and controlled, nonemotional and nonpassionate ones.

It is because of the Stoics' rejection of passions and emotions as, without exception, bad states of feeling—shocking evidence of serious moral, and intellectual, failure—that we have come to think of Stoics as people altogether without affect in the conduct of their lives, as people who go through life passively and hard-heartedly accepting everything that happens to them, and not caring about anything one way or another, while nonetheless carrying forward their lives on the basis of some misguided, humanly empty, idea of duty. In fact, however, as I have already explained, the Stoic life is by no means without affect—without felt engagement, in a perfectly natural human way, both with the doing of one's duties and with all aspects of normal human relationships to other people and to one's own bodily and psychological satisfactions. However, the seriousness of the Stoic rejection of emotions or passions, and its consequences for the Stoic theory of morality and for the Stoic way of life, is not to be underestimated, or swept under the rug. The feelings that motivate Stoic actions and that Stoics feel in response to significant events in their lives are not in any way equivalent to the emotions or passions we experience, and some people treasure, in our own ordinary human lives.[75] It is not at all only insignificant differences of terminology, as is sometimes said, that separate the Stoics from either the Aristotelian ethical theory and way of life, or any way of life that nowadays most people would recognize as decently human. True Stoics do not grieve (at all) when their child dies, they do not become angry (to any degree) when someone grossly insults or mistreats them, or mistreats someone they care about and have some responsibility for; they do not have any degree of pity, in sympathy for someone who suffers pain or poverty or overwhelming loss; they do not have any elated feelings if they win some competition, or get vindicated, or simply are favored with something they were hoping against hope for; they do not fall in love, if that means becoming bound to and infatuated with some single other person's company, and sexual intercourse with that person, as a condition of their own continued functioning and happiness in life.

---

[75] As to the ways they feel instead, see endnote 25.

It is true that Stoic virtuous people do not feel nothing if their child dies. (Similarly, mutatis mutandis, for the other cases I have just gone through.) They know that, if their child dies, they have lost something that belongs to the natural ideal for a human life that nature itself aims at as a norm, and something that, for that reason, they themselves have been attempting to secure and retain for themselves. Accordingly, there must be some feeling in recognition of that loss. However, this feeling is accompanied and imbued with the full recognition that the event of loss and the child's death are things that contribute positively to the overall good state and history of the whole world (though one never knows anything much, at all, of how this is so), about which they care ultimately much more than they care for their own petty affairs. And whatever this feeling is, it is not grief (of any degree). It is important, in fact, to emphasize this difference, and not to downplay it. Grief, on Stoic theory, as I have said—and they seem right about this—involves a feeling that something good that one possessed has been lost, and it represents the thought that, in being now denied that thing, one's life has been diminished, and is from now onward, or at least for a long time hereafter, much worse, or even terribly blighted. Stoic virtuous people, whatever they do feel, do not feel in any such way at all—even mildly, or moderately, or with reservations.

Nor are the Stoics idiosyncratic in placing the essence of a passion or emotion in a thought about the feeling's object as something bad (or good). Aristotle, as we have seen, clearly agrees with them about this. And, as we also saw, Aristotle's theory of value supports his own view that emotions and passions are not at all, as such, bad things to experience (even though excesses or defects of them are bad, however common, and even commonly approved, such deviations may be)—just as the Stoics' theory of value is positively bound up with their wholesale rejection of them.[76] We are faced here with a fundamental, and serious, disagreement in ethical and psychological theory. Exactly those conditions of mind, some of which Aristotle thinks not only not bad, but positively good, to experience (because he thinks them entirely appropriate to the particular circumstances in which they arise, and entirely approved by reason), the Stoics think are uniformly, and in all instances, bad things to feel, blights to one's life. And they are agreed in giving the same ordinary names to these conditions: grief, anger, pity, pleasure (at

---

[76] Aristotelians also disagree with the Stoics on secondary points: they do not agree that all emotions or passions are excessive, nor that all are "disobedient to reason" (in that they depart from reason's own standards about how it is right to feel about things). These secondary disagreements depend upon the fundamental difference between Aristotle and the Stoics, over whether the things that the Stoics call merely naturally valuable or disvaluable are instead (to some degree, in some way) good or bad.

something's having happened), fear, and so on. They differ only in their views on how to analyze and place these sorts of experience correctly within an overall theory of the human soul. Aristotle's theory holds that moderate degrees, on suitable occasions, of all these passions are good to feel (and that it is bad and a mark of vice not to feel them then). The Stoics hold that any and all instances of any of these feelings are thoroughly bad, indelible marks of moral vice.

As I have indicated, this disagreement is ultimately grounded in the two differing theories of value. We have already seen how and why the Stoics are convinced that nothing in human life except the condition of one's mind, as one either lives in agreement with Zeus or nature, or does not, could possibly be either good or bad. Other things in or affecting a human life have a very different sort of value, as either naturally valuable or disvaluable. Aristotle, by contrast, adopts the (for us nowadays) more commonsensical view that while virtue is the greatest good, all the Stoic naturally valuable things are good too. Therefore, their presence or absence makes some difference to the goodness and happiness of a life. The respective Stoic and Aristotelian positions on passions or emotions follow quickly from this division of opinion about the nature of value and goodness. Clearly, the issues at stake in this disagreement over values are difficult matters of high theory. They are therefore quite remote from easy adjudication on the basis of agreed or commonsensical principles derived directly from our own experience of life. What should (or does really) count as good for or in a human life? Virtues only? Or also pleasures, worthwhile accomplishments, loving relationships, deserved recognition? These are hard questions calling for a good deal of systematic and careful reflection. By contrast, the opposed positions about emotions, as sometimes good, or as always bad, are apparently more immediately accessible to adjudication, directly from our experience of them. On that basis, it is easy to think that Aristotle's position on emotions wins hands down against the Stoics': it is normal in our cultures to think that emotions, properly calibrated and controlled, do have an important role to play in anything we can readily recognize as a good human life. They show a full and, it might seem, properly human engagement with life, with other people, and with ourselves as agents.[77] The Stoic preference for calm and unpassionate feelings about oneself

[77] On the other hand, there is one feature of the Stoic theory that should make it seem in fact more attractive than the Aristotelian one. For the Stoics, when people suffer from moral lack of control, getting "carried away" by emotion or another passion of the moment, it is they, in the fullest sense, who are the agent: they decide to act as they do, so as to obtain the pleasure or whatever else is the objective they adopt, and pursue under the influence of the passionate state of their minds. This makes them directly and fully responsible agents in their action. The Aristotelian view makes the agent only at some second remove responsible: it is not they (their decision, their choice) who act, but only some nonrational power belong-

and one's life, and about naturally valuable but not *good* things in life (including friends and people you love) is among us a minority attitude, to say the least. But, given the priority of those issues of high theory for deciding about emotions and their value, we must not allow ourselves simply, on that basis in ordinary intuition, to dismiss the Stoic position, as counterintuitive, outrageous, and unacceptable. This is what many (including ancient critics, but many others since then who have paid attention to the Stoic outlook) have always done.

Instead, we must take very seriously the much more fundamental disagreement between Stoics and Aristotle in the general theory of values. Each of their respective theories is a coherent and impressive development, deriving from a sharply different, but, in itself, each an impressive and coherent general outlook on the world of nature, to which we human beings belong. Each has its attractive aspects, as I hope I have brought out in my expositions above and in the previous chapter. Each gives an intelligible and indeed, from the moral point of view, a conceivably correct, account of the nature and place of emotions in human life—even if the Stoic view is a morally more challenging and demanding one for us, given our commonsensical ideas: it is not easy for us to accept that we really ought not ever to get angry, or be moved by pity or grief, or elation when things go well for us in some important part of our lives. Being, as I said, matters of high theory, these issues about values and goodness in human life require, for any satisfactory settlement, a comprehensive consideration of values in general, and goodness in particular. My own impression is that each theory provides a viable, and indeed a deeply interesting, outlook on human life—and, as part of that, on the place of emotions within it. I would find it very hard to decide between them, on the appropriate grounds, that is, on grounds of philosophical theory concerning value. Each seems quite conceivably right—even though, of course, they cannot both be right.

Yet it may seem, and has seemed to many, both in antiquity and in modern times, that the Stoics' position on emotions is vulnerable, and the Aristotelian position much more successful, when confronted with one ordinary, and undeniable, type of human experience. If that should be so, one would have strong indication in favor of the Aristotelian, and against the Stoic, theory of values,

---

ing to their souls that they have, no doubt both regrettably and irresponsibly, simply failed to get properly trained and under their reason's control. One clear, and clearly undesirable, consequence of the Aristotelian view is that it enables miscreants to say it wasn't really their fault, something just carried them away, they couldn't really help it, and so on, when they act in that out-of-control way. (On acting out of control, see below in my main text.)

too, given that the Stoic position on emotions is so closely insinuated and intertwined with their general theory of values. The issue here has to do with the common experience we all sometimes have of acting against our own better judgment, or (in the frequently used terminology of contemporary philosophy) with weakness of will—moral lack of control. The experience, common to all of us, of losing control to our emotions and acting badly as a result, is often thought to be something the Stoics simply cannot account for. As I will argue, that is in fact far from clear.

Still, the Stoics do face a legitimate challenge here. As we experience them, emotions are ways that we feel ourselves affected—moved from without—by how things and events strike us, as either good or bad for us, or from our point of view, in one way or another. We feel ourselves—certainly in cases of the more powerful instances, but also, I would grant, in milder ones—to be not so much agents in experiencing them, but passive. In fact, the Stoics do not disagree with that characterization. It is true that, as we have seen, for them emotions are ways that we, as agents, affect ourselves. But even if in fact, on their theory, it is we who are deciding to feel that way, the active role of our power of reason in generating these states may be disguised from us when we experience them, as Chrysippus himself insists.[78] Emotions are, he says, (typically) "runaway" feelings, feelings that, once we are in their grip, carry us away and are then well out of our control. They are felt as assailing us. This is especially clear in cases of moral lack of control (what the Greeks called ἀκρασία). We decide, for reasons that we give ourselves, and honestly do accept as good reasons, not to do some sort of thing, and we try to train ourselves not, on the spur of the moment, to feel a strong temptation (of appetite, or an angry emotion, say), or at any rate not to yield to those feelings and act in that way. Yet, as we all know, sometimes we fail. We feel the temptation, and yield to it, with a sense of powerlessness in the face of the desire (our desire) that is moving us. We try not to do whatever it is, we continue (or at least, we seem to ourselves to keep on) deciding not to do it, but we do it anyway. Here, it appears, we have clear evidence that emotions really are nonrational states of motivation: we have a clear conflict between a reason-generated motivation (the decision not to do what one does), active all the while that an emotional one, driving us toward action, causes us to act against it. Since the desire we end up acting on is opposed by the reason-generated one all the way,

---

[78] See Ar. Did. 10a (Long and Sedley, *The Hellenistic Philosophers*, 65 A5), with Galen in Long and Sedley, *The Hellenistic Philosophers*, 65 J4–9. For discussion on the possible lack of self-conscious knowledge of what we are doing, and on emotions as runaway and out of control desires, see endnote 26.

straight through to the action, it cannot come from the same rational source. We cannot simultaneously, in effect, both be deciding not to do an action of ours, while also deciding to do it: that could only lead to inaction. The desire that we act from must be a nonrational motivating state, as Aristotelian theory makes it out to be, and not the reason-generated thing that Chrysippus and the other Stoics maintain.

However, all the Greek philosophers, beginning already with Socrates in Plato's *Protagoras*, found the phenomena of uncontrol, as so described, both fascinating and highly problematic. Except (as it appears) for Plato in *Republic* book IV, they all rejected, on somewhat different grounds, the description I have just given of what we experience in these cases. On that description, we experience a simultaneous opposition of two motivating states, one evidently coming from a judgment belonging to our power of reason, and the other, therefore, equally evidently nonrational in origin. The Greek philosophers' unwillingness simply to go along with that account (however convincing it may seem to the ordinary moral consciousness) is quite understandable. One is entitled to be suspicious of people's recollections of what they experience when subject to the sorts of stresses that admittedly accompany the sorts of conflicts and mental struggles that are involved in such situations. The clarity of mind that one reasonably demands, if one is to accept honest later reports of details of one's experiences as containing the truth about them, is certainly lacking here. Accordingly, Socrates maintained that in all such cases what really happens is that, under the pressure of temptation, we change our minds at the last moment before action, and decide to do the thing after all. As we do it, and in doing it, we are deciding to do it. Only afterward do we come to regret it, as we reflect more soberly, again, on the circumstances and our own system of values.[79] Aristotle, in his discussion of uncontrolled actions in *Nicomachean Ethics* VII 3, maintains that there are opposing motivations (during the time of struggle, as one fights against the power of temptation), one rational and the other emotional and nonrational. But he denies that it can ever happen that, precisely while acting on the emotion or appetite, having given in to temptation, agents do retain in force their reason's commitment or decision against the precise action, the very thing, that they then do

[79] The initial temptation, to which one gave in, in deciding after all to do the thing, need not have been itself a nonrational motivation (a force in the soul pulling one toward the action); it may have consisted only of a series of alluring and enticing representations you were giving yourself of the pleasures or other (as you think) values to be achieved if one does act. These would only be inclining you toward the action, i.e., toward deciding to do it. They would not yet be full motivations, that is, movements in the soul toward the action. See my discussion in section 2.2.

do.[80] They do not (contra Socrates) decide to go ahead and do it, but they also cease to decide against it—that is, they cease to decide that way, as and while they act. We may think, looking back, that sometimes we do act while keeping on deciding not to act that way, but Aristotle is sure we are misremembering or misreporting to ourselves what did go on, under those confusing and confused occasions.

Chrysippus simply goes further, and differently, down this same Aristotelian line. He argues that at times what happens that appears to us, at least in recollection and maybe even at the time of action, as being pulled simultaneously in two directions, and acting on one impulse while the other continues to pull in the other direction, is in fact something quite else. It is in fact a rapid switching back and forth of our reason's ideas about what to do (and why).[81] There occurs a rapid oscillation in our minds. First we feel emotionally moved to act, while accepting some alluring impression of what will result if one does (we picture the immediate bodily pleasure we will experience, say). But then we switch: we become rationally moved not to act, while withdrawing our acceptance of the alluring impression, and endorsing a conflicting different one that represents abstention as right. We go back and forth during the period of struggle. But when, having finally given in to temptation, we act to indulge ourselves, only the one impulse, the emotional one, continues in existence. Obviously, again, we could not do anything while deciding both to act and not to act. But so rapid and sharp is the changing back and forth, while we experience the struggle, that it can nonetheless seem to us that the two thoughts about action, and the two impulses, exist simultaneously, and that they actually pull us, at one and the same time, in both directions, as we act. As to the claim that once the action begins, only the one impulse (the emotion or appetite) is in existence (unless, even while doing it, the agent stops for a mini-second and draws back, proceeding only jerkily to do whatever it is), this does not go further than Aristotle himself already went. For all we can reasonably claim to know, then, as it seems to me, Chrysip-

---

[80] There is a huge philosophical and scholarly literature dissecting Aristotle's discussion in detail, and offering analyses of his ultimate account. However, my point here seems clearly a correct characterization of his view, and is widely accepted in the literature (even in connection with otherwise different and even opposing overall accounts).

[81] See Plutarch's report in his little essay *On Moral Virtue*, chap. 7, 446F–447A (in Helmbold, *Plutarch's Moralia* VI). Plutarch immediately objects (447B–C) that our experience shows us that this is not what happens, but he does not begin to take seriously the real difficulty of being sure what our experience does show us. He is so committed to the truth of the Platonic psychology that he does not pause to think clearly about whether Chrysippus's proposal might be a viable alternative analysis in some cases.

pus may be right that in cases of akratic struggle we do not, after all, find clear evidence showing that the emotions and appetites we are sometimes motivated by, and act upon, whether in akratic situations or not, are nonrational in their constitution. So far as our own experience of such cases goes, we cannot firmly deny that they are instead, as Stoic theory maintains, simply judgments of the agent's reason as to the goodness or badness of something, colored by a special sort of reason-generated feeling.

It seems, then, that the appeal to what we clearly do experience, in the case of uncontrolled acts, cannot suffice to prove, for a reasonable and open-minded psychologist, or to ordinary introspection, that there really are, as the Platonic-Aristotelian moral psychology maintains, nonrational motivations at work in the lives of adult human beings. Accordingly, we cannot honestly say that we know just from this experience that less prominent instances of what Aristotle and Plato count as nonrational desire really are nonrational, and not instead reason-generated desires: for example, when we act from a desire for food, upon getting bodily hunger signs, or for drink, upon getting signs of the need for water. In the case of the virtuous, such desires will of course be formed with the conception of their objects as naturally appropriate to consume, not as good. For the nonvirtuous, they may well betray a conception of the objects as in fact good to have or enjoy; and in those cases the desires will be defective and bad and, as the Stoics say, overblown and excessive. Hence they might be counted as "emotional" (perhaps sometimes rather mild cases of emotion). The main point is that we have not come across any strong experiential evidence that tells us, one way or the other, whether the Aristotelian theory that the desires of the virtuous agent, in doing virtuous actions, include a mix and combination of nonrational desires with rational wishes and decisions, is more acceptable than the Stoic one, according to which all the desires and decisions the agent ever acts upon are exclusively reason generated.

4.9. The Stoic Way of Life

In the preceding sections, I have explained and discussed the Stoics' theories of human nature, human morality, and the good human life. I have placed these theories in the context of their overarching theory of the world of nature, of which human beings and human life are integral parts. As we have seen, for the Stoics the world is dependent upon the activities of a deity that, with the power of its thoughts, shapes the world in all its details, sustains it in existence, and causes all the events that make up world history. In going in some detail into this cosmic context for Stoic ethical theories my conviction has been that we cannot properly understand, and appreciate, the Stoic way of life that we read about in ancient Stoic authors, such as Seneca and Epictetus, or in Cicero, without thinking carefully about these details and taking them into account. On their surface, and if taken simply on their own, many of the Stoic theories in ethics (the ethical "doctrines" of the school) are hard to grasp, and even extremely counterintuitive. They approach being simply unbelievable (both to us nowadays and to ancient audiences). It was common coin in antiquity to refer to the "paradoxes of the Stoics": Cicero is the author of a work with that title, an oratorical display piece devoted to the challenging task of defending them, paradoxical or no.[82] We have touched on all these "paradoxes" in our discussion above. By showing how they follow from reasonable philosophical first principles (however, nonetheless, disputable, as everything in philosophy is) concerning human nature and our natural place in the organization of the world of nature as a whole, I have sought to make these "paradoxical" doctrines intelligible, and to show why they deserved to be taken seriously in antiquity—and even nowadays, too.

Most of the authors we rely upon for our knowledge of ancient Stoicism are affiliated with other philosophical schools (or even the Christian religion); they are committed to other approaches than the Stoic one to questions of human life. They do not try to understand and evaluate fairly the philosophical positions the Stoics adopt that lead them to these "paradoxes." They just want to highlight what from their own point of view are blank errors. So we get instead, as I mentioned in section 4.2 above, works such as Plutarch's *On Stoic Self-Contradictions*, bent on portraying Chrysippus and other Stoic authorities as simply incompetent at philosophy and indeed even at consecutive reasoning. Plutarch wants to show them contradicting themselves in their analyses at every turn. The impression the reader is left with, and this is not unintended, is that one should not waste time considering Stoicism as a guide for one's life. There can be no final merit in a philosophy that consists of a mass of self-contradictions! I have tried to show that, time and again, when one takes proper account of the full

---

[82] Cicero lists six "paradoxes." They are (loosely translated) as follows: virtue and virtuous action are the only good; virtue is by itself sufficient for living happily; all moral violations are equally bad, and all fully right actions are equally good; every unwise person (i.e., every nonvirtuous one) is mentally deranged; the wise person alone is a free man, every unwise person is a slave; and only wise people are wealthy.

background, in their philosophy as a whole, for the major elements in their ethical theory that seem paradoxical and hard to accept, their theories turn out to have quite a lot of philosophical (and even psychological) merit. The contrasts with the corresponding Aristotelian analyses and theories that I have drawn out along the way serve both to highlight what is unusual, but philosophically and ethically interesting, in the Stoic point of view, and to emphasize the viability, at least in terms of the ancient philosophical tradition, of both these contrasting outlooks. I have wanted to suggest, as well, that the Stoic and the Aristotelian outlooks both have considerable merit for us, too, in reflecting on our own lives and helping to shape them.

In turning now to consider Stoic philosophical theory as grounding the Stoic way of life, we need to recall the main elements of philosophy conceived as a way of life that Socrates introduced into the history of thought. For Socrates, philosophy alone is the ultimate authority for deciding what life is best for a human being, and how we ought individually to live, both in general terms and in as much detail as it is possible to specify that life. But it is not just a set of prescriptions, based on fully elaborated reasons; it is also, as I have put it, a basis of thought which, internal to that best life, provides the constant motivation from which it is to be, and is, led. Finally, for Socrates, the activities of philosophical argument, analysis, and so forth—the activities constituting philosophy as a subject of study—occupy a central and constant place at the center of the best life. We have seen that, in taking over, applying, and developing this Socratic perspective, Aristotle follows Socrates on all three points, but with one prominent twist. He accepts fully that philosophy is the sole final authority for how we should live, and he defines the best life as one in which philosophical thought (practical philosophy) pervades, directs, and provides the full motivating basis on which the best life is led. The twist is that, for Aristotle, it is only in one of his two ways of life, the contemplative life, that the study and active, constant pursuit of the formal practices of philosophical theorizing become a central occupation. In his secondarily happy life, of the virtuous political leader or of the virtuous ordinary citizen, any devotion to formal philosophical study, whether of a practical or a theoretical kind (apart from during one's preparation while young for adult life), is optional and ancillary. The Stoics, as I will explain below, appear to go one step further even than Aristotle has gone in restricting the place of formal philosophical study in the best life. For them, in effect, all of philosophy becomes practical, with the result that though, indeed, philosophy is for them too the sole authority, and pervades the best life by providing the motivating thoughts on which it is led, the formal study of philosophy, as an ongoing, day-by-day occupation, drops aside or becomes totally ancillary, or, at any rate, it becomes, in principle, optional.

What, then, would it be like to lead one's life as a fully informed, fully educated and persuaded, Stoic—one who does not just act the way a Stoic does, doing "duty for duty's sake," never complaining about what happens to one, and never getting upset or elated, but keeping one's life on an even keel, finding one's happiness simply in the thought that one has done one's best? I am referring here to someone who knows and accepts the Stoic "paradoxes," but does so because they have a full understanding of them, based upon an understanding and acceptance of the Stoic philosophical first principles, on which Stoic theory rests them.[83] It is these that make the ethical doctrines worth accepting, even if they might be not only paradoxical, but indeed morally revolutionary. How would philosophy—Stoic philosophical thought—shape such a life? Living virtuously, or as nearly so as one can achieve, is at the center of the Stoic way of life. That goal provides the needed organization for, and oversight over, all one's practical interests and pursuits—just as for Aristotle. But living virtuously on the basis of Stoic philosophy is a significantly different thing. Aristotelian virtuous persons will understand themselves, and engage with other people and with their daily tasks, while holding constantly in mind Aristotle's analyses and insights: but these are limited to those belonging to Aristotelian practical philosophy. While for Aristotle these will include, in a very general way, the overall world scheme that Aristotelian metaphysics and natural philosophy endorse, no technical details of his physical or metaphysical theory, or his epistemological or logical views, will be included. As we saw in chapter 3, Aristotelian practical philosophy is a specific, dedicated, and largely self-standing, inquiry into the human good, in light of basic features of human nature and the human soul; it does not include or require the studies contained in such works of Aristotle as his *On the Soul* or *Physics* or his biological or logical writings.

By contrast, Chrysippus and other Stoics make it a fundamental requirement for being virtuous and living virtuously—in other words, for being a truly just and temperate and courageous person, and leading a good moral life[84]—that one

---

[83] The contrast I have in mind here with the Stoic who understands Stoic first principles, and lives on the basis of that understanding, is one who lives "Stoically" on the basis of graphic rhetorical inducements to adopt a life of Stoic resignation and avoidance of emotion (we find this in the writings of familiar Roman Stoics, particularly Marcus Aurelius and Epictetus), appealing to imagination rather than reasoning and understanding as a basis for a "Stoic" life. See below, p. 222f.

[84] In my discussion of the Stoic theory of virtue, I have spoken of Stoic virtue throughout as a single

know, all the way down to its grounding in fundamental principles about being and nonbeing, the whole of Stoic physical theory, as well as dialectic (logical theory, epistemology, and philosophy of language). For them, following Socrates, you cannot have any single virtue without having them all,[85] and among the virtues are, as they hold, physics (knowledge of the whole correct theory of the universe and its constitution) and dialectic.[86] In fact, Diogenes Laertius tells us that the Stoics hold that we human beings were endowed by nature with reason "as a more perfect form of governance" for our lives than nature gives to animals through their instinctive, and other, nonrational desires.[87] The point, then, of any use of reason in a Stoic life is toward governing our lives in the right way: that is, so as to live always in agreement with nature. Reason and its activities have no other point for the Stoics. Hence, on Stoic principles, all of philosophy, however theoretical some parts of it may seem, are for the practical end of living well and happily, through making the contribution to the life of the cosmos that we, and only we, can make, through our decision making as we do all our actions and live our own individual lives. All philosophy is practical. There is no separate, nonpractical, part of philosophy, a theoretical and higher one, as there is for Aristotle.[88]

The result is that in living the Stoic life we must bear constantly in mind, whether in the forefront or only in the back of our minds—what comes to the forefront depends upon the specific situations and circumstances of the moment—the totality of Stoic philosophical theory, in metaphysics and physics, in logic and theory of knowledge, as well as in ethics, more narrowly conceived. True Stoics have fully understood, on the full basis of philosophical argumentation on which Chrysippus and Zeno based it, the Stoic conception of the world

---

condition of mind, in which one possesses the full knowledge of all the natural norms for the "natural" life that Zeus or nature itself intends for human beings to live, and for individual humans at least to always try for. It's the virtuous life, as a whole, that Stoic theory focused upon. They seem not to have devoted detailed attention to specific virtues such as justice, temperance, courage, etc. in the manner of Aristotle in *NE* III–V with his eleven moral virtues. Still, the Stoics did recognize many more different virtues than even Aristotle did (indeed, as Plutarch complains in his *On Moral Virtue*, 441b, they recognized a whole "swarm" of them). For a detailed account, see sect. V of Cooper, "The Unity of Virtue," in *Reason and Emotion*, pp. 96ff.

[85] On Socrates's reasons for holding the "unity of virtue" (i.e., of the virtues), with the consequence that no one can possess any one of them without possessing them all, see section 2.4. For the Stoics' rather different way of understanding this philosophical thesis, and grounding it in their analysis of the different virtues, see the previous note, and the reference there.

[86] For physics and dialectic as virtues, see Cicero, *On Moral Ends* III 72–73.

[87] Diog. Laert. VII 86.

[88] This is certainly Chrysippus's view. On Posidonius's position, see endnote 27.

as governed by the mind of Zeus or nature, and of the human species as created by that mind, as part of its plan to create a world, and a life for that world, that will be maximally well-ordered and therefore the best conceivable. Part of that maximal well ordering is to have in the world some other rational beings than itself, individual rational animals whose nature would be fulfilled through developing and choosing for themselves lives in full agreement with Zeus's own thoughts in carrying out this plan. True Stoics have deeply embedded this outlook in their minds, through accustoming themselves over long years of active life to habits of thinking and reacting in the ways that this outlook implies, to people and events in their lives—and to themselves, as objects of self-scrutiny. They have come always to think and react, in all their daily circumstances, in terms of this conception. They also, of course, work out on its basis any answers to practical questions that may arise that might need to be specially thought over, or thought through, before reaching a conclusion.

They do not think of this self-training, and the condition of virtue that results if, or to the extent that, they may succeed, as involving the habituation by practice of a special nonrational set of capacities that they possess for feeling motivated and acting, in addition to the power of thinking about good and bad and deciding how to act in the light of those thoughts. Rather, in accordance with the Stoic theory of the psychology of human motivation, they regard their self-training in terms of establishing in themselves certain patterns of thinking about good and bad, or more generally about things of value—together with ways of feeling that are consequent upon, or part of, those ways of thinking. It may take time and effort to instill these patterns of thinking fully in one's mind. Part of this effort must concern training oneself, so far as this is possible, not to allow oneself, as one goes about one's daily rounds and finds oneself confronted with various shifting situations and possibilities of action, to receive the sorts of misleading impressions that ordinary people receive, of things that are only of *value* in a human life, and not either good or bad—impressions that represent them as good or bad and endow them with the sorts of alluring features that would require great effort to resist, as one then forms the desires and other motivations that will lead one to act. One must train out of oneself any tendency to have feelings even of inclination, which is, as I have suggested, what for the Stoics these impressions actually are, to pursue or enjoy something that is only normally of value, with ways of feeling and desiring that would thus be excessive or otherwise inappropriate. It takes time and practice to break the habits of forming such impressions that, at least for most of us, have been engrained in us through our upbringing. On the positive side, Stoic ideas about good and bad, and about the merely valuable, differ greatly from the ones current in the societies we are brought up in. We need to become completely convinced of and totally familiar with the highly unusual Stoic ideas. We also need to train ourselves to experience impressions of all the things that are merely of value, when we confront them, that represent them not at all as good or bad for us to have and enjoy or undergo, but merely of natural positive or negative value. If we succeed, we become able smoothly and easily to react with properly calibrated, virtuous, ways of feeling and desiring, or other virtuous motivations, in the pursuit and enjoyment of all the ordinary objectives of daily life. We need to become completely used to thinking and perceiving according to these patterns, so that we can trust ourselves to have spontaneous resort to them in all the circumstances of life. In all these tasks we need to strengthen our minds, so as to make ourselves react spontaneously, properly focus our attention, and bring into play as needed all the conceptual and moral distinctions we have learned to draw, and the reasons lying behind and supporting them. This requires habituation, but of our minds, our power of reason, our ways of thinking—not, as with Aristotle, some supposed power of desire and motivation lying outside the scope of reason.

At the center of their habituation, Stoics accustom themselves to thinking that their only good, just as with the overall good of the world and its life, consists in the good order they have established among, on the one hand, the external objects and circumstances they attempt to bring about or to preserve, and to make use of and enjoy, and, on the other, their own attitudes and ways of approaching them. Crucial to the latter is the conviction that contributing to the wonderfully beautiful, well-ordered life of the whole world is their highest objective. They see, and feel, their own particular detailed objectives, selected in accordance with the natural ideal for the lives of human animals that I described above, as worth having only if having them turns out to fit in properly with that highest objective. Intimately connected to this central idea of human beings' highest good consisting in their living in such a way as to make their fullest contribution to the good of the whole world is the further idea that in making that contribution we become god's coworkers. Taken together, these two central components of the Stoic outlook on life determine the structuring principles for the Stoic way of life.

Most notably, this outlook leads to a deep sense of respect, even awe, for human beings as such—all human beings—which was quite new to the ancient world. In the Stoic view, we are all equally, by nature, helpers (even partners) of the cosmic god, created as parts of himself, so as to occupy the central, and an independent, place in the unfolding, and in the active achievement, of the divine plan for the world. That, as I said earlier, is a remarkably high calling for us—for each of us, no matter what our circumstances of life might be. Our humanity is capable of being fully realized no matter what station in life we occupy. For the Stoics, more privileged positions (as we normally think them) in regard to health or wealth or social standing, and the like, do not constitute, to any extent, a more complete fulfillment of our human potential; these have no bearing whatsoever in that regard. Provided that we do live in agreement with nature—something that is, in principle, just as possible for a slave as it is for a Roman senator (perhaps more so)—we fulfill our natures. This remarkable underlying moral egalitarianism provides the basis for a conception of the dignity of human beings, simply as rational beings, and for nascent ideas of human rights. On the other hand, it was also overlaid with a sharp recognition of the miserable failures that most, even perhaps virtually all, human beings in all ages have made of their lives. Hence their moral egalitarianism did not lead Stoics, for example, to advocate democratic forms of government. They saw no reason to suppose that such government would have any good effects (quite possibly, it might have bad ones), in relation to the only thing that really does matter in human life, namely, personal moral reform.[89] Their moral egalitarianism may have had some effects in the development among the members of the Roman ruling elite of ideas of shared humanity and dignity among all the world's peoples. Many of this class were Stoics during the establishment of the empire and the first centuries of imperial rule (including, famously, the emperor Marcus Aurelius in the second half of the second century). But it was not until early modern times, long after the Stoic way of life had ceased to be widely practiced, that this heritage of Stoicism began to find any political voice.

The Stoic conception of human beings as the only other rational beings except god, and his/its coagents in governing the world, has further important consequences for the way fully committed, fully knowledgeable Stoics lead their lives. All the desires that Stoics experience, all their interests and attachments, all their moral and other undertakings, all their reactions to events and circumstances in their lives and the lives of others to whom they may have, and feel, bonds of attachment, are of the nonemotional sort I discussed above. They re-

---

[89] On Stoic political ideas, one could consult the texts collected in Long and Sedley, *The Hellenistic Philosophers*, chap. 67.

quire this of themselves because they understand precisely and firmly just what sort of value these objectives of daily life and action possess—and what sort does not belong to them at all. Virtue, as they conceive it, requires (indeed it largely consists in) being motivated in this nonemotional way with respect to everything that they do care about. As we saw earlier, they experience, or do their best to experience, no emotions whatsoever—no anger, no grief, no fear, no terror, no outrage, no pity, no sadness or depression, no feelings of exultation or elevation when things "go their way," no hatred of any other person however malignant and obstructive, no disgust at anyone's malfeasances or outrageously unmerited successes, no malice. Their philosophical studies and the self-training of their minds described in the previous sections have taught them not to feel in these ways.

It is clear, then, that the Stoic way of life depends upon, and incorporates into itself, a lot of sharp, striking, and unusual philosophical conclusions about human life. It even incorporates a great deal of detailed philosophical analysis and argumentation of a surprising and challenging kind, across many areas of inquiry besides the ethical. An active understanding and full awareness of these analyses and arguments is often required in order to form proper evaluations and think through the proper course of action, in response to the unexpected or unusual circumstances that frequently arise for any human being. You never know when you might need to recall and employ Stoic analyses of logical paradoxes, or matters of intricate physical theory, in order not to be fooled into misjudging what Stoic duty requires of you at some moment. This is not a way of life led by people who have simply been inspired by Stoic models of duty for duty's sake or for serene restraint, and set out to inspire themselves through a superactive imagination to keep on following some heroic, Stoic-looking, way of living. Such flights of imagination may highlight the Stoic life's attractiveness to people who have not tried seriously to study Stoic philosophy and to learn its lessons. But whatever does come of such people's lives as a result, they are not leading their lives in the way that Stoic theory requires. What is required are improvements in one's own understanding of how things are, through a philosophically reasoned grasp of a large body of essential truths about human nature and the cosmic context of human life. This understanding could not possibly be achieved by such flights of imaginative self-identification.

This is worth emphasizing, because a good deal of what the famous Roman Stoics, who are for us the most accessible way into Stoicism, write emphasizes precisely rhetorical inducements, aimed at providing materials for such flights of imagination.[90] They offer encouragements for a better life, one without ups and downs, without wrenching decisions or wrenching consequences of decisions made—in short, ones shaped in the Stoic way. But they downplay or even, sometimes, omit altogether the philosophical argumentation and analysis that Stoic theory makes clear is the only possible avenue for true improvement. Such rhetorical appeals to the attractive peacefulness, even serenity, of the Stoic life, by contrast with the frenetic character of other ways of life, especially altogether nonphilosophical ones, may have their proper place, especially in the early stages of winning someone over to Stoicism, or to philosophy itself. But they are not, and on Stoic principles they cannot be, the substance of any final inducement to the Stoic way of life. For that, the arguments and philosophical analyses I have been presenting and discussing in this chapter are indispensable.[91]

We have explained, then, how philosophy does play an essential role in the Stoic way of life. It provides the basic principles used in continuously structuring that life, and providing the motivating thoughts and desires on which it is led, day-by-day. This corresponds to the first two roles noted above for philosophy as a way of life, as Socrates originally proposed it. But Socrates also made the constant practice of philosophical discussion and inquiry a third component of philosophy as a way of life: for him, to live the life of philosophy meant making philosophical inquiry and discussion one's main daily occupation. Here, it seems, Stoicism departs from the Socratic paradigm. As we have seen, the Stoics make all of philosophy, even its most abstruse and theoretical parts, an enterprise aimed at living any human life properly, and they allow, or even insist, that a full Stoic life is open even to a slave, even though slaves are occupied in menial or other tasks as their principal occupations, on a full-time basis. There could hardly

---

[90] See Marcus Aurelius's *Meditations*, and Epictetus's *Discourses*. The *Moral Essays* and *Moral Letters* of Seneca, while they do contain many extended and rather detailed expositions of Stoic philosophical theory, frequently accompany those with such rhetorical appeals, as providing grounds for believing the principal doctrines of Stoic moral theory. For further discussion, see Cooper, essays on "Moral Theory and Moral Improvement" in Seneca, Marcus Aurelius, and Epictetus, *Knowledge, Nature, and the Good*, chaps. 12 and 13, and Scaltsas and Mason, *The Philosophy of Epictetus*, 9–19.

[91] This is true even, or especially, for the Stoic life of one who, in Stoic terminology, is "progressing" toward virtue and is not (anyhow, not yet) virtuous and wise, as virtue and wisdom are defined in their theory. In fact, almost everyone who did in fact live the Stoic way of life would fall into this category, given the paucity of wise people. On Stoic theory, as we have seen, any life except that of a wise person is not a fully happy one; it is to some degree, as they say, "miserable." But anyone who understands enough of the Stoic philosophy to lead a life devoted to duty in the Stoic way, lives a vastly improved life over that of an ordinary person, with the fundamentally mistaken orientation to things of human value that we have discussed, and the deeper one's understanding and more constant, as a result, one's effective commitment to the Stoic life goes, the more improved it is, and in that sense, the better.

be time in such a life for any constant devotion to explicit, formal, continued philosophical study and investigation. Thus, so far as concerns particular professions and lines of work, social roles, and other functions, which inform one life in comparison with another, and give so much of the substance to individual lives, Stoic theory seems to dictate a largely noncommittal position. If any and every human life, in whatever station and external circumstances, can be a Stoically well-lived one, a life devoted to philosophy, in the sense of a special sort of intellectual's life, must be, at best, one among indefinitely many coequally good Stoic lives.

Hence there seems to be no place in Stoic theory for regular and constant daily involvement in the activities of investigating and studying mathematics or metaphysical or natural philosophy—or teaching it—as part of the happy and best life for a human being. This is not a required part of the life lived in agreement with nature. If some persons, professional philosophers or natural scientists, have the talent and personal predilection to allow them to elect to devote themselves largely to these activities, as others do to a career of business or art or music, that should, of course, be perfectly acceptable from the Stoic point of view. It might even be something "preferable" for all of us, in more than one way, to choose such a life. Still, the activities of reasoning about philosophical matters, exploring in a systematic way the nature and structure of the universe, and taking part in activities of thought that exhibit in a specially salient way the logical connectedness and coherence of whatever makes any activity good, are surely among the most choiceworthy ones to make as much room for as possible in a human life. And, in any event, the rest of us may owe these philosophers a debt of gratitude if, as a result of their teaching and writing, we can learn better how to live ourselves (in our own, nonphilosophical, careers). But it is clearly not part of the Stoic life, as such, to live a theoretical or "philosophical" life, as opposed to a more practical one, devoted mostly to public and private affairs that do not include extensive engagement with further philosophical study and discussion, after one has come to understand adequately, and to embed in one's own mind, the truths on which the Stoic way of life itself rests, with a ready grasp of all its principles and arguments.

In summary and conclusion, then, it is true that the Stoic way of life admittedly, as I have emphasized, requires extensive study of and practice in philosophical argument and analysis, as a necessary preparation. And it also requires constant and conscious reference, as one leads one's life, to philosophical principles and to specific philosophical conclusions, together with the reasoning on which they rest. If true Stoics are to maintain their complete and active grasp of all the complicated philosophical grounds on which their way of life rests, then, it seems reasonable to hold, they must keep up their studies and their practices of discussion, if not in anything like the full-time endeavor that Socrates himself made it, or as an Aristotelian contemplative might do—but still, as a regular part of their lives. Even some slaves might have time for that. What other humanly available way is there of keeping one's knowledge sufficiently fresh and alive, so that it can play the role required of it in the Stoic way of life? Thus, at least the constant replenishment of insight and understanding from its philosophical fountainhead would be required in a true Stoic life. We do not find evidence from what we know of the Stoics' writings that they saw this consequence, or, certainly, that they emphasized it. And it is true that, if in this way the Stoic life does require regular engagement in philosophical study and discussion, this comes about as an incidental result. It is not (so to speak) of the essence of the Stoic way of life that it includes constant devotion to the practice of philosophy as a form of study, discussion, and inquiry. In that way, as I have said, the Stoic life departs from the Socratic paradigm of philosophy as a way of life.

We will see, in the next chapter, that this departure from Socratic ideals holds also, though for different reasons, for the Epicurean way of life—that is, for the sharply opposed, other main Hellenistic school of philosophic thought.

CHAPTER 5

The Epicurean and Skeptic Ways of Life

5.1. Introduction

Despite their many individual differences, for all the philosophers we have discussed in previous chapters—Socrates, Aristotle, and the Stoics—a devotion to reason lies at the center of the best way of life. The same is true, of course for Plato and, as we will see in the next chapter, for the tradition of Platonism, based on Plato's works, that came to dominate philosophy in late ancient times. For these philosophers, the best life is not merely the one that philosophical reason explains and justifies to us. Reason also guides people as they go about leading that life, in that they act as they do for reasons, drawn from philosophical thought, that they are prepared (up to some point) to explain and defend, so that the reasons that they act upon derive from their own reasoned understanding—they are not taken over "on faith," or by just following a pattern laid down by some guru. But, in addition, all these philosophers hold that human reason is a preeminently valuable power, and especially worthy of our adherence, indeed our devotion, because of its divine origins and/or its affiliations to the divine. It is because of this high status assigned to reason that all these philosophers—they constitute the "main line" of the ancient philosophical tradition—agree, in their different ways, that engagement in philosophical argumentation and investigation is an essential component of the best life (or, for the Stoics, an incidental, but necessary, and especially good, one, exhibiting to the highest degree the value of order in complexity). This connection to the divine is part of the reason why, in their different ways, for all these philosophers, philosophy does not just authoritatively specify some way of life as best for us, but the very practice of philosophical study and inquiry is included within the best way of life.

Neither Epicurus (and his many followers) nor the ancient skeptics, both Academic and Pyrrhonian, accept this conception of human reason, as having divine affiliations that give it some unique power and value. They do not accept, with these mainline philosophers, that human reason has powers of insight and judgment sufficient of themselves to go behind appearances and reach a divinely ordained truth about reality, so as to decide authoritatively about human good and bad, and to discover the true scheme of values for a human life. I reserve further discussion of the skeptics' attitude to reason and its value to later in this chapter.[1] As for Epicurus, he adopts a conception of reason as a purely naturally arising power of humans (and, with limitations and gradations, of some other animals, as well) that is firmly grounded in, and strictly limited by, our powers of sensation and feeling.[2] It has no authority whatsoever except what derives from these sources. Ultimate "truth" is found only in sensation and in naturally unavoidable feelings of attraction or aversion.[3] Where questions of good and bad and how to act are concerned, reason and philosophy are limited to working out, from those bases, correct ways of thinking and feeling, both about particular objects in particular circumstances and in general theory. Reason itself properly consists simply in exercises of memory, and of restrained, wary generalization from sensory experience to what cannot be observed (e.g., the world of atoms, which Epicureans hold forms the basis of all reality)—it has no powers of independent insight into the truth.[4] It has no possible legitimate ambitions to reach some divinely given "essences" of things, by starting from such sensory inputs and working upon them with some inherent, divinely affiliated, powers of insight into divinely constituted reality. In Epicurus's world, there is no cosmic reason, of either a Platonic or Aristotelian or Stoic sort, for human reason to have affiliations to.[5]

Correspondingly, reason becomes just another animal power belonging to our animal nature. It is not something that raises us, as we plan and lead our lives,

---

[1] See sections 5.5–5.7 below.

[2] For information about our sources of knowledge of Epicurus's philosophy, see endnote 28.

[3] This is the burden of Epicurus's doctrine of the "criteria of truth"; see Long and Sedley, *The Hellenistic Philosophers*, sect. 17.

[4] See Frede, "An Empiricist View of Knowledge: Memorism," pp. 225–50, discussing the views of medical theorists belonging to the "empiricist" school of medicine, as well as Epicurean theories.

[5] That does not mean that he accepts no gods, but, as we will see, Epicurean gods have no cosmic function. They are to be conceived as rational animals of the same sort as we, with no greater powers—except that, as it happens, they are to be conceived as never dying.

above the rest of the animal realm, in ways that are crucially important, from the cosmic point of view, as we have seen for Aristotle and the Stoics. The world for Epicurus is a totally material one; everything in it is not just bodily (as for the Stoics), but constituted from material atoms. Such order as the world contains, such natural laws as there are governing the behavior of material stuffs and types of object, living or inanimate, result from random ways in which atoms swirling in the void happened to come together in the formation of our given world, and to hold together in sustaining it in existence. Atoms just happen to come together to form the particular world we live in (there are others), with its particular emergent laws and principles of operation. In order to learn what these may be, there is, therefore, no recourse except to sensory observation and memory of that world, and of how it can be seen to operate, plus modest extensions from that through cautious generalization, so as to cover parts of the world one has not had any sensory experience of, because of distance away or subperceptible size. This capacity for retention of experience by memory and for mundane generalization to what may not have been, or even cannot be, experienced, is what human beings possess under the name of reason. This name, so freighted in the mainline tradition with divine, superhuman pretensions, is applied in Epicurean theory to a diminished, modest set of human animal functions.

This "empirical" understanding of human reason, as opposed to the main line "rationalist" one,[6] led Epicurus to a vision of the best human life as one authorized by reason (as he understands reason), and lived through guidance by reason. But with his reduced and modest conception of reason, he could make no special place within the best life for the practice of philosophizing, of philosophical thinking and understanding, as something to be prized as part of our highest good. Reason was valuable simply because of how it enabled us to get around more effectively in the world, and for figuring out (I will say more about this just below) how we should organize and lead our own lives, in view of what we can learn from our sensory experience and innate patterns of feeling. But its value was wholly instrumental. This was as true of philosophical as of any other sort of legitimate reasoning.

---

[6] The contrast between empiricism and rationalism in philosophical theories of epistemology is best known to us nowadays through our study of the philosophers of the early modern period—Descartes and his successors, on the British Isles (the "British empiricists") and the continent of Europe (the "Continental Rationalists"). However, the terminologies of "empiricist" and "rationalist," and the two associated attitudes to reason and its bases and powers, go back to debates among medical writers of the third century BCE. See the discussion in Frede, "An Empiricist View of Knowledge: Memorism," p. 225.

Thus the Epicurean way of life, a distinctive and even socially prominent way of living for several centuries after Epicurus's death, depended crucially upon his own philosophical arguments and conclusions—as with Aristotle and the Stoics. But it did not require a full mastery of those, as a prerequisite to living the Epicurean life of virtue and happiness. As we will see, so long as one kept a grasp of the fundamental doctrines of Epicurean theory well fixed in one's memory, one could live virtuously and happily on the basis of the knowledge that that organized set of memories would provide. Thus the Epicurean life, the life in which the Epicurean philosophy is lived, does not include the third component I have identified as belonging to Socrates's initial conception of philosophy as a way of life. It did not make the active engagement in philosophical study and inquiry itself in any way an essential part of the best life. Epicurus, with his reduced conception of what reason is, takes a further step beyond the Stoics, in reducing the importance to the well-lived life of philosophical study and inquiry. As we saw at the end of the last chapter, it is needed in any Stoic life at least incidentally, as a means of sustaining one's happy life activities of virtuous behavior, and, besides, it has a high value in itself, as an outstanding example of highly ordered, complex, mental activity, deserving of high rank among preferred activities in which to engage. But for Epicurus, as we will see, active engagement in philosophical analysis and argument is not necessary, even in order to achieve the Epicurean knowledge of the human good and of human life that the Epicurean life does require, and on which it is based.

5.2. Epicurus's Theory of the Human Good: "Kinetic" and "Katastematic" Pleasure

Everyone today who knows Epicurus's name knows that Epicurus had a high regard for pleasure. In fact, as he seems to have thought, experience teaches us that pleasure is the only thing in human life that has value just in itself. It is the only thing that, by and in its own nature, is a good thing. Thus he was a hedonist in ethical theory.[7] Cicero reports as the "beginning" of Epicurus's ethical doctrine his famous "cradle" argument. This deduces that pleasure is the highest, and only intrinsic, good from what we adults can allegedly see going on in the instinctive

---

[7] On normative versus psychological hedonism, see endnote 29.

behavior of all newborn animals.[8] The subsequent discussion in Cicero makes one think, however, that Epicurus did not in fact offer this as a sound argument proving this conclusion.[9] Rather, the appeal to newborn animals' behavior was meant as a sort of reminder to us adults of what Epicurus thinks we in fact know, and instinctively knew already immediately after birth, as soon as we experienced any desires at all, and got them satisfied. We do know this, even now, however much our culture, through our upbringing, has made us forget or deny it, Epicurus insists. Our feeling of desire, from the outset, he thinks, was a feeling of attraction to pleasure anticipated in the desire; in satisfying the desire we felt delight in pleasure, and therein felt pleasure to be good in itself, and in fact to be our highest good, because we felt, so to speak, intrinsic goodness as simply amounting to pleasantness. Those naturally arising feelings of pleasure in the satisfaction of desire tell us (authoritatively, Epicurus thinks) that pleasure is our "natural good," as he describes it.[10] As adults, we only need to attend to what nature (our nature) was telling us when initially we felt desire and experienced its satisfaction, and what it continues to tell us, precisely in our current experiences of having these feelings, if only we will listen. If we do, we will overthrow our culturally prejudiced downgrading of pleasure as a value, and come to know self-consciously what we already knew implicitly at the beginning, in desiring and pursuing things, and what we continue to know implicitly even now. We will recognize that pleasure is our only intrinsic good.

Unfortunately, we come to hide this knowledge from ourselves in the course of our upbringing. By introducing new and different ideas about our good from this "natural" one, our socialization corrupts us with a corruption that newborns are necessarily free from. That is why the "argument" from the cradle can have its

---

[8] See Cicero's On Ends I 29–30 (also, much more briefly, Diog. Laert. X 137 and Sextus Empiricus, Outlines of Pyrrhonism III 194). For more on the "cradle" argument, and whether, as Epicurus thinks, his highest good has to be the only intrinsic good, see endnote 30.

[9] Considered as an argument to that conclusion, it is pretty feeble. The Stoics, arguing not from observation, but from their first principles concerning nature and its operations, claim that the "first impulses" of newborns are for self-preservation (newborns have an innate sense, as yet completely inarticulate of course, of themselves as living things of a particular sort, with certain limbs and organs and certain needs, and an innate desire to sustain themselves as things of that sort). They add that if anyone thinks the first impulse is for pleasure, they are mistaking something that is first experienced after desires begin to be satisfied, as a subsequent by-product to obtaining the object of the desire (viz., self-preservation). See Diog. Laert. VII 85–86. The major premises of the Epicurean argument (that newborns go for pleasure as their ultimate good) is, therefore, not only disputed, but in itself quite uncertain. Certainly, one cannot have direct empirical evidence that with newborns that is how it is. No one remembers what they felt and perceived in the first moments after birth.

[10] See Principal Doctrines 7, Letter to Menoeceus 129, 133.

restorative effect: it brings us to identify with the "child" within us, stripping away from our experience of desires all these later accretions, and enabling us to experience desires in the same way as newborns (allegedly) do, as desires for pleasure and not for any culturally recommended things instead (virtue, power, learning—cultural accomplishments in general). As we grow up we are taught to disparage pleasure, particularly bodily pleasure, because of our need, evident to our parents, to learn to postpone gratification. A timeworn technique in this process is to try to get children to think of, and desire, their health, or other valuable things, as good in themselves, and as more important goods than any immediate pleasure. In this process we tend to forget that (as Epicurus insists) any other such good, more important though it certainly may be than a given immediate pleasure, is itself of value only for helping to secure later and greater pleasures, which are of course immediate ones at some later time or other, namely, the times when they occur. Attending to what Epicurus tells us about the desires of infants (and other newborn animals) allows us to recover, and hold self-consciously onto, that original knowledge of pleasure as our highest good. Knowing that, and keeping the knowledge of it centrally in mind, we can conform our desires to it by self-consciously desiring nothing but pleasure for its own sake, and making sure that anything else we also desire, we desire as and because it helps to produce pleasure, in the present or on some future occasions.[11]

Anyone who knows a little more about Epicurus than just his name knows also that he held quite unusual views about when we are (or are not) experiencing pleasure, and, in particular, about when the pleasure we experience is at its greatest (because purest, or most unadulterated). There is a great deal of confusion in our sources about just what Epicurus's ideas here were, and how he thought he could argue successfully for them. Cicero, for example, makes much, in both his positive presentation of Epicurus's theory and his derisive criticisms

[11] Although our sources do not make this seem to have been a major topic for Epicurus, he, like the Stoics, adopts the Socratic rather than the more complex Platonic-Aristotelian view on the varieties of human desire. He too assumes that all desires are judgments of reason as to the value of the thing desired: evaluative judgment produces or by itself constitutes the motivating impulse in every case of mature human desire (or aversion), and every voluntary action. There are, in that sense, no nonrational desires that would need to be stripped away, before this reform could take effect in the life of a person brought up, as virtually all of us are, to desire other things than pleasure as good in themselves. Those erroneous desires (as Epicurus thinks them) were themselves nothing but evaluative judgments; once the knowledge that pleasure is the sole intrinsic good is firmly in place, they simply cease to occur. In that sense (through changing our minds, and holding different evaluative views), we have the power to make ourselves desire pleasure as Epicurus's tenets tell us to, and to prevent ourselves from experiencing any desires not in conformity with them.

of it, of the two kinds of pleasure that he alleges Epicurus maintained that there are. One of these, Cicero says, we are all quite familiar with, and everyone will grant that these experiences correctly count as experiences of "pleasure." This is what we feel for example in the pleasures of sex, or, less dramatically, when we enjoy the taste of our food in eating it, or feel the warmth of the sun on our bare arm on a cool day. And there are analogues when what we enjoy is some experience or activity of the mind, rather than the body. The other supposed *kind* of pleasure is just an arbitrary renaming, Cicero charges, of a certain other state of consciousness (if ever we could experience it). This would be a state of consciousness in which we were undergoing neither any such (genuinely) pleasurable experiences, nor any opposite feelings of pain or discomfort, physical or mental. Epicurus, on Cicero's account, classed as a second kind of pleasure this mere bodily-cum-mental condition of the complete absence of both pleasure (of the first sort—the only sort there actually is, according to Cicero) and pain. For short, on Cicero's account, Epicurus paradoxically and illegitimately also counted the total absence of both pleasure and pain as pleasure!

Cicero is wrong about this, however, and we cannot understand and appreciate the full force of Epicurus's ideas about the human good without seeing clearly where Cicero goes wrong. It seems clear enough even from evidence that lies somewhat submerged within Cicero's own account, that Epicurus did not intend to distinguish pleasure into two *kinds* at all.[12] Instead, he distinguished two significantly different types of circumstances or conditions in which, he claimed, a single type of feeling (of pleasure, he argued) arises, and on which it is conditioned in the two different sorts of circumstance. In the first set of circumstances, the feeling of pleasure comes into being because of, and in accompaniment with, bodily and psychic *movements*: the movements in the flesh (sometimes rapid and intense, in other cases smooth and gentle) in sexual intercourse, or when swal-

---

[12] Torquatus, Cicero's Epicurean spokesman, initially presents "katastematic" pleasure (for this terminology, see just below in my main text) as the pleasure "which is felt when all pain is removed," and he adds that "when we are freed from pain, we take delight in that very liberation and release from all that is distressing" (*On Ends* I 37, trans. Woolf). In suggesting that the pleasure being indicated here is just a feeling of relief from prior distress, Torquatus and Cicero are inaccurate and misleading (as I will argue), but it is clear from this quotation that Torquatus intends to count as pleasure some feeling that being rid of pain causes in us, or sets free in us. He is not counting the bare condition of absence from pain, itself, as a pleasure: that is only, for him, the cause of this feeling. It is in that sense that one must understand Torquatus's repeated statements, beginning already in I 37, that "every release from pain is rightly termed a pleasure." Cicero's attack on Epicurus's recognition, or attempted establishment of, katastematic pleasure turns wholly on the misconstrual of Torquatus's and Epicurus's view as simply claiming that absence of pain, just in itself, is a pleasure. Epicurus is not proposing the condition of absence of pain as a kind of pleasure, but as one distinct kind of circumstance or cause of a certain feeling, the feeling of pleasure.

lowing one's tasty food, or even when the sun shines pleasantly on one's bare arm, together with the accompanying movements in one's sensory awareness of these events (in some cases, movements of lively excitation). (There are analogues in cases of mental, non-bodily-pleasurable movements: for example, excited movements in your thoughts when you've just learned something that you've eagerly been seeking.) In such a case, the pleasure can be called, in English, a "kinetic" pleasure, as Epicurus apparently did, using adverbial phrases employing a Greek word for "movement."[13] But here the term "kinetic" is not applied to the pleasure in such a way as to indicate an allegedly distinct *kind* of pleasure. Rather, this term marks a special circumstance—that of bodily and/or psychic movement, sometimes quite lively and excited—in which a single sort of feeling comes into being, the one that Epicurus identified as our highest good and called pleasure. This is the same feeling that he took newborns to experience as good in itself and as the highest good. It clearly is, as Cicero says, something we are all familiar with, and that we can all agree with Epicurus in recognizing as a feeling of pleasure.

To grasp and appreciate the second set of circumstances for the arousal of allegedly the same feeling, we need some background considerations concerning human psychology. Epicurus held that waking awareness (which is essentially a general sensory awareness of ourselves and of our openness to perception of our environs) must always possess some hedonic tone, as one could put his point. Either one's consciousness is afflicted by painful or distressed states of feeling, or accompanied by a feeling of pleasure, or, of course, perhaps by both at the same time. This does not seem an unreasonable generalization from what we retain in memory about our states of awareness when we experience them. They always do seem to be other than hedonically neutral in the way we experience them. It seems, really, that there is no possibility of waking awareness, for a human being or other animal, that is experienced as in no way either good or bad, but just flat and neutral. Feelings of liking or disliking, welcoming or rejecting what we experience, just seem integral to waking awareness like ours, an awareness of ourselves and of our openness to outer experience—whether or not our consciousness is being currently acted upon by outside stimuli. This means that even when one is completely free from all the sorts of bodily and psychic movements in which kinetic pleasure (or the corresponding pain) arises—when one's awareness of

---

[13] See κατὰ κίνησιν ("on the basis of movement") in Diog. Laert. X 136, quoting from Epicurus's work titled *On Choices* (περὶ αἱρέσεων); other writers in this context sometimes use instead ἐν κινήσει ("in movement").

oneself and of one's openness to sensory movement is accompanied by no excitements of feeling, and there are no movements in the body or the mind of which one is currently aware—one must nonetheless be in a state of feeling of some level and kind of hedonic tone. In fact, it seems evident that such a condition of awareness must be one of completely positive hedonic tone; any pain or other negative feeling would seem to require some movement in one's awareness itself, perhaps one deriving from some movement felt in the body. An awareness altogether without any feeling of movement, psychic or bodily, would have to be somehow pleasant, because it would be completely relaxed and undisturbed.

In fact, what we are talking about here will be an awareness of one's living organism in repose, that is, in its naturally self-maintaining condition of active readiness for sensory engagement, on the basis of a complete absence of physical deficiencies (which would cause bodily movements of a negative sort, giving rise to excitations of pain). It would be a condition of no pleasure and no pain classifiable as kinetic, but it would by no means be a condition of no pleasure and no pain at all. It would in fact be a condition of pleasure arising from the simple, undisturbed, undistracted, awareness of oneself, and of one's openness to the world through specific sensory inputs, but without being currently engaged with any. It would be an active awareness of one's constitution as a particular sort of animal—a constitution for such sensory engagement. And, as I mentioned, one would not be experiencing this pleasant awareness unless one's condition were one of normal healthiness and ongoing natural functioning: if one's condition were not such, one would be experiencing some disturbing movements in one's consciousness—unhealthy or disturbed and distorted functioning is just what does cause kinetic pain. Accordingly, to pleasure arising in this second set of circumstances for the arousal of pleasure, Epicurus gave the name "katastematic," drawing upon a Greek term for a condition or state, or for the constitution, of a thing.[14] It is called "katastematic" not so as to indicate a special *kind* of pleasure, any more than kinetic pleasures are a kind of pleasure, but rather so as to draw attention to the special *circumstances* of pleasure's arousal, on which it is condi-

---

[14] Rather than attempt a translation of the Greek word here in question (καταστηματικός, used in one fragment we possess from Epicurus's own work, quoted by Diog. Laert. X 136), I simply offer a transliterated version of it in my discussion, as if it were an English word. For the connection of this adjective to the stable constitution of our organism, see Plutarch's quotation from Epicurus's *On the End* in his anti-Epicurean essay *That a Pleasant Life Cannot Be Led on Epicurus' Principles*, 1089d. One common translation, "static," is very seriously misleading and should be avoided. The katastematic pleasure is taken in an active awareness of one's constitution (if you like, of one's stable, ongoing "state"). It is a pleasure in something stable and balanced, but not thereby anything itself static, as opposed to dynamic.

tioned, in the case of this pleasure. We could describe this pleasure as pleasure in the awareness of the healthy functioning of one's own natural constitution, physical and psychic.

In presenting Epicurus's conception of katastematic pleasure so far, I have idealized it, so as to bring out clearly its essential character. I have spoken of a pleasure in or from one's awareness of one's healthy natural constitution, regarded in abstraction from other objects of awareness—ones brought into consciousness through sensory input from outside. But of course this awareness, and its pleasure, can perfectly well be present even while one is not merely open to such sensory inputs, as depicted in the abstract account I have given above, but actively engaging oneself in receiving them. Indeed, the pleasure of this awareness can be present even while one is engaged in consequent pursuits and actions of a complex kind, all guided by such perceptual reception. For example, people in this condition of pleasant active awareness, experiencing no sources, bodily or mental, of kinetic pleasure or of pain, might fill that awareness by attending to something that interests them that is taking place in their environment. They would then continue to experience katastematic pleasure, but now katastematic pleasure focused upon and in part derived from those events and their own focused experience of them. Provided that such additional functions of focused awareness, sensory or mental, do not inhibit or impair what one could call one's katastematic awareness itself, then katastematic pleasure is perfectly possible outside the idealized conditions in which I have introduced and explained Epicurus's idea. One can have katastematic pleasure in, or including, activities of sense and/or thought, when those activities derive from the exercise of a katastematically pleasant state of consciousness. I will return to this important point shortly.

Our sources do not indicate on what basis of empirical argument Epicurus adopted the complex analysis concerning human psychology that I have just sketched, and proposed his theory of the nature of pleasure as a particular sort of feeling that humans and other animals experience in their awareness of their healthy and undisturbed natural state. In our sources it is presented, at best, tricked out with ancillary and confirmatory observations, but not with direct arguments or other sorts of appeal to evidence. We are not told how Epicurus thought other reasonable and open-minded people might be legitimately persuaded of its truth. Like so much of our evidence about Epicurus's ethical views (by contrast with his physical doctrines), what we learn on this topic consists very largely in reports of his doctrines, delivered as if from an oracle. Apparently,

Epicureans were supposed to accept Epicurus as a great genius, the savior of humankind through his insights, which were to be simply taken in gratitude, and used by them in planning and leading their lives. They were not required to inquire into any reasons that might be offered in explanation and defense: they needed only to give them their credence, and all would be well with them and their lives. I will return in the next section to this aspect of Epicureanism.

It is not difficult, however, to sketch how (in accordance with his understanding of the human mind and its legitimate functions) Epicurus arrived at this doctrine, as a carefully prepared generalization from his own varied experiences of pleasure—and, he assumed, other people's too, if only they would attend to them with an open mind. He seems to have regarded in this way his account of pleasure as a single state of feeling, of which we can be immediately aware, and such that in being aware of it we can know its goodness immediately, simply by perceiving it. But we can observe, he thinks, that this state of feeling has two quite different sources: certain perceived movements, especially the more active and excited ones, in body and mind, on the one hand, and our simple awareness of ourselves as sensory and thinking beings, when awake and functioning in normal health. In popular speech and the common understanding, people do not regard the pleasure that, as newborns, they knew as good in itself and indeed as the highest good, as the same feeling (differing only in strength or other incidental features) that they have when they are in (approximately) the conditions Epicurus specifies for the arousal of katastematic pleasure. But that is no obstacle. It may well be that people restrict talk of pleasure only to the excited states of feeling that they imagine newborns feel when getting pleasure from eating when ravenously hungry, and other similar ones open to us as adults. It may be that they talk of the feeling one gets in repose and freedom from all such exciting experiences (whether painful or pleasurable) as something quite else, not "pleasure." That simply shows how we become corrupted in being brought up in communities with misguided sets of values—all, not surprisingly, accompanied by culturally acquired conceptual apparatus that backs them up. Careful and controlled inference from what we do experience shows, he thinks, that the feeling in both cases is the same feeling—of pleasure—differing only in strength or other incidental features (intensity, for example, which is notably present in many kinetic pleasures but apparently absent from katastematic).

I mentioned above that, armed with this analysis concerning the two sources of pleasure, Epicurus went on to count the katastematic pleasure as the greatest that can be experienced. What leads him to that conclusion? To begin with, katastematic pleasure is purest, because one's awareness is then free of any and all disturbances that cause pain, distress, or discomfort (bodily or mental): one's pleasure is accompanied by, and diminished or distracted by, no pain at all, the contrary and opposite of pleasure. But, equally important, in the idealized state I presented it in above, all *pleasurable* excitations, and even milder pleasurable movements, are also absent. Pleasures involving excitement coming from intense desire (which is a common sort of excitement in these cases) do certainly involve the feeling of pleasure, but it is compromised by the stressful state of mind always associated with intense desires. In such a case, the pleasure (even if experienced as intense, for example, in sexual orgasm) is one thus mixed with pain (i.e., with the stressful feeling of need and still-frustrated dissatisfaction that immediately precedes and even accompanies them).[15] Hence, in being free also from all kinetic pleasures, the katastematic pleasure of complete repose is also free of pleasure that is impure, because bound up in the way such intensely desired and intensely experienced pleasures are with the discomforts of stress. Because of katastematic pleasure's uniquely guaranteed purity, it is in that pleasure that we would achieve the goal we would set before ourselves in accepting Epicurus's theory of the good, and in desiring pleasure as our highest good. It is only then that we experience in a pure and unadulterated way what is good, and what we feel to be good, about pleasure. Having, so to speak, the full presence of pleasure—the good—open to us in our consciousness, we are then in a condition of pleasure in which the pleasure and good that is experienced could not be exceeded. It can, if we are lucky, be stretched out into the future. But the experience of pleasure that we have in such circumstances cannot be exceeded, in quantity or level of pleasure experienced, at any other time, under any other circumstances. When experiencing katastematic pleasure, we experience pleasure, and derive for ourselves what is good in pleasure, at its fullest. Nothing is missing of or about pleasure and about its value for us, that we could hope to attain at any other time or in any other circumstances.

If people commonly think that it is greater intensity of pleasure, as experienced at some moment, that brings the greater quantity of pleasure, that is just another harmful confusion, induced by our upbringing in misguided cultural communities; true philosophy, Epicurus argues, shows the error of any such view. Philosophy shows that extreme intensity of pleasure is caused by the stress-

---

[15] Plato's *Philebus*, which of course was available to Epicurus when he was working out his theories, is the classic source for this sort of analysis of desire for kinetic pleasure.

ful intensity of the desire at work in its pursuit, which in turn causes the excited psychic movements that give rise to it. Because of the pain or distress caused by the intense desire, the pleasure is mixed with pain, and its intensity is no more than a consequence of the fact that one's state of consciousness, in experiencing the pleasure, is mixed in that way. To take intensity as a measure of quantity of pleasure is just a delusion. What we should be interested in, and should use in organizing our lives, is how to achieve the greatest actual quantity, the highest level, of pleasure—both at each moment, so far as that might be possible, and for the longest time. That highest quantity is reached when we achieve katastematic pleasure. In that condition we experience as much pleasure, at a single moment, as it is in the nature of things possible to experience. For that reason, Epicurus made the goal of a well-lived life—that is, of a life successfully aimed at pleasure as the highest good—to live always, so far as possible, in the katastematic condition of freedom from all pain, bodily or mental, and from all pleasures, too, that is, ones that bring distress with them to any significant degree. Such pleasures, based in harmful intense desires, prevent or destroy katastematic pleasure.

One can, of course, as I said above, experience katastematic pleasure not just while enjoying one's healthy state of consciousness in a state of repose, but also while engaged in all sorts of activities, led by desires for their particular further pleasures—that is, for the experiences of pleasure to which they give rise—and while experiencing such further pleasures. This is, for the Epicurean theory of happiness, a crucially important point. All of the additional pleasures will, I take it, be kinetic pleasures: they will be pleasures deriving from movements in body or mind of which we are conscious.[16] Some of them may, and presumably will, be at least somewhat mixed with pain, as the extremely intense ones are, but not because, as with the latter, the pain is self-inflicted through pursuing the pleasures with a pointlessly intense, stressful, desire. Here one may think of such normal, frequently recurring pleasures as those of eating when hungry, hunger being a distressful state, though only mildly so when the hunger is relatively slight and not prolonged. But others may be completely free of distressed desire, as I will explain below. Epicurus speaks here of "variation" in one's pleasurable consciousness, and, in considering the Epicurean way of life, his doctrine of this variation is a crucially important one for us to grasp.[17] Those who successfully follow Epicurus's doctrines about pleasure as our highest good, and the only thing good in

[16] So Cicero implies: *On Ends* II 10.
[17] See *Principal Doctrines* 18 and 9; Cicero, *On Ends* I 38.

itself for us, achieve katastematic pleasure as an ongoing pleasurable awareness of their own healthy, well-functioning natural constitutions as sentient beings. This may be threatened by physical or even mental illness (conditions that are out of one's direct control); I will say something shortly about how for Epicurus such threats are to be dealt with, or managed. But leaving such threats aside for the moment, we can consider this pleasurable consciousness as a kind of platform on which to settle the whole pattern of one's feelings and desires, in relation to all the things that concern one in life. It is in this way that one introduces variations into one's pleasurable katastematic consciousness, once that is achieved and sustained. One settles onto this platform desires for a whole array of kinetic pleasures, derived from a large variety of activities involving different agreeable, but mostly distress-free, movements of body and mind.

The most important thing, Epicurus thinks, in achieving this constant and continuing pleasurable awareness, is not to create desires in oneself that, because of their intensity and peremptoriness, lead inevitably (and needlessly) to pain and distress that are great enough (both in experiencing them, and in case the desires end up being frustrated), so as to undermine one's katastematic pleasure, altogether or to a significant degree. Epicurus calls such desires "empty" or "groundless," because they rest on what his theory reveals as groundless evaluative opinions about the things they are desires for, as sources of pleasure.[18] He speaks here especially of infatuated desires, or addictions, as we sometimes speak of them: desires for certain (as he calls them, extravagant) foods or drinks or for other practices, for example, for sex of certain sorts or with certain particular people. As to empty and groundless desires for sex, we can think especially of desires based in one's having fallen in love, where that means an attachment that makes one feel that one's life will be ruined, cannot go on in any way happily, without one's being with and having sexual relations with the loved person. For a different example, suppose you like lobster quite a lot; it is one of your favorite foods, something you dote on. In light of that, you might, on some occasion, conceive a desire for a lobster dinner (you might create this desire in yourself, as Epicurus will say) that is so intense and peremptory that, when you go to the restaurant and discover that they are fresh out of these crustaceans, you become quite upset, thoroughly disappointed and frustrated. You had been planning on lobster, you had anticipated with relish all day long the pleasure of eating it: you

---

[18] See *Principal Doctrines* 29 (the content of which is stated somewhat differently, and better, in *Letter to Menoeceus* 127) and 30, with the important scholium to 29 printed in most translations.

now feel and think that you *need* lobster for your dinner. You cannot enjoy the meal that you go on to have anyhow (since, after all, it is dinnertime and you are hungry): no substitute will do. ("Crayfish? Crab? Atlantic salmon? Foo.") Now, this gourmand's way of desiring a lobster meal on such an occasion is not just material for a comedian's skit. It is emblematic of many of the desires that make up the emotional life of many people. They, like him, are out of sorts, if what they want is denied them, or even while desiring it in the first place. Their way of desiring things is needlessly intense and peremptory. By desiring something in that way, they undermine and make impossible the katastematic pleasure that they previously experienced, or would have been able to experience if they had not had desires of this sort. These desires are self-defeating, if one conceives one's desires, as for Epicurus one ought to, as aimed ultimately at the highest good—at pleasure, not just of some moment, but at every moment over a whole lifetime.

Instead, even if one does have favorite foods or drinks (that is perfectly natural, after all), or ways of having sex or people to have it with, or other favorite practices or activities, one can desire them without the intensity, or the peremptoriness, that marks desires as groundless and empty. That nonintense, nonperemptory way is how one will desire them, if one takes seriously Epicurus's analysis of the nature of pleasure, and recognizes katastematic pleasure as one's highest good. In that case, one will treat all such favorites as among one's preferred ways of satisfying naturally arising hunger or thirst or sexual desire, or of spending one's time interestingly and with satisfaction, both at work or in other obligations, and at leisure. But one will recognize that the pleasures that can be gotten from these favorites, if experienced, are only variations—preferred ones, to be sure—on one's state of consciousness in enjoying one's katastematic awareness of one's healthy normal condition or constitution as a sentient being. That is, these pleasures are only preferred variations on one's highest good of katastematic pleasure. One's katastematic pleasure is not increased by the addition of the pleasure of enjoying the favorite food or activity, and one is not deprived of that highest state of pleasure by, as it may happen, being blocked from having that added pleasure on some occasion when one particularly wanted it. With enough reasonable ingenuity in planning one's life, there are plenty of other undisturbing ways and things to eat or drink, or ways to engage one's energies in some activity of sufficient interest to oneself, so as to keep up an active life without succumbing to boredom (that, of course, is a severely distressing condition, and would detract from one's katastematic pleasure), even if one were deprived on some occasion, or even often, of one's favorite ways of getting pleasure. One can always eat or drink something else healthy and tasty enough to be satisfying, or, as the case might be, one can engage in some other interesting enough activity, in place of the one that has been prevented or interrupted. All the pleasures that these other ways of engaging oneself provide are alternative variations, not perhaps among one's favored ones, but good enough nonetheless—anyhow, in a pinch. Their availability makes it entirely misguided to desire one's favorites in the way that my gourmand desired his lobster, and that many people desire just about everything they desire.

All such variations (whether favored ones or not) are, as I said, particular kinetic pleasures that are "additions" to the katastematic pleasure. I place scare quotes around that word here because these do not *increase* the pleasure in one's overall state of mind. As I have explained, pleasure is a single type of feeling (it is not necessary to think of it as a sensation, as if always coming from bodily processes that affect consciousness through sensory stimulation). To vary the pleasure that you are constantly experiencing if you are living well and happily—that is, the one that is based in katastematic awareness—is to bring it about that that pleasure now comes to have among its sources also the particular movements in the soul (often associated with further movements in the flesh of the body) that give rise to the pleasure of the food or drink or of the other activity that you then engage yourself with. The pleasure does not increase, but it comes to have new, additional sources, and in that sense one experiences a second pleasure, the pleasure from that source, deriving from the focused use of one's pain-free and pleasurable awareness of one's sentient self. These additional sources of pleasure are among your favorite ways of engaging yourself, or else, when circumstances and availabilities make that difficult or impossible, less favored but nonetheless perfectly satisfactory ones. In either case, the result of varying the basic, katastematic, pleasure with some kinetic variation is an experience of pleasure that has its own particular character: the awareness of the kinetic activity as part of the source of the pleasure on that occasion, colors it with a particular character, different ones for each. The pleasure a fully accomplished Epicurean gets from a meal of lobster differs in its felt character from that of listening to a symphony, or reading a book. But even the less interesting ways of engaging yourself help to reinforce and keep up one's katastematic pleasure, by giving sustained pleasure in the active use of your healthy human constitution and consciousness.

Nonetheless, it is through having learned to enjoy and take a vital interest in a number of what are for the given individual favorite ways of varying one's pleasure that, for Epicurus, the happy life is to be attained. This is a fundamental point for Epicurus in working out his theory of human happiness. What you can look forward to with zest, as you contemplate and form expectations for tomorrow, and what sustains your ability to continue feeling katastematic pleasure throughout your days, are these favorite pursuits. If deprived of them, to any significant degree, for a time or on some occasion, one can, as Epicurus emphasizes, still find ways not to fall into pain or distress and lose one's grip on pleasure. But that is a second-best situation, and one that might very well become impossible to maintain, if it continued for a long time. Having the spice of favorite variations on pleasure in one's life makes it stably and securely worth living; one may manage without them, but one does not want to live that way. Any ordinary well-lived Epicurean life will be full of vitality and interest, because of the regular and continuing presence in it of such favorite ways of engaging one's consciousness of one's active nature. It is important to bear in mind that, although all the sources of these variations, whether favorite ones or not, are of the kinetic type—consisting in movements of mind, and usually of body, too, rather than in the repose of katastematic pleasure on its own—not all of them are *mixed* pleasures (involving some degree of distress or pain), though of course some of them will be, in particular the pleasures of eating favored foods when hungry. The pleasure of eating food, whether it is a favored food or not, when hungry is, as I explained above, a mixed pleasure, because the experience of pleasure then is mixed with the experience of the pain of need for the removal of the distress of elevated hunger. Most crucially, none of them are mixed to such a degree that the desire for them, which motivates and guides the experience of them, is characterized by intensity and peremptoriness: in the happy Epicurean life, groundless and empty desires are totally absent.

It is admittedly impossible not to feel bodily, and even mental, discomfort, to some degree, if one is hungry or thirsty, or sexually deprived for any sufficient period of time. Such naturally arising desires, which lead to such discomfort if unsatisfied, Epicurus classifies as not only natural ones (and therefore perfectly acceptable in a well-lived life) but also necessary: they arise inevitably in all of us at intervals, and if they go unsatisfied bodily pain and discomfort of a demanding and very distracting sort are also soon inevitable.[19] Indeed, the experience of hunger or thirst, or other natural and necessary desires, always carries with it some degree of discomfort—that is one way that nature ensures that we take proper

---

[19] See *Letter to Menoeceus* 127 and *Principal Doctrines* 29. For further discussion, see Cooper, "Pleasure and Desire in Epicurus," pp. 498–508.

care of our bodily needs. Hence in enjoying eating or drinking when hungry or thirsty (the normal circumstance for having these pleasures), and in having other similar enjoyments, one cannot avoid having a mixed pleasure. That is why a prudent Epicurean will take care, to the extent possible, to avoid ever becoming extremely hungry or thirsty or sexually deprived. (I will have something to say below about what one can do to maintain one's katastematic pleasure if, despite one's best efforts, one does fall into a condition of extreme need, causing serious distress, or into bodily pain caused by disease or physical injury.) Some of many people's favored activities (e.g., running, or other strenuous exercises, or games) also inevitably involve pain and discomfort, mixed with the pleasure. That need not disqualify them from inclusion on good Epicureans' list of planned-for variations of their pleasure. The pain mixed into the experience may be of such a sort as to be tolerable, as one consequence of the overall movements of body and mind that give rise to the pleasure of variation. What matters most—but this matters crucially—is that the commitment people have to these as favorite ways of enjoying the exercise and functioning of their natural constitutions should not be accompanied by the sort of intense and peremptory desire to engage in them that immediately and necessarily undermines their katastematic pleasure. Also, of course, an activity involving pain or distress in the mixed pleasure that it gives rise to, that is so great that the pain is inevitably very distracting, and therefore significantly undermines, of itself, one's katastematic pleasure, would have to be dropped from the list. And, of course, it should go without saying that in all one's choices, whether of food and drink or of activities of whatever sort to engage in, one must, in deciding on a pleasure of the moment, take rigorously into account possibly countervailing consequences for pleasure in the future, or for being beset afterward by unmanageable pain.

Many, or even the vast majority, of the favorite pleasures of variation in any normal human being's life will not be mixed with pain in any of the ways I have mentioned, though they too will be kinetic pleasures. If one is fond of music (either for playing or singing oneself, or for listening to), the pleasure is of the sort "which stirs our nature with its sweetness and produces agreeable sensations in us," which is Cicero's first characterization of what he later calls pleasure "in movement."[20] The organ of hearing and the central organ for sensing are stimu-

---

[20] *On Ends* I 37, trans. Woolf; for "in movement" see II 8ff. If my interpretation of Epicurus's theory is right, Cicero gets the order of causation backward here. It's not the pleasure that causes movements or produces sensations; the movements that stir our nature with sweetness thereby produce the pleasure, by

lated with smooth and orderly movements, which give rise to smooth and pleasant movements in the soul or mind, so that the pleasure we experience is aptly characterized, as Epicurus and Cicero both characterize it, as a kinetic pleasure, or pleasure in movement or movements (bodily and psychic). Yet these are not in any way disturbing or distressing or painful movements; the pleasures they cause are not mixed pleasures at all. The same holds, in most cases, for the pleasures of conversation with friends, or of reading and studying, or going to the theater, or even of watching television (provided the program's subject or the images conveyed are not distressing in themselves). The pleasures of caring for a garden, or of all sorts of social games and interactions (the ones that are pleasant, I mean) are similar. All these combine physical activities with ones of mental engagement, and those activities give pleasure through the pleasant character of the psychic movements—the feelings—to which they give rise.

Although Epicurus describes katastematic pleasure as experienced in the absence of pain or discomfort in the body and of mental distress, he does not, as I will explain shortly, hold that a person must cease to experience katastematic pleasure, if there is pain in the body, even, possibly, quite serious pain. Mental distress, at least if at all significant in degree and extent, is another matter. That does undermine the feeling of well-being and well-functioning that is at the core of the katastematic pleasurable self-awareness. But it is also something that (on Epicurean principles) we can rid ourselves of, if we understand correctly and well why being severely distressed or upset is never justified, and indeed why mental upset is nothing but self-inflicted harm. Bodily pain and discomfort, by contrast, are often not something we cause directly in ourselves, or that we can rid ourselves of simply by thinking straight about what is good and bad for us (in any event, thinking straight might be difficult, under some circumstances of pain). Epicurus claims, and stresses, however, that, even if one is in extreme pain, one's overall state of mind can be one of pleasure, that is, katastematic pleasure, varied by some suitable kinetic ones. This is so partly because, as he himself is quoted as saying on his deathbed, one can "array in opposition" to the pain (or, in Cicero's translation, "counterbalance" it with) extremely pleasant memories of past pleasures, both katastematic pleasure and kinetic ones that varied it.[21] In Epicurus's

---

producing certain sensations. This is typical of Cicero's lax concern to understand Epicurus's theories with precision.

[21] At *On Ends* II 96, Cicero translates from a letter that Diogenes Laertius quotes (X 22) as having been addressed to Epicurus's friend Idomeneus on what Epicurus said in the letter was his last day. He had been suffering for some days from severe bladder disease.

case, these were recollections of philosophical discussions in his school and its garden with friends and colleagues. But one can also distract oneself from the pain, often enough, simply by engaging one's consciousness in favorite activities still available despite the pain and injury or illness. The resulting kinetic pleasures can serve to sustain, as they vary, your katastematic pleasure. The pain may remain, but it recedes into the background of your consciousness, which is focused instead on, and occupied by, the kinetic pleasures you draw upon as variations of your katastematic pleasure.

It also can aid one in such emergencies, Epicureans thought, to keep repeating to oneself (obviously, as an item of belief) a celebrated abbreviation of one of Epicurus's most famous *Principal Doctrines* (however wildly overoptimistic), concerning bodily pain: "Short if it's severe; light if it's long."[22] Apparently Epicurus felt it important to claim that, on his principles, it is just as possible for someone to live in continuous happiness, right up to the end, as for Aristotelians and Stoics. Even if that is not always so (because bodily pain can be so severe for so long that no one can sustain katastematic pleasure in the face of it), it does seem fair to claim, as Epicurus does, that, on his account, we do have psychological resources sufficient to sustain our katastematic pleasure, and so our grasp on our highest good, even under many of the most threatening conditions of painful illness, disease, and injury. True, perhaps things can get so bad that one loses the capacity to retain one's pleasurable state of self-awareness even by attempting whatever variations on it one can manage. But the important point is that Epicurus sets up for human life an objective that does not, for most people most of the time, lie beyond human capacities. An Epicurean way of life seems quite possible, humanly speaking, despite the uncontrollable risks we all face of illness, injury, and pain, and despite the (thankfully rare) circumstances when illness so defeats even the strongest-minded among us that continuing to live happily and overall pleasantly is simply no longer even possible. When that happens one can, and should, just end one's life, Epicurus points out. No one has to live unhappily, at least not for long.

The Epicurean life, then, is one of continous katastematic pleasure, sustained through the constant variation in the active employment of one's natural powers of sense and thought in favored activities, a life in which one engages these natural powers in ways that one finds particularly interesting—or, in exigent circumstances, in other ways that might be available to one. It is a life of few exigent

---

[22] See Cicero, *On Ends* II 95; this abbreviates *Principal Doctrines* 4.

needs, since one is always ready to make do with a simple diet and lack of luxury, even if some of one's favored activities do require more than minimal life resources. It is a retired, private life, as we will see toward the end of the next section, spent in shared enjoyments within a close community of friends. One final point about the Epicurean life, as we have so far unfolded it, deserves emphasis. Epicurus, like Aristotle and the Stoics, directs each of us to be ultimately concerned in all our actions for our own happiness. Epicurus's theory of our highest good—notoriously, in fact—focuses upon our own pleasure, not on acquiring and exercising virtues. It is true, of course, that, on Epicurus's theory, we should seek always the katastematic pleasure given to us when we attend to our own sensory and mental constitution, as it is exercised under pain-free and undistressed circumstances; the Epicurean life is not one of sexual or any other sort of debauchery—indeed, it firmly rules out all such behaviors, because of the pervasive pain and distress they inevitably entail. Still, as we have so far examined it, an Epicurean's does appear an extraordinarily self-absorbed existence (as the Aristotelian's and the Stoic's lives are decidedly not). Does Epicurus really argue that we should each sink into a private world of our own, enjoying our own bodies and minds, with no other concerns? In the uncompromisingly egoistic Epicurean value system, how can there be room for any concern at all for other people—beyond, I mean, warding them off, or appeasing them, in case they might pose obstacles to ease of access to that private world? In fact, Epicurus argues that, when the nature of katastematic pleasure, and the natural requirements for attaining it, are taken into account, a life devoted to our individual pleasure turns out to be one not only full of deep personal friendships—it involves a shared life of common activities among one's friends—but one governed by the same virtues of temperance, courage, and justice, with all the concern for other people's welfare that at least courage and justice imply, that we find highlighted in the Stoic, Aristotelian, and Socratic ways of life. In the following two sections, beginning with the question of justice and the other virtues, I explain how Epicurus thinks this is so.

5.3. The Epicurean Way of Life: Virtue, Irreligion, Friendship

Following moral conceptions current in wider Greek culture, the philosophical tradition that Epicurus inherits recognizes four principal virtues: (practical) wisdom, temperance or moderation, courage, and justice. In turning now to consider the way of life to which the Epicurean theory of the human good leads, the first thing to note is that, according to what Epicurus says, at any rate, the Epicurean life is a fully virtuous one. One of the virtues (practical wisdom) is a general virtue for thinking well about action in whatever context, the other three (courage, justice, and temperance) are virtues with specific application to different aspects of moral or ethical action or challenges in life. Epicurus's theory of the human good, examined in the previous section, tells us about the knowledge of human values that we need in order to live well and happily. Most fundamentally, this is, according to him, the knowledge that katastematic pleasure, varied suitably with kinetic pleasures, is our highest good. This corresponds, unproblematically, to the first of the four traditional virtues just listed: the state of mind constituted by the possession of this knowledge, when it is deeply ingrained in one's practical consciousness and in one's habits of feeling and desiring, is Epicurus's candidate for the virtue of practical wisdom (φρόνησις), traditionally recognized by Greek philosophers.[23] Hence, in that sense and to that extent, a well-lived Epicurean life will clearly be one governed by virtue. But what about courage, justice, and temperance? Are those also involved? Yes, or so Epicurus claims. He famously said in his *Letter to Menoeceus* that

> practical wisdom is that from which all the other virtues grow, since it teaches that it is impossible to live pleasantly without living wisely, finely, and justly, and impossible to live wisely, finely, and justly, without living pleasantly. The virtues grow up in union with living pleasantly, and living pleasantly is inseparable from them.[24]

Unfortunately, except for justice, to which I will return below, we do not find in our sources for Epicureanism any worked-out account of how Epicurus explicated this claim, and how he defended it against obvious possible objections. Unlike for both Aristotle and the Stoics (with less differential detail than Aristo-

[23] Note that practical wisdom, for Epicurus, as for the rest of the Greek tradition, is not the same as mere knowledge (the philosophically well grounded ability to reason correctly about values and value questions). That is why, in the sentence of *Letter to Menoeceus* 132 immediately preceding the passage quoted just below in my main text, Epicurus says that practical wisdom is a more valuable thing than philosophy. Sextus Empiricus (*Against the Ethicists* 169) reports Epicurus as saying, "[P]hilosophy is an activity which by arguments and discussions brings about the happy life." Practical wisdom is the firmly established reformation of one's habits of desire and feeling when the knowledge of philosophy's conclusions about life and about human values is grasped and held firmly in one's memory. So it is a better good.

[24] *Letter to Menoeceus* 132; also, in shortened form, in *Principal Doctrines* 5. The word translated "finely" here, καλῶς, is the same word Aristotle uses in claiming that the inherent goal for all virtuous actions, as such, is "the fine."

tle provides), it appears that Epicurus developed no detailed theory of what (apart from justice) each of these moral virtues is, that is, of what the specific psychological state is in which a person is entitled to be called a courageous, or a temperate person, on proper philosophical consideration.[25] We just get the blank assertion that a pleasant life requires it to be a virtuous one, that is, a courageous, temperate, and just one (and one possessing such other moral virtues as there may be). In what follows I will attempt to fill this gap by drawing upon my account in the previous section of Epicurus's views on pleasure itself, and on the psychological dangers we face in pursuing it.

One important point should be clear already. If virtue, or any virtue, has any value for us at all, it must be entirely as a means to pleasure in our lives—in particular, of course, as a means to our attaining in the first place, and then sustaining, katastematic pleasure in our consciousness of ourselves as organisms and agents. Only pleasure is good in itself; so if virtues are good, too, they can be so only in this indirect and secondary way. For philosophers of the Greek philosophical main line, it would seem a flat impossibility that virtue could have only such value. For them, the very concept of a human virtue rules this out. For Aristotle and the Stoics, and Socrates and Plato too, the human virtues (under the names of those traditionally prized qualities just mentioned) were to be conceived as perfections of our very natures as rational beings; it is of their essence to be conditions under which our power of reason is brought to its fullest natural realization, and set in charge of our lives. As such, virtues were necessarily good in themselves, whatever further productive effects they might have for our acquiring and enjoying other things of legitimate independent value. For these mainline philosophers, being virtuous is, for us, what our being good, and so our own good, consists in. Likewise, acting virtuously constitutes our happiness. For such philosophers, a conception of virtue that gave it only the instrumental value

---

[25] Cicero provides for his Epicurean spokesman in *On Ends*, Torquatus, brief explications of how temperance and courage are, for Epicurus, closely linked to maintaining one's katastematic pleasure, but these explications do not seem to rest on, or reveal, any analysis or definition of either virtue in terms of its specific psychological constitution. See I 47–49. Even in Torquatus's account of how being a just person is necessary for a pleasant life (50–53), Cicero omits to report the theory of what justice is that we learn about from Epicurus's maxims (on this, see below). Cicero's whole account of Epicurean virtues shows signs of having been improvised by himself, drawing on various scattered bits of Epicurean theory, rather than worked up from any specific Epicurean text dealing with the topic of what the virtues are and how, given that, they are linked to happiness. His principal theme is to show that for Epicurus, the virtues, as popularly conceived, are in fact valuable solely as means to katastematic pleasure, and not at all "in themselves."

that Epicureanism gives it, would simply be an unacceptable (mis)conception of what virtue itself is.

The same may presumably be said also for what one might call Greek moral common sense. It is certainly a view that Cicero vociferously maintains as his own, and thinks belongs to the Roman elite's moral common sense. On that basis, he castigates Epicurus mercilessly for violating this view in his theories. Rather, from the point of view of the mainline philosophers, and that of common opinion, if this is how Epicurus proposed to value virtue, and to recommend it to people as part of the happy life of pleasure, then he was simply declaring to be of value something other than virtue—some surrogate, perhaps with some external resemblance to true virtue, but something altogether else. For Epicurus, in fact, to speak the plain truth, they would say, virtue was not merely not a good thing; it was something thoroughly bad: on his view it is a bad failure of understanding if one values virtuous behavior as a good in itself. And, indeed, on Epicurus's view, true virtue, as these people think it—as a good in itself—is bound up with—it is an essential and inseparable part of—a thoroughly mistaken understanding of human nature and human values, a thoroughly mistaken and harmful view about how human beings should conceive of themselves, and about how they should relate to other people, to their own pleasures, and to all their own concerns and pursuits in life. For Epicurus, such regard for virtue is based on the chimerical, morally puffed-up delusion that there is something of intrinsic value except pleasure. If virtuous behavior is an important good in life at all, as he and they evidently agree that it is, it cannot be conceived as having any such value. We must reconceive, and explain, virtue—its value, and the virtuous life—in some different way.

Many people in antiquity were prepared to reject Epicurean ethics as false, and to disparage the Epicurean way of life, simply because it did not allow for the intrinsic goodness of virtue and virtuous action. So strong was their intuitive sense that virtue is of higher value than pleasure or any other good. Since Epicurus's theory clearly had that unacceptable consequence, they thought, one could simply dismiss in advance, without seriously confronting them, Epicurus's reasons for thinking that pleasure really is our highest, and only intrinsic, good. I will set aside for now the question of the virtues' intrinsic value. I will return to it in the next section, after we have seen how Epicurus did think that what he was willing to call justice, courage, temperance, and other moral qualities played a central role in governing a well-lived and happy life. I will attempt to show that, when all his philosophical views are taken into account, his theory does allow for something, from his opponents' perspective, surprisingly close to the sort of intrinsic value of virtuous action that their intuitions demand. Whether that would be sufficient to mollify them, I will leave an open question. But first, let us consider in its own terms Epicurus's theory of the moral virtues, and their place in the happy life.

Since, as I said, Epicurus seems not to have offered his own theories of the psychology—the specific attitudes and spirit of behavior—of the different types of virtuous person, we can begin by thinking of the various virtues simply in terms of the ranges of behavior that are associated with them in popular thought and ordinary concepts.[26] Thus temperance consists, in practice, we could say, in not overindulging in bodily pleasures of eating, drinking, and sex, and showing a general restraint when it comes to assessing the value of immediately available pleasure in relation to potentially damaging consequences. In popular morality, those who are seen to behave in those ways consistently are to be regarded as temperate, particularly if they seem to privately make a point of it. Courage involves not being dissuaded from tasks one reasonably sees as important merely because, as may happen, they turn out to involve threats of bodily harm or pain, or may even threaten one's own life. In particular, courage is shown when people refuse to betray family members, friends, or their country so as to avoid a personal threat of harm to themselves. Again, in popular terms, those who stand up to such tests count as courageous people, especially if they seem to make an unobtrusive point of doing so. As for justice, that implies first of all avoidance of criminal activities of all sorts—robberies, murders, financial fraud, abuse of office—and beyond those, lying and deceit and shirking responsibilities, cheating in games or in more important parts of life, or sharp dealing in one's business. Just people are ones who, while frequently enough seeing opportunities to benefit themselves in these ways at others' expense, regularly refrain from doing so, and unobtrusively make a point of refraining. The first question we need to address, on Epicurus's behalf, is whether or not his theory of happiness as continued katastematic pleasure can reasonably be claimed to imply that everyone has good reason to possess these qualities of justice, courage, temperance, and other associated virtues, understood simply in these behavioral terms.

Now, one could accept without much difficulty that living pleasantly (on the

---

[26] This seems to be Cicero's procedure in his discussion in *On Ends* I 47–54.

basis of Epicurus's theory of pleasure) involves constant and regular temperate behavior. It is clear that Epicurean practically wise persons will choose and act temperately as a matter of principle: they will see clearly why such habitual behavior is a good thing, and their temperate way of life will express that understanding, and be based upon a system of desires derived from it. They will understand that kinetic pleasure in general is of a very secondary value, as providing means of varying katastematic pleasure. They will understand that kinetic pleasures of an intense bodily kind (in eating, drinking, and sex), or involving extreme physical exertions, for example in getting the high that long-distance running is reported to give, are impure and bound up with pain in the very experience of them, and, very often, pain as a later consequence. The pursuit of such pleasures, often enough, also involves desires for pleasure that are mentally distressing states of mind. They will know that all pain or distress, physical and mental, has the potential either to disrupt totally one's katastematic enjoyment of one's natural capacities of sense and thought, or to place severe pressure on one's ability to hold onto it. Hence neither will they be given to excesses of bodily indulgence as a general part of their way of life, nor will they ever seek to vary their katastematic pleasure through an intense and unseemly pursuit of those, or any other, kinetic pleasures. If we conceive temperance solely in the popular behavioral terms specified above, then, there seems no doubt at all that, on Epicurus's theory, temperance is clearly required as one organizing component of a truly happy life. Temperance is necessary for happiness, conceived as continuous katastematic pleasure over a whole adult lifetime.

But will the Epicurean wise person regularly and on principle engage in actions recognized as characteristic of courage and justice? Here, I think, matters are really quite a bit less clear. Before attempting to answer this question, we need to recognize, and bear in mind, that, as I have argued in discussing the Socratic, Aristotelian, and Stoic philosophies, any ethical theory is entitled, as part of philosophy's authority for guiding our lives, to extend or trim and adjust our initial or intuitive conception of what truly is characteristic behavior for particular popularly recognized virtues. Thus Socrates insisted that justice required him to remain in prison and face his state-ordered fatal poison; Aristotle developed accounts of whole new virtues that in popular thought did not even have names; the Stoics redefined even the most prominently recognized virtues, so as to turn them away from being conceived as each concerning a different area of life, and into different aspects of the psychology of a virtuous approach to *each* action, whatever the circumstances and in whatever area of life—eating and drinking and sex, or facing risks of harm in order to achieve more important goals, and so on.[27]

To begin with courage, then. Epicurus is entitled, in approaching the question of the place of courage in a happy life, to reconceive this virtue in terms that suit the quiet and rather retiring life that his theory argues is the best one for us. Even under the common conception, courageous people do not run foolish risks, and a distinction between courage and bravado is recognized; perhaps Epicurean courage would move quite a number of actions counted in the popular conception as brave ones off toward the foolhardy, bravado end of the spectrum. Nonetheless, the ineliminable core of courage is the willingness to risk serious harm to oneself, in one's own private longer-term interest, but notably also in the interests of one's family, friends, and country. Does the Epicurean conception of courage preserve this core? Well, what serious risks of harm or loss, at all, would an Epicurean run? Ordinary courageous persons think the threats they face are threats to something that is of real and important value to them (their property, their family's well-being, their country's continued dominance of trade, or simple dominion over a wartime enemy, or the avoidance of the woes of invasion by an enemy). Can Epicurus reasonably show that such value survives reinterpretation in terms of a tight relation to the courageous person's katastematic pleasure?

It is true, to begin with, that Epicurus tells us that bodily pain and injury (such as a courageous person may face and risk) can be endured, and that they do not necessarily undermine our continuing katastematic pleasure. But what reasons would there be for an Epicurean's risking pain or injury in the first place? There can be no doubt that having to put up with these pains, while exercising the skills of self-distraction and so forth that enable one to endure them, is an effort. Why risk having to do that? Further, on Epicurean theory, we do not need, or even have any strong legitimate interest in, any of our property or possessions—the sorts of things that courage is most typically exercised in order to defend. His doctrine is that all these are of use merely to allow or enable continued pleasure, and his doctrine also holds that we do not really need them, since we can maintain a pleasant life on very minimal resources. As he says, "[S]imple flavors bring pleasure equal to those of an expensive table, once the pain of want has been removed; bread and water [can] provide the highest pleasure."[28] Is it

---

[27] See above section 2.4; section 3.6; section 4.9, and n. 86.

[28] *Letter to Menoeceus* 130–31.

reasonable to run serious risks of harm to life or limb just in order to ensure a more constant availability of one's preferred and favorite variations on the katastematic pleasure? Or consider risks run to save other people's lives or injury to their property, and especially the more dramatic incidents of physical courage that take place in wartime. It is true that Epicurus perfectly reasonably insists that not life alone but a good and happy life of pleasure is worth having and continuing, and he can point to his doctrine (I have not mentioned it so far) that "death is nothing to us," because, being composed of atoms, both our souls and our bodies will disperse after we die, removing at the moment of death all possibility of any experience at all, whether of pleasure or pain, and all consciousness.[29] But will knowing these things encourage an Epicurean warrior to seriously risk dying for his country?[30] Why risk the permanent loss of pleasurable consciousness that death entails? What good would Epicureans think they would get from doing that, sufficient to make the risk worth running? It may well seem doubtful that they would see any.

But there is another consideration I have not mentioned so far, and this needs to be included, in order to argue with any hope of success, that courage (conceived in reasonable behavioral terms) is an integral part of the Epicurean happy life. Epicurus must maintain that our future security in seeking to maintain a life of pleasure is of supreme importance to us. We need to have, and to maintain, a reasonable prospect of continued security in having what we need, by way of material and human surroundings, so as to make the continuance of our katastematically happy lives possible (if we have achieved that status). We need to secure the ready availability to us of all the material and human resources we rely on to make our usual favorite activities and practices of life available. This, he could argue, does depend heavily on the stable projection into the future of all the structures of support for our lives provided by our property, families, friends, and country. Our lives will surely be severely disrupted if our normal expectations as to our customary daily circumstances are suddenly un-

---

[29] *Principal Doctrines* 2. See below, pp. 261–62.

[30] Cicero puts Torquatus, his Epicurean spokesman in *On Ends* I, through hoops (I 34–36; cf. 49) to explain on Epicurean grounds, and in the end not quite convincingly, his ancestor's famous courageous deed in fighting and killing a Gaulish warrior in single combat (see I 23). But that may only show Cicero's own lack of understanding or sympathy. It is true that, in this story, the brave ancestor survived without serious injury, so that he lived on (possibly quite happily), and got that benefit from his extraordinary effort, as Torquatus points out. But what if he had died? Would it have been worth the effort, from his personal point of view, properly considered in Epicurean terms, to make the attempt, in that case? If not, then it wasn't worth it in the actual case either.

dermined. If we lost all our property to some bully, or we saw our family destroyed, or we lost our friends through betraying them, or our country fell into the kind of disarray that befell Germany after the First World War, we would certainly face very severe strains, and difficulties in keeping our lives on an even keel. Perhaps Epicurus thinks that no human being, even the wisest among us, could in fact fail to fall into despair or at least suffer very great anxiety (sufficient to make katastematic pleasure no longer sustainable), as one faced the prospect of continued life under such circumstances: the need to make new friends, acquire substitute property, a new family, and so on, and the difficulty of doing so successfully. If so, then all the normally recognized courageous acts, even ones of facing death for country or family and friends, might arguably be found in the Epicurean well-lived life. And that would be so despite the fact that all these things are solely of instrumental value, for Epicurus, in relation to one's own state of happy consciousness, and therefore in principle substitutable for by replacement provisions in like kind.

The situation with justice is apparently more severe, though here again consideration of the important value of security in one's way of life helps to support Epicurus's claims. Justice requires that each person should pursue their own financial and material interests, and those of their friends and family, only to the extent that fair consideration of the interests of others permits. It is true that Epicurean agents place low value, in any event, on money and material resources. One does not need a lot of money or land or other resources in order to support, with reasonable confidence, as satisfactory a range of favorite pursuits as one could wish for; large resources would be needed only in order to satisfy appetites of an excessive and intense kind, harmful to one's happiness, and Epicureans rule such appetites out of court from the outset. So Epicureans would be free from any of the more extreme desires for money and other resources that cause the more spectacular injustices—robberies, murders, embezzlements, even petty thieveries or mere chiseling and sharp business practices. And, as we have seen, the Epicurean doctrine of the possibility of continued happiness, even without any resources beyond a bare minimum, can also legitimately be appealed to in favor of the claim that Epicureans will not do these or other acts of injustice, either: certainly, they will not think they absolutely need any of the things unjust action might get for them. But in addition, Epicurus, in his own theory of justice, emphasizes its role in providing for security of possessions, and thereby of the material means for sustaining life itself, on a mutually acceptable basis, among all those who live and work together in a community. He identifies justice as a pledge or pact among members of society not to harm, and so not to be harmed by, one another.[31] And, following the commonsense ideas about just behavior and what it is to be a just person that I mentioned above, he insists that justice requires that one keep to the pact, pretty much come what may. The security against invasions of one's privacy and disruption of one's life by other human beings (an especially rich potential source of such destabilization) provided by such a pact, if effective, Epicurus thinks, is especially desirable from the Epicurean point of view. (I will come back to this point below.) If such an agreement is in force and generally respected, especially by those who do not share the Epicurean freedom from the pursuit of intense and expensive pleasures, it frees one from major grounds for worry. One can make plans for the short- and the longer-term future, in pursuit of continued katastematic pleasure, with assurance that it will not be disrupted by alien violence or other interference, and with confidence that material possessions and other means needed for one's favorite activities will be available, when called upon for varying one's katastematic pleasure.

On the other hand, the provisions of the pact need to be quite stringent, as I mentioned (and Epicurus clearly recognizes this). Otherwise—if people are free, under the agreement, to pursue their perceived interests to the detriment of others' when they are extremely needy, or when their own interests are extremely threatened, or when they think no one will know what they have done—this beneficial effect is significantly undermined. It is essential to justice that it requires people to adhere quite strictly to the rules defining the terms of the agreement, and that the terms be drawn in such a way as to favor peaceful retention of the privileges of a private life, and to bar outright physical harm to others. Here is where one may doubt whether accepting the Epicurean theory of value can provide the basis needed for being a just person, understood simply, as we have so far been understanding it, in behavioral terms. We can assume, for the sake of argument, that Epicurus's pact does specify as just actions pretty much all those characteristic actions of justice (and avoidance of unjust ones) that I mentioned above. But being a just person, on Epicurus's theory, requires accepting the terms of the agreement with full stringency. That means that one will never contravene these terms, even when one perceives one's interests as extremely at risk, or, especially, when one can be confident that no one will know what one has done, if

---

[31] See *Principal Doctrines* 31–33, and Lucretius V, 1011–27. Epicurus thus comes close to endorsing the theory of justice provisionally advanced by Glaucon and Adeimantus at the beginning of book II of Plato's *Republic*. That is presumably not an accident, or unpremeditated. Epicurus wants to revive and defend the egoist, quid-pro-quo approach to justice that Glaucon and Adeimantus want Socrates to knock down.

one behaves unjustly. Just persons must be ready to allow their own financial and other material interests to be overridden in cases where their interests conflict with the interests of others, if those others' interests prevail under the rules of justice. Both the Stoic and the Aristotelian theories of virtue permit Stoic philosophers and Aristotle to satisfy this condition: a just person, on their theories, recognizes that to have attitudes of regard for other people and their interests at this level of stringency, and to act from them, is good in itself. It is an immediate fulfillment of one's own nature's perfection to have these attitudes and to act upon them. It is true that in doing acts of justice, Stoic and Aristotelian just persons act for the sake of their own happiness, as their ultimate end, just as much as the Epicurean does. But their theories make it clear that, even under circumstances when one's own financial and material interests suffer greatly, or when one could avoid the self-sacrifice involved in acting justly, because no one would know what one has done, it is still for one's overall good to act justly. Whatever financial and material interests would be sacrificed cannot be worth the cost in one's own lost natural good of virtuous behavior if one should act the other way.

But, for Epicurus, happiness is just a continuing feeling in one's own mind. We can certainly grant that in order to maintain that feeling in existence we do not need much by way of financial or material resources. But Epicurean justice's emphasis on the importance of stability and security, as to whatever possessions and other resources for supporting one's active life one may have in place, attaches a positive value, for each person, in holding on to them, if not also in extending one's stock. And it must surely happen that, given one's special favorites among activities with which to vary that feeling, and the great importance, as we have seen it is, of being able easily to vary it, sometimes one will have quite strong reasons to cheat on the agreement. By doing so, with only a very modest degree of luck one will preserve or obtain resources needed to continue one's pleasure in a secure way, by helping to guarantee one's access to those favorite activities. Most notably, one may be quite sure, and reasonably so, that no one else will ever know what one has done, if one does an injustice in such circumstances. Justice—the stringency of the rules defined in the agreement—and self-interest may conflict. In such a circumstance, what can Epicurean theory say, except that in the pursuit of one's own happiness one must do the unjust act? But to say that is to recommend that one not be a just person. It recommends only that one act as if one were one, all the while being prepared, under some circumstances, to violate the pact defining justice. When and if such circumstances do arise, one will act unjustly, while hiding it from others, especially from those socially appointed to punish violators of the pact—such punishment, of course, being a bad thing, because of the serious obstacle to continued katastematic pleasure that we have to assume it will constitute.

Epicurus appears to attempt to avoid this conclusion by insisting that no one ever can be sure that any act of injustice that recommended itself under such circumstances would go undetected. He says (with quite ludicrous caution),

> It is impossible for one who violates any of the things agreed to for the sake
> of not harming or being harmed by one another to be confident that he
> will escape detection, even if from the present time[32] [forward] he has tens
> of thousands of escapes. For it is unclear up to death whether he will in fact
> escape detection.[33]

The consequence is that one must never do any injustice whatsoever, even when one has good reason (from the point of view of one's own future pleasure) to consider doing it, and even when one is in fact very unlikely to be found out (and so to suffer punishment or other damaging effects). That is so because, Epicurus seems to think, once one does knowingly do an injustice, one's mind will be racked with fear of exposure, and its expected bad consequences, and this will do away with one's katastematic pleasure, or will too severely interfere with it.[34] Accordingly, it can never be the Epicurean right thing to do, knowingly to do any injustice. And so, Epicurean theory does, after all, Epicurus claims, offer a firm basis for holding that the practically wise person will also be a truly just one— not merely one who pretends to be, while harboring the intention to cheat if ever (however rare and special the circumstances would have to be) a justified occasion arises.

Surely Epicurus goes too far here. There surely are in everyone's life, if not plenty, at least some occasions when one could do something unjust knowing one would not be caught, and when one has some reason (acceptable from the Epicurean point of view) for doing it. A just person would refrain, nonetheless. Why would Epicurean wise people refrain in these cases? It cannot be fear of being caught, unless they are pathologically cautious—and of course no wise person could be subject to any sort of psychic pathology. It seems clear that they

---

[32] The manuscripts offer a choice of several different prepositions here. I read and translate ἀπό, with J.-F. Balaudé, in *Diogène Laërce*. Other choices, less suitably, would have the text say "at the present moment."

[33] *Principal Doctrines* 35.

[34] See *Principal Doctrines* 34 and *Vatican Sayings* 70.

would not hold back, or not by considering such reasons alone. To uncover a deeper reason why they might nonetheless refrain, we can begin by noting that Epicurus seems to think it right to place a very high premium on the stability of one's life, not just the security of one's possessions and other means to one's pleasures. The Epicurean ideal for human life is one in which each person works out for himself or herself, on the basis of their own experience and whatever appropriate opportunities present themselves, an individual mode of life that suits their particular personality and talents, in which they achieve and sustain katastematic pleasure over their adult lifetime. Each such life consists of an individually selected and assembled set of favorite activities ample enough to allow sufficient variation in the steady pleasure of enjoying one's natural constitution, so that life goes forward always smoothly and easily, without having to face sources of untoward stress and strain—unless some emergency falls, of the sort that can afflict any human life.

Once we have achieved this condition (which is not hard to do, Epicurus insists), the most important concern for each one of us is to stabilize this life by providing stability in its surrounding and enabling circumstances. Our concern is simply to sustain that given way of life, and the particular material and other resources on which it is based. We do not seek to expand our resources, or seek new ones needed for engaging in new activities, even if opportunities presented themselves to do so—whether or not we could expand our resources only by acting unjustly. Our whole concern is to have our way of life, whatever it is, stable and secure: all we want is to continue in the happy and pleasant life that we already have.[35] The point of the pact concerning justice, then, is to enable each of us to enjoy such a stable basis of life with confidence and security, at least so far as disruptions from other people in our community might be concerned—these being the principal sources of potential destabilization that we might face. (Natural disasters, of one's personal health or in the wider environment, are mostly beyond our control, and have to be endured as best we can manage, through the psychological strategies Epicurus specifies for distracting ourselves from their potential ill effects on our continued katastematic pleasure.) So the reason why an Epicurean wise person will never do any act of injustice, as defined by this

---

[35] Of course any life grows and changes over time, with new interests and occupations taking the place of old ones, and in response to changing circumstances: part of the stability of life envisioned in my idealization here of the Epicurean life is the ready evolution from the stable basis at any one point in time, to a future transformation that is in close accord, and continuity, with it. The main point is that the psychological strengths of the Epicurean wise person are all that is needed to make such transformation possible, no matter what befalls.

pact, is that sustaining the practice of justice, established in one's community through the existence of this pact, when it is agreed to by all, is the only stable means—that is, the only means acceptable to all—by which to secure the stable life one already leads, and to which one is deeply and permanently attached. They feel no temptation at all to act otherwise, under any circumstances.[36] They do not, in fact, as one might suppose given what Epicurus says in *Principal Doctrines* 35, quoted above, refrain out of fear of getting caught.[37]

We can conclude, then, that not only temperance (temperate behavior) among the standard Greek moral virtues, but courage and justice also, have an arguably firm basis in the happy life of Epicureanism. In the latter two cases, as we have seen, the high premium Epicurus places on stability, not only on security of access to the means of life, in any katastematically pleasant life plays the crucial role in the argument, given the prominence in any pleasant life of the variations on pleasure needed in order to sustain it over time, lest it fall victim to boredom or emptiness. I will return to this theme at the end of this section, when I turn to the importance in the Epicurean life of friends, with whom to share one's pleasantly varied activities. But first we need to address three features of the Epicurean life, beyond its virtuousness, that are especially emphasized by Epicurus himself and reported in all our later sources. Epicurus highlights the first two features—its irreligion and its freedom from fear of death—by mentioning and elaborating on them as the first things he advises Menoeceus (and other readers of his letter to him) to put into practice in their lives. His readers are to hold onto them, and memorize them, as "elements" or basic building blocks of living well. These also have pride of place as the substance of the first two of the forty *Principal Doctrines*. Ancient Epicureans appealed to these two doctrines as the principal benefits for humankind deriving from the Epicurean philosophical system. Taken together, they free us once and for all from the su-

---

[36] Thus one could say that the Epicurean will always act justly and never unjustly on principle. The principle is that the stability of one's present and future katastematically pleasant life demands this commitment, since that stability itself is of premium value.

[37] In the preceding discussion I have spoken of the Epicurean just person's behavior under "ideal" conditions for justice, where the pact is openly acknowledged as generally binding on everyone and is seen to be adhered to by most people most of the time. Under less ideal ones, where injustice is widespread, I take it that the Epicurean reasoning I have reconstructed and outlined will lead such a person to do what they can to help both to spread understanding of justice as a pact for mutual self-protection, and, by their own just behavior, and avoidance of unjust, to encourage others to follow suit in theirs. If things got bad enough, perhaps even the Epicurean wise persons might not feel bound by the pact, but the tendency of their thinking would be to vastly prefer life under the pact; and they would still see little good reason to violate its terms.

perstitions of religion and from fear concerning our own deaths. Thus the Epicurean life involves rejecting the traditional Greek gods (and, by extension, the Jewish, the Christian, and the Muslim ones too) and all the religious practices that go along with belief in those religions; it is a life of irreligion. And, as a result, Epicureans live cheerfully, right up to the end of their lives, completely free from any and all concern regarding any afterlife.

First, Epicurus's epistemological and physical theories show that human beings have nothing at all to fear, or to be in any way concerned over, so far as concerns the gods and their possible interventions in our lives—whether favorable, in return for our devotions, or vengeful or otherwise adverse action in our regard. Gods there may be, but there is only one concept of gods that we have a right to trust, because this is the only one that human beings everywhere seem to come to by mere natural, unprejudiced openness to the world as we experience it. All other concepts of gods, or additions to this one, derive simply through socially induced, erroneous passing on of traditionally established cultural falsehoods. The true concept presents gods simply as sublimely happy and deathless beings, rather like ourselves in all other respects. Accordingly, since, as Epicurus argues, happiness means continuous katastematic pleasure, the gods, being blessedly happy, cannot have concerns for the whole world and its workings—as if they were creators, and/or enablers of its operations. Nor can they concern themselves with wickednesses or virtuous actions of humans, or wish for devotions from them, and then take the trouble to punish people in case they don't do their part. Such concerns would inevitably be burdensome impositions and would distract the gods from their own preferred pleasurable activities, whatever those might be. All such concerns are incompatible with the gods' essential happiness. And in any event, we know that the world and its contents are the product of nothing but random bumpings together of atoms moving in the void, and that the world and its contents behave according to purely natural principles deriving from the natures of those atoms and from their atomic movements. No gods could have any involvement in the world's formation or its laws of operation. Nor can the gods ever get upset at anything that we might do (supposing, which there is no reason to do, that they could even be aware of it), and cause hidden retributions to befall us. It is totally beneath them to take any interest whatsoever in any of our human malfeasances, or our moral accomplishments, either. Thus, popular religion, with its claims for divine control over the world of nature, and divine moral oversight, and punishment for wrongdoers, in this world or an afterlife, is pure superstition. Its claims (frightening, and therefore disruptive to any decently pleasant human life) cannot possibly be true.

It may surprise us to find Epicurus and Epicureans giving such prominence to the damage that religious superstition can do to people's lives, and claiming Epicurus's own philosophy as a great benefactor because it immunizes us against it. It is impossible to imagine that Socrates or Plato or Aristotle or Chrysippus were subject to superstitious, or any, terror at the prospect of what the gods might do; they, and their followers, did not need the Epicurean doctrine of divinity as happy and immortal, and unconcerned with us, or with the world of which we and it are part, to ward off such debilitating afflictions. So Epicurus could not claim any advantage for his own theory over those of these other philosophers in this regard. That Epicurus lays such emphasis on these benefits of his doctrine does, however, strongly suggest that, at his time, and perhaps increasingly as time went on, many uneducated people, whom his philosophy was also aimed at benefiting, were in fact afflicted by superstitious fear concerning the gods. It is worth noting that the other ancient philosophies did not put themselves forward at all, as Epicureanism did, as having this benefit. Their authors may not have concerned themselves as much as Epicurus apparently did to engage with ordinary, unsophisticated, and uneducated people and their concerns.

Second, Epicurus emphasizes that, on his theories, there are no grounds for being terrified, or even more mildly disturbed simply by fear, in realizing that we are going to die some day. Hence there are no grounds for allowing the fact of our mortality to deprive us, or interfere with the fullest enjoyment, of the pleasures that life provides us.[38] His atomic theory of material stuffs and material objects as all that exists applies just as much to our souls as it does to our bodies. He argues that there cannot exist any noncorporeal spirits of the sort Platonists believe in; such an idea is the merest chimera. Accordingly, our deaths are the permanent end of our natural existences. The atoms making up our souls and keeping us alive are necessarily disarranged and dispersed when we do cease to live. We possess consciousness entirely in virtue of our souls' presence in our bodies, and the functioning arrangements of its atoms, in relation to our bodily or-

---

[38] Thoughts about possibly painful processes of dying are another matter. The remedy against anticipatory distress on such a basis has already been explained (see the last two paragraphs of the previous section); you have no good reason to think that such pains will deprive you of your happiness (if you can attain it), if they do arise. If we do experience such distress, it is our own fault. It is self-caused, not necessary, and not rational, just as much so as fear of death because of what we might suffer after dying.

gans; so our deaths, and the dispersal of our souls' atoms, are the permanent end of our consciousness.[39] Once dispersed, they can never come back together in just the way required so as to sustain life in a human body, and even if they did, they would no longer cause the same consciousness as before to exist. There would be no same self-awareness preserved across this span of time. Epicurus may be going too far when he puts his point by saying that our deaths (in prospect) are *nothing* to us,[40] since his own theory certainly does hold that we have reason to want to keep on living and enjoying the pleasures that only life can bring us. When we die, we do lose something that we want, namely, to be alive, and, like any other fact relevant to our lives, we have reason not to forget this, or act in prospect as if it is not a fact. But Epicurus's theory does show clearly how foolish it would be to become actually upset with fear or sadness when recalling, or bearing in mind, that one is going to die—and thus that one is going to cease to have the pleasures of living. As he says, "[W]henever we exist death is not present, but when death is present we do not exist." We ought not in any way to allow that prospect to undermine our fullest commitment to, and maintenance of, an untroubled consciousness, suffused with katastematic pleasure and varied with our favorite ways of interestingly spending our time. Of course you are going to die sometime and cease totally to exist! All the more reason to live the life you have with full devotion to its pleasures, without distraction through dwelling on that knowledge.

Here, too, it may seem curious that Epicurus should place such emphasis on this benefit of his theories. It does not seem that Aristotle's or the Stoics' theories leave room (though they do not go on about the matter, as Epicurus does) for any actual fear of death, or for any disturbance of our consciousness at all, as a result of recognizing that we are going to die some day. And Socrates in Plato's *Apology* gives his own philosophical reasons for not being concerned over his own death, reasons that apply equally to everyone else too.[41] Perhaps, just as with religious fear of the gods, the debilitating effects of supposing we might somehow live past death and into an afterlife were widespread among unsophisticated people of Epicurus's time and later in antiquity, under the influence of religious myths of punishment in the afterlife. Such myths were spread even by well-enough-meaning philosophers like Plato, as a means of scaring people into be-

---

[39] This consequence of Epicurus's theory of nature is beautifully (even, perhaps paradoxically, rather pathetically) presented in book III 830ff., of Lucretius's poem *On the Nature of Things*.

[40] *Letter to Menoeceus* 125, and (more pithily) *Principal Doctrines* 2.

[41] *Apol.* 40c–41b.

having better than they otherwise might. If so, Epicurus is, here again, wishing to address, not the followers of other philosophies, claiming an advantage for his own system over theirs, but, rather, uneducated people frightened by myths that no philosopher could take seriously anyhow.

The third feature of the Epicurean life I mentioned above is not one that we find expressed clearly in any of Epicurus's *Principal Doctrines* or in his *Letters*. We learn about it from Plutarch, who tells us that Epicurus was famous for the maxim "live unnoticed" (λάθε βιώσας). This striking expression, a second-person singular imperative, addressed presumably to some individual person, perhaps in a letter also meant for circulation, is a splendid addition to the other maxims found in the *Principal Doctrines* and *Vatican Sayings*.[42] To "live unnoticed" means to live a completely private life, with no involvement, beyond what might be obligatory for all citizens, in the public life of one's community or country,[43] and also with no ambitions for making a mark in any other public realm—in any of the arts or professions, for example.[44] One easily sees how Epicurus might have thought his own theory of the human good leads to this advice. For Epicurus, the only criterion for deciding on one's way of life is what will work out best from the point of view of one's own pursuit of a continuous experience of katastematic pleasure, varied suitably so as to conform to one's own, perhaps somewhat idiosyncratic, preferences among sources of kinetic pleasure. It seems obvious that the more exposed one's life is to the attentions of the public, and, in general, to those of any wide circle of nonintimates, the more risks one runs of potential harmful interference from them. The general run of people are more inclined to envy and ingratitude than to honoring honest good services, or sim-

---

[42] Plutarch wrote a short essay arguing against this Epicurean advice, *Is "Live Unknown" a Wise Precept?*.

[43] Diog. Laert. (X 119) says flatly that the true Epicurean will not engage in politics. But Seneca's fragmentary essay *De otio* (*On Leisure* or, better, *On the Private Life*) gives a more nuanced view: under some conditions, an Epicurean would become politically involved. Like Diog. Laert. (VII 121), he tells us that Chrysippus said (not all that differently) that virtuous people would take a leading role in politics, unless some obstacle to this arose (e.g., if political life were too irreversibly corrupted for them to do any good).

[44] As ancient critics were quick to point out, this aspect of the Epicurean philosophy marked it off, much to its detriment, as they thought, from both Aristotelianism and Stoicism. This Epicurean advice is manifestly inconsistent with both of Aristotle's two ideal lives. The second happiest Aristotelian life is devoted to the public affairs and the government of a city constituted so as to advance the virtuous lives of all one's fellow citizens. The absolutely best, contemplative life is equally clearly one of active involvement in cutting-edge philosophical writing and discussion with other like-minded philosophical experts, which would quite naturally lead to recognition as a cultural leader (in the way, in fact, that Epicurus himself became recognized, already in his own lifetime). The Stoics, too, with their emphasis on the importance of the public good as an object of each human being's legitimate concern, promote and specially recommend a life of public service in a political position.

ply reciprocating favors, and, besides, people who set out to distinguish themselves in public life are sure to acquire plenty of enemies. And, in any case, as
Epicurus says in another context, "There is no need for things that involve struggle and conflict (ἀγῶνας)."[45] Moreover, any human life is more vulnerable to the
harms of interference than it is open to helpful advancement through strangers'
good will. On the positive side, life is truly one's own to make something of (and,
as we have seen, it does not require more than ordinary external resources); on
the negative side, intrusions can pose serious obstacles that one has to work hard
to overcome. The pact of justice is one source of self-protection; living unnoticed
is a second step in the same direction.

Still, in *Principal Doctrines* 7 Epicurus seems to recognize (quite appropriately) that one ought not to generalize too readily on such a matter: there might
be, for some people, in some communities and in some personal circumstances,
acceptable Epicurean reasons to opt to live a political life. He says,

> Some people have wanted to become highly reputed and acclaimed, think-
> ing that this is the way to obtain security from others. If such persons' life
> was secure, they attained the natural good. But if it was not secure, they do
> not have that for the sake of which they strove from the beginning, in ac-
> cordance with what naturally suits [a human being].[46]

Thus for Epicurus the default position is to live a life of devotion to one's private
affairs, letting public and political interests take care of themselves, or rather letting them get taken care of by those foolish enough to go in for such things. The
hope is that by keeping out of the limelight one can live happily, in peace and
quiet, surrounded, and both protected and advanced in one's pursuit of pleasure,
by one's family, and by a circle of intimate, like-minded friends.

Epicureans were in fact famous in antiquity for forming little societies, perhaps on the model of life during Epicurus's time in the Epicurean community of
his school at Athens, with its famous garden. There seem to have been many
common meals (including annual celebrations of Epicurus's birthday), and
shared pastimes (intellectual and other), as well as philosophical study and discussion. These were communities of friends, who lived and ate together, and

---

[45] *Principal Doctrines* 21.

[46] Seneca cites as Epicurus's principle, not the unqualified advice (reported in Diog. Laert. X 119) not
to live a life of public service, but rather to do so (only) when something comes up that would make it
acceptable or desirable (*On the Private Life* 3.2). We have no other source to such an effect, but it does
perhaps support a noncommittal reading of this *Doctrine*. See also *Principal Doctrines* 14, which seems to
go in the same direction.

shared their life in all its main aspects. In fact, whether in connection with such a fully merged life together or not, Epicurus placed a heavy emphasis on the presence and value of friendship in making possible the life of katastematic pleasure. The remarkable number of *Principal Doctrines* and *Vatican Sayings* that relate to the topic of friendship testifies to its importance for the Epicurean life.[47] Epicurus valued friendship so highly that he declared that, among all the things that wisdom, that is, philosophical knowledge, provides to make one's whole life blessed, the having of friends is by far the greatest.[48] That marks it as the greatest resource one can have for obtaining and preserving continuous katastematic pleasure in one's life.

Of course, that friendship is the greatest resource does not make it a greater good than practical wisdom itself or the other virtues,[49] since these are causally more fundamental to our ability to live a happy life at all, with or without friends. But in assigning it that high status Epicurus does emphasize how crucially important friendship is for achieving a stable and mutually secure form of pleasurable existence, one that is full of richly interesting activities with which to vary, and thereby most easily to sustain, that pleasurable consciousness. Diogenes Laertius reports that for Epicurus, friendship "is constituted by a partnership of those who are fulfilled in their pleasures."[50] Our nature is such that we all need like-minded friends to share our interests, and to engage with us in mutually favored joint activities, as well as for the open and free conversation that we all need but that are possible only with people we like and trust. Friends are also needed, of course, for mutual assistance in illness or in disappointments, or in other circumstances that, if we had to deal with them all on our own, might lead to disturbed states of mind incompatible with katastematic pleasure. It is in these ways that, for Epicurus, friendship is the greatest resource for living a blessed life.

Cicero, and apparently others in antiquity, doubted or disputed Epicurean theory's ability to support, or even to permit, the assignment of this high value to friendship. For them, Epicurus's theory could not justify the role of friendship in the lives Epicureans seem actually to have lived, allegedly under its banner.[51]

---

[47] See *Principal Doctrines* 27, 28, and 40, and *Vatican Sayings* 23, 28, 34, 39, 52, 56–57, 66, and 78: this is more than a tenth of the total preserved "maxims" of Epicurus.

[48] *Principal Doctrines* 27.

[49] Epicurus declares practical wisdom, as root and origin of the other virtues, to be the greatest good (i.e., the greatest good that is not the feeling of katastematic pleasure); see *Letter to Menoeceus* 132.

[50] Diogenes Laertius X 120.

[51] Cicero's exposition of Epicurean theory on friendship is found in *On Ends* I 67–70, at the very end of his account of Epicurean ethics. His criticisms are lodged in II 78–85.

Cicero does not dispute that Epicurus and Epicureans lived lives of devotion to their friends, but, in this as in other respects, he thinks that they were, and lived, both inconsistently with their philosophy, and better than it told them to live. Cicero insists that friendship (true friendship, not some perversion or fraud) requires loving another person for that person's own sake (*ipsum propter ipsum*). And he claims that if one establishes and maintains a relationship of mutual attention, shared activities, and mutual assistance, "for one's own advantage" or because of its usefulness or expediency (*utilitas*), that cannot be a friendship at all.[52] In linking friendship to each partner's pursuit of their own pleasures, in the way that we have seen Epicurus does, Cicero thinks he is grounding friendship (self-contradictorily) in just that self-advantage or expediency, rather than in care for the other person for that person's own sake. Hence, for Cicero, if, as Epicurus does seem to hold, true friendship makes the greatest, and a virtually essential, contribution to the life of pleasure, he is simply admitting (with Plutarch in the essay I mentioned above) that it is impossible to live pleasantly according to his own theory. To live pleasantly one needs friendship, Epicurus says; but friendship is impossible unless one has other values than pleasure (the friends' good for their own sake), and assigns that value weight independent of any relation to one's pleasure. The good of some other persons (the ones one makes friends with) must be of value to oneself, independently from its effects on one's own pleasure.

But it seems likely that Cicero, and perhaps other ancient critics, Plutarch among them, did not appreciate the subtlety of Epicurus's analysis. Epicurus is not saying that true friendships should or could be initiated, and maintained, by people looking solely to their profit or advantage, measured in material terms, or their self-advancement in society—or with a view solely to such things as one's sexual pleasure or even mere entertainment or amusement. Those may be the sorts of things one would first think of when told that Epicurus recommended friendship as being to one's advantage, or for its "utility."[53] But those are cases of using other people (whether acceptably or not) for one's personal (perceived) benefit. Certainly, if this benefit was all you cared about in a relationship, it would not be a friendship, at least not on your side. But there is no good reason to think Epicurus would have wanted to deny this. If we are to understand and

[52] *On Ends* II 78.
[53] See *Vatican Sayings* 23, 34.

appreciate Epicurus's theory properly, we must keep in mind that the good that a person derives from an Epicurean friendship lies in their achievement and maintenance of their katastematic pleasure, suitably varied. It is not profit or advantage conceived in the crude material ways I mentioned above, as Cicero seems to misunderstand it, that an Epicurean aims at through friendship. Continued katastematic pleasure, suitably varied, is what each friend is seeking, and this fact is of course well and mutually understood among any group of Epicurean friends. It forms the basis of Epicurean friendship on both sides of the friendship.

Moreover, the activities belonging to the friendship that are of such great value to the friends, as providing variations of pleasure, require mutual intimacy and the interest in and concern on the part of each for the well-being and pleasure of the other. (I do not say it requires interest and concern for the other "for the other's own sake," in the way Cicero demands. I have more to say about that just below.) What Epicurus envisages are two or more people who have come to be capable of, and to enjoy, sharing with one another activities of mutual interest on a common basis of mutual trust, exchange of intimacy, concern for the equal enjoyment of the other person, and mutual support for the things that one finds interesting and worthwhile, in part by finding them endorsed and shared by another. Among these activities might be some that one could also engage in and enjoy with strangers or other nonintimates (e.g., certain games or other leisure activities). But, Epicurus is suggesting, even these activities have an enhanced interest, and so give a distinctively interesting variation on one's pleasure, if they are engaged in with intimate friends on a basis of shared mutual concern. It is, one might suggest on Epicurus's behalf, the added complexity of the activities, when they are engaged in as part of such a relationship, that lies at the core of their special appeal when so engaged in, as variations on one's katastematic pleasure. One has more to think about, more to pay attention to, more to integrate into the overall experience, in engaging one's self-conscious experience of one's natural constitution and its capabilities, and therein varying one's katastematic pleasure, as one participates in such shared activities with friends, with a mutual concern for one another's pleasure in the activity, than when one engages in them with relative strangers where that concern is absent.

It is, I suggest, this added complexity that makes the activities of friendship so engaging and interesting—in fact, so enjoyable. If one has no friends, and is left wrapped up in the privacy of one's self, the pursuit of pleasure, when that is understood Epicurus's way, can become cloying and may lose its appeal. One will be stuck in a round of solipsistic pursuits of not very wide scope, that carry the risk of becoming boring, or coming to seem empty and pointless. If one opens oneself up to other people, and makes possible the more complex engagement with one's life that having friends makes possible in part through their interest in oneself and one's life, one's activities in varying the katastematic pleasure (assuming one achieves it) are greatly expanded in interest and indeed in variety. One comes to take pleasure in tending to the needs of one's friends, when they are in need, and to take a special, and added, pleasure even in receiving their attentions, when one is in need oneself. And in being engaged in conversation or other activities of social life with them, one has the added pleasure of anticipating their thoughts, bringing to bear memories of previous conversations and of other accumulated and pleasant knowledge of them. One can relate what one is doing oneself to what they are doing, in a common activity that is aimed equally, by all participants, at the pleasure of all parties. And so on. The central and crucial point, on Epicurus's theory of friendship and its value, is that friends mutually enjoy, in a direct and immediate way, their friends themselves, their friendships, and all the shared and mutual pleasure-seeking activities that make their friendships up. And they do so in a specially strong way: friendship provides the context for many or most of the activities of life that they find most appealing and challenging, and that they place in the first rank among their favorite ways of varying their katastematic pleasure.

It is certainly true, then, that when Epicureans engage with a friend in some common activity, or offer the friend assistance in some situation of legitimate need, they act for the sake of their own pleasure. But the pleasure is an immediate one, the pleasure of the particular thing one is doing—the pleasure of the shared activity, the pleasure of helping the friend when the friend is in need, the pleasure of seeing and hearing and interacting with the friend as they reciprocally do their part in the friendship. It is not only, and cannot be primarily, a pleasure to be obtained in the future (say, the pleasure got from the friend's later helping you out in some way); that would be an abuse, or would at the least tend to compromise the friendship. They are not using the friend for their benefit, when they engage with the friend in the common activities of friendship. They are seeking the friend's pleasure, as part of the objective of the activity itself that they are engaged in. They are seeking that pleasure for the sake of their own pleasure in seeking it, and in achieving it, insofar as they make friendship and its activities among their own favored variations on their katastematic pleasure. They enjoy doing all the things that friendship demands, and consists of. That is, they enjoy seeing to their friend's pleasure, and they see to the friend's pleasure because they do enjoy doing so.

Is Cicero right, even on this better understanding of Epicurus's theories of pleasure and of friendship, that a relationship of Epicurean friendship is a perversion of true friendship, or a fraud, just because it and its constituent activities are entered into always for the sake of the agent's own pleasure as their ultimate end? I think this is very doubtful. The immediacy of the pleasures that are taken, in an Epicurean friendship, in the shared activities of the friends, including the concern of each for the pleasure of the other in their shared participation in them, makes a huge difference. Cicero thinks it is essential to true friendship to care for the other person for that other person's sake (and independently from any relationship to your own pleasure—out of "duty," he says).[54] By that he understands that friends value their friend's good as an end in itself for them, a direct contribution to their own good, capable of motivating actions of friendship even in the absence of any relation to one's own pleasure. This understanding of friendship derives from, or, anyhow, is part of the Stoic and the Aristotelian conceptions, as developed on the basis of their own ethical theories. Plainly, Epicurus's ethical theory cannot support any such relationship.[55] But are we entitled to take it as a pretheoretical datum, a requirement that any acceptable theory of friendship must preserve, that friends love one another in that dutiful, "for their own sake" way? What if, with Epicurus, we do not love them and act on their behalf in that way, but only because we find it immediately pleasant to love them and act for their pleasure? On a different understanding from Cicero's of what could be meant by "for their own sake," could it not be said that one does then love them and act on their behalf for their own sake, just because of this immediate pleasure taken in their pleasure? That is, one acts not, or not only, because of any longer term or future benefits in one's own later pleasures, but for the direct

[54]"Officium" is Cicero's word here for duty: see, e.g., *On Ends* II 81.

[55]In *Vatican Sayings* 23, in what seems certainly the correct Greek text, Epicurus does say that "[e]very friendship is worth choosing for its own sake (δι' ἑαυτήν), though friendship has its origins in its benefits." I take this to mean that true friends value both their friend and the activities constituting the friendship, each for its own sake. Understood Cicero's way, this manifestly contradicts Epicurus's fundamental theory of pleasure as the whole of the human good (everything else having only productive value in relation to that experience). This could be simply an intentionally provocative overstatement of Epicurus's actual view. But in what follows in my main text I suggest another way of understanding Epicurus's claim in *Vatican Sayings* 23 that friendships are worth choosing "for their own sake."

and immediate pleasure one takes in loving them and in so acting. Perhaps that is, after all, enough to preserve whatever truth about friendship one may legitimately have had in mind, in laying down as a pretheoretical datum to govern all acceptable theories of friendship, that friends love and care for one another "for their friend's own sake." To seek a friend's pleasure for the pleasure of doing so certainly does not seem damagingly self-seeking.

Epicurus emphasizes that for Epicureans friendship is a source of each person's security. Indeed, as he puts it in *Principal Doctrines* 28, it is the easiest such source, living as we do among the bad things that can afflict any human life, and the danger of suffering them that arises from the malevolence of many other people. In this security he certainly includes protections of an ordinary sort: friends rely on one another to ward off physical dangers or threats and they help each other in need. But as we have seen, the mutual security of friendship consists more fundamentally in the assurance that living in close union with people who are one's friends provides for the constant maintenance of one's own katastematic pleasure, suitably and interestingly varied day by day. Living among friends, one can be securely confident that one will be able readily to fill up one's days with activities and pursuits of the very special degree of complex interest that friendship makes possible.

In addition, Epicurus strikingly declares friendship "an immortal good," in comparison with wisdom (σοφία), the knowledge and understanding of human nature and the human good that is the goal of philosophy. Wisdom, he says, is only a mortal good.[56] That friendship is an immortal good must mean, for Epicurus, that it is through our friends' fond memories of us and of our good times together, and their continuing love for us after our deaths, that we obtain immortality (insofar as human beings can be immortal at all). To the extent that people like to think they are immortal, then, it is friendship, and only friendship, that can give us what we want, in an Epicurean world. It is in this way, as a reference to friendship and its benefits, that we should presumably understand the closing words of Epicurus's *Letter to Menoeceus*:

> Practice these precepts, and ones related to them, day and night, by yourself and with a like-minded friend, and you will never feel troubled either when awake or when asleep. You will live among human beings as a god: a human being living surrounded by immortal goods is in no way like a mortal animal.

[56] *Vatican Sayings* 78.

5.4. The Epicurean Life: Concluding Summary

Let us, then, draw together the threads of the Epicurean way of life that we have been sorting through in the previous two sections. Epicureans live convinced of the truth of Epicurus's theory of nature, which makes physical reality all the reality there is. All that is real is ultimately made up exclusively of material atoms moving in an infinite void, by chance at some places and times forming worlds, such as our own. Epicurus made major points in this theory available for memorization in his published *Letter to Herodotus*, a pupil. Having memorized these major points, one could readily call them to mind, thereby renewing one's convinced belief in their truth, in case something might happen to make one waver, and thus threaten one's steady and pleasure-filled state of mind by some foreboding or worry about nature's operations. In particular, this theory makes it completely clear that, though gods do exist, they do not and cannot affect human life, or the world and its operations, in any way, through any actions of their own. Their own long-lasting lives of supreme katastematic bliss, effortlessly and beautifully varied in their communal activities, make them paragons and paradigms of that immortal blessedness that we ourselves attain through the immortal good of friendship. Except in that way, that is, as models of long-lasting and continuous happiness for us to aspire to, the gods play, and can play, no role in our lives—unless, that is, we are foolish or deluded enough to imagine one for them to play, as many people, including philosophers like Plato, Aristotle, and the Stoics do. Likewise, Epicurus's theory of nature shows that our physical deaths are the permanent end to our consciousness, and so to our very existence, as agents and seekers of happiness.

Holding firmly to a convinced belief in these truths, Epicureans concentrate the whole of their attention on the here and now, seeking to live their lives by following Epicurus's ethical precepts as outlined in the *Letter to Menoeceus*, and in the *Principal Doctrines* and other collections of maxims. These collections too are ready for memorization, and for subsequent use in the same way as the *Letters*. They are a handy resource for renewing or strengthening one's ethical beliefs in case something arises that might threaten one's equanimity. Epicureans know that pleasure is the sole thing good in itself, or think they do, because this is something, as Epicurus has taught, that they can directly feel, and therefore know, every time they experience pleasure, if only they will strip away, and keep at bay, contrary beliefs belonging to the surrounding culture. They also accept, as an item of firm belief, that their greatest pleasure is a feeling given by the steady experience of a healthy and normal state of self-consciousness, to the achievement and maintenance of which they bend their efforts. They experience this as living, waking, agents in touch with the world around them, with which they interact, as it presents itself to them through the use of their senses. They make it their highest and constant objective in life to attain and then sustain in existence that state of pleasurable self-consciousness. They know that all this knowledge, just summarized, is the result of philosophical investigations conducted by Epicurus, handed on to them for their benefit, and they honor him for it in special memorial observances. Leaving aside for the moment (I return to it below) the question whether they have engaged to any significant extent in philosophical study themselves in order to acquire it for themselves, they possess this knowledge in such a way as to have transformed their own motivations and desires so that those are in full conformance with it. It is held in their minds as practical knowledge, knowledge of value, embedded in their desires and directed at the management of their lives. It is not theoretical knowledge about value.

This practical wisdom, governing their lives, leads them to keep away from the competitive life of politics or indeed any life of competition with others, in which, whether by winning or losing, they will become so distressed that katastematic pleasure will either never be attained or will be lost. They retreat from the big world, if possible into a small one of their own construction as a bulwark for their pursuit of pleasure, accompanied by like-minded friends and family. There they exercise a virtuous concern for the well-being of others, and exercise (an Epicurean version of) the virtues of temperance and courage and justice (and honesty and due compassion, and sociability, and all the rest of the virtues philosophers such as Aristotle or the Stoics recognize). These virtues, especially justice, control also their interactions with people outside their own circle. They firmly believe that nothing good for themselves can be gained by contravening the rules of justice, or the principles of any other of the standard virtues. In fact, they think, their own good (the final good consisting in their continued katastematic pleasure) is, and can only be, served by observing them.

Thus the virtues are for Epicureans, among other things, a form of self-protection from outside interference. In fact, however, though we have no evidence that Epicurus or other Epicureans after him developed this as an articulated doctrine, it seems quite clear that the virtues, and their exercise in individual actions, should be regarded by those leading the Epicurean life as among their favorite ways of varying their katastematic pleasure—just as we saw that the activities constituting their friendships become for them, as well.[57] This applies most notably within their inner circle, but also outside it, in their interactions with people in the big world. They come to enjoy acts of justice, or acts of temperate management of their diets, or honest speaking, or courageous defense of their property and of their own practical principles, or other actions of Epicurean virtue. These they regard as interesting activities involving their own special complexities, and involving intricacies of thought and feeling (i.e., certain special intricate movements of the mind or soul). In this way Epicureans can rebuff critics like Cicero, who say that Epicurus makes virtues handmaidens of pleasure, and that, as a result, on Epicurus's views the virtues become things of no intrinsic value, mere neutral tools for self-aggrandizement.[58] Instead, handmaidens though they are, the virtues and their practical expression in action are valued, as the Epicurean can say, as I suggested above, in themselves, or for their own sake—that is, insofar as they are immediately pleasant. It remains true, of course, that an Epicurean cannot value just action, say, as a good in itself in some other way, without reference to pleasure, as the Stoics and Aristotle can and do. But, as I said above concerning friendship, it is not so clear that pretheoretical experience or opinion validly requires acceptable ethical theories to make room for that way of valuing virtuous action.[59] This Epicurean way of valuing it may make their theory a distinct and legitimate contender among theories of virtue, and of its proper role in our lives. It may be that Cicero and others would refuse to be mollified in their insistence that no theory of virtue can begin to be acceptable that did not value virtuous action for it own sake in the stronger interpretation of what that requires. But it is not clear that they would be on strong ground in doing so.

It is very clear that the life I have described was, and was conceived by Epicureans as they led it as, a philosophical way of life. It was grounded in a distinctive

[57] Cicero unwittingly leaves us a hint in this direction. In *On Ends* I 25 he reports that what most has turned large numbers of uneducated, ordinary people into Epicureans is their belief that Epicurus "said that . . . pleasure consists in performing right and moral actions for their own sake." Cicero is contemptuous of the idea that Epicurus did say such a thing: but if one understands "acting virtuously for its own sake" as acting that way for the immediate pleasure of doing so, then the ordinary people Cicero looks down on were not off base at all in finding Epicureanism attractive in the way Cicero says they did.

[58] See *On Ends* II 69.

[59] Epicurus is quoted by Athenaeus (end of the second century CE) in his *Learned Banquet* (Δειπνοσοφισταί) XII 547a, as saying, "I spit upon the fine and those who emptily admire it, whenever it brings no pleasure." Thus he spits on Stoics and Aristotle, as well as on their puffed-up conception of the value of virtuous action, and on actions done on the basis of that conception.

set of tenets of philosophical theory. Its ultimate psychological motivation was provided through the knowledge of (i.e., the firm belief its adherents gave to) Epicurus's theory of the human good that constituted their practical wisdom, lodged firmly in their philosophically informed minds. Epicureanism's radical departures from typical ancient attitudes and ways of conducting oneself in life (and from our contemporary ones perhaps even more) are a clear mark—perhaps the clearest we have—of how philosophy in antiquity could transform people's lives. But was there a place in the Epicurean way of life, as there was in the Socratic, Aristotelian, and Stoic lives (and, as we will see in the next chapter, the Platonist one), for philosophical argument and theorizing, of one's own, as a necessary part of it? Two questions here must be recognized and distinguished. First, do those who successfully lead the Epicurean life have to have studied, at some point, presumably in early maturity, Epicurus's philosophy so thoroughly that they understand for themselves, in terms of Epicurus's own or other similarly fundamental arguments that allegedly establish them as true, the major tenets of the Epicurean worldview and Epicurean ethical doctrines? Must one leading this life successfully do so on the basis of a personal conviction, based in deeply grounded philosophical reasons grasped fully by oneself, both that and why the Epicurean life is the best way of life? Second, does this way of life require as a necessary component philosophical discussion or other regular activity as a practicing philosopher?

We do not find clear statements addressing either of these questions in any of our sources for Epicureanism. However, as to the first question, Epicurus's naturalized conception of reason and knowledge makes it doubtful that for him the best way of life requires having studied philosophy to the point of learning thoroughly, not only the central practical tenets of the school, but also, and in real critical depth, the reasons on which their (alleged) truth rests. For Epicurus, as I have said, all knowledge, including philosophical, is arrived at through a very conservative extension beyond sensory experience, with the results retained in memory; and, of course, for Epicurus, there is no value in any exercise of reason except for the pleasure that one attains in or by it. A deeper understanding is no better than a weaker or less extensive one, provided both support a pleasant life. To know the truths of Epicurean theory requires (on Epicurus's own theory of knowledge) that one believes them, and does so with a psychological firmness that allows one regularly and reliably to retain them in mind, as needed, so as to apply them in action, in accordance with the circumstances of action on particular occasions. But this, in turn, requires only a felt commitment, a feeling of conviction sufficient to fend off doubts or other disturbances to one's katastematic pleasure. This might, but need not, depend upon, and derive from, an exploration and acceptance of the reasons that Epicurus advances for their truth. Psychologically, such conviction could rest on no more than a habituated feeling of their truth. That is why Epicurus, as I mentioned, provides his summaries of the doctrines, and emphasizes so much the importance of memorizing them. He does not believe human reason is a faculty of divine provenance, providing insight into the structure of the world or into human nature and the human good. In order to function adequately in directing a human being's life, there is no requirement that it do so on the basis of knowledge of the reasons why the truths about pleasure and virtue and the other matters that are crucial, according to his analysis, for a well-lived human life, are *truths*. Memory of them, and a solid feeling of conviction of their truth, is enough. That is all, as it turns out, that Epicurean practical wisdom, as "that from which all the other virtues grow," need amount to.[60]

Accordingly, the emphasis placed in Stoic theory on achieving and retaining a grasp on the chains of reasoning, and a fully critical grasp of alternative lines of thought, backing one's philosophical conclusions in ethics, seems not to be part of the Epicurean conception. There is no special value in reason or reasoning in itself, as for the Stoics, to be realized in this way. So long as one knows, that is, firmly believes the bottom-line Epicurean tenets about the human good and how to achieve it—a psychological state of mental commitment to using the information contained, where relevant—and so long as one has a strong grasp in memory on them, one is as equipped to live the Epicurean life to perfection as anyone needs to be. This is why the Epicurean movement was so open to people of little or no education. It did not require a lot of study or learning to be a good Epicurean.

Hence, a fortiori, there is no room in the Epicurean life for that constant ethical inquiry that for Socrates placed philosophical discussion and argument and analysis at the very center of the best life. Obviously also, there is no special place provided in the Epicurean life for Aristotelian theoretical investigations for their own sake: people who have a special liking for that sort of thing are invited to make it prominent among the ways they vary their katastematic pleasure, but

---

[60] For the quote see *Letter to Menoeceus* 132.

that is entirely an optional matter.[61] The Epicurean life can be led perfectly well and happily without it. Nor is there room for philosophizing in the manner of Aristotle's second-best life, in which, as we saw, the exercise of the practical virtues is in itself a kind of philosophical thinking. Moreover, the Epicurean life does not require constant or regular activities of philosophical argument and discussion even in the way we saw in the Stoic life, where the knowledge needed to live the Stoics' way needs constantly to be renewed through exercise in philosophical discussion.

If this analysis is correct, it seems that the Epicurean life, however much grounded in the results of philosophical analysis and argument, and however much the psychological motivation provided by firm belief in these results steers Epicureans in living their life, that life cannot be said to involve, in any essential way, the practice of philosophy, that is, of philosophical reflection, analysis, discussion, and argument. When Epicurus says in an often-quoted *Vatican Saying* that "[o]ne must philosophize and at the same time laugh and take care of one's household and engage in the rest of one's personal functions, and never stop proclaiming the utterances of correct philosophy,"[62] the philosophizing he has in mind consists simply in making evident in one's own happy life the truth of the tenets of Epicurean philosophy, on the basis of which one is living it—whether with a philosophically reasoned understanding, or merely a convinced and ready memory, of these tenets.

5.5. Ancient Skepticism: Living without Believing Anything

Nowadays, philosophical skepticism functions primarily, or even solely, as a force in epistemology—as indeed it has done ever since the Renaissance. The central question for skeptics today is, what are the legitimate requirements one must satisfy in order actually to know something? Skeptics doubt that any human being ever does satisfy these requirements, whatever exactly they are. They doubt, on principle, whether we actually do know anything. They may even hold the philosophical position that, because of certain specifiable features of our situation in confronting the presumed external world, knowledge is actually unattainable—that is, unattainable by human beings. (God's knowledge is another

---

[61] See *Vatican Sayings* 27.
[62] *Vatican Sayings* 41. Translation adapted from Inwood and Gerson.

matter.) That is how Descartes, at the beginning of the modern tradition in philosophy, conceived the skeptic. He used skepticism, so conceived, as a foil for use in his own ambition to establish philosophy on a new, post-Aristotelian and post-medieval—and unassailably sound—foundation of basic knowledge. This was knowledge of our own individual existences as inquiring minds. Descartes thought that, with this foundation in place, we could establish on its basis much wider claims to knowledge, as well, through modern, mathematical-scientific investigations, when rigorously carried out. Specialists in early modern philosophy are well aware that Descartes, and other early modern philosophers who discussed skepticism, did so primarily on the basis of two ancient skeptics' writings, Cicero's and Sextus Empiricus's. These specialists also read other ancient writers, besides these two, who were familiar with skepticism in antiquity. It must nonetheless come as a shock to most contemporary philosophers when they first realize that our richest source for ancient skepticism, Sextus Empiricus, presents it as primarily a set of ideas about how to live one's life, not about epistemological theory.[63] This is not something one would be likely to know simply from early modern and later presentations of skepticism. Yet it is a fundamental fact about ancient skepticism as a philosophy that it presented itself in the guise of a way of life. Much of its philosophical interest and value are lost if it is too readily assimilated to its early modern and later descendants.

The skeptical philosophy, for Sextus, like all the other main schools of philosophy at his time (last half of the second century CE), aims at helping people to achieve the ethical "end" for human beings. This, he thinks (in a special, skeptical way about which I will say more below), is a life completely free from any but naturally arising and inevitable disturbances—a life of serene acceptance and tranquility (ἀταραξία), as one makes one's way through one's daily rounds, as well as through any crises that might arise.[64] In taking the "end" that makes possible a good and happy human life to be tranquility—total absence of (avoidable) disturbance—Sextus allies his skepticism most closely to Epicureanism, among the

---

[63] See *Outlines of Pyrrhonism* (also sometimes called *Pyrrhonian Sketches*) I 25–30 (with 21–24); the best translation is that of Annas and Barnes, using the title *Outlines of Scepticism*. The *Outlines* (in three books) provides a comprehensive and detailed account of ancient skepticism. In quoting it I follow Annas and Barnes's translation, but with alterations (not always explicitly noted). On Cicero's *Academica*, his account of skepticism, see below, note 72. I focus my discussion of ancient skepticism and skepticism as a way of life, in this and the next two sections, on Sextus's presentation. For reasons explained below, I leave aside the other principal ancient representatives of skepticism, the Academics of the third to first centuries BCE.

[64] For discussion of the "end" skeptics set themselves and for textual references, see endnote 31.

nonskeptical, "dogmatic" philosophies of antiquity. Epicureans, too, place a lot of emphasis, as we have seen, on keeping away so far as possible from disturbances of one's equanimity. But for the Epicureans that tranquility is merely the fundamental means for attaining happiness: happiness is the pleasure that results. For Sextus, tranquility itself is the end. As we will see, for Sextus the means to that end include adopting a special understanding of philosophy itself, and special techniques of philosophical argument. This understanding and these techniques assure the skeptics who possess them, Sextus claims, of achieving, and securely retaining their grip on, this ethical end. He also thinks application of these skeptical techniques of argumentation can raise very serious doubts about the correctness of the ends proposed by all the other ancient schools of philosophy, doubts that the members of those schools must, by their own standards for what legitimately casts doubt, take very seriously—with disturbing effect. By contrast, the skeptics' way of accepting tranquility as their end leaves immune to doubt both it, as the correct end, and one's own achievement of it through the skeptical philosophy.

Thus the epistemological issue of the possibility of knowledge, and the skeptic stance in relation to this issue, are, for Sextus, a secondary matter: doubts about knowledge (or even, more radically, about the mere truth of any assertion) are only a means to achieving the ethical end. The good and happy life that skepticism makes possible is indeed one led without claims to know anything—in particular, to know what is good and bad, in general, or to know that the way one is living really is the best one, the most suitable or proper one for a human being to aim at living. In Sextus's philosophy, the skeptics do have doubts about knowledge (of a certain rather delicate kind, as we shall see), and, in fact, they doubt the propriety of claiming even that any of anyone's beliefs are true. They live their lives, or so they say, without so much as believing anything at all, however mundane and apparently obvious.[65] But they live contentedly with their doubts

[65] Below, in section 5.7, I explain why it would be entirely appropriate, despite this denial, to say that the skeptic has (and lives according to) beliefs—in one way that ordinary language in both English and Greek makes available to us of using the terms "belief" and "opinion." As I will explain more fully below, what the skeptic eschews is holding any view about anything whatsoever, however recondite, scientific, or philosophical, or straightforward and apparently obvious, in such a way as to rest your view on, or in any way open yourself to giving, *reasons* why your view is correct, or why others should accept it too. You don't even think, when you can see with your very eyes that it is now nighttime, that your seeing what you see is any reason for holding that that is so; nonetheless, when you do see what you see, if you are a skeptic, you not only can but you do hold the view that it is nighttime: that shows in how you then behave. You believe (in this distinctive, nonreasoning way) that it is nighttime, and act accordingly.

about whether anything is true, and with their total lack of beliefs (at any rate, on standard philosophical accounts of what a belief is, as I will explain below); indeed, they say, they live on the very basis of that lack. Our next task, then, in this and the next two sections, is to examine the skeptics' version of living one's philosophy and of philosophy as a way of life.

Before we begin, we need to place Sextus's skepticism and his skeptic way of life briefly in the larger context of skeptical thinking in Greece, which had roots going back as far as Socrates, and, in some ways, further back even than that. Sextus speaks of his own philosophy simply as that of skepticism, without a qualifier.[66] But he is classed nowadays, as indeed he was already in later antiquity, as a "Pyrrhonian" skeptic.[67] This classification is intended to distinguish him from the earlier movement of "Academic" skepticism, so called because it developed in Plato's Academy, beginning with Arcesilaus in the third century BCE. Arcesilaus was an older contemporary of Chrysippus who engaged extensively in critical, and negative, examination of the Stoics' doctrines in all parts of philosophy.[68] Pyrrho, for whom Pyrrhonian skepticism is named, is a shadowy figure, active in mainland Greece (at Elis, near Corinth) during the forty years or so following Aristotle's death. This was the period when Zeno the Stoic and Epicurus founded their schools in Athens. Pyrrho left no writings of his own, but his legend was promoted in the extensive writings of a follower called Timon. It was through the work of an Academic philosopher named Aenesidemus, active at Athens and later at Alexandria in the mid-first century BCE, that Pyrrho's name became associated with skepticism as a philosophy.[69] Aenesidemus appears to have ap-

---

[66] For some details about Sextus's life and work, see endnote 32.

[67] Sextus himself accepts the propriety of the name "Pyrrhonian" for his type of philosophy (see *Outlines* I 11, and his occasional use thereafter of "the Pyrrhonian philosopher" in reference to the skeptic). But that is only because, as he says, Pyrrho (on whom see further below in my main text) "appears to us to have attached himself to Scepticism more substantially and conspicuously than anyone before him" (I 7, trans. Annas and Barnes, with one change). Thus, Sextus does not link his own philosophical views or practices to any "doctrinal" inheritance from Pyrrho; Pyrrho is a retrospective, honorary figurehead for the "school," quite different from Plato in relation to later Platonists, or Aristotle to the Peripatetics, or Zeno and Chrysippus to the Stoics.

[68] Sextus rejects the claim of Academic "skeptics" to be true skeptics. See endnote 33.

[69] My authority here is Aristocles of Messene, the first or second century CE Peripatetic author of a large work, *On Philosophy*, which seems to have been a comprehensive, critical history. Aristocles is reported to have said that it was Aenesidemus who "revived" Pyrrhonian skepticism, after it lapsed upon Timon's death. His authority is more highly regarded by scholars than whatever authority Diog. Laert. may have had for his contradictory claim (IX 115) that Ptolemy of Cyrene had already revived it half a century earlier.

pealed to Pyrrho, through his legend, as a suitably "ancient" sponsor—a contemporary of Zeno and Epicurus, founders of rival Hellenistic schools—for Aenesidemus's own philosophical views and practices.[70]

As this historical sketch indicates, it was, in fact, to Aenesidemus that the skepticism of Sextus and his contemporaries looked back for their most fundamental ideas and, in particular, for their technique of using philosophical argument in supporting a skeptical way of life. Aenesidemus started, as I just said, as an Academic philosopher, but he became disillusioned with both of the opposed ways that his elders in the Academy had come to interpret their Academic heritage. These elders were his principal teacher, Philo of Larissa, but also a well-known rival of Philo's named Antiochus, of Ascalon.[71] Everyone in authority in and around the Academy, Aenesidemus thought, had lost the philosophical insights, and abandoned the skeptical philosophical practices of their predecessors of the previous two centuries, the "Academic skeptics." Philo had even begun to deny that any of his Academic predecessors ever had these insights and practices in the first place! Philo argued (to us, somewhat obscurely) for acceptance of the possibility, and even the actuality, of human knowledge, as something essential to the whole prior Academic tradition, stretching back to Plato. Antiochus, while accepting the skeptical character of the Academy after Arcesilaus, repudiated it, in favor of returning to the positive doctrinal stance that he attributed (as we usually do too) to Plato (in his works other than the Socratic dialogues), to Aristotle, and to their immediate successors down to Arcesilaus. Under these circumstances, committed skeptic that he was, Aenesidemus understandably came to feel no longer at home in the Academy.

The earlier Academic skeptics, beginning with Arcesilaus, and including most notably Carneades in the second century BCE, had insisted on a philosophically reserved, always questioning, way of doing philosophy: they never asserted, much less pontificatingly set forth, philosophical doctrines of their own. They limited themselves to critically examining the views of their contemporary Stoic

---

[70] It is a typical feature of ancient thought, especially prominent in later ancient times, to look back, for authorization of one's own views, to some famous ancient thinker: the more ancient the better, since then the closer one could claim to come to acquaintance with the original and divine truth of things, known by some or other wise persons of old and passed on somehow to these famous "ancient" intermediaries (on this original truth see below, section 6.1). Diogenes Laertius's *Lives* is organized on a system of pedigrees starting in as ancient times as can be decently managed, given various bits of sometimes hearsay evidence, for each of several general "schools" of philosophical thought—pre-Socratic, post-Socratic, and Hellenistic.

[71] Cicero heard Philo's lectures on Academic skepticism as a young man, in Rome in 88/87 BCE. He later also heard lectures of Antiochus, at Athens (79–77).

and Epicurean rivals (and, of course, to finding them unsatisfactory, in terms of the standards and principles for satisfactoriness prevailing among these other philosophers)—very much as Socrates had done with the fifth century Sophists and other claimants to wisdom of his own time.[72] It seemed to Aenesidemus that, under Philo and Antiochus, Academic philosophers were, as he put it, in their different ways, just "Stoics fighting with Stoics."[73] He wished to return to the reserved, skeptical way of doing philosophy that he thought Arcesilaus and Carneades had practiced (though now Philo was denying that they had). So he decamped and established his own school, no longer under the banner of these famous Academics, or of Socrates or Plato, but of Pyrrho. Nevertheless, it seems, in fact he embarked simply upon a continuation of Academic skepticism, but now under this different name. There is, however, one important difference between Academic skepticism as it had existed in the third and second centuries BCE, and the Pyrrhonian skepticism introduced by Aenesidemus. We have no evidence linking the skepticism of Academics such as Arcesilaus, Carneades, and Philo with the promotion of any particular total way of life. We do not hear of any of these philosophers proposing the idea of living one's philosophy, in the way we have seen Socrates did, or that Aristotle and the third and second century Stoics did—not even in some less assertive and more circumspect way.[74] When, by contrast, Sextus not only presents as an essential component of the skeptical tradition that he codifies, but sets at its center, this "ethical" concern, we are entitled to regard this feature of his skepticism as an innovation of Aenesidemus's.[75] The skeptical philosophy as a way of life was Aenesidemus's invention.

---

[72] The most accessible, and the best, source for the Academic skepticism of Arcesilaus and Carneades, down to the time of Aenesidemus's teacher Philo, including Antiochus' revolt, is found in Cicero's *Academica* of 45 BCE. The best translation is by Brittain, *Cicero on Academic Scepticism*. For more on Antiochus, see also Cicero, *On Ends* V.

[73] Aenesidemus's principal work, in eight books, titled *Pyrrhonian Discourses*, is lost, but there is a very interesting summary of it by Photius, a ninth century Byzantine Patriarch of Constantinople, from which this quote is taken. See Long and Sedley, *The Hellenistic Philosophers*, 71C, 72L.

[74] Of course, the Academics were serious about their philosophical work, and were not just playing argumentative games. They certainly expected anyone who listened similarly seriously to them, not to accept the prescriptions for life of any of what they called the "dogmatic" philosophers. This was the skeptics' label for philosophers who thought they could establish, however open-mindedly and even tentatively, solidly grounded knowledge of their own specific philosophical first principles, and of the deductive consequences of these as to how to live. But we have no evidence that the Academics formulated an alternative skeptic way of life, or tried self-consciously to lead one themselves.

[75] Or perhaps it is due already to Pyrrho? We cannot rule that out; and indeed reports reaching us of Pyrrho's life do emphasize his living his "philosophy" (such as it may have been). But see Diog. Laert. IX 62, where Aenesidemus is cited as denying that Pyrrho lived in the way his philosophy implied he should.

5.6. The Pyrrhonian Skepticism of Sextus Empiricus

Let us set aside these questions of historical context, and turn now to discuss Sextus's philosophy, as he presents it in his *Outlines*. Sextus tells us that the "causal origin" of skepticism as a philosophy, and as an intellectual skill, lay in the anxiety caused in certain smart and energetic people's minds by what he calls "the anomaly in things."[76] (Dumb or lazy people do not bother about such things, apparently.) All kinds of things that we have to deal with in life have conflicting aspects (hence the anomaly Sextus refers to). Under some circumstances, one would ordinarily think of these things in one way, but in others in another. A tower viewed from a distance, to take one of Sextus's favorite examples, may look round, but look flat-sided from close at hand.[77] Well, which is it? Round or flat-sided? In ordinary life (and so, for dumb or lazy people) it might not seem to matter: mostly, at any rate, when we deal with towers it is from up close, and then we can treat them (successfully enough) as flat-sided, if that is how they look then. Generally speaking, we need not worry about their different look from afar, because mostly we do not do anything with towers from that distance. Or, if ever we do interact with a tower from a distance, we can learn pragmatically (or be told by others) how things will go when we do—so far as our interests, then and later, are concerned. We can take it to be flat-sided, even when viewed from a distance, or just not care about how it actually is, so long as, when we follow our pragmatic expectations, things go well. All we need to know is how to deal with it, whether at a distance or up close, so that our interests are satisfied. Anyhow, if, as a result of inexperience with distant towers, we mess things up, how important is that likely to be? That is no doubt how dumb or lazy

---

[76] Or rather, he places the origin in the desire or hope of getting rid of the anxiety. From this hope the practices and principles of skepticism arose. They are means of achieving that goal of ridding oneself of this anxiety; see *Outlines* I 12. It is in this way that the "end" or "goal" for a skeptic, in living a skeptic life, comes to be tranquility—freedom from this disturbance (and, in fact, from other disturbances too, since once this one goes away, others can be avoided). My description of these predecessors as "smart and energetic" glosses Sextus's own description of them as μεγαλοφυεῖς (lit. "great-natured"), rendered by Annas and Barnes rather blandly by "men of talent." I should add that when Sextus refers to the origins of skepticism, he probably intends to speak also of how others than the original skeptics, in fact skeptics in general, come to be skeptics. They too began with worries about anomalies, undertook to investigate in a positive philosophical spirit how things actually stand, one way or the other, and then found the sought-for tranquility through the unexpected means of suspension. But in my main text I follow Sextus's lead in speaking about how the skeptic system got established in the first place, as something then for later worriers to avail themselves of.

[77] See *Outlines* I 32, 118; II 55.

people might react to such anomalies. They would, in effect, just shrug if someone pointed these anomalies out.

But Sextus's original skeptic predecessors, being smart and energetic, did not
just shrug and try to do their best to muddle through somehow. They felt it to be
important which way the tower is in its own self, in its nature: it must be because
of how it is, they thought, that it is experienced in those anomalous ways. What
reasons do we have, or could we develop, if we thought about our experiences
(which are initially all we have to go on), for holding it to be in itself the one way
or the other? What is *it*, that it has these two appearances? And how, on the basis
of how it actually is, can one then understand that, and why—for what reasons—it does have both? Only by knowing those things, they felt, could one
proceed with confidence to deal with the tower, whether from afar or up close. If
one is smart and energetic, one sees (or, not to prejudge, thinks) that it is important what the tower is in itself, in its nature, since (it must surely seem, they
thought) it is that nature that grounds its behavior in relation to our own apprehension of it through the use of our senses.

Of more fundamental importance, of course, than these anomalies in the
physical properties of objects, are questions about what is of value in and for
human life. What is good for us, and what is bad? What really matters if it happens to us, or if it does not? Here too there are anomalies: things have conflicting
aspects, being or seeming good in one way, but bad in some other. Sextus's smart
and energetic people were made even more anxious by these anomalies concerning whether something is good or bad, or in general of positive or negative value,
for human life, than they were by those presented by towers, and other similarly
"factual" anomalies, as one could classify them—the famous straight stick under
water, where it appears bent, to mention another well-worn ancient skeptics' example. When something has conflicting value aspects, or "appearances," which is
the more important or authoritative under the given circumstances? What, overall, is the correct thing to say—what is there the best reason to say—about
whether it (the thing) is good or bad (then or ever)? If something is quite pleasant, but harms our health, what is one to say about it? How is it right to treat it?
Why is that the right way? People may say, well, unless it's very pleasant, leave it
alone—or if your health won't suffer greatly, then go ahead. But how does one
decide what's pleasant enough, or what's a small enough bad effect on the health?
Only, it can seem, if we know the answers to these questions can we proceed with
confidence to make our decisions, and conduct our lives. At any rate, that is how

it seemed to Sextus's smart and energetic persons. They wanted to lead their lives in what they thought a responsible way, with due application and individual attention to all the practical problems that face us, and they wanted to be able, so far as that might be possible, to understand the *reasons* why what was right or best was indeed right or best. A self-respecting person, it seemed to them, could do no less. So they suffered anxiety. Until they could resolve the anomalies about values, by figuring out what the truth is in each case (Is it really good? Is that its nature? How good is it?), by working out a satisfactory account of the relevant reasons that support the claim to truth, they could not live responsibly and securely.

Now, it is philosophers who take it upon themselves to investigate and develop answers to such questions as these. They are the ones who profess to know how to investigate the natures of things and how to resolve these questions in terms of reasoned-out theories of how things are. Indeed, it is presumably they who introduced into human life for the first time the very idea of there being a nature of things underlying how things appear to us in practical life, or at any rate to have developed the idea of a disciplined use of reasoning to figure out what does belong to things by their natures. This means that, in beginning by experiencing anxiety at the anomalies in things, an anxiety caused by worrying over why (for what reasons) things appeared so anomalously, Sextus's proto-skeptics were already bitten by, or had bitten themselves with, the philosophy bug. They were not willing to deal merely pragmatically with these anomalies, as of course dumb or ordinary people somehow manage to do. They were not willing just to muddle through however, in ordinary life, people manage to do that. They accepted the distinction—we will see later that Sextus thinks this was the highly questionable root of all their troubles—between appearance and reality, that is, reality in the nature of things, that philosophers had articulated, and insisted upon. They wanted to know the answer, in each case, as to which of the conflicting sides of any such anomaly (if either) is the *true* one, and which the only apparent—whether this was a question of pressing practical concern, or only something quite remote from daily life, but nonetheless beset by anomalous appearances. How does sweat get onto the skin when it is hot? Does it come through the skin? How? Or does it precipitate from the surrounding wet air? Here too appearances seem to point in different directions. But it has to be some one way or another! About all such questions, of course, dumb or lazy people simply shrug: since the possible answers do not matter to our lives, or seem, at least, not to matter, such people simply pay them no attention; no pragmatic response is called for. Not so for our proto-skeptics! They wanted to know how the truth gave rise to, and otherwise related to, the appearances: what are the reasons, in the natures of things, for these anomalies? They felt the need to know the answers, because otherwise they felt they could not proceed with adequate confidence in the conduct of their daily lives, or rid themselves of worries concerning such matters as how sweat gets onto skin. So they sought, from philosophy, a means of ridding themselves of their anxiety, and so of making possible an anxiety-free, unperturbed life, in which, by knowing the answers, they could rely on themselves to deal correctly in making their decisions and choices, and leading their lives, and could feel satisfied about the other, more remote, matters of fact and theory that attracted their notice.

Thus the goal for Sextus's proto-skeptics became to obtain tranquility through philosophy—that is, through positive philosophy, as one could put it. Positive philosophy provides definite answers, one way or the other, through a devoted and critically self-conscious use of our native rational powers, to all the questions that arise when one begins to worry about anomalies, whether ones with practical effects on life or ones bearing solely on more purely theoretical questions, and when one seeks to understand how appearance and reality work together to constitute our world. Once, through such a critically self-conscious—philosophical—use of reason, they had achieved the answers they were seeking, they could then proceed with their lives with confidence, or could live them so for the first time, and without these perturbing worries over what the natures of things they have to deal with in daily life actually are, or those other perturbing worries concerning matters of theory. So, these proto-skeptics undertook philosophical studies, by engaging with the arguments and theories given in the various schools of positive philosophy: Platonic, Aristotelian, Epicurean, Stoic, and any others they might find. These schools' views, or some revision of one or more of them produced by their own positive philosophical reasoning, they hoped, would lead them to their goal of tranquility. They embraced critical, philosophical reason, and accepted its authority, as a means to their own salvation.

Philosophers, of course, notoriously disagree with one another about just about everything, and that was true in antiquity too, as these original Pyrrhonian skeptics soon discovered. One group said pleasure was our highest good, others that it was virtue; one said reality was atoms and void and nothing else, others that nothing is real but intelligible and bodiless Forms, others that reality is the creation of god's mind, which is itself a body acting on preexisting matter. Starting from their different sets of ethical or metaphysical starting points, they also gave divergent answers to virtually every question about which our proto-skeptics were worried. Moreover, by the principles and standards these philosophers had worked up for deciding the correct answer when we attempt to use our minds to discover the truth about how the world itself, and human values are, in the nature of things, it seemed that all these theories had good arguments for them—but also good ones against them, too. (After all, different philosophical schools, using their common tool of disciplined reasoning, reached incompatible conclusions.) And where the ancient schools of positive philosophy might agree, still, it seemed to these proto-skeptics, philosophical reason, better prepared in accordance with the self-developed standards of positive philosophizing, might well show that one could not say with the full support of critical reason that things are, in their natures, as these positive philosophers might wish to say, on their own positive theories, as they had so far worked them out. There always remains, it seemed to them, something countervailing on the other side of any and every question investigated by philosophers, if you are as inventive as possible in your philosophically disciplined inquiries.

Thus these proto-skeptics developed what Sextus describes as the specific skill of the full-blown skeptic. This the Pyrrhonian skeptics conceived as the highest development, indeed the perfection, of the power of self-consciously critical, philosophical, reasoning. It is skill in being able always to find an opposition, of appearance to appearance, or philosophical thought to appearance, or one philosophical thought to another philosophical thought, of such a sort as to cause any rationally well-prepared mind, committed to following reason wherever it leads, to withhold a final judgment (to "suspend," as they said) on any question of philosophical theory.[78] Hence, having discovered this skill, the proto-skeptics themselves neither affirmed nor denied anything, on whatever the matter under investigation and inquiry might be. They recommended this "suspension" also to any positive philosophers they may have been conducting their inquiry with and questioning them about their school's views. That is what, as it seemed to them, philosophical, critically self-conscious reason itself, the pride of all positive philosophers, demands.[79] Thus, having begun their study of philosophy in order to

[78] For more on this special skill and the "modes" of skepticism, see endnote 34.

[79] Since the skeptic's method is intended for use on all and sundry who are given to holding opinions and making definite assertions about how things actually are, holding them for reasons that they think support the claim that their opinions are true, whether they are philosophers or not (see below), Sextus explains (see *Outlines* III 280–81) that it includes the flexibility needed to lead someone to suspend even by presenting weak, or indeed fallacious, arguments on one or the other side. Whatever might work with

relieve their anxiety, by arriving at definite answers to their questions about reality and appearances, they found themselves frustrated at every turn. Time after time, and without exception, they kept finding that, on any issue that they investigated in their search, reason itself, employed in accordance with the principles and standards for reasoning that the positive philosophers themselves promoted, led them to suspend judgment. This applied both to matters of more or less pure theory, and to ones of practical interest in leading one's daily life.

Hence, as time went on, these proto-skeptics began, and continued, to expect, even before beginning a new inquiry, that they would be rationally driven to suspension: it would seem to them very likely that the rationally demanded result would be a stalemated lack of success in arriving at any definite conclusion of the question at issue, one way or the other. Reason, when used according to the standards of philosophy for its proper use, would dictate suspension—as it seemed to them. They reached a point of near despair. Sextus continues his narrative by telling how then, on some occasion of failure, all of a sudden, each proto-skeptic got possessed by a feeling of tranquility, instead of a repeat of their prior near despair. This tranquility seemed to them to just follow suspension "as a shadow follows a body."[80] All of a sudden, one would seem to see (one would now feel) that one does not need the assurance of positive philosophy about the natures of things, and about how and why they have any of the anomalies that they do, in order to proceed with one's life in an unperturbed state of mind, as well as to just stop worrying about what the truth might be among the conflicting possible theories that could explain the more theoretical anomalies they had been worrying over. The simple condition of sustained suspension turns out (as it seems to oneself) to provide one with what one was seeking to achieve only through getting final, definitive answers from positive philosophy about how the things one has to deal with in life are, in themselves and in their natures, or about those other more theoretical matters. One loses the anxiety, but not by learning the truth, and the critically developed reasons that show it to be the truth, as one initially thought one would have to, if one was ever going to rid oneself of it. One loses one's anxiety by renouncing the ambition to live positively on the basis of

---

a particular interlocutor is good enough, and acceptable to the committed skeptic, since the controlling ethical objective is to bring them to suspend. It does not really matter how. The account in my main text is an idealization, representing the special case of suspension in discussions with expert positive philosophers.

[80] The quotation is from *Outlines* I 29. For the continuation of the narrative from I 12, see I 26ff.

critical reason at all (though, as I will explain, without renouncing the commitment to keep on engaging in critical rational inquiry about these matters). Thus one achieves the initial goal of one's philosophizing, not by getting answers, but by always refusing prematurely (which means, in actual effect, ever) to accept any answer (or, of course, by the same token, to deny any). One becomes a full-blown skeptic. Their experience with critical reason itself, when using it on the assumption that it is our authoritative guide to the truth, has led the skeptics to suspension, and through suspension, as a body is followed by its shadow,[81] to the goal of unperturbedness that they were all along seeking.

Having achieved their goal of unperturbedness via suspension, skeptics quite naturally want to keep on suspending—if possible: that is, so long as reason doesn't tell them to accept some argument and some conclusion, whether factual or to do with questions of value, and whether it concerns some purely theoretical issue or something with evident practical bearings. They remain open to the possibility that new considerations might be brought to their attention, or reconsideration of old ones might lead them to think some matter actually settled: perhaps a really convincing final argument might be invented by an Epicurean to show that reality really is just atoms and void, and thus provide a good basis for settling our questions about what is real and what is only appearance, and how the one accounts for the other. But, for the interim, they suspend, and they expect to keep on suspending, so that they can keep themselves free from perturbation by that means. They are now ready to live in a fully satisfied way, since to live without perturbation, as we have seen, is what seemed to the proto-skeptics, as they evolved into skeptics, to be all they required in order to find satisfaction with their lives.

So far I have been summarizing and commenting upon Sextus's account in the early chapters of his *Outlines* of the intellectual origins of Pyrrhonian skepticism, the train of thought that leads to skepticism. Sextus offers this in the guise of a narrative history of the experiences of those who became the first to practice the skeptic philosophy. Here we should recall that Sextus's proto-skeptics took themselves to positive philosophy because they were anxious about anomalies that were evident already to them in their daily, ordinary lives. They wanted those to be resolved. They wanted to decide which appearance of the tower

---

[81] Or, in Sextus's famous image, in the way that the painter Apelles "painted" the foam on a racehorse's mouth by throwing his sponge at the painting, in desperation and annoyance, after being unable to produce the foam by normal painterly means. *Outlines* I 28.

showed how it is (flat-faced), and which (round) was only an appearance: flat-faced things normally do look round from such distances. But philosophy introduced them to many other worrying anomalies, too, ones, as I have said of a purely theoretical sort, remote from any issue of daily practical concern. It also introduced them to philosophical theories attempting to dissipate these worries, but which were in conflict with one another, and very hard to choose between on an adequate basis of reason. These too they wanted to resolve.

Hence their suspension over all and every philosophical theory about appearance and reality, and how the one causes or otherwise relates to the other, is linked with suspension from taking a position on the anomalies arising in ordinary life that initially set the proto-skeptics off in their quest. They suspend from saying that the tower is flat-faced, but only appears round from a distance, or that pleasure is good, or not good, or that health is better, or to be preferred over pleasure, in case some pleasure will harm your health. But hanging out with philosophers, as we have seen, alerts you to new and previously unnoticed or unsuspected anomalies even where everyday matters are concerned—indeed, they seem to be everywhere you look. Is the door to your room actually, in fact, open, when it seems perfectly obvious that it is, and you can see that it is? Well, it might just *look* that way: if you are a philosopher, it is not hard to think up some consideration that could suggest that, really, it's closed (but because, say, of some so far unnoticed temporary derangement in your vision, or some unusual reflection of the light through your window, it looks open while in fact being shut). When (or if) you say, in response to these anomalies, that the door really *is* open (you've checked, and your eyes are fine; there are no unusual reflections; you really can see that it is open), you are claiming to have adequate reasons for saying that. Thus in becoming skeptics the proto-skeptics come to suspend on all matters, whether of philosophical theory, or the simplest and most straightforward points of everyday life, agreed to by everybody. They suspend, that is to say, on all claims or assertions that, like all assertions of philosophical theory, and the ones I've just illustrated from ordinary life, are asserted for *reasons* that, you think, show what you say to be true—or, in being made, are intended to be understood as open to critical scrutiny as to the reasons why they should be believed.

But on what basis, then, positively speaking, do skeptics live, once they suspend over all matters? If they have no opinions or beliefs, and never have any reasons for anything that they think, what determines their decisions, choices, preferences, and actions? Life requires discriminations, options, holding back sometimes and going forward at others, doing this now, instead of that. I mentioned above that skeptics do not renounce their commitment to the regular practice of philosophical inquiry and to critical reasoning concerning both the questions of philosophy and those concerning everyday anomalies (I will say more about that in the next section); so, much of their daily life is devoted to this philosophical avocation (Sextus expounded in writing and maybe taught the skeptical philosophy to students). But like everyone else skeptics spend much of their time in eating and drinking and sleeping, they have some profession or work (Sextus was a doctor), they have families, including perhaps spouses and children, and engage in all the obligations and practices of life in a civilized community. How do skeptics manage all that? That requires at every turn making discriminations, taking options, doing one thing rather than another, moment by moment. Without any beliefs as to how things truly are, and eschewing doing anything ever for any reason, what can lead them to act at all? Sextus's answer, though this raises a lot of questions we will have to go into, is that skeptics live on the basis of "appearances" (φαινόμενα), instead of "opinions" or "beliefs." The skeptic's basis for acting, Sextus says, is not beliefs as to how things are, resting on reasons that show them true (the tower being actually round or flat-faced), but only how things appear at a given moment to the one who has to act. Sextus formulates the skeptic life like this: to live following (i.e., "adhering" or "attending" to)[82] the "appearances," without holding any opinions. But what should we take that to mean? We must turn to this in the next section.

One thing is already clear. What Sextus is suggesting is that we should simply not fall victim to the naturally understandable human tendency to react to the anomalies among the appearances of things, both factual and normative, by supposing that there must be some way the tower is in itself, for example, and that the other, different, ways it appears are appearances only, to be explained, one hopes, on the basis of the way it really is (and its connections to the way other things that surround it really are). Living by following the appearances is living without falling victim, to any degree, to that natural temptation (the temptation the proto-skeptics fell victim to in going to philosophy to resolve their worries about anomalies). It is, somehow, leaving the appearances, all of them, *alone*, just taking them as they come—without subjecting any of them to rational criticism. This may not be easy, but that, it seems, is what Sextus tells us skeptics manage to do. It is what the skeptic philosophy requires.

---

[82] The Greek is προσέχοντες. See *Outlines* I 23.

5.7. The Skeptic Way of Life

But what does Sextus's formula of living according to appearances (alone) entail?[83] Surely, when skeptics view the tower from a distance, and it looks round to them, they do not "follow" that appearance, and make plans to approach it on the basis that it is round and will be correctly treated as round upon approach. If they did, they would clearly make a mess of things (bringing curved ladders with them, say, that would not fit, as they attempted to climb up). And, at least next time, if they were not totally stupid, they would not act in that same way, even though it surely would still have that same appearance for them. This shows, or suggests, that even skeptics can learn from experience. When the tower looks round to them from a distance, once they have learned by experience about towers, they will also have a further appearance about it, that it is flat-sided, or may very well be. (It is perhaps too far away still to tell—that it is too far away to tell is something else that will appear to them, after experience.) And it will appear to them that it is *this* appearance—that it is flat-sided—that is to be followed, not the first one. Hence, it seems clear that a skeptic will not follow every appearance (indeed that would be impossible, since one can, as just mentioned, have conflicting appearances at the same time about the same thing). The ones they do follow will be the ones that it appears to them are the ones *to* follow, on that occasion and under those (apparent) circumstances.

The crucial point is that, in this whole account, it is always and only appearances, of this or of that, that skeptics consider and then act on. They do not act on assertions as to how things actually are, in truth or in the nature of things, where those assertions are based on reasons why (as they think) the one appearance is to be followed and the others not, whether this "truth" and "nature" is understood in a philosophically laden way or not. They do not have, or think they have, reasons of a critically reflective kind for what they do, or for which appearance they follow; it only appears to them that following *this* one or *that* one is the thing to do, and they follow it in that spirit. It is, for them, appearances all the way down, so to speak. They never have any reasons for what they do, at

---

[83] There has been much dispute by scholars over the answer to this question. Some argue that living by appearances means making no assertions at all, beyond acknowledging one's private sensations and other impressions (appearances) about things; others hold that the easygoing following of one's impressions that Sextus is describing includes making assertions as to how things are, given, and on the basis of, one's impressions. See the articles collected in Burnyeat and Frede, *The Original Sceptics*, and the bibliography there. The interpretation I present below is closer to the Frede side of the controversy than the Burnyeat and Barnes one.

all: it was by accepting that one ought to have reasons that the proto-skeptics bit themselves with the full-blown skeptics' now-renounced philosophy bug—the bug that led them naively (as Sextus thinks) to think that philosophy contained the answers to their dilemmas. That eschewal is part, indeed the essential core, of the skeptics' practice of suspension of judgment. Their practices of behavior, in accepting some appearances but not others, have just grown up with them, individually, in whatever way they have, as they have experienced whatever they have experienced in their lives. All skeptics adhere to their own practices of following these but not those of their appearances, just because they are their own practices, *their* ways of responding to appearances (unless, of course, they change their practices in some way, on the basis of additional, new appearances that they begin to have and to accept, after further experience).

One should notice here that, when skeptics do act on some appearance (say the appearance of the tower as flat and square, despite looking round from where they are standing), they act on the appearance that something is so and so—that the tower is flat and square. An appearance of the tower merely as looking or seeming square—where that is to be interpreted as looking to them the way that square towers usually look (from up close)—would not yet, of itself, lead to any action at all, if "accepted." To accept (or report) that that is how it looks or seems just invites the question, "So what?" It is perhaps an interesting report on your state of consciousness that you accept that that is how it looks or seems to you, but it goes no further than that. It has no definite implications for action. Instead, the appearance that skeptics accept, and incorporate into their "action plan," is of the tower *as* square.[84] It is on that appearance, if on any, that they act, when they proceed to approach the tower and deal with it in the square-tower ways that they then do. Thus when skeptics get an appearance from afar of a tower that looks round from there but that also appears to them, given their prior experience, as flat-sided and square, and when they proceed to obtain an ordinary ladder (not a rounded one) and approach the tower with the intention of climbing it, they act taking it that a ladder is to be found where they go to look for one (they have a memory appearance to go on here that leads them to take it that that is where to look for one), taking it that this is a square tower before them as they approach it, and similarly taking things to be some given way all through the series of ensuing actions. However, unlike other people at least some

---

[84] See endnote 35 for the philosophical distinction between "epistemic" and "nonepistemic" appearances.

of the time, they do all these things without thinking at all that they have any *reason* for so taking any of the things in question. If challenged ("Maybe there is no ladder there, maybe you're deceived?"), they may very well just wave it off (or if they pause to think again and check their memory, they only do that, again, because it appears to them that, under these circumstances of challenge, that is the thing to do, and they accept and follow that appearance). They never offer (or in their thoughts hold) *anything* as a reason for taking *anything* to be the way they do take it to be, and for treating it that way.

Given all this, in fact, I see no obstacle to using the ordinary-language word "belief" here to describe what skeptics have in accepting and following appearances. It is true that in philosophical analyses of belief, and in many applications in ordinary life of the term "belief" (or "opinion"), a belief is understood to be a claim that something is true in fact, where that claim is put forward as based on and supported by reasons of some appropriate sort. But if skeptics act on ways they take things to be, without holding that they have any justification at all for taking things so, ordinary usage surely authorizes describing those acts of taking things to be so as beliefs. That is how they *think* things are; if you asked them what they were up to, they would perfectly naturally say either that they thought, or that they believed, or that it was their opinion, that things are so and so: that they ought to take a rounded ladder, because the tower is round, that there is a rounded ladder in a certain place, and so on. They do believe all these things, although, perhaps unusually for people in their societies, they are clear and explicit to themselves (and to others, if questioned) that they do not have, and are by no means claiming, any reasons whatsoever for believing what they do. They just *do* believe them.[85]

The appearances that skeptics live by, on Sextus's account, then, all have an individual, conceptually articulated content—each one is an appearance of something as being a certain way: a tower appears to be flat and square, a pleasure seems good to have, health seems threatened, and, accordingly, some possible action seems a bad one, or a good one. Skeptics do not live by *all* the appearances they receive, either in the use of their senses, or in recalling things they earlier got such perceptual appearances of, or in their thoughts as they reflect upon things, but only by the ones they accept, in the way I have described. Those are the ones that may lead to action, or may help to shape actions that they then undertake.

[85] For comment on these Pyrrhonian "beliefs" and on the differences between them and Socrates's ideas about what a "belief" commits one to, see endnote 36.

In the acceptances themselves, the skeptics are active, and not passive, as they are simply in receiving perceptions or when memories come to mind. Nonetheless, whenever they do accept an appearance, they never do so because they think they have any reason to do so. They just find that, for given ones, they do feel driven to accept them (what else is one to do, when things appear to you like that, they think—the way they now do?), and, in fact, they just *do* accept them— for no *reason* at all.[86] They may review and reflect upon an appearance that is a candidate for acceptance (the human mind evidently has that capacity),[87] before accepting it (or rejecting it). But in this as in all other respects, their behavior is driven simply by habits of response that have been built up over time, and in consequence of earlier experiences, going back all the way to early childhood. In that sense, acceptances too are, and feel, passive, as well; they are, as one could say, from the agent's perspective, quite automatic occurrences. They do them, but while being swept along in ways they habitually do get swept along.

Given the enormously varied history of childhood and later experiences that different individuals undergo, one might think that the actual patterns of life among a group of skeptics would vary enormously, to the point of not really constituting any skeptic "way of life," beyond the simple, but enormously variable, common feature of acting always only on appearances and never on reason-based beliefs, as I have explained. One might expect that the differing sets of early and later experiences of sensory perception, bodily feelings, memory, and thought, occasioned by these individuals' varying exposures to environing conditions, would produce habits of response, via automatic and non-reason-based acceptances, to the array of appearances that any adult would be subject to, so individually tied to their own past that no single pattern would be discernible among the whole class of skeptic philosophers. But, in fact, Sextus makes quite strong claims about universally applicable constraints of action, in any and every skeptic life, which would establish a markedly distinct way of life for skeptics. He lists fourfold "everyday observances" that skeptics, following appearances, use to give structure to their life:

> Thus, attending to that which appears, we live in accordance with everyday observances, withholding opinions—for we are not able to be utterly inactive. These everyday observances seem to be fourfold, and to consist in

[86] See *Outlines* I 19 and I 193, where Sextus emphasizes the sense of necessitation with which skeptics accept and follow the appearances that they do accept.

[87] I take Sextus to be taking notice of this fact when he lists in *Outlines* I 23–24 (quoted just below) as part of "direction by nature" in a skeptic life our engaging in thought.

(1) direction by nature, (2) necessitation by passive affection, (3) handing down of laws and customs, and (4) teaching of professional occupations: (1) by nature's direction, insofar as we are naturally such as to engage in perceiving and thinking; (2) by the necessitation of passive affection, insofar as hunger conducts us to food and thirst to drink; (3) by the handing down of customs and laws, insofar as we accept, in an everyday way, that acting piously is good and acting impiously bad; (4) by teaching of professional occupations, insofar as we are not inactive in those which we accept. And we say all this not as expressing our opinions.[88]

The first two of these "observances" are fairly straightforward. First, in reverse order, as for the necessitation of passive affection, everyone from time to time gets hungry and thirsty, and gets turned on for sex, and when they do they receive appearances of various objects, and things to do in relation to them, as appropriate to those feelings. Then those things and actions appear to them as attractive. Likewise, given their particular bodily constitutions, they have passive affections that generate other appearances presenting other objects and actions in an attractive light. Moreover, they find themselves inclined (indeed, in the way we have seen, actually driven) to accept, and they do accept, many of these appearances (but not others): the ones they accept are the ones they have, through experience, become habituated to accept. Second, so far as direction by nature goes, they constantly interact with their environments in the various modes of perception natural to human beings, and they do so (as I mentioned above) by gradually acquiring concepts and then applying them to what they perceive; they also think conceptually in other ways, in response to their current surroundings as they perceive them. They receive conceptually structured appearances in perception and thought, as a matter of how human nature operates;[89] and, again, they find themselves inclined to accept, and they do accept, many (but not all) of these. Sextus implies, quite reasonably, that, despite the huge variations between individual

---

[88] *Outlines* I 23–24, translation based on Annas and Barnes, but with many changes. The numbering of the separate points is my addition.

[89] The appearances of thought referred to here will include many activities of reasoning, such as when, having the question before one's mind, how much is 30 divided by 6? one then experiences the appearance that 30 divided by 6 is 5. One will have learned about these matters as one grows up, and that will give one tendencies to receive such appearances, and to accept them, under such circumstances. Such "ordinary" uses of reasoning are by no means excluded for skeptics when they eschew the critical use of reason, in evaluating appearances and deciding, on bases provided by standards of such reasoning, what the truth is. That is why in the preceding I have often added the qualifier "critical" to reason when speaking of it as rejected by skeptics.

human beings, given their differing environments and particular natural endowments, and the resulting history of their experiences, there will be a very significant commonality, in these respects, among all skeptics, as they come to maturity and continue their lives thereafter. They do not question their appearances, or try to find reasons why one should act on them (or should not), or which ones to act upon; they just follow the appearances, and the tendencies for acceptance of appearances, which they find themselves with.

The third and fourth observances are more interesting, and much more far-reaching. Here Sextus seems to assume that among the other effects of being raised in any human community are appearances that everyone receives, as they grow to maturity, that relate to cultural norms of behavior, first in what we can think of, broadly, as the moral realm, and secondly in relation to particular occupations and work that individually people find themselves attracted, or otherwise directed, to. Here again, his claim is (and reasonably so) that whatever the community may be in which one is brought up, one comes to receive appearances indicating that some behaviors are OK and others not, as one learns to live in the community. And, as one finds one's way into some field of work or occupation (among those on offer in the community), one also comes to receive appearances, provided through one's interaction with the established practitioners with whom one comes into contact, indicating that some behaviors are OK or required, others not OK or forbidden. Many of these appearances, these cultural neophytes find themselves inclined (in a way, even driven) to accept; and they find that they do accept them. Here again, we find a very significant commonality in skeptics' appearances, acceptances, and behaviors, despite the huge individual differences in localities and in details of people's experiences in growing up. Other people being raised in their communities may come to question the appearances they receive, and may look for reasons for or against conforming, but skeptics (once grown up and committed as skeptics) resolutely do not do that. They just follow these appearances that their upbringing has left them with, by sticking to the habits of acceptance that grew up in their minds as they matured.

On Sextus's representation, then (rather surprisingly, if one considers the usual conception of a skeptic as an inveterate doubter), skeptics question nothing that is authoritatively accepted in their community: they come, through their own upbringing and the appearances and acceptances that that engenders in them, to blend in seamlessly with whatever is authoritative where they live, both in morals and religion and in every other aspect of life. Skeptics accept instruction in their profession, and then act unquestioningly in accordance with its standards. They accept whatever the prevailing ethical and moral standards are in the traditions of their community.[90] They otherwise live quiet and compliant lives. They are compliant and conformist in all these ways because in each case they get and accept the appearance that that is how to behave: they act on appearances to them to behave in those ways, appearances that seem to them forced upon them in the way I have indicated. It is not ruled out, I take it, that individual skeptics might begin to get appearances about things that would depart from existing standards in one area or another, even perhaps in ethics or morals, or religion. These could lead to innovations in their behavior (in relation to what is standard or customary in their communities or profession), and perhaps also in the behavior of those around them, due to their influence; and they could even help to change community life to what eventually becomes a new traditional standard of behavior, by aligning their own behavior, and explanations of it, with some new moral or social movement. They are, of course, members of their communities and participate in the human perspective on the world and on human life that their community's practices define. Hence their fundamental conformity. But by the same token, their own innovative appearances and consequent behaviors will participate in the constant reshaping that any such socially determined perspective must undergo. Moral or other revolutionaries, however, they decidedly are not. They never claim that there is any reason to make a change in religion or morals or in the conduct of their profession, for example because something is false or wrong in current practices. It just strikes them that something else than the heretofore usual thing might go better, that is, might go in such a way that one would, if one adopted it, then be struck with the impression that this was better, or more equitable, or whatever. And, obviously, they do not bring to the moral life, or to the satisfying life as proposed by themselves, any innovations involving some special spirit in which to act, or some special conception of oneself and others, deriving, as with Aristotle, the Stoics, Epicurus, and

[90] Under the heading of "laws and customs" Sextus mentions only pious and impious behavior—respectfully performing or attending civic temple rites and the like. But included are, presumably, behavior in accord with all the moral norms of one's society (the ones brought together by philosophers under headings drawn from the names of the traditional virtues and vices of justice, temperance, courage, etc.)—as well, of course, as all the more important, and more or less universally respected, customs, traditions, and laws of one's society. It is noteworthy that Sextus has nothing to say here, in sketching the skeptic guides for living, about the virtues themselves, which figure so grandly in all the ethical theories of the "positive" philosophies we have been examining in this book. As we have seen, especially in discussing the ethical theories of Aristotle and the Stoics, the aspiration to virtue is a mark of an elitism (a moral elitism, to be sure, not a matter of social or class distinction) to which skeptics, with their wish not to distinguish themselves from the run of life around them, must renounce.

Plotinian Platonists, from positive philosophical theory. They have learned to avoid any and all theses of positive philosophy, because those are presented as based on reasons. For the most part, they do not stand out from the rest of society in any way (except, perhaps, for their constant practice of philosophical investigation, as an avocation alongside whatever their professional work may be: more on that below). They are quite content to blend in, unquestioningly, with whatever is normal where they live. They are satisfied, even happy, to do so.

I have just reminded the reader that the skeptic life, beyond its conformism so far as issues of daily life, morality, religion, politics, and so on, may go, also includes a devotion to philosophical discussion and investigation. I will say more about that shortly, in concluding this chapter. As to the rest of their life (the conformist part), it might seem that Sextus's skepticism returns its adherents to the paradisiacally innocent position they would have been in, if, like the dumb and lazy people Sextus contrasts his proto-skeptics with in his narrative, they had never begun to entertain worries about those anomalies from which his narrative took its start. Those people just go with the flow, never questioning anything to find out reasons why things are, and need to be, the way they are, they just deal pragmatically with any conflicts or anomalies they might face in their experience of things. Aren't Sextus's skeptics supposed to live, to a significant extent, just as those dumb and lazy people? No. In fact, there is quite a large difference between the two ways of life, despite the similar outward appearances of the behaviors that might be found in each. Skeptics may follow the same traditional standards in morals, professions, and in all other respects, as these others, and, like them, they will do so docilely and without question. But they remain smart and energetic, and the others are still dumb and lazy. This means several things.

To begin with, skeptics carry within themselves a strongly self-conscious understanding of how they are living, in living this way. They are living according to what they themselves conceive to be appearances (not that they have or live with any theory as to what these appearances are, as such). They live while constantly eschewing any opinions or beliefs that go beyond an easy acceptance of those appearances. They do not think they have a grounding for human life in reasons why their life and their actions are right and best—as the Stoics and Aristotle, with their theory of a god-given and god-supervised reality, do, in their different ways, for the Stoic and Aristotelian lives, or as Epicurus does for his life of pleasure. But they have an intimate familiarity with the theories of those who do regard human life in this way, and they are also acutely conscious of the failings of these theories, as it appears to them, in regard to the very standards for theory construction that are appealed to by these philosophers in setting them out. None of this is true of the dumb and lazy people. The skeptics' philosophical suspension of belief in all these theories, and in all those ways of life, is active in the way they do live, and that produces a large difference for them from the way the dumb and lazy live. Most decisively for the way they lead their skeptic lives, having started out as full believers in the power and authority of reason in shaping our lives, they know from their personal experience (and bear constantly in their minds as they live their lives) the full allure of that idea. That is to say, it appears strongly and forcibly to them that they used to be such believers, and the idea of this authority was and remains alluring, just as it appears forcibly to them that all the theories of life proposed by the other schools of philosophy have failed in the way I have indicated.

All this must affect their daily actions in many ways, as they self-consciously bear it all in mind in doing them. Their lives are much the richer for their disappointed love affair with philosophy than any ordinary person's who lives, to an external view, according to many of the same patterns. They, no less than the Aristotelian or Stoic or Epicurean or Platonist, live their philosophy—their skeptical life of suspension of reason-based belief and conformity to the traditions that are authoritative in their society. Their philosophical views are the source of their life; those views are their life's ultimate steersman—even if, for the most part, in a negative and warning way, rather than, as with the other ancient philosophies, a positively prescriptive one. And, of course, with the skeptics, unlike with the other philosophies, all their philosophical views are held only as accepted appearances that have arisen in their minds through their experience, both in investigating philosophical arguments and in their experience of daily life. They do not hold any philosophical views for any reason, including those they live by adhering to.[91]

This allure, for Sextan skeptics, of the idea of critical reason as authoritative for human life deserves more extended attention in this connection. It is not merely that skeptics (as it appears to them) used to fall to that allure and used to spend lots of time looking for the truth through positive philosophical efforts to discover it, firmly believing in the authority of reason (and of its handmaiden, philosophy) to tell us what we ought to believe, what we ought to do, how we

---

[91] That is the force of Sextus's remark, in the passage from *Outlines* I 23–24 quoted above in which he sets out the "fourfold" direction of a skeptic's life, that he states there no opinions, i.e., nothing for which he can be expected to give any reasons. He reports only appearances that he accepts in so describing their life.

ought to live. Even after they have settled into skeptical living according to appearances (alone), they retain a certain allegiance to the authority of reason and
philosophy. It's just that what started out being a fully committed acceptance of
that authority now becomes a conditional one. Their experience in philosophy
has left them with the strong impression, which they cannot but accept, so strong
is it, that critical reason does not lead to any decisive result, and, to all appearances, never will succeed in doing so. So we could put their current attitude like
this: if there is any authority for how to live, reason and philosophy are certainly
it—nothing else could possibly be (as it seems to them) an authority for living.
But, it appears, even reason and philosophy, if pursued with the greatest rigor
and vigor, as they themselves pursue it, fail to deliver any authoritative instructions for how we should live (or, more generally, what we should believe or dis-
believe, in the sense of accepting and acting on it). Hence, we have to live what,
from the point of view of that conditional attitude, is a second-best way of life—
one that, nonetheless, in its own terms is perfectly satisfying: a life spent suspending belief and reason, led according to appearances alone, instead. This is a
life not with a different authority (e.g., tradition), it is a life altogether without
any authority for it. It's just a life that one leads.

Still, the skeptic does not at all give up on reason—on looking for an authoritative set of instructions for life, with the intention of living according to them
(if found). That is why it is a crucial part of skeptics' lives to spend lots of time in
their avocation of investigating philosophical questions, examining them anew,
looking for previously unexplored possible ways through and away from the
anomalies in human experience—while, as has happened at least so far, reaching
no acceptable conclusion, one way or the other, on the questions investigated,
but suspending. They keep this up because of their continued (skeptical) hope of
success. If reason should after all, eventually, produce reason-certified instructions about how to live, or, in general, what to believe, one would certainly be
foolish (as it seems to them) not to follow those instructions. So, as Sextus says
at the beginning of the *Outlines*,

> When people are investigating any subject, the likely result is either a dis-
> covery, or a denial of discovery and a confession of inapprehensibility,[92] or
> else a continuation of the investigation. This, no doubt, is why in the case

---

[92] The Greek word here is ἀκαταληψία, an especially Stoic term. To confess inapprehensibility is to
conclude, on the basis of one's failure in inquiry, that the matter is not capable of being settled (by us); it
is permanently beyond our grasp.

of philosophical investigations, too, some have said that they have discovered the truth, some have asserted that it cannot be apprehended, and others are still investigating. Those who are called Dogmatists in a specialized
sense of the word think that they have established the truth—for example,
the schools of Aristotle and Epicurus and the Stoics, and some others. The
schools of Clitomachus and Carneades, and other Academics, have asserted that things cannot be apprehended. And the Skeptics are still
investigating.[93]

The skeptic keeps on investigating, however, as I have said, not merely for
the formalistic reason, perhaps suggested here, that a "committed" skeptic must
take great care to remain a skeptic, on pain of falling into the second of Sextus's
classifications, that of a special kind of skeptically "dogmatic" philosophers—
"negative" dogmatists, who assert that the truth is beyond our powers to discover
(on the ground that repeated failure has shown this to be so). They must take
care not to fall victim to the (to them) all too tempting thought that, because
they have examined millions of philosophical arguments, their failure to find
even one completely sound one (of other than trivial consequence) is some
ground (even a probabilistic one) for thinking that philosophical arguments are
always flawed. It is true that they must do this in order to remain skeptics (something that seems to them essential for the tranquility they now enjoy). But they
must not keep on investigating just as a charade engaged in so as to keep, or pre-
tend to keep, an open mind, while secretly being pretty well convinced that critical reason and philosophy really are frauds—simply so as not to fall into negative
dogmatism, instead of remaining tranquil skeptics. No, the reason they keep investigating is a quite positive one. It is because they remain positively committed
to follow reason as the true authority (that seems to them the thing to do), if
only it can (seem to) prove itself to be capable of giving authoritative instructions for what to believe and how to live. Having that commitment, they cannot
(as it seems to them) fail to keep giving it a try.

This implies that, even after having achieved the tranquility that comes from
universal suspension of judgment, skeptics will, as a regular part of their life,
continue to investigate questions of philosophy, with interest and an open mind.
They have the special skill I referred to, of being able always to counterpose to
any (reason-based) claim as to the truth, an equi-balanced counterclaim. So they
will continue to use that skill even after they have examined enough positive

[93] *Outlines* I 1–3, trans. Annas and Barnes, with three changes.

philosophy, its claims and arguments, to suspect that it is all a will-o'-the-wisp, and that even about ordinary matters of daily fact one is never going to establish any truth or falsehood, according to philosophical standards of truth and falsehood, based on valid reasons for holding them true or false. Skeptics may and presumably will take great pleasure in their philosophical work of argument, analysis, and discussion, about human nature and human values, among other questions. They will, of course, sustain their own tranquility in their life of suspension so long as they do keep on failing to be satisfied with their results. And the loss of tranquility looms, as it seems to them, if they ever cease to suspend on any question: then they would revive their old worries. But the hope of sustaining their tranquility, which rests on not asserting that positive philosophy is hopeless (the reasons for saying that are all too inadequate), is not a motive, for them, in trying to make every investigation turn out fruitless. The greater motive is the hope that philosophy will succeed, not that it will fail. Of course, if it ever does, and skeptics learn about and can certify that fact, they will forthwith cease to be skeptics—whether they have to shoulder ensuing worries or not.

The fact remains, however, that it must seem to skeptics that their tranquility and happiness in life do depend on continually finding fault with any and every philosophical argument and thesis. It must seem to them that if ever they do find philosophy succeeding in establishing even one claim, they will then have to recognize that critical reason and philosophy have been vindicated; and even if that recognition is only the acceptance of the appearance, to them, that critical reason has been vindicated, once they have reached it, surely they will then become worried about all the other anomalies (the ones not settled in whatever argument they now find acceptable): what prevented worry was the unexpected effect of *universal* suspension. Having recognized that critical reason *can* establish truths that one ought to believe (witness the given case), for the reasons it proposes, wouldn't it now seem to them that philosophy isn't a will-o'-the-wisp, after all, and that it might, despite earlier apparent failures, succeed in other areas where anomalies arise? And that would now take away their tranquility: they would feel the need to try to extend philosophy's success into the area of questions, beset by anomalies, concerning how one ought to live one's life. In short, they would cease to be skeptics, and become returned to the anxious state they were in when they were proto-skeptics—until, they might hope, they could settle those anomalies, and so achieve tranquility by this alternative route of positive, committed philosophical theory. Thus, as it seems, skeptics will live their lives in a very delicate balance between living as Sextus describes, following his fourfold direction (and also devoting lots of attention to philosophy), and worrying about what would happen to their lives if ever their skill of counterbalancing arguments should fail to undermine an argument of philosophy. Could they really maintain the perfect tranquility that Sextus claims for them by living according to appearances only? Wouldn't living that way actually lead them to start worrying, precisely because of what would seem to them the need to make their method succeed every time they applied it? If so, then it would seem doubtful, to us neutral observers, that the skeptic philosophy does, after all, enable us to achieve the skeptic's stated goal of tranquility.

Two further questions might occur to one in assessing the viability of the skeptic way of life. Consider the skeptic demand that we live our lives with no reliance on critical reason at any point or circumstance, and while holding no reason-based beliefs about anything. Here two sets of questions arise. First, how realistic is the skeptic's impression that, if one did sometimes or often rely on reason in figuring out how things are and how it makes best sense to behave in relation to them, one would suffer from anything like the seriously disturbing anxiety that his proto-skeptics began from? How much, in fact, does it matter, if we did rely on reason, that we could never be certain we were right about anything? Sextus's smart and energetic proto-skeptics were racked with anxiety caused by the anomalies, he says. But is it reasonable to think that, if we—the ones he wants to persuade to become skeptics too—did permanently bear the burden of uncertainty that caused them this anxiety, we would suffer at all greatly in our life? Couldn't we still live at least decently happily, even by the skeptic lights that make happiness consist of unperturbedness? How perturbed would one have to be, just because one did seek reasoned beliefs with which to decide on, explain, and defend one's choices (or, at any rate, some of them—the more important ones), without being able decisively and for sure to assert that one's way of life was the right one? Maybe one could be satisfied, well enough, with having some good reasons for being a Stoic, say, even if one might dither between that and Aristotelianism? Isn't Sextus's going on so about the seriousness of the anxiety in people's lives who do accept critical reason, and reason-based belief, more than a bit exaggerated?[94]

[94] See *Outlines* I 27 (trans. Annas and Barnes): "[T]hose who hold the opinion that things are good or bad by nature are perpetually troubled. When they lack what they believe to be good, they take themselves to be persecuted by natural evils, and they pursue what (so they think) is good. And when they have acquired these things, they experience more troubles; for they are elated beyond reason and measure, and in fear of change they do anything so as not to lose what they believe to be good." Really? He adds (I 30) that when they are afflicted with some ordinary and inevitable bodily distress (e.g., shivering in the cold) such

Second, how possible is it, really, to give up our human practice of using our powers of reason to subject ourselves and others to criticism, and to judge, on the basis of reason, what to think about the facts and also about norms for decision? Even if it is possible, as Sextus insists, to live following the appearances, instead, and only thereby to achieve tranquility, should one really want to? Maybe such perturbation as this practice really may entail (setting aside Sextus's exaggerations) is worth it, for other reasons; one might think it important to have such vindication as one could find for one's beliefs and actions. Maybe that is worth the less than fully tranquil but still *relatively* tranquil life one might then lead. In fact, when Sextus includes among his "fourfold observances" that guide skeptic lives the "direction by nature," many readers might expect that this direction would include results of the fact, as it does seem to many people, even if Sextus denies it, that it belongs to our nature as rational beings to seek for our own reasons for believing things, and to attempt to satisfy ourselves as to which is the right thing to believe, given what appears to be the case. If so, we can't give this up, once we mature to the point where this part of our nature is present, and "revert" to living on appearances, and on habits of acceptance, alone. Also, even if we waive that objection, it might seem that, under his third "observance," the handing down of customs and laws, the skeptic's banned practices of critical reasoning would find a way back in. It does seem that we are customarily brought up to think of ourselves as rational beings of just that critical, and self-critical, sort.[95] Moreover, it may seem to many that there is an honor and dignity involved for us in having such a nature (if it is our nature), or at least in our having, as a species, developed our cultures to the point where we inculcate into the young this self-conception as part of what they acquire as they grow into maturity. If so, it might very well seem that, even if some perturbation, or some degree of anxiety, unavoidably does go along with preserving, and living with, this self-conception, and acting upon it quite often, it is not for that reason to be renounced.

"ordinary people are afflicted by two sets of circumstances: by the feelings themselves, and no less by believing that these circumstances are bad by nature." *Afflicted* by thinking that? Really?

[95] This must have been so in ancient Greece, too, long before Sextus's time, and perhaps even before philosophy came on the cultural scene. Sextus's apparent idea of a paradisiacal time when ordinary people (his dumb and lazy folk) were not affected with worries about anomalies seems a motivated projection from his own skeptical philosophical position. In any event, as I argued above, Sextus's skeptics do not "return" to the life that any such dumb and lazy persons would have led.

CHAPTER 6

Platonism as a Way of Life

6.1. Introduction: Pythagoras, Plato, and Ancient Greek Wisdom

In the last two chapters we have discussed the main philosophical movements of the Hellenistic period—skipping ahead in time to include the Pyrrhonian skepticism of Sextus Empiricus. We have discussed their respective conceptions of philosophy itself (philosophical understanding, philosophical thinking) as fundamental for the specific ways of life associated with each of these philosophies. The third century BCE saw the establishment of three Hellenistic "schools" of philosophy, each on its own firm and complete philosophical foundations, each formally organized with its own central place of instruction in Athens: the Epicurean Garden, the Painted Stoa, and the skeptical Academy that Plato's own school in Athens became under the headship of Arcesilaus.[1] As noted above, during the third and second centuries, and even later—into the first centuries of the new era of Roman domination of the Greek-speaking eastern Mediterranean—Stoic, Epicurean, and skeptical philosophy constituted the main options for those attracted to philosophical studies. All three seem to have had many adherents, not only among the more educated classes of Greek and Roman society, and the upper classes of the Hellenized peoples of North Africa and the

---

[1] There existed in the third century (and later, too, though with increasing etiolation) also what scholars call a "Peripatetic" school, the continuation of the research and advanced teaching institute that Aristotle established at Athens and headed in his later years. (See above, chapter 4, note 2.) After the death of his friend and successor as head of the school, Theophrastus (d. 287/286 BCE), the Peripatos was not the prominent force in Greek intellectual life that these three new schools were. (On these Athenian schools for philosophical study, see above, section 4.1.)

Middle East, but also among the masses (especially, as we saw, in the case of Epicureanism). Nonetheless, Stoicism was the standard-bearer for philosophy as a whole in this period: the Epicureans' and skeptics' deeply thought out and in fact carefully considered rejections of rationalist ideas about the vast extent of the human power of reason and of its divine origins made them minority outriders. The Stoics were the ones with prestige.

One common feature, not emphasized so far, stands out in all the ancient philosophers we have discussed. This is in sharp contrast to the philosophers to whom we now turn, in this last chapter: Plotinus and the other Platonist philosophers of late antiquity. As we have seen philosophy becomes a way of life in this whole tradition, these late Platonists included, because of the relationship the Greek philosophers see between the highest human good, or eudaimonia, and philosophy: for them, philosophical thought and understanding, which bring to human life, as they think, a full grasp of the ultimate truth about human nature and the human good, is a necessary, and if brought to completion, a sufficient, source of fulfillment and happiness for us. The key contrast I just alluded to concerns the relationship that late Platonists see between human nature and happiness, on the one hand, and, on the other, our life as human animals. As human animals we have needs and interests, both physical and social, and a good, that we pursue in a life of quite a short duration. We grow to maturity within a family, and live out our lives, right through until the moment of our deaths, within a social and political context of constant interaction with others (and at the best, of mutual cooperation) in shaping our lives. For the philosophers of the classical and Hellenistic periods, the good that we achieve with philosophy's help at least includes goods existing or taking place within that embodied animal life: either our pleasures or at least our virtuous attitudes and evaluations as we decide and act, in dealing with our circumstances and with events arising in our lives as such animals, count for all these philosophers as crucial, indeed central, elements in the human good. Our happiness is found, at least in part, within a well-lived animal life.[2]

In turning to Plotinus and late Platonism, we step into a different philosophical world. The value and function of philosophy for these Platonists is not to

[2] This includes Plato himself, I would argue (though Plotinus, and Platonists before and after him, would not agree with me). It also includes Aristotle, even though Aristotle, as well as Plato, recognizes a human capacity for being in intellectual touch with a higher, nonphysical realm, and even though Aristotle too may accept that human beings can survive death in some etiolated way as pure intellects. On Plato and Aristotle see below.

enrich and deepen our life as animals, but, much more, to disengage us, and take us away, from it, even while we are (perforce) living it. In Plotinus's theories of human nature—the human essence—and, as a result of that, of human happiness or the human good, as we will see, we, the human persons that we are, who live either well or badly as embodied living beings, are not in fact embodied things at all; our life lies not at all in acts or experiences of the senses, or in the choices and actions that make up our daily lives in our families, with our friends, and in our societies. *Our* life, Plotinus thinks, lies exclusively in activities of pure intellectual thinking that we, all of us, engage in all the time, most of us without even realizing it; our task is to become as self-conscious as possible of this activity, and to constantly focus our minds upon it (something we can, in principle, do even while, qua embodied animals, living an embodied life). If we do this, we lift ourselves altogether out of the physical world, and up to a world of pure intellectual thinking, in which our true life has, all along, been taking place. But now, if we reach the final goal of self-purification, our life consists in a full and active understanding of the intelligible objects of that intellectual thought. We self-consciously and actively live that life of the intellect. That, for Plotinus, is the human good and human happiness. Philosophy's task—one that only philosophy can perform—is to make us truly alive, and to keep us alive, in that self-consciously intellectual way. Human happiness requires not regarding yourself as an animal at all; your animal life, however well lived, is not part of your good, the human good.

In Hellenistic and early imperial times, as I said, Stoicism was the most prestigious philosophy; its doctrines were the base line from which the other philosophies represented themselves as departing. Ironically, the seeds were already well sown among Stoics of the late second and the first half of the first centuries BCE for a momentous new growth that before long came to overtop and deprive the Hellenistic philosophies of all their light.[3] Increasingly philosophy itself simply became a "Platonist" endeavor, and also a way of life—a life founded in ideas about the human soul (human nature), and about what Platonists regarded as reality itself (the reality behind or above things as they appear), that made both of them out to be fundamentally spiritual in nature, to be sharply set off from and contrasted with everything bodily. Many philosophers became dissatisfied with the materialist or corporealist assumptions of Epicurus and the Stoics,

---

[3] See chapter 4, notes 2 and 3. For historical details on the origins and progress of the movement to recognize Plato as an important authority in philosophy, see endnote 37.

which seemed to them unresponsive to their own personal sense of their status as beings of a spiritual, and not at all a bodily, order.[4] For these philosophers, such spiritualist ideas found their most powerful and persuasive presentation in Plato's dialogues—hence the classification of their philosophical movement as Platonism.

But Platonists (both "middle," as scholars refer to them, from the first century to the early third century, and late ones, such as Plotinus) actually claimed to trace these ideas themselves back ultimately to Pythagoras and the Pythagoreans of southern Italy in the sixth and fifth centuries BCE—indeed further back, to a postulated primordial, rather mystical "wisdom" of "the ancients." This "wisdom" was supposedly available to these most ancient of thinkers, long shrouded in the mists of prehistory, because of their nearness, in those earliest days of the world, to the gods—authors, in some way, of all (besides themselves) that there is. On this widely shared account, fanciful though it was and based on little or no evidence, the primordial wisdom was handed down to, or rather recovered in historical times by, insightful thinkers such as Pythagoras and Parmenides. At last, dressed up in the proper philosophical format of argument and analysis through the philosophical genius of Plato, it was made available to posterity in Plato's dialogues. Late Platonists, therefore, thought of philosophy as grounded in a primordial wisdom discovered by the most ancient Greeks, and recovered for humankind in more recent times by Pythagoras (who left no writings) and formulated by Plato in his dialogues, though incompletely and often in superficially misleading ways. Their own work, as original philosophers themselves, consisted in continuing this task of recovery by explaining, interpreting, and arguing for this alleged Greek wisdom, while defending it from objections and updating it for their own times by drawing upon more recent philosophy (especially Aristotle and the Stoics), where that seemed compatible and helpful.

The crucial point of this wisdom was the recognition that the whole of what we ordinarily take for real—the physical world as a whole, all its contents, including our own bodies—are misleading derivations from a higher realm of true being. We ourselves—our souls, the seats of our consciousness—are immaterial spirits, allied in their nature to this immaterial true being, this real reality. The study and knowledge of true being (including the knowledge of our own souls as

---

[4] The "spiritualist crisis," mentioned in section 1.2, that afflicted intellectuals across the Greco-Roman world during the early centuries CE, had a lot to do with this growing dissatisfaction with the "shallowness" of the Hellenistic philosophies.

spiritual allies of the true being) becomes the ultimate and proper task of philosophy. At the same time, this study is the only completely proper occupation of our souls themselves, too. By the middle of the third century CE, and continuing thereafter until Greek philosophy's effective end, by the seventh century, philosophy considered as an independent source of authoritative ideas about the world and about human life, just meant a commitment to this Platonist philosophy—in one form or another, with varying details. It consisted in putting ourselves in touch intellectually with true being, and, as we will see below, in living wholly for our own "return" to our origin, as intellects and consciousnesses, in that being, upon death.

Now, despite its Platonic roots, about which I will have more to say shortly, this late Platonist philosophy was, in effect, something fundamentally new in the world of Greek thought. Its difference from all the philosophy that preceded is worth considering in some detail, in the remainder of this section. As I said above, Greek philosophers in both the classical and Hellenistic periods, including Plato himself, as I will argue below, conceived philosophy and its task as addressing human beings and human life in full commitment to their lives as animals, in this world—a world of personal, social, and political issues to be lived through on a philosophically informed and principled basis, leading to a this-worldly happiness that only philosophy could provide (even if, for Plato in the myths he appended to some of his dialogues, such a happy life would be rewarded with an even happier afterlife as a spirit). The Stoics, Epicurus, and Pyrrhonian skeptics do not even so much as envision any sort of other, nonworldly life for a human being at all.[5] For them philosophy is aimed at helping us live the lives we all know we have got, in the here and now. Philosophy helps us to live our worldly lives without reference to a supposed afterlife, or even to any realm of alleged being outside the physical world itself, and beyond whatever the inherent principles may be for the world's constitution and operation over time. Aristotle too confines his attention in his moral philosophy to our lives as physically embodied, living substances, with minds and souls that organize and direct a life for us that comes to an end with our deaths. Our whole happiness, or failure to achieve it, is to be found in that life, including our emotional and appetitive and, in general, our animal lives.

As for Aristotle, it is true that he assigns to human reason, as an aspect or part of the overall human soul, a special and anomalous status. In its fundamental

[5] For Hellenistic philosophers' views on souls' continuance after death, see endnote 38.

account, a soul, even a rational human one, is, as Aristotle puts it, the "form" or "actuality" of a physical and material entity that, when having that form to animate it, counts as a living being. The "forms" of material substances are principles of organization for relevant sorts of materials; a soul gives a living material thing its capacities as something with a life to live. The idea of an unembodied bodily life capacity, for example the capacity for sense perception, does not make much sense. So it makes no good sense to think of a soul, in general, as surviving the animated being's death, or having any possibility of a further life, so to speak, of its own. However, Aristotle does allow at least some vaguely indicated possibility of an exceptional status for one of the rational powers that human beings possess.[6] For Aristotle, the capacity to grasp in thought the essences or natures of whatever belongs to the constitution of the world (including the natures of the various different sorts of living things as well as of god), is to be conceived not as a capacity of an embodied living thing at all. Rather it is a capacity that belongs to human beings, along with their other, embodied, capacities, in some way that involves the animation of no bodily part, and requires no connection to a body in order to function. The exercise of this unembodied capacity is required for, and central to, the activity of theoretical knowing or understanding that Aristotle identifies as the absolutely highest good of, and for, a human being.[7] Moreover, as Aristotle emphasizes in his discussion of the theoretically contemplative philosopher's happiness in *Nicomachean Ethics* book X, this activity is the one that brings us closest to the pure activity of thought that, on Aristotle's analysis, is the very essence of god. God's activity of thought, while standing metaphysically outside and beyond the physical world, is the original source of being for all things that have being at all, in whatever way they do possess it. For Aristotle, then, in our own active knowing and understanding, insofar as its ultimate completion is found in the knowledge of god's activity of pure thought as the origin of being, we realize our highest good. At the same time we exercise what counts as most divine in us, because of this direct relationship of knowledge that it makes possible for us to the divine, transcendent source of all being. This one soul capacity that human beings have, then, on Aristotle's view, the one making possible for us theoretical understanding of the natures of things, including that of god, might perhaps persist in existence after a person's death (however difficult it might be to conceive the manner of its disembodied existence).

[6] See Aristotle, *On the Soul*, esp. III 4.
[7] See section 3.4.

Nonetheless, whatever thin idea of an afterlife, or even of immortality, Aristotle's carefully hedged account of this unembodied human capacity may hold out for us, these aspects of his theories do not compromise, much less in any way undermine, his focus, as with his predecessors' and his Hellenistic successors', on our this-worldly life and on the pursuit of our happiness within it. His ethical theory has no regard to any such bare theoretical possibilities. God's goodness does lie at the ground of all goodness, including the goodness of the happy human life; the goodness of a good human life is a quality such a life comes to possess, and in possessing it a good human life is dependent on god's goodness. For Aristotle, god—god's thought—is good simply and immediately as the activity of thought that it is. It is the very essence of goodness, as it is of being. But god's goodness—that pure and perfect activity of thought—remains a distinct thing of its own, and exists apart on its own. Our goal, our good, consists in our activity, in our this-worldly life, of relating ourselves to that good in a proper way. We do that, principally, through our contemplative-theoretical activities of thinking (if we possess the virtues needed for that); but, in any event, we relate ourselves to that good, as well, through our virtuous or decent personal and social lives, as embodied rational animals, in our families, our work, and our political communities.

Likewise for Socrates—that is, for the notional Socrates of this book, the Socrates of Plato's, Xenophon's, and other surviving Socratic writings by people who knew him personally. As we saw in chapter 2 Socrates, on something approaching principle, eschewed inquiry into, and made no assumptions about, such metaphysical questions as those that lie at the center of the Platonist philosophy—questions about true being versus unreliable appearance, or about the nature of the soul. In particular, Plato himself makes clear, Socrates included in this banned territory ideas about whether our souls survive our deaths or not: at his trial Plato has Socrates go out of his way, in his final remarks to the jurors, to indicate that he did not think he knew anything about that—and he is not in the least worried by not knowing.[8] For him, the crucial point is that people are responsible individually for the state of their own mind and soul, for better or worse. If one cares for one's soul in the proper philosophical way, by understanding virtue itself as the highest good, and seeing all other human goods and ills as only of secondary and inessential concern, then one can be sure that nothing

---

[8] See Plato, *Apology of Socrates* 40c–41b. For the contrasting ideas about the soul and immortality expressed by the character Socrates of the *Phaedo*, see endnote 39.

that happens to oneself, whether in life or (in case there is any continuing existence for a person) after death, can actually harm one. This, as we saw, he does know, because the good reasons that support this view are so extensive and deep. Your virtue is a guarantee that, however other things may stand, things will go well for you, for so long as there is any of you at all to be concerned over.

It is true that, for Socrates, virtue itself, since it consists in a full and final knowledge of the whole realm of human values, is something that, as it seems, no human being will ever achieve. Only god has that knowledge: god has it, because it is something essential to the nature of divinity, on Socrates's pious belief. But there is nothing to be done about the inevitable falling short of any and every effort, however persistent, actually, finally, and fully, to achieve our highest good. No prolongation of our lives into some afterlife could change that: Socrates is not one to engage in fantasies about some fundamental transformation of a human being into something else. After death, in case our consciousness does continue, Socrates says in this passage of the *Apology*, there may be extremely interesting and pleasurable conversations with wise men and heroes of old: but, however attractive and desirable such a prospect may be, such a continued life would be a good one on no other basis than the goodness of the life one was already leading before one's death—provided, always, one really is as good a person as possible in one's lifetime. There is no fundamental improvement to be anticipated. For Socrates, then, there is no getting round the fact—or beyond it—that the philosophical life has its full and exclusive focus on this-worldly concerns, concerns, to be sure, for the intellectual value of rational understanding of our good, but also for our animal lives in applying that knowledge to our circumstances as embodied beings.

In fact, basically the same thing is to be said also about Plato. If we agree to accept the views of Plato's lead characters in his non-Socratic dialogues as Plato's own, then Plato does indeed think, as the later Platonists did too, that human souls are bodiless spiritual entities, with no possibility of either coming into being or passing away.[9] Only material bodies can do either of those things. Souls are only temporarily lodged in particular living bodies, giving those their life powers of sensation and other aspects of human consciousness, so long as those bodies are materially so conditioned that the living things that they constitute can remain alive with the help of these souls. Plato agrees with the Platonists that

---

[9] I have in mind here such dialogues as *Symposium*, *Phaedo*, *Phaedrus*, and *Timaeus*, as well as *Republic*.

souls have a metaphysical status, as spirits, that relates them in an essential way to the true reality and being of Platonic Forms—that is, to the natures themselves of all the objects existing in the world and formed by nature, of all mathematical entities and relationships, and of all the natural properties of natural objects, including most particularly everything to do with goodness, happiness, virtue, and other human values, all conceived as natures that actually exist elsewhere than in the natural world.[10] Souls in fact, for Plato, have as their highest and most essential function, the rational activity of thinking, even knowing, Forms. Souls and Forms jointly constitute "intelligible" reality, which is to say, true being. The physical world and everything in it derives from this reality by a relationship of projection by Forms of the natures that they are onto the materials that offer a basis for reception in the physical world of the "reflections" that result from that projection. In all I have said in this paragraph, Plato and the philosophers of late Platonism can be seen as in agreement.

Yet, for Plato, the pursuit of philosophy and the value for a human being in engaging in it is just as this-worldly as it is in the rest of the philosophical tradition of classical and Hellenistic Greece as so far discussed in this book. Knowledge of Forms, on which philosophy concentrates, is, for us human beings, fundamentally aimed at allowing us to grasp and make sense of the world we live in as embodied rational animals—that is, the physical world—and of the natural and social events, and changing circumstances, that provide us with all the work of living our lives, as we pursue our own animal interests and our efforts to direct our nonrational desires and emotions and to do our actions in as virtuous a way as possible. In the imagined ideal city of the *Republic* the most intelligent and otherwise suitable young people are sought out and given a complete mathematical and philosophical education, reaching to a full and final grasp of the Forms—all of the Forms, including the most important and indeed fundamental one, the Form of Goodness. The point of this education is to qualify them to be rulers in the city, implementing their knowledge of Forms in forming and sustaining the institutions and practices of this ideal community. Thereby they can enable everyone living in it, including themselves, to live a happy and fulfilled life, to the degree allowed by their own natural endowments of intelligence and strength of character, as those affect their capacities in making their own decisions, as em-

---

[10] Here I follow the late ancient Platonist understanding of Plato's theories; Plato's own writings leave many details of his theory of Forms open to alternative and more limited accounts of the characteristics and extent of the Forms than the late Platonist regimentation of Plato's philosophy allows (see, e.g., the discussion between the characters Parmenides and Socrates in Plato's *Parmenides*, 130a–e).

bodied animals, and living according to them. That is, the rulers can enable all the citizens to live a life of decency or virtue. These rulers, once their education is complete, may have legitimate cause, just because of the excellence and highest value, to them, just in itself, of the activity of thinking and knowing Forms, to regret the (intermittent) work they do as rulers. They may legitimately prefer to have lived instead, if only the general circumstances of human life permitted it (as they do not), while giving much more nearly full-time devotion to their philosophical and theoretical pursuits—that is, to the cultivation of their pure intellects, while reducing the time spent on and active interest in the emotional satisfactions of virtuous actions in other areas of private and social life.[11] Even so, such a potentially better life for them would be one lived in the there and then; their knowledge of Forms, and of the Forms' divine value, would be implemented in a this-worldly life for themselves of a particularly exquisite and good sort. On either alternative—the life of ruling, or the life of contemplation—it is a this-worldly happiness that Plato is concerned with. It is a life of full engagement in activities of this-worldly living: sitting in one's study thinking, or explaining one's ideas to someone else, are, of course, just special cases of virtuous this-worldly activity, with its special animal satisfactions.

In the *Phaedo* Plato has Socrates complain and lament most copiously over the body's pleasures (and pains), and the body's other annoying effects on our consciousness: it throws up insurmountable obstacles to our getting to know Forms, and to spending time thinking and knowing them once we do grasp them. Even there, however, Socrates's principal aim is to underline the fact that virtue (virtuous behavior in living our embodied animal lives, with our animal interests and concerns) is an incomparably greater good than any bodily pleasures or any other of the "goods of life." It is with knowledge of Forms in its function of providing us with virtues in living our lives that Socrates in the *Phaedo* is concerned throughout.[12] It is certainly true that when he agrees with the popular judgment that philosophers might as well be dead (so little do they get of the

---

[11] Aristotle's unPlatonic separation of practical wisdom from theoretical wisdom, and the attainability, for him, of the former even without the latter, make it possible to envisage this alternative as a practicable ideal, as for Plato in the *Republic* it is not. On Aristotle's view, a well-functioning city can see to the happiness of ordinary citizens (at the highest level that their capabilities permit) through the practical wisdom of the political leaders, while also providing, for the theoretically inclined full philosophers, the freedom to live a retired, studious happy life in which their theoretical wisdom plays the dominant role. See sections 3.4 and 3.8 above. For these issues in the *Republic*, see VII, 519b–521b.

[12] See *Phaedo* 64a–69d, 80a–84b. I discuss these passages further in section 6.4 below, where my aim is to explore Plotinus's own use of Socrates's laments so as to bolster his own very different concerns, as a Platonist, for the problems posed by the fact that we have bodies.

alleged good things of life), and when he provocatively insists that any true philosopher spends as much of his time as he can "in training for being dead,"[13] Plato does have Socrates stress the value of the afterlife. That is the time when, if ever, philosophers finally achieve their highest ambition of fully knowing the Forms. Before death, our bodies prevent us from attaining our highest good. But earlier in the dialogue Socrates has refused to endorse the idea that it could be right to take one's own life just in order to enjoy, at the soonest, the goods only fully available to us then:[14] he thinks one should remain in life, and remain committed to life in this material world and to legitimate animal and social satisfactions, so long as one's life happens to last.

Even in this earlier discussion about suicide, Plato does disparage embodied life, however well lived, and he makes the Socrates of the *Phaedo* seem dissatisfied or even disgruntled with having to be alive at all, even if he thinks it wrong to commit suicide rather than await whatever death one may happen to meet, without doing anything untoward to cause it. One might find this disparaging attitude to life reprehensible. It is in any event at odds with the zest for life we see in the Socrates of Plato's and Plato's contemporaries' Socratic dialogues—a zest that reveals on Socrates's part a healthy and happy concern for all the goods of ordinary human life, so long as they are limited by appropriate measures, to make sure that they are pursued and enjoyed virtuously.[15] Still, it would be a distortion to allow Socrates's disparagement of life in the *Phaedo* to cloud out the main argument of the dialogue, whose effect is to emphasize the philosopher's resoluteness in the face of death, just as philosophers are equally resolute in living their life as an animal. Philosophers refuse to regard their deaths as a bad thing, as anything at all to be lamented, and Socrates does not lament his

[13] See *Phaedo* 64b and 67e. At 67e Socrates speaks of training for death, i.e., for dying (ἀποθνῄσκειν), but at 64a5–6, where he introduces the topic of philosophers' attitude to death, he says that the true philosopher is always practicing "to die and to be dead" (τεθνάναι). Being dead, not the event of dying, is the principal thing the philosopher practices so far as he can, and trains for.

[14] See *Phaedo* 61c–62c. Socrates is cautious in speaking against suicide, however; he does not endorse personally the reasons that he cites here for never thinking suicide might be rationally allowable under any circumstances (desperate ones of one sort or another). He finds them interesting and suggestive, but no more. In any event, the commitment to life he expresses in this passage, and evinces throughout this last day of his life, in his devotion to his friends and to the good of philosophical discussion with other human animals, would by itself deter him from any suicide except one somehow forced on him, such as (if one counts the Athenian judicial administration of poison as involving suicide at all) what he faced at the end of this day.

[15] These are the principal passages of the *Phaedo* that the late Platonists emphasized in their reading of it. They unreservedly welcomed this disparagement, and think that it is the dialogue's main message. See my discussion below, section 6.4.

own impending death. But he is also in no way halfhearted in his commitment to life (witness the warmth and loving attention to his friends so evident in Plato's account of this last day of his life). So long as one is a good and virtuous person, which the true philosopher of whom Socrates is speaking necessarily is, anyone should be as joyful in their life as they are in their death, and for the same reason: they know their life has been and is going well, and does not need to be prolonged while waiting for it to begin to do so, or in the hope it might get better! For an unprejudiced reader, that is the main message the Socrates of the *Phaedo* leaves his friends, and us, with.

Despite its manifest, and manifold, Platonic roots, the philosophy of late Platonism, which I began this chapter by characterizing briefly, conceives its role in improving our lives significantly differently from how Plato himself in *Republic*, *Phaedo*, and other non-Socratic dialogues, does. The value and function of philosophy for these Platonists is not to enrich and deepen our this-worldly life, but, as we will see, and as I have suggested above, much more to disengage us and take us away from it. In the remainder of this chapter I focus on the seminal writings of Plotinus, from the last half of the third century CE.[16] I will attempt to explore and explain the philosophical analyses and argumentation that provided the theory of the virtues and of human happiness that Plotinus erected on the foundations of the ancient "wisdom" that he and the other Platonists found reflected and articulated in Plato's works. Plotinus's works are essays or "treatises," of widely varying length. They were written, beginning in 253, at Rome, where Plotinus, himself educated in philosophy in the Greek city of Alexandria in Egypt, had moved and began to teach ten years earlier. The last was written in the year of his death, in 270, at the age of about sixty-six. Some thirty years later, Plotinus's pupil Porphyry collected and published Plotinus's writings in the form of fifty-four individual works, to which he gave titles, divided into six sets of nine (i.e., in Greek, into six "enneads"). This complete edition has survived almost intact.[17]

I have two principal reasons, in explaining and discussing the Platonist philosophy and way of life, for focusing my discussion on Plotinus's accounts. Not before Plotinus do we find a full and philosophically rich, self-critically alert,

[16] For information on Plotinus's predecessor Platonists in the Roman era, see endnote 40.

[17] It is available in a modern English translation, with the Greek text facing, by Armstrong, *Plotinus*; this edition includes, in vol. 1, Porphyry's *Life of Plotinus*, in which he explains his editorial practices and lists the fifty-four treatises in their chronological order of composition (see sections 4–6 and 24–26). My translations from Plotinus are based on Armstrong's, but with many departures, usually not specifically marked.

exposition of late Platonism; most of what does survive is in fragmentary form. It is true, on the other hand, that numerous works of Platonists after Plotinus survive (including some quite massive ones).[18] But, though many of these later philosophers disagreed with or departed from Plotinus in some points of theory, they all worked within the basic framework of Platonist metaphysics and theory of the soul that he had elaborated. Second, the depth and subtlety of Plotinus's grasp of the many intricate philosophical problems a Platonist confronts in explicating and defending the basic elements of the Platonist worldview far exceeded these later thinkers'. For that reason, Plotinus's version of Platonism has much greater philosophical merit, and is, as well, more suitable for the sort of philosophically detailed treatment that I am seeking to provide in this book. Hence, for the most part, I leave aside special features, or departures from Plotinus, in the work of Platonists after him—as I also do for earlier Platonists (the ones referred to in modern scholarship as "middle Platonists"), on whose work Plotinus built in developing his own philosophical system, and in addressing the many difficult issues that he faced in explaining and defending it adequately in philosophical terms.

6.2. Plotinus's Platonist Metaphysics

Porphyry collected and arranged Plotinus's works on topics concerned with ethics in the first *Ennead* of his edition. Quite appropriately, Porphyry placed first a work titled *What Is the Living Being, and What Is the Human Person?*[19] Here Plotinus lays the groundwork for his accounts of the human virtues and human happiness by working out a novel, and quite extraordinary, theory of human nature—in particular, an extraordinary and unprecedented theory of what a human person is. This theory also grounds the Platonist conception of philosophy itself as a central and crucial component of the best, most humanly fulfilling, way of life. At its core, this theory claims that, because of humans' possession of the ability to engage in theoretical reasoning about the natures of things, a human being, a human person, is in fact, in full truth, simply identical with the

[18] I could mention here works of Porphyry himself, as well as Iamblichus, in the fourth century, and Proclus and Damascius in the fifth and sixth, respectively. There are also many commentaries on works of Aristotle by Platonist teachers, such as by Ammonius, son of Hermias, in the fifth and Simplicius in the sixth century. (On these Platonist successors of Plotinus, see further below, section 6.7.)

[19] For discussion of the literal translation of Porphyry's title, and on the chronological place among his works of Plotinus's treatises on ethical topics, see endnote 41.

capacity of intellect and power of rational insight that human beings by their nature inevitably possess—however well or poorly it is developed and exercised by individual human beings. It is in our intellectual self-awareness, not in our animal, embodied consciousness, that our selves are to be located. For Plotinus, as we will see, our selves become these bare centers of intellectual activity, through which we are, in fact, constantly in touch with the higher reality of true being.

In order to come to grips with Plotinus's theory of human nature we will need to attend first to his wider theory of the whole realm of the "intelligible," or true and real, being, of which the ordinarily accepted "perceptible" or "sensible" world, on Platonist analysis, is only a derivative and very inadequate representation. This will involve reference to many other treatises in the *Enneads*, especially ones in *Ennead* IV, which collects Plotinus's treatises concerning the soul—both the human one and the soul of the whole world, which, on Platonist analysis, as on the Stoic account, is responsible for all the workings of nature, apart from whichever ones are immediately involved in, or immediately derive from, human decisions and actions. On Plotinus's theory, human persons are just one part of their individual souls, namely their reason or intellect. Other parts of their soul derive their being (in some way to be investigated and explained below) from this "higher" part (Plotinus sometimes calls it a "higher soul"); these other parts are responsible for all the other activities of a human consciousness—the appetitive and spirited desires, the emotional and bodily feelings. Plotinus uses this theory of the human person and the human soul as his framework in developing his Platonist account of the virtues, human happiness, and the human good. As we will see, he does this always with explicit or implicit reference to the previous philosophical tradition (especially Aristotle and the Stoics). He points out what he regards as the philosophical and spiritual merits of this framework, which he thinks make his account of these ethical matters vastly superior to those of Aristotle and the Stoics.

Our ultimate focus must be on Plotinus's theory of the human soul, since, as we have seen, it is common coin in ancient philosophy that it is with our souls that we live. Fundamentally, the condition of our soul determines whether we live happily or not. But first we must properly situate our discussion of the human soul within the larger context of Plotinus's metaphysical theory. Souls are, for Platonists, metaphysically very special sorts of entities, and we need to grasp their natures in relation to the other metaphysically basic entities recognized in the Platonist version of the primordial wisdom that I referred to above. In what follows in this section (and into the following one) I attempt to do this, with as little use as possible of the elaborate and jargonized technical terminology, and special conceptual apparatus, that Platonists developed. My intention is to explain as well as I can Plotinus's fundamental philosophical ideas, using philosophical terms and concepts familiar in contemporary and traditional modern English-language philosophy. The Platonist metaphysical system depends upon highly abstruse, and, to us, strange-seeming, distinctions and theories, and my hope is to guide the reader quickly and as untechnically as I can to grasp (and acquire some philosophical appreciation for) the importance and role of these background ideas into which Plotinus's theory of the human soul is situated. These ideas center upon the great triad of basic Substances postulated by Platonist metaphysical theory (they are Platonism's divine Trinity, rival to the Christian one): the One, Intellect, and Soul. As you would expect, it is with Soul that we will be most concerned, but, in Plotinus's and Platonist theory, Soul ranks in reality third in this sequence, below the other two. So we must start with Intellect and the One, and only proceed to Soul after that.

The philosophical principle at the basis of Platonism as a whole is the claim that the natures or essences of all natural objects, and of all the natural properties (including mathematical ones) of any natural object, are not located in the world of nature at all—in the world that we humans, and other animals, have access to, initially, only through the use of our senses. There are in the world things and properties that have these natures, and we can examine and learn about them— about how they behave, how they may be connected and related to one another—by observation and study and experience, using our memories and making projections from the past to the future, and so on. But, Platonists claim, the natures themselves are not there, to be learned about by any use, however extensive and effective, of our senses and memories and powers of generalization and of effective projection to the future, from data we might collect about things or properties *of* those natures. We can find out all kinds of things about dogs, individually or as a group, or about the color red, in that sort of "empirical" way. But we cannot find out in such ways what it is to be a dog (what the dog's nature or essence is) or what the color red is in its essence or nature. Those natures are, as one may say, "instantiated" in the natural world, but they are not there, in themselves. To be sure, other animals don't at all need to know about, or even to have any idea about, the nature of anything that they deal with in their daily lives— they don't even have the concept of a nature. They can get along perfectly well without it, simply on the basis of learning what they need to learn in the empirical way I have roughly indicated just now. Human beings can do likewise: you can live a contented and, in physical terms, quite successful life without ever knowing or thinking or even caring at all about any thing's or any natural property's nature or essence. But it is an undeniable fact that human beings, apparently alone among the animals, do possess the concept or idea of the nature of something, and so human beings can become engaged in investigating the whole issue of the natures of things. For Platonists, the impulse that leads to and makes philosophy possible, for those to whom it might be of some concern, is precisely the impulse to wonder what the nature of something is, or indeed in general to wonder about what a nature could possibly be.

For Platonists, following Plato's own usage, these natures are what we traditionally refer to as Forms (with a capital letter)—Platonic Forms. The crucial feature of a Form is that in order to be the nature of something (say, the nature of humankind), that is, in order to be what it is to be human, it must itself be human in a complete and perfect way. The Platonists think that the essence of humanity can only (as it must) be the principle for organizing and otherwise disposing some physical substances into a physical human being, and for sustaining them in that status, if it really and fully *is* human itself. It is not another human being, maybe a "super" one, wonderfully powerful, and so on. But it has to, and can only, provide and sustain that organization by *being* what it is making them be— human. That means that it must itself be human, in a special and perfect or complete way of being human, quite different from the way any physical human being is human. It is essentially, in its very nature, human, and being human is all that it is. Physical human beings are material objects, made of physical substances of various sorts disposed and organized, held together, and made to function in certain ways by the presence to them of this Form. Physical human beings are lots else besides being human: they have many properties and characteristics, some related to their humanity (such as their shapes and sizes and their possession of certain organs and other physical parts), others not, or not so much so (e.g., chemical and other physical properties belonging to the materials making them up). Furthermore, the underlying materials that make up a human being are not essentially human. They are not, even taken together as a whole, and structured in such a way as to make up a human being, human in their natures: in their natures, they remain the particular specific materials, or complex of materials, that they are (and even such natures belong to them only contingently).[20]

---

[20] In Aristotelian terms, for Platonists, no physical human being is essentially a human being at all: all the properties any human being possesses, including its humanity, are instead properties of the matter that makes up the human being. In fact, all the substantial things (whether objects or physical stuffs) and all

By contrast, the Form is not a material being at all, and it has no other sort of "substrate" (to speak again in Aristotelian terms) characterized by the term "human." Each Form is what it is essentially, and is solely that one thing: human, or red, or tall, or beautiful or ugly, and so on, depending on the particular Form that might be in question. No physical thing is anything essentially.

Each Form is therefore a being, in the strictest and strongest sense: it is, in its nature and essentially, something in particular. One Form is human, another is canine, another is beautiful, another is double, yet others are respectively tall or short, heavy or light, round or square, red or green or blue, and so on. No physical thing is anything at all, in this strong, strict, and proper sense. Each predicate we employ in speaking truly of any natural object is something that belongs to it not by or in the nature of that object; each term we predicate indicates instead some nature, some Form, that the object only "instantiates." Collectively, then, we can say that the Forms, in being the natures of the natural objects and of their natural properties, are also the only true, strict, and proper beings that exist. Taken together, they constitute "that which is." The physical world, by contrast, and everything in it, is no being at all; the physical world instantiates myriad beings, but to instantiate something is not at all to be that thing, as we have seen— indeed, it precludes it. The physical world, without any doubt, exists, and by all means it is not nothing; but it would be a mistake to consider it as a collection of beings, of things that fully are any of the things we may (correctly) describe them as. What then are these physical things, if not beings? They are mere reflections, or shadows, cast upon and into the matter from which the world is formed: this happens, as we will see below, by the agency of the world soul.

Before turning to the world soul and its agency, two further important points about these beings, these Forms, must be noted. First, we can see from their effects in the physical world that taken altogether, as a whole, the set of beings constitutes a well-integrated, intimately closely bound together, unified system of entities. The physical world is a marvelously well-ordered thing, with all its parts and all their distinctive properties working together in such a way as to maintain and sustain a single ongoing and recurrent "life" over the days, years, centuries, and millennia of its essentially temporal existence. This makes it clear that the beings, too, on which this world depends through the process I have called instantiation, are a unified, well-ordered, integrated set of entities. Each of

---

the natural properties to be found in the physical world, belonging to those things, are Aristotelian "accidents" of particular bits of the world's matter. Any physical thing is only contingently whatever it is.

the natures of the different Forms—what the different ones of them are in their natures—is linked to each of the other natures in such a way as to constitute a single system. Hence, one will not succeed in fully grasping any single Form (say, the nature of a dog, or the nature of red color) except by grasping closely related ones as well (the natures of other animals, the natures of other colors), in their relationship to it. To be sure, one might perfectly reasonably think of the task of grasping the natures of things as a one-by-one process: one investigates the nature of dogs, and other animals, or of the varied types of material stuff, or the human soul and its virtues, one by one or area by area of investigation. But ultimately one cannot grasp any specific nature except by grasping it along with all the rest, as a unified whole system. One must see any given Form in the context of the whole system of Forms of which it is just one part, in order finally and fully to understand any of them.

The second point concerns what the Platonists call the exclusively "intelligible" character of Forms. Physical objects and their properties, themselves, can be seen or heard, or otherwise taken note of, and investigated, through the use of the senses. But their natures, as I explained above, are not found in the physical world at all. These natures must therefore be grasped, investigated, and learned about solely through intellectual means, not at all by sensory ones. One must approach them through pure thought, starting from what we see or hear, but in attempting to grasp essences and natures, we must consider them as intellectual principles of organization, that is, as intellectual structures *for* ordering, each in specific ways, the "sensible" or perceptible materials that the world provides. Since these entities are essentially "intelligible," and in no way "sensible," we can say that they exist in and for the understanding, in and for being grasped intellectually. The Forms retain their inherent connection to being understood, even if none of us has ever grasped, or is currently grasping, them, in thought. As such, as "intelligible," they must, in existing, also be understood. They are not merely *capable* of being understood. Their existence includes, or even in some sense is, their being understood, being grasped intellectually through pure thought. Hence, Platonists think, we must conceive this organized system of beings, the Forms, as, in their very natures, constant objects of thought; they are the contents of an intellect whose whole existence is, reciprocally, to be thinking the Forms and understanding them, in a full and total grasp of their individually and systematically connected natures. Thus, for Forms to exist is the same thing as for there to exist an Intellect, a universal Intellect, or Intellect of or in the universe, which is, and is nothing but, the timeless act of thinking and fully understanding all the Forms.

By the train of thought set out in the previous five paragraphs we have arrived at one of the three "Substances" (or, in technical Platonist terms, three "hypostases") that make up true being or reality, the reality ultimately lying behind and responsible for the physical world. The universal Intellect, this entity whose whole nature it is to actively think the whole system of Forms, in its full and explicitly laid out orderly intellectual interconnection—and in that sense can be said to *be* the Forms—is one of the three basic realities that make up Plotinus's and the other Platonists's metaphysical system. What I have already said about Forms leads us quickly and easily to a second of these Substances: the "first" or "highest" or ultimate Substance, or first god. This is the source of the reality of Intellect (and so, of the existence of the physical world itself, too, since that, in turn, derives wholly from Intellect or Forms). I have emphasized the essential unity of the set of beings or Forms, in that they constitute a single, fully interconnected system of separate beings, each of them a distinct and different, single nature from the others, but such that the essence of any nature ultimately consists in its mutual interrelationships with all the others. Thus, this set of beings is what we could call a unity in plurality. That is, it is a unified set of many distinct things. These many are, however, a definite, fully determinate number of unitary entities. Thus, each of these "units" in the set is, in a different way, a unity on its own. Each nature is one unified thing: the canine nature, the nature of the color red, the nature of beauty, and so on across the vast whole set of Forms, are each a single coherent whole nature. Even if, when we humans grasp a nature, we grasp it in some articulated set of ideas (say, in traditional terms, by thinking of the human as the featherless, biped animal), this does not mean that human nature itself is divided into separate and assembled parts; our thought just expresses the singleness and unity of human nature in an articulated way, which enables us to relate it to and distinguish it from other similar natures, seeing them all as distinct parts of the whole set of Forms.[21]

In these two ways, unity is essential to being. Each being is in a strong way a unity—each is a single nature, one unit in the overall set of Forms—and this whole set of beings is strongly a unity (a unity in plurality, in this case), too. In being "units" and a unit, in these ways, in fact, the Forms are exhibiting a feature

[21] In speaking here of the articulated thinking of Forms that we humans engage in I do not mean to say that Forms, as they exist in Intellect, are in the same way given articulation in Intellect's thought of them. There, according to Plotinus, thought is pure and directly intuitive: the system of Forms is grasped as a single whole of many interrelated unitary parts, each of which is grasped equally as a single thing, and all the relationships among them are grasped in the same single, unarticulated, act of thinking. The articulated, detailed, thinking of Forms one by one and all together is instead a function of Soul (see below).

of them that is essential to their status as beings. Beings, just as such, are unities, and, just as such, they are altogether a systematic unity in plurality. But, Plotinus thinks, that beings are of this character must depend on something beyond them, in fact on something whose (if one could put it this way) very nature is to be one, to be a unit, to be unified. Just as the physical dogs depend upon the canine nature, which, unlike them, is in its nature canine, so the Forms depend for their unity on an entity that is one, in a complete and final way, and nothing but one: it is the paradigm of unity; it is what it is to be one; being one just is the whole of it.[22] The being of the Forms, therefore, implies the existence of a further Substance, the One, as Plotinus sometimes calls it (but often, because of its character as the ultimate reality, he does not name it at all, but just points to it as "the highest" or "the first").[23] Thus the One is the ultimate reality in the Platonist metaphysical system: it is responsible for the possibility of beings (since they are, and have to be, unified in the ways I have indicated), and for the particular ways that these different beings differ from one another. Indeed, in some way that is "beyond" any kind of causation, the One brings Intellect and the Forms into existence. As an absolute, self-contained and totally independent, eternal reality, something so to speak real to its very core, actively "turning in" to itself just on its own, it is so "overfull" of reality that it "overflows" and therein "generates" being and beings.[24] First it generates Intellect, and then through a further process of what in discussions of Plotinus and late Platonism is usually referred to as "emanation" (from the Latin for "overflowing"), Intellect, in a further act of the fullness of the One's reality, generates a third eternal entity and Substance, Soul, to which I will turn in a moment.

---

[22] Actually, this formulation is faulty (as indeed, according to Plotinus, any formulation in language and thought would inevitably be): the One is "beyond being" and therefore it is inaccurate to say, as I do here, even that it *is* one.

[23] On these questions of terminology concerning the One, see *Enn*. II 9, 1.1–19. (For references to the *Enneads* I cite first, in Roman numerals, the ennead (here, the second), followed by the number within that ennead of the treatise being referred to (here, the 9th), adding after a comma the chapter number of the treatise and, where needed, the line numbers of the citation in the Oxford Classical Texts edition of Plotinus's works by P. Henry and H.-R. Schwyzer.) This highest substance is also called the Good: it is the ultimate and undivided source of being, and thereby also of goodness to all that has being and so is, in some specific way special to itself, good. It is the highest divinity or god. (Intellect and Soul, the other substances in the system, are additional gods, because eternal, living things: their "life" consists in the fact that these entities are at bottom activities of pure intellectual thinking. On this see further below.)

[24] See *Enn*. V 1, 6–7; also V 2, 1 for the striking images of the One as overfull of reality, and overflowing into Intellect, the home of being. For the generation of Intellect and Soul from the One, Plotinus usually speaks, rather than of an emanation, of how Intellect or Soul "proceed," or "take their way onwards" (πρόοδος) from their predecessor in the emanative series, and ultimately from the One: see, e.g., IV 8, 6.

The One and Intellect, then, are two of the three basic Substances in Plotinus's metaphysical system. In Intellect, Forms are thought not only in a timeless way, in a single, undivided thought, but entirely in themselves, with no thought of their role as the natures of physical things. They are thought as a single unified set of ordered, mutually interrelated, intellectual structures. However, of course, Forms are ordered structures *for* organizing matter; this is something, as we could loosely say, essential to them. But what explains this further step in the functioning of Forms—that they are natures of things in the physical world? That does not derive from Intellect: Intellect is the thinking of Forms on their *own*, as a system of intellectual structures, all interconnected and interrelated simply as such structures. This function belongs, for Platonists, instead, to Soul. Soul, a third Substance in addition to the One and Intellect, possesses a full understanding of the whole system of Forms, as Intellect does too, but now we find a fully articulated understanding of each and of all of them, as the specific nature each one is within the overall system, *in* their relationship to the physical world. Soul's understanding thus includes full, spelled-out "definitions" of each Form. Thus—and this is a crucial point for Plotinus's theory of the human soul—Soul, no less than Intellect, consists in an act of understanding, an act of thought; however, its way of thinking Forms, as a whole system, is one in which they are grasped specifically and fully as principles *for* organizing the physical, material world, in a virtual infinity of specific ways, distributed across specific places at specific times, into a maximally well-ordered system of its own. Unlike Intellect, Soul thinks Forms as instantiable and for instantiation—for being participated in in the material, physical world. Thus, whereas Intellect thinks Forms in a way that sees them as mathematical structures, making up a mathematically unified system, Soul thinks them concretely, as Red, or Dog, for example: that is, in terms of a linguistically elaborated definition of what it is to be red or a dog. Moreover, in doing so, and because it does so, it is moved to create the physical world, and to shape, organize, and direct everything in it.[25] It does this, as I indicated above, by casting reflections of relevant Forms onto and into the cosmic

[25] As part of this function it also somehow gives rise to matter, the blank sheet, so to speak, onto which its organizing powers are directed, and which it requires for its work. Though the relation of matter to Soul, and to the other Substances, was a subject of much debate and disagreement among Platonists, both early and later, and a very important one in the theological debates into which Platonists were drawn with opposing and competing cultural and religious forces in late antiquity, I do not need to pursue this question in addressing Plotinus's ethical theories and his ideas about the role of philosophy in the best human life. It suffices to say, simply, that matter exists because Soul needs it, in order to do its work of expressing the being of Forms in a derived, physical world.

matter, and by overseeing the coming and going of these reflections—the coming and going that constitutes, and then destroys, all the physically existent things, and that brings about all the events making up the history of the world. For Platonists, it belongs to the very nature of Soul to move itself toward creation: this is what it is to *be* soul.

So much, then, for the three basic Substances of Plotinian metaphysics. We need now to carry our discussion forward by addressing further questions about Soul, this "lowest" of the three Substances. Our specific topic, Plotinus's account of the human soul and of the human person, precisely concerns ways in which, in developing his account of the Substance, Soul, he relates us humans to that Substance—and, through it, to the higher Substances of Intellect and the One, from which it devolves.

6.3. Plotinus's Theory of the Human Person

To be precise about it, there are for Platonists no additional entities that are souls, human souls for example, beyond this Soul Substance.[26] What there are, are distinct and distinguishable ways that Soul works in creating, organizing, maintaining, and so to speak operating the created world and everything in it. Soul does all this at several quite different levels, however, and our (and Plotinus's) habit of speaking as if there are a lot of distinct individual things that are souls derives from considering Soul, working at these different levels, as involving a plurality of distinct souls: each "soul" that he refers to is just a way of speaking of Soul insofar as it performs some specific, importantly distinguishable function in organizing and making the world do what it does. And of course, when it comes to ourselves, considering the world from our own individual points of view, it is completely natural for us to think of our own consciousness, our actions, and indeed our life overall, as being due to a unique and special entity—my soul, distinct from yours, and distinct from all other souls of different animal kinds, belonging to distinct individual animals. In my discussion below I will follow this highly convenient way of speaking and thinking. In fact, how-

[26] I am speaking here, and in the remainder of this section, solely of Plotinus, and even with him not everything is as clear as one might like. I offer what, despite wavering forms of expression at many places in his works concerned with Soul and souls, seems the clearest and most plausible way of understanding him—plausible, I mean to say, in relation to the major controlling principles of Platonist thought, that is, the basic Platonist assumptions about the three Substances, about Forms, and about instantiations of Forms.

ever, to repeat, the real truth, for Plotinus, is simply that Soul, the Substance, works in relation to the physical world and to its various living and nonliving parts at several importantly distinguishable levels.

The most pervasive function of Soul is the one that Platonists, beginning with Plato himself, associate with what, in discussions of Platonism, we traditionally refer to as "the world soul."[27] For Platonists, Soul pervades the world and is everywhere in it. It does not do so literally, of course: Soul, being an entity with an eternal existence, exists outside time as well as outside body-filled space; it cannot occupy even a point in the physical world. (In this respect, the world soul of the Platonists differs fundamentally from that of the Stoics.) Literally, Soul's power is simply *exercised* everywhere. It causes the matter of the world to possess its differential properties spread out across different places, by bringing about instantiations of Forms in different locations at different times, and in different combinations at those locations and times. The world soul is Soul carrying out those functions, in constituting and characterizing the natural world. First, it creates, and sustains in existence, all the different kinds of stuffs, and all the different natural objects, including plants and animals, too. But in this last case, the world soul is active, at this first level, just insofar as concerns the bodily structures—the combinations of materials needed to constitute all the organs and other parts, distributed appropriately across their bodies—of the various plants and animals. It is also responsible for bringing about all the changes, of place and in size, qualities, and so on, that take place over time anywhere in the natural world, in accordance with what we think of as the operation of "natural laws" concerning how matter and its various different kinds act and interact under varying conditions. So at this first level, Soul is responsible for all the ways that nonliving materials are constituted and behave, as well as for the materials making up living things, insofar they are put together and make up the given animal or plant body, with its specific bodily structures and organs.

Soul works also at a second level where living things, both animals and plants, are concerned. Different forms of living matter (flesh, bone, animal organs) behave in special and different ways, depending not only upon their particular material constitution but also upon their functional roles in maintaining the ongo-

---

[27] It is interesting to observe that we never find either in Plato or in Plotinus any phrase that speaks precisely of a "world soul" (ψυχὴ τοῦ κόσμου). The closest term can find, and that quite rare in Plato though fairly common in Plotinus, is a phrase literally translatable as "soul of the All" (ψυχὴ τοῦ παντός)—soul of the universe. See Plato's *Timaeus* 31b–37a, where in his myth of creation Timaeus describes the creator god's creation of the world's body and (beginning at 34b) its soul. As a whole, the world is to be conceived as a vast, single living animal; see above, section 4.3.

ing life of the organism to which they belong.[28] Soul therefore has to operate in living bodies in ways that maintain and continue the automatic life functions of nutrition, breathing, heart beat, heat maintenance, growth, the maintenance of all the equilibriums of health, and so on, appropriate to each life form. This is a second function Soul performs, limited to the world's living things, both animals and plants.[29] Soul works also, however, at a third level with animals, since they possess consciousness, as plants, though alive, do not. Each animal controls some of what it and its body do through its conscious states of perception of its surroundings, and through related conscious desires and bodily feelings, plus feelings of arousal, and interest in and seeking after satisfactions. In general, animals cause their voluntary actions through their conscious responses (desiderative and emotional) to what they perceive (i.e., to ways in which their bodies and the things that environ them act on their consciousness).[30] This shows that Soul, in order to function as it needs to, so as to direct all the operations of nature, works in a quite particular, and additional, further way in regulating the life of animals, beyond the "automatic" aspects of being alive, shared by plants as well as animals. It provides animal perception, desire, and emotion wherever they are found.

Human beings are a special case of this. Human beings not only are conscious and react in their consciousness to changes in their bodies and in what environs them, as other animals do, in such a way as to give rise to voluntary bodily movements through animal-like desires and feelings of emotional arousal. They also cause these movements, often, on the basis of reasoned thoughts (thoughts about

---

[28] Platonists, like Aristotle, think that the "natural laws" of the behavior of matter, as such, are too weak to explain these particular movements of animal bodies.

[29] For our purposes we do not need to force Plotinus to clarity and consistency about in what capacity Soul performs this second function. He sometimes seems to suppose that, just as at the first level, it is again directly as world soul that it performs it. There are suggestions, however, in some of Plotinus's writing of a sort of "trace" of soul, imparted by the world soul, that are responsible, at this second level, where automatic life functions take place, including the bodily changes that constitute bodily pain and pleasure, for their occurrence. (These soul "traces" are to be distinguished from the "soul-images" created by individual human souls, not by the world soul, discussed below.) See *Enn*. IV 4, 18.1–9, for example. We do not need to go into such questions of detailed interpretation.

[30] Again, Platonists, like Aristotle, think that the "natural laws" of the behavior of matter, as such, even if taken together with the "plant-like" functions of merely being alive, are too weak to explain these particular movements of animal bodies. Conscious states and perceptual responses of animals themselves to what is in, and what takes place in, their environments, are needed to explain these effects. For animals other than human beings, Plotinus seems to offer two possibilities: either they have their consciousness through the world-soul's "illuminating" their bodies with an image of itself (on this see below); or they have within their bodies individual souls of their own, consisting in images of an individual intellect (such as the one each of us possesses) which, however, is "there without being there for them," i.e., it is inoperative and dormant, because of the particular kinds of bodies they possess. See *Enn*. I 1, 11.8–15. For humans, see below.

what there is reason to do or not do, and about why those proposed reasons really do count as reasons). They consciously decide, often, what to do, and their decisions are then the causes of what they go on to do—often, at any rate, or even usually. They also have reasoned thoughts about other matters than what to do or not do: they make inferences from what they perceive, and form general and specific views about what surrounds them and how to expect it to behave, on the basis of reasons that they accept. Given this special feature of human mental and bodily self-movement, as opposed to the self-movement of other animals, we need to recognize in the case of humans a fourth level at which Soul operates, in giving structure and content to the world of nature, and in regulating and directing the total life of the world-animal, of which the human animals are parts. At this level, Soul is responsible for human capacities of reasoned thinking about the surrounding physical world and reasoned action.

So far, then, we see that Soul functions at four levels in human bodies, three of these levels being involved also where other animals are concerned, and two where plants are concerned, too. With human beings there is also a fifth level, to which I will turn in a moment: at this level we can locate the capacity for abstract, theoretical thinking about the natures of things. In order to summarize and review these first four levels of Soul's operations in human bodies, let us shift now to the natural and convenient, though potentially misleading, way of speaking that I mentioned above, in which we conceive not of Soul, the Substance, as carrying out all these functions, but of some or other distinct soul—the world soul, or an individual human soul—as doing various ones of them. First, the world soul constitutes the particular material stuffs making up a human body, which as mere stuffs are inanimate things, operating as such by the natural laws of material interaction. Whenever a human body does or undergoes something in no way differently from how a nonliving, inanimate, thing would be affected or behave under relevantly similar conditions (given its weight, external pressures or impacts, material consistencies, etc.), that is the work of the world soul. The laws governing these behaviors are established by Soul's pure thought of Forms (the Forms of these distinct material natures). It is these thoughts, being applied in the physical world at all the relevant places and times by the world soul, that create, keep in existence, and cause the various movements and interactions of the different material stuffs, both simple and compound.

Second, world soul has additional thoughts, affecting only the places in the physical world where living entities exist, giving them their special characteristics as living things, with various sorts of organic matter and various organs being formed and behaving according to the special laws that apply to such kinds of material. A special set of these thoughts is at work in all the places where human bodies are located. These thoughts govern the specific behaviors of the specific organs and the organic materials making human beings up, so far as the automatic or "plant-like" functions of nutrition, respiration, heat maintenance, and so on, are concerned. At these first two levels everything is done exclusively by the world soul and its consciousness.[31] The individual human consciousness—something in some important ways unique to each person—functions crucially at each of the remaining two (as well as at the fifth level mentioned above, concerned with the capacity for abstract, theoretical thought). Thus, at the third level, we have perceptions, nonrational desires, and emotions. At the fourth, we have the power of reasoned thought and decision making about events in the physical world and about their significance for our physical life. The Substance, Soul, endows us with these powers when the world soul constitutes us as the particular sort of animal that we are. These are ones that belong squarely to our individual consciousnesses: they are functions, when they operate, of our own consciousnesses, our own individual souls, not the world soul's.

The fifth level is in fact the most fundamental one, and the most important when it comes to considering Plotinus's theory of the human person, to which we now turn. We must bear firmly in mind that Soul, the Substance, is a purely intellectual, conscious entity: it consists of a single, eternal activity of pure, self-conscious thinking. As for the world soul, it is also a unified thought of the Forms, in their full articulation as organizing principles for all the various kinds of stuff and objects that the physical world contains and consists of, and for all their natural properties. It is the expression of Soul's creative impulse toward the instantiation of these principles in the physical world, and toward the maintenance and management of the resulting instantiated entities. Thus the world soul works through its conscious, creative, purely intellectual thought of the Forms. We can conceive of the world soul itself, as I have done above, as thinking

---

[31] Many or most of these functions take place without our being conscious of them, but some, as for example breathing, we may be aware of as they occur (except when asleep), and so can have some conscious control over. Because of this openness of these functions to our consciousness, Plotinus sometimes speaks unclearly about these functions, sometimes suggesting that even these automatic life functions belong to the individual soul of the particular human being (or particular other animal), rather than to the world soul. This is a fine point we need not concern ourselves with. Our being conscious, or not, of these automatic life functions is insignificant: our consciousness is not required for them to take place, and we do not, normally, have any conscious control over them. The correct Plotinian view is that they belong to the world soul.

certain relevant Forms in relation to specific locations and times in the physical world, as Soul expresses its essentially creative nature. Thereby world soul causes all the physical states and events that result.[32] But, for Plotinus, the soul of human beings too, as we will see in detail shortly below, is in its essence a purely intellectual entity, just as Soul and the world soul are. Its essence consists in thinking and understanding the Forms (even if we may not be aware of ourselves as doing that). Yet the human consciousness, and so, speaking in broad terms, the human soul, encompasses much, much more than purely intellectual conscious states and activities. Among the principal difficult issues Plotinus faces in developing and applying the Platonist basic principles of One, Intellect and Soul to human life is to explain how it can be that a purely intellectual entity—an "intelligible," as he puts it—can possess and function, as humans do, with animal perceptions and desires, and with elaborated trains of thought that seek and give reasons for a particular person's doing or not doing specific things in specific observed circumstances. We know that Soul must operate in those ways in organizing and directing the lives of human beings; the difficulty is to figure out and understand how it can operate in those ways, if it is something thoroughly and solely engaged in pure, abstract thought about nothing but the natures of things.

The nub of the problem is that all the functions of perception and desire, shared with animals, as well as those special ones to do with human (as one could say) empirical reasoning, are in a certain essential way shared with the body. When we perceive, we use our bodily organs; when we are hungry or our foot gets stepped on we experience something, in experiencing which some corresponding bodily affection is (at least normally) required. Indeed, in some crucial sense the bodily affection is *part* of the overall conscious state or act. When we are angry, to draw on a famous analysis of Aristotle in his *de Anima*, there is blood boiling around the area of the heart, and in no mere coincidental way;[33] when we remember something there are traces in our minds from bodily experiences; when we think out concrete plans for action we have in some way to visualize or otherwise represent in our minds what we are to do. In all these cases the conscious experience is linked with bodily states and events, in such a way that, following Aristotle (on whom Plotinus bases this part of his theory), we need to think of these activities of consciousness as ones that, in some way, are "com-

[32] This does require willingness to swallow without choking the idea of something completely spiritual and totally bodiless as having causal relations with matter, though without any reciprocal causing of effects upon it in the process. But we can leave worries about that to one side.

[33] See *On the Soul* I 1, 403a25ff.

mon" to body and soul—they are not wholly "soul phenomena" at all. But how can a purely intellectual thing, something essentially self-contained and occupied in its thoughts with nonbodily entities, the Forms, share its operations with anything bodily? It is one thing to suppose Soul can creatively cause physical objects, sustain them in existence, and cause their varied movements. But the states and activities here concerned are ones where consciousness is itself mutually affected through its interactions with the body, as it causes our movements of perception, feeling, and action. When we feel a pain in our foot, some state of the body is what we are feeling, and indeed that state of the body is what gives us this feeling. Correspondingly for the other cases. How, then, can we possibly make sense of the human soul as being so linked to the human body that some of its operations are ones that have a physical, bodily side to them?

Plotinus's ingenious solution is to suppose that in animating human beings (as well as other animals) Soul provides a special sort of "illumination" in their bodies (Plotinus constantly expresses his views here in heavily metaphorical language). Soul casts a certain "image" of itself (another metaphor) into the bodies of these living things. It is this image or illumination in the body which, taken together with the body, constitutes it as a "living being" (in Greek, a *zôon*).[34] This image is animal consciousness (including perceptual and desiring and emotional consciousness). The living being itself, constituted by this consciousness in that body, possesses the powers of sensation, physical desire, and emotional reaction, all of which have both bodily and conscious components, and it does so because of the soul-image animating and "illuminating" it, and so, making it conscious. The point we need to notice is that Plotinus, by attributing the powers of sense perception and sensory memory, bodily desire, and emotion to this soul-image, can avoid having to think of Soul itself as directly providing or grounding these activities, ones that are so evidently alien, and contrary, to its own nature. Soul itself, and therefore all particular souls, being purely spiritual, thinking, "intelligible" entities could not possibly be "affected" by anything bodily, as this soul-image is, when it activates all these powers.[35] However, it is not difficult to conceive of an *image* of Soul, just because as an "image" it is darker and more obscure, and somewhat deformed, as something mingled in precisely such ways with the body that it animates. We can suppose (even if we do not fully understand it) that this image can make us conscious with these sorts of bodily consciousness.

---

[34] See *Enn.* I 1, 7 and 10; the language of a "soul-image" is found at 11.11–14, as well as in other treatises.

[35] Plotinus has a whole treatise on *The Impassibility of the Bodiless, Enn.* III 6.

It is the basis for a human being's engaging in these particular forms of conscious experience.

The Substance, Soul, or equivalently our soul (a purely intellectual and intelligible thing), creates this image of itself when it "comes down" (another metaphor) into a human body, in order to animate it. We, like other animals, need to have powers of individual consciousness, in order to observe our particular surroundings and obtain food, avoid danger and harm, and interact in the social ways with members of the same species or other species that are natural to the animal kind to which we belong. This has to include desires for certain sorts of food and other nourishment, and emotional responses to perceived dangers or prospects of harm, as well as emotions and desires to give us interests in, and to motivate us to engage in, our various natural activities of social life. Each animal has to have its own complete system of such forms of consciousness, and Soul provides us with an appropriate human soul-image, which gives us the forms of consciousness we need in order to grow up properly, reproduce, and thrive and flourish, according to our own physical nature as the kind of animal we are. Each animal has charge of very significant parts of its own life through its use of its powers of embodied consciousness, which therefore must be a fully integrated, developing, and sustained system for its whole life span. Thus, we can say generally that the forms of consciousness belonging to the soul-image of any given animal are provided to it for the sake of its taking care of itself, and adequately providing for its physical life, and for seeing to it that, so far as outer circumstances make possible, it thrives, reproduces, raises offspring so that they too will be able to thrive, and so that it lives a naturally effective whole physical life.

The soul-image focuses exclusively, then, on the single individual animal in which it is lodged, enabling and directing that animal to be concerned for itself and its physical life. This soul-image simply is, in nonrational animals, their soul, their consciousness. It is the result of Soul's creative work at the third of the levels I have enumerated above. In human beings, this animal consciousness is certainly part of a human soul. But, because we are *rational* animals, in constituting the sorts of animals that we are Soul has to work at a fourth level, as well, as we saw. In receiving *our* soul-image we must also acquire the further powers of empirical inference and ordinary reasoning about what to do, and why, in particular empirical circumstances: we have to notice things, draw inferences, think about what is good for us, or bad, and plan out courses of action. We do not, as other animals do, possess only what I have called "animal" consciousness, with nonrational forms of perception, desire, and feeling. We have powers of rational

thought too; we conceptualize, seek and give reasons through which to understand what we are affected by perceptually and through which to shape our feelings and desires. Plotinus seems, however, not entirely clear, or perhaps even
quite consistent, about these additional powers and their operation. Since they
clearly do depend upon our being conscious of, and making reference in our
thoughts to, physical entities as such, they must be somehow aspects of the soul-
image given by Soul to human beings as part of their nature—they involve embodied events that are jointly conscious and bodily. On the other hand, Plotinus
seems to say that even reasonings about particular matters of fact are activities
of the "higher" soul, the fifth level of Soul's work in constituting human beings,
to which we will come shortly.[36] That is because, according to Plotinus, even
such "empirical" reasonings come "from" the Forms, or rather from our implicit
awareness of them—an awareness that, in itself, is totally a matter of abstract,
purely intellectual thinking. We have to be thinking implicitly of Forms in order
to classify the physical things being thought about under their natural kinds, and
so, in fact, to think about them at all, even in a merely empirical way. We need to
pause briefly to consider how Plotinus resolves this tension in his account.

To begin with, why does Plotinus think that, in order to engage in reasoning,
even empirical or decision-making reasoning, one has to possess the higher
power of being able to question and think about the natures of things? His reasoning seems to be along the following lines. Language, he thinks, is the necessary vehicle for considering and proposing and acting on reasons, and for giving
reasons in connection with thinking about empirical questions. Yet, in using language to classify and provide conceptual connections between different kinds of
things and their properties, we necessarily rely implicitly upon ideas about the
natures of those things and properties. Language users are implicitly, and perhaps unconsciously and unknowingly, making use, when they learn a language
and use it, of a power they possess that is directed toward Forms, that is, toward
these natures. This power may, or may not, be exercised, so to speak, in itself, that
is, for investigating and thinking about Forms and about what particular ones
among them are by their nature. But it is being used in a minimal way even when
we classify something in our immediate experience as a thing of a certain kind
(i.e., as falling under a given Form), or remember that something or other happened to us, or think of some future prospect as threatening or offering some
pleasurable enjoyment—even more so, when, on such a basis, we think out con-

---

[36] See, e.g., *Enn.* I 1, 7.14–24.

sequences and consider what might be good or bad about them for us, and whether they are in fact good or bad. Such "discursive" reasoning, in other words, is considered by Plotinus to depend upon and presuppose a higher intellectual or reasoning power, a power that consists in at least the ability to inquire into Forms, and the ability, in principle, actually to come positively to grasp them. This higher power is something, therefore, that all human beings must possess—since, as is evident, all human beings, being rational animals, certainly do engage in empirical reasoning, applying Forms to things, throughout all their daily life.

Still, even if it presupposes that higher power, the more mundane uses of reason so far in question deserve to be counted as a separate, fourth, product of Soul's work in constituting human beings, as a special sort of animal, as I have said. These activities, of empirical reasoning and action planning and execution, are hybrids, in which our senses and feelings, and emotional and other nonrational desires—that is, elements of consciousness belonging to our soul-image—combine with the pure thinking involved, implicitly, in our acts of classification under Forms. The result is acts of what Plotinus speaks of as "discursive" thinking, remembering, choosing, deciding, which draw both on the soul-image and the consciousness it provides to us, along with the higher consciousness (in this case, only implicit) provided at the fifth level. Because of their first aspect, these acts are expressions of the powers of consciousness we are endowed with by our soul-image. They are ones we possess as part of the enriched embodied life for which Soul provides us with capacities, including our empirical reasoning capacity, so that we can live and function effectively in the physical world, with a view to our thriving, reproducing, raising offspring so that they too will be able to thrive, and living a naturally effective whole physical life. Just as we saw for our soul-image, these hybrid activities, too, focus exclusively on the single individual animal in which the image is lodged. That image directs the human animal to be concerned for itself and its life. The individual consciousness that comes with the soul-image, including these hybrid activities of empirical reasoning and reason seeking and reason giving, is focused on some particular human being and its life.

Our power of reason has a higher use, as well, in which we can engage our minds instead upon the project of self-consciously grasping, in pure thought, the fully articulated definitory accounts of the natures, themselves, that Soul possesses, and uses in constituting the physical world. A human consciousness is therefore quite a complex thing. We can become aware, through the powers of our soul-image and these hybrid activities, of things we perceive, of nonrational desires and urges, of pleasures and pains in our bodies, of memories, of implications for the future of what we think we see happening now, of problems we face in achieving our objectives, of ways we can think of for getting round them, of decisions and choices we make in response—and we can have a full range of thoughts of all sorts, theoretical as well as practical, concerning physical objects and their affections and behaviors. But we can also become self-consciously aware, through our intellectual powers, of Forms, their individual natures, and their relationships. It is with a single, psychologically unified consciousness that each of us does any and all of these things. Nonetheless, our capacities of pure intellect stand aside from and "above" all the other activities of awareness, both the nonrational and the rational ones. In fact, the pure intellect of a human being consists, Plotinus thinks, essentially in nothing but the same power of abstract thought that belongs to Soul, the Substance, itself. In providing that intellect to a human being, Soul simply, as one could say, gives *itself* to that person. In this regard, Soul works in relation to us quite differently from the way it works in providing to us our other powers of awareness. It provides those not through itself, but only via a sort of image of itself—something derived and obscure, not the reality itself of which the image is a mere reflection. In our individual soul, therefore, there is one element, what we can call our intellect, that is Soul active in us simply and directly, and that element, therefore, is something fully real in us. The rest of our consciousness and its contents, including our empirical reasonings and decision makings, are no more than *reflections* of something real. The intellect in us belongs to the eternal realm of "intelligible" entities, real and true beings. It is a being. Our other powers belong to nature: they and the activities to which they give rise are "appearances," not beings at all.

This last observation has momentous implications for Plotinus. I mentioned in chapter 1 the "spiritual crisis" that intellectuals of the first centuries CE faced, as Christians and pagans alike began to worry about their own consciousness— their self-consciousness as rational beings, possessed of a consciousness that sets us apart from other animals.[37] They experienced this as something alien to the

---

[37] In Plotinus's terms, animal consciousness occurs at the third of the levels I set out above at which Soul works in creating and sustaining the physical world. The constant dependence of animal consciousness on, and constant use of, bodily organs and other bodily features of animals involves nothing problematic, from the philosophical point of view. But at levels 4 and 5 worries arise about what our consciousness can even be: this is where both empirical reasoning and abstract theoretical grasp of Forms take place. What are we, that we can do these things? What is this bare "I" that seems, to those afflicted with this worry, a bright beacon and center of oneself, the light of reason within this body?

physical world—not a "natural" phenomenon, but something set aside from, and, for one experiencing it, above the world of nature.[38] The crucial contribution of Plotinus and his fellow Platonists to resolving this crisis—to the "salvation" of those afflicted by it—lies in the claim, based in the philosophical theories we have just been examining, that the root and origin of our human consciousness—of all of it—is in our intellects, our active (implicit) knowing of Forms, which allows us, if we concentrate resolutely upon the task, to actively grasp their natures in a completely explicit way.[39] On Plotinus's theory, what I am conscious of when I am conscious of my consciousness is my intellect. Thus each of us, the human person we individually are—this worrisome consciousness we have that, for Platonists, is no part of the natural world—is, and is exclusively, this part of "our" soul, that is, this part of our consciousness. We, what Plotinus calls the "true human beings,"[40] are our intellects. The soul-image is not *us*, it is only *ours*:[41] it is ours, because in some sense we (we as intellects) created it, when Soul endowed the living being whose consciousness is our consciousness with its life. On Plotinus's account, when Soul lodged an intellect in our bodies, that lodged intellect illuminated that body with that image of itself.

So *we* are exclusively our power of abstract thought about the natures of things, the Forms. Our own life, properly speaking, then, is the life—the activity—of that power. And that life consists in thinking and understanding the Forms. Thus, *we* only and fully live in actively and attentively thinking of Forms, grasping the natures of physical things that the Forms constitute in their individuality and as a total system. The rest of "our" life is a life dependent on and expressing, not us, but this image of us, that animates the living body. Our consciousness as animals and as embodied living beings is just an offshoot of our real consciousness, the consciousness that comes to us because we are intellects. Hence, all of what we do and feel and think that depends in any way on our lower consciousness—all our emotions, our feelings, our practical actions (i.e., the ones not consisting in just directing our attention in thought to the Forms)—

---

[38] See section 1.2.

[39] Notoriously, St. Augustine, around the turn of the fifth century, tried this Platonist solution, but was not satisfied. He, and increasingly many others, felt they needed a more personal savior than the Platonist One, to be the ground of all being, with a nature cognate to one's own, in which one could engulf oneself, and find salvation from the anxieties caused by the "alien" physical world.

[40] In Greek, ὁ ἀληθὴς ἄνθρωπος. For this phrase see *Enn*. I 1, 7.20, 10.7; but see the whole of chapter 7 in order to grasp more fully what this entails.

[41] *Enn*. I 1, 7.17.

all that constitutes not our true life: it is only an image of life, of living. True, real life is found only in the activities of Intellect as it thinks and knows the Forms. We truly live only insofar as we, too, engage in those activities.

It is important to emphasize that for Plotinus "our" life is an explicit, active thinking about Forms. As I have said, Plotinus holds that all human beings (at any rate, once they have come to maturity) possess an ongoing and active process of intellectual contact with Forms, but that activity of thought is not the activity that Plotinus has in mind as constituting "our" life.[42] The common and constant contact with Forms is required for all uses of language and all thinking, even in everyday activities in conducting one's life in the physical world—eating and drinking, having conversations, doing one's work. But such constant contact with and reference in our thoughts to Forms is one of which we are not self-aware as we put it to use. It is entirely implicit in the operations of which we are aware: thinking our thoughts about what is going on around us, or remembering incidents, or making judgments and plans. It is likewise only implicit, not self-conscious, even in doing bits of "scientific" investigation such as trying to figure out, by experimentation and theory construction, how some complicated medical or atomic-physical phenomenon is to be explained and perhaps controlled. One can engage fully and successfully in those operations without thinking or knowing anything about the natures of things (in the sense in which a nature is, on Platonist theory, something abstract and completely nonbodily). One need not hold or so much as take for granted even that there are such entities. By contrast, our life, in the sense of the life activity that belongs to us as what we are—which belongs to our "true" selves—is an activity of explicit acceptance that there *are* such natures, and of self-aware, self-directed thought about them, or about some of them in particular (inquiring into what it is to be a human being, or what it is to be the color red, for example).[43] That is what realizes our nature,

[42] For Plotinus this provides the basis for the celebrated Platonic theory of knowledge, i.e., knowledge of basic necessary truths such as about the natures of things, as coming about by "recollection" from our souls' preexistence. See Plato, *Meno, Phaedo,* and *Phaedrus.* Plotinus alludes to this theory of recollection fairly frequently. He often presupposes it as a matter of course, especially in contexts concerning *erôs* and the attractions of beauty and beautiful things, but he relies little on it as a theory of knowledge, and he does not discuss or present and defend it as his own theory of knowledge. It is a mistake to think of our souls, for Plotinus, as some commentators suggest, as containing only obscure "traces" of Forms, derived from our preexistence, in the manner described by Socrates in these dialogues of Plato. For him, Soul is always, i.e., eternally, knowing the Forms in themselves and fully, so that even our souls are always knowing Forms themselves, not at all traces of them left in our souls; we just need to turn our attention to and become aware of what is already fully in us.

[43] Plotinus speaks quite strikingly (*Enn.* I 1, 9.13–15) of the implicit use of our power of abstract thought about Forms as one in which we "have" the Forms, deal with them, but do not have them "to

and makes us fully alive. The rest of the life we live is, as I said, a life of the soul-image that organizes and constitutes the living body in which our total consciousness is lodged. Our physical life, including our social and "applied" intellectual life of empirical inquiry, is not lived by *us*, but by something, as Plotinus once puts it, merely "attached" to us.[44]

In sum then, within a human consciousness taken as a whole, we should identify as the person himself or herself, their intellect. This alone, in human consciousness, is the Substance, Soul, in itself, insofar as Soul gives itself intact and unadulterated—not via an "image"—to this place where we are, so as to create the particular kind of living being that a human animal is. Among animals, only human beings, Plotinus assumes, are self-conscious, that is, not just conscious of whatever "objects" of consciousness (feelings, sensations, perceptions, memories, say, or theoretical thoughts) they may be aware of moment by moment, but conscious of oneself as something conscious of those objects. If we ask what we, the subjects of our consciousness—that is, the objects of our *self*-consciousness—in fact are (i.e., what this thing is that is active in our being conscious of ourselves in being conscious of objects), Plotinus's answer is that it is our intellect. Indeed, it is because of and from our intellect, through its "image," that we have the rest of our consciousness, what he calls our "lower" consciousness, at all.

Nonetheless, any human consciousness does contain, quite explicitly, a lot of other experiences than acts of an intellectual sort—whether intellectual acts only implicit (as when we apply a Form to something empirical so as to classify and deal with it) or also explicit ones, in which we think about Forms as they are in themselves. In fact we are always, while awake and even to some extent sometimes while asleep, active with our senses and with their effects in memory. We can hardly prevent that: to be conscious at all, for us, is to be open via our senses to the world surrounding us, and responsive in our consciousnesses to what we perceive. And we are also filled with feelings of pleasure and pain and, depending on the particular characters of our soul-images, and all kinds of emotional reaction and response to what we perceive and the desire that arise as a result. These too we can hardly prevent experiencing, if we are conscious at all—or, at any rate, it requires an effort not to do so. Still, it is, at least to a significant extent, up to us what to give our *attention* to, what to focus on—or else, to ignore and consciously look away from, and, perhaps, reduce their felt effects in our conscious-

hand"—only in the explicit, actively theorizing mode of our higher soul's thought do we have them "to hand."

[44]*Enn.* I 1, 9.25.

ness. Here, at last, we reach the point of connection from Plotinus's metaphysical theory of the human person and the issues of human virtue, self-fulfillment, and happiness that are our principal concerns in this chapter.

For Plotinus, in giving itself to us, Soul makes us—that is, our *intellects*—in charge of our lives. It gives us the power to determine how our life is to be conducted and lived—even if, of course, a good deal of the life of a human animal is lived through the activities of the soul-image (i.e., through bodily feelings, emotions, empirical inquiry and information gathering, ordinary daily decision making). We exercise this leadership through the capacity, essential to an individual human intellect, lodged in a certain body at a certain place, to direct our intellectual attention explicitly and self-consciously, as Plotinus picturesquely puts it, "upward" toward Forms and/or "downward" toward the life of the soul-image. To turn upward is to attend with our consciousness to and exercise our powers as pure intellects, with concentration, and without attending to anything involving, or having to do essentially with, bodies—with our own, or ones surrounding us—even if and while one may still be *aware* of them. To turn downward is to attend to, and focus our consciousness upon, the life of daily activities and concerns, the life we possess insofar as we are embodied things. This orientation of our attention, of the focus of our consciousness, is something for us, our individual intellects, to decide. It is in that power of our intellects to focus our attention that our essential freedom as agents resides, on Plotinus's view.

Now in fact, so long as we are alive at all, we cannot fail, as I have said, to be conscious of what is "below," and it would be quite unreasonable, if not entirely impossible, to attempt either to be actually unaware of what goes on down there, or, as a general policy, just to distract and hold one's attention away from it, in favor of looking exclusively upward, toward Forms. The two alternatives—keeping our attention directed upward, and directing it downward—cannot be treated as mutually exclusive. Even if we follow Plotinus and accept that our true selves are our intellects, we must somehow combine an interest in what is above with one in what is below in our lives. One can on some occasions and for some periods of time distract oneself, and train oneself so that for those times one hardly even notices what is below, as one concentrates one's attention upward. As we will see, Plotinus definitely does recommend doing that, since it is exclusively in those activities of explicit and devoted abstract thinking that our true good lies, on his view. But, in our lives as a whole, we must divide our attention, whether at different times or even simultaneously; we must be attentive to and concerned for what is below—not just be conscious of it—as well as for the above. The principal question of ethics, for Plotinus, then, concerns the principles on which, and the spirit in which, one ought to effect this division. What reasons are there, lying in one's own nature and in the nature of reality, that could determine how one should combine holding one's attention, as a regular practice, below, with also, as a regular practice, turning it and holding it above? This question concerns one's basic, constantly maintained, practical assumptions, one's worked-out thoughts, convictions, and attitudes, about the values for oneself—namely for an individual intellect—in such concerns. What basic outlook ought one to adopt, in governing one's use of one's natural power (belonging, Plotinus insists, to one's intellect) to focus one's consciousness and pay attention either upward or downward or both, in the course of one's life? What should one care about in the exercise of one's lower powers of consciousness? How should one relate those cares to the consummate and final value that one places in the exercise of one's higher power, when it is being exercised to perfection?

To pursue these questions, and Plotinus's answers to them, we need to turn to his theories concerning the human virtues: it is through possessing the virtues that, on Plotinus's theories, one combines attention upward with attention downward, in the whole of one's life, in the naturally proper way.

6.4. Three Levels of Human Virtues: "Civic," "Purifying," and "Intellectual"

In the whole Greek philosophical tradition, as we have seen, the human virtues lie at the center of ethical theory, because it is agreed on all hands—and the wider culture of preclassical and classical Greek cities, surviving even in later times, supported this idea—that only through possessing and using the virtues in all that one does can one perfect one's soul, one's nature as a human being, and so achieve one's natural good, happiness.[45] Plotinus clearly belongs in this tradition, even though, under Roman domination, Greek cultural life and, even more, the social and political lives of the citizens of Greek cities, had altered in many highly significant ways by the third century CE. For Plotinus, as for Aristotle and the Stoics, the path to the virtues and to virtuous living begins with acquiring an understanding of the human soul. Since Plotinus holds that what *we* are is only *one* of our soul capacities, our intellects, for him whatever conditions of our souls can count as virtues for us, and so enablers of our happiness,

---

[45] At *Enn.* I 4, 2.42–3 Plotinus says that virtue just is the perfection of reason (see also 2.25).

must stem from a firm and fundamental awareness of our selves—the "I" of our most intimate self-consciousness—as our intellects exclusively. We are no other element in our consciousness; the rest of our consciousness belongs to us, and in that sense is ours, but it is not us. On the other hand, the life human beings actually lead, until and unless they have learned that Platonist lesson, derives entirely from desires, emotional reactions, sensory experiences, decisions, and so on, belonging to our lower consciousness, not this higher one. Moreover, even after you have achieved the Platonist insight into our true selves, you continue to have a lower consciousness, and continue to need to take care of your body's needs and the physical and social life of the embodied animal that you, loosely speaking also are.

So, for Plotinus, human virtue, overall, must be a complex thing, including both specific conditions that structure the direct uses of our intellect in addressing its specific task of knowing Forms, and ones belonging to the lower consciousness, governing its (and, more crucially, our intellect's) relations to the physical and material world and to our embodied lives. The first are virtues that concern our activities "above," as we actively exercise our higher capacities; Plotinus calls them the "greater" virtues. The second concern our activities as we and our intellects look down into the physical world, and relate to our life "below." So, as will see in detail as we proceed, Plotinus works out a theory of the human virtues that includes both an account of the virtues our intellects need in order to perfect our intellectual lives (I will call these, on his behalf, the "intellectual" virtues), and an account of the virtues of our lower consciousnesses, as we experience, react to, and make our choices concerning our physical and social environments in the proper and best ways; these are needed for us to make that life, too, as good a life as possible.[46] In that connection he develops a theory of what he calls these the "political" or "civic" virtues. In fact, as we will see, Plotinus thinks we must recognize a third level of virtues as well: ones that belong to the intellect, and not the lower consciousness, but concern the conditions in it that are needed to enable us to draw ourselves away from the (wrong) sort of active, self-identifyingly engaged involvement in and concern for the life "below" that ordinary people evince. These virtues enable us to focus our attention, with increas-

---

[46] Actually, as we will see, it seems that these virtues apply only to people who live the lower life in the wrong way, by holding that the lower consciousness is one's true self (or, at least, part of it)—with the result that the apparent goods and bads in that lower life become, for them, their *own* goods and bads. They think their happiness is to be found in a decent, humanly responsible way of living a life on that fundamentally wrong basis. The truly virtuous Platonist's attitude toward the lower life is anything but zestfully committed, as these people are, even when it is being lived well and correctly (see the next paragraph).

ing strength and effectiveness, upon what is "above." These he calls the "purifying" virtues.

The key point, for Plotinus, in the theory of virtue is that because of what we are, our calling is to a life above. The essential and sole activity of the virtue of the human person, as such, is actively contemplative understanding of what lies above, in the Intellect, and that our own intellects enable us to access. A Platonist's real and sole interest, therefore—the sole source of satisfaction and fulfillment in life—is in looking away from, and infinitely far above, the physical life below. It lies in a deeply enthralled love of theoretical thinking, and (equivalently, as we have seen) a love of the true reality that such thinking brings us fully into touch with. Our only true good is to be found there, in understanding the Forms. So far as the life below goes, the correct attitude is to regard oneself as a caretaker appointed to oversee the life of the individual embodied rational animal that one is. One is to see that it gets the foods and other physical care it needs, to see that it relates to other human animals in morally and socially proper ways. But one does these things always from the emotional distance required, for Plotinus, by faithfulness to one's true identity as an intellect. So far from showing a virtuous disposition of mind, as Aristotle thinks, to identify ourselves in any way or degree with the lower consciousness, and to take a direct and zestful interest in its states, or in objects of pursuit for its life, to think that anything either good or bad for one's self and one's life, occurs there—all that is incompatible with virtue. If, whether by our action or not, our physical and social life flourishes, the "goods" of our bodies and of our soul-image so attained are not, and must not be regarded as bringing us, any intrinsic satisfaction. Or so the Platonist has come to think. The lower consciousness and what it undergoes or accomplishes do matter to us insofar as they are *ours* (though that consciousness is not *us*). But since they are imposed on, or joined to, us—the intellects that we are—they are given to us solely to take care of, to offer our leadership over—so long as we are physically alive (that too is something imposed upon us). True virtue involves accepting and understanding this relationship between ourselves and everything else—bodily and spiritual—that is in this external way ours.

In summary, then, the root of a Platonist life is in maintaining an infinite distance between oneself and everything bodily or physical. Not only does Plotinus follow Plato in making the human soul something entirely disjoint from everything bodily—a purely spiritual entity, something of a totally different substance from anything physical. He also understands the soul, given that difference, as something that properly keeps itself psychologically disengaged from all aspects of human consciousness that relate to our lives as embodied, physical entities.[47] Here we see an especially sharp contrast with both Aristotle and the Stoics, though in a great deal of his theory Plotinus does in fact follow the Stoics, with their similar conception of duty as imposed from above by the cosmic mind. In their different ways, both Aristotle and the Stoics regard every virtuous agent as psychologically fully committed to the intrinsic good of a well-lived life of practical virtue (as well, for Aristotle, as a life of the virtues of theoretical thinking that belong to the happiest human life). For Plotinus, the spiritualizing of human nature carries with it a fundamental reorientation in the conception of the human virtues, and of the virtuous human life. The sole true good is one we only experience while looking away from the lives we lead over time, in the physical world. We look away to an eternal life that, on his theory, we can live without regard to any passage of time.

In turning now to consider in detail Plotinus's theories of the virtues (in the remainder of this section) and human happiness (in the next section), we will be concerned principally with two treatises of the first *Ennead*, I 2 *On Virtues* and I 4 *On Happiness*.[48] As for the individual virtues, at each of the three levels he distinguishes, Plotinus simply takes over ready-made the Platonic summation, in the *Republic*, of the whole of virtue as consisting in four interconnected and interlocking psychic conditions. To these the Socrates of that dialogue gives the names of temperance (or moderation), courage, wisdom and justice, and Plotinus follows him.[49] Plotinus offers no basis in his own Platonist theories for recognizing these as four "cardinal" virtues, indeed as the only ones he seems to recognize at all.[50] Notably, without independently examining, explaining, and defending them in his own (or indeed, any) terms, he also accepts the famous thumbnail accounts that Socrates offers in summary terms in *Republic* IV of pre-

---

[47] Even in the *Phaedo*, where Socrates presages Plotinus's ideas here about the purely intellectual character of the soul, Socrates remains to the end (the conversation of the *Phaedo* is represented as his last one, before dying by hemlock poisoning) fully and zestfully committed to his physical life, as a source of goods as well as evils, and to his love of his friends.

[48] Armstrong translates the Greek title of I 4, Περὶ εὐδαιμονίας, as *On Well-Being*, explaining his reasons in a footnote. In fact, for Plotinus, as for Aristotle and the Stoics, εὐδαιμονία is an activity, not a state or standing condition. Well-being, however one interprets it, is a condition of a person or their life. The traditional English translation as "happiness" is not ideal, but it can be made to carry the appropriate sense and nuance, as I have tried to make clear in earlier chapters. Hence my preferred translation for the title of I 4.

[49] In Greek, σωφροσύνη, ἀνδρεία (ἀνδρία), σοφία or φρόνησις, δικαιοσύνη.

[50] He has a precedent in this in Chrysippus, who took over the Platonic fourfold classification, treating it merely as providing the basic genera for the great multitude of particular virtues he recognized. But Chrysippus offered his own, very counter-Platonic, Stoic account of what these four consist in.

cisely which psychic conditions these virtues consist in, one by one—"justice" consists in each part of the soul "doing its own," and so on.

To this extent, Plotinus follows the Platonic account blindly.[51] However, Plotinus uses this unargued framework in highly original and quite striking and interesting ways. Looking to the demands of his own theory of the human person—concerning both the soul-image belonging to the body, and the "higher" soul of intellect in us—he uses the Platonic framework to propose his own quite distinctive Platonist theory of the virtues. For Plotinus, the Platonic distinction of four psychic conditions, and the terms in which in Plato they are set out, applies in fact with instantiations at three distinct levels—not just one, as we find worked out in the *Republic*.[52] First there are temperance$_3$, courage$_3$, (practical) wisdom$_3$, and justice$_3$. These belong to our soul-image. They correspond, though only roughly, to the actual four virtues as Plato intended to describe them, when he discusses the psychological conditions that constitute the virtues of justice, courage, temperance, and wisdom, as those exist in the individual person.[53] Plotinus refers to these as "civic" or "political" virtues[54]—they are virtues dealing with our feelings and emotions and the decisions and actions of daily life. Virtue as a whole, for Plato—these four virtues, taken together—constitutes a balanced, well-ordered set of standing and effective relationships among the three kinds of motivation that Plato and Platonists (along with Aristotle) assign to human beings:[55] nonrational types of desire (appetite) and emotional feeling (spirit), plus reasoned desires representing the agent's convictions about what is good for human beings. From these three sources of motivation, practical decisions and rational actions derive.

[51] See endnote 42 for more comments on the chronology of Plotinus's writings on ethics.

[52] We will see below that Plotinus makes a great deal of a passing reference in *Republic* VI, 500d, that seems to imply that Socrates there conceives of a second, lower level of psychic conditions, different from the ones formally and officially defined as "justice," "wisdom," "courage," and "temperance" and employed in the dialogue's main argument about justice and happiness. These would then count as a distinct second and lower sort of justice, wisdom, courage, and temperance—providing textual support for Plotinus's own distinction between "greater" and "lesser" justice, wisdom, courage, and temperance.

[53] The correspondence is rough, because (1) in the *Republic* the virtues described are true virtues; they define the fully correct way to engage with the nonrational aspects of one's soul, and with one's ethical life as an embodied animal—whereas in Plotinus's exposition they turn out to depend upon the common and ordinary, wrong view of human identities as including the lower soul; (2) in developing his theory Plotinus blends the *Republic* account with themes drawn from the *Phaedo* that, in Plato's conception, do not belong together with it. On these points see below in this section.

[54] I.e., πολιτικαὶ ἀρεταί, cf. *Enn.* I 2, 1.16. This terminology has its basis in Plato's texts jointly in *Rep.* IV, 430b (and VI, 500d), and in *Phaedo* 82a (see also, for the phrase πολιτικὴ ἀρετή, *Protagoras* 322e).

[55] See I 2, 2.13–18.

As for the four constituent virtues, following Plato's words very closely, Plotinus describes practical wisdom (significantly, he uses the Aristotelian term φρόνησις here, where Plato mostly speaks of σοφία) as a possession of the "reasoning part."[56] This wisdom₃, for Plotinus as for Plato, consists in the ability of one's reason to perform well the tasks of figuring out what is best for the person to do, in general and in particular circumstances, and with what additional motivating impulses, nonrational ones, to do it. Courage₃ he describes as possessed by spirit. With courage₃, spirit is so disciplined that it does not cause the agent to feel afraid or upset about any bodily or external harm, or about any denial of bodily or other gratification, when reason decides it is best to endure them. Moderation₃ and justice₃ are matching conditions that complete the balance, or good order, just referred to: moderation₃ is a sort of "agreement and harmony" of the nonrational and the rational parts in accepting that reason is the proper authority in all cases where action is called for, justice₃ a more positive condition in which (here Plotinus quotes Plato) each of the parts works together with the others in "doing its own work where ruling and being ruled are concerned."[57]

The other two sets of virtues consist, on Plotinus's account, in rather forced and contrived replications of this fourfold scheme (I won't take the trouble to report them fully here), at two distinct levels of the use of our intellects, our true selves.[58] Before proceeding to a summary presentation of these virtues, I need to say something about a severe complication, and even confusion, in Plotinus's theory of the virtues₃. As I mentioned above, Plotinus's virtues₃ are only roughly equivalent to Plato's *Republic*'s virtues of justice, courage, moderation, and wisdom in the individual good person. On the one hand, Plotinus does describe his virtues₃ as *virtues*. This indicates that he does wish to capture, somehow, with these terms and under the descriptions of them I have just reported, a proper and correct way of using our intellects to control and oversee our lower life, through the use of our soul-image and its feelings, emotions, decisions, and everyday actions. Yet, as we will see, he also disparages them, as unworthy of the truly happy and truly virtuous person: such a person lives beyond them.[59] In a nutshell, for Plotinus the problem is this: the truly virtuous person (whose whole life is fully

---

[56] I.e., τὸ λογιζόμενον, recalling the standard Platonic term τὸ λογιστικόν—i.e., what calculates and thinks discursively.

[57] See I 2, 1.17–21.

[58] Porphyry expands his own account of virtue into four levels, adding one to Plotinus's three. Augustine and other later Platonist and Christian philosophers adopt other related theories of the levels of virtue, all of which take off from Plotinus's account.

[59] See, most strikingly, Plotinus's account at the end of I 2 (at 7.19–30) of the truly virtuous person as

characterized by the remaining two sets of virtues, to be gone into shortly) continues, as I remarked above, to have a lower consciousness and to live a life of embodied action, as Plotinus clearly recognizes; yet, virtuous persons live turned away from, and without involvement in that life in any way that would betray the slightest acceptance of anything that it brings or involves as being either good or bad for themselves personally, as the person that they are. Thus Plotinus needs a set of virtues for the truly good and happy person to possess and use for their virtuous oversight over their life below; yet what he actually describes under the title of the virtues₃ is the life of someone who lives decently, but nonetheless with a wrong conception of their own identity and their own good, as including the life of their soul-image. This puts Plotinus's interpreters in the awkward position of having to find in his descriptions of the virtues₃ materials for working out a set of related true, fully spiritual virtues, possessed by the truly virtuous and happy person—a person whose life Plotinus describes in *Enneads* I 4—that nonetheless differ in important ways from the "official" virtues₃, as described in *Enneads* I 2. I will come back to this problem in the next section. Meanwhile, the reader must bear in mind Plotinus's schizophrenia on the status of the virtues₃ and on whether they really are virtues at all, as we proceed to discuss the remaining two levels of virtue.

As to the additional two levels of virtues that Plotinus recognizes, there is first of all (at the top level) a replication of Plato's fourfold scheme from the *Republic*, described above, for the use of intellect in explicit, purely theoretical investigation and contemplative thinking about Forms. Versions of temperance, courage, justice (and, of course, wisdom) are in use, Plotinus holds, when fully engaged and committed, successful Platonist philosophical thinkers concentrate their full attention in contemplating the Forms, and engage in what we can think of as actively concentrated philosophical thought. These are "intellectual" versions of the four virtues: they are virtues of our intellects (not, as with the virtues₃, of our soul-images).[60] Here, Plotinus intends us to find the same basic pattern of balance, good order, and harmoniousness that constitutes virtue at the "civic" level. But at that level it involves interlocking conditions of and on each of three distinct "parts" of the soul (i.e., for Plotinus, of the soul-image). Here, however,

having gotten beyond the civic virtues, having left them behind, and using different measures than the ones provided in the principles of those virtues for making practical decisions.

[60] In I 2 Plotinus himself refers to them simply as "greater" virtues, greater because they are virtues of the human intellect or true self—by contrast to the "lesser" ones of the mere and not fully substantial soul-image.

balance, order and harmony must be thought of as applying exclusively to something that is wholly simple and single, without independently operating parts—our pure intellect. In this case, wisdom$_1$ is the human intellect's "looking toward" and understanding the Forms, as they exist in Intellect, the Substance. Justice$_1$ is its activity in going back toward Intellect (the soul's, and Soul's, origin). Here, Plotinus presumably means its "going back" without any distraction of its energy toward things below—when it does that, our soul is doing its own work, and not doing the work of anything else, namely, the soul-image. Moderation$_1$ is our intellect's "turning inward toward Intellect"—in doing so, I take it Plotinus means, it expresses its agreement with, or acceptance of, Intellect's priority and authority for Soul's own activity. Courage$_1$ is our intellect's freedom from affect in being made like that toward which it looks: by its own nature, Intellect is without affect, and when our intellect "turns" upward and is made like Intellect, it does so without anything resembling emotional excitement. Moreover, we should recall that "civic" courage is the standing condition of not being affected with fear under certain circumstances and in relation to certain things: our intellects, in engaging virtuously in concentrated abstract thinking, are holding back from involvement with the body and with the soul-image, an involvement that would bring psychical affections to it—we are "courageously" avoiding that affection.[61]

But in addition, Plotinus proposes a third, intermediate version, of temperance, courage, wisdom, and justice. He classifies the "intellectual" virtues just discussed as ones possessed by a soul when, and insofar as, it is already purified from all interested involvement with the body and its life (wrongly taking its life as one's own), and with the practical decision making of the soul-image: it can, at will, withdraw into itself, into its own nature as intellect, so as to know and contemplate the Forms. Those virtues are exercised whenever (but only when) one whose intellect has been perfected, so that it has reached, or come near to reaching, a full understanding of all the Forms in their complete, systematic, "unfolded," and fully articulated relationships to one another, turns to and engages in the activity of contemplation. As we will see in the next section, Plotinus

---

[61] For these definitions of the intellectual virtues, see I 2, 6.11–27, esp. 23–27, plus (for wisdom$_1$), 7.6–7. The interpretative glosses are my own speculation. Plotinus is quite notably lax in offering these definitions and explicating them: it is as if he isn't interested in how the details of the idea of order and harmony might apply, so as to yield four cooperating and interlocking different conditions when our higher souls have their specific virtue. Perhaps this, and similar laxity elsewhere in I 2, may be among the reasons why Porphyry speaks of the chronologically first twenty-one treatises, which include this one, as showing less accomplished ability than the middle twenty-four.

considers that a person can be engaged in that contemplative activity not only when explicitly occupied fully in the work of thinking Forms, but also—even unconsciously so—while being occupied with other "lower" matters (though, of course, un-self-interestedly so).

There are virtues also that are used in the process of purifying ourselves—of reaching the capacity to withdraw fully into oneself, into what one truly is, an intellect, and to act as such, by actively understanding the whole system of Forms. Plotinus locates these at the level, described above, where we may use (or fail to use) our powers of intellect so as to draw ourselves away, and keep ourselves away, from the wrong kind of attention to our soul-image's life. These virtues he calls "purifications."[62] They are functions of the intellect's self-purification from the bad effects on their intellects that all ordinary, nonphilosophical people impose on themselves through their way of life. With their inappropriate and wrong zest for and interest in the body and its experiences (assuming that they contain things good or bad for oneself), even if they live as decent people without what is conventionally regarded as actual vices, ordinary, nonphilosophical people are ignoring and denying their true selves. They are denying their intellect's hegemony and rightful leadership in their lives. The intermediate, "purifying" virtues of moderation$_2$, courage$_2$, wisdom$_2$, and justice$_2$ are the ones that we need in order to exercise fully and appropriately our intellect's powers of looking upward, firmly and without letup, not downward—for not focusing our inner attention on the animal and its body, its needs and experiences, physical and social, in such a way as to treat them as if they were *us*, or of any intrinsic interest to us, any part of what is good or bad for us. Instead, we look upward and aspire and strive to be, in full and actual fact, what we are in our essences: intellects. Through that concentrated aspiration, we work hard at thinking about Forms, and make progress toward the final possession of a full understanding of them, in which we will then possess and be able to exercise the "intellectual" virtues. I will return to these "purifying" virtues below.

In working out this three-level theory, especially as concerns the intermediate level, Plotinus combines reference to two discussions about virtues in Plato. He refers extensively, first, to the theory of the virtues in the *Republic*, and, second,

[62] In fact, as I understand him, Plotinus speaks of both the intellectual and these intermediate virtues as "purifications," but in different ways. For the intellectual virtues as purifications in the sense that they consist in a state of having-been-purified, see I 2, 7.8–10 (cf. 4.4). For the distinction between virtues in this sense and the process sense that holds for the intermediate virtues, see 4.1–5 (where I follow an alternative emendation of the text from the one translated by Armstrong; this was proposed by Igal and adopted by Kalligas).

to the apparently independent, and not overtly related, set of reflections on the virtues that Socrates enters into in two passages of the *Phaedo*. Plotinus combines the two discussions in interesting and striking ways. The result is, as I have said, a truly novel and quite ingenious Platonist theory of the human virtues, differing markedly from Plato's own, standardly cited one, in the *Republic*. Before discussing further Plotinus's "purifying" virtues, it will be helpful to consider at some length these sources in Plato's texts for Plotinus's three-level theory. This will require detailed discussion, on our own, of Plato's accounts of the virtues in *Phaedo* and *Republic*, before we turn to see what use Plotinus makes of these passages. But this digression will provide us with an illuminating perspective on the intellectual context of Plotinus's own theory. It will also, incidentally, show an example of how subtly and ingeniously Plotinus, and other Platonists, often interpret Plato, so as to find their own ideas adumbrated in his texts. Often it seems that securing that authorization is at least as important in winning adherence to their theories as the philosophical arguments on which they officially base them. It meant a lot to Plotinus and his contemporaries (and his predecessor Platonists) if something could be claimed, via Plato, to be part of the primordial wisdom revealed to the ancients that these later philosophers thought they were recovering.

It is in the *Phaedo* (and not at all in the *Republic*) that Socrates speaks of true virtue (he mentions specifically true moderation, justice, courage, and wisdom) as a "purification" of the soul—specifically, as the purging away of pleasures, pains, fears, "and all such things."[63] For Socrates in the *Phaedo*, purging these away means not having, or ceasing to have, any "willing association with the body," and "keeping away from" the desires and passions of the body,[64] or at least

---

[63] *Phaedo* 69b8–c3: Socrates uses two linguistically related terms for this, κάθαρσις (Plotinus's term) and καθαρμός. He does so with specific reference to, and on the basis of some comparison with, the rites of the Greek mystery cults. By taking part in certain ceremonies concluding in some sort of religious vision, and having been "purified" by this vision, an "initiate" is guaranteed entry into Hades after death on especially favorable terms. Socrates first speaks of purification a bit earlier, at 67c5 (with related terms at 67a5 and a7): what is in question there is purification from the body in not using the senses at all in connection with efforts to understand truth and reality, but using only our minds and their independent powers of insight into Forms. In this paragraph and the next three I am drawing on and summarizing the whole context, 65e6–69d6, in common with a later passage of the work (see the next note but one). (In my translations from the *Phaedo* I follow the translation of G.M.A. Grube in Cooper, *Plato: Complete Works*, with modifications.)

[64] Here Socrates, if taken literally, identifies the body as what desires (and what experiences other passions), and by implication as what experiences bodily pleasure. However, in the immediately preceding sentence he has spoken of us, our souls, as being "filled with appetites, fears, all sorts of illusions" by the body (just as earlier at 65a7 he speaks of "the pleasures that come through the body"). So probably he

"mastering" them and (crucially) "not handing oneself over to them."[65] (As to what exactly this means for the way one will lead one's life when "purged," we will see shortly.) Socrates says that it is only philosophers who engage in this purgation, because only they even know that there are Forms: only they know that truth and reality are to be found in Forms, and in them alone. Philosophers are "lovers of learning," and they realize that to attain their goal of knowing the natures of things through grasping the Forms, they must "separate [their] soul as far as possible from the body and accustom it to gather itself and collect itself out of every part of the body and to dwell by itself, as far as it can . . . freed from the—as it were—bonds of the body."[66] Philosophers do not think anything in our physical lives, our lives in human society, is of supreme intrinsic value or interest; for them, the highest good for a human being simply lies elsewhere, in our minds and intellects.

These lovers of learning or wisdom hold themselves back, and do not make the desires and pleasures of the body or of ordinary social life their own. They regard them as lying outside themselves, even if they do have to experience them all the time. Socrates sharply contrasts the lovers of wisdom with "lovers of the body," including "lovers of wealth" or of "honors." In fact, for Socrates everyone not properly attuned to philosophy and its overriding importance for human life is, in one way or degree or another, a lover of the body. Such people think, or take it for granted, that our worldly life, both physically and in our social circumstances, is of supreme intrinsic value and interest, worthy of full personal satisfaction if it goes well, or, in the opposite case, worth bitter disappointment. They live their lives on that basis. Some of them, to be sure, are better people than others—not every lover of the body has to be a glutton or sex maniac, or an insensitive or cruel brute, or murderer or thief, or languid sybarite. But even the decently behaved ones have, at best, what Socrates describes as a "shadow drawing,"

---

means "desires and passions of the body" as shorthand for desires and passions that arise in us because of things going on in the body. That is, in any event, how in the *Republic* Socrates thinks about appetitive desires. His own very briefly sketched conception of virtue as purification from bodily involvement, little elaborated as it is, can be understood sufficiently without the need to press him on this point. However, Plotinus's own theory of purification, largely developed out of reflection on these *Phaedo* passages, definitely does assign functions to an animal body that are tantamount to this literal assignment of desires, pains, and pleasures to it, and not to the soul (even in the case of the souls of bad people, which join forces with the body in these experiences). On this see, e.g., *Enn.* I 1, 4.5–10.

[65] The quotations in this sentence are from *Phaedo* 80e3–4 and 82c3–4. At 79e8–84b8 Socrates takes up again the themes of purification and the virtues' role in it, which he introduced at 65e6. He dropped it at 69e5, to allow and respond to an intervening objection from his interlocutor Cebes.

[66] *Phaedo* 67c6–d2.

or illusory appearance, of virtue. They cannot have what Socrates thinks should count as true virtue: only the philosopher can have that. In ordinary usage— usage that grew up among, and is authorized by, ordinary people, all of whom are body lovers—people apply virtue terms to one another on the wrong basis. The ordinary conception of virtue is just completely wrong and mistaken (I will say just below what Socrates thinks the basic error is). Anyone with "virtues" so conceived has what Socrates describes as mere *popular or civic* virtue, a wrongly so-called virtue, developed through habit and practice alone, without philosophy and true understanding.[67] Their alleged virtues are, as I said, only "shadow-drawings" of the real thing, that is, of the true virtue that only philosophers possess.

Precisely because they do regard our physical life as of supreme and true interest and value, and do not recognize (indeed, they hardly have an inkling of) the independent, spiritual use of our minds, and its superior intrinsic value, such people can reach the decent behavior that they may attain only by illegitimate means. They measure and "trade off" pleasures foregone now, or pains endured now, for greater pleasures or lesser pains later; or they trade honor now not given, or belittlement received now, for greater honor later; or they stand up to fear of harm now so that later they won't have greater things to fear. Or they trade off some mixture of these values and disvalues against one another. Ordinary usage may call such behavior, by making such trade-offs, wise and knowledgeable control over human life, but in fact it does not show wise control at all: it betrays the false view that only bodily and social goods are goods for a human being. These body-loving people behave decently in many or most respects, but, as I said, they do not reach any sort of true virtue. That, Socrates claims, requires the recognition of all of physical human life as having in itself only minimal real value; only intellectual activity has any really important intrinsic value for us. The *true* virtues of moderation, courage, justice, and wisdom are based on this recognition. The truly virtuous person selects among pleasures and pains, present in relation to future, or among honors or fears, or any combination of these, solely on the ground that knowledge of Forms, as guides to our physical life, indicates that these are the appropriate choices for an embodied soul to make in directing one's physical life, and in taking care of the body and sustaining social relationships. They do their practical actions solely for the sake of instantiating

---

[67] For the terms quoted in the last two sentences, see *Phaedo* 69b7 and 82a11–12. "Popular or civic virtue" translates τὴν δημοτικὴν καὶ πολιτικὴν ἀρετήν. The italics are mine.

these intellectually valuable Forms in their lives—and, in the process, achieving just those pleasures and honors, and other goods of an embodied life, that do count as worth something, of some (minor) intrinsic value for a human being. Far from taking our physical life, and anything that is done or achieved in it, as having any important intrinsic value, or being the legitimate source of serious personal satisfaction (or disappointment), such truly virtuous people know that for a human being supreme value and interest is found only in the properly focused use of our powers of theoretical understanding of the natures of things (including, of course, an understanding of what actions are good and bad in the oversight of a human physical and social life). The rest of our life consists of things that it falls to us to do or experience, or try to achieve, simply because, and while, we are embodied, and while, as such, we have to find a suitable way in which to conduct ourselves, in recognition of the severely limited values to be achieved and maintained in our embodied lives.[68]

Plotinus quite naturally sees a connection between Socrates's remarks in the *Phaedo*, with their emphasis on true virtue as consisting in the purification of the soul, and his own ideas about virtue and purification. But when in the *Phaedo* Socrates calls the faux virtue of decently behaved ordinary people "popular or civic 'virtue,'" Plotinus also sees a connection between these ideas in the *Phaedo* and what Plato has Socrates say at two widely separated places in the *Republic*.

In book IV, in describing the virtues, not of individual persons, but of whole cities (i.e., virtues consisting in the organized behavior of the different "classes"

---

[68] In presenting Socrates's rather spare contrast between the lives of the body lovers and the embodied lives of the philosophical lovers of learning, I interpret him as regarding the pleasures and other goods (and bads) of our physical life as being of some value to each person: the legitimately experienced ones of these count as truly good or bad for oneself—even if they can be of only relatively minor value for a person, in comparison to the supreme value in the mere understanding of Forms. Socrates is not in the thrall of late Platonist ideas about our lower consciousness as belonging not to our souls but to a soul-image: he clearly assumes (without its occurring to him to say so explicitly, so evident is it to all his friends, and to all Plato's intended readers) that it is *we* who experience bodily pleasure and pain, emotions, and nonrational desires, and who make decisions and carry out actions that are virtuous or vicious. Hence, if *we* live truly virtuously in selecting actions as well as pleasures and honors, etc., by following the guidance of the Forms of justice, or moderation, and so on, those virtuous actions are true goods for us, they contribute to our overall good. (Compare my account in section 2.2, of Socrates's views on virtue and goodness in the *Euthydemus*.) By imposing his Platonist ideas about the soul-image upon Socrates's account, Plotinus is able to read Socrates as rejecting as no true virtue not only the debased calculations of the decently behaved lover of the body, but also the virtues that Socrates in fact does endorse, the true justice, moderation, and courage in which the morally legitimate goods of physical life get counted as one's own goods, though, of course, minor goods compared with the good of knowing Forms. This results when, as we see below, Plotinus identifies the true virtues of the *Republic* (which one could reasonably identify with Socrates's true virtues in the *Phaedo* passage), in effect, with his "shadow-drawing" ones.

into which the citizens of the ideal city have been divided for political reasons),
Socrates speaks of the "political" or "civic" courage exhibited by the city's "auxil-
iary" or administrative cadres, including military and police forces, in making
their specific contribution to the justice of the whole civic order.[69] Thus, Plotinus
finds Socrates in *Republic* IV speaking of a "political" virtue (Plotinus's own label
for the virtues at his lowest level), and this is one of the two terms Socrates uses
in the *Phaedo*, as we have seen, for the "shadow-drawings" of virtue possessed by
decent nonphilosophers. This serves for Plotinus as a hinted link between the
two discussions of virtue, in *Phaedo* and *Republic*. The "political" courage, discussed in *Republic* IV, is, of course, a psychic condition of the individual souls of
properly educated and functioning auxiliaries: it is, Socrates says, because of the
presence of this psychic condition in the souls of the auxiliaries that the city itself
counts as a courageous one. This condition, he argues, does not consist merely in
some system of emotional feelings. The administrators of the ideal city are
brought up in the regimen of physical and musical education that Socrates has
earlier described, which he has said they need for the sake of the city's good, and
which is also suitable for their own human growth and development. So they
will certainly feel emotional attachments toward acting rightly. But their courage, as Socrates defines it, consists, rather, in a firmly implanted set of *beliefs*—
that is, considered views and opinions that they have come to hold, and must
have regularly reflected upon, as they go about their administrative work (including their work as magistrates and judges), in applying the laws.[70] These are
beliefs about the true nature of goodness—in particular, they are applications of
that nature, specifically, to what is best for the ideal city as a whole, both in its
internal procedures of orderly social, political, and economic life, and in its ways
of behaving in relation to other cities and their citizens.[71] The beliefs that constitute the auxiliaries' courage are, in sum, beliefs in the correctness of the constitution and laws of the ideal city, insofar as those specify, for the members of each
class within it, a certain way of life as best for themselves. These include beliefs
about certain ways of being related to other cities and their citizens, through the

---

[69] *Republic* IV, 430b–c. The word translated "civic" here is the same one used in the *Phaedo* passage
just cited: πολιτική. For what follows in this paragraph and the following one, see the whole context,
429a–430c.

[70] He formally defines this courage at 430b2–5 in terms of "correct belief," ὀρθὴ δόξα—in the definition he omits mention of emotional feelings.

[71] Thus these auxiliaries correspond to Aristotle's decent, but not fully virtuous persons, as described
above, chapter 3.

official policies, and the decisions, that are made not by these administrators, but by the philosopher-rulers of the city.

Due to their upbringing, these beliefs and commitments, as Socrates says, are strongly "dyed into" the minds of the auxiliaries. So when it is their turn to perform any one of their administrative functions—in management of the marketplace, or as policemen and in minor judicial contexts, or when serving in the military—they do not, and psychologically cannot, allow prospects of pleasure or harm, or possible honors or disgraces, to themselves personally, or prospects of disappointment or satisfaction in their personal hopes or wishes, to dissuade them from performing their proper duties. They are convinced that their specific, politically assigned, way of living and working, is the best life for them personally, and they never waver from the certainty of that commitment. They show their "civic" courage in this specific strength of character for resisting both threats and inducements. They are so firmly convinced of the truths in which they believe, concerning the goodness of the constitution under which they live, that their own "spirited parts" support their reasons' committed acceptance of these beliefs, with the additional motivational power of their spirited emotions and desires.

This system of beliefs, Socrates emphasizes, is, however, not the true virtue of courage. It is only, he says, "political" or "civic" courage. It is a certain quality of mind existing in the members of one class of the city, and that quality of mind in them constitutes the city's courage. Courage itself (courage without the qualification of "civic"), he says in *Republic* IV, he and his friends can discuss at some later time: just then, in the conversation of the *Republic*, their concern is, instead, with justice. And in fact, later, in *Republic* VI, Socrates returns to speak of the virtues, but this time specifically of the virtues of the philosopher-rulers. In doing so, he implicitly makes good on his suggestion that he and his friends might sometime discuss full or complete, true courage: as we will see, he tells us that it is possessed by the rulers.[72] In this same context he also once refers, disparagingly, to "popular" virtues, thus using the same term in reference to virtue that Plotinus has linked with "political" or "civic," when he labels the virtues at his own lowest level "popular and civic." In the earlier discussion, in book IV, Socrates has said that any ideally good city, in seeing to the happiness of its citizens, must not only be courageous (in the way I have discussed—through fixed

---

[72] See *Republic* VI, 500b–e. In this paragraph and the next I am summarizing and interpreting that very short passage. The reference to "popular" virtue comes at 500d; the term used is δημοτικὴ ἀρετή, the same one used in *Phaedo* 82a11–12, cited above. On this sort of virtue, see further below.

and fast beliefs of the auxiliaries), but also wise. (It has to be just and temperate too.) There, he identifies any truly ideal city's wisdom as devolving to it from the wisdom in the minds of the rulers. But, unlike his reference to courage, in discussing the city's wisdom in book IV, he enters no qualification of what the quality is in the rulers' souls that makes the city wise. It is not, in parallel with the true beliefs of the auxiliaries, a special case of wisdom ("political" or "civic" wisdom—something that makes the city "politically" wise). In fact, though Socrates does not make a point of saying this there, in book IV, it is actual, unqualified wisdom itself, the full human virtue, consisting in a final and complete knowledge of the whole system of Forms, and, especially, knowledge of that system as having at its apex the Form of the Good. (Socrates could not say that yet, in book IV, because the theory of Forms had not yet been introduced into his discussion, as it has been, with great celebration at the end of book V and in the early part of book VI.)

When Socrates comes back to discuss the virtues in the later passage, in book VI, he says that, through knowing the Forms in their full perfection and paradigmatic mutual organization and orderliness (i.e., through their wisdom), properly prepared philosophers will at once wish to imitate the Forms by maintaining a corresponding orderliness and proper organization within their own soul. Though Socrates does not pause to spell this out, he means that complete philosophers will bring about within themselves, through this finally acquired knowledge, an ordering of the three parts of their soul—reason, spirit, and appetite—in which they become just, courageous, and moderate, in accordance with the rough specifications provided at the end of book IV of what these virtues of internal order for an individual soul are.[73] Hence, these rulers will have full and true courage because, instead of mere true beliefs about goodness, such as the auxiliaries operate with, they will know the Good itself, the Form of the Good, and will do so in its relationships to all the other Forms, also similarly known in the same intellectual grasp. Their strength of character, in resisting all threats and all morally objectionable inducements—provided by their full knowledge of the Forms, and supported by the spirit within them, the ally of their knowledgeable reason—is, therefore, true courage. (This knowledge also gives them true justice and true moderation.)

This same knowledge, Socrates adds, will suffice for the rulers, in doing the work of ruling that political necessity has imposed upon them, and in thereby

---

[73] See *Republic* IV, 441c–442d.

achieving the final natural end of a city, the happiness of all the citizens, so far as their natural endowments make them capable of it. By "looking to" the Forms (in particular to that of the Good), the rulers will be able to work into the characters of other people (all the ones not rulers, that is, all those not qualified by knowledge of Forms for ruling)—both individually and as a populace, four virtues of a different form from the ones their knowledge allows them to shape within their own souls: these will be "popular" virtues, Socrates calls them.[74] Here he uses the same term as Plotinus found him using in the *Phaedo* passage I have discussed above: Plotinus finds in it another hint toward the identification of these popular virtues both with the "civic" virtues he finds hinted at in book IV's "civic courage," and with the debased shadow-drawings of virtue in the *Phaedo*. Socrates, however, says nothing further about these "popular" versions of justice, moderation, courage, and wisdom. In particular he says nothing about their similarities to, or differences from, the true virtues based on full knowledge of Forms, as first set out at the end of book IV. He alludes just this once to these "popular" virtues that the rulers will instill by education in all the citizens, of both lower classes. He drops them from further discussion.[75]

It is reasonable enough of Plotinus to align this passage of *Republic* VI (speaking of "popular" virtue) with those of *Republic* IV where the virtues of city and individual are explained, and where we find the reference, discussed above, to "civic" courage. When Socrates in *Republic* VI refers to "popular" virtues, it seems not unreasonable to think he intends these at least to include the "political" or "civic" courage that the auxiliaries exhibit as the principal quality of character that is needed for members of their class in the ideal city, so that they will perform well their specific political function—the courage that makes the whole city courageous. (But, as we have seen, in book IV Socrates does not speak at all of a parallel "civic" justice or moderation, and the wisdom he discusses there is definitely not a lesser version of the true wisdom he later attributes to the philosopher-rulers; it is precisely that true wisdom.) But Plotinus goes beyond any-

---

[74] Thus we see that, in the view of Socrates in the *Republic*, the true and full virtues of justice, moderation, courage, and wisdom (possessed by the philosopher-rulers) are virtues of practice, of engagement in practical affairs, both in their personal lives, and in their work as rulers. They are not, as are the true virtues of Plotinus's theory, even though it is partly grounded in what Socrates says about true virtue in *Republic* VI, purely intellectual virtues—virtues displayed solely in acts of pure intellection and contemplation of Forms. For Socrates, the wisdom of the rulers does, of course, despite being a virtue of practice, also include the sort of intellectual activities of contemplation that Plotinus assigns to his wisdom$_i$.

[75] For further discussion of the "popular" virtues of all the ordinary citizens of Socrates's kallipolis, see endnote 43.

thing Plato's text indicates, and in fact goes on to conflict with it.[76] Socrates in the *Republic* does seem to imply that the nonruling citizens of the ideal city will possess "popular" versions of the four virtues. But Plotinus sees Socrates as pointing to a second whole set of four virtues, denominated both "popular" and "civic" or "political," possessed individually by all the nonphilosophers in the ideal city, but also, in general, by decent people under whatever constitution they may live. Thus Plotinus finds in Plato not just a "civic" courage (one not quite identical, in fact, with the civic courage Socrates actually mentions, belonging exclusively to the auxiliaries), but also a "civic" justice, a "civic" moderation, and, it would seem, a "civic" wisdom ("practical" wisdom) as well—belonging to all the nonruling citizens.[77] Plato's text gives no warrant for this. Plato's texts do not warrant the attribution to him of a theory of "popular" virtues, possessed individually by all the nonruling citizens in some form, that are also to be denominated "civic" or "political" virtues.

But Plotinus goes even further. He also aligns these two *Republic* passages, from IV and VI, with the *Phaedo* passages discussed above. And in fact, as we have seen, at *Phaedo* 82a Socrates does speak of the so-called virtue of ordinary people, who have no inkling of the human intellect, or of philosophy and its value, as "civic or popular" "virtue"—thus using, in reference to some misguided shadow-drawing of virtue the same pair of adjectives that Plato uses separately in these separated *Republic* passages in speaking of less-than-full virtue.[78] By aligning the *Republic* passages with those in the *Phaedo*, Plotinus makes it possible to use the *Phaedo*'s emphasis that true virtue consists in purification of the soul (something nowhere alluded to, or so much as hinted at, in the *Republic*), to es-

---

[76] It is in conflict because it sees "political" courage as found not just in the auxiliaries, but in all the citizens except the rulers.

[77] It is noteworthy and significant that in Plotinus's own theory of the virtues all reference to Plato's ideal city drops out of the picture. He refers to these passages of *Republic* IV and VI simply in order to give support from "the ancients" for his own distinction between "greater" and lesser or "civic" virtues, as distinct internal conditions of psychic order for different parts of our souls—our intellects, on the one hand, and the "soul-image" on the other. Plotinus, with his lack of interest in any details of our this-worldly life, has no interest in following Plato's Socrates in the devotion and care with which Socrates places his account of the psychic virtues of individual persons within the context of their contribution to a common and shared social and political life—ideally, the life of the *Republic*'s "kallipolis."

[78] Socrates does not totally disparage these popularly conceived so-called virtues. He speaks at *Phaedo* 82 of how such people will, by having lived in their decently behaved, however fundamentally misguided, way, win a subsequently reincarnated life for their souls as gentle social animals—bees or wasps or ants—or else as the same sort of human person as they have just succeeded in being. They won't be reincarnated, as the gluttons and drunks will, as donkeys or similar animals—or, as the thieves and murderers or tyrants and temple robbers will, as wolves and hawks and kites.

tablish his own sharp distinction between "civic" virtue (which he explains on the basis of *Republic* IV's theory of virtue as inner harmony) as a lesser form of virtue than true virtue, while true virtue itself (closely involving knowledge of the Forms) consists in purification of the soul from any involvement with the body beyond, as Socrates puts it in the *Phaedo*, "what is absolutely necessary."[79] Plato's texts do not warrant this either.

The most important point to keep in mind is that for Socrates in the *Phaedo* the "popular and political virtue" he refers to there is not a deficient form of true virtue. It derives from a totally misguided approach to life. It involves making decisions about what to do on a debased calculus in which one pleasure (in fact an unworthy and illicit one) is avoided only in order to obtain greater pleasures (of a nonillicit kind), or to obtain nonillicit honors or other social goods in the future. This method of moral reasoning derives from the totally inadequate, indeed thoroughly mistaken, idea that the whole of what has any intrinsic value for a human being is found in bodily and social experience. These agents see their "virtuous" actions solely as wisely selected means to attain an overall pleasurable and respected life. They behave decently, but they do not do so as truly decent people. Truly decent people value virtue for its own sake and regard moral value as something beyond, and humanly more important than, pleasures and honors—even if they may not have a full understanding of what makes something morally right, or why it truly is morally right, or of why, precisely, moral value does have this higher standing. In the *Republic*, however, when Socrates refers to the "civic" virtue of courage, and when he refers by implication in book VI to the psychic justice of economic producers or of auxiliaries, he seems quite clearly not to be thinking of these as leading merely to decent *behavior*, but rather to include true decency. The auxiliaries whose "civic" courage he describes in book IV have a true belief about the goodness of the laws and the constitution of the ideal city, because of the order and orderliness that laws impose upon their own lives and upon the lives of those whom they manage and control as soldiers and policemen. Socrates could not describe these virtues as "shams," as he virtually does those of ordinary people who have only the nonvirtues that ordinary usage, as he perhaps hypercritically insists, calls virtues.

The result for Plotinus of his effort to ground his theories of the virtues in Platonic texts is an uneasy—in fact, as we will see, an ambivalent, or even, as I put it above, a schizophrenic—attitude to what he calls civic virtues. On the one

[79] *Phaedo* 67a4.

hand, he wishes to follow Socrates in the *Phaedo* and reserve this term for a way of leading one's life that no truly virtuous person would tolerate: these virtues are possessed only by ordinary people of no account at all, mere lovers of the body, even if they may behave decently enough. On the other hand, he clearly envisages virtues of engagement with our physical and social lives in connection with truly virtuous people's ordinary daily life, and their oversight of it—the life of the one who lives according to the second of the three levels I have distinguished for Plotinus above, the level of the purifying virtues of justice$_2$, wisdom$_2$, courage$_2$, and temperance$_2$, and, in general with the "higher" virtues, those of the intellect.[80] In turning now to say more about these crucially important intermediate virtues, we will be forced to sort out for Plotinus some issues concerning the relationship between these intermediate ones and the lesser, civic ones, that Plotinus seems not to have worked through properly for himself.[81]

The crucial point to bear in mind is that the civic virtues are, for Plotinus, virtues of what Plato (and Aristotle) call the nonrational desires of appetite and spirit. This follows from his characterization of these virtues as ones that result from "habits and exercises," as opposed to thought and reasoned learning.[82] Equivalently for Plotinus, they belong, if possessed at all, to a person's soul-image, not to their soul, properly speaking.[83] The purificatory or purifying virtues belong, by contrast, to one's intellect, one's capacity for thought about

[80] A good part of *Enn.* I 4, *On Happiness*, is devoted to discussing the way of life of the "virtuous person" (in Greek, the σπουδαῖος), because of course such a person is happy and lives completely happily. Beginning at chapter 4.25, and carrying through the last chapter, chapter 16, Plotinus describes such virtuous people's life in terms that make it clear that in engaging with the life of their soul-image and lower consciousness they are exercising virtues: see, e.g., the discussion of how they react to a friend's death (they might feel some grief, but only in the soul-image, without taking that up or identifying themselves with it, 4.30–36), or the description of their way of seeing to their body's needs, chapter 7, or of their sympathetic and helping relations with friends, 15.21–25. See section 6.5 below.

[81] At any rate, he had not done so even in writing *Enneads* I 4, one of the final nine treatises sent to Porphyry in the last two years of his life: the ambivalence I have referred to is very prominent in that treatise, as we will see in section 6.5.

[82] See *Enn.* I 1, 10.12–13. In endnote 44 I provide textual support for this inference.

[83] In the passage of *Enn.* I 1, 10 cited in the last note, Plotinus assigns the virtues that for him result from habituation to "the common" or "joint" thing, i.e., the living body joint with the soul-image. Confirmation that he thinks of practical wisdom as among these virtues comes in I 1, 12, where Plotinus tells us that what gets punished in our afterlife for sins we committed in the present one is "another form of soul" than our individual intellect, by which he means to refer to the soul-image. Whatever does get punished has, of course, to include the person's practical reason, in assenting to or deciding to do what unruly and bad appetites or emotions suggest to them to be desirable and good. In fact, that is what preeminently deserves punishment, if any punishment at all can be due. No one would think it reasonable to punish a badly behaved animal in its afterlife, if it had one: that is the equivalent of punishing people for their bad nonrational desires, leaving out of account their practical reason.

Forms. The purification these virtues provide is a process wherein we turn our souls, that is to say our intellects, gradually upward and away from the downward focus of attention that brings us, if we are not careful, into contact and active—collusive and zestful—cooperation with the soul-image and its embodied nonrational desires and feelings, and their representations of some physical things and experiences as actually good for you.[84] At the same time, purification involves also a purified way of turning our attention downward. As what I have just said implies, we must continue, while being purified (and so while progressively turning our soul's attention upward), in some way and to some extent, to focus our intellect's attention also downward. While being purified, and once fully purified, our intellects must continue to have concern for, and at least some sort of active cooperation—albeit a noncollusive one—with the needs of the body and of our social lives. Hence, even then, we must continue to work with and use the desires and feelings of the body and its soul-image. How then do the purifying virtues, wisdom$_2$-justice$_2$-moderation$_2$-courage$_2$ relate to the civic ones, wisdom$_3$-justice$_3$-moderation$_3$-courage$_3$, in bringing about a purified way of looking downward with one's intellect?

Clearly, Plotinus defines the civic virtues so as to make them belong to a soul (the soul-image) that is by its very nature turned toward the body and its needs, as well as toward the ordinary needs of any human being for social interaction and involvement in a common life with other people. Its desires are desires for bodily and other gratification, responses to bodily harms or perceived threats to the body, as well as desires and responses related to social standing and respect (or violations of it). Its virtues (if they truly are virtues, not shams) must consist in a proper and orderly way of, so to speak, having these desires and feelings "scheduled": the civic virtues schedule the arousal of these desires and feelings so that the body's true needs are seen to, and so that extraneous and unnecessary, or harmful, desires and feelings have either been trained out of the system, or are kept at low enough levels so that they are controllable, in the first instance, by other desires or feelings that have been trained in and have grown strong. Decent behavior, with decent motivations, is civic virtue's aim, and its whole concern. We should note that, as mentioned above, one of these civic virtues is what Plotinus calls "practical" as opposed to "theoretical" wisdom: φρόνησις vs. σοφία.

---

[84] The "intellectual" virtues, wisdom$_1$, justice$_1$, moderation$_1$, and courage$_1$, are ones we possess only when we may have completed a full purification and are no longer using our intellects in any way except to contemplate and know Forms. I described these above, at the beginning of this section, and will not discuss them further here. I return to them below, section 6.5.

This distinction makes good sense, from Plotinus's point of view, since the behavior we are talking about is entirely a matter of action, as opposed to contemplation or theorizing. Acts of pure thought are not in a strict and narrow sense actions at all, since actions at least typically result, and certainly result insofar as the civic virtues are concerned with them, at least in part, from one's particular nonrational states of desire and feeling: these are, or are among, the causes of actions. For example, when you are thirsty and take a drink, or when you are moved to assist someone in need, upon noticing their distress, the action you take is partly motivated by nonrational feelings and desires. On the other hand, actions will also often or usually, and always so where a (civically) virtuous agent is concerned, have among their causes an "assent" or "decision" by the person in favor of doing them. The action may be done partly from fear or irritation or an appetitive arousal for some gratification, but it will also be done from (and actually be in part caused by) an assent or decision the agent makes, distinct from the mere desire or feeling, to do what he or she then does. This is where practical wisdom for Plotinus comes in. Wisdom$_3$, practical wisdom, is the virtue that schedules the way we assent and decide for (or against), and in consequence do (or refrain from doing), an action.

But what within us, in our consciousness, is the source of these assents or decisions? According to Plotinus, it is a kind of reasoning power, one concerned with proposing and considering reasons for action, and for empirical evaluations and judgments, from a practical point of view, about current or future likely states of affairs. Reason, in all its forms and applications, on Platonist principles, derives from our intellects. We, or our intellects (our true selves), have the power to turn our attention upward, toward Forms, seeking to understand them in their full systematic interrelationship. But we (our intellects) can also attend downward, toward our bodies, and to the operations of our soul-image, in its concern for our embodied life as living beings. For Plotinus, the assents and decisions I have just mentioned result from our intellects' attention in looking downward, bringing to the animal-like functions (the nonrational desires and perceptions) of the soul-image the added feature of reasoning about action, and indeed more generally, empirical reasoning about current and expected future circumstances and events. This addition is part of the "illumination" given to the living body of human beings by reason's (i.e., intellect's) being lodged within it.

For Plotinus, the central issue for morality and virtue, at the level of the civic virtues, concerns the manner with which this downward attention of intellect is given to the body and to the experiences and operations of its image (the lower consciousness). (Practical) wisdom₃ (if, again, it is truly a virtue and no sham) results from this attention's being given in the right way. So long as we are alive at all (I mean, alive as individual animals in this world), we pretty well have to think in the empirical and action-oriented way I have described, much if not all the time we are awake. Not to do that would mean that we, our self-conscious intellectual selves, would abdicate our control, and allow our purely animal consciousness, and so our nonrational desires and feelings, to initiate all our bodily movements, unsupervised and unattended to. When we attend in the right way, in accordance with the principles of (practical) wisdom₃, we are employing our power of empirical, action-oriented reasoning, a power that belongs to our soul-image as illuminated by intellect. Hence, for Plotinus, practical wisdom₃, though the reasoning that it consists in derives from the intellect, is a quality belonging to the soul-image, and not to the soul (the intellect) itself. This civic virtue, too, then, along with temperance₃, courage₃, and justice₃, is a virtue of the soul-image—although, crucially, it is a virtue of the soul-image that results from the activity of the intellect *itself* in looking down, so as to bring about a proper way of one's soul-image's concerning oneself with one's embodied, physical, and social life.

What I have just said raises the questions of what the right way is for turning our attention (our selves' attention, our intellects') downward, and of how that way of attending downward relates to the more important matter of our selves', our intellects', upward attention to the Forms, and beyond them, to the ultimate origin of being, the One. To answer these questions, we need to turn now to Plotinus's account of the human good, human happiness.

6.5. Virtue and Happiness

In his essay *On Happiness*, *Enneads* I 4, Plotinus follows the ancient philosophical tradition, especially prominent in Aristotle, of regarding happiness (eudaimonia) as essentially not a state or condition of one's person or one's life, or any possession or combination of possessions, but an activity—in fact, the activity of "living well."[85] But which activity is the one in which we "live well" (i.e., in which we, our human persons, live well)? Plotinus takes it for granted that this is an activity "of virtue"—as again the whole prior tradition has maintained (with

---

[85] In Greek εὖ ζῆν. As we have seen in earlier chapters, in understanding happiness as an activity the Stoics follow Aristotle, and Aristotle follows hints in Plato and the Socrates of Plato's Socratic dialogues.

some exception or qualification needed where Epicurus and the Pyrrhonists are concerned, as we have seen). But activity of which virtue—that is, virtue at which of Plotinus's three levels? Activity of all of them? As we have seen, Plotinus has argued that we ourselves, the consciousnesses that we both *are*, and are aware of when we are conscious of ourselves, are, in reality, our intellects. Our lower consciousness is only a temporary offshoot of this basic one. So our activity of living, the living that belongs to us as intellects, and that we ourselves engage in, is an activity of intellectual thinking, directed at Forms. Hence, for us human beings, for the *persons* and consciousnesses that we are, living well must consist in the activity of intellectual thinking, thinking of Forms, when that is done with full attention, as well as through, and on the basis of, the intellectual virtues, the virtues$_1$, as described above.

Much of the rest of what "we" do (i.e., of what we do or experience that our consciousness is crucially involved in), including all the "practical" actions and activities of our daily lives as embodied living beings, and all our feelings and emotions, are not things that we, ourselves, the selves of which we are self-conscious, do. To be sure, there are virtues involved when all those other things are done in the ways that they ought to be, and are done well (and we must not neglect them, in considering Plotinus' theory of happiness). But these lowest, "lesser" virtues, and a person's active employment of them, cannot be any part of one's happiness. For Plotinus, these activities are not even, as they are for Aristotle, the agent's "secondary" happiness—where the "primary" part, or the essence, of their happiness is found in excellent and fine intellectual activities. On Plotinus's theory, human happiness, for those who manage to achieve it, to whatever degree they may do so, and for however long, consists exclusively of their activities of pure, fully attentive, absorbed, and concentrated, thinking of the natures of things. No involvement in ordinary human affairs, however right and good and virtuous that might be, is itself a "happy" activity, to any degree or in any way. Our human happiness consists entirely in an activity in which we take ourselves away from all such involvement. I will return to this fact later, and consider some of its more salient consequences for the conduct of one's life.

For Plotinus, intellectual thinking about the natures of Forms, in their systematic differentiation and unity, is the activity of real or true or full living. It is the life of our soul—the only real thing in us, the being that we have and are. In this real life, if we can achieve it, but only in it, are we truly "made like" to god. The god that we are made like, according to Plotinus, is, in the first instance, Intellect (the Substance), since our intellect, or Soul in us, itself, in thinking Forms with the virtues₁, is engaging in the activity that Intellect itself is.[86] This is true even though Soul thinks in a slightly derivative and "reflected" or "imitating" sort of way (as explained above): that is, with full articulation of the Forms in their readiness to be embodied in the physical world. We are made like this god, Intellect, by very closely imitating the very activity that that god not only does, but is. That god is itself an "overflowing" of being and goodness from the One, or First god, so that its own activity is one of imitating the One. This activity of Intellect is essentially one of "returning" to and becoming, in some strange way, the One itself. So we are also, in our own activity of excellent pure thinking, becoming that First and highest god, in that strange way.

One point of detail in Plotinus's theory of the activity of the virtues₁ is especially worth noting. With other human activities, one can distinguish and describe the activity itself, while leaving aside any consideration of whether it was done well or badly, that is, was a good or bad instance of its kind. One can walk across a room, say, or saw a tree down, or read or write something, or again, play a game, or engage in other actions and activities in which one relates oneself to other people—and one can do all these things either well or badly. Whether it is a good or a bad instance of its kind, what one does remains an activity of some specific kind that in itself is a neutral thing.[87] Likewise, both morally good or acceptable, and bad and vicious acts, say, of killing a human being, are acts that belong to the kind, killing a human being; moral or other evaluations of a particular act, on some occasion or in some circumstance, is evaluation, whether favorable or unfavorable, of acts of some same basic kind. With pure acts of thinking and understanding Forms, however, Plotinus argues, this distinction does not apply. You cannot be actually thinking of Forms, on some occasion well or on others badly. Either you are understanding them, and then you are achieving your natural good in doing so, or you just aren't engaging in any activity at all that can correctly be described as understanding Forms. You may be *trying* to think of Forms and understand them, but you haven't got there yet. Whatever it may be that you are doing is simply not the same kind of thing as *actually* thinking Forms while *actually* grasping them. That is a sui generis kind of thing to do. This follows, for Plotinus, from the fact that this activity of ours is the activity in which Soul (what we ourselves truly are) and Intellect (in their different, but essentially related ways) actually consist. It is not some activity of some generic

---

[86] See *Enn.* I 4, 6 and I 2, 1.

[87] Some kinds, say doing a murder, are not neutral in this way; but there is nonetheless, in such cases, a neutral kind to which one might assign it: killing a human being.

kind, extremely well executed, and thereby made to be a good thing. Rather, it is an activity that in itself, as the very activity that it is, is the very essence of goodness. As Plotinus puts it, happy persons *are* the good that they *have*: they are this activity that they engage in, an activity that is good in itself, good simply as what it is as an activity. It is not at all good as having something added to an activity that stood in need of some addition, in order to make it perfect of its kind.[88] Its very kind of thing is a good for anyone who engages in it.

Happy persons, then, for Plotinus, are happy, and live happily, entirely through having acquired, and through using, their "intellectual" virtues, in active contemplation of Forms. In fact, Plotinus maintains, once a person has reached that state of final human perfection, they can and will engage in that activity at every moment thereafter. They will be doing this no matter what else they are doing at the same time: in this respect they will be multitasking at every moment. They will be actively and deeply contemplating the complete system constituting the natures of things, even if they are asleep, or have gone mad and cannot think straight, so far as ordinary consecutive attention to local matters of fact and reasonable inferences from them might go. Such deranged conditions, or being asleep, only imply that one may be unconscious of oneself as engaging in the activity of contemplating Forms. This activity is, of course, essentially an exercise of consciousness: in engaging in it, one is necessarily conscious of the Forms, in their full, complex reality. But it is only one's personal self-consciousness, consciousness of oneself as conscious and active, that sleep or such derangement affects. Those conditions do not, and could not possibly, Plotinus argues, affect one's power of contemplation itself, once it is fully achieved. That power remains intact and active under all conditions, once one has come to possess and use the virtues₁ in the first place, through the concentrated force of one's innate power to think Forms, and through turning your full attention upward to them.[89] You can be active with them, and you might therefore be living happily, even if you were totally unconscious of your body and of your empirical surroundings through an "out-of-body" experience of willed self-absorption into Soul, and Intellect. You might even in some mystical way experience self-absorption into the One itself—the ultimate reality, the source of both Soul and Intellect.[90]

[88] *Enn.* I 4, 4.18–19, 3.28–30; also, 9.17–25.
[89] See *Enn.* I 4, 9–10.
[90] Porphyry reports that, while he was working with Plotinus in Rome, Plotinus himself achieved this goal on four occasions. See *Life* 23.

Nonetheless, so long as one is alive as an individual at all—and this applies to happy persons and to their activity of contemplation as much as to any other human being—one will only occasionally have any such act of thinking as the sole object of one's consciousness. All of us are aware, most of the time that we are awake, of our bodies and our empirical surroundings. We are necessarily occupied in myriad varying ways, most of the time, in conducting our ordinary lives: eating, drinking, playing, going to entertainments, raising our children, helping various of our fellow citizens in various ways, doing our shopping, perhaps teaching philosophy. If we do these things well, then, as the Stoics describe it, we do all our daily duties, in response to the varying circumstances of daily life. Such will be the daily life of the happy person. Happy persons will only occasionally, and presumably for only relatively short periods of time, be conscious of their contemplative thinking and of nothing else. How then—with what attitudes and thoughts—does a happy and virtuous person go about leading their daily life? Here is where the other levels of virtue, and their place in the happy person's life, come in. As I have said, activities of the lower levels of virtue are no part of the happiness of the happy life, but they are nonetheless good things, at their levels, and happy persons will necessarily be concerned to live all of their life, in all its aspects, as well as is humanly possible. They will acquire the appropriate additional virtues and approach their bodily and social needs with the appropriate virtuous ways of engagement with the issues that come up in connection with daily events and their effects on those needs.[91]

As I mentioned above, Plotinus's key idea is that the correct, and virtuous, way of approaching daily life—the part of our lives in which we turn our attention as intellects downward, to the physical world—is in the spirit of caring for our bodies and their proper place and role in the natural world, including the social world of other embodied human beings, but caring for them as something other than ourselves. As Plotinus puts it, when people have passed over into identity with Intellect, through possessing and exercising the true and final virtues of a human being, the "intellectual" ones, then their bodies are things that they are merely "surrounded by" or that they "wear." They have them as their "neighbors," as it were, as other persons they live with—but they are decidedly

[91] In what follows I first describe in broad strokes the virtues of the happy person that are relevant to daily life and social life. I leave for later questions about how to situate these on Plotinus's triple scale of virtues. They are distinct from the "intellectual" virtues, of course. But questions remain as to how they relate to the "civic" and the "purifying" virtues outlined in the preceding section.

not in any way *them*.[92] The key idea here, as I have emphasized already more than once, is that we should exercise this responsibility of "caring for" this alien thing without compromising our status as separate and distinct entities, that is, as intellects. We must not enter into the life of the body, and into our social and physical needs and relationships, by treating the desires and emotions that, at the level of the compound of soul-image and body, drive that life as, even partly, belonging to us. As Plotinus puts it, happy persons do not will to be engaged in that life (they do not think it is a good thing for them to have those feelings, nor do they think that satisfying or relieving them is in any way good for them). They accept the bodily and social life, gladly enough, indeed with serenity, but only as something they have to deal with so long as they remain physically alive and have charge over the animated life of their living bodies. When, as might happen even to a truly virtuous and happy person, one's embodied consciousness becomes affected by hunger, or bodily pain, or feelings of anticipation or hope, or of irritation and annoyance, one must not add to the turmoil or excitation of these feelings by, as Plotinus once puts it, having one's intellect, in its supervisory care of, and attention to, bodily and social requirements, itself "get riled up along with them."[93]

In part, and up to a point, Plotinus is simply agreeing with the Stoics here—and self-consciously so. He is also disagreeing with Aristotle, also self-consciously. (In fact, though he would not wish to acknowledge this, in disagreeing with Aristotle, Plotinus is disagreeing with Plato too, in dialogues such as the *Republic*.) As Porphyry rightly says, Plotinus's "writings are full of concealed Stoic and Peripatetic doctrines," adopted and developed in his own Platonist way; and Plotinus often, more overtly, but often still not with any clear acknowledgment of the fact, develops his own doctrines in close and attentive criticism of these two predecessors' views. In fact, in his theories of the virtues and happiness, and their interconnections, as in other parts of his work, Plotinus is the self-conscious inheritor of the whole prior tradition of Greek philosophy, not just of Plato. It will put Plotinus's view of the happy life in illuminating perspective if we pause to consider in some detail these agreements and disagreements with the Stoics and with Aristotle.

Like the Stoics, Plotinus holds that, given the nature and essence of human beings, the human good can consist only in acts of thinking (ones in which vir-

---

[92] See, e.g., *Enn.* I 4, 4.13–17; for the image of neighbors or housemates see I 2, 5.21–31.
[93] *Enn.* I 2, 5.13.

tue is exercised): no bodily event or experience, and no outward event, or circumstance or achievement, in the physical world or its social component can possibly be either good or bad for a person at all. (Aristotle and Plato, of course, count as goods or bads, in addition to virtuous actions, favorable or unfavorable bodily states and external conditions and circumstances: these all contribute to the good or bad, the happiness or unhappiness, in a human life.) And, again like the Stoics, Plotinus regards as an unmitigated bad our mind's (our reasoning power's) "getting riled up," to whatever degree and in whatever circumstances that might occur. To do so would be to experience what the Stoics define as a "passion," or emotional feeling or desire. Instead, both for Stoics and for Plotinus, any action one might rightly undertake—for example, to eat some food, or to take steps to remove some bodily pain, or again to retaliate against someone who has done something morally offensive or physically harmful to you—should be done for some good reason, some reason other than the felt need to vent, or to extinguish, some disturbed state of one's consciousness. On the other hand, the Stoics, as we have seen in chapter 4, have a complete system of ideas concerning what is natural for human beings to do both in terms of general rules and in various circumstances: these are actions "according to nature," that are to be undertaken because these are the ones that Zeus wants us to do, in furtherance of his plans for the ongoing life of the whole cosmos. We are to undertake them as part of our own efforts to function well as his "assistants." In each case, the reason for action, when it is in fact correct to do the given act of eating or whatever it might be, will derive from this system of ideas. The desire to do the act will be in fact a decision made for those reasons. We will do it for those reasons and for them alone, and altogether without any agitation of feeling, whether positive and uplifting, or negative and distressing. Though Plotinus agrees that the happy person never experiences, or acts with, agitated feelings, his conception of reason as transcending the physical world and as having higher functions than to create and sustain it, entails a different relationship of ourselves, and our actions, to god's activities.

Plotinus departs from the Stoics in one other important respect. In Stoic theory our consciousness, as agents, is thoroughly "rational": all desires and even all "impulsive impressions" are states of our power of reasoning; no desires, or feelings oriented to action, are nonrational (as those of young human beings and all other animals' are). Every adult human desire contains conceptual characterizations of its object and is based on our acceptance, maybe wholly implicit, of certain reasons that we see as adequate for feeling it. Plotinus, by contrast, as we have seen, accepts the Aristotelian and Platonic theory of the psychology of human action. According to this conception we do have "rational" desires that, as for the Stoics, are decisions to do something. But we also have nonrational ones that are not at all, as the corresponding states of feeling are for Stoics, agitations in or of our reasoning power itself.[94] For Plotinus, these desires and emotional feelings belong not to the intellect (reason), but to the soul-image that animates the body. So he can speak of these desires and feelings as belonging to the body (i.e., the living body), not to the soul (the intellect or reason)—that is, not to the true "us."[95] Nonetheless, they belong to our unitary consciousness, and in that less strict sense they do belong to us: in Plotinus's terminology, they too are "ours."

Aristotle, as we saw in chapter 3, thinks of moral virtue as consisting in certain scheduling conditions into which these types of desire and feeling can be brought. These are achieved by good upbringing leading to assiduous control over these desires by our reasoning power. This control is itself achieved through attentive practice and "persuasion" on our part, even after reaching adulthood. Through this practice and self-persuasion we come not, or no longer, to desire bad kinds of gratification, or other gratification more strongly than is proper. (Plato's view in the *Republic* does not differ in these respects.) We possess each and all of the many Aristotelian moral virtues when we feel these desires, and in fact act upon them, in accordance with our practical reason's judgment that it is appropriate and fitting to feel and, other things being equal, to act upon them. The properly "measured" and "intermediate," virtuous desires for food or drink or sex, or for any other physical or social good, are ones that we have come to feel under our reason's control and direction, and virtue also entails our not feeling them when they are inappropriate, or in degrees or amounts that overdo or underdo what is (correctly) judged to be correct by our rational evaluations of good and bad and right and wrong.

Plotinus, however, makes a much sharper separation than Aristotle does between the "lower" part of the soul (where Aristotle's nonrational desires are located) and its "higher" one of reason (i.e., in Plotinian terms, the separation between the soul-image and the soul proper). In doing so, he establishes a momentous psychological distance, in overall effect quite new to Greek philoso-

---

[94] So, as we saw, Plotinus's ban on "getting riled up" is a ban on agitated states of reason—however exactly agitated states of the intellect are to be conceived.

[95] Plotinus even speaks of the body as having "opinions," such as for example the opinion that the pleasures of eating or sex are good for oneself, good to have. See, e.g., *Enn.* I 2, 3.11–14.

phy, between us, if we are truly virtuous, and any and all such feelings. For Plotinus, as for Stoics, a truly virtuous, happy person never acts except out of a reasoned decision to do whatever it may be: the Plotinian virtuous agent never acts at all, even in any small or contributory part, out of the sorts of properly conditioned and scheduled rise and fall of feelings that for Aristotle (and Plato) are integral elements in each and every truly and fully virtuous action. However much these feelings and desires are felt in our unitary consciousness and in that sense are ours, they are nonetheless alien to the true us, our intellects. *We* do not feel them, and if we are virtuous we by all means do not adopt or "share" them. To do so would involve us in sharing also the evaluations of the pleasures or satisfactions that they can lead to, which, in feeling these desires, the animated body itself endorses: we would think them good for us. In fact, Plotinus is quite skeptical of the ambitious Aristotelian idea that it belongs to human nature to be able,[96] even in the case of a completely perfect specimen human being, to "master" these nonrational desires and feelings by bringing them into the (as he sees it) very optimistically ideal Aristotelian situation of never feeling too strong or too weak, or otherwise inappropriate, nonrational desires.[97] The living body, to which these belong, is simply too independent from our control and too essentially unruly for that to be possible. Hence, for Plotinus, while the virtuous, happy person will not feel, even in their lower consciousness, extremes of bodily and social desire, or other extremely unruly ones, he does not require the complete subordination of these to the "dictates of reason," as Plato and Aristotle do. On Plotinus's analysis, unruly states, of less than extreme kinds, may be caused, simply and inevitably, by the conditions of the body that act on that consciousness—no matter how truly and fully virtuous a person might be.

The fundamental point of the virtue of the happy person for Plotinus, in this regard, is not (as with Aristotle and Plato) to have and act on these desires when they are correctly and perfectly disciplined, alongside and in conjunction with reason-based decisions. Rather, the point is not to associate oneself in action with nonrational desires and feelings, at all. If a virtuous, happy person is hungry (I mean, if in their living body they have a nonrational appetitive feeling, driving toward eating and the pleasure to be gotten from it) they will take food because, as they think this hunger shows, their body needs replenishment; or if they act to alleviate a pain, it will be because (as they think) the pain indicates something

---

[96] It is also a Platonic one, though Plotinus does not, and would not, acknowledge that.
[97] See *Enn.* I 4, 4.34–36, 5.16–21.

going wrong in the body that might threaten its continued ability to function as a living organism. And the same goes for more complex social decisions: when to retaliate, when to go to someone's aid, when to take exercise or relax in the garden. As I said above, fully virtuous agents see themselves (their intellect or reason) as having charge of the living bodily thing that it accompanies (and that it illuminates with the lower consciousness). They, their pure reason, duly and dutifully see to this thing's varied needs in keeping it alive and well functioning, both physically and socially. But they decidedly do not "mix" with the body by feeling these desires as desires of their selves, and adopting them and (as Plotinus puts it) their body's ideas about values into the psychological basis of their action.

It is worth noting that Plotinus says extremely little about either substantive general principles or any detailed directives for action that reason may give us in this connection. Unlike the Stoics, with their elaborate, detailed theories of what is "according to nature," and why it does accord with nature to think those specific actions and attitudes are "appropriate," and unlike Aristotle with his lengthy and subtle discussions of the principles of evaluation a virtuous person will use in assessing which among conflicting values, or legitimate interests for human life, to favor in given recurrent types of situation, Plotinus just leaves the whole matter at a bare and abstract level: reason sees itself as being charged with keeping the living body and its social relationships healthy. As for what that may entail, he says virtually nothing beyond platitudes.[98] There is a reason for this. Unlike both the Stoics and Aristotle, for whom attention to these matters of daily and wider social life is the very essence of human living, for Plotinus human living lies starkly and decisively elsewhere: in contemplating the whole system of Forms. Plotinian virtuous and happy persons do indeed occupy themselves with daily and social concerns, but they do so without finding any inherent satisfaction or self-fulfillment in doing so. In this respect even Aristotle, who shares the Platonist high evaluation of pure theoretical thinking and knowing, retains the idea that human beings as such belong to this world, the physical world. For him, since there are no Forms existing as some true reality accessible only through

---

[98] For example, he reasonably says (*Enn.* I 4, 15.21–25) that on his theory virtuous, happy persons will not be unfriendly or unsympathetic types, and will furthermore "render to their friends all that they render to themselves" (i.e., they will actively tend to the needs of a friend's living body in just the way and in the same spirit as they tend to their own body's needs), even while being focused in their life on their own intellectual activity. Part of taking care of one's living body, though Plotinus does not pause to spell this out at all, is to tend properly to its social context, and this sort of attention to the needs of others is part of that.

concentrated, purely intellectual activity, the exercise of both the practical and the intellectual virtues fulfills human nature, and both are required for a completely happy life. Human nature is something belonging to this world and human beings have no other substantial place to be. (Even if for Aristotle we do "assimilate" ourselves to god by intellectually virtuous pure thought, we cannot ever *become* such thought, "residing" where it is, off in an intellectual realm of pure form.) For Plotinus, by contrast, daily life and social life are of very little moment. They hold little interest. What does interest him about daily life is the idea of purification, in which one learns and sustains a complete lack of personal investment in what goes on in one's ordinary, this-worldly, life. Platitudes suffice, for Plotinus, for describing the soul's caring concern for the living body that it merely accompanies or is surrounded by, because his thoughts, like the thoughts of his truly virtuous and happy person, are elsewhere—"above."

The fundamental point of moral and social virtue in the happy life for Plotinus, then, is indeed not to "mix" one's true self with the animated body and its life. But there is more to moral and social virtue for him than that—even if, as I have said, Plotinus has no interest in either general principles or details of just which actions will be favored or avoided by the happy person. The "more" I am speaking of concerns the virtuous person's attitudes to the sorts of things our living bodies themselves, as he puts it, want, and the strategies happy persons will adopt in dealing with the living body's desires and emotions. This has two aspects. On the one hand, Plotinus says that the happy person will actually despise all the bodily and social so-called goods (which as we have seen are strictly speaking no goods at all on Plotinus's stoicized ethical theory): health, freedom from pain, all other such "goods." The happy person thinks we should seek these only as what can reasonably be called "necessities," in that if we lack them and find ourselves instead faced with their opposites, we are in danger of ourselves becoming distressed. Experiencing these opposites tends to tempt us to fall back into the common way people have of adopting the desires of the body as desires of their own.[99] The happy person seeks and accepts these "goods" as necessary, given our actual embodiment, in order to enable us with serenity and concentration to engage in the activities of pure thought in which our happiness consists. Indeed, we would rather not need to avoid their opposites, and when we do possess these "goods" we nonetheless do not will to have them and to enjoy their use. We *will* only to engage in those activities of thought, and in fact we prefer not to

---

[99] See *Enn.* I 4, 6.24–32.

have these mere necessities along with the latter true goods. We would much rather have the true good entirely on its own.[100] Similarly, a happy person considers death as better than life with the body—and so, he or she can hardly regard the death of a friend or family member with anything but total equanimity.[101]

The other aspect of social and moral virtue that is important for the happy life concerns the discipline that happy persons will try to impose on the desires belonging to their soul-image. If one's concern, as the Plotinian happy person's is, is to purify oneself—one's intellect—from all association or "mixture" with the living body's desires, one must certainly, first of all, do what one can to minimize their occurrence. When our unified consciousness is affected by appetitive or spirited desires of any sort, that experience does not merely give one (i.e., one's power of thought and decision) some prima facie reason to decide in favor of doing what will satisfy them. It also, as we have seen, puts pressure on our reason, as it looks down and concerns itself with the agitation in the desires and with the needs of the living body that they connote. It invites, and even seduces, reason to adopt as our own those desires—after all, this is a unitary consciousness that is experiencing them—and, along with the desires, to adopt the evaluative opinions of the living body contained in them. To be sure, part of the effect of the moral and social virtues is a strong power of resistance, lodged in our reasoning power, against such desires as might arise that it holds are contrary to correct reason to satisfy, either in general or in the given circumstances. Plotinus emphasizes this fact. And Plotinus does think that a happy person might continue to experience bad appetitive or spirited desires (I mean, ones that it is wrong to satisfy)—this is part or a consequence of his skepticism concerning Aristotle's and Plato's ideal of getting the lower parts of the soul so exquisitely trained that, in the virtuous person's case, nothing but correct nonrational desires would be experienced. So there is some important use for such strength of resistance.

However, even if that Aristotelianly near-ideal situation obtained, one would still face serious moral danger, in the very fact that one continued to experience at all appetitive and spirited impulses (even apparently innocuous ones). One would need to keep exercising special care so as not to be sucked into regarding those desires as one's own. As a general rule, it would simply be better not to experience them at all, leaving it to the intellect, in its reasoned concern for the living body, to see to its needs through the soul-image's practical reason, all on its

---

[100] *Enn.* I 4, 7.1–10.
[101] *Enn.* I 4, 7.22–26.

own. Hence Plotinus emphasizes that, in being purified, the happy person's soul will "get rid of feelings of spirit as completely as possible, altogether if it can, but if it cannot, at least it does not get riled up along with them."[102] Any remaining spirited desires will be "small and weak." Likewise, Plotinus reasonably says that the happy, in being purified, will have rid themselves, pretty much, of all fear: what could one's reason have to fear? Plotinus grants that, perhaps, a fear "that does not involve any decision" (a decision to be afraid—because one thinks something bad is looming) might pop up in an unguarded moment (perhaps, you look up from your thoughts as you are walking home and suddenly see a truck bearing down on you), but quickly the happy person will see the situation aright, as one not calling for fear at all (merely, presumably, for immediate avoidance behavior), and will promptly and easily calm down the nonrational part that reacted in this way to the sudden vision.[103]

Appetite is apparently a more difficult customer than spirit. Our living bodies seem simply ineradicably given to experiencing appetitive desires for food and for the pleasures of eating, and many other such gratifications, whenever deprived to any significant degree of what they need. Sex, for example. Here, Plotinus claims only that the happy person will have no appetitive desires for anything actually bad: he thinks the soul-image of the virtuous and happy person may retain normal and natural desires for food, drink, and I suppose sex too. Even so, a happy person's soul proper, their intellect, will not itself have such desires. Nor will the practical reason attached to the soul-image do so. It will generate appropriate decisions as to what to do, but it will not cause in itself any inflated feelings of desire: or, if, presumably while still in the gradual process of being purified, it may come to feel desires on its own, these will be natural responses to very salient and obvious forms of needed gratification.[104] Even if happy persons may feel grief, in their nonrational feelings, when a close friend dies, they, their intellect, will not share in these feelings, or feel any grief of their intellect's own.[105] In all these cases—spirited impulses, fear, appetitive desires, including grief at the death of our friends—and other related ones, the virtuous person's aim is to make the nonrational, soul-image parts of their consciousness as pure as they are capable of being made. They will give only "slight shocks," eas-

---

[102] *Enn.* I 2, 5.11–16. (In lines 15–16 I am accepting a textual transposition and emendation offered by Kalligas.)

[103] *Enn.* I 4, 15.16–21.

[104] *Enn.* I 2, 5.17–21.

[105] See *Enn.* I 4, 4.34–36.

ily allayed by the nearby, neighborly, presence of the well-developed intellect of the virtuous person. For the most part they will simply keep quiet, posing no possible disturbance to the serenity of the soul, and to its governance even over our daily and social lives. That quietude is the nonrational parts' own purified condition, corresponding to the purified condition of the soul proper. Happy persons make this quietude their aim as regards the nonrational parts, because of their wish to avoid so far as possible all moral dangers potentially posed by the nonrational parts, even when those are purged of all bad and seriously inappropriate desires. As I have said, the cardinal point for moral and social virtue on Plotinus's theory is that our souls proper must not adopt as our own any impulses at all that might arise in the lower soul.

So far, in discussing Plotinus's theory of the moral and social virtues as possessed by the happy person I have left aside questions concerning how these fit into Plotinus's scheme of the three levels of virtue.[106] Are these "civic" virtues—justice$_3$, (practical) wisdom$_3$, moderation$_3$, and courage$_3$—or "purifying" ones, virtues$_2$? Or do they involve both in some way? Before turning now to consider these questions it will prove worthwhile if we reiterate and expand upon what I have said about Plotinus's departures from the Aristotelian (and Platonic) theory of these virtues, and about his adaptation of them, so as to accommodate elements of the Stoic theory that he found attractive and persuasive.

With his theory of our intellects as our true selves, Plotinus found very appealing the Stoic theory of adult human agency as through and through an affair of reason. For him, as for the Stoics, if not every human action, then certainly every fully virtuous one, finds its motivating psychological impulse in, and solely in, a reason-based assent to some impressions concerning what has some value for us. If we are our intellects, then if we act, it ought to be solely from some state of mind or impulse arising there, in our reasoning power: we assent to an impression, and act on the decision that that assent constitutes. And as in Stoic theory,

---

[106] In the later chapters of *On Happiness*, in describing the way of life of the happy person, beginning in chapter 5, Plotinus speaks constantly of the person it describes simply as a σπουδαῖος, a virtuous person, without further specification in terms of particular virtues. I have followed Plotinus's practice in my report and discussion of this part of the treatise in the preceding paragraphs: I have reported various aspects of the way of life of a virtuous and happy person, according to what Plotinus says in these chapters, without going into such details. In what follows, I address the question of how to add the needed specification of this person's virtuousness, in terms of the particular virtues provided in Plotinus's scheme of three sets of four specific virtues (some sort or other of practical wisdom, courage, moderation, and justice at each of the three levels), as described in the previous section.

Plotinus recognizes that many human beings (not of course the virtuous ones), in assenting and deciding, and so also in actions, do so with excessive enthusiasm. They generate agitated or riled up feelings in their very intellects, because of false and misguided estimates of the nature and character of the values for oneself that are pursued and, one hopes, achieved in the given action. On the other hand, as a Platonist, Plotinus also accepted the tripartite division of the soul adopted in Plato's *Republic* and Aristotle's *Ethics*. In addition to our soul proper we also possess a soul-image, where additional impulses toward action arise in our consciousness (appetites and spirited, emotion-laden desires). (This the Stoics denied, as we have seen in chapter 4.)

This leads Plotinus to recognize, or to postulate, what amounts to two kinds of emotions and appetites—two kinds of feelings of uplift or depression, of positively or negatively disturbed, agitated mental states. On the one hand, as with the Stoics, there exist in many human consciousnesses reason-based emotional feelings—ones belonging to their reasoning and decision-making power, involving and deriving from a decision to feel that way. These people estimate the positive or negative values being pursued or avoided in their actions as ones properly to be regarded as good or bad for oneself, so that it seems right and appropriate to them to feel in those agitated, emotional ways. On Plotinus's theory, as on the Stoic, the truly virtuous person (the one who is happy and lives happily) never experiences any of these emotions, to any degree and extent. But what about the other, the nonreasoned, nondecided, purely nonrational, emotions—the desires and feelings of the Platonic and Aristotelian tripartite moral psychology's nonrational parts? As we have just seen, Plotinus holds that the ideal of virtue is to eliminate or reduce even all these feelings as far as, in one's individual case, one can manage. The hallmark, or anyhow the ideal, of the happy person's virtue is quietude in this part of one's consciousness. For Plotinus, a truly virtuous and so happy person (i.e., intellect) must, of course, not, in its oversight of the living being's life, "mix," in their actions, with the living body and its desires or emotions, by endorsing them as belonging to oneself and enlisting them as coagents of the action also decided on by practical reason and endorsed by intellect. Such an agent will also, from the outset, experience few and weak such motivations—no spirited desires, no fear, few and weak appetites.

Here we see Plotinus's most striking departure from the Aristotelian (and Platonic) theory of the virtues. Aristotelian virtuous agents do rationally endorse their disciplined and duly measured appetites and spirited impulses, and accept them as their own.[107] Most of the time when they act virtuously, part of what is virtuous about their action is that it is done out of—motivated by—appetitive and/or spirited impulses. (Actions are also, as a separate matter, decided on and done from the decision.) From the Aristotelian point of view it would be a moral failure both not to feel significantly strong appetitive enthusiasm for one's food and not to act, in eating, out of a felt motivation for the food as pleasant and appetitively satisfying. Of course, one ought also to act (perhaps only implicitly) from a decision in which such action is endorsed and supported as appropriate and good. For Plotinus, however, this idea is anathema—it is *morally* anathematic. The happy person's virtuous pursuit of food must not involve endorsement and "mixing" with appetitive desires of the living body. The hallmark of the happy person's moral virtue for Plotinus is to will not to act from appetite, at all, ever. A pure, unemotional, Stoic-style act of reasoned assent is to be the sole psychological cause involved in the production of any happy person's virtuous action. For Plotinus, a person with the character of an Aristotelian virtuous agent is certainly not really virtuous at all, in the way that his own happy person is. To be really happy, by Plotinus's lights, requires complete disengagement in one's actions from appetites and spirited feelings (to the small or much reduced extent that appetites and spirited feelings are any longer even experienced by the Plotinian happy person).

How, then, does Plotinus use his categories of civic versus purifying virtues in accounting for these attitudes of the happy person toward daily life and toward human social relationships? Or, perhaps rather, how might he use them, if he properly attended to this question? This is of course a rather scholastic issue, concerning as it does technical details of Plotinus's philosophical system. The overall conception, as set out in the preceding discussion, gives us what we need for our narrower purposes—enough so as to understand and explore the place of philosophy itself in the happy life according to Plotinus's view. Moreover, as it seems, Plotinus's writings do not give us adequately determinate answers to the scholastic questions we would need to pursue if we wanted to find a fully worked out Plotinian account.[108] However, I will conclude this section with a proposal for how Plotinus's theories of the civic and the purifying virtues can be seen as

---

[107] For Aristotle, all adult appetites and spirited desires or emotions, including those of the virtuous, are voluntary (even if passively felt) (they are "up to us") both to experience and to act upon. See *NE* III 1, 1109a30–31, and III 5.

[108] Certainly, he does not give us such an account anywhere in the treatises of *Ennead* I.

the background needed for understanding happy persons' attitudes to their embodied life.

The purifying virtues, as we have seen, consist in the power of our intellect, even while being aware of and attending appropriately to the life of the living body, not to "share its experiences or have the same opinions as it," but rather to keep itself focused on its own proper work of pure thinking and understanding the natures of things.[109] The soul we speak of here includes both that of the happy person, possessed of the intellectual virtues, and a soul that may still be in the course of being purified, and so may not yet have achieved the final condition of full knowledge of the whole system of Forms. Clearly, then, the purifying virtues are required for, and are prominently displayed in, the happy person's moral and social virtues as described above: happy persons do resolutely refuse to "share" their living body's feelings. But, formally speaking, they concern the power of the virtuous intellect to keep away, as it does look to the life of the living body, and not to involve itself in that life by adopting any of its functions as one's own. As described by Plotinus, these virtues do not provide directives for, or active involvement in decision making as to, actions that are to be taken in overseeing the needs of the living body. It seems clear that, in some way, the latter, more positive, activity of the virtuous intellect must come under the general umbrella of Plotinus's civic virtues, including prominently practical wisdom$_3$. It is through practical wisdom$_3$, in union with the other virtues$_3$, that virtuous decisions and actions are produced. Here however we run into the difficulty that Plotinus seems, without acknowledging it, to work with a double conception of civic virtue. In one way, the practices described earlier in this section, of disciplining the living body so that one comes to experience no or only weak appetitive and spirited desires and emotions, and so that one comes to engage in daily activities of eating, drinking, relaxing, and so on, and perform one's other moral and social duties, in a spirit of complete personal disengagement, are indeed, for Plotinus, exercises of what one can only regard as some sort of civic virtues. These activities plainly derive from the condition of justice$_3$ as Plotinus describes it, in which reason, spirit, and appetite all "do their own proper work where ruling and being ruled are concerned."[110]

On the other hand, as I remarked above, Plotinus also sometimes speaks in very derogatory terms of the civic virtues as ones that a happy, truly virtuous

[109] See *Enn.* I 2, 3.13–19.
[110] See *Enn.* I 2, 1.20–21.

person would in fact disavow.[111] They will "altogether not live the life of the good person which civic virtue deems worthy. The happy person will leave that behind and choose another, the life of the gods."[112] And, in the peroration to *On Happiness* Plotinus distances his virtuous and happy person from a merely decent person, "a mixture of good and bad, living a life that is also a mixture of good and bad," having no greatness in their character. This is a "life of the joint entity"— the compound of soul-image and body.[113] Virtuous persons will have different "measures" for the appetitive and spirited parts of their own soul-image than such a merely decent, civically "virtuous" person will have. Here Plotinus seems to be considering, and rejecting, precisely the person Aristotle (and Plato too in the theory of virtue proposed by the Socrates of the *Republic*) describes as virtuous: a person whose life consists in a full endorsement of and participation in the life of appetitive and emotional desire, who actively retains those impulses as crucial parts of their motivating attachments to physical life itself, and to the social relationships and the accompanying duties that they regard as self-fulfilling to perform. Indeed, they regard acting with those attachments as constituting happiness (at least, happiness in Aristotle's "second" degree). Plotinus is expressing his disapproval and rejection of such a conception of moral and social virtue and such an ideal of life, by calling such a person merely "decent," and "a good person" only according to the totally inadequate standards of what he here calls "civic" virtue.[114]

The result is that we have to recognize in Plotinus a double conception of the civic virtues. Rejected, as no true virtuous life at all, is the life of someone who zestfully lives a decent bodily and social life, falsely affirming to themselves the goodness of bodily and social values. Such a person knows nothing of their true self, nothing of the true good in human life, the activity of fully understanding and contemplating Forms. But in happy persons' conduct of their daily and social lives, based upon precisely that missing understanding, we find at work a

---

[111] See n. 59 above, and the main text there.

[112] *Enn.* I 2, 7.24–27.

[113] *Enn.* I 4, 16.4–9.

[114] In this rejection of civic virtue, we see a vestige of Plotinus's efforts to integrate Plato's *Phaedo* account of the incorrect and inadequate conception of virtue his Socrates found among ordinary, nonphilosophical, people, with the *Republic*'s fourfold theory of the virtues of the citizens of the ideal city. (See above, section 6.4.) Plotinus need not be interpreted as accepting Socrates's account of these "virtues" (wrongly so called) as resting merely on calculations of how to get the most pleasure in life; rather, he replaces that idea with his own rejection of the Aristotelian theory on the ground that it retains a full "mixing" of the "virtuous" person's intellect with the desires and practical evaluations of the living body itself. It is that "mixing" that makes these "virtuous" persons for Plotinus not truly virtuous at all.

refined and purified version of those same virtues$_3$. These virtues result, as I have suggested, from the happy person's application to their daily and social life of the effects of their purifying virtues$_2$. The virtuous, happy person, whose approach to their daily and social life I have described in this section, then, does combine both Plotinian purifying virtues and some version of his civic ones.

6.6. Philosophy: The Sole Way Up to Life Itself

It is through philosophy, the disciplined use of our native human powers of understanding the truth, that one comes to see and accept as true all the basic propositions underlying and supporting the Platonist way of life that we have been discussing throughout this long chapter. It is philosophical argumentation and analysis that provide for us the fundamental knowledge about the derivative character of the world of nature itself, and about Forms, and the theories of human nature, the human good, and the virtues that I have been presenting and discussing in earlier sections. True philosophy, Plotinus is convinced, reveals to us something that we would never even begin to suspect, if we just accepted life as it comes to us when we are introduced to the practices of human life as they have taken shape and been passed on to new generations of human beings from prior ones. It is philosophy that reveals and explains that, and why, we have the best possible reasons for believing that the physical world is a derivative existence, derivative from and modeled upon purely intelligible principles that constitute the whole of true reality. True (i.e., Platonist) philosophy establishes for us that we ourselves are pure intellects, and therefore have our own existence as elements within that intelligible, spiritual, true reality, turned in consciousness to it. The contents of the rest of our consciousness consist of intrusions from the physical world, of which we are no part. Philosophy teaches us that our good, therefore, can consist only in the active life of our intellects; and that the virtues that perfect us, so that we can live that life, include dispositions of our consciousness affecting not only our intellectual activities of pure thought, but our ways of approaching and conducting our daily and social lives in our human communities in this physical world. Platonists must understand and bear constantly in mind all these philosophical truths as they lead their lives, engaging in and planning the varied activities that make them up, both those of the embodied animals that they somehow remain and those of intellectual contemplation and thought. Their life is a life of philosophy, from beginning to end, and in all its aspects.

The central moral truth that Platonist philosophy reveals (or claims to) is that our true life and our true good consist in a constant effort of ascension from our physical embodiment—an active and full "return" to our intellectual and spiritual origin in the Substances, Soul, Intellect, and the One. The One is the single origin of all of reality, and ultimately also of the rest of what exists, the physical world. That ascension and return can be achieved only through, and in, perfected pure thought. That thought and its processes are themselves exercises in completed philosophical understanding. Philosophy itself, however, taken as a whole, consists of a good deal more than the metaphysical grasp of Forms in which this return consists: there are detailed investigations of logic, physical theory, even moral philosophy, as well (to the extent that, for Plotinus, there remains any serious philosophical work to do, beyond the general theories I have explained in previous sections, in examining and justifying principles of action and behavior for our bodily and social lives). But, as Plotinus argues, the essential and best part of philosophy, presupposed by and applied in these elaborations, is what, following Plato, he calls "dialectic." This is the study of the whole realm of Forms, working out in full detail all the relationships in which the various ones of them stand to one another.[115] So the rise to full life, in our self-absorption into our intellectual origins and natures, is itself an exercise of philosophy, of philosophy at its essential core of active knowledge of Forms.

Even, however, when pursuing philosophical studies of matters outside this core we are also engaged in activities of self-purification and return. Plotinus emphasizes in his treatise on *The Living Being and the Human Person* that the very thing that is carrying out the investigation contained in that treatise is our intellect. This activity of investigation and thought, which we engage in as we think out, and think through, all the arguments and propositions making up the content of the treatise, is part of the higher life of the soul that the treatise's purpose is to make clear to us, and to invite us to aspire to.[116] Likewise for all the rest of philosophical study—in the philosophy of nature, in mathematical theory, in ethics and moral philosophy. In pursuing these studies we engage our intellects in their essential activity of pure thought, and we help to train and purify them so that we/they will be able to approach our daily and social lives in the correct, virtuous spirit of refusing to "mix" with the life of our living body, the living being that most people think we are, while nonetheless continuing to concern

[115] See *Enn.* I 3, 3–6.
[116] See *Enn.* I 1, 1.9–11, and I 1, 13.

ourselves with the living being's needs and legitimate interests. Later Platonists, in their commentaries on Aristotle's works in logic, philosophy of nature and metaphysics, follow Plotinus in this, as we can see from the Introductions or Prologues to some of these works. Thus Ammonius, the fifth to sixth century Platonist who taught in Alexandria, explains that the study of Aristotle's writings is useful because in studying them we are brought to "ascend to the common principle of all things and to be aware that this is the one goodness itself, incorporeal, indivisible, uncircumscribed, infinite and of infinite potentiality."[117] Similarly his pupil, the great Aristotelian commentator Simplicius, maintains that the study of Aristotle's *Physics* not only helps us bring our souls into good and virtuous order, but that "it is the finest path to grasping the nature of the soul and to the contemplation of the separate and divine Forms."[118] For Platonist philosophers, it seems, all of philosophy, whatever the specific topic and however much focused directly on mundane and physical matters, has its principal value in its uplifting force, and in the reorientation of our lives away from our physical life and toward making our true selves fully real.

Thus philosophy, and only philosophy, can prepare us adequately for our true life, a life consisting of contemplation of Forms, in self-absorption into Intellect and into Intellect's own origin, the One. Furthermore, this very contemplation, which constitutes both our natural good and our true life, is an exercise of completely achieved philosophical understanding. For Plotinus, and the late ancient Platonists in general, philosophy is the sole road to happiness, and also its very essence. Thus the Platonist way of life is doubly a philosophical life. The practice of philosophy is the sole necessary means to happiness. Moreover, the highest level of active philosophical understanding is happiness. It is the very essence of happiness.

6.7. Epilogue: The Demise of Pagan Philosophy, and of Philosophy as a Way of Life

After Plotinus's death, Porphyry seems to have remained in Italy (Sicily or Rome), where he wrote and taught philosophy as a close adherent of Plotinus's

---

[117] Ammonius, *On Aristotle's* Categories, 6.10–12 in the edition of the Greek text by Busse, *Ammonius, In Aristotelis categorias commentarius.*

[118] See the prologue to Simplicius, *Commentary on Aristotle's* Physics, 4.17–5.25; the quotation translates 5.11–12.

Platonist philosophical system.[119] But Plotinus's other closest associate, Amelius, who alongside Porphyry was most responsible for making Plotinus's work known outside Rome's intellectual circles, was already living, and presumably teaching, in the city of Apamea in Syria. This was the birthplace of Plotinus's most important, and very highly regarded, Platonist predecessor, Numenius.[120] Another famous Platonist philosopher, Iamblichus, who had studied with Porphyry, followed Amelius there later on. Thus began the post-Plotinian so-called Syrian Neo-Platonism, which diverged in momentous ways from the purely rationalist, traditionally Greek-philosophical spirit of Plotinus's (and Porphyry's) work. This revised and extended Platonism affected the whole later history of Platonist philosophy, as it was taught in both Athens and Alexandria, the two major centers of the Greek-speaking world for philosophy during the fifth and sixth centuries, until its ultimate demise. Before and during Iamblichus's lifetime (he died ca. 325, during Constantine's reign as Roman emperor, with his seat by that time in the new city of Constantinople), Platonist theological ideas were in vigorous competition not only with those of the intellectualized and philosophized Christianity that had been taking shape partly under the influence of Platonism for the past two centuries.[121] Already Plotinus had contended against the theology of so-called Gnostic thinkers, and against the secret religious rituals they based upon them, as means of personal salvation: to one of the treatises in his collection of *Enneads* (II 9) Porphyry gave the title *Against the Gnostics*.

The Christian orthodoxy then in formation, Gnosticism, and Platonism all three shared a belief in a single first god, union with which would be salvation for human beings, conceived as bare self-conscious "I's" imprisoned in an alien material world.[122] We have seen that for Plotinus (and for Porphyry) this salvation was to be attained—and could only be attained—through patient, concentrated efforts to understand the truth, in terms of philosophical argument and

---

[119] On Porphyry one can consult Eyjólfur Emilsson's *Stanford Encyclopedia of Philosophy* article (http://plato.stanford.edu/entries/porphyry/).

[120] Amelius wrote a work (now lost) devoted to showing that Plotinus's system differed significantly from Numenius's: Porphyry in his *Life of Plotinus* 17 reports that word was circulating in Greece that in his Roman seminars Plotinus was passing off Numenius's philosophy as his own. (On Numenius, see George Karamanolis's article in the *Stanford Encyclopedia of Philosophy* [http://plato.stanford.edu/entries/numenius/].)

[121] See my discussion above, section 1.2.

[122] The Gnostics specialized in seeing the material world as not only alien but potentially fatally hostile, whereas for Plotinus, though we human minds are not at home in the material world, the world is not hostile to us and not bad, but in fact good—as the necessary product of the One's necessary but free overflowing into being: matter may be bad, but the material world is not.

analysis, and to achieve virtue, leading ultimately to a reasoned, contemplative insight into the One itself. Though Iamblichus continued to philosophize in the same way as earlier Platonists had done, with expanded theories about the three Substances, the human soul, virtue, and happiness, he added to Platonism, in a way not essentially different from the Gnostics, ritualistic utterances and performances of a religious and (in the sense of the earlier philosophical tradition from Socrates to Plotinus) unphilosophical kind.[123] For him, salvation of our souls did not depend on depth and completeness of philosophical understanding of reality, leading to a progressive separation of our consciousness from concern for and attention to the physical world, as with Plotinus and Porphyry. Instead, it depended on a different kind of connection to the gods, and ultimately to the first god—through what the modern scholarly tradition calls "theurgical" ritual utterances and performances. In short, for Iamblichus, salvation depended on pagan religious magic.[124] Ironically, Iamblichus had philosophical reasons for this. He believed that the soul was damaged in its metaphysical "descent" into the material world and into the individual human body, so that reascent would not be possible by purely intellectual means, as Plotinus had assumed: theurgical practices step in to make up for the deficiency caused by this damage.[125] In Iamblichus's view, the ancient Egyptians, Chaldeans, and Assyrians handed over to the

[123] On Iamblichus's philosophy one might consult A. C. Lloyd, "Porphyry and Iamblichus," chap. 18 in Armstrong, *Cambridge History of Later Greek and Early Medieval Philosophy*, pp. 283–301. For his theurgical ideas and practices, see Shaw, *Theurgy and the Soul*. Shaw is a historian of ancient religions, not a philosopher; from that perspective, he writes as an enthusiast for Iamblichus's theurgical soteriology based on religious sentiment and ritual, the alleged "deeper significance" of which, to his credit, Iamblichus supposedly recognized, thus downgrading and rejecting the "excessive rationalism" (as Shaw describes it) of Plotinus and Porphyry (see Shaw, *Theurgy*, pp. 4, 14). Where Shaw sees in Iamblichus the liberation of Platonism from its shallow rationalist past and a renewed openness to the depths of experience and of true life that religious rituals and devotions alone make possible, I see its degradation and loss of intellectual nerve.

[124] A distinction is sometimes attempted so as to separate magic (conceived as the manipulation of natural processes or forces with a view to getting spirits or gods to intervene in the world and our lives) from Iamblichean and other pagan Greek theurgy, since the latter involves rising above nature to obtain union or at least spiritual contact with the supernatural origins of nature. I disregard this distinction. For my purposes, a ritualistic way of achieving such union or contact counts as magic, since it contrasts with the sober thought processes Plotinus calls for, even if the ultimate step in them is a mystical experience of reversion to and identification with the One.

[125] One of Iamblichus's works that survived into medieval and modern times is his *On the Mysteries*, in which he gives a lengthy defense of reliance on theurgy in the process of salvation. This work (in ten books) was written as a riposte to one of Porphyry's (his *Letter to Anebo*, now known only in fragments), in which the latter attacked Iamblichus's contamination of philosophy with theurgy. There is a translation, with introduction and notes, of Iamblichus's *On the Mysteries* by Emma C. Clarke, John M. Dillon, and Jackson P. Hershbell.

Greeks in distant times just the correct rituals of utterance and performance that are needed to bridge this gap; his adoption of such rituals into philosophical Platonism thus became at the same time a vindication of what he regarded as his own life project of revivifying the mystic rites, the other rituals, and the prayers that belonged to the whole hoary, ancestral tradition of polytheistic Hellenic cult and piety, by placing them on this new philosophical foundation.

Iamblichus's ideas, both the philosophical extensions and the theurgical additions to Plotinus, spread to Athens, if not with the revival of Platonism in the school founded there by Plutarch of Athens in the late fourth century,[126] then through his successor Syrianus, and after that through Syrianus's famous pupil Proclus, in the fifth.[127] Proclus wrote voluminously and was the teacher at Athens of Ammonius son of Hermias, who was himself responsible, upon his return to Alexandria and through his teaching there, for the outburst of Platonist commentary writing (by Simplicius, Philoponus, and others) on the works of Aristotle in the fifth and sixth centuries. Thus, after Iamblichus, Platonism became as much a religious as a philosophical movement. The contamination of Greek philosophy into the Christian religion, as it spread from its origins as a local cult in Palestine and became a religious movement pervading the whole Roman Empire, became matched by a reverse contamination of philosophy by religion—this time from a revival, or rather an extension and renewal, as well as defense, of traditional pagan Greek theological ideas and religious practices. The presence within it of these superstitions made pagan philosophy's sole remaining representative, Platonism, less and less distinguishable as a special sort of intellectual movement, distinguishable both from pagan and Christian religions, as a basis for one's way of life. Platonism now looked like nothing more than another religious movement (though containing an intellectual component), competing for adherents both with the varied strands of Gnosticism and with the varied strands of intellectualized Christianity passing through the spiritual turmoil of late-antique life.

That is how Platonism looked to Augustine of Hippo (d. 430) when, in the late fourth century, he became dissatisfied with what he regarded as his own previous materialistic way of life and sought a better way of living, one that recognized and attended to spiritual values. That is to say, Augustine felt he needed a life that attended to his anxieties in thinking of himself as a pure, blank, self-

---

[126] This Plutarch is to be distinguished from the first to second century author of the *Parallel Lives*.

[127] On Proclus, see the entry in the *Stanford Encyclopedia of Philosophy* by Christof Helmig and Carlos Steel (http://plato.stanford.edu/entries/proclus/).

conscious "I," contending with life in an alien material world. Augustine says he first took himself to the work of Platonist philosophers, in fact Plotinus and Porphyry but also Iamblichus and his followers.[128] Augustine admired the purity of the Platonists' commitment to self-salvation but remained dissatisfied. A life based on philosophical thought and understanding (as even Iamblichus's version of Platonism was, despite its heavy burden of pagan ritual) did not suffice. Augustine felt he needed a personal god and father, of the kind that only the Christian religion could give him. He became a Christian. But by his time, with Iamblichus's innovations, and certainly by the end of the sixth century when pagan philosophical schools had been closed by the Emperor Justinian's orders, and pagan philosophizing had ceased to exist, Platonism, the last philosophy of Greek rationalism, had already effectively brought itself to an end. What, after all, would have happened if Iamblichean and Proclan Platonism had defeated, or reached a standoff with, Christianity, so that both survived? Suppose the Byzantine emperor had given his support for the old pagan religion, as revised, spiritualized, and provided with a philosophical foundation in the manner of these post-Plotinian Platonists. Emperor Julian ("the Apostate") tried to do just that in the late fourth century, using Iamblichus's works as his guide. Even so, philosophy in the old sense, going back to Socrates and continuing through Plotinus, of a life led on the basis of, and exclusively from, a rationally worked out, independent and authoritative, account of reality (including an account of the nature and characteristics of divinity) would not have survived. It was already dead. All that remained was a philosophized pagan religion, facing, and losing out to, a philosophized Christian one.

Too bad.

[128] See Augustine's *Confessions*, VII.9.13.

FURTHER READINGS

READINGS FOR CHAPTER I

Appiah, K. A. *Experiments in Ethics* (Cambridge, Mass.: Harvard University Press, 2008).

Aristotle. "Metaphysics," in Jonathan Barnes (ed.), *The Complete Works of Aristotle*, vol. 2 (Princeton: Princeton University Press, 1995).

Cooper, John M. "Socrates and Philosophy as a Way of Life," in Dominic Scott (ed.), *Maieusis: Essays in Ancient Philosophy in Honour of Myles Burnyeat* (Oxford: Oxford University Press, 2007), chap. 2.

Hadot, Pierre. "La fin du paganisme," in *Études de philosophie ancienne* (Paris: Les Belles Lettres, 1998), 341–74.

Hadot, Pierre. *Philosophy as a Way of Life: Spiritual Exercises from Socrates to Foucault*, translated by Michael Chase and edited with an introduction by A. I. Davidson (Oxford: Blackwell, 1995). A rearranged and expanded translation of Pierre Hadot's *Exercices spirituels et philosophie antique*, 2nd ed. (Paris: Études Augustinennes, 1987).

Hadot, Pierre. *The Present Alone Is Our Happiness: Conversations with Jeannie Carlier and Arnold I. Davidson*, translated by Marc Djaballah (Stanford, Calif.: Stanford University Press, 2009). Translation of *La philosophie comme manière de vivre. Entretiens avec Jeannie Carlier et Arnold I. Davidson* (Paris: Éditions Albin Michel, 2001).

Hadot, Pierre. *What Is Ancient Philosophy?*, translated by Michael Chase (Cambridge, Mass.: Harvard University Press, 2002). Translation, with some corrections by Hadot, of *Qu'est-ce que la philosophie antique?* (Paris: Gallimard, 1995).

Jaeger, Werner. "On the Origin and Cycle of the Philosophic Ideal of Life," appendix II in *Aristotle: Fundamentals of the History of His Development*, 2nd ed., translated, with the author's corrections and additions, by Richard Robinson (Oxford: Oxford University Press, 1948), 426–61.

"Philosophy," in *Random House Webster's Unabridged Dictionary* (New York: Random House, 2001).

Plato. *Protagoras*, in John M. Cooper (ed.), *Plato: Complete Works* (Indianapolis: Hackett, 1997).

READINGS FOR CHAPTER 2

Ahbel-Rappe, Sara, and Rachana Kamtekar, eds. *A Companion to Socrates* (Malden, Mass.: Wiley-Blackwell, 2009).

Aristophanes. *The Acharnians; The Clouds; Lysistrata*, translated by Alan Sommerstein (London: Penguin, 1981).

Aristotle. *Nicomachean Ethics* and *Politics*, in Jonathan Barnes (ed.), *The Complete Works of Aristotle*, vol. 2 (Princeton: Princeton University Press, 1995).

Benson, Hugh, ed. *Essays on the Philosophy of Socrates* (Oxford: Oxford University Press, 1992).

Benson, Hugh. *Socratic Wisdom: The Model of Knowledge in Plato's Early Dialogues* (Oxford: Oxford University Press, 2000).

Brickhouse, Thomas, and Nicholas Smith. *Plato's Socrates* (Oxford: Oxford University Press, 1994).

Burnyeat, M. F. "The Impiety of Socrates," in *Ancient Philosophy* 17 (1998), 1–12.

Cooper, John M. "Socrates and Philosophy as a Way of Life," in Dominic Scott (ed.), *Maieusis: Essays in Ancient Philosophy in Honour of Myles Burnyeat* (Oxford: Oxford University Press, 2007), chap. 2.

Cooper, John M. "The Unity of Virtue," in *Reason and Emotion* (Princeton: Princeton University Press, 1999), chap. 3.

Forster, Michael. "Socrates' Demand for Definitions," in *Oxford Studies in Ancient Philosophy* 31 (2006), 1–47.

Forster, Michael. "Socrates' Profession of Ignorance," in *Oxford Studies in Ancient Philosophy* 33 (2007), 1–35.

Galen. *The Best Doctor Is Also a Philosopher*, in Peter N. Singer (ed.), *Galen: Selected Works* (Oxford: Oxford University Press, 2002).

Irwin, T. H. *Plato's Ethics* (Oxford: Oxford University Press, 1995).

Lane, Melissa. *Plato's Progeny: How Plato and Socrates Still Captivate the Modern Mind* (London: Duckworth, 2001), esp. chap. 1.

Lear, Jonathan. "Socratic Method and Psychoanalysis," in Sara Ahbel-Rappe and
    Rachana Kamtekar (eds.), *A Companion to Socrates* (Malden, Mass.: Wiley-
    Blackwell, 2009).

Leibowitz, David. *The Ironic Defense of Socrates: Plato's* Apology (Cambridge, Eng.:
    Cambridge University Press, 2010).

MacPherran, M. L. *The Religion of Socrates* (University Park: Penn State University
    Press, 2006).

Morrison, Donald, ed. *The Cambridge Companion to Socrates* (Cambridge, Eng.: Cam-
    bridge University Press, 2011). Includes extensive, topically organized bibliography.

Nails, Deborah. "Socrates," in Edward Zalta (ed.), *Stanford Encyclopedia of Philosophy*
    (http://plato.stanford.edu/archives/spr2010/entries/socrates/). Includes an exten-
    sive bibliography.

Nehamas, Alexander. *The Art of Living: Socratic Reflections from Plato to Foucault*
    (Berkeley: University of California Press, 1999).

Plato. *Apology, Euthyphro, Crito, Alcibiades, Charmides, Laches, Lysis, Euthydemus, Pro-
    tagoras, Gorgias, Meno, Greater* and *Lesser Hippias, Ion, Menexenus, Clitophon,
    Minos, and Republic book I*, in John M. Cooper (ed.), *Plato: Complete Works* (Indi-
    anapolis: Hackett, 1997).

Prior, William J. "Socrates Metaphysician," in *Oxford Studies in Ancient Philosophy* 27
    (2004), 1–40.

Reeve, C. D. C. *Socrates in the Apology* (Indianapolis: Hackett, 1989).

Rudebusch, George. *Socrates* (Malden, Mass.: Wiley-Blackwell, 2009).

Sedley, David. *Creationism and Its Critics in Antiquity* (Berkeley: University of Califor-
    nia Press, 2007), chap. 3, "Socrates."

Vlastos, Gregory. *Socrates: Ironist and Moral Philosopher* (Cambridge, Eng.: Cambridge
    University Press, 1991).

Waterfield, Robin. *Why Socrates Died: Dispelling the Myths* (New York: Norton,
    2009).

Wilson, Emily. *The Death of Socrates* (Cambridge, Mass.: Harvard University Press,
    2007).

READINGS FOR CHAPTER 3

Anagnostopoulos, George, ed. *A Companion to Aristotle* (Malden, Mass.: Wiley-
    Blackwell, 2009).

Aristotle. *Aristotle: Nicomachean Ethics*, translated by T. H. Irwin, 2nd ed. (Indianapo-
    lis: Hackett, 2000).

Aristotle. *Aristotle: Nicomachean Ethics*, translated by Christopher Rowe with an introduction and commentary by Sarah Broadie (Oxford: Oxford University Press, 2002). Includes a topically organized bibliography.

Aristotle. *Nicomachean Ethics, Eudemian Ethics, Politics, Magna Moralia,* and *On the Soul,* in Jonathan Barnes (ed.), *The Complete Works of Aristotle,* vol. 2 (Princeton: Princeton University Press, 1995).

Aristotle. *Politics,* translated by C. D. C. Reeve (Indianapolis: Hackett, 1998).

Bobonich, Chris. "Aristotle's Ethical Treatises," in Richard Kraut (ed.), *The Blackwell Guide to Aristotle's Nicomachean Ethics* (Malden, Mass.: Blackwell, 2006), chap. 1.

Broadie, Sarah. *Aristotle and Beyond* (Cambridge, Eng.: Cambridge University Press, 2007). Chaps. 7–11 concern Aristotle's ethics.

Broadie, Sarah. *Ethics with Aristotle* (Oxford: Oxford University Press, 1991).

Burnyeat, Myles. "Aristotle on Learning to be Good," in Amélie O. Rorty (ed.), *Essays on Aristotle's Ethics* (Berkeley: University of California Press, 1980).

Chappell, Timothy, ed. *Values and Virtues: Aristotelianism in Contemporary Ethics* (Oxford: Clarendon, 2006).

Cooper, John M. "De Motu Animalium 7 (through 701b1): The Role of Thought in Animal Voluntary Self-Locomotion," in *Aristotle's De Motu Animalium,* edited by Oliver Primavesi and Christof Rapp (Oxford: Oxford University Press, forthcoming).

Cooper, John M. "Plato and Aristotle on 'Finality' and '(Self-)Sufficiency,'" in *Knowledge, Nature, and the Good* (Princeton: Princeton University Press, 2004), chap. 11.

Cooper, John M. "Political Animals and Civic Friendship," in *Reason and Emotion* (Princeton: Princeton University Press, 1999), chap. 16.

Cooper, John M. "Reason, Moral Virtue and Moral Value," in *Reason and Emotion* (Princeton: Princeton University Press, 1999), chap. 11.

Gill, Christopher, ed. *Virtue, Norms, and Objectivity: Issues in Ancient and Modern Ethics* (Oxford: Clarendon, 2005).

Kraut, Richard. "Aristotle's Ethics," in Edward N. Zalta (ed.), *The Stanford Encyclopedia of Philosophy* (http://plato.stanford.edu/archives/sum2010/entries/aristotle-ethics/). Includes an extensive bibliography.

Kraut, Richard. *Aristotle on the Human Good* (Princeton: Princeton University Press, 1989).

Kraut, Richard, ed. *The Blackwell Guide to Aristotle's Nicomachean Ethics* (Malden, Mass.: Blackwell, 2006).

Lear, Gabriel Richardson. *Happy Lives and the Highest Good* (Princeton: Princeton University Press, 2004).

Lorenz, Hendrik. "Virtue of Character in Aristotle's *Nicomachean Ethics,*" in *Oxford Studies in Ancient Philosophy* 37 (2009), 177–212.

MacIntyre, Alasdair. *Dependent Rational Animals: Why Human Beings Need the Virtues* (Chicago: Open Court, 1999).

Miller, Fred. "Aristotle's Political Theory," in Edward N. Zalta (ed.), *The Stanford Encyclopedia of Philosophy* (http://plato.stanford.edu/archives/spr2011/entries/aristotle-politics/). Includes an extensive, topically organized bibliography.

Reeve, C. D C. "Aristotle on the Virtues of Thought," in Richard Kraut (ed.), *The Blackwell Guide to Aristotle's Nicomachean Ethics* (Malden, Mass.: Blackwell, 2006), chap. 9.

Rorty, Amélie O., ed. *Essays on Aristotle's Ethics* (Berkeley: University of California Press, 1980).

Schofield, Malcolm. "Aristotle's Political Ethics," in Richard Kraut (ed.), *The Blackwell Guide to Aristotle's Nicomachean Ethics* (Malden, Mass.: Blackwell, 2006), chap. 14.

Sedley, David. *Creationism and Its Critics in Antiquity* (Berkeley: University of California Press, 2007), chap. 6, "Aristotle."

Sedley, David. "The Ideal of Godlikeness," in Gail Fine (ed.), *Plato 2: Ethics, Politics, Religion, and the Soul* (Oxford: Oxford University Press, 1999), 309–28.

READINGS FOR CHAPTER 4

Algra, K., J. Barnes, J. Mansfeld, and M. Schofield, eds. *The Cambridge History of Hellenistic Philosophy* (Cambridge, Eng.: Cambridge University Press, 1999).

Arnim, H. von. *Stoicorum Veterum Fragmenta* [Fragments of the Early Stoics] (Leipzig: Teubner, 1903–5; vol. 4 indexes by M. Adler, 1924).

Baltzly, Dirk. "Stoicism," in Edward N. Zalta (ed.), *The Stanford Encyclopedia of Philosophy* (http://plato.stanford.edu/archives/win2010/entries/stoicism/). Includes a concisely annotated bibliography.

Bobzien, S. *Determinism and Freedom in Stoic Philosophy* (Oxford: Oxford University Press, 2001).

Brennan, T. *The Stoic Life: Emotions, Duties, Fate* (Oxford: Oxford University Press, 2005).

Cicero. *On Ends* [*De Finibus*], translated by H. Rackham (Cambridge, Mass.: Loeb Classical Library, Harvard University Press, 1914). Books 3 and 4 concern Stoicism.

Cicero. *On Moral Ends* [*De Finibus*], translated by Raphael Woolf and edited by Julia Annas (Cambridge, Eng.: Cambridge University Press, 2001). Books 3 and 4 concern Stoicism.

Cicero. *On the Nature of the Gods*; *Academica*, translated by H. Rackham (Cambridge, Mass.: Loeb Classical Library, Harvard University Press, 1933). Book II of *On the Nature of the Gods* concerns Stoicism.

Cicero. *Tusculan Disputations*, translated by J. E. King (Cambridge, Mass.: Loeb Classical Library, Harvard University Press, 1927).

Cooper, John M. "The Emotional Life of the Wise," in *Southern Journal of Philosophy* 43, suppl. (2005), 176–218.

Cooper, John M. "Moral Theory and Moral Improvement: Marcus Aurelius," in *Knowledge, Nature, and the Good* (Princeton: Princeton University Press, 2004), chap. 13.

Cooper, John M. "Moral Theory and Moral Improvement: Seneca," in *Knowledge, Nature, and the Good* (Princeton: Princeton University Press, 2004), chap. 12.

Cooper, John M. "Stoic Autonomy," in *Knowledge, Nature, and the Good* (Princeton: Princeton University Press, 2004), chap. 9.

Cooper, John M. "The Unity of Virtue," in *Reason and Emotion* (Princeton: Princeton University Press, 1999), chap. 3.

Cooper, J. M., and J. F. Procopé, eds. and trans. *Seneca: Moral and Political Essays* (Cambridge, Eng.: Cambridge University Press, 1995).

Diogenes Laertius. *Lives of Eminent Philosophers*, 2 vols., translated by R. D. Hicks (Cambridge, Mass.: Loeb Classical Library, Harvard University Press, 1970). The life of Zeno contains an account of Stoic "logic" (7.41–83), ethics (7.84–131), and physics (7.132–160).

Epictetus. *Discourses* and *The Encheiridion*, translated by W. A. Oldfather, 2 vols. (Cambridge, Mass.: Loeb Classical Library, Harvard University Press, 1925–28).

Galen. *On the Doctrines of Hippocrates and Plato*, edited and translated by P. De Lacy (Berlin: Akademie Verlag, 1978–80). Books 4 and 5 contain many quotations from Chrysippus's works, dealing with the psychology of emotions.

Inwood, Brad, ed. *The Cambridge Companion to the Stoics* (Cambridge, Eng.: Cambridge University Press, 2003). Includes an extensive bibliography.

Inwood, Brad. *Reading Seneca: Stoic Philosophy at Rome* (Oxford: Oxford University Press, 2005).

Inwood, Brad, and L. Gerson, eds. *Hellenistic Philosophy: Introductory Readings*, 2nd ed. (Indianapolis: Hackett, 1997).

Irvine, William B. *A Guide to the Good Life: The Ancient Art of Stoic Joy* (Oxford: Oxford University Press, 2009). Treatment with popular appeal.

Long, A. A. *Epictetus: A Stoic and Socratic Guide to Life* (Oxford: Clarendon, 2002).

Long, A. A. *Hellenistic Philosophy* (Berkeley: University of California Press, 1986). An introduction to Stoicism, Epicureanism, and ancient skepticism.

Long, A. A. *Stoic Studies* (Cambridge, Eng.: Cambridge University Press, 1996).

Long, A. A., and D. N. Sedley, eds. *The Hellenistic Philosophers*, 2 vols. (Cambridge, Eng.: Cambridge University Press, 1987). Vol. 1 contains Stoic sources in translation with commentary; vol. 2 has the original texts as well as an extensive bibliography.

Marcus Aurelius. *Marcus Aurelius*, edited and translated by C. R. Haines (Cambridge, Mass.: Loeb Classical Library, Harvard University Press, 1916).

Miller, Jon. "Stoics and Spinoza on Substance Monism," in Olli Koistinen (ed.), *Cambridge Companion to Spinoza's Ethics* (Cambridge, Eng.: Cambridge University Press, 2009).

Nightingale, A., and D. N. Sedley, eds. *Ancient Models of Mind: Studies in Human and Divine Rationality* (Cambridge Eng.: Cambridge University Press, 2010). Chaps. 7–11 concern Stoicism.

Nussbaum, M. *The Therapy of Desire* (Princeton: Princeton University Press, 1994).

Plutarch. *On Stoic Self-Contradictions* and *Against the Stoics On Common Conceptions*, in *Plutarch's Moralia* XIII: Part 2, edited and translated by Harold Cherniss (Cambridge, Mass.: Loeb Classical Library, Harvard University Press, 1976).

Salles, Ricardo, ed. *God and Cosmos in Stoicism* (Oxford: Oxford University Press, 2009).

Scaltsas, Theodore, and Andrew S. Mason, eds. *The Philosophy of Epictetus* (Oxford: Oxford University Press, 2007).

Schofield, M. *The Stoic Idea of the City* (Cambridge, Eng.: Cambridge University Press, 1990).

Sedley, David. *Creationism and Its Critics in Antiquity* (Berkeley: University of California Press, 2007), chap. 7, "Stoics."

Sedley, David. "Stoicism," in E. Craig (ed.), *Routledge Encyclopedia of Philosophy* (London: Routledge, [1998] 2005; http://www.rep.routledge.com/article/A112). Contains a briefly annotated bibliography.

Sellars, John. *Stoicism* (Berkeley: University of California Press, 2006). An introduction to Stoicism.

Seneca. *Epistles*, 3 vols., translated by Richard Gummere (Cambridge, Mass.: Loeb Classical Library, Harvard University Press, 1917–25).

Seneca. *Moral Essays*, 3 vols., translated by John W. Basore (Cambridge, Mass.: Loeb Classical Library, Harvard University Press, 1928–35).

Sharples, R. W. *Stoics, Epicureans and Skeptics* (London: Routledge, 1996).

Vogt, Katja Maria. *Law, Reason, and the Cosmic City: Political Philosophy in the Early Stoa* (Oxford: Oxford University Press, 2008).

READINGS FOR CHAPTER 5

Algra, K., J. Barnes, J. Mansfeld, and M. Schofield, eds. *The Cambridge History of Hellenistic Philosophy* (Cambridge, Eng.: Cambridge University Press, 1999).

Allen, James. "Pyrrhonism and Medical Empiricism: Sextus Empiricus on Evidence and Inference," in *Aufsteig und Niedergang der Römischen Welt*, II, 37, 1 (Berlin: De Gruyter, 1993), 644–90.

Annas, J., and J. Barnes, eds. and trans. *Sextus Empiricus, Outlines of Scepticism* (Cambridge, Eng.: Cambridge University Press, 2000). This is also sometimes called *Pyrrhonian Sketches*.

Barnes, J. *The Toils of Scepticism* (Cambridge, Eng.: Cambridge University Press, 1990).

Bett, Richard, ed. *The Cambridge Companion to Ancient Scepticism* (Cambridge, Eng.: Cambridge University Press, 2010). This includes an extensive bibliography.

Bett, Richard, ed. *Pyrrho, His Antecedents, and His Legacy* (Oxford: Oxford University Press, 2000).

Bett, Richard, trans. *Sextus Empiricus: Against the Ethicists* (Oxford: Oxford University Press, 1997).

Blank, D. L., ed. and trans. with commentary. *Sextus Empiricus: Against the Grammarians* (Oxford: Oxford University Press, 1998).

Bobzien, Susanne. "Did Epicurus Discover the Free-Will Problem?" in *Oxford Studies in Ancient Philosophy* 19 (2000), 287–337.

Brunschwig, J. "The Cradle Argument in Epicureanism and Stoicism," in M. Schofield and G. Striker (eds.), *The Norms of Nature* (Cambridge, Eng.: Cambridge University Press, 1986), chap. 5, 113–44.

Burnyeat, M. F., and M. Frede, eds. *The Original Sceptics: A Controversy* (Indianapolis: Hackett, 1997).

Cicero. *On Academic Scepticism*, translated by Charles Brittain (Indianapolis: Hackett, 2006).

Cooper, John M. "Pleasure and Desire in Epicurus," in *Reason and Emotion* (Princeton: Princeton University Press, 1999), chap. 22, 485–514.

Diogenes Laertius. *Lives of Eminent Philosophers*, II: Books 6–10, translated by R. D. Hicks (Cambridge, Mass.: Loeb Classical Library, Harvard University Press, 1925). Book 10 concerns Epicurus.

Epicurus. *Letter to Menoeceus, Letter to Herodotus,* and *Principal Doctrines,* in Brad Inwood and Lloyd Gerson (eds. and trans.), *The Epicurus Reader: Selected Writings and Testimonia* (Indianapolis: Hackett, 1994).

Fish, Jeffery, and Kirk Sanders, eds. *Epicurus and the Epicurean Tradition* (Cambridge, Eng.: Cambridge University Press, 2011).

Frede, M. "An Empiricist View of Knowledge: Memorism," in S. Everson (ed.), *Companions to Ancient Thought I: Epistemology* (Cambridge, Eng.: Cambridge University Press, 1990), chap. 11.

Inwood, Brad, and Lloyd Gerson, eds. and trans. *The Epicurus Reader: Selected Writings and Testimonia* (Indianapolis: Hackett, 1994).

Konstan, David. "Epicurus," in Edward N. Zalta (ed.), *The Stanford Encyclopedia of Philosophy* (http://plato.stanford.edu/archives/spr2009/entries/epicurus/). This includes an extensive, topically organized bibliography.

Long, A. A., and D. N. Sedley, eds. *The Hellenistic Philosophers*, 2 vols. (Cambridge, Eng.: Cambridge University Press, 1987). Vol. 1 contains Greek and Latin sources in translation with commentary; vol. 2 has the original texts as well as an extensive, though by now dated, bibliography.

Lucretius. *On the Nature of Things*, translated with facing Latin text by W. H. D. Rouse and revised by Martin F. Smith (Cambridge, Mass.: Loeb Classical Library, 1924).

Lucretius. *On the Nature of Things*, translated by Martin Ferguson Smith (Indianapolis: Hackett, 2001).

Perin, Casey. *The Demands of Reason: An Essay on Pyrrhonian Scepticism* (Oxford: Oxford University Press, 2010).

Plato. *Philebus*, in John M. Cooper (ed.), *Plato: Complete Works* (Indianapolis: Hackett, 1997).

Plutarch. *Is "Live Unknown" a Wise Precept?* and *That Epicurus Actually Makes a Pleasant Life Impossible*, in Plutarch's *Moralia* XIV, edited and translated by B. Einarson and P. De Lacy (Cambridge, Mass.: Loeb Classical Library, Harvard University Press, 1967).

Sedley, David. "Epicurus' Theological Innatism," in Jeffrey Fish and Kirk Sanders (eds.), *Epicurus and the Epicurean Tradition* (Cambridge, Eng.: Cambridge University Press, 2009).

Seneca. *Moral Essays*, 3 vols., translated by John W. Basore (Cambridge, Mass.: Loeb Classical Library, Harvard University Press, 1928–35).

Striker, G. "Historical Reflections on Classical Pyrrhonism and Neo-Pyrrhonism" in *Pyrrhonian Skepticism*, edited by W. Sinnott-Armstrong (Oxford: Oxford University Press, 2004), chap. 1.

Thorsrud, H. *Ancient Scepticism* (Berkeley: University of California Press, 2009).

Vogt, Katja. "Ancient Skepticism," in Edward N. Zalta (ed.), *The Stanford Encyclopedia of Philosophy* (http://plato.stanford.edu/archives/sum2010/entries/skepticism-ancient/). Contains an extensive bibliography of recent articles and books.

Warren, James, ed. *The Cambridge Companion to Epicureanism* (Cambridge, Eng.: Cambridge University Press, 2009). This includes an extensive bibliography.

Warren, James. *Facing Death: Epicurus and His Critics* (Oxford: Clarendon, 2004).

Wilson, Catherine. *Epicureanism at the Origins of Modernity* (Oxford: Oxford University Press, 2008).

READINGS FOR CHAPTER 6

Aristotle. "On the Soul," in Jonathan Barnes (ed.), *The Complete Works of Aristotle*, vol. 1 (Princeton, Princeton University Press, 1995).

Aubry, Gwenaëlle. *Plotin, Traité 53 (I, 1)*, introduction, translation, commentary and notes (Paris: Cerf, 2004).

Bonazzi, M., and C. Helmig, eds. *Platonic Stoicism—Stoic Platonism. The Dialogue between Platonism and Stoicism in Antiquity*. Ancient and Medieval Philosophy, Series I, 39 (Leuven: Leuven University Press, 2007).

Boys-Stones, G. R. *Post-Hellenistic Philosophy. A Study of Its Development from the Stoics to Origen* (Oxford: Oxford University Press, 2001).

Dillon, John, and Lloyd Gerson, trans. *Neoplatonic Philosophy. Introductory Readings* (Indianapolis: Hackett, 2004).

Edwards, Mark. *Culture and Philosophy in the Age of Plotinus* (London: Duckworth, 2006).

Emilsson, Eyjólfur. "Porphyry," in Edward Zalta (ed.), *Stanford Encyclopedia of Philosophy* (http://plato.stanford.edu/entries/porphyry/).

Gerson, Lloyd P., ed. *The Cambridge Companion to Plotinus* (Cambridge, Eng.: Cambridge University Press, 1996).

Gerson, Lloyd P. *Plotinus* (London: Routledge, 1994).

Helmig, Christof, and Carlos Steel. "Proclus," in Edward Zalta (ed.), *Stanford Encyclopedia of Philosophy* (http://plato.stanford.edu/entries/proclus/).

Henry, P., and H. R. Schwyzer. *Plotini Opera*, 3 vols. (Oxford: Clarendon, 1964–82).

Iamblichus. *On the Mysteries [De Mysteriis]*, translated with introduction and notes by Emma C. Clarke, John M. Dillon, and Jackson P. Hershbell (Atlanta: Society of Biblical Literature, 2003).

Karamanolis, George. "Numenius," in Edward Zalta (ed.), *Stanford Encyclopedia of Philosophy* (http://plato.stanford.edu/entries/numenius/).

Karamanolis, George. *Plato and Aristotle in Agreement? Platonists on Aristotle from Antiochus to Porphyry* (Oxford: Oxford University Press, 2006).

Lloyd, A. C. "Porphyry and Iamblichus," in A. H. Armstrong (ed.), *The Cambridge History of Later Greek and Early Medieval Philosophy* (Cambridge, Eng.: Cambridge University Press, 1970), chap. 18, 283–301.

O'Meara, Dominic. *Plotinus: An Introduction to the Enneads* (Oxford: Oxford University Press, 1993).

Plato. *Apology, Parmenides, Phaedo, Phaedrus, Republic, Symposium*, and *Timaeus*, in John M. Cooper (ed.), *Plato: Complete Works* (Indianapolis: Hackett, 1997).

Plotinus, *Enneads. Plotinus*, 7 vols., edited and translated by A. H. Armstrong (Cambridge, Mass.: Loeb Classical Library, Harvard University Press, 1966–88). Greek with facing English translation. This edition includes, in vol. 1, Porphyry's *On the Life of Plotinus and the Order of His Books*.

Porphyry. *On the Life of Plotinus and the Order of His Books*, in *Plotinus*, vol. 1, translated by A. H. Armstrong (Cambridge, Mass.: Loeb Classical Library, Harvard University Press, 1969).

Remes, Pauliina. *Plotinus on Self. The Philosophy of the "We"* (Cambridge, Eng.: Cambridge University Press, 2007).

Schniewind, Alexandrine. *L'éthique du sage chez Plotin: le paradigme du Spoudaios* (Paris : Vrin, 2003).

Shaw, Gregory. *Theurgy and the Soul: The Neoplatonism of Iamblichus* (University Park: Penn State University Press, 1995).

Slaveva-Griffin, Svetla. *Plotinus on Number* (Oxford: Oxford University Press, 2009).

ENDNOTES

1. It is true that one might, and some people presumably do, read and study literature (novels or poetry) for the sake of finding models and inspiration for one's own life; mimicking the term "philosophy as a way of life," used so influentially by Pierre Hadot (see p. 8 and n. 12 below), one could speak of "literature as a way of life." Still, as I explain as we proceed, the ancient idea of philosophy as a way of life included crucially the idea that one's intellectual grasp of philosophy should itself be the direct source of the motivation that leads to the actions making up your life. If one lives one's life on the basis of literary models or ideas found in literary works, however, one's impulse to do that does not come merely from the activities of reading and understanding and otherwise grasping literary works. Any use you make of such writings is another matter.

2. In speaking summarily here and in the remainder of this chapter about "the ancient philosophers" (from Socrates onward) I include the ancient Pyrrhonian skeptical philosophers, but naturally, as skeptics about philosophy's positive claims, their commitment to the value of philosophy and their understanding of how it might function in giving shape to one's life differ in fundamental ways from those of the other philosophers, who all espouse and defend positive philosophical analyses and positions. What I have to say here and in what follows about ancient philosophy is framed so as to apply strictly only to the latter group; I ignore the qualifications that would have to be made in order to fit what I say to Pyrrhonian skeptics. On the skeptics, see sections 5.5–5.7.

3. That Plato was responsible for establishing this understanding of philosophy was the view of W. Jaeger in his 1928 article, later reprinted in English translation by Richard Robinson, "On the Origin and Cycle of the Philosophic Ideal of Life,"

appendix II in Jaeger, *Aristotle: Fundamentals of the History of His Development*. The term "philosopher" itself seems to date from the middle to late fifth century. In establishing this exclusive meaning for philosophy in subsequent times Plato had to defeat his contemporary Isocrates's rearguard counterefforts to deny the word to logico-scientific writers and to reserve it for a person, like himself, devoted to general culture including a close knowledge of Greek history and, especially, the cultivation of language and style in speaking—abilities that, he thought, were of some actual *use*, and therefore worth honoring with such a title of distinction, by contrast with logic, physics, and metaphysics, which were of no use at all to anyone. (See below, section 2.2, and Cooper, "Socrates and Philosophy as a Way of Life," n. 5.)

4. For Hadot's reference to St. Ignatius, see p. 82 of "Way of Life"; he says that these exercises are "nothing but a Christian version of a Greco-Roman tradition" in philosophy. His reference to Seneca comes at p. 85, n. 45 (he is thinking of *De ira* III 36). It is a striking fact that in the whole of Hadot's sweeping account of Hellenistic philosophy (pp. 83–89), claiming that Hellenistic philosophies "consist essentially in spiritual exercises" (p. 86), almost all his references are to writings from the late second century and afterward. No relevant ones are to fourth- or third century BCE writings, except to Epicurus, a very special case (see below in my main text). Obviously, especially given what I say (p. 20), following Hadot himself, about the new conception of the self that originated and took hold only in imperial times, one must not assume that what goes for Marcus Aurelius or Plutarch or Galen goes for Chrysippus or Epicurus or those who followed the Stoic or Epicurean philosophies four to six centuries earlier! Even so, a great many of the alleged "spiritual exercises" Hadot instances in his discussion of Hellenistic philosophy are no more than perfectly ordinary ways of getting oneself to understand the real meaning and implications of philosophical arguments and philosophical positions, to fix them in one's mind and make oneself ready to apply them smoothly to situations of life as they may arise. These are parts of the intellectual training required to live philosophically; there is nothing at all "spiritual" in Hadot's sense of the term about them. They have no affinity with St. Ignatius's meditations on sin and on the passion of Christ.

5. In his conversations first published in French in 2001, looking back over his career, Hadot defines spiritual exercises as "voluntary, personal practices, intended to bring about a transformation of the individual, a transformation of the self" (*The Present Alone Is Our Happiness*, p. 87). Yet, later in the same conversation, titled "Philosophical Discourse as Spiritual Exercise," he stretches the application of the term to cover *any* activity of living, for example activities of daily life in which one infuses one's actions with one's knowledge of Stoic logic or Stoic physical theory, as well as Stoic ethical theory, thinking Stoic thoughts in directing one's daily life. Applied as widely as that, engaging in spiritual exercises would simply be synonymous with liv-

ing one's philosophy. When I speak here and elsewhere in this book of spiritual exercises, and reject the idea that ancient philosophy, except in its last phase, adopted them, I use the term in the narrower and more useful sense that Hadot gave it in his writings.

6. Xenophon too wrote such an *Apology* (but Plato was present at the trial, while Xenophon was not). It is clear that Xenophon wrote later than Plato. He was familiar with Plato's text (so, at least, internal evidence suggests) and wrote (as he almost says himself) with a view to correcting what he thought were unflattering and, he alleged, incorrect impressions about the historical Socrates conveyed in Plato's work. Both *Apologies* were central elements in later generations' construction of my notional Socrates, but Plato's clearly weighed more heavily. Readers should bear in mind what I said above, that the Socrates whose philosophy I discuss in what follows is this notional Socrates. I do not attempt, to any degree, an account of my own of the historical Socrates. Moreover, since for my purpose it is Plato's Socrates who counts most, I focus for the most part in my discussion on those of Plato's dialogues that were thought of already in antiquity as offering a portrait of the historical Socrates. These are the ones we nowadays refer to as Plato's "Socratic" dialogues. But I take into account also Xenophon's Socratic writings, especially, besides *Apology*, his *Memorabilia*. As Socratic dialogues of Plato I have in mind *Euthyphro, Apology, Crito, Alcibiades, Charmides, Laches, Lysis, Euthydemus, Protagoras, Gorgias, Meno, Greater* and *Lesser Hippias, Ion, Menexenus, Clitophon*, and *Minos* (on the assumption that they are all genuine works of Plato). To these one might add *Republic* I. In this last case, as in several of the others (notably *Protagoras, Meno, Gorgias*, and *Euthydemus*), one must be prepared to find suggestions of ideas and concerns of Plato's own, going beyond those of the character Socrates as presented in *Apology* and in the bulk of Plato's Socratic dialogues—ideas and concerns that we can see further developed and pursued in non-Socratic works of Plato. So the division between Socratic and non-Socratic dialogues is not absolute, and has to be treated with circumspection. See further Cooper, "Socrates and Philosophy as a Way of Life," p. 22 and n. 3.

7. Xenophon, too, reports (in his own *Apology of Socrates* 14–16) that Chaerephon consulted the Delphic oracle concerning Socrates, but he includes other qualities besides wisdom, among those the oracle's response attributed to him. Xenophon gives evidence that the historical Socrates was already well established and active in philosophical discussion and "teaching" at Athens as young as his mid-thirties: in his *Memorabilia* I 2, 39–46, Xenophon tells a story about the notorious Athenian politician Alcibiades's political ambitions while still in his teens, when Socrates was "teaching" him, or trying to, in the second half of the 430s (Socrates was born ca. 469). In any event, when Chaerephon consulted the oracle, Socrates must already

have acquired a widespread reputation in Athens for extraordinary philosophical ability through public discussion; otherwise Chaerephon would not have consulted it, or if he did the oracle would not have heard enough about Socrates to respond as it did. We do not have evidence about how early in his life Socrates began to engage in public philosophical discussion and "teaching," but it may well have been in his twenties. At any rate, he certainly did not begin his philosophical career only after Chaerephon consulted the oracle, as readers of Plato's *Apology* sometimes wrongly infer.

8. One of the main differences between the Platonic and the Xenophontic Socrates is that in Xenophon, while Socrates most often does appear as questioner (and cf. *Mem.* I 2. 36, where an enemy notes his "habit" of asking questions when he already knows the answer), sometimes he is the answerer instead. See *Mem.* III 8, IV 4. Socrates is also depicted frequently just explaining to his young men, on vaguely philosophical grounds, various things about life and about the virtues, and encouraging them outright toward specific behaviors: see *Mem.* I 5, I 7, II 4, III 9. Xenophon does not make a principled avoidance of taking a position in argument, or of direct instruction of the young, any part of his Socrates's persona. Plato's Socrates is always self-consciously strict with himself in these regards. See further Cooper, "Socrates and Philosophy as a Way of Life," 33–35 and n. 17. Here, I follow the main philosophical tradition in making these aspects of Plato's Socrates canonical for the notional Socrates whose philosophy we are examining.

9. I mentioned above that in his defense in the *Apology* Socrates suppresses this part of his philosophical activities. This is understandable. In defending himself against the charge of corruption, Socrates reasonably avoids mention of discussions on moral questions with the young men, since those discussions were clearly aimed at helping them to think for themselves, and not to merely piously follow their fathers' (the jurymen's) instructions, or their elders' general ideas about how to behave. And, in thinking for themselves, the young men might reach conclusions that would go contrary to the traditional morality of the Athenians—and though that is not necessarily something Socrates himself would disapprove of, it would be impolitic to bring that to the attention of these elders (including the jurymen). One of the main charges against Socrates that Xenophon attempts to rebut in his *Memorabilia* is that Socrates taught his young men to think they were wiser than their fathers and to show contempt for them: see I 2, 49–50 and II 2. If that was a significant part of Socrates's reputation, there is good reason for Socrates, in Plato's account, to omit altogether mention of any conversations directly with his young men, and indeed, as we have seen, to leave the impression that any bad influence of that sort that he may have had on them came from their reaction to seeing Socrates explode puffed-up, allegedly wise people and their opinions (*Apology* 23c).

10. In *Apology* 22d–e Socrates speaks of wise "craftsmen" (χειροτέχναι) as one group he went to to see if any of them really were not only wise in their own crafts (that he does not dispute), but wise with the special wisdom that he considers a human virtue, wisdom about human affairs and human life. Often in his philosophical discussions (indeed notoriously so) he draws upon an analogy with such crafts (and with other specialist areas of knowledge, such as medicine or arithmetic) in order to work out a proper conception of the structure and functions, and relationship to its object, of this relatively less familiar, though grander, sort of wisdom, or of other virtues such as justice and so on with which he identified it (on this identification, see below, section 2.4). He assumed that all these "wisdoms" must be similar to one another, so that such more ready-to-hand crafts as carpentry or medicine could serve both as models and, sometimes, as instructive contrasts in relation to human wisdom, courage, justice, etc., which formed the central topics of his discussions. See, e.g., *Euthyphro* 13–14, *Laches* 191b–193d, *Protagoras* 356e–357e, *Lesser Hippias* 373c–374b, *Charmides* 165e–166b, *Republic* I, 340d, 349e–350d, among many other contexts in Plato's Socratic dialogues. See also Xenophon, *Memorabilia* 1.2.37, where Socrates responds to the contemptuous dismissal of what an interlocutor alleges are his favorite topics (cobblers, metal workers, even cowherds) by saying that these are necessary illustrations for the virtues.

11. The corpus of Aristotle's writings contains in fact three complete and comprehensive ethical treatises. Besides the *Nicomachean* we have also the *Eudemian Ethics* (which shares three of its eight books with the ten of the *Nicomachean*). And then there is a shorter work, in two books, called by its Latin title *Magna Moralia*, given to it because of the unusual length of each of its books. Scholars have debated the relationships of these works to one another, and have proposed guesses as to how it came about that there were three versions of lectures on ethics that survived among Aristotle's papers at his death. The consensus, which I share, is that the other two treatises derive from an earlyish period in Aristotle's career as a teacher, with the *Nicomachean* coming toward the end of his life. Only the *Nicomachean* relates itself explicitly to the *Politics*, which however appears to have been written earlier, perhaps in the same period as the *Eudemian Ethics*. It is the mature *Nicomachean* conception of ethics as part of political theory that I make the basis of the following discussion.

12. On the account I am offering in this section of the Aristotelian idea of "practical knowledge" (as consisting in a *mere* grasp of truths about human values that is also in itself a motivating force for choices and actions), I am drawing on Aristotle's theory, adumbrated below in this section, that rational animals have, in addition to the nonrational sources and states of motivating desire that he calls appetite and spirit, also a further source of motivation, belonging to their power of reason, which

he dubs "wish." When Aristotle speaks of this explicitly rational sort of desire or motivation, interpreters sometimes suppose that on Aristotle's view the asserted thought of something that it is *good* for you *triggers* a motivating desire to choose or do that thing in a separate "part" of your soul, a "desiderative" part, where "wishes" reside or arise. (The idea would be that it is just a fact about the rational nature of human animals that we are provided, by nature, with a desiderative part, which is so keyed to our reasoning power that all one has to do, in one's "reasoning part," is to *think* that something is good, for the desiderative part to respond by generating a rational *desire* in favor of that thing.) I think, instead, that Aristotle considers the reasoning power, all by itself, and directly, as the source of the motivations he calls wishes; they do not reside in some other part of the soul, a separate "desiderative" one. That is to say, according to my interpretation, which I follow in this section, to refer to a "wish" is to refer simply and directly to the exact same occurrent state of mind that is also the mere "intellectual" *thought* that the thing wished for is good, in some way, or to some extent, for oneself. For more details, see Cooper, "*De Motu Animalium 7.*"

13. That Aristotle thinks of what he is helping his hearers to acquire through their studies with him as practical wisdom may seem surprising to hear, even for scholars and advanced students of Aristotle's *Ethics*. Aristotle does not say any such thing in any of the passages where his topic of discussion is the virtue (practical wisdom) itself; indeed he notoriously suggests in the chapter expressly defining practical wisdom (VI 5) that it is a quality possessed by people of especially extensive practical experience in politics, such as Pericles, the Athenian leader of the mid-fifth century BCE. However, it may reduce one's surprise at reaching this conclusion, as I have done in the preceding by working out fully the implications of what Aristotle says in the opening chapters of *NE* and elsewhere about the requirements for and benefits of a rigorous philosophical study of ethics, if one takes note of his identification in *NE* VI 8 of practical wisdom with the same state of mind as also constitutes political knowledge or science (πολιτικὴ ἐπιστήμη). Given his broad understanding of political knowledge, as explained in I 1–2, it is clear that he does expect his hearers to be acquiring political knowledge through learning for themselves the full truth about the matters investigated and discussed in the *Ethics* (and continued in the *Politics*). But from this it follows, however little explicit he is about this, that he is expecting them to acquire through their philosophical studies the very same state of mind that is practical wisdom. On Aristotle's view, the body of knowledge, so to speak, that they are acquiring *is* the knowledge that constitutes practical wisdom, just as much as it constitutes political science.

14. Somewhat artificially, he assigns authority over two distinct stages in the performance of an action respectively to virtue of character or feeling and to virtue of

thought: "[V]irtue of character makes the target [of action] correct, while practical wisdom makes what leads to it correct" (1144a7–9). He does not, however, intend to exclude the virtue of thought from selecting, on the basis of its own independent understanding, the target of the action as being good and properly to be acted for in the circumstances—as if the goal is selected independently by one's feelings and then all that practical reasoning does is to figure the steps of action out through which to achieve it. Only a little earlier he has said that the virtue of a good deliberator, as such, concerns the means for achieving ends that practical wisdom has a true grasp of (1143b32–33). So, for Aristotle, reason grasps ends too, with its own understanding. His point in assigning to virtue of character the role of "making the target correct" is that if an agent's nonrational feelings do not support doing what reason prescribes, then there is a strong and real likelihood that the agent will not in fact make what reason prescribes a target of his action at all; in his reason, he will know what to do, but his adverse feelings will interfere with this knowledge, which, being a case of practical knowledge, involves its own motivation for acting. His adverse feelings will prevent him from acting on reason's prescriptions. These feelings can do this by temporarily converting the rational grasp of the end into something merely theoretical. As a result, the agent will act, instead, on appetite or spirit and not do the right thing. This is how Aristotle analyzes in *NE* VII 3 people who lack self-control and in their actions go astray from their own practical judgments about what to do. See VI 5, 1140b11–13, where Aristotle approves an etymology of the Greek word for temperance, one of the virtues of character, as indicating that it is what "preserves practical wisdom." Temperance, or in fact virtue of character in general, preserves practical wisdom by keeping appetites moderate through correct training, so that they are always in line with reason's correct judgments of value; if appetites were not in that condition, the agent would, despite knowing what the right thing to do is, sometimes not do it, by losing reason's *practical* grasp of the right ends as targets, that is, as things to be *acted* for. It is only in that sense that virtue of character (as against practical reason) makes the target correct.

15. Here and in what follows, in speaking of the "virtuous person" I mimic Aristotle's practice of speaking of an ideal type, that is, of a person with a perfect and absolutely steadily maintained good character (composed of all the virtues of practical thought plus those of nonrational feeling), and whose character unfailingly brings them to do the morally right thing in all circumstances. It is important to observe, however, that in actual fact, as Aristotle recognizes, people who have some virtues of character may not possess them all (at least not to the same high degree), and may not possess them in this once-for-all sort of way. They may occasionally depart from what is best to do in some circumstance, and they need not possess their virtues as permanent possessions, once attained. For the latter point, about impermanence,

one could note Aristotle's discussion in *Categories* 8 (8b26–9a13) of the class of "qualities" that he calls ἕξεις or "states" (in the *Ethics* Rowe translates this as "dispositions"). Aristotle's "definition" of virtues of character in *NE* II 5–6 defines them as "states" of a certain sort, and in the *Categories* virtues (ἀρεταί) count as one of two illustrations he gives of this class of qualities. There he mentions specifically justice and temperance "and all such things" (8b33–34). The essential points distinguishing "states" from another allied group, which Aristotle calls διαθέσεις or "conditions," include that "states," such as the virtues, are "more stable and longer lasting" (8b28); they "are not easily changed" (οὐκ εὐκίνητον οὐδ᾽ εὐμετάβολον, 8b34–35) because, in effect, they have "become, through length of time, part of one's nature, and irremediable, or exceedingly hard to change" (9a2–3). The crucial point to notice is that Aristotle does not say here that one who has a virtue *cannot* lose it, or lapse from it—as if it would not count, for Aristotle, as *having* a virtue at all if one were subject to such losses or lapses. Here he mentions, vaguely, that changes from being in a state might be brought about by "illness or some other such thing" (8b31–32). In *NE* II 4, 1105a28–33 Aristotle makes it a condition on virtuous actions, i.e., the actions *of* virtuous persons, deriving from their virtues, that these actions be done "from a firm and unchanging disposition" (βεβαίως καὶ ἀμετακινήτως ἔχων), and that passage is sometimes taken to say that, according to Aristotle, a virtue, once fully acquired, is an unfailingly possessed and activated quality of one's soul. In light of this *Categories* passage it seems best, instead, to understand "unchanging" here as meaning (this is common with words having the alpha-privative prefix) not absolutely unchanging, but only unchanging under normal conditions—unchanging except, in other words, under the influence of illness or "some other such thing." "Unchanging" here in the *NE* just means "not easily changed," as he explicitly says of virtuous dispositions in the *Categories* passage.

16. These routine sensory or bodily pleasures, Aristotle explains, do not include all pleasures in the use of the senses. Some of the other pleasures might accompany or be integrated with the routine ones, but Aristotle leaves any such connections aside in his discussion: for example, relishing the flavors of wines, or those of gourmet meals. No doubt those too might be regarded and pursued as having more importance than they do in fact have, as might also the pleasures of seeing or hearing involved in the appreciation of drama or music (as Aristotle notes himself, 1118a3–6). But Aristotle does not work out the basis on which one could explain the virtuous person's attitudes in these regards. If pressed, he would presumably say something about the place and importance in a well-lived, naturally fully developed and equipped, human life of the full development and exercise of our powers of sensory discrimination, and of the values inherent in human activities of representation and the enjoyment of their products. Such a story would without doubt be complex and

complicated; but one can see, in general outlines at least, how one could derive from it the same sorts of guidelines for what would be or is too much and too little, as Aristotle sets out in discussing these routine sensory pleasures.

17. See *Pol.* I 4, which concludes with the summary statement that a slave is a human being that is a piece of property (i.e., a possession for use in actions, 1254a2), which is a tool, and separate (from the human being whose tool it is—a human being's hand is a tool for actions that is *not* separate). See esp. 1254a1–8, contrasting slave tools (tools that *do* actions) to physical tools, such as shuttles: just as it is the weaver who does some weaving *with* a shuttle (while the shuttle weaves only in an extended or secondary sense), or, to choose a different contrast, just as it is people using their fingernails who do the scratching, so the master uses the slave tool to sweep the floor or cook the meals, or dig the trenches for a barn's foundations, etc. In all these cases, the agent, or primary agent, in the actions is the one that uses the tool, not the tool, even in the case of the slave, who, being a human being, is also an agent active in the doing of the action. One should compare so-called master-craftsmen (ἀρχιτέκτονες) in relation to undercraftsmen or assistants (ὑπηρέται) who do the actual labor of the craft under the hands-off direction of the masters (see 1253b38–1254a1). On Aristotle's view "even in the case of actions involving external objects [such as weaving some cloth or sweeping a floor] the one who does them, in the fullest sense, is the master craftsman who directs them by means of his thought" (VII 3, 1325b21–23); Aristotle expresses the same view more compactly at I 13, 1260a18: "the work that is done is in the first instance that of the master craftsman."

18. See his discussion in *NE* X 9. Here one needs to bear in mind a distinction Aristotle seems to draw at 1179b7–20 among three classes of people: (1) the "many" who are permanently only ever going to behave decently through legal requirements, backed by pleasurable incentives and painful sanctions; (2) the people who, having been habituated well, can come to acquire "some share of virtue" through argument, and so become decent people living decently from their own inner resources; and (3) the ones who can become truly and fully good because they have a native love of the fine that permits argument to make virtue take possession of their souls. (See also 1180a10–18.) It seems possible that Aristotle thinks that group 3, which will include his authorized hearers, might reach a point in their ethical-political development where they are no longer subject to any attractions of immediate pleasure in circumstances where acting as it would incline them to would lead them to depart from virtuous action. This could happen either because they would not find any pleasure in acting that way then, or because their inner psychology is sufficient to reliably give them strong enough other motivations, so that they never do depart from virtuous action (except, as noted above, n. 59, in case of illness or something similar). On the other hand, at *Pol.* III 16, 1287a30–32 he says that "appetite is like a beast, and

spirit (θυμός) corrupts rulers, even if they are the best men"—which is why "law [rule by which is better than by absolute rulers] is understanding without desire." That even the best men in ruling are subject to corruption (and so, give way to vicious action in some circumstances) suggests that even group 3 people remain actively vulnerable to being carried away by appetite or spirit into acting unvirtuously. If so, then the moral support given to decent people, which I go on to describe, by living a fundamentally communal decent life, would be required even for these paragons of the human virtues. They too could not consistently and constantly engage in virtuous activity without that moral support, and so without joining their lives with those of the others (including the merely decent people) in their polis κοινωνία by making the virtuous life of the whole community their objective in their pursuit of their own good through virtuous activity.

19. Skepticism in antiquity had its vicissitudes, and I need to say something briefly here about those, in order to orient the reader to my discussion below, sections 5.5–5.7. I have already mentioned the Academic skepticism of Arcesilaus and his successors in the Hellenistic Academy. As we learn primarily from the philosophical dialogues that the Roman statesman Cicero wrote at the end of his life, in the 40s BCE, the early decades of the first century BCE were tumultuous ones in the teaching of the Academy at Athens. Philo of Larissa, then head of the school, developed the skeptical philosophy of Arcesilaus and Carneades, his most distinguished predecessors, in directions that led to two "defections" from the school. Antiochus of Ascalon, a former student and younger associate of Philo's, opened a rival school of his own in Athens. His intention was to revive the "old" Academic, nonskeptical philosophical doctrines, as he thought, of Plato in his dialogues (as refined by the first two generations of Plato's successors). He thus joined a movement already under way among some Stoics, of regarding the (by that time) "ancient" philosophers, Plato especially, but also Aristotle, as having very special authority when it comes to establishing the truth on all questions of philosophy. So began the lengthy and gradual conversion of philosophy among the Greeks to a sort of "Platonism" that included Aristotle too as a worker in the Platonist camp and that eventually became coextensive with philosophy itself. I discuss this late ancient Platonism in chapter 6. The other "defection" from the Academy under Philo came with Aenesidemus, from Cnossos in Crete. Aenesidemus thought Philo's "skeptical" teaching had eventually lost its Socratic edge. With repeated refinements to its epistemological underpinnings, Philo's philosophy came, Aenesidemus thought, to be merely a fussily qualified endorsement of Stoic theories: Philo disagreed with the Stoics over the proper standards for claiming to have knowledge of any truth, but on his own relaxed standards for knowledge, he too endorsed all the same substantive doctrines as they. Aenesidemus, outraged, reverted to a strict skepticism—no longer under the

Socratic banner of Arcesilaus, however. He selected as his "founder" an obscure figure, suitably contemporary with the other founders of the Hellenistic schools, Epicurus and Zeno—Pyrrho. Pyrrho was reputed to have eschewed all beliefs, as involving rash commitment to the truth of something that is in itself permanently obscure, and to have championed a life led while holding oneself back from belief about anything. Aenesidemus is reported to have taught, at least for some time, in Alexandria, the Hellenistic port city of Egypt (we know about his defection not through Cicero but through later Greek writers). I discuss Pyrrhonian skepticism in sections 5.5–5.7.

20. A continuing commitment to a distinctive, basic perspective on the world and on the place of human beings in it, first worked up by Zeno, provided the essential unity and continuity of the Stoic movement throughout its long history. But, so far from being something taken in any way "on faith," this commitment entailed an independently thought through acceptance of this perspective, by successive writers and teachers. They based their commitment on philosophical reasons that they understood individually, as independent philosophical thinkers, and accepted because they thought they saw reasons that showed that this worldview was *true*. It would betray a serious misunderstanding of the philosophical enterprise itself (both in antiquity and nowadays), and especially of philosophy as conceived by the Stoics themselves, to speak of Zeno's writings during any period as the Stoic "gospel," as scholars sometimes do. One must not imagine that instruction by a Stoic teacher (anyhow if presented according to the standards of the Stoic philosophy itself) had any purpose except to help students to understand, for themselves, *why* the Stoic outlook was correct and why the Stoic doctrines were true. Only such an independent understanding, as Stoic theory itself implied, could do anyone any real good: acceptance of some Zenonian "gospel" on any other basis would be a waste of time and effort. If Stoic teachers taught Zeno's (and his successor Chrysippus's) works, offering commentaries on passages as they were successively read out in their classes, especially at later stages (in the time of Epictetus, second century CE), this was always a search for the truth, never an attempt to find out "what Zeno said," as if that by itself was dispositive of anything. Nor was it aimed at bringing people to live the way Zeno teaches us to live, if that were achieved by any means other than improved understanding of the reasons why living that way is good for us. Philosophers often, of course, have hangers-on who are not philosophically skilled, or perhaps interested enough to take this philosophical attitude to what they are teaching and learning; they may be satisfied to take things on faith, and to imitate the life of those who live philosophically, while missing its substance. It is important not to confuse such hangers-on with true members of the Stoic school—that is, with fully qualified, or nascent, *philosophers*.

21. I should mention here also Chrysippus, who was later regarded as having constructed in his own voluminous writings, upon the Zenonian foundations, the final, "orthodox" version of the system. Chrysippus was a younger contemporary of the academic skeptic Arcesilaus. He was a student and associate in the Stoic school at Athens of Cleanthes, Zeno's own student, and successor as its head. Arcesilaus's skeptical examination, as a teacher in the Academy, of Zeno's and Cleanthes's doctrines was an important stimulus to Chrysippus's work in formulating and arguing for all the elements of the resulting "orthodox" system of Stoicism. This included a complete logic and philosophy of language, a complete philosophy of nature, and ethical philosophy. This formed the target for the renewed skeptical attacks of the Academic Carneades in the next century, the second BCE. But the main "repairs" to Zeno's system, if such were needed, had already been implemented by Chrysippus. It seems that the result of Carneades' highly inventive, and philosophically very rich, skeptical engagement with the Stoic system was effectively a standoff. At any rate, so far as its principal doctrinal content goes, Stoicism was fixed for later times through Chrysippus's writings, despite Carneades's attacks. Chrysippus's system did not go unquestioned or even uncontradicted, on detailed points, by all later Stoics, but it did form the basis for Stoic teaching, and for writers like Cicero, Seneca, Epictetus, and Marcus Aurelius, it was the basis for presenting the Stoic philosophy, and for encouraging their readers to the Stoic way of life.

22. There is scholarly dispute about whether the convergence between the Stoics and Aristotle on the "definition" of happiness derives (along with other aspects of their theories, in ethics and elsewhere, where some have seen evidence of Stoic knowledge of Aristotle's work) from Zeno's or Chrysippus's having read Aristotle's philosophical treatises. It is widely agreed that, unlike Plato's dialogues, Aristotle's treatises were not issued for general circulation and were not available in bookshops in Athens or elsewhere during this period. It seems certain, however, though this too has been disputed, that these works were available for reading and study in Aristotle's own school in Athens. Both Zeno and Chrysippus could have consulted them there, and it seems hard to believe they would not have availed themselves of the opportunity. That, so far as we know, neither made specific reference in their writings to Aristotle or his views, as they did to Plato's, could be explained not by their ignorance, but by the special difficulties entailed by this limited access: one did not have one's own copy, and neither did one's intended readers.

23. Here we skirt a complicated aspect of Stoic theory (much disputed over both in antiquity and in modern scholarship), namely their doctrine of "fate." According to this, the whole history of the world is determined from the beginning through a "chain" of causes that control all events, down to the smallest particulars, from the first event extending down to the last in the whole history of the world. The Stoics

identify this fate with Zeus or reason or nature. In considering this theory, and its consequences for human action and human responsibility, one must understand that we, as minds, are actually parts of the world-mind (as indeed the Stoics emphasized): the "chain" of causes includes the contributions we individually make to the causal history of the world. That everything is determined from the outset does not mean that we are not free at every moment to do whatever it is we decide to do (so far as the initiation within our souls of a process aimed at bringing about some outcome goes): whatever we decide (for the reasons that we do decide it) then becomes part of the subsequent history of the world. Zeus's role (understanding "Zeus" now to refer to the world-mind minus us human minds that are very subordinate parts of it) is to take as given, from the outset, so to speak, whatever it is that we *will* (i.e., do) decide on any occasion. Then, in planning the sequence of world-events that he or it will determine from the very beginning of the world, Zeus structures the world and sets it to behave in such a way that the overall maximally good order and history of total events will be the result—the events caused by us in deciding what to do being included. On this, see "Stoic Autonomy," in Cooper, *Knowledge, Nature, and the Good*, pp. 204–44.

24. Given the radical difference between reason as a cause and causation through material objects and laws and their (derived and instilled) power of causation, the Stoics hold that our growth to maturity, however gradual it may be in all other respects, is punctuated by a fundamental shift, at some time around the age of fourteen, from being nonrationally governed animals, to being rational ones. They need not, and do not, deny that, for example, the acquisition of language (the hallmark of rationality) is extremely gradual, and begins at a very early age, when we are still infants. Extensive expansions of our grasp of the world around us proceed only through the use at many points in our early life, including infancy, of our incomplete but growing linguistic and associated conceptual powers (ones that, it seems, already far outstrip those of any other nonrational animal, however mature). It is merely that at some point our voluntary behavior began, by a permanent shift in our natural constitutions, to be governed through rational thoughts and decisions, and no longer by naturally implanted, nonrational, desires, however much developed and overlaid by conceptual structuring and by self-conscious means-ends calculation it might already be. On all this, see Cooper, "Stoic Autonomy," in *Knowledge, Nature, and the Good*, pp. 213–18, and the passages from ancient authors cited there.

25. Chrysippus sketched a whole theory, of which we hear some few details (see Diog. Laert. VII 116 and Cicero, *Tusculan Disputations* IV 12–14), of what he called "good ways of feeling" (εὐπάθειαι), which he held that the virtuous, and only they, do experience. They respond with "joy" in being aware of and attending to Zeus's and their own good and orderly thoughts and actions—as opposed to the emotional, over-

blown, and bad sort of elation that ordinary people feel at their achievements or at simple good luck. They have feelings of "caution" (not fear) in dangerous situations (especially, perhaps, morally dangerous ones), and pursue the naturally valuable things of life with "wishes"—never with appetitive desires for any of them. More generally, as I explained above, section 4.6, they have a variety of appropriate affective feelings of desire or aversion, and of response to events, suited to the levels and importance of the various items in the list of naturally valuable and disvaluable things. The pursuit and enjoyment, or avoidance, of these make up the substance of any human daily and social life, and this is as true of the Stoic virtuous person as it is of anyone else. For further discussion, see John M. Cooper, "Emotional Life of the Wise," pp. 176–218.

26. Chrysippus and other Stoics, so far as we have evidence, did not devote much attention to explaining and defending the claim that reason's activities in forming our desires are hidden in such cases from the agent's awareness. This must apply, of course, to (some) desires of all types, including not only emotional ones but also even some of the virtuous agent's, in for example eating a meal with pleasure or having sex, or any energetic activity involving liking or enthusiasm for what one is doing. The judgment, in such circumstances, that it is appropriate to have such states of affect need not, on Stoic theory, be overt and conscious, as perhaps the decision to eat or have sex might be. Those judgments are made automatically, and on the basis of long familiarity with situations like the ones one finds oneself in. In any event, there is nothing to recoil from in the idea that our power of reason can work in shaping our lives in ways that we are not aware it is doing. Once having become angry, in this unreflective way, one will not—given the force with which, in accepting to *be* angry, one has endowed one's desire to lash out—be able to put an end to one's desire or stop oneself from behaving in regrettable ways, *simply* by suddenly deciding that feeling and acting in these ways is a bad idea. It may well take a little time actually to *cease* feeling the effects of the impression on the rejected desire you are acting upon. This is why Chrysippus calls emotions "runaway" desires.

27. It is true that in a passage of the Christian Father of the Church, Clement of Alexandria's late second or early third century CE *Miscellanies*, the first century BCE Stoic Posidonius is quoted (his fragment 186 in the edition of Edelstein-Kidd) as declaring the "end" or highest good of human life to be "living studying the truth and orderly arrangement of the universe" and *then* helping to implement this so far as one can. We cannot tell from the (very bare) quotation what Posidonius himself intended by this. We do not know whether he was consciously wishing to revise classical Stoic doctrine by putting knowledge of nature on its own or for its own sake first, and then the use of that knowledge in structuring and directing our lives second. That would establish, or at any rate *claim*, a closer affinity of Stoic doctrine

with Aristotelian (and Platonic) perspectives. Still, it is worth observing that, in itself, Posidonius's mention of study, and his placing it first, in his official "formula" for the highest good (if that is what Clement is citing) does not imply any assignment of value to study *except* for enabling us to govern our own lives well. And that does not depart at all from Chrysippus's view, except perhaps in emphasis. Chrysippus's view is quite clear: knowledge of nature is part of our highest good because of its contribution to our living in agreement with nature—not at all for its own sake alone.

28. Unlike for the Stoics, several complete, but rather short, writings, surveying Epicurus's main philosophical theses, with some (but not much) indication of the philosophical arguments and analyses on which he rested them, have come down to us bearing Epicurus's name. They survived because Diogenes Laertius quoted them in full in his *Lives and Opinions of the Eminent Philosophers*, book X. These are in the form of three "Letters" to named recipients. Of special interest to us in this book is much the shortest of these, the *Letter to Menoeceus*, dealing with Epicurus's ethical theory; this runs to only about four printed pages. In addition we have (also quoted in full by Diogenes Laertius) forty short sayings or "maxims," almost all deriving from Epicurus's ethical theory, which circulated widely in antiquity (Cicero quotes from them frequently in his account of Epicurean ethics in *On Ends* I and II: at II 20 he says that every Epicurean must learn them by heart, so important are they to living the good Epicurean life). These, the so-called *Principal Doctrines*, presumably consist of excerpts from more substantial writings (including further Letters now lost). Furthermore, a medieval manuscript at the Vatican Library in Rome contains some sixty-two additional, similar ethical maxims drawn from Epicurus's writings (it also repeats some of the *Principal Doctrines*, and has some others that scholars regard as not by Epicurus but by his pupil and assistant Metrodorus, or by Hermarchus, to whom Epicurus bequeathed his school and his books). In addition, we have the Latin poem of Lucretius (contemporary of Cicero), *On the Nature of Things*; but its intention is to set out the Epicurean theories of physics and of the origins of human civilization, rather than the ethical theory (which it rather presupposes, while drawing on it in the proems to the poem's six books). For that part of Epicurus's philosophy, we have also his own *Letter to Herodotus*. A number of ancient writers (all hostile, with the exception of Diogenes Laertius) have quotations or paraphrases from Epicurus that give some help in the task of philosophical reconstruction, as Diogenes Laertius also does with the Stoics. Portions of Epicurus's major work of physical and psychological theory, his thirty-seven books *On Nature*, survive in damaged papyrus remains from an Epicurean Library of the first century CE in Herculaneum, south of Naples. These have little to say about ethical matters. Although some writers after Epicurus contributed developments and

extensions of Epicurus's theories (notably the first century BCE Philodemus, who lived in southern Italy), the basic doctrines were not disturbed. In my own discussion, I limit myself to presenting and interpreting the Epicurean philosophy and way of life, as Epicurus himself set it out, without later accretions. Besides Epicurus's *Letter to Menoeceus* and his *Principal Doctrines*, I draw heavily upon Cicero's exposition of Epicurean ethics in *On Ends* I and his scathing criticism of it in *On Ends* II. For translations from Epicurus's writings I follow (with many unmarked changes) those of Inwood and Gerson in *The Epicurus Reader*; for translations from Cicero I follow Woolf in his translation of *On Moral Ends*, again with many changes.

29. Commentators have usually (but without much thought) classed Epicurus also as a hedonist in psychological theory—one who holds that human desire is by its nature aimed always at obtaining pleasure, and at nothing else, except such things as may seem to the desirer to be means of one sort or another to obtaining it. On the theory of psychological hedonism, such other things can be desired derivatively, together with, and in subordination to, the pleasure they are expected to lead to (but not otherwise). That attribution is probably a mistake. It seems very likely that Epicurus was a hedonist only in a normative sense—as to what is worth desiring—and not as to the facts of human psychology. See John M. Cooper, "Pleasure and Desire in Epicurus," in *Reason and Emotion*, pp. 485–514, sect. 1. In any event, all that matters in considering the Epicurean way of life is Epicurus's normative hedonism. Whether he regards it as psychologically possible, for example, for Stoics or Aristotelians actually to desire virtuous activity for its own sake, in the way they *say* they do—because of its intrinsic qualities in perfecting our nature—we need not decide.

30. As we have already seen with Aristotle, that something or other is the highest good does not immediately imply that it is the only intrinsic good. Something chosen or pursued for its own sake alone, and for the sake of which everything else is pursued, i.e., a candidate for being the highest human good, need not have an exclusive claim to pursuit for its own sake. Epicurus, however, seems not to consider or allow that anything might be pursued for the sake of pleasure except by being sought in one way or another as a means of producing or obtaining it. We see this clearly enough in his remarks on the value of virtue and virtuous action, which he says have no intrinsic value of their own, but are of value only because they produce pleasures. (I return to this in section 5.3 below.) See, e.g., Cicero, *Tusculan Disputations* III 41–42, translating two passages from Epicurus's lost treatise *On Ends* into Latin verbatim (these are included in Long and Sedley, *The Hellenistic Philosophers*, as 21L). On the "cradle" argument there is an interesting article, Brunschwig, "The Cradle Argument in Epicureanism and Stoicism."

31. In *Outlines* I 25 Sextus tells us what the "end" (τέλος) is for the skeptic way of life, which he defines, following Aristotle and the Stoics, as "that for the sake of which everything is done ... while it is not done for the sake of anything [else]" or "the final object of desire": in other words, as for the other philosophers, happiness (though Sextus refrains from specifying the end sought in skepticism with that term). He says that the skeptic "end"—their implicit conception of happiness—is lack of disturbance or tranquility "in matters of opinion" and "moderation of feeling in matters forced on us." As he explains, if, like the skeptic and unlike Aristotelians or Stoics or other proponents of positive philosophical doctrines, you live without beliefs or opinions (I will explain what this means below) about whether anything that happens is either good or bad *for you*, then, even if you, like any human can be made to suffer physical pain or get physical pleasure when you do something or something happens, and even psychological disappointment or satisfaction when other things happen, you will not increase these enforced feelings, positive and negative, by adding the gratuitous further disturbance or elation that anyone in your circumstances would feel if they thought something good or bad *for them* had occurred. Thus for Sextus "moderation of feeling in matters forced on us" is not a parallel, independent second part of the skeptic's "end," alongside lack of disturbance in "matters of opinion"; in fact, it is a natural consequence of the fundamental objective of lack of disturbance in those matters. Hence in my main text I speak simply of tranquility (in matters of opinion, but also, as a result of that, so far as feelings go, too) as the skeptic's idea of happiness. Even when you feel pain or disappointment, you accept those with equanimity and tranquility, if you are a skeptic: your feelings in such cases are always "moderate."

32. Sextus lived in the second half of the second century CE (he is mentioned by Diogenes Laertius as a recent teacher of skeptical philosophy). Like many of the skeptic philosophers (and teachers) from as far back as the first century BCE, he was also a medical doctor of the so-called Empiric school of medicine (his commonly used second name indicates this). (See Diog. Laert. IX 116.) In treating illness, these doctors favored careful attention to facts of observation and simple predictions from carefully recorded experience; they eschewed anatomical and physiological theory, since those appeal to unobservable entities and processes. (You can see inside an animal only after it is dead, and what you see then may well be different from its insides while alive.) The Empirics' reliance on experience (on the "appearances") and their mistrust of medical theory are links between medical Empiricism and skepticism. However, Sextus himself denies that the skeptic philosophy and the "philosophy" of the Empiric school are the same. (See *Outlines* I 236–41).

33. Sextus rejects the claims of the principal Academic skeptics, Arcesilaus, Carneades, and Philo of Larissa, to have been at all what *he* counts as a skeptic (see *Outlines* I

232–34, 226–31, 236, respectively). Below, I indicate why I think, as many other scholars nowadays do too, that Sextus overstates, and even misstates, the differences. The evidence about Carneades in particular, the most impressive of the Academics, is divided and unclear on essential points, and already was so by Cicero's time less than a century later. It seems that Sextus is following Aenesidemus (on whom see below in my main text) in accepting an interpretation that does fairly decisively make Carneades appear nonskeptical in essential attitudes. Carneades's philosophy, under that interpretation, was a central aspect of Aenesidemus's rejection of the Academic philosophy of his own time (early to mid-first century BCE), as having abandoned skeptical principles. Thus, a desire for product differentiation played some role in the attitudes to the Academics of later philosophers of the skeptic tradition, such as Sextus. Sextus is notably more kind, from his own Pyrrhonian point of view, about Arcesilaus's ways of philosophizing than he is about Carneades's. Indeed, he admits that Arcesilaus "certainly seems to me to have something in common with Pyrrhonian ways of arguing, so that his way of philosophizing (ἀγωγή) and ours are pretty much the same" (I 232). For more on the Academic skeptics see section 4.1 and n. 3.

34. Sextus describes this ability to find oppositions as the specific skill of the skeptic at *Outlines* I 8. Aenesidemus is credited with having worked out ten "modes," or different ways or bases, for bringing to light, with regard to at least some such question, such a balanced set of considerations on either side, leading to suspension of judgment upon it. See I 36–163. Sextus also speaks of a different set of five modes (see I 164–77) that he says can be used for "every object of investigation" in science or philosophy. For application of the skeptic's skills to questions about good and bad, and other ethical topics, see *Outlines* III 169–278, and the more extensive exposition in book XI of Sextus's other work, sometimes very misleadingly called in English *Against the Mathematicians* or *Against the Professors* (its Latin title is *Adversus Mathematicos*). A more accurate title would be *Against the Theoreticians*. Book XI is available in a contemporary translation by Bett, in *Sextus Empiricus: Against the Ethicists*.

35. Philosophers sometimes distinguish two distinct sorts of appearances or impressions (especially sensory ones): epistemic (an appearance of something as *being* something or other, or being somehow or other) and nonepistemic (an appearance of something as *looking* the way something or other typically looks). In J. L. Austin's example, one can say that, from far above, men on a playing field may look like so many ants (a nonepistemic appearance), without looking as if they *are* ants (an epistemic one). Furthermore, expressions of epistemic appearances ("It appears to me that those are ants down there," said by someone looking over at a nearby mound of earth) are often taken to be mere polite or reserved positive assertions expressing

what that person takes to be the facts, and, as such, as requiring to be backed up by *reasons* they have for so thinking ("I know what ants look like, and those *look* like ants; so, they *are* ants!"). Sextus's skeptic appearances are not of either of these two sorts. Each Sextan appearance has a single "content," which one could state as the appearance of something *as* such and such (the tower as round), or equivalently the appearance that it *is* such and such. In that respect they look like "epistemic" ones. But Sextan appearances do not imply that the one having the appearance, or accepting it, thinks, in any way, that there are *reasons* for thinking those things. In that respect they resemble "nonepistemic" appearances (when the men on the field look like ants to you, you normally don't have any *reason* for thinking that; they just do). (Of course, in saying this, I do not mean to attribute to Sextus any *theory* of appearances and acceptances of them. I offer this bit of positive philosophy of my own, as making the best sense of Sextus's assumptions about appearances, and about their role in the skeptic life.) When, in acting, skeptics accept an appearance, whether a sensory one or one in their thoughts, what they accept is that the thing in question is somehow or other, or is something or other—but the appearance includes and implies no apparent reasons, and accepting it does not include accepting that there are any reasons why, in accepting it, they think things are so. That is what matters for Sextus's purposes.

36. I should emphasize that in saying that skeptics have beliefs I offer an interpretation of Sextus's views; it is I who say that, in an acceptable, ordinary way of thinking and speaking in both English and Greek, skeptics' attitudes constitute beliefs and that skeptics believe all the things that appear to them and on which they act. I do not claim that Sextus himself makes it a part of his account of skepticism that, according to one acceptable usage of the terms "belief" and "believe" (or δόξα and δοκεῖν or δοξάζεσθαι), skeptics hold beliefs. In any event, the notion of belief that I say applies to the skeptic is markedly different, in its commitments, from the Socratic beliefs on moral subjects discussed in chapter 2. For Socrates, if his interlocutors were serious in asserting something as a belief of theirs, they automatically became subject to questioning, to discover whether their reasons for holding it could stand up to rational scrutiny: belief, understood in this Socratic way, carries with it a commitment to be able to explain and defend it. If you refuse to answer when questioned, or just walk away, that is at least some indication that they you are not a serious person, not worth paying attention to. Skeptics, in accepting an appearance, can say, truthfully, that they are serious about believing what they think (look at how they go on to behave!) without in any way opening themselves to answering questions aimed at discovering and examining their *reasons* for holding it. Skeptics have no reasons, but their refusal to answer when asked for some does not in the least show them up as unserious in holding it. They are *serious* about not having any reasons: besides their

behavior, their, or their predecessors', history of unhappy engagement with philosophy is evidence enough of their seriousness. Socrates's assumptions about what holding a belief commits a person to are the beginnings of the philosophical conception of belief that I have contrasted with the skeptic one. From the beginning (with Pyrrho and the Academic skeptics, as well as the Pyrrhonians) the opponents of skepticism constantly objected that skepticism is an unacceptable philosophy, because the universal suspension of judgment it recommends would render us altogether incapable of action: no beliefs, no actions, they said. (See, e.g., Cicero, *Academica* II 61–62.) My analysis in the last two paragraphs shows that action does not require belief, construed as holding something as true on some grounds of reason, as these opponents, especially the Stoics in their attacks on the Academics, in fact argued that it did; the sort of accepted appearance that, as I have argued, Sextus actually relies on would be enough to support action. If, as I have also argued, we are entitled to call such an accepted appearance a belief (but one that does not claim or require to be backed up by any reasons for thinking what one thinks), then the "no belief, no action" thesis may well be true, but it does not have the anti-antiskeptic implications these opponents thought it did. On two sorts of belief, see *PH* I 13.

37. Panaetius, head of the Stoic school in Athens from 129 BCE (d. 110/109) is reported to have assigned special authority in philosophical matters to Plato and Aristotle, alongside his Stoic authorities Zeno and Chrysippus. Posidonius (d. ca. 51 BCE), who studied with Panaetius and later had a famous and influential school of his own in Rhodes, developed theories concerning the psychology of action—while remaining a fully committed Stoic—that were much indebted to the Platonic and Aristotelian acceptance of nonrational desires. (On the Stoic theory of human desires, and their seat in the power of reasoning, see sections 4.4 and 4.8 above.) From the side of the Academy, Posidonius's contemporary Antiochus (d. 69/68), on whom see chapter 4, notes 3–4, eventually abandoned skepticism and revived the study of "dogmatic" Platonism. He helped to initiate the program in later Platonism of looking to the "ancients," Plato and also Aristotle, as fonts of wisdom. However, this revival of interest in Plato's work, and the authority accorded by these thinkers to Plato's epistemological, metaphysical, and ethical views, only laid the groundwork for the coming into being of what I am calling Platonist philosophy. These Hellenistic philosophers concentrated on aspects of Plato's thought that could be brought into close connection with the dominant philosophy of their time, Stoicism. By contrast, the movement referred to in scholarship as "middle Platonism," beginning in the first to second centuries CE, began to focus on the spiritualist and otherworldly aspects of Plato's work, especially as seen in dialogues such as *Phaedo, Phaedrus, Parmenides, Timaeus,* together with isolated passages of other dialogues that

scholars classify as "middle-period" and "late" works, selected and read for their spiritualist and otherworldly aspects.

38. The fourth century Christian bishop Eusebius (*Preparation for the Gospel*, XV 20.6, excerpted in von Arnim as fragment II 809 and translated in Long and Sedley, *The Hellenistic Philosophers*, as passage 53W) reports as Stoic doctrine that human souls survive a person's death (though nonrational animals' do not), as separate physical substances on their own, for some varying period of time—in the case of virtuous persons, right up until the conflagration in which the whole world-order itself is consumed. Apparently, rational souls are so strongly constructed entities—like all entities, for the Stoics they are bodily ones—that the best among them, those of fully virtuous people, will not only not come apart immediately at death, but are such well constructed and self-coherent stuffs that they hold together till the world's own end. But this physical survival of the stuff in question does not mean any personal afterlife, nor do we have any evidence that any Stoic held out the prospect of such survival as in any way an object or goal, or any sort of prized benefit of living one's own this-worldly life as well as possible. For Epicurus any soul (for him too, of course, a material body or stuff) reaches its permanent end upon the death of the animal whose body it animated (see Epicurus's *Letter to Herodotus* 63–67, and for the ethical implications that Epicureans drew from this thesis, see Lucretius III, 417ff.). Skeptics, of course, take things as they come and resolutely do not worry themselves over any such questions.

39. Plato presents Socrates, in the *Phaedo*, arguing strenuously that the soul *is* immortal, and that its true home, which can be reached only after death, and from which it is blocked while lodged in a body, because of the ineliminable distractions of sensory consciousness that the body provides, lies in purely intellectual communion with Platonic Forms. In doing so, it seems, Plato shows that he thinks Socrates's famously passionate commitment to the supreme value for a human being of philosophical thinking and discussion about human virtue and the human good requires supplementation by and ultimate grounding in such philosophical doctrines of Plato's own: doctrines of the immortality of the soul, the existence of Forms as the only true beings, the misleading character of the senses, and the fundamental unsatisfactoriness of ordinary sensory consciousness. These ideas (and the text of the *Phaedo*) are central elements in the late Platonists' program of finding and recovering the ancient wisdom in Plato's works. But we have no reason at all to think that Socrates himself agreed, or would have agreed, about any need to ground his own moral and philosophical commitments in any such metaphysical speculations!

40. The information that has come down to us about the beginnings of spiritualist Platonism as an ongoing philosophical movement is not plentiful, much of it is obscure,

and there are gaps. Hence, one cannot do more than trace Platonism's origins vaguely to the first centuries BCE and CE. We see it clearly in the work of the prolific philosophical and religious or theological writer Philo of Alexandria (d. 39/40 CE), a Jewish but thoroughly Hellenized writer of Greek (he seems to have had little or no Hebrew). Philo adopts the later Platonists' ideas about an ancestral "wisdom" outlined above, but traces it back, quite unbelievably, through Plato and Pythagoras, to Moses, the presumed author of the Hebrew bible's first five books, from whom these Greeks were supposed somehow to have learned it. Moses thus becomes the fountainhead of both Greek philosophy and the Jewish religion and its customs. Of the important Platonist teachers before Plotinus (except for Plutarch, the author also of the famous *Parallel Lives*, who lived at the end of the first century and the beginning of the second CE) we have little but bare-bones summaries of relevant doctrines, bolstered by short quotations from long-lost writings. About Plotinus's own teacher at Alexandria, Ammonius Saccas, we have even less than that to go on. (For accounts of all these figures one could consult Dillon, *The Middle Platonists*.)

41. Literally, the title asks about "the animal" and "the human being"—the *zôon* and the *anthrôpos*. In fact, the treatise concerns only human beings, not other animals, and in Plotinus's usage the two Greek terms that Porphyry puts in this title refer respectively to two levels or stages in the constitution of a human being: the animal that each of us is, and, above that, the person or self, which Plotinus locates in our capacity for reasoning about the natures of things, that is, our intellects. Hence my choice of translation. In identifying the "human being" (perhaps surprisingly) with intellect or reason (and not with the emotions, senses and pleasures of the "animal") he seems to be following a hint in Plato, *Republic* IX, 588d 3–4. It may be worth adding that this treatise, on which I base most of what I say in section 6.3 below about Plotinus's theory of the human soul and the human person, is the next to last in Porphyry's chronological list, no. 53. So it constitutes a kind of looking back over the most important results of Plotinus's prolonged and profound reflections on the human soul over his long career. It draws together, in brief and pithy statements, in specific application to human life, many ideas about the soul that are investigated and debated at much greater length in earlier works of his most productive period (especially in the very great, major work *Perplexities Concerning Soul* that Porphyry broke up into three treatises, *Enn.* IV 3–5). Porphyry himself says (*Life* 6.34–37) of the last nine treatises, and especially of the last four (of which no. 53 is of course one), written in the years of his last illness, that they show his powers already failing. I must say that I cannot find in this marvelous treatise any signs of anything like senility, so far at least as the depth and acuity of its ideas go (the qualities of the writing are another matter!).

42. It is a curious fact that, with one small exception (the very short I 5, which can be seen as a supplement to I 4, though written earlier), all Plotinus's treatises on ethical matters, collected by Porphyry into *Enneads* I, belong either to the first group of twenty-one, written before Porphyry arrived in Rome to study with Plotinus, or to the last group of nine that Plotinus sent to him after Porphyry left Rome to live in Sicily. Porphyry, as noted above (section 6.2, note 16), thought the last nine (which include I 4 and I 1) showed a decline in their author's capacities; he also thought the first twenty-one, including I 2 and I 3, showed less accomplished power than the middle ones, to which I 5 belongs. That during this "middle" period Plotinus devoted his writing almost exclusively to nonethical matters (metaphysics, theory of the soul, physical theory) may indicate the greater depth of his interest in those latter matters, and his sense of their more crucial importance for a Platonist. His treatment of ethical matters is quite curtailed (if, e.g., one compares Plato's own writings with Plotinus's), and, quite noticeably, there is no concentrated attention at all to questions of political theory; Plotinus's conceptions of the human person and of the low value and importance of our physical lives made political questions philosophically insignificant. In my discussion here and in the following section, besides I 2 and I 4, I rely also on I 3 and I 5, as well as, to a lesser extent, I 7 and I 8, both of which, like I 4, belong to the last four treatises that Plotinus sent to Porphyry— indeed, I 7, *On the First Good and the Other Goods*, is the fifty-fourth and final treatise he wrote. Apparently, as he knew the end of his life was approaching, Plotinus felt a need to engage more directly with questions of ethical theory than he had been doing in the great major works of his middle period.

43. Apparently, Socrates thinks that if a city is to be happy, and make its citizens as happy as, group by group, given their natural endowments, they can become, *all* the citizens need to have all the four virtues at least in some diminished form. Economic producers and workers have to be just, and so do the auxiliaries, even though this cannot amount to the true justice, based on a personal knowledge of Forms, possessed by the complete philosophers. And they need other virtues of character, in order to *want to do*, and to keep successfully focused on, their own work, carried out with respect for others, and with due restraint. They need some sort of courage, and some sort of temperance, and some sort even of wisdom (*some* reflective true beliefs), in order to become as happy as they can be—happiness only coming through virtue, as Socrates argues. And likewise, though somewhat differently in details, for the auxiliaries. *Their* justice includes a willing acceptance of their political role as not merely just for them to perform, but also one that fulfills and makes them happy. This will be based on a much more actively reasoned grasp of why the laws are good for everyone to live by: themselves, as well as the others. And the special "civic" form of courage that Socrates refers to at 430b, based on this true

belief, supported by their spirited and outgoing feelings for active involvement in the administration of the city and the defense, when necessary by force, of its political and moral principles, is the version of courage that *they* need in order to do their own specific political work. (Plotinus's Platonist assumptions about soul-images badly mislead him here, if we wish to take him as offering an interpretation of Plato's intentions.)

44. With the phrase I quote, Plotinus cites *Republic* VII, 518e1–2; the wider context, from 518b to 519d, is important to him. Plato's Socrates argues there that moral education consists in the training of the nonrational desires and feelings in such a way that, having thereby come to possess the virtues of courage, moderation, and justice, they will, in their quietude and orderliness, allow the mind to develop its innate capacity for knowledge of Forms by turning its attention upward toward Forms. Thereby education can complete the virtues by adding wisdom (σοφία) to the other three. Plato can speak of just three of the virtues in the *Republic*'s system (justice, courage, moderation) as being due to habituation and training, since the "wisdom" he counts as the fourth really is, despite its use in the practical activities of directing the life of the city, a work of pure understanding, acquired through philosophical study of mathematics and "dialectical" discussion of ethical questions. While Plotinus can follow Plato in thinking of theoretical wisdom, such as Plato speaks of there, as being a matter of pure thought alone, he needs to distinguish from it a practical form of wisdom, concerned with practical matters (matters of "action"). This practical wisdom belongs in some way (I go on in the main text to try to clarify and specify what this way is) to the soul-image, not, strictly or entirely, to the soul itself; for Plotinus, it too is the result of habituation and training.

BIBLIOGRAPHY

Ammonius. *Ammonius, In Aristotelis categorias commentarius*, edited by A. Busse (*Commentaria in Aristotelem Graeca 4.4*; Berlin: Reimer, 1895).

Ammonius. *On Aristotle's* Categories, translated by S. M. Cohen and G. B. Matthews (London: Duckworth and Cornell University Press, 1991).

Appiah, K. A. *Experiments in Ethics* (Cambridge, Mass.: Harvard University Press, 2008).

Aristotle. *Aristotle: Nicomachean Ethics*, translated by T. H. Irwin, 2nd ed. (Indianapolis: Hackett, 2000).

Aristotle. *The Complete Works of Aristotle*, edited by Jonathan Barnes, 2 vols. (Princeton: Princeton University Press, 1995).

Aristotle. *Politics*, translated by C. D. C. Reeve (Indianapolis: Hackett, 1998).

Arius Didymus. *Epitome of Stoic Ethics*, edited and translated by Arthur J. Pomeroy (Atlanta: Society of Biblical Literature, 1999).

Armstrong, A. H., ed. *The Cambridge History of Later Greek and Early Medieval Philosophy* (Cambridge, Eng.: Cambridge University Press, 1970).

Arnim, H. von. *Stoicorum Veterum Fragmenta* [Fragments of the Early Stoics] (Leipzig: Teubner, 1903–5; vol. 4 indexes by M. Adler, 1924).

Arnim, H. von. "Über Einen Stoischen Papyrus der Herculanensischen Bibliothek," in *Hermes* 25 (1890), 473–95.

Athenaeus. *Learned Banqueters*, 7 vols., edited and translated by S. Douglas Olson (Cambridge, Mass.: Loeb Classical Library, Harvard University Press, 2007–11).

Bett, Richard, trans. *Sextus Empiricus: Against the Ethicists* (Oxford: Oxford University Press, 1997).

Brittain, Charles. *Cicero on Academic Scepticism* (Indianapolis: Hackett, 2006).

Brunschwig, J. "The Cradle Argument in Epicureanism and Stoicism," in M. Schofield and G. Striker (eds.), *The Norms of Nature* (Cambridge, Eng.: Cambridge University Press, 1986), 113–44.

Burnyeat, M. F., and M. Frede, eds. *The Original Sceptics: A Controversy* (Indianapolis: Hackett, 1997).

Chiesara, Maria Lorenza. *Aristocles of Messene: Testimonia and Fragments* (Oxford: Oxford University Press, 2001).

Cicero. *On Duties*, edited by M. T. Griffin and A. M. Atkins (Cambridge, Eng.: Cambridge University Press, 2000).

Cicero. *On Ends* [*De Finibus*], translated by H. Rackham in *Cicero* vol. 17 (Cambridge, Mass.: Loeb Classical Library, Harvard University Press, 1914).

Cicero. *On the Making of an Orator* (*De oratore*), books 1–2, translated by E. W. Sutton and H. Rackham in *Cicero* vol. 3 (Cambridge, Mass.: Loeb Classical Library, Harvard University Press, 1948).

Cicero. *On the Making of an Orato* (*De Oratore*), book 3; *On Fate; Stoic Paradoxes; Divisions of Oratory*, translated by H. Rackham in *Cicero* vol. 4 (Cambridge, Mass.: Loeb Classical Library, Harvard University Press, 1942).

Cicero. *On Moral Ends* [*De Finibus*], translated by Raphael Woolf and edited by Julia Annas (Cambridge, Eng.: Cambridge University Press, 2001).

Cicero. *On the Nature of the Gods; Academica*, translated by H. Rackham in *Cicero* vol. 19 (Cambridge, Mass.: Loeb Classical Library, Harvard University Press, 1933).

Cicero. *Orator*, translated by H. M. Hubbell in *Cicero* vol. 5 (Cambridge, Mass.: Loeb Classical Library, Harvard University Press, 1939).

Cicero. *Tusculan Disputations*, translated by J. E. King in *Cicero* vol. 18 (Cambridge, Mass.: Loeb Classical Library, Harvard University Press, 1927).

Clement of Alexandria. *The Stromata or Miscellanies*, 8 vols. (Whitefish, Mont.: Kessinger Publishing, 2004).

Cooper, John M. "De Motu Animalium 7 (through 701b1): The Role of Thought in Animal Voluntary Self-Locomotion," in *Aristotle's De Motu Animalium*, edited by Oliver Primavesi and Christof Rapp (Oxford: Oxford University Press, forthcoming).

Cooper, John M. "The Emotional Life of the Wise," in *Southern Journal of Philosophy* 43, suppl. (2005), 176–218.

Cooper, John M. *Knowledge, Nature, and the Good* (Princeton: Princeton University Press, 2004).

Cooper, John M. "*Metaphysics* A 10: Conclusion—and Retrospect," in C. Steel (ed.), *Aristotle's Metaphysics A: Symposium Aristotelicum* (Oxford: Oxford University Press, 2012).

Cooper, John M. *Reason and Emotion* (Princeton: Princeton University Press, 1999).

Cooper, John M. "Socrates and Philosophy as a Way of Life," in Dominic Scott (ed.), *Maieusis: Essays in Ancient Philosophy in Honour of Myles Burnyeat* (Oxford: Oxford University Press, 2007), chapter 2, 20–43.

Dillon, John. *The Middle Platonists* (Ithaca, N.Y.: Cornell University Press, 1977).

Diogenes Laertius. *Lives and Opinions of the Eminent Philosophers*, 2 vols., translated by R. D. Hicks (Cambridge, Mass.: Loeb Classical Library, Harvard University Press, 1970).

Diogenes Laertius. *Vies et doctrines des philosophes illustres*, translated into French under the direction of Marie-Odile Goulet-Cazé with introductions, translations, and notes by J.-F. Balaudé, L. Brisson, J. Brunschwig, T. Dorandi, M.-O. Goulet-Cazé, R. Goulet, and M. Narcy (Paris: Hachette, 1999).

Döring, K. "The Students of Socrates," in Donald Morrison (ed.), *The Cambridge Companion to Socrates* (Cambridge, Eng.: Cambridge University Press, 2011).

Epictetus. *Discourses* and *The Encheiridion*, translated by W. A. Oldfather, 2 vols. (Cambridge, Mass.: Loeb Classical Library, Harvard University Press, 1925–28).

Epicurus. *Letter to Menoeceus, Letter to Herodotus, Principal Doctrines*, and *Vatican Sayings*, in Brad Inwood and Lloyd Gerson (eds. and trans.), *The Epicurus Reader: Selected Writings and Testimonia* (Indianapolis: Hackett, 1994).

Frede, M. "An Empiricist View of Knowledge: Memorism," in S. Everson (ed.), *Companions to Ancient Thought I: Epistemology* (Cambridge, Eng.: Cambridge University Press, 1990), chap. 11.

Galen. *On the Doctrines of Hippocrates and Plato*, edited and translated by P. De Lacy (Berlin: Akademie Verlag, 1978–80).

Geuss, Raymond. *Public Goods, Private Goods* (Princeton: Princeton University Press 2001). Chap. 2 discusses Diogenes the Cynic.

Hadot, Pierre. "La fin du paganisme," in *Études de philosophie ancienne* (Paris: Les Belles Lettres, 1998), 341–74.

Hadot, Pierre. *Philosophy as a Way of Life: Spiritual Exercises from Socrates to Foucault*, translated by Michael Chase and edited with an introduction by A. I. Davidson (Oxford: Blackwell, 1995). A rearranged and expanded translation of Pierre Hadot's *Exercises spirituels et philosophie antique*, 2nd ed. (Paris: *Études Augustinennes*, 1987).

Hadot, Pierre. *The Present Alone Is Our Happiness: Conversations with Jeannie Carlier and Arnold I. Davidson*, translated by Marc Djaballah (Stanford, Calif.: Stanford University Press, 2009). Translation of *La philosophie comme manière de vivre. Entretiens avec Jeannie Carlier et Arnold I. Davidson* (Paris: Éditions Albin Michel, 2001).

Hadot, Pierre. *What Is Ancient Philosophy?*, translated by Michael Chase (Cambridge, Mass.: Harvard University Press, 2002). Translation, with some corrections by Hadot, of *Qu'est-ce que la philosophie antique?* (Paris: Gallimard, 1995).

Hauser, Marc. *Moral Minds: How Nature Designed Our Universal Sense of Right and Wrong* (New York: Ecco/HarperCollins, 2006). Also published in paperback under the title *Moral Minds: The Nature of Right and Wrong* (New York: Ecco/HarperCollins, 2006).

Henry, P., and H. R. Schwyzer. *Plotini Opera*, 3 vols. (Oxford: Clarendon, 1964–82).

Iamblichus. *On the Mysteries [De Mysteriis]*, translated with an introduction and notes by Emma C. Clarke, John M. Dillon, and Jackson P. Hershbell (Atlanta: Society of Biblical Literature, 2003).

Inwood, Brad, and L. Gerson, eds. *Hellenistic Philosophy: Introductory Readings*, 2nd ed. (Indianapolis: Hackett, 1997).

Jaeger, Werner. "On the Origin and Cycle of the Philosophic Ideal of Life," appendix II in *Aristotle: Fundamentals of the History of His Development*, 2nd ed., translated, with the author's corrections and additions, by Richard Robinson (Oxford: Oxford University Press, 1948), 426–61.

Kahn, Charles H. *Plato and the Socratic Dialogue* (Cambridge, Eng.: Cambridge University Press, 1996).

Kalligas, P., ed. and trans. into modern Greek. *Plotinus: First Ennead: Ancient Text, Translation, Notes*, 2nd ed. (Athens: Center for Research on Greek and Latin Philology, 2006). In the modern Greek language.

Lear, Gabriel Richardson. *Happy Lives and the Highest Good* (Princeton: Princeton University Press, 2004).

Long, A. A., and D. N. Sedley, eds. *The Hellenistic Philosophers*, 2 vols. (Cambridge, Eng.: Cambridge University Press, 1987). Vol. 1 contains sources in translation with commentary; vol. 2 has the original texts as well as an extensive bibliography.

Lucretius. *On the Nature of Things*, translated with facing Latin text by W. H. D. Rouse and revised by Martin F. Smith (Cambridge, Mass.: Loeb Classical Library, 1924).

Lucretius. *On the Nature of Things*, translated by Martin Ferguson Smith (Indianapolis: Hackett, 2001).

Marcus Aurelius. *Marcus Aurelius*, edited and translated by C. R. Haines (Cambridge, Mass.: Loeb Classical Library, Harvard University Press, 1916).

Plato. *Plato: Complete Works*, edited by John M. Cooper with associate editor D. S. Hutchinson (Indianapolis: Hackett, 1997).

Plotinus, *Enneads. Plotinus*, 7 vols., edited and translated by A. H. Armstrong (Cambridge, Mass.: Loeb Classical Library, Harvard University Press, 1966–88). Greek with facing English translation.

Plutarch. *Lives*, 11 vols., translated by Bernadotte Perrin (Cambridge, Mass.: Loeb Classical Library, Harvard University Press, 1914–26).

Plutarch. *Moralia* [Philosophical Essays], in 15 vols. (Cambridge, Mass.: Loeb Classical Library, Harvard University Press): vol. 6, *On Moral Virtue*, translated by W. C.

Helmbold; vol. 13, pt. 2, *On Stoic-Self-Contradictions* and *Against the Stoics on Common Notions*, edited and translated by Harold Cherniss; and vol. 14, *That Epicurus Actually Makes a Happy Life Impossible, Reply to Colotes, Is "Live Unknown" a Wise Precept?* and *On Music*, edited and translated by Benedict Einarson and Phillip H. DeLacy.

Posidonius. *Posidonius*, 3 vols., edited by L. Edelstein and I. G. Kidd (Cambridge, Eng.: Cambridge University Press, 1972–99).

Random House Webster's Unabridged Dictionary of the English Language (New York: Random House, 2001).

Raphael, D. D. *British Moralists, 1650–1800*, selected and edited with comparative notes and analytical index, 2 vols. (Oxford: Clarendon, 1969).

Rowe, Christopher, trans. *Aristotle: Nicomachean Ethics*, with an introduction and commentary by Sarah Broadie (Oxford: Oxford University Press, 2002).

Scaltsas, Theodore, and Andrew S. Mason, eds. *The Philosophy of Epictetus* (Oxford: Oxford University Press, 2007).

Seneca. *Ad Lucilium Epistulae Morales* [Epistles or Moral Letters], 3 vols., translated by Richard Gummere (Cambridge, Mass.: Loeb Classical Library, Harvard University Press, 1917–25).

Seneca. *Moral Essays*, edited and translated by John W. Basore, 3 vols. (Cambridge, Mass.: Loeb Classical Library, Harvard University Press, 1928–35). Latin with facing English translation.

Seneca. *Seneca: Moral and Political Essays*, edited and translated by J. M. Cooper and J. F. Procopé (Cambridge, Eng.: Cambridge University Press, 1995).

Sextus Empiricus. *Adversus Mathematicos* [Against the Theoreticians], in R. G. Bury (trans.), *Sextus Empiricus*, vols. 2–4 (Cambridge, Mass.: Loeb Classical Library, Harvard University Press, 1935–49).

Sextus Empiricus. *Outlines of Scepticism*, edited and translated by J. Annas and J. Barnes (Cambridge, Eng.: Cambridge University Press, 2000).

Shaw, Gregory. *Theurgy and the Soul: The Neoplatonism of Iamblichus* (University Park: Penn State University Press, 1995).

Simplicius. *Commentary on Aristotle's* Physics, 7 vols., translated by various scholars (London: Duckworth and Cornell University Press, 1989–2001).

Traversa, Augustus, ed. *Index Stoicorum Herculanensis* (Genoa: Istituto di filologia classica, 1952).

Xenophon. *Memorabilia. Oeconomicus. Symposium. Apology*, translated by E. C. Marchant and O. J. Todd (Cambridge, Mass.: Loeb Classical Library, Harvard University Press, 1923).